Middle School 2-2
학교시험 완벽대비

KB087725

2학기 전과정

적중 100 plus

영어 기출문제집

중2

지학 | 민찬규

Best Collection

구성과 특징

교과서의 주요 학습 내용을 중심으로 학습 영역별 특성에 맞춰 단계별로 다양한 학습 기회를 제공하여 단원별 학습능력 평가는 물론 중간 및 기말고사 시험 등에 완벽하게 대비할 수 있도록 내용을 구성

Words & Expressions

Step1 Key Words 단원별 핵심 단어 설명 및 풀이
Key Expression 단원별 핵심 숙어 및 관용어 설명
Word Power 반대 또는 비슷한 뜻 단어 배우기
English Dictionary 영어로 배우는 영어 단어

Step2 실력평가 단원별 수시평가 대비 주관식, 객관식 문제풀이

Step3 서술형 대비 학업성취도 및 수행능력평가 대비 서술형 문제풀이

Conversation

Step1 핵심 의사소통 의사소통에 필요한 주요 표현 방법 요약
핵심 Check 기본적인 표현 방법 및 활용능력 확인

Step2 대화문 익히기 상황에 따른 대화문 활용 및 연습

Step3 기본평가 시험대비 기초 학습 능력 평가

Step4 실력평가 단원별 수시평가 대비 주관식, 객관식 문제풀이

Step5 서술형 대비 학업성취도 및 수행능력평가 대비 서술형 문제풀이

Grammar

Step1 주요 문법 단원별 주요 문법 사항과 예문을 알기 쉽게 설명
핵심 Check 기본 문법사항에 대한 이해 여부 확인

Step2 기본평가 시험대비 기초 학습 능력 평가

Step3 실력평가 단원별 수시평가 대비 주관식, 객관식 문제풀이

Step4 서술형 대비 학업성취도 및 수행능력평가 대비 서술형 문제풀이

Reading

Step1 구문 분석 단원별로 제시된 문장에 대한 구문별 분석과 내용 설명
확인문제 문장에 대한 기본적인 이해와 인지능력 확인

Step2 확인학습A 빈칸 채우기를 통한 문장 완성 능력 확인

Step3 확인학습B 제시된 우리말을 영어로 완성하여 작문 능력 키우기

Step4 실력평가 단원별 수시평가 대비 주관식, 객관식 문제풀이

Step5 서술형 대비 학업성취도 및 수행능력평가 대비 서술형 문제풀이
교과서 구석구석 교과서에 나오는 기타 문장까지 완벽 학습

Composition

|영역별 핵심문제|
단어 및 어휘, 대화문, 문법, 독해 등 각 영역별 기출문제의 출제 유형을 분석하여 실전에 대비하고 연습할 수 있도록 문제를 배열

|서술형 실전 및 창의사고력 문제|
학교 시험에서 점차 늘어나는 서술형 시험에 집중 대비하고 고득점을 취득하는데 만전을 기하기 위한 학습 코너

|단원별 예상문제|
기출문제를 분석한 후 새로운 시험 출제 경향을 더하여 새롭게 출제될 수 있는 문제를 포함하여 시험에 완벽하게 대비할 수 있도록 준비

|단원별 모의고사|
영역별, 단계별 학습을 모두 마친 후 실전 연습을 위한 모의고사

INSIGHT
on the textbook ....

교과서 파헤치기

- **단어Test1~2** 영어 단어 우리말 쓰기와 우리말을 영어 단어로 쓰기
- **대화문Test1~2** 대화문 빈칸 완성 및 전체 대화문 쓰기
- **본문Test1~5** 빈칸 완성, 우리말 쓰기, 문장 배열연습, 영어 작문하기 복습 등 단계별 반복 학습을 통해 교과서 지문에 대한 완벽한 습득
- **구석구석지문Test1~2** 지문 빈칸 완성 및 전문 영어로 쓰기

이책의 차례 Contents

Lesson 5

I Don't Have a Clue

 의사소통 기능

- 설명 요청하기
  Can you explain how to use the buttons?

- 열거하기
  First, fold the paper in half. Second, turn it over.
  Then, draw a face.

 언어 형식

- 수동태
  The cheese **was eaten by** a mouse.

- 조동사의 수동태
  Bright stars **can be seen** at night.

Words & Expressions

Key Words

- **accident** [ǽksidənt] 몡 사고
- **bat** [bæt] 몡 배트, 방망이
- **bean** [biːn] 몡 콩
- **block** [blɑk] 몡 구역, 블록
- **bottom** [bɑ́təm] 몡 맨 아래 (부분)
- **button** [bʌ́tən] 몡 단추
- **candle** [kǽndl] 몡 양초
- **clue** [kluː] 몡 단서, 실마리
- **congratulation** [kəngrætʃuléiʃən] 몡 축하
- **cross** [krɔːs] 몸 건너다
- **delete** [dilíːt] 몸 삭제하다
- **detective** [ditéktiv] 몡 탐정, 형사
- **disappear** [dìsəpíər] 몸 사라지다
- **dragon** [drǽgən] 몡 용
- **enter** [éntər] 몸 입장하다, 들어가다
- **escape** [iskéip] 몸 탈출하다
- **explain** [ikspléin] 몸 설명하다
- **finally** [fáinəli] 몸 마침내
- **fold** [fould] 몸 접다
- **half** [hæf] 몡 반, 절반
- **hide** [haid] 몸 숨기다, 숨다

- **inside** [ìnsáid] 몐 ~의 안에, ~의 내부에
- **lie** [lai] 몸 거짓말하다
- **luckily** [lʌ́kili] 몸 다행히
- **none** [nʌn] 몐 하나도 ~ 않다
- **outside** [áutsàid] 몐 ~ 밖에 몸 밖으로, 밖에
- **prize** [praiz] 몡 상
- **riddle** [rídl] 몡 수수께끼
- **safely** [séifli] 몸 안전하게
- **scene** [siːn] 몡 장면
- **solve** [sɑlv] 몸 해결하다
- **somewhere** [sʌ́mhwɛ̀ər] 몸 어딘가에
- **space** [speis] 몡 공간, 우주
- **stamp** [stæmp] 몡 우표
- **straight** [streit] 몸 똑바로, 일직선으로
- **strange** [streindʒ] 몡 이상한
- **suspect** [səspékt] 몡 용의자
- **thief** [θiːf] 몡 도둑
- **throw** [θrou] 몸 던지다
- **triangle** [tráiæ̀ŋgl] 몡 삼각형
- **twice** [twais] 몸 두 번, 두 배
- **win** [win] 몸 얻다, 이기다

Key Expressions

- **at the time of**: ~이 일어나던 때에
- **catch a thief**: 도둑을 잡다
- **fill A with B**: A를 B로 채우다
- **for free**: 공짜로

- **help yourself**: 마음껏 드세요
- **make it to** ~: ~에 이르는 데 성공하다
- **turn over**: ~을 뒤집다
- **write down**: ~을 적다

Word Power

※ 서로 반대되는 뜻을 가진 단어

□ **appear** 나타나다 ↔ **disappear** 사라지다

□ **top** 맨 위 ↔ **bottom** 맨 아래쪽

□ **throw** 던지다 ↔ **catch** 잡다

□ **win** 이기다 ↔ **lose** 지다

□ **dark** 어두운 ↔ **bright** 밝은

□ **inside** ~의 안에 ↔ **outside** ~의 밖에

□ **safe** 안전한 ↔ **dangerous** 위험한

□ **special** 특별한 ↔ **general** 일반적인

□ **straight** 똑바른, 일직선의 ↔ **curved** 굽은

□ **fold** 접다 ↔ **unfold** 펴다

English Dictionary

□ **accident** 사고
→ an event in which a car, train, plane, etc. is damaged and often someone is hurt
자동차, 기차, 비행기 등이 손상되고 때로는 누군가가 다치는 사건

□ **bat** 방망이, 배트
→ a long wooden stick with a special shape that is used in some sports and games
몇몇 스포츠와 게임에서 사용되는 특별한 모양을 가진 긴 나무 막대

□ **bean** 콩
→ a seed or a pod that comes from a climbing plant and is cooked as food
덩굴나무에서 나오며 음식으로 요리되는 씨앗 또는 꼬투리

□ **bottom** 맨 아래 (부분)
→ the flat surface on the lowest side of an object
물체의 가장 낮은 부분의 평평한 표면

□ **clue** 단서, 실마리
→ an object or piece of information that helps someone solve a crime or mystery
누군가가 범죄나 미스터리를 풀도록 도와주는 물체나 정보

□ **cross** 건너다
→ to go from one side of something such as a road, river, room, etc. to the other
길, 강, 방 등과 같은 무언가의 한 쪽에서 다른 쪽으로 가다

□ **delete** 삭제하다
→ to remove something that has been written down or stored in a computer
적어 놓았거나 컴퓨터에 저장해 놓은 무언가를 제거하다

□ **detective** 탐정
→ someone who is paid to discover information about someone or something
누군가 또는 무언가에 대한 정보를 발견하도록 돈을 받는 사람

□ **enter** 입장하다
→ to go or come into a place
한 장소로 들어가거나 들어오다

□ **escape** 탈출하다
→ to leave a place when someone is trying to catch you or stop you, or when there is a dangerous situation
누군가가 당신을 잡으려 하거나 당신을 멈출 때, 또는 위험한 상황이 있을 때 한 장소를 떠나다

□ **half** 반, 절반
→ exactly or about 50% of an amount, time, distance, number, etc.
양, 시간, 거리, 수 등의 정확히 또는 거의 50%

□ **riddle** 수수께끼
→ a question that is deliberately very confusing and has a humorous or clever answer
의도적으로 매우 혼란스럽게 하는 그리고 재미있거나 재기 넘치는 대답을 갖는 질문

□ **suspect** 용의자
→ someone who is thought to be guilty of a crime
어떤 범죄의 죄가 있다고 생각되는 사람

□ **thief** 도둑
→ someone who steals things from another person or place
다른 사람이나 장소로부터 물건들을 훔치는 사람

01 다음 짝지어진 단어의 관계가 같도록 빈칸에 알맞은 말을 쓰시오.

agree: disagree = appear : _____

02 다음 영영풀이가 가리키는 것을 고르시오.

to remove something that has been written down or stored in a computer

① enter   ② delete   ③ shift
④ throw   ⑤ cross

03 다음 중 밑줄 친 부분의 뜻풀이가 바르지 않은 것은?

① Clues can be found <u>somewhere</u> inside the room. 어딘가에
② <u>Luckily</u>, he wasn't badly hurt. 다행히
③ The thief <u>escaped</u> from the police station. 탈출했다
④ Where did you <u>hide</u> your gold? 찾다
⑤ The players are dragons and <u>seahorses</u>. 해마

04 다음 우리말에 맞게 빈칸에 알맞은 말을 쓰시오.

(1) 나는 셜록 홈즈가 위대한 탐정들 중 한 명이었다고 생각한다.
   ➡ I think Sherlock Holmes was one of the greatest _____.
(2) 수건을 반으로 접으세요.
   ➡ _____ the towel in _____.
(3) 그는 1분 만에 수학 퍼즐을 해결했다.
   ➡ He _____ the math puzzle in just one minute.

05 다음 문장의 빈칸에 들어갈 말을 〈보기〉에서 골라 쓰시오.

┌─ 보기 ─┐
made it to / turn over / help yourself / for free

(1) The soccer team _____ the finals.
(2) I got this T-shirt _____.
(3) You should _____ the sweet potato before it burns.
(4) _____ to anything you like on the table.

06 다음 주어진 문장의 밑줄 친 suspects와 같은 의미로 쓰인 것은?

The detective met some <u>suspects</u> and asked questions.

① The spoiled food is <u>suspected</u> of causing food poisoning.
② Who is the <u>suspect</u> in the crime?
③ I <u>suspected</u> that he stole my wallet.
④ The police <u>suspect</u> that he is a spy.
⑤ We <u>suspected</u> him to be a liar.

07 다음 문장에 공통으로 들어갈 말을 고르시오.

• There is enough space for three people to _____ down.
• I don't want to _____ to my parents anymore.
• I promise not to _____ again.

① explain   ② solve   ③ throw
④ win   ⑤ lie

01 다음 짝지어진 단어의 관계가 같도록 빈칸에 알맞은 말을 쓰시오.

> top : bottom = inside : _____

02 다음 우리말에 맞게 빈칸에 알맞은 말을 쓰시오.

(1) 너는 이것을 일주일에 두 번 볼 수 있다.
➡ You can see this _____ in a week.

(2) 그녀는 사고가 일어나던 때에 아침을 만들고 있었다.
➡ She was making breakfast _____ _____ of the accident.

(3) 당신은 우리 가게에서 일곱 가지 상품을 무엇이든 무료로 고를 수 있다.
➡ You can choose any seven items from our store _____.

03 다음 우리말을 주어진 어구를 배열하여 영작하시오.

(1) 그 이야기를 제게 설명해 주실 수 있나요?
(you / me / to / the story / can / explain)
➡ _____

(2) 너는 하루에 두 번 약을 먹어야 한다.
(twice / a day / the pills / should / you / take)
➡ _____

(3) 나는 빵을 삼각형으로 잘랐다.
(triangles / the bread / into / I / cut)
➡ _____

04 다음 우리말에 맞게 빈칸에 알맞은 말을 쓰시오.

(1) 그녀는 어제 차 사고를 당했다.
➡ She got in a car _____ yesterday.

(2) Mary가 게임하는 중에 다쳤니?
➡ Did Mary get _____ during the game?

(3) 경찰이 오후에 용의자를 심문할 것이다.
➡ The police will _____ the suspect in the afternoon.

(4) 네 컴퓨터에 공간을 만들기 위해 모든 사진을 지워야 한다.
➡ You should _____ all of the pictures on your computer to make more space.

05 다음 우리말을 주어진 단어를 이용하여 영작하시오.

(1) 경찰은 도둑을 잡을 수 있을 것이라고 확신했다. (catch, sure)
➡ _____

(2) 페이지를 넘겨 그림을 보세요. (turn, look)
➡ _____

(3) 이 병을 물로 채워 주시겠어요? (would, fill, with)
➡ _____

06 다음 대화의 빈칸을 완성하시오.

> A: Try to solve this riddle.
> B: Sure.
> A: This has three to four legs but it can't walk. Can you explain why?
> B: Yes! It's because it's a _____.

Conversation

교과서

① 설명 요청하기

Can you explain how to use the buttons? (버튼 사용법을 설명해 줄 수 있니?)

■ 'Can you explain ~?'은 '너는 ~을 설명해 줄 수 있니?'라는 뜻으로, 상대방에게 설명을 요청할 때 쓰는 표현이다. 'Can you explain' 다음에 'how to ~' 표현을 사용하여 어떤 절차나 방법을 물어볼 수 있다.

설명 요청하기

• I don't get it. Can you explain why? (이해가 안돼요. 이유를 설명해 줄 수 있나요?)
• Can you show me how to use this machine? (어떻게 이 기계를 사용할 수 있는지 보여줄 수 있나요?)
• Can you tell me how to draw this character? (이 캐릭터를 어떻게 그릴 수 있는지 말해 줄래요?)
• Let me know how to make the cookies. (쿠키 만드는 법을 알려 주세요.)

핵심 Check

1. 다음 우리말과 일치하도록 빈칸에 알맞은 말을 쓰시오.

(1) A: Can you _____ a little bit more? (좀 더 설명을 해 주시겠습니까?)

B: No problem. (그럼요.)

(2) A: _____ how to use the copier. (복사기 사용법 좀 알려 주세요.)

B: Sure. Look at this. (물론이지. 여기를 봐.)

(3) A: _____? (어제 무슨 일이 일어났었는지 말해줄 수 있니?)

B: Well, I got hurt in a car accident. (차 사고로 다쳤어.)

❷ 열거하기

First, fold the paper in half. Second, turn it over. Then, draw a face.
(먼저, 종이를 반으로 접어. 두 번째로, 뒤집어. 그리고 나서, 얼굴을 그려.)

■ 서수를 사용하여 어떤 절차의 순서를 열거할 수 있다. 이때, 'Second, Third' 대신에 'Next, Then'을 쓸 수 있다.

열거하기

• First, draw a circle. Second, put a star inside. Then, put a triangle on top of the circle.
(첫째로, 원을 그리세요. 둘째, 안에 별을 놓으세요. 그리고 나서, 원의 맨 위에 삼각형을 놓으세요.)

• First, he looked around the school. Then, he met some suspects and asked questions. Finally, he found the thief. (첫째로, 그는 학교를 둘러봤어. 그리고 나서, 몇몇의 용의자를 만나서 질문을 했지. 마침내, 그는 도둑을 찾았어.)

핵심 Check

2. 다음 우리말과 일치하도록 빈칸에 알맞은 말을 쓰시오.

(1) **A:** Can you explain how to make a taco? (타코 만드는 법을 설명해 주실 수 있어요?)

B: _____, fill your tortilla with vegetables and meat. _____, add some sauce on the top. (먼저, 토르티야를 채소와 고기로 채워. 그 다음, 위에 약간의 소스를 추가하렴.)

(2) **A:** _____, the farmer buys a fox, a duck, and a bag of beans. _____, the farmer needs to cross a river. (먼저 농부는 여우, 오리, 콩 자루를 하나씩 사. 그리고 나서, 농부는 강을 건너야 해.)

B: What's the problem? (뭐가 문제인데?)

(3) **A:** _____, fold a paper in half to make a triangle. _____, fold the top of the triangle to the bottom line. _____, fold both ends of the bottom line to the top to make ears. _____, turn it over and draw a face. (먼저, 종이를 반으로 접어서 세모를 만들어. 두 번째로, 세모의 꼭대기를 맨 아랫선 쪽으로 접어. 세 번째로, 맨 아랫선 양쪽 끝을 위로 접어서 귀를 만들어. 그리고 나서, 그것을 뒤집어서 얼굴을 그려.)

B: That sounds easy. (쉽구나.)

Listen and Speak 2-B

Jane: Minsu, do you know the TV show about the student ❶detective?

Minsu: Yes. I love ❷that show, but I didn't see ❷it this week. What was ❷it about?

Jane: Well, all of the bikes at school disappeared.

Minsu: So, what did ❸he do?

Jane: ❹First, he looked around the school. ❹Then, he met some suspects and ❺asked questions. ❹Finally, he found the thief. The thief was....

Minsu: No, don't tell me! I'll watch it later.

Jane: 민수야, 학생 탐정이 나오는 TV쇼를 아니?

Minsu: 응, 나는 그 쇼를 아주 좋아하지만 이번 주에는 못 봤어. 무슨 내용이었어?

Jane: 음, 학교의 모든 자전거들이 사라졌어.

Minsu: 그래서 그가 무엇을 했어?

Jane: 첫째로, 그는 학교를 둘러봤어. 그러고 나서, 몇몇의 용의자를 만나서 질문을 했지. 마침내, 그는 도둑을 찾았어. 도둑은...

Minsu: 안 돼, 말하지 마! 내가 나중에 볼 거야.

❶ detective: 탐정
❷ that show와 it 모두 the TV show about the student detective를 가리킨다.
❸ he는 the student detective를 가리킨다.
❹ 학생 탐정이 한 일을 열거하고 있다.
❺ met과 병렬구조이다.

Check(√) True or False

(1) Minsu loves the TV show about the student detective.　　　T ☐ F ☐

(2) Jane knows who the thief was.　　　T ☐ F ☐

 Real Life Communication

Emily: Junsu, do you want to solve a riddle?

Junsu: Sure, what is ❶it?

Emily: There is a farmer. First, the farmer buys a fox, a duck, and a bag of beans. Then, the farmer needs to cross a river.

Junsu: What's the problem?

Emily: The boat can only hold the farmer and one more thing.

Junsu: ❷Are you saying that the farmer can take only one thing ❸at a time?

Emily: Yes. Also, the fox will eat the duck or the duck will eat the beans if the farmer isn't there. Can you explain how to move everything across the river safely?

Junsu: Hmm ....

Emily: 준수야, 수수께끼 하나 풀어볼래?

Junsu: 물론이지, 뭔데?

Emily: 한 농부가 있어. 먼저 농부는 여우, 오리, 콩 자루를 하나씩 사. 그러고 나서, 농부는 강을 건너야 해.

Junsu: 뭐가 문제인데?

Emily: 보트는 단지 농부와 한 가지만 더 옮길 수 있어.

Junsu: 농부가 한 번에 오직 한 가지만 옮길 수 있다는 말이니?

Emily: 응. 또한 만약 농부가 없다면 여우가 오리를 먹거나, 오리가 콩을 먹을 거야. 전부를 강 건너로 안전하게 옮길 방법을 설명할 수 있겠니?

Junsu: 음....

❶ it은 riddle(수수께끼)을 가리킨다.
❷ 자신의 이해를 한 번 더 점검하고 있다.
❸ at a time: 한 번에

Check(√) True or False

(3) The farmer should cross a river with only one thing.　　　T ☐ F ☐

(4) Without the farmer, the fox will eat the beans.　　　T ☐ F ☐

Listen and Speak 1-A

Jimin: Do you want to play the new game ❶that I bought?

Brian: Sure, what is it, Jimin?

Jimin: It's ❷like a soccer game but the players are dragons and ❸seahorses. You need to use these buttons to play.

Brian: That sounds fun. ❹Can you explain how to use the buttons?

Jimin: Sure.

❶ that은 목적격 관계대명사로 which로 바꾸어 쓸 수 있다.
❷ like는 전치사로 '~와 같은'을 뜻한다.
❸ seahorse: 해마
❹ 버튼 사용법에 대한 설명을 요청하는 표현이다. how to+동사원형: ~하는 방법

Listen and Speak 2 -A

Tom: Yujin, ❶look at my paper fox.

Yujin: That's cute. How did you make ❷it?

Tom: First, ❸fold a paper ❹in half to make a triangle. Second, fold the top of the triangle to the bottom line. Third, fold both ends of the bottom line to the top to make ears. Then, ❺turn it over and draw a face.

Yujin: That sounds easy.

❶ look at: ~을 보다
❷ it은 Tom's paper fox를 가리킨다.
❸ 동사로 시작하는 명령문이다.
❹ in half: 반으로
❺ turn over: 뒤집다

Listen and Speak 1-B

Jack: Kelly, here's a riddle. You can see this twice in a week, once in a year, but never in a day. What is this?

Kelly: ❶I have no idea.

Jack: It's the letter "E."

Kelly: ❷I don't get it. Can you explain why?

Jack: Well, there are two "E"s in the word "week," one "E" in the word "year" but no "E"s in the word "day."

Kelly: Aha! ❸Now I get it.

❶ I have no idea. = I don't know.
❷ I don't get it. = I don't understand.
❸ I get it. = I understand. = I see.

Let's Check

Minjun: Wow! Something smells really good, Mom. What is it?

Mom: We're going to have tacos for dinner. ❶Help yourself.

Minjun: Can you explain how to make a taco?

Mom: First, ❷fill your tortilla with vegetables and meat. Then, add some sauce on the top.

Minjun: ❸Sounds delicious!

Mom: Would you like some cheese?

Minjun: No, thanks.

❶ Help yourself.: 마음껏 드세요.
❷ fill A with B: A를 B로 채우다
❸ Sounds delicious.: 맛있을 거 같아요.

● 다음 우리말과 일치하도록 빈칸에 알맞은 말을 쓰시오.

Listen & Speak 1 - A

Jimin: Do you want to play the new game _____ I _____?

Brian: Sure, what is it, Jimin?

Jimin: It's _____ a soccer game but the players are _____ and _____. You _____ _____ _____ these buttons _____ _____.

Brian: That _____ fun. _____ _____ _____ _____ _____ _____the buttons?

Jimin: Sure.

해석

Jimin: 내가 산 새로운 게임을 하고 싶니?

Brian: 물론이야. 그게 뭐니, 지민아?

Jimin: 축구 시합 같은 것인데 선수들이 용과 해마야. 게임을 하려면 이 버튼들을 사용해야 해.

Brian: 재밌을 거 같아. 버튼 사용법을 설명해 줄 수 있니?

Jimin: 물론이지.

Listen & Speak 1 - B

Jack: Kelly, here's a _____. You can see this _____ in a week, _____ in a year, but _____ _____ _____ _____. What is this?

Kelly: _____ _____ _____ _____.

Jack: It's the letter "E."

Kelly: I don't _____. _____ _____ _____ _____ _____?

Jack: Well, there are two "E"s in the word "week," one "E" in the word "year" but no "E"s in the word "day."

Kelly: Aha! Now I _____ _____.

Jack: Kelly, 수수께끼가 있어. 넌 이것을 1주에 두 번, 1년에 한 번 볼 수 있어. 하지만 1일에는 전혀 볼 수가 없어. 이게 뭐게?

Kelly: 전혀 모르겠어.

Jack: 알파벳 'E'야.

Kelly: 이해가 안 가. 이유를 설명해 줄 수 있니?

Jack: 음, 단어 week에는 'E'가 2개 있고, 단어 year에는 'E'가 1개 있고, 단어 day에는 'E'가 없잖아.

Kelly: 아! 이제 이해했다.

Listen & Speak 2 - A

Tom: Yujin, _____ _____ my paper fox.

Yujin: That's cute. _____ _____ _____ _____ _____ _____?

Tom: _____, fold a paper _____ _____ to make a triangle. _____, fold the top of the triangle to the _____ _____. _____, fold _____ _____ of the bottom line to the top to make ears. _____, _____ it _____ and draw a face.

Yujin: That sounds _____.

Tom: 유진아, 내 종이 여우를 봐.

Yujin: 귀엽다. 어떻게 만들었니?

Tom: 먼저, 종이를 반으로 접어서 세모를 만들어. 두 번째로, 세모의 꼭대기를 맨 아랫선 쪽으로 접어. 세 번째로, 맨 아랫선 양쪽 끝을 위로 접어서 귀를 만들어. 그리고 나서, 그것을 뒤집어서 얼굴을 그려.

Yujin: 쉽구나.

Listen & Talk 2 - B

Jane: Minsu, do you know the TV show about the student _____?

Minsu: Yes. I love that show, but I _____ _____ it _____ _____. What was it _____?

Jane: Well, _____ _____ the bikes at school _____.

Minsu: So, what _____ he _____?

Jane: _____, he _____ _____ the school. _____, he met some _____ and asked questions. _____, he found the _____. The thief was ....

Minsu: No, _____ _____ me! I'll _____ it _____.

Real Life Communication

Emily: Junsu, do you want to _____ a riddle?

Junsu: Sure, what is it?

Emily: There is a farmer. _____, the farmer buys a fox, a duck, and _____ _____ _____ _____. Then, the farmer _____ _____ _____ _____ _____.

Junsu: What's the problem?

Emily: The boat can only _____ the farmer and _____ _____ thing.

Junsu: Are you saying that the farmer can _____ only one thing _____ _____ _____?

Emily: Yes. Also, the fox will eat the duck or the duck will eat the beans if the farmer isn't there. _____ _____ _____ _____ _____ _____ _____ the river safely?

Junsu: Hmm ....

Let's Check

Minjun: Wow! Something _____ really _____, Mom. What is it?

Mom: We're _____ _____ have tacos _____ _____. _____ _____.

Minjun: _____ _____ _____ _____ _____ _____ a taco?

Mom: _____, _____ your tortilla _____ vegetables and meat. _____, add some sauce _____ _____ _____.

Minjun: Sounds _____!

Mom: _____ you _____ some cheese?

Minjun: No, _____.

해석

Jane: 민수야, 학생 탐정이 나오는 TV 쇼를 아니?

Minsu: 응, 나는 그 쇼를 아주 좋아하지만 이번 주에는 못 봤어. 무슨 내용이었어?

Jane: 음, 학교의 모든 자전거들이 사라졌어.

Minsu: 그래서 그가 무엇을 했어?

Jane: 첫째로, 그는 학교를 둘러 봤어. 그리고 나서, 몇몇의 용의자를 만나서 질문을 했지. 마침내, 그는 도둑을 찾았어. 도둑은....

Minsu: 안 돼, 말하지 마! 내가 나중에 볼 거야.

Emily: 준수야, 수수께끼 하나 풀어볼래?

Junsu: 물론이지, 뭔데?

Emily: 한 농부가 있어. 먼저 농부는 여우, 오리, 콩 자루를 하나씩 사. 그리고 나서, 농부는 강을 건너야 해.

Junsu: 뭐가 문제인데?

Emily: 보트는 단지 농부와 한 가지만 더 옮길 수 있어.

Junsu: 농부가 한 번에 오직 한 가지만 옮길 수 있다는 말이니?

Emily: 응. 또한 만약 농부가 없다면 여우가 오리를 먹거나, 오리가 콩을 먹을 거야. 전부를 강 건너로 안전하게 옮길 방법을 설명할 수 있겠니?

Junsu: 음....

Minjun: 와! 뭔가 정말 좋은 냄새가 나요, 엄마. 뭐예요?

Mom: 우리는 저녁 식사로 타코를 먹을 거야. 맘껏 먹으렴.

Minjun: 타코 만드는 법을 설명해 주실 수 있어요?

Mom: 먼저, 토르티야를 채소와 코기로 채워. 그 다음, 위에 약간의 소스를 추가하렴.

Minjun: 맛있을 것 같아요!

Mom: 치즈 좀 줄까?

Minjun: 아뇨, 괜찮아요.

01 다음 대화가 자연스럽게 이어지도록 주어진 문장을 알맞게 배열하시오.

> (A) Sure, what is it, Jimin?
> (B) That sounds fun.
> (C) It's like a soccer game but the players are dragons and seahorses. You need to use these buttons to play.
> (D) Do you want to play the new game that I bought?

➡ _____

[02~04] 다음 대화를 읽고 물음에 답하시오.

> Tom: Yujin, look at my paper fox.
> Yujin: That's cute. How did you make it?
> Tom: First, fold a paper in half to make a triangle. (A)둘째, fold the top of the triangle to the bottom line. (B)셋째, fold both ends of the bottom line to the top to make ears. Then, turn it over and draw a face.
> Yujin: That sounds easy.

02 위 대화에서 다음의 영영풀이가 가리키는 말을 찾아 쓰시오.

> a shape that is made up of three lines and three angles

➡ _____

03 위 대화에서 (A)와 (B)의 우리말을 영어로 쓰시오.

➡ (A) _____ , (B) _____

04 위 대화의 내용과 일치하지 <u>않는</u> 것은?

① Yujin은 Tom에게 종이 여우 만드는 법에 대해 물어보았다.
② 종이 여우를 만들기 위해 먼저 종이를 반으로 접어서 세모를 만들어야 한다.
③ 두 번째로, 맨 아랫선을 사용하여 세모로 접어야 한다.
④ 세 번째로, 맨 아랫선 양쪽 끝을 위로 접어 귀를 만든다.
⑤ 네 번째로, 귀를 만든 면을 뒤집어 얼굴을 그린다.

[01~02] 다음 대화를 읽고 물음에 답하시오.

Jimin: Do you want to play the new game that I bought?

Brian: Sure, what is it, Jimin?

Jimin: It's like a soccer game but the players are dragons and seahorses. You need to use these buttons to play.

Brian: That sounds fun. (A)Can you explain how to use the buttons?

Jimin: Sure.

01 위 대화의 밑줄 친 (A)와 의도가 다른 것은? (2개)

① Would you show me how to use the buttons?

② Do you understand how to use the buttons?

③ Can you tell me how to use the buttons?

④ Let me know how to use the buttons, please.

⑤ Why don't you explain how to use the buttons?

중요

02 위 대화의 내용과 일치하지 않는 것은?

① Jimin bought the new game.

② Brian wants to play soccer with Jimin on the playground.

③ The game is similar to a soccer game.

④ The dragons and seahorses are the players in the new game.

⑤ The buttons are used to play the game.

[03~04] 다음 대화를 읽고 물음에 답하시오.

Jack: Kelly, here's a riddle. You can see this twice in a week, once in a year, but never in a day. What is this?

Kelly: I have no idea.

Jack: It's the letter "(A)_____."

Kelly: (B)I don't get it. Can you explain why?

Jack: Well, there are two "(A)_____"s in the word "week," one "(A)_____" in the word "year" but no "(A)_____"s in the word "day."

Kelly: Aha! Now I get it.

서답형

03 위 대화의 빈칸 (A)에 공통으로 들어갈 수수께끼의 답을 쓰시오.

➡ _____

04 위 대화의 밑줄 친 (B)와 바꾸어 쓸 수 있는 말은?

① Not at all.

② I don't understand.

③ It doesn't matter.

④ I can't believe this.

⑤ It's not fair.

[05~07] 다음 대화를 읽고 물음에 답하시오.

Tom: Yujin, look at my paper fox.

Yujin: That's cute. How did you make (A)it?

Tom: First, fold a paper in half to make a triangle. Second, fold the top of the triangle to the bottom line. Third, fold both ends of the bottom line to the top to make ears. Then, turn it over and draw a face.

Yujin: That sounds easy.

서답형

05 위 대화에서 밑줄 친 (A)it이 가리키는 것을 찾아 쓰시오.

➡ _____

서답형
06 To make the paper fox, what should Yujin do after making a triangle by folding a paper in half?

➡ _____

서답형
07 What should Yujin make just before drawing a face?

➡ _____

[08~09] 다음 대화를 읽고 물음에 답하시오.

> Jane: Minsu, do you know the TV show about the student detective?
> Minsu: (A) Yes. I love that show, but I didn't see it this week. What was it about?
> Jane: (B) Well, all of the bikes at school disappeared.
> Minsu: (C) So, what did he do?
> Jane: (D) Then, he met some suspects and asked questions. Finally, he found the thief. The thief was ....
> Minsu: (E) No, don't tell me! I'll watch it later.

중요
08 위 대화의 (A)~(E) 중 주어진 문장이 들어가기에 가장 적절한 곳은?

> First, he looked around the school.

① (A) ② (B) ③ (C) ④ (D) ⑤ (E)

09 위 대화를 읽고 대답할 수 <u>없는</u> 것은?

① What show does Minsu like?
② What happened at school?
③ Who was the thief who had stolen all the bikes at school?
④ What did the student detective do to catch the thief?
⑤ Why didn't Minsu want to know who the thief was?

[10~13] 다음 대화를 읽고 물음에 답하시오.

> Minjun: Wow! Something smells really good, Mom. What is it?
> Mom: We're going to have tacos for dinner. (A)Help yourself.
> Minjun: (B)<u>타코 만드는 법을 설명해 주실 수 있어요?</u>
> Mom: First, fill your tortilla (a)____ vegetables and meat. Then, add some sauce on the top.
> Minjun: Sounds (b)_____!
> Mom: (C)<u>Would you like some cheese?</u>
> Minjun: No, thanks.

서답형
10 위 대화의 밑줄 친 (A)의 의미를 우리말로 간략히 쓰시오.

➡ _____

서답형
11 위 대화의 밑줄 친 (B)의 우리말을 〈보기〉에 주어진 단어를 배열하여 완성하시오.

> ┤ 보기 ├
> make / how / a taco / can / to / you / explain

➡ _____

12 위 대화의 밑줄 친 (C)와 바꾸어 쓸 수 있는 것은?

① Do you want some cheese?
② Do you like cheese?
③ Have you tried some cheese?
④ Do you know some cheese?
⑤ Do you mind if I have some cheese?

서답형
13 위 대화의 빈칸 (a)에는 알맞은 전치사를, (b)에는 대화의 흐름에 어울리는 d로 시작되는 단어를 쓰시오.

➡ (a)_____, (b) _____

Conversation 서술형 시험대비

[01~04] 다음 대화를 읽고 물음에 답하시오.

Emily: Junsu, do you want to solve a riddle?

Junsu: Sure, what is it?

Emily: There is a farmer. First, the farmer buys a fox, a duck, and a bag of beans. Then, the farmer needs to cross a river.

Junsu: What's the problem?

Emily: The boat can only hold the farmer and one more thing.

Junsu: Are you saying that the farmer can take only one thing at a time?

Emily: Yes. Also, the fox will eat the duck or the duck will eat the beans if the farmer isn't there. Can you explain (A)옮길 방법 everything across the river safely?

Junsu: Hmm ....

01 What did the farmer buy before crossing the river?

➡ _____

02 How many things could the farmer load on the boat at a time?

➡ _____

03 What will happen to the fox and the duck if the farmer isn't there?

➡ _____

04 밑줄 친 우리말 (A)를 move를 이용하여 3 단어의 영어로 쓰시오.

➡ _____

05 다음 대화가 자연스럽게 이어지도록 순서대로 배열하시오.

(A) Can you explain how to make a taco?

(B) We're going to have tacos for dinner. Help yourself.

(C) First, fill your tortilla with vegetables and meat. Then, add some sauce on the top.

(D) Wow! Something smells really good, Mom. What is it?

➡ _____

06 다음 대화를 읽고 대화의 내용과 일치하도록 빈칸 (A)~(C)를 명령문 형태로 완성하시오.

Tom: Yujin, look at my paper fox.

Yujin: That's cute. How did you make it?

Tom: First, fold a paper in half to make a triangle. Second, fold the top of the triangle to the bottom line. Third, fold both ends of the bottom line to the top to make ears. Then, turn it over and draw a face.

Yujin: That sounds easy.

⬇

How to make a paper fox
Fold a paper in half to make a triangle.
(A) _____
(B) _____
(C) _____

Grammar

1. 수동태

> The author **wrote** many books. 그 작가는 많은 책을 썼다. 〈능동태〉
> Many books **were written by** the author. 많은 책이 그 작가에 의해 쓰여졌다. 〈수동태〉

- 수동태는 'be+p.p.+by'의 형태로, 행동의 주체보다는 행동의 대상에 초점을 맞춘다. 'by+행위자'는 동작의 주체가 일반인이거나 막연한 사람일 때, 그리고 동작의 주체가 명확하지 않을 때 생략한다.
  - Jerry **was taken** to the hospital **by** Tom. Jerry는 Tom에 의해 병원으로 데려가졌다.
  - Nelson **is loved by** many people. Nelson은 많은 사람들에게 사랑받는다.
  - All the flowers **were planted** yesterday. 어제 모든 꽃들이 심어졌다.

- 4형식 문장의 수동태는 두 가지 형태를 갖는다. 직접목적어를 주어로 한 수동태에서는 간접목적어에 특정한 전치사를 쓴다. 전치사 to를 쓰는 동사는 'give, tell, teach, show, bring' 등이고, 전치사 for를 쓰는 동사는 'buy, make, cook, get' 등이며, 전치사 of를 쓰는 동사는 'ask'가 있다.
  - A picture **was given to** me. 사진 한 장이 내게 주어졌다.
  - A chicken soup **was cooked for** Jimmy. Jimmy를 위해 닭고기 수프가 요리되었다.

- 5형식 문장의 목적격 보어가 원형부정사인 경우, 수동태 문장에서는 to부정사로 바뀐다. 그 외에는 모든 목적격 보어를 그대로 쓸 수 있다.
  - Mom **allowed** me **to hang** out with my friends. 엄마는 내가 친구들과 놀도록 허락하셨다.
    (= I **was allowed to hang** out with my friends by Mom.)
  - He **made** me **do** the job. 그는 내가 그 일을 하게 했다.
    (= I **was made to do** the job by him.)

- by 이외의 전치사를 사용하는 수동태에 유의한다.
  - Jane **is interested in** playing tennis. Jane은 테니스를 치는 것에 흥미가 있다.
  - Cheese **is made from** milk. 치즈는 우유로 만들어진다.
  - Katherine **was surprised at** the news. Katherine은 그 소식을 듣고 놀랐다.

핵심 Check

1. 다음 우리말과 같도록 빈칸에 알맞은 말을 쓰시오.
   (1) 우리는 그 벽을 칠했다.
      ➡ The wall _____ _____ _____ us.
   (2) 나는 그에게서 영어를 배웠다.
      ➡ I _____ _____ English by him.

2 조동사의 수동태

> • We **can delay** the plan. 우리는 그 계획을 연기할 수 있다. 〈능동태〉
> • The plan **can be delayed**. 그 계획은 연기될 수 있다. 〈수동태〉

■ 조동사의 수동태는 '조동사+be+p.p.+by ~'의 형태로, 수동태 구문 앞에 조동사를 넣어 사용한다.

- A pizza **will be delivered**. 피자가 배달될 것이다.

- Many messages **must be deleted**. 많은 메시지들이 지워져야 한다.

- Any puzzle **can be solved** by Jason. 어떠한 퍼즐이든 Jason에 의해 해결될 수 있어.

■ 조동사 수동태의 부정문은 조동사 뒤에 not을 붙여 '주어+조동사+not+be+p.p.(+by 행위자)'를 쓴다. 의문문은 '조동사+주어+be+p.p.(+by 행위자)?' 형태로 쓴다.

- The information **will not be provided**. 그 정보는 제공되지 않을 것입니다.

- It **cannot be completed** in an ordinary way. 그것은 평범한 방법으로 완성될 수 없다.

- **Will** the bike **be bought** by Jerry? Jerry가 그 자전거를 살까?

- **Can** the book **be borrowed** by any student? 어떤 학생이건 그 책을 빌릴 수 있나요?

- **Should** the car **be parked** by me? 내가 그 차를 주차해야만 하나요?

핵심 Check

2. 다음 우리말을 능동태와 수동태로 쓰시오.

(1) 나는 그 방을 청소할 거야.

➡ I _____.

➡ The room _____.

(2) 우리는 우리의 숙제를 해야만 한다.

➡ We _____.

➡ Our homework _____.

(3) 그가 그녀를 도와 줄 거야.

➡ He _____.

➡ She _____.

01 다음 문장에서 어법상 <u>어색한</u> 부분을 바르게 고치시오.

(1) My sweater made in England.

_____ ➡ _____

(2) The building will complete next month.

_____ ➡ _____

(3) Careless driving is caused many accidents.

_____ ➡ _____

(4) The window can't open by me.

_____ ➡ _____

02 주어진 동사를 어법에 맞게 빈칸에 쓰시오.

(1) The car _____ last weekend. (steal)
(2) The letter should _____ by this Friday. (send)
(3) Hundreds of people _____ the place every day. (visit)
(4) The Olympic Games _____ every four years. (hold)
(5) Karl _____ as a great teacher now. (look up to)
(6) The children will _____ with toys. (play)
(7) Badminton can _____ by two or four people. (play)

03 주어진 단어를 바르게 배열하여 다음 우리말을 영어로 쓰시오. 필요하다면 단어를 변형하거나 추가하시오.

(1) 그 교실은 매일 청소된다. (clean / every day / the classroom)
➡ _____

(2) 이 건물은 언제 지어졌니? (when / build / this building / was)
➡ _____

(3) 우리는 그에게서 표를 받지 못했다. (tickets / give / were / we / not / him / by)
➡ _____

(4) 이것은 오늘 밤이 되기 전에 되어져야만 해. (tonight / this / do / must / before)
➡ _____

(5) 그 문은 10분 후에 닫힐 겁니다. (10 minutes / the door / close / will / in)
➡ _____

01 다음 괄호 안의 동사의 알맞은 형태를 고르시오.

> Two people (injure) in the accident yesterday.

① injure
② injured
③ is injured
④ was injured
⑤ were injured

02 다음 빈칸에 들어갈 말로 가장 적절한 것은?

> Meat _____ in a refrigerator, or it will spoil.

① was kept
② keeps
③ kept
④ must be kept
⑤ must keep

03 주어진 문장과 같은 의미의 문장은?

> You should return these books by next Wednesday.

① You return these books by next Wednesday.
② These books should return by next Wednesday.
③ These books should be returned by you by next Wednesday.
④ Next Wednesday is returned by you these books.
⑤ These books are going to be returned by you by next Wednesday.

04 다음 두 문장이 같은 의미가 되도록 빈칸에 알맞은 말을 쓰시오.

> The noise did not wake me up.
> = I _____ by the noise.

05 다음 중 우리말을 영어로 바르게 옮기지 <u>않은</u> 것은?

① 그 사진은 내 남동생이 찍은 거야.
　→ The picture was taken by my brother.
② 그 나무를 너의 부모님이 심으셨니?
　→ Was the tree planted by your parents?
③ 나는 아침마다 오렌지 주스를 마셔.
　→ I drink orange juice every morning.
④ 우리는 그 노래를 불렀다.
　→ The song sang by us.
⑤ 그가 상자를 옮길 거야.
　→ The box will be moved by him.

06 다음 빈칸에 들어갈 말이 바르게 짝지어진 것은?

> My car _____ last month, but the next day it _____ by the police.

① is lost – is found
② lost – found
③ was lost – was found
④ was lost – was founded
⑤ was lost – will be found

07 다음 중 밑줄 친 부분을 생략할 수 <u>없는</u> 것은?

① The moon can be seen <u>by us</u> at night.
② Lots of bikes are ridden <u>by people</u> in China.
③ My pencil case was stolen <u>by someone</u>.
④ BTS is loved <u>by people</u> all over the world.
⑤ The vase was broken <u>by Thomson</u>.

서답형

08 주어진 문장을 수동태로 쓰시오.

> She will cook the fish.

➡ _____

09 다음 빈칸에 들어갈 말로 가장 적절한 것은?

> The hospital was _____ down for a day.

① shutting　　② shutted　　③ shut
④ shuted　　⑤ shutten

서답형

10 주어진 어구를 바르게 배열하여 다음 우리말을 영어로 쓰시오. 필요하다면 단어를 변형하시오.

> 그 편지가 올바른 주소로 보내질까?
> (the right address / the letter / send / will / to / be)

➡ _____

11 다음 중 빈칸에 들어갈 단어 play의 형태가 다른 하나는?

① The game is _____ on a court.
② Boys are _____ on the playground.
③ The role is _____ by a British actor.
④ The audio is _____ from the beginning.
⑤ A violin is _____ with a bow.

서답형

12 주어진 단어를 활용하여 다음 우리말을 영어로 쓰시오.

> 너희들은 그 선생님에게 벌 받을 거야.
> (punish)

➡ _____

13 다음 우리말을 영어로 바르게 옮긴 것은?

> Julia의 친구들은 그녀에 대해 좋게 말한다.

① Julia's friends speak well with her.
② Julia is spoken well with her friends.
③ Julia's friends are spoken well of by her.
④ Julia is spoken well of by her friends.
⑤ Julia is talked about by her friends.

14 다음 빈칸에 들어갈 말로 가장 적절한 것은?

> It was cold, so the heater was turned _____ Jason.

① on at　　② at by　　③ on by
④ off by　　⑤ into by

15 다음 중 어법상 바르지 않은 것은?

① The woman typed all the reports.
② My father was born in Canada.
③ A book must be written by him by tomorrow.
④ The glass was filled with chocolate milk.
⑤ James is interested by taking pictures.

16 다음 중 수동태로의 전환이 바르지 않은 것은?

① Someone ate my sandwich.
　→ My sandwich was eaten by someone.
② Mom made me a candy bar.
　→ A candy bar was made for me by Mom.
③ Ms. Han runs a restaurant.
　→ A restaurant is ran by Ms. Han.
④ A stranger spoke to me.
　→ I was spoken to by a stranger.
⑤ Melisa prepared an interview.
　→ An interview was prepared by Melisa.

17 다음 대화의 빈칸에 알맞은 말을 쓰시오.

> A: Who takes care of your children while you are here?
> B: My children _____ my mother.

18 다음 빈칸에 공통으로 들어갈 말로 가장 적절한 것은?

> • The restaurant is crowded _____ many people.
> • Are you satisfied _____ your birthday present?

① at ② by ③ from
④ about ⑤ with

19 주어진 문장을 수동태로 바르게 전환하시오.

> They sell stamps in a post office.

➡ _____

20 다음 우리말을 수동태를 활용하여 영어로 쓸 때 다섯 번째로 오는 단어는?

> 많은 사람들이 이 공연을 볼 거야.

➡ _____

21 다음 문장을 능동태는 수동태로, 수동태는 능동태로 전환하시오.

(1) I saw him dancing.

➡ _____

(2) Jack will buy the cake.

➡ _____

(3) Did you drink the juice?

➡ _____

22 다음 중 어법상 바르지 <u>않은</u> 것은?

① The car was repaired by a man.
② A terrible accident was happened last night.
③ The illness was cured by a doctor.
④ A boy was hit by a truck.
⑤ The package was delivered by a young girl.

23 다음 중 빈칸에 들어갈 말로 가장 적절한 것은?

> Do your brothers help you?
> = _____ your brothers?

① Do you help ② Are you helping
③ Were you helped ④ Are you helped
⑤ Are you helped by

24 다음 빈칸에 공통으로 들어갈 말로 가장 적절한 것은?

> • Were the pants bought _____ you?
> • Was the chocolate made _____ his mother?

① for ② to ③ about
④ of ⑤ in

25 주어진 문장과 같은 의미가 되도록 빈칸에 알맞은 말을 쓰시오.

> I will take care of your cats.
> = Your cats _____.

26 주어진 단어를 활용하여 다음 우리말을 다섯 단어의 영어 문장으로 쓰시오.

> 이 다리는 수리되어야만 해. (repair)

➡ _____

01 다음 문장을 수동태로 쓰시오.

We will not give up the project.

➡ _____

02 다음 문장에서 어법상 틀린 것을 바르게 고쳐 올바른 문장으로 다시 쓰시오. 중요

My parents will be used the treadmill.

➡ _____

03 다음 대화의 빈칸에 알맞은 말을 쓰시오.

A: How many solutions will they offer?
B: As far as I know, three solutions _____ _____ _____ by them.

04 같은 의미의 문장이 되도록 빈칸에 알맞은 말을 쓰시오.

David put on the pants.
= The pants _____.

05 괄호 안에 주어진 단어를 어법에 맞게 고쳐 쓰시오. 중요

A: You are going to throw a party for Jenny, right?
B: Yes. A cake will (make) by me, some balloons will (buy) by James, some friends will (invite).

➡ _____

06 주어진 동사를 어법과 내용에 맞게 빈칸에 쓰시오. 중요

arrest / cut / serve / laugh at / eat

(1) Julia _____ by her classmates. She was really embarrassed.
(2) Don't worry. I'm sure that the suspect will _____ by the police.
(3) My dog _____ all the pizza on the table last night.
(4) The news that tuition fees will _____ in half makes me happy.
(5) The cook _____ customers himself. So they feel satisfied.

07 다음 대화의 빈칸에 알맞은 말을 쓰시오.

A: Who will write a script for our play?
B: A script _____ by Colin. He is good at writing.

08 주어진 단어를 활용하여 다음 우리말을 영어로 쓰시오. 중요

이 집은 언제 지어졌니? (build)

➡ _____

09 같은 의미의 문장이 되도록 빈칸에 알맞은 말을 쓰시오.

Someone should tell James the news
= James _____.

10 다음 각 문장을 능동태는 수동태로, 수동태는 능동태로 전환하시오.

(1) The company may offer Chris a job.

➡ _____

➡ _____

(2) You must send this letter before June 1.

➡ _____

(3) The electric light bulb was invented by Thomas Edison in 1879.

➡ _____

(4) I will divide the class into two sections.

➡ _____

(5) Rice is grown in many countries by people.

➡ _____

11 두 문장이 같은 의미가 되도록 빈칸에 알맞은 말을 쓰시오.

We must wear seat belts during takeoff and landing.
= Seat belts _____ during takeoff and landing.

12 주어진 단어를 활용하여 대화를 완성하시오.

A: Andy, your chores (should, finish) by the time I get home.
B: Don't worry, Dad. I'll do everything you told me to do.

➡ _____

13 주어진 단어를 어법에 맞게 빈칸에 쓰시오.

Jim is wearing a gold band on his fourth finger. He (marry).

➡ _____

14 주어진 단어를 어법에 맞게 빈칸에 쓰시오.

introduce / originate / grow

Bananas _____ in Asia but now _____ _____ by people all around the world. They _____ to the Americas in 1516.

15 주어진 어휘를 활용하여 문장을 완성하시오.

When we are in the middle school, we _____ (require / to wear uniforms).

➡ _____

16 같은 의미의 문장이 되도록 빈칸에 알맞은 말을 쓰시오.

Timmy dropped a plate after dinner last night.
= A plate _____.

17 다음 문장을 수동태로 전환하시오.

(1) You must not bring food into the lab.

➡ _____

(2) You should turn off cell phones.

➡ _____

(3) We cannot explain UFO sightings.

➡ _____

The Great Escape

Welcome to the Escape Tower. You will enter the first room in our
〜에 들어가다(타동사)

tower. You need to solve some riddles to escape. Clues can be found
〜해야 한다(= have to. should) 〜하기 위해서(to부정사의 부사적 용법) 조동사의 수동태는 '조동사+be+p.p.' 형태임

somewhere inside the room. So, are you ready to think like Sherlock
〜처럼 생각하다

Holmes?

Room #1

Mr. Doodle was hit by a car on Sunday afternoon. Luckily, he wasn't
〜에 의해 …되다   문장 수식 부사: 운 좋게도

badly hurt, but he didn't see the driver. Three suspects were questioned
(= A police officer questioned three suspects.)

by a police officer. Ms. A said she was reading a book at the time of

the accident. Mr. B said he was walking his dog. Ms. C said she was
        said (that): 명사절 접속사 that 생략

making breakfast. Who hit Mr. Doodle? Can you explain why? Do you

have the answer? Write it down. Then you can move to the next room.
       down이 부사이고 목적어가 인칭대명사이므로 it이 동사와 부사 사이에 위치함

Clue The accident happened in the afternoon.
                    자동사(수동태 불가능)

Congratulations! You made it to the second room. However, the

second room is much harder to escape than the first one. Good luck!
        비교급 강조 부사 '훨씬'(= still. far. even. a lot)   =room

---

escape: 탈출하다	
riddle: 수수께끼	
clue: 단서	
somewhere: 어딘가에	
be ready to: 〜할 준비가 되어 있다	
hurt: 다친	
suspect: 용의자	
question: 심문하다	
at the time of: 〜이 일어나던 때에	
accident: 사고	
write down: 적다	
make it to: 〜에 이르는 데 성공하다	

📎 확인문제

● 다음 문장이 본문의 내용과 일치하면 T, 일치하지 <u>않으면</u> F를 쓰시오.

1 You should solve some riddles to escape from the tower. ☐

2 Clues will be given to you by the tower manager. ☐

3 The car accident happened on Saturday afternoon. ☐

4 If you write down the answer to the first riddle, you can escape from the tower. ☐

Room #2

Jay gets an email from his favorite clothing store. The title reads "You
won our Lucky Day event!" Jay is surprised. He quickly opens it.

JayJr@kmail.com

You won our 'Lucky Day' event!

Congratulations!

You have won a special prize. During our Lucky Day event, you
can choose any seven items from our store for free! Come to our store
on November 31. We can't wait to see you.

Truly yours,

Kay Brown

However, Jay thinks that the event isn't real and deletes the
email. Can you explain why?

Clue There are usually 30 or 31 days in a month.
Do you have the answer? Write it down and then you are free to go!

title: 제목
win: 얻다, 이기다
event: 행사, 이벤트
for free: 무료로
delete: 삭제하다
real: 진실한, 사실의
write down: ~을 적다

확인문제

● 다음 문장이 본문의 내용과 일치하면 T, 일치하지 않으면 F를 쓰시오.

1 Jay gets many emails from his favorite clothing store. ☐

2 Jay is surprised at the title of the email. ☐

3 Seven items can be chosen by Jay on November 30. ☐

4 Jay wants to meet Kay Brown. ☐

5 Jay thinks the event is not true. ☐

6 Jay deletes the email before reading it. ☐

우리말을 참고하여 빈칸에 알맞은 말을 쓰시오.

The Great Escape

1 Welcome _____ the Escape Tower.

2 You will _____ _____ _____ in our tower.

3 You need _____ _____ _____ _____ to escape.

4 Clues can _____ _____ somewhere _____ the room.

5 So, _____ you ready _____ _____ like Sherlock Holmes?

Room # 1

6 Mr. Doodle _____ _____ _____ a car _____ Sunday afternoon.

7 _____, he wasn't _____ _____, but he didn't _____ the driver.

8 Three suspects _____ _____ _____ a police officer.

9 Ms. A said she was _____ _____ _____ at the time of _____ _____.

10 Mr. B said he _____ _____ his dog.

11 Ms. C said she _____ _____ _____.

12 _____ _____ Mr. Doodle? Can you _____ why?

13 Do you have the answer? _____ _____ _____.

14 Then you can _____ _____ the next room.

15 **Clue** The accident _____ _____ the afternoon.

16 Congratulations! You _____ _____ _____ the second room.

대탈출

1 '탈출탑'에 오신 것을 환영합니다.

2 당신은 저희 탑의 첫 번째 방에 들어갈 것입니다.

3 당신은 탈출하기 위하여 몇 개의 수수께끼를 풀어야 합니다.

4 단서들은 방 어딘가에서 발견될 수 있습니다.

5 그러면 당신은 셜록 홈스처럼 생각할 준비가 되었나요?

방 # 1

6 Doodle씨는 일요일 오후에 차에 치였습니다.

7 다행히 그는 심하게 다치지 않았으나 그는 운전자를 보지 못했습니다.

8 세 명의 용의자들이 경찰에게 심문을 받았습니다.

9 A씨는 사고가 일어난 시간에 책을 읽고 있었다고 말했습니다.

10 B씨는 그의 개를 산책시키고 있었다고 말했습니다.

11 C씨는 아침을 만들고 있었다고 말했습니다.

12 누가 Doodle씨를 치었을까요? 왜 그런지 설명할 수 있나요?

13 답을 가지고 있나요? 적어 보세요.

14 그런 다음, 당신은 다음 방으로 갈 수 있습니다.

15 단서: 사건은 오후에 일어났습니다.

16 축하합니다! 당신은 두 번째 방에 오는 데 성공하셨습니다.

17 However, the second room is _____ _____ _____

_____ _____ the first one. Good luck!

Room #2

18 Jay _____ an email _____ his favorite clothing store.

19 The title _____ "You _____ our Lucky Day event!"

20 Jay is _____. He quickly opens it.

21 JayJr@kmail.com

You _____ our 'Lucky Day' event!

22 _____! You _____ _____ a special prize.

23 _____ our Lucky Day event, you can _____ any seven items

_____ our store _____ _____!

24 Come _____ our store _____ November 31.

25 We can't _____ _____ _____ you.

26 _____ _____, Kay Brown

27 _____, Jay thinks that the event _____ _____ and

_____ the email.

28 _____ you explain _____?

29 **Clue** _____ 30 or 31 _____ in a month.

30 Do you _____ _____ _____?

31 Write _____ down and then you _____ _____ _____

_____!

17 그러나 두 번째 방은 첫 번째 방
보다 탈출하기 훨씬 더 어렵습
니다. 행운을 빕니다!

방 # 2

18 Jay는 그가 가장 좋아하는 옷
가게로부터 이메일을 받습니다.

19 제목은 "당신은 '행운의 날' 행
사에 당첨되었습니다!"라고 적
혀 있습니다.

20 Jay는 놀랍니다. 그는 재빨리
그것을 엽니다.

21 JayJr@kmail.com
당신은 우리의 '행운의 날' 행사
에 당첨되었습니다!

22 축하합니다! 당신은 특별한 상
품을 받게 되었습니다.

23 '행운의 날' 행사 동안, 당신은
우리 가게에서 일곱 가지 상품
을 아무거나 무료로 선택할 수
있습니다!

24 11월 31일에 우리 가게로 오
세요.

25 우리는 몹시 당신을 보기를 기
대합니다.

26 안녕히 계십시오, Kay Brown

27 그러나 Jay는 그 행사가 사실이
아니라고 생각하고 이메일을 삭
제합니다.

28 왜 그런지 설명할 수 있나요?

29 단서: 한 달은 주로 30일 또는
31일이 있습니다.

30 답을 가지고 계신가요?

31 그것을 적으면, 당신은 자유롭
게 가실 수 있습니다!

• 우리말을 참고하여 본문을 영작하시오.

The Great Escape

1 ▶ '탈출 탑'에 오신 것을 환영합니다.

➡ _____

2 ▶ 당신은 저희 탑의 첫 번째 방에 들어갈 것입니다.

➡ _____

3 ▶ 당신은 탈출하기 위하여 몇 개의 수수께끼를 풀어야 합니다.

➡ _____

4 ▶ 단서들은 방 어딘가에서 발견될 수 있습니다.

➡ _____

5 ▶ 그러면 당신은 셜록 홈스처럼 생각할 준비가 되었나요?

➡ _____

Room #1

6 ▶ Doodle씨는 일요일 오후에 차에 치였습니다.

➡ _____

7 ▶ 다행히 그는 심하게 다치지 않았으나 그는 운전자를 보지 못했습니다.

➡ _____

8 ▶ 세 명의 용의자들이 경찰에게 심문을 받았습니다.

➡ _____

9 ▶ A씨는 사고가 일어난 시간에 책을 읽고 있었다고 말했습니다.

➡ _____

10 ▶ B씨는 그의 개를 산책시키고 있었다고 말했습니다.

➡ _____

11 ▶ C씨는 아침을 만들고 있었다고 말했습니다.

➡ _____

12 ▶ 누가 Doodle씨를 치었을까요? 왜 그런지 설명할 수 있나요?

➡ _____

13 ▶ 답을 가지고 있나요? 적어 보세요.

➡ _____

14 ▶ 그런 다음, 당신은 다음 방으로 갈 수 있습니다.

➡ _____

15 ▶ 단서: 사건은 오후에 일어났습니다.

➡ _____

16 ▶ 축하합니다! 당신은 두 번째 방에 오는 데 성공하셨습니다.

➡ _____

17 그러나 두 번째 방은 첫 번째 방보다 탈출하기 훨씬 더 어렵습니다. 행운을 빕니다!

➡ _____

Room #2

18 Jay는 그가 가장 좋아하는 옷 가게로부터 이메일을 받습니다.

➡ _____

19 제목은 "당신은 '행운의 날' 행사에 당첨되었습니다!"라고 적혀 있습니다.

➡ _____

20 Jay는 놀랍니다. 그는 재빨리 그것을 엽니다.

➡ _____

21 JayJr@kmail.com
당신은 우리의 '행운의 날' 행사에 당첨되었습니다!

➡ JayJr@kmail.com _____

22 축하합니다! 당신은 특별한 상품을 받게 되었습니다.

➡ _____

23 '행운의 날' 행사 동안, 당신은 우리 가게에서 일곱 가지 상품을 아무거나 공짜로 선택할 수 있습니다!

➡ _____

24 11월 31일에 우리 가게로 오세요.

➡ _____

25 우리는 몹시 당신을 보기를 기대합니다.

➡ _____

26 안녕히 계십시오, Kay Brown

➡ _____

27 그러나 Jay는 그 행사가 사실이 아니라고 생각하고 이메일을 삭제합니다.

➡ _____

28 왜 그런지 설명할 수 있나요?

➡ _____

29 단서: 한 달은 주로 30일 또는 31일이 있습니다.

➡ _____

30 답을 가지고 계신가요?

➡ _____

31 그것을 적으면, 당신은 자유롭게 가실 수 있습니다!

➡ _____

[01~03] 다음 글을 읽고 물음에 답하시오.

Welcome to the Escape Tower. You will enter the first room in our tower. You need (A)to solve some riddles to escape. Clues can be found somewhere inside the room. So, are you ready to think like Sherlock Holmes?

01 다음과 같이 풀이되는 단어를 위 글에서 찾아 쓰시오.

something that helps a person find something, understand something, or solve a mystery or puzzle

➡ _____

02 다음 중 위 글의 내용과 일치하지 <u>않는</u> 것은?

① There are some riddles to solve.
② In order to escape, you need to solve some riddles.
③ It is necessary to find clues inside the room.
④ Clues are hidden inside the room.
⑤ Sherlock Holmes used to think many things in the tower.

03 다음 중 밑줄 친 (A)와 쓰임이 같은 것은?

① Is there anything <u>to eat</u>?
② She hopes <u>to meet</u> you someday.
③ Bradley woke up early not <u>to be</u> late.
④ Kathy is happy <u>to see</u> him.
⑤ He must be generous <u>to buy</u> you shoes.

[04~08] 다음 글을 읽고 물음에 답하시오.

Room #1
Mr. Doodle (A)_____ by a car on Sunday afternoon. ①<u>Unfortunately</u>, he wasn't badly hurt, but he didn't see the driver. Three suspects were questioned by ②<u>a police officer</u>. Ms. A said she was reading a book at the time of the accident. Mr. B said he was walking his dog. Ms. C said she was making breakfast. ③<u>Who</u> hit Mr. Doodle? Can you explain why? Do you have the answer? Write it down. Then you can ④<u>move</u> to the next room.
Clue: The accident happened ⑤<u>in the afternoon</u>.
Congratulations! You made it to the second room. However, the second room is much harder to escape than the first one. Good luck!

04 다음 중 빈칸 (A)에 들어갈 말로 가장 적절한 것은?

① is hit   ② hit   ③ hits
④ was hit   ⑤ can be hit

05 다음 중 위 글을 읽고 답할 수 <u>없는</u> 것은?

① When was Mr. Doodle hit by a car?
② Why didn't Mr. Doodle see the driver?
③ What was Ms. A doing on Sunday afternoon?
④ What was Mr. B doing at the time of the accident?
⑤ How many people were questioned by a police officer?

서답형

06 ①~⑤ 중 글의 흐름상 어색한 것은?

①   ②   ③   ④   ⑤

서답형

07 How many suspects are there? Answer in English with a full sentence.

➡ _____

서답형

08 다음 물음에 완전한 문장의 영어로 답하시오.

> Q: After you escape from the first room, where do you have to go?

➡ _____

[09~14] 다음 글을 읽고 물음에 답하시오.

Room #2

Jay gets an email from his favorite clothing store. The title reads "You won our Lucky Day event!" Jay (A)_____(surprise). He quickly opens (B)it.

JayJr@kmail.com

You won our 'Lucky Day' event!

Congratulations!

You have won a special prize. During our Lucky Day event, you can choose any seven items from our store for free! Come to our store (C)_____ November 31. We can't wait to see you.

Truly yours,
Kay Brown

However, Jay thinks (D)that the event isn't real and deletes the email. Can you explain why?

Clue: There are usually 30 or 31 days in a month.

서답형

09 빈칸 (A)에 괄호 안에 주어진 동사를 어법에 맞게 쓰시오.

➡ _____

서답형

10 밑줄 친 (B)가 가리키는 것을 위 글에서 찾아 쓰시오.

➡ _____

11 다음 중 빈칸 (C)에 들어갈 말로 가장 적절한 것은?

① in   ② at   ③ on   ④ by   ⑤ to

12 다음 중 밑줄 친 (D)와 쓰임이 다른 하나는?

① Did you just say that she loves me?
② The fact that you stole it doesn't change.
③ Jason knew that they couldn't arrive in time.
④ Where is the box that came yesterday?
⑤ It is impossible that they come together.

서답형

13 According to the email, what can Jay do during their Lucky Day event? Answer in English with eleven words.

➡ _____

14 다음 중 위 글의 내용과 일치하지 않는 것은?

① Jay's favorite clothing store sent an email to Jay.
② The email that the clothing store sent had no title.
③ The person who sent Jay an email is Kay Brown.
④ Jay didn't believe what the email said.
⑤ The email was deleted by Jay.

[15~22] 다음 글을 읽고 물음에 답하시오.

Welcome to the Escape Tower. You will enter the first room in our tower. You need to solve some riddles to escape. ⓐClues can be found somewhere inside the room. So, are you ready to think like Sherlock Holmes?

Room #1

Mr. Doodle was hit by a car on Sunday afternoon. Luckily, he wasn't badly hurt, but he didn't see the driver. Three suspects were questioned by a police officer. Ms. A said she was reading a book ⓑ_____ the time of the accident. Mr. B said he was walking his dog. Ms. C said she (A)[was making / was made] breakfast. Who hit Mr. Doodle? Can you explain why? Do you have the answer? Write (B)[it / them] down. Then you can move to the next room.

Clue: The accident (C)[happened / was happened] in the afternoon.

15 밑줄 친 ⓐ와 같은 의미의 문장이 되도록 빈칸에 알맞은 말을 쓰시오.

You _____ .

16 다음 중 빈칸 ⓑ에 들어갈 말로 가장 적절한 것은?

① on   ② at   ③ to   ④ in   ⑤ by

17 (A)~(C)에서 어법상 옳은 것끼리 바르게 짝지어진 것은?

① was making – it – happened
② was making – them – happened
③ was making – it – was happened
④ was made – them – happened
⑤ was made – them – was happened

18 위 글의 내용에 맞게 빈칸에 알맞은 말을 쓰시오.

Q: Did Mr. Doodle see the driver?
A: No. The driver _____ Mr. Doodle.

19 What was Ms. A doing when Mr. Doodle was hit by a car? Answer in English with a full sentence.

➡ _____

_____

20 다음 중 위 글의 내용과 일치하지 <u>않는</u> 것은?

① Solving some riddles lets you get away from the room.
② A car hit Mr. Doodle on Sunday.
③ Mr. Doodle was hardly hurt.
④ According to Ms. C, she was making breakfast when Mr. Doodle was hit by a car.
⑤ Mr. B has a dog.

21 위 글의 내용에 맞게 빈칸에 알맞은 말을 쓰시오.

If the right answer _____ , you can move to the next room.

22 다음과 같이 풀이되는 단어를 위 글에서 찾아 쓰시오.

a sudden event that is not planned and that causes damage or injury

➡ _____

[23~30] 다음 글을 읽고 물음에 답하시오.

Congratulations! You made it to the second room. (A)_____, the second room is much harder to escape than the first one. Good luck!

Room #2

Jay gets an email (B)_____ his favorite clothing store. The title reads "You won our Lucky Day event!" Jay is surprised. He quickly opens it.

JayJr@kmail.com

You won our 'Lucky Day' event!

Congratulations!

You have won a special prize. During our Lucky Day event, you can choose any seven items from our store (C)for free! Come to our store on November 31. We can't wait to see you.

Truly yours,

Kay Brown

However, Jay thinks that the event isn't real and deletes the email. Can you explain why?

Clue: There are usually 30 or 31 days in a month.

Do you have the answer? Write it down and then (D)당신은 자유롭게 가실 수 있습니다!

23 다음 중 빈칸 (A)에 들어갈 말로 가장 적절한 것은?

① Therefore ② For example
③ However ④ On the other hand
⑤ As a result

24 다음 중 빈칸 (B)에 들어갈 말로 가장 적절한 것은?

① to ② about ③ in
④ from ⑤ by

25 밑줄 친 (C)의 의미로 가장 적절한 것은?

① freely ② for yourself
③ at no cost ④ with paying money
⑤ for anything

26 주어진 단어를 활용하여 밑줄 친 우리말 (D)를 영어로 쓰시오.

```
free
```

➡ _____

27 글의 내용에 맞게 다음 물음에 대한 대답을 완성하시오.

Q: By whom is the email deleted?
A: It _____.

28 다음 중 위 글을 읽고 답할 수 <u>없는</u> 것은?

① From whom did Jay get an email?
② What is the title of the email?
③ How many items can Jay choose from the store on the event day?
④ What does Jay think about the email?
⑤ When did Jay get the email?

29 글의 내용에 맞게 빈칸에 알맞은 말을 쓰시오.

Q: Why doesn't Jay believe the email?
A: It's because the event is _____ but there are only _____ in November.

30 글의 내용에 맞게 빈칸에 알맞은 말을 세 단어로 쓰시오.

The second room is not as _____ as the first room.

[01~03] 다음 글을 읽고 물음에 답하시오.

Welcome to the Escape Tower. (A)You will enter into the first room in our tower. You need to solve some riddles to escape. You can find clues somewhere inside the room. So, are you ready to think like Sherlock Holmes?

01 What do you need to do to escape from the tower? Answer in English with a full sentence.

➡ _____

02 밑줄 친 (A)에서 틀린 곳을 고쳐 다시 쓰시오.

➡ _____

03 글의 내용에 맞게 빈칸에 알맞은 말을 쓰시오.

In order to _____ from the room, you should think _____.

[04~08] 다음 글을 읽고 물음에 답하시오.

Room #1

(A)Mr. Doodle was hit by a car on Sunday afternoon. Luckily, he wasn't badly hurt, but (B) he didn't see the driver. Three suspects were questioned by a police officer. Ms. A said she was reading a book at the time of the accident. Mr. B said he was walking his dog. Ms. C said she was making breakfast. Who hit Mr. Doodle? Can you explain why? Do you have the answer? Write it down. Then you can move to the next room.

Clue: The accident happened in the afternoon.

Congratulations! You made it to the second room. However, (C)두 번째 방은 첫 번째 방보다 탈출하기가 훨씬 더 어렵습니다. Good luck!

04 밑줄 친 (A)를 능동태로 전환하시오.

➡ _____

05 다음은 밑줄 친 문장 (B)와 같은 의미의 문장이다. 빈칸에 알맞은 말을 쓰시오.

The driver _____.

06 What was the second suspect doing when Mr. Doodle was hit by a car?

➡ _____

07 According to the passage, what happened to Mr. Doodle on Sunday afternoon? Answer in English.

➡ _____

08 주어진 어구를 바르게 배열하여 밑줄 친 우리말 (C)를 영어로 쓰시오.

(the first one / the second room / than / is / harder / escape / much / to)

➡ _____

_____

[09~13] 다음 글을 읽고 물음에 답하시오.

Room #2

Jay gets an email from his favorite clothing store. The title reads "You won our Lucky Day event!" Jay is surprised. (A)He quickly opens it.

JayJr@kmail.com

You won our 'Lucky Day' event!

Congratulations!

You have won a special prize. During our Lucky Day event, you can choose any seven items from our store for free! Come to our store on November 31. We can't wait to see you.

Truly yours,
Kay Brown

However, Jay thinks that the event isn't real and deletes the email. Can you explain why?

Clue: (B)한 달은 주로 30일 또는 31일이 있습니다.

Do you have the answer? Write it down and then you are free to go!

09 다음 빈칸에 알맞은 말을 써서 밑줄 친 (A)와 같은 의미의 문장을 만드시오.

It _____ .

10 주어진 단어를 활용하여 밑줄 친 우리말 (B)를 영어로 쓰시오.

there

➡ _____

11 According to the email, what did Jay win?

➡ _____

12 What does Jay do after reading the email? Answer in English with a full sentence.

➡ _____

13 글의 내용에 맞게 빈칸에 알맞은 말을 쓰시오.

Q: What surprises Jay?
A: He _____ the title of the email.

[14~17] 다음 글을 읽고 물음에 답하시오.

It was last Sunday. Dohun was at home. Suddenly, (A)he heard a sound in the next room. When he went into the room, the window was broken. When he looked outside, Sujin was holding a baseball bat and Ted was throwing a ball to his dog. (B)Who broke the window? How can it be explained?

14 밑줄 친 (A)를 수동태로 전환하시오.

➡ _____

15 When was the window broken? Answer in English with five words.

➡ _____

16 밑줄 친 (B)와 같은 의미의 문장이 되도록 빈칸에 알맞은 말을 쓰시오.

By whom _____ ?

17 What was Sujin holding? Answer in English with a full sentence.

➡ _____

해석

Listen and Speak 1-C

A: Try to solve this riddle.
　try to: ~하려고 노력하다 try ~ing: 시험 삼아 ~해 보다
B: Sure.

A: Four people are under one umbrella, but nobody gets wet.
　　　　　　　　　　　　nobody는 부정대명사로 3인칭 단수 취급하여 동사에 –s가 붙는다.

　Can you explain why?
　　　　　　　　=why nobody gets wet
B: Yes! It's because it's a sunny day!
　　　A가 말한 내용　　비인칭 주어

구문해설　• riddle: 수수께끼　• wet: 젖은　• explain: 설명하다

A: 이 수수께끼를 풀어봐.
B: 그래.
A: 4명의 사람들이 하나의 우산 아래 있는데 아무도 젖지 않아. 이유를 설명할 수 있겠니?
B: 응! 왜냐하면 맑은 날이기 때문이야.

Let's Write

It was last Sunday. Dohun was at home. Suddenly, he heard a
비인칭 주어
sound in the next room. When he went into the room, the
　　　sound를 수식하는 형용사구
window was broken.
　　행위자가 불분명 할 때 'by+행위자' 생략
When he looked outside, Sujin was holding a baseball bat and
　　　　　　　　　　　　　과거진행형
Ted was throwing a ball to his dog. Who broke the window?
　　　　　　　　　　　～에게
How can it be explained?
　　주체가 행위의 대상이 되므로 수동태를 씀

구문해설　• suddenly: 갑자기　• break: ~을 깨뜨리다 (–broke–broken)　• hold: ~을 쥐다, 잡다
　　　　• throw: ~을 던지다　• explain: ~을 설명하다

지난 일요일이었다. 도훈이는 집에 있었다. 갑자기, 그는 옆 방에서 나는 어떤 소리를 들었다. 그가 그 방으로 갔을 때, 창문이 깨져 있었다. 도훈이가 밖을 보았을 때, 수진이는 야구 방망이를 들고 있었고 Ted는 그의 개에게 공을 던지고 있었다. 누가 창문을 깼을까? 그것은 어떻게 설명될 수 있을까?

Culture & Life

This is the famous riddle of the Sphinx. Oedipus needs to solve it to go into
　　　　　　　　　　　　　　　　need to V: V할 필요가 있다　부사적 용법(목적)
Thebes. This is the question that the Sphinx asks him.
　　　　　　　　　　　　목적격 관계대명사
Which creature walks on four legs in the morning, two legs in the afternoon,
의문형용사로 creature 수식
and three legs in the evening?

구문해설　• famous: 유명한　• solve: 해결하다　• question: 질문　• creature: 생명체

이것은 스핑크스의 유명한 수수께끼이다. 오이디푸스는 Thebes에 들어가기 위해 그것을 풀어야 한다. 이것은 스핑크스가 그에게 묻는 질문이다.

어느 생명체가 아침에는 네 다리로 걷고, 오후에는 두 다리로 걷고, 저녁에는 세 다리로 걷는가?

영역별 핵심문제

01 다음 영영풀이가 가리키는 것을 고르시오.

> someone who steals things from another person or place

① detective   ② liar
③ thief   ④ police
⑤ prosecutor

02 다음 중 밑줄 친 부분의 뜻풀이가 바르지 <u>않은</u> 것은?

① She was reading a book at the time of the <u>accident</u>. 사고
② Sujin was holding a baseball <u>bat</u>. 방망이
③ The duck will eat the <u>beans</u>. 콩
④ Do not <u>cross</u> the river by yourself without your parents. 건너다
⑤ Did you watch this week's TV show about the student <u>detective</u>? 회장

03 다음 우리말과 일치하도록 주어진 단어를 사용하여 영작하시오.

(1) 첫 번째, 원을 그리세요. (draw)
➡ _____

(2) 두 번째, 원 안에 별을 놓으세요. (put, inside)
➡ _____

(3) 그리고 나서 원의 맨 위에 삼각형을 놓으세요. (then)
➡ _____

04 다음 문장의 빈칸에 들어갈 말을 〈보기〉에서 골라 쓰시오. 필요하면 어형 변화를 하시오.

> ┤ 보기 ├
> delete / clue / suspect / escape

(1) The thief _____ from the police station last week.
(2) The _____ lied to the police officer.
(3) The detective looked for _____ at the scene.
(4) Don't open emails with strange titles. _____ them at once.

05 다음 우리말에 맞게 빈칸에 알맞은 말을 쓰시오.

(1) 나는 이 도시를 떠날 준비가 되어 있다.
➡ I'm _____ leave this city.
(2) 나는 축제가 일어나던 때에 아팠었다.
➡ I was ill _____ the festival.
(3) 여기에 당신의 주소를 적으세요.
➡ _____ your address here.

06 다음 주어진 문장의 밑줄 친 cross와 같은 의미로 쓰인 것은?

> My parents needed to <u>cross</u> a river.

① I want to <u>cross</u> the road as soon as possible.
② I drew a <u>cross</u> on the map to mark my office.
③ I want to have a <u>cross</u> as a small tattoo on my hand.
④ You can mark it by a <u>cross</u>.
⑤ My mother always keeps her <u>cross</u> necklace.

Conversation

[07~08] 다음 대화를 읽고 물음에 답하시오.

Jimin: Do you want to play the new game ⓐwhat I bought?

Brian: Sure, what is it, Jimin?

Jimin: It's ⓑlike a soccer game but the players are dragons and seahorses. You need to use these buttons ⓒto play.

Brian: That sounds ⓓfun. Can you explain how ⓔto use the buttons?

Jimin: Sure.

07 위 대화의 밑줄 친 ⓐ~ⓔ 중 어법상 어색한 것을 찾아 바르게 고치시오.

➡ _____

08 위 대화를 읽고 대답할 수 <u>없는</u> 것은?

① What are Jimin and Brian going to do?

② What type of game are Jimin and Brian going to play?

③ What role do dragons and seahorses play in the game?

④ Why does Brian need to know how to use the buttons?

⑤ Why did Jimin buy the game similar to a soccer game?

[09~10] 다음 대화를 읽고 물음에 답하시오.

Jack: Kelly, here's a riddle. You can see this twice in a week, once in a year, but never in a day. What is this?

Kelly: (A) I have no idea.

Jack: (B) It's the letter "E."

Kelly: (C) Can you explain why?

Jack: (D) Well, there are two "E"s in the word "week," one "E" in the word "year" but no "E"s in the word "day."

Kelly: (E) Aha! Now I get it.

09 위 대화에서 다음 영영풀이가 나타내는 말을 찾아 쓰시오.

a difficult question that is asked as a game and that has a surprising or funny answer

➡ _____

10 위 대화의 (A)~(E) 중 주어진 문장이 들어가기에 적절한 곳은?

I don't get it.

① (A) ② (B) ③ (C) ④ (D) ⑤ (E)

[11~12] 다음 대화를 읽고 물음에 답하시오.

Tom: Yujin, ⓐlook at my paper fox.

Yujin: That's cute. How did you make it?

Tom: First, fold a paper ⓑin half to make a triangle. Second, fold the top of the triangle to the bottom line. (A)Third, fold both ends of the bottom line to the top ⓒto make ears. Then, ⓓturn it over and ⓔdrawing a face.

Yujin: That sounds easy.

11 위 대화의 ⓐ~ⓔ 중 어법상 어색한 것을 찾아 바르게 고치시오.

➡ _____

12 위 대화의 (A)와 바꾸어 쓸 수 있는 것은?

① Next ② Besides ③ After
④ Before ⑤ Close

[13~14] 다음 대화를 읽고 물음에 답하시오.

Minjun: Wow! Something smells really good, Mom. What is it?

Mom: We're going to have tacos for dinner. Help yourself. (A)

Minjun: Can you explain how to make a taco? (B)

Mom: First, fill your tortilla with vegetables and meat. (C)

Minjun: Sounds delicious! (D)

Mom: Would you like some cheese? (E)

Minjun: No, thanks.

13 위 대화의 (A)~(E) 중 주어진 문장이 들어가기에 적절한 곳은?

Then, add some sauce on the top.

① (A)   ② (B)   ③ (C)   ④ (D)   ⑤ (E)

14 위 대화의 내용과 일치하지 <u>않는</u> 것은?

① 민준이는 좋은 냄새를 맡았다.

② 엄마와 민준이는 저녁식사로 타코를 먹을 것이다.

③ 타코를 만들 때 토르티야와 채소와 고기가 필요하다.

④ 타코 위에 약간의 소스를 추가하여 만든다.

⑤ 민준이는 치즈를 더 원한다.

Grammar

15 다음 중 빈칸에 들어갈 말이 <u>다른</u> 하나는?

① The mountain is covered _____ snow.

② Helen is not satisfied _____ the result.

③ My eyes were filled _____ tears.

④ Terry was surprised _____ his letter.

⑤ He was pleased _____ many gifts.

16 다음 중 어법상 바르지 <u>않은</u> 것은?

① Windows are made of glass.

② The store will be closed at 9 o'clock.

③ Something sad happened last night.

④ A postcard was given to me by Jane.

⑤ Hundreds of people were died in the tornado.

17 다음 빈칸에 들어갈 말로 가장 적절한 것은?

People made fun of him
= He _____ people.

① was made fun   ② is made fun

③ was made fun of   ④ made fun of

⑤ was made fun of by

18 주어진 단어를 활용하여 다음 우리말을 영어로 쓰시오.

언제 그 음식이 배달될까? (deliver)

➡ _____

19 다음 중 문장의 전환이 바르지 <u>않은</u> 것은?

① The students use the computer.

→ The computer is used by the students.

② Does Vicky help you?

→ Are you helped by Vicky?

③ They asked me a question.

→ A question was asked to me by them.

④ Stars can be seen at night.

→ We can see stars at night.

⑤ Is this umbrella carried by you?

→ Do you carry this umbrella?

20 다음 빈칸에 들어갈 말이 바르게 짝지어진 것은?

• Vietnam _____ in Southeast Asia.

• I think life will _____ on other planets.

① located – existed

② locates – exist

③ located – be existed

④ is located – exist

⑤ is located – be existed

21 다음 밑줄 친 ①~⑤ 중 어법상 틀린 것은?

> According to our teacher, ①all of our compositions ②should write ③in ink. He won't accept ④papers ⑤written in pencil.

22 다음 문장을 수동태로 전환하시오.

> Studying English interests us.

➡ _____

23 다음 문장과 같은 의미의 문장을 모두 고르시오.

> Mr. Kim teaches students Korean.

① Students are taught to Korean by Mr. Kim.
② Students are taught Korean by Mr. Kim.
③ Korean teaches students to Mr. Kim.
④ Korean is taught to students by Mr. Kim.
⑤ Korean is taught students by Mr. Kim.

24 다음 중 어법상 옳은 문장의 개수는?

> ⓐ The pencil will sharpen by Tom.
> ⓑ Did the flowers picked up?
> ⓒ Your dog was taken from a hospital.
> ⓓ Can the concert be canceled?
> ⓔ The piano played by James these days.

① 1개　② 2개　③ 3개　④ 4개　⑤ 5개

25 다음 중 빈칸에 들어갈 말로 가장 적절한 것은?

> Shakespeare wrote *Romeo and Juliet*.
> = *Romeo and Juliet* _____ Shakespeare.

① is written　　② was written
③ is written by　④ was written by
⑤ were written by

26 다음 각 문장을 능동태는 수동태로, 수동태는 능동태로 전환하시오.

(1) We must pick up trash.

➡ _____

(2) Kelly is looked down on by Peter.

➡ _____

Reading

[27~30] 다음 글을 읽고 물음에 답하시오.

> Welcome to the Escape Tower. You will enter the first room in our tower. You need to solve some riddles (A)to escape. Clues can be found somewhere inside the room. So, are you ready to think like Sherlock Holmes?
> Room #1
> Mr. Doodle was hit by a car on Sunday afternoon. ① But he didn't see the driver. ② Three suspects were questioned by a police officer. ③ Ms. A said she was reading a book at the time of the accident. Mr. B said he was walking his dog. ④ Ms. C said she was making breakfast. Who hit Mr. Doodle? ⑤ Can you explain why? Do you have the answer? Write it down. Then you can move to the next room.
> **Clue:** The accident happened in the afternoon.

27 다음 중 주어진 문장이 들어가기에 가장 적절한 곳은?

> Luckily, he wasn't badly hurt.

①　　②　　③　　④　　⑤

28 다음 중 밑줄 친 (A)와 쓰임이 같은 것은?

① Jason told them not to do it again.
② I just did it to help your mother.
③ Helen needs something to wear.
④ It was easy to handle the situation.
⑤ Tamia was happy to hear the news.

29 According to the clue, when did the accident happen?

➡ _____

30 다음 탐정 수첩에서 위 글의 내용과 일치하지 <u>않는</u> 것을 두 개 찾아 바르게 고쳐 쓰시오.

> First Riddle
> • Mr. Doodle was hit by a bike.
> • The accident happened on Sunday afternoon.
> • Ms. A was reading a book and Mr. B was walking his dog. Ms. C was making dinner.

➡ _____

➡ _____

[31~34] 다음 글을 읽고 물음에 답하시오.

    Congratulations! You made it to the second room. However, the second room is much harder to escape than the first one. Good luck!
Room #2
Jay gets an email from his favorite clothing store. The (A)_____ reads "(B)<u>You won our Lucky Day event!</u>" Jay is surprised. He quickly opens it.
JayJr@kmail.com
You won our 'Lucky Day' event!
Congratulations!
You have won a special prize. During our Lucky Day event, you can choose any seven items from our store for free! Come to our store on November 31. We can't wait to see you.
                    Truly yours,
                    Kay Brown
However, Jay thinks that the event isn't real and deletes the email. Can you explain why?
  Clue: There are usually 30 or 31 days in a month.
Do you have the answer? Write it down and then you are free to go!

31 다음과 같이 풀이되는 말을 빈칸 (A)에 쓰시오.

> the name given to something such as a book, song, or movie to identify or describe it

➡ _____

32 밑줄 친 (B)를 수동태로 전환하시오.

➡ _____

33 다음 중 위 글을 읽고 답할 수 <u>있는</u> 것은?

① How hard it was to escape from the first room?
② Where is Jay's favorite clothing store?
③ When did Jay get the email?
④ When did Kay Brown send the email to Jay?
⑤ What do you have to do if you have the answer?

34 다음 중 위 글의 내용과 일치하지 <u>않는</u> 것은?

① The first room is much easier to escape than the second room.
② Jay has his favorite clothing store.
③ Jay deletes the email because he doesn't like the special prize.
④ Jay opens the email with surprise.
⑤ You are free to go if you solve the riddle.

[01~02] 다음 대화를 읽고 물음에 답하시오.

Emily: Junsu, do you want to solve a riddle?

Junsu: Sure, what is it?

Emily: There is a farmer. First, the farmer buys a fox, a duck, and a bag of beans. Then, the farmer needs to cross a river.

Junsu: What's the problem?

Emily: The boat can only hold the farmer and one more thing.

Junsu: (A)Are you saying that the farmer can take only one thing at a time?

Emily: Yes. Also, the fox will eat the duck or the duck will eat the beans if the farmer isn't there. Can you explain how to move everything across the river safely?

Junsu: Hmm ....

출제율 90%

01 위 대화의 밑줄 친 (A)와 바꾸어 쓸 수 있는 것은?

① Do you mean that the farmer can take only one thing at a time?

② Why do you say that the farmer can take only one thing at a time?

③ Why do you think the farmer must take only one thing at a time?

④ Do you know that the farmer can take only one thing at a time?

⑤ Have you heard about that the farmer can take only one thing at a time?

출제율 100%

02 위 대화의 내용과 일치하지 <u>않는</u> 것은?

① Emily는 준수에게 수수께끼를 내주었다.

② 농부는 여우한 마리, 오리 한 마리, 콩 한 자루를 샀다.

③ 농부는 강을 건너야 한다.

④ 배는 한 번에 농부와 두 가지 더 옮길 수 있다.

⑤ 농부가 없다면 오리가 콩을 먹거나 여우가 오리를 먹을 수 있다.

[03~04] 다음 대화를 읽고 물음에 답하시오.

Jane: Minsu, do you know the TV show about the student detective?

Minsu: Yes. I love that show, but I didn't see it this week. What was it about?

Jane: Well, all of the bikes at school disappeared.

Minsu: So, what did he do?

Jane: First, he looked around the school. Then, he met some (A)_____s and asked questions. (B)Finally, he found the thief. The thief was ....

Minsu: No, don't tell me! I'll watch it later.

출제율 90%

03 위 대화의 빈칸 (A)에 다음의 영영풀이가 가리키는 말을 고르시오.

> a person who is believed to be possibly guilty of committing a crime

① lawyer　　　　② suspect

③ victim　　　　④ merchant

⑤ prosecutor

출제율 95%

04 위 대화의 밑줄 친 (B)와 바꾸어 쓸 수 있는 것을 <u>모두</u> 고르시오.

① Though　　　　② Eventually

③ Nevertheless　　④ At last

⑤ Initially

[05~06] 다음 대화를 읽고 물음에 답하시오.

Jack: Kelly, here's a riddle. You can see this twice in a week, once in a year, but never in a day. What is this?

Kelly: I have no idea.

Jack: It's the letter "E."

Kelly: I don't get it. (A)이유를 설명해 줄 수 있니?

Jack: Well, there are two "E"s in the word "week," one "E" in the word "year" but no "E"s in the word "day."

Kelly: Aha! Now I get it.

출제율 90%

05 위 대화에서 밑줄 친 (A)의 우리말을 4단어로 영작하시오.

➡ _____

출제율 85%

06 위 대화의 내용과 일치하는 것을 고르시오.

① Kelly solved the riddle with the help of Jack.

② Kelly asked Jack to give him a hint for the answer.

③ Kelly didn't understand the answer at first.

④ The riddle Jack gave to Kelly is about the diary.

⑤ Jack was confused when he got to know the answer to the riddle.

[07~08] 다음 대화를 읽고 물음에 답하시오.

Minjun: Wow! Something smells really good, Mom. What is it?

Mom: We're going to have tacos for dinner. (A)맘껏 먹으렴.

Minjun: Can you explain how to make a taco?

Mom: First, fill your tortilla with vegetables and meat. Then, add some sauce on the top.

Minjun: Sounds delicious!

Mom: Would you like some cheese?

Minjun: No, thanks.

출제율 95%

07 위 대화의 밑줄 친 (A)의 우리말을 두 단어로 영작하시오.

➡ _____

출제율 90%

08 위 대화의 내용과 일치하도록 민준이의 일기를 완성하시오.

Sun, Sep 8th, 2019

I had (A)_____ for dinner with Mom. It was so delicious. I wondered how to make tacos. Mom told me that (B)_____ first, and then (C)_____. Next time, I'll try to make them by myself.

출제율 100%

09 다음 대화가 자연스럽게 이어지도록 순서대로 배열하시오.

(A) That sounds easy.

(B) Look at my paper fox.

(C) That's cute. How did you make it?

(D) First, fold a paper in half to make a triangle. Second, fold the top of the triangle to the bottom line. Third, fold both ends of the bottom line to the top to make ears. Then, turn it over and draw a face.

➡ _____

출제율 90%

10 다음 대화에서 수수께끼의 답이 'E'가 되는 이유를 우리말로 설명하시오.

Jack: Kelly, here's a riddle. You can see this twice in a week, once in a year, but never in a day. What is this?

Kelly: I have no idea.

Jack: It's the letter "E."

Kelly: I don't get it. Can you explain why?

Jack: Well, there are two "E"s in the word "week," one "E" in the word "year" but no "E"s in the word "day."

Kelly: Aha! Now I get it.

➡ _____

11 다음 중 밑줄 친 부분을 생략할 수 있는 것은?

① Was the vase broken by Katherine?
② The door was locked by my parents.
③ The gold mine was discovered by someone in 1890.
④ The water was boiled by your sister.
⑤ A doll was made by my friend.

12 다음 중 문장의 전환이 바르지 않은 것은?

① Julia will help the poor.
= The poor will be helped by Julia.
② I must do my homework.
= My homework must be done by me.
③ Bob drew many paintings.
= Many paintings were drawn by Bob.
④ The result disappointed me.
= I was disappointed by the result.
⑤ Brad gave me some chocolate.
= Some chocolate was given to me by Brad.

13 주어진 단어를 활용하여 다음 우리말을 영어로 쓰시오.

식탁이 차려지고 양초들에 불이 켜졌다.
(the table / set / light)

➡ _____

14 빈칸에 들어갈 말이 바르게 짝지어진 것은?

• The building _____ by the earthquake last year.
• The plane _____ behind a cloud.

① was damaged – was disappeared
② is damaged – was disappeared
③ damaged – disappeared
④ is damaged – is disappeared
⑤ was damaged – disappeared

15 다음 우리말과 같은 의미의 문장을 모두 고르시오.

그 소녀는 공에 맞았다.

① The ball hit the girl.
② The ball was hit by the girl.
③ The girl was hit the ball.
④ The girl hit the ball.
⑤ The girl was hit by the ball.

16 다음 빈칸에 알맞은 말을 쓰시오.

Someone will deliver the package to your apartment.
= The package _____ to your apartment.

17 다음 각 문장을 수동태로 전환하시오.

(1) Someone told the kids to leave.
➡ _____
(2) Thomas heard me singing in my room.
➡ _____

[18~22] 다음 글을 읽고, 물음에 답하시오.

Welcome to the Escape Tower. You will enter the first room in our tower. You need to solve some riddles to escape. Clues can be found somewhere inside the room. So, are you ready to think like Sherlock Holmes?
Room #1
Mr. Doodle was hit by a car on Sunday afternoon.
(A) Who hit Mr. Doodle? Can you explain why? Do you have the answer? Write it down. Then you can move to the next room.

(B) Ms. A said she was reading a book at the time of the accident. Mr. B said he was walking his dog. Ms. C said she was making breakfast.

(C) ⓐLuckily, he wasn't badly hurt, but he didn't see the driver. Three suspects were questioned by a police officer.

Clue: The accident happened in the afternoon. Congratulations! ⓑ당신은 두 번째 방에 오는 데 성공하셨습니다. However, the second room is much harder to escape than the first one. Good luck!

출제율 100%

18 자연스러운 글이 되도록 (A)~(C)를 바르게 나열한 것은?

① (A)-(C)-(B)　　② (B)-(A)-(C)

③ (B)-(C)-(A)　　④ (C)-(A)-(B)

⑤ (C)-(B)-(A)

출제율 90%

19 다음 중 밑줄 친 ⓐLuckily를 대신하여 쓰일 수 있는 것은?

① Especially　　② Recently

③ Fortunately　　④ Suddenly

⑤ Particularly

출제율 85%

20 주어진 어구를 바르게 배열하여 밑줄 친 우리말 ⓑ를 영어로 쓰시오.

(the second / you / to / made / room / it)

➡ _____

출제율 90%

21 위 글의 내용에 맞게 빈칸에 알맞은 말을 각각 두 단어로 쓰시오.

A: Do you know that there were _____ in Mr. Doodle's accident?

B: Yes. Actually a police officer _____.

출제율 95%

22 다음 중 위 글의 내용과 일치하지 <u>않는</u> 것은?

① Clues for riddles can be found inside the room.

② Mr. Doodle didn't know who hit him.

③ Ms. A was reading a book on Sunday afternoon.

④ Mr. B was with his dog when Mr. Doodle was hit by a car.

⑤ The second room is as difficult to escape as the first room.

[23~25] 다음 글을 읽고 물음에 답하시오.

It was last Sunday. Dohun was at home. Suddenly, he (A)[heard / was heard] a sound in the next room. When he went into the room, the window (B)[broke / was broken]. When he looked outside, Sujin was holding a baseball bat and Ted was throwing a ball to his dog. Who (C)[broke / was broken] the window? How can it be explained?

출제율 100%

23 (A)~(C)에서 어법상 옳은 것끼리 바르게 짝지은 것은?

① was heard – broke – broke

② was heard – broke – was broken

③ heard – broke – broke

④ heard – was broken – was broken

⑤ heard – was broken – broke

출제율 90%

24 What was Ted doing when Dohun looked outside? Answer in English with a full sentence.

➡ _____

출제율 95%

25 다음 중 글의 내용과 일치하지 <u>않는</u> 것은?

① 도훈은 지난 일요일에 집에 있었다.

② 누군가가 창문을 깼다.

③ 도훈이가 있던 방의 창문이 깨졌다.

④ 도훈은 창문이 깨진 것을 보고 밖을 보았다.

⑤ 도훈은 창문이 깨지는 소리를 들었다.

[01~03] 다음 대화를 읽고 물음에 답하시오.

> Jimin: Do you want to play the new game that I bought?
> Brian: Sure, what is it, Jimin?
> Jimin: It's like a soccer game but the players are dragons and seahorses. You need to use these buttons to play.
> Brian: That sounds fun. (A)버튼 사용법을 설명해 줄 수 있니?
> Jimin: Sure.

01 위 대화의 밑줄 친 (A)의 우리말을 주어진 〈보기〉의 단어를 모두 배열하여 영어로 쓰시오.

> ┌─ 보기 ┤─
> the buttons / how / use / the / can / to / you / explain

➡ _____

02 What are Jimin and Brian going to do together?

➡ _____

03 How can Jimin and Brian play the game?

➡ _____

[04~05] 다음 대화를 읽고 물음에 답하시오.

> Jane: Minsu, do you know the TV show about the student detective?
> Minsu: Yes. I love that show, but I didn't see it this week. What was it about?
> Jane: Well, all of the bikes at school disappeared.
> Minsu: So, what did he do?

> Jane: First, he looked around the school. Then, he met some suspects and asked questions. Finally, he found the thief. The thief was ....
> Minsu: No, don't tell me! I'll watch it later.

04 What was the TV show that Minsu had missed about?

➡ It(=The TV show) was about the case that

_____

05 What did the student detective do to find the thief?

➡ _____

_____

06 다음 문장을 수동태로 전환하시오.

(1) Someone already made the coffee.

➡ _____

(2) Did you return the book?

➡ _____

(3) I will invite my friends.

➡ _____

07 다음 빈칸에 알맞은 말을 쓰시오.

> Wild animals attacked the villagers.
> = The villagers _____
>   wild animals.

08 다음 대화의 빈칸에 알맞은 말을 쓰시오.

> A: Who will make the decision?
> B: The decision _____
>   our CEO.

09 주어진 어구를 활용하여 다음 우리말을 영어로 쓰시오.

> 실종 소녀가 어제 경찰에 의해 발견되었다.
> (the missing girl, the police)

➡ _____

10 주어진 단어를 어법에 맞게 활용하여 빈칸에 알맞은 말을 쓰시오.

> **A:** Is the train going to be late?
> **B:** No. It _____(expect) to be on time.

[11~13] 다음 글을 읽고 물음에 답하시오.

Welcome to the Escape Tower. You will enter the first room in our tower. You need to solve some riddles to escape. Clues can be found somewhere inside the room. So, are you ready to think like Sherlock Holmes?
Room #1
   Mr. Doodle was hit by a car on Sunday afternoon. (A)Lucky, he wasn't badly hurt, but he didn't see the driver. (B)A police officer questioned three suspects. Ms. A said she was reading a book at the time of the accident. Mr. B said he was walking his dog. Ms. C said she was making breakfast. Who hit Mr. Doodle? Can you explain why? Do you have the answer? Write it down. Then you can move to the next room.
Clue: The accident happened in the afternoon.

11 밑줄 친 (A)를 알맞은 형으로 고치시오.

➡ _____

12 밑줄 친 (B)와 같은 의미의 문장을 완성하시오.

> Three suspects _____ .

13 Where can you find clues? Answer in English. (7 words)

➡ _____

[14~16] 다음 글을 읽고 물음에 답하시오.

   It was last Sunday. Dohun was at home. Suddenly, he heard a sound in the next room. When he went into the room, (A)the window was broken. When he looked outside, Sujin was holding a baseball bat and Ted was throwing a ball to his dog. Who broke the window? (B) How can it be explained?

14 빈칸에 알맞은 말을 써서 밑줄 친 (A)와 같은 의미의 문장을 완성하시오.

> someone _____

15 Where was Dohun last Sunday? Answer in English with a full sentence.

➡ _____

16 주어진 문장의 빈칸에 알맞은 말을 써 넣어 밑줄 친 (B)와 같은 의미의 문장을 완성하시오.

> How can you _____ who broke the window?

01 다음 대화의 내용과 일치하도록 빈칸을 완성하시오.

> **Jane:** Minsu, do you know the TV show about the student detective?
> **Minsu:** Yes. I love that show, but I didn't see it this week. What was it about?
> **Jane:** Well, all of the bikes at school disappeared.
> **Minsu:** So, what did he do?
> **Jane:** First, he looked around the school. Then, he met some suspects and asked questions. Finally, he found the thief. The thief was ....
> **Minsu:** No, don't tell me! I'll watch it later.

⬇

> I was fascinated by the TV show about the student detective. I was happy when I heard that Minsu also loved that show. This week, the episode was so exciting. The show was about the crime that (A)_____. I also had the experience of losing my bike, so it was more interesting. When I talked about it to Minsu, he said that he (B)_____ this episode. I told him what (C)_____ had done to find the thief. I know who (D)_____ was, but Minsu didn't want to know it. He said he would watch it later.

02 다음은 Mr. Doodle 사고의 용의자 심문 내용이다. 빈칸에 알맞은 말을 쓰시오.

> A police officer: Ms. A, you said you were reading a book at the time of the accident. Where (A)_____ by you?
> Ms. A: I read the book at a cafe.
> A police officer: Okay. Then Mr. B, nobody saw you walk your dog. It means you (B)_____ to walk your dog by anyone. How can you prove it?
> Mr. B: I went to a pet shop to buy my dog a gum. Ask the clerk who worked on Sunday.
> A police officer: I'll check that out. Ms. C, you said you were making something. What (C)_____ you?
> Ms. C: Breakfast was made by me.

03 주어진 동사와 수동태를 활용하여 다양한 문장을 쓰시오.

> send   see   show   eat   borrow

(1) _____

(2) _____

(3) _____

(4) _____

(5) _____

단원별 모의고사

01 다음 짝지어진 단어의 관계가 같도록 빈칸에 알맞은 말을 쓰시오.

> win : lose = s_____ : dangerous

02 다음 영영풀이가 가리키는 것을 고르시오.

> an object or piece of information that helps someone solve a crime or mystery

① clue
② accident
③ fact
④ prize
⑤ scene

03 다음 문장의 빈칸에 들어갈 말을 〈보기〉에서 골라 쓰시오.

> ┌─ 보기 ├─
> case / candle / triangle / hide

(1) The thief couldn't _____ under the table because there wasn't enough space.
(2) The _____ was solved by the police.
(3) The _____ will be put inside the box.
(4) Fold the opposite corners together to form a _____.

04 다음 문장에 공통으로 들어갈 말을 고르시오.

> • The police officer found the clues in the _____ of the crime.
> • The movie opens with a _____ in the Museum of Modern Art.
> • I was fascinated by a beautiful _____.

① prize
② scene
③ bean
④ space
⑤ stamp

[05~07] 다음 대화를 읽고 물음에 답하시오.

Jane: Minsu, do you know the TV show about the student detective?
Minsu: Yes. I love that show, but I didn't see it this week. What was it about?
Jane: Well, all of the bikes at school (A)[appeared / disappeared].
Minsu: So, what did he do?
Jane: First, he looked around the school. Then, he met some (B)[suspects / suspends] and asked questions. Finally, he found the (C)[thief / chief]. The thief was ....
Minsu: No, don't tell me! I'll watch it later.

05 위 대화에서 다음의 영영풀이가 가리키는 말을 찾아 쓰시오.

> a police officer who investigates crimes and catches criminals

➡ _____

06 위 대화의 흐름상 (A)~(C)에 들어갈 말로 적절한 것끼리 바르게 짝지어진 것은?

	(A)	(B)	(C)
①	appeared	suspects	thief
②	appeared	suspends	chief
③	disappeared	suspects	chief
④	disappeared	suspends	thief
⑤	disappeared	suspects	thief

07 위 대화의 내용과 일치하지 <u>않는</u> 것은?

① Minsu missed the TV show about the student detective this week.
② Jane told Minsu about the episode of the TV show.
③ The TV show dealt with the crime of stealing bikes.
④ The student detective investigated the school and some suspects.
⑤ Minsu asked Jane to let him know who the thief was.

[08~10] 다음 대화를 읽고 물음에 답하시오.

Emily: Junsu, do you want to solve a riddle?

Junsu: Sure, what is it?

Emily: There is a farmer. First, the farmer buys a fox, a duck, and a bag of beans. Then, the farmer needs to cross a river.

Junsu: What's the problem?

Emily: The boat can only hold the farmer and one more thing.

Junsu: Are you saying that the farmer can take only one thing at a time?

Emily: Yes. Also, the fox will eat the duck or the duck will eat the beans if the farmer isn't there. (A)전부를 강 건너로 안전하게 옮길 방법을 설명할 수 있겠니?

Junsu: Hmm ....

08 위 대화의 밑줄 친 우리말 (A)를 〈보기〉에 주어진 단어를 모두 배열하여 완성하시오.

┌─ 보기 ┤
explain / to / the / across / river / can / how / move / you / safely / everything
└─────

➡ _____

_____

09 위 대화를 읽고 대답할 수 없는 질문은?

① What is the riddle Emily gave to Junsu?

② What did the farmer buy?

③ Why should the farmer cross the river?

④ Why shouldn't the farmer leave the fox and the duck together?

⑤ How many things could the boat hold at a time?

10 위 대화에서 제시된 수수께끼의 해결책을 완성하시오.

Junsu: First, the farmer crosses the river with the duck. Second, he comes back and takes (A)_____. Third, he leaves the fox and comes back with (B)_____. Then, he leaves the duck and takes (C)_____. Next, the farmer should leave the beans with the fox. Then, he comes back and crosses the river with (D)_____.

11 다음 대화가 자연스럽게 이어지도록 순서대로 배열하시오.

(A) It's the letter "E."

(B) I have no idea.

(C) I don't get it. Can you explain why?

(D) Well, there are two "E"s in the word "week," one "E" in the word "year" but no "E"s in the word "day."

(E) Kelly, here's a riddle. You can see this twice in a week, once in a year, but never in a day. What is this?

➡ _____

12 다음 짝지어진 대화가 어색한 것은?

① A: Did I draw it correctly?
   B: No, you didn't.

② A: Where did you hide your gold?
   B: It is in the building on your right.

③ A: Can you explain how to buy a train ticket?
   B: First, choose the station. Then, put in the money.

④ A: Would you like some cheese?
   B: No, thanks.

⑤ A: How did you make it?
   B: That sounds interesting.

13 다음 빈칸에 들어갈 말로 가장 적절한 것은?

> I will not forget their stories.
> = Their stories _____.

① are not be able to be forgotten
② is not forgotten by me
③ won't be forgot to me
④ don't have to be forgotten by me
⑤ won't be forgotten by me

14 다음 중 어법상 바르지 <u>않은</u> 것은?

① What happened to you last night?
② This key is belonged to your brother.
③ The party will be held in Jin's garden.
④ A job at a local bank was offered to me.
⑤ This symptom can't be explained.

15 다음 문장을 수동태로 전환하시오.

> Hundreds of fans surrounded the rock star outside the theater.

➡ _____
_____

16 다음 빈칸에 들어갈 말로 가장 적절한 것은?

> The noise annoys me.
> = I _____ the noise.

① am annoyed to
② am annoyed of
③ am annoyed in
④ am annoyed with
⑤ am annoyed from

17 주어진 단어를 어법에 맞게 활용하여 문장을 완성하시오.

> Hudson's house burned down. The fire
> _____. (cause / lightning)

➡ _____

[18~23] 다음 글을 읽고 물음에 답하시오.

> Room #2
>   Jay gets an email ①from his favorite clothing store. The title reads "You won our Lucky Day event!" Jay is ②surprised. He quickly opens it.
> JayJr@kmail.com
> You won our 'Lucky Day' event!
> Congratulations!
> You have won a special prize. ③During our Lucky Day event, (A)you can choose any seven items from our store for free! Come to our store on November 31. We can't wait to see you.
>   Truly yours,
>   Kay Brown
>   However, Jay thinks that the event isn't real and ④delete the email. Can you explain why?
> Clue There are usually 30 or 31 days ⑤in a month.
>   Do you have the answer? Write it down and then you are free to go!

18 밑줄 친 문장 (A)를 우리말로 옮기시오.

➡ _____
_____

19 ①~⑤ 중 어법상 바르지 <u>않은</u> 것은?

①   ②   ③   ④   ⑤

20 다음 중 위 글의 내용과 일치하는 것은?

① Jay deletes the email because he isn't interested in shopping.
② The email was sent to Jay from Jay's favorite shoe store.
③ The email has no title at all.
④ Jay opens the email as soon as he sees it.
⑤ Jay is looking forward to going shopping at the store.

21 다음은 위 사건의 탐정 수첩이다. 글의 내용과 일치하지 <u>않는</u> 것을 두 군데 찾아 바르게 고치시오.

Second Riddle
• Jay will get a special prize.
• The event is on November 30.
• Jay kept his email because it was not true.

➡ _____

➡ _____

22 다음 물음에 완전한 문장의 영어로 답하시오.

Q: How many items are free during the Lucky Day event?

➡ _____

23 다음 중 위 글을 읽고 답할 수 <u>없는</u> 것은?

① Where does Jay get email from?
② Why is Jay surprised?
③ How many people get the email besides Jay?
④ When is the 'Lucky Day' event?
⑤ What do we have to do if we know the answer?

[24~25] 다음 글을 읽고 물음에 답하시오.

It was last Sunday. Dohun was at home. Suddenly, he heard a sound in the next room. When he went into the room, the window was broken. When he looked outside, Sujin was holding a baseball bat and Ted was throwing a ball to his dog. Who broke the window? (A) _____

24 다음 중 위 글에서 찾아볼 수 <u>없는</u> 것은?

① Dohun who was resting at home on Sunday
② a noise from the next room
③ a ball which was thrown to Dohun's home
④ a girl who was holding a baseball bat
⑤ Dohun looking outside to see who broke the window

25 주어진 단어를 바르게 배열하여 빈칸 (A)에 들어갈 말을 완성하시오. 필요하다면 어형을 변형하시오.

(be / how / explain / it / can)

➡ _____

Lesson 6

We're Here to Dance

 의사소통 기능

- 의견 표현하기
  In my opinion, he really enjoys dancing.

- 확실성 정도 표현하기
  I'm sure you'll feel great.

 언어 형식

- so ~ that ...
  The dance is **so** popular **that** everybody learns it.

- 원급 비교
  The dancers looked **as** beautiful **as** flowers.

Words & Expressions
교과서

Key Words

- **bee**[bi:] 몡 벌
- **behind**[biháind] 젠 ~ 뒤에
- **between**[bitwíːn] 젠 ~ 사이에
- **brave**[breiv] 혱 용감한
- **bright**[brait] 혱 (색상이) 밝은
- **character**[kǽriktər] 몡 등장인물
- **cheer**[tʃíər] 됭 응원하다
- **comfortable**[kʌ́mfərtəbl] 혱 편안한
- **communicate**[kəmjúːnəkèit] 됭 의사소통하다
- **couple**[kʌ́pl] 몡 두 사람, 남녀
- **costume**[kɑ́stjuːm] 몡 의상, 복장
- **doll**[dɑl] 몡 인형
- **drop**[drɑp] 됭 떨어뜨리다
- **enemy**[énəmi] 몡 적
- **express**[iksprés] 됭 표현하다
- **fan**[fæn] 몡 부채
- **female**[fíːmeil] 혱 암컷의, 여성의
- **field**[fiːld] 몡 들판, 경기장
- **fight**[fait] 몡 싸움, 다툼
- **gracefully**[gréisfəli] 붑 우아하게
- **hide**[haid] 됭 숨다
- **hold**[hould] 됭 열다, 개최하다

- **interestingly**[íntərəstiŋli] 붑 흥미 있게도
- **male**[meil] 혱 수컷의, 남성의
- **movement**[múːvmənt] 몡 움직임, 동작
- **nowadays**[náuədèiz] 붑 오늘날에는
- **opinion**[əpínjən] 몡 의견
- **originally**[ərídʒənəli] 붑 원래, 본래
- **perform**[pərfɔ́ːrm] 됭 공연하다
- **popular**[pápjulər] 혱 인기 있는
- **powerful**[páuərfəl] 혱 강한, 힘 있는
- **rugby**[rʌ́gbi] 몡 럭비
- **scared**[skɛərd] 혱 겁먹은, 무서워하는
- **scary**[skɛ́əri] 혱 무서운
- **strength**[strenkθ] 몡 힘
- **sure**[ʃuər] 혱 확실한
- **through**[θruː] 젠 ~을 통해
- **totally**[tóutəli] 붑 완전히
- **traditional**[trədíʃənl] 혱 전통적인
- **uniform**[júːnəfɔ̀ːrm] 몡 제복, 유니폼
- **wild**[waild] 혱 야생의
- **windy**[wíndi] 혱 바람이 많이 부는

Key Expressions

- **be allowed to** ~이 허용되다
- **be good at** ~을 잘하다
- **catch a cold** 감기에 걸리다
- **give up on** ~을 포기하다
- **good and evil** 선과 악
- **have fun** 즐거운 시간을 보내다
- **in my opinion** 내 의견으로는

- **keep up the good work** 계속 열심히 하다
- **look like** ~처럼 보이다
- **make a sound** 소리를 내다
- **on time** 정시에
- **sound like** ~처럼 들리다, ~일 것 같다
- **take a look** 살펴보다
- **try one's best** 최선을 다하다

Word Power

※ 서로 반대되는 뜻을 가진 어휘

- □ **bright** 밝은 ↔ **dark** 어두운
- □ **comfortable** 편안한 ↔ **uncomfortable** 불편한
- □ **good** 선 ↔ **evil** 악
- □ **sure** 확실한 ↔ **unsure** 불확실한
- □ **enemy** 적 ↔ **friend** 친구

- □ **brave** 용감한 ↔ **cowardly** 비겁한
- □ **male** 수컷의, 남성의 ↔ **female** 암컷의, 여성의
- □ **popular** 인기 있는 ↔ **unpopular** 인기 없는
- □ **behind** 뒤에 ↔ **ahead** 앞에
- □ **powerful** 강한, 힘 있는 ↔ **weak** 약한

English Dictionary

- □ **behind** 뒤에
  → at or towards the back of a thing or person
  물건이나 사람의 뒤쪽 또는 뒷부분을 향해

- □ **brave** 용감한
  → dealing with danger, pain, or difficult situations with courage and confidence
  용기와 자신감을 갖고 위험, 고통 또는 어려운 상황을 다루는

- □ **cheer** 응원하다
  → to shout as a way of showing happiness, praise, approval, or support of someone or something
  누군가 또는 무언가에 대한 행복, 칭찬, 승인 또는 지지를 보여주는 방식으로 소리치다

- □ **comfortable** 편안한
  → making you feel physically relaxed, without any pain or without being too hot, cold, etc.
  어떠한 고통이나 너무 뜨겁거나 차가움 없이 신체적으로 편안하게 느끼도록 만드는

- □ **drop** 떨어뜨리다
  → to stop holding or carrying something so that it falls
  무언가가 떨어지도록 그것을 쥐거나 나르는 것을 멈추다

- □ **express** 표현하다
  → to tell or show what you are feeling or thinking by using words, looks, or actions
  말, 표정 또는 행동을 사용하여 당신이 느끼고 있거나 생각하고 있는 것을 말하거나 보여주다

- □ **fan** 부채
  → a flat object that you wave with your hand which makes the air cooler
  당신이 손을 움직여 공기를 더 시원하게 만드는 평평한 물체

- □ **field** 들판
  → an area of land in the country, especially one where crops are grown or animals feed on grass
  특히 곡식이 자라거나 동물들이 풀을 먹는 시골에 있는 땅의 한 지역

- □ **movement** 움직임
  → an act of moving
  움직이는 행동

- □ **originally** 원래, 본래
  → in the beginning, before other things happened or before things changed
  맨 처음에, 다른 일들이 발생하기 전이나 상황이 변하기 전에

- □ **popular** 인기 있는
  → liked by a lot of people
  많은 사람들이 좋아하는

- □ **strength** 힘
  → the physical power and energy that makes someone strong
  누군가를 강하게 만들어 주는 신체적인 힘과 에너지

- □ **uniform** 제복
  → a particular type of clothing worn by all the members of a group or organization such as the police, the army, etc.
  경찰, 군인 등과 같이 집단 또는 조직의 모든 구성원들이 입는 옷의 특별한 종류

- □ **wild** 야생의
  → living in a natural state, not changed or controlled by people
  자연 상태에 사는, 사람들에 의해 바뀌거나 통제되지 않은

서답형

01 다음 짝지어진 단어의 관계가 같도록 빈칸에 알맞은 말을 쓰시오.

man : woman = male : _____

02 다음 영영풀이가 가리키는 것을 고르시오.

dealing with danger, pain, or difficult situations with courage and confidence

① brave
② comfortable
③ scared
④ sure
⑤ traditional

중요

03 다음 중 밑줄 친 부분의 뜻풀이가 바르지 않은 것은?

① Nowadays, many people want to be Youtubers. 오늘날에는
② When did you drop your glasses? 떨어뜨리다
③ I'm interested in Chinese traditional dancing. 전통적인
④ I couldn't sleep well after watching a scary movie. 무서운
⑤ Before the speech, I wrote my opinions about the issue. 사실

서답형

04 다음 우리말에 맞게 빈칸에 알맞은 말을 쓰시오.

(1) 너는 그녀 뒤에 많은 팔들이 보이니?
➡ Do you see many arms _____ her?
(2) 힘이 넘치는 춤꾼들의 힘을 느껴라!
➡ Feel the _____ of the powerful dancers!
(3) 무용수의 우아한 움직임을 보아라.
➡ Look at the _____ movements of a dancer.
(4) 우리는 종종 우리의 손님들을 위해 전통적인 한국 음식들을 요리한다.
➡ We often cook _____ Korean meals for our guests.

05 다음 주어진 문장의 밑줄 친 character와 같은 의미로 쓰인 것은?

I love this cartoon because of its unique characters.

① This book describes the writer's character.
② Generosity is part of American character.
③ She is going to play a main character in the play.
④ The most important thing is the character.
⑤ Tom revealed his real character when he was upset.

중요

06 다음 문장에 공통으로 들어갈 말을 고르시오.

• I have read many stories about _____ and evil.
• Harry is _____ at playing soccer.

① good
② best
③ better
④ bad
⑤ worse

01 다음 짝지어진 단어의 관계가 같도록 빈칸에 알맞은 말을 쓰시오.

> bright : dark = _____ : friend

02 다음 문장의 빈칸에 들어갈 말을 〈보기〉에서 골라 쓰시오.

┌─ 보기 ├─
enemy / expressed / originally / strength / perform
└──────────────────────┘

(1) He _____ an interest in meeting her yesterday.

(2) The singers will _____ at Carnegie Hall.

(3) The school _____ belonged to Mr. Bower.

(4) The boxer had no _____ left to punch.

(5) Who is our _____ during the war?

03 다음 주어진 말을 이용하여 우리말에 맞게 빈칸에 알맞은 말을 쓰시오.

(1) 끝날 때 당신은 함께 춤추는 것이 허용된다. (allow)
➡ You _____ dance together at the end.

(2) 몇몇 물고기들은 소리들을 낼 수 있다. (make)
➡ Some fish can _____.

(3) 만약 네가 최선을 다하면 불가능한 것은 없다. (best)
➡ Nothing is impossible if you _____.

04 다음 우리말과 일치하도록 주어진 단어를 모두 배열하여 영작하시오.

(1) 내 의견으로는 무용수들이 인형만큼 귀여워 보인다.
(dancers / my / look / in / opinion / as / as / dolls / cute)
➡ _____

(2) 소년의 신발이 매우 편안해서 그는 그것들을 하루 종일 신을 수 있었다.
(comfortable / are / the boy's / he / can / them / all day / that / wear / shoes / so)
➡ _____
_____

(3) 너는 연기자들 뒤에 많은 사람들이 보이니?
(see / the / many / do / people / behind / actors / you)
➡ _____

05 다음 우리말을 주어진 단어를 이용하여 영작하시오.

(1) 그 춤은 아주 인기 있어서 모두가 이것을 배운다. (so, everybody)
➡ _____

(2) 본래 헝가리에서 공연되었던 이 멋진 공연을 놓치지 마라. (miss, which, great, performed, originally)
➡ _____

(3) 나는 나의 감정을 표현하기 위해 몸을 움직인다. (feelings, move)
➡ _____

Conversation

1 의견 표현하기

> **In my opinion, he really enjoys dancing.**
> (내 의견으로는, 그는 정말로 춤을 즐겨.)

■ 'In my opinion, …'은 '내 의견으로는, …'라는 뜻으로 자신의 의견을 표현하는 말이다. 유사한 표현으로는 'I think that …', 'I believe (that) …', 'I would say that …', 'To my mind', 'In my view', 'In my eyes' 등이 있다.

의견 표현하기

- I think that we should have homework because it helps with learning.
  (나는 숙제가 학습에 도움이 되므로 숙제가 있어야 한다고 생각해.)

- I believe that we should not have homework because it takes away our free time.
  (나는 숙제가 우리의 자유 시간을 뺏기 때문에 숙제가 없어야 한다고 믿어.)

- I would say that we should work hard to achieve our goals.
  (나는 우리가 우리 목표를 성취하기 위해 열심히 노력해야 한다고 말하고 싶다.)

- To my mind, wearing a school uniform every day is boring.
  (내 생각에, 교복을 매일 입는 것은 지루해.)

- In my view, it's easy to learn and it's also beautiful. (내가 봤을 땐, 그것은 배우기 쉽고 또한 아름다워.)

- In my eyes, my English teacher is an intelligent person.
  (내가 보기에는, 나의 영어 선생님은 똑똑한 사람이야.)

핵심 Check

1. 다음 주어진 우리말과 일치하도록 빈칸에 알맞은 말을 쓰시오.

   (1) **A:** _____ _____ _____ _____ _____ Jenny? (Jenny에 대해 어떻게 생각해?)

   B: Jenny? _____ _____ _____, she's a nice person.

   (Jenny? 내 의견으로는, 그녀는 좋은 사람이야.)

   (2) **A:** What do you think about _____ _____ _____ _____?

   (너는 교복을 입는 것에 대해 어떻게 생각하니?)

   B: _____ _____ _____ we _____ _____ _____ _____ _____
   _____ because it's more uncomfortable.

   (나는 교복이 더 불편하기 때문에 교복을 입지 말아야 한다고 생각해.)

2 확실성 정도 표현하기

I'm sure you'll feel great. (나는 네가 기분이 좋을 것이라고 확신한다.)

■ 'I'm sure ~'는 '나는 ~을 확신한다'라는 뜻으로 자신의 추측이나 생각의 확신을 표현한다. 'I'm certain ~'으로 바꿔 쓸 수 있다.

확신 말하기

- I'm sure (that) ~: 나는 ~을 확신한다
- I'm certain (that) ~: 나는 ~을 확신한다
- I have no doubt that ~: 나는 ~에 대해 의심치 않는다

A: Jane has a great voice. (Jane은 좋은 목소리를 갖고 있어.)

B: I'm certain she will be a great singer. (나는 그녀가 좋은 가수가 될 거라고 확신해.)

A: Jack studies all day. (Jack은 하루 종일 공부해.)

B: I have no doubt that he will get a good grade on the test. (나는 그가 시험에서 좋은 성적을 받을 것이라고 의심치 않아.)

핵심 Check

2. 다음 우리말과 일치하도록 빈칸에 알맞은 말을 쓰시오.

(1) **A:** I'm going to a _____ _____ in our town next weekend. Do you want to join me? (나는 다음 주말에 우리 마을에서 열리는 문화 행사에 갈 거야. 나와 같이 갈래?)

B: Sounds _____. (재미있겠다.)

A: We can enjoy dances from many countries. _____ _____ we'll have a lot of fun. (우리는 많은 국가에서 온 춤들을 즐길 수 있어. 우리는 매우 즐거울 거라고 확신해.)

(2) **A:** I think Sejun's photo is very funny. (나는 세준이의 사진이 매우 재미있다고 생각해.)

B: _____ _____ he'll win the school photo contest.

(나는 그가 학교 사진 대회에서 우승할 것이라고 확신해.)

Listen and Speak 1-B

Emily: Hojun, did you know that some male birds dance?

Hojun: ❶No. Why do ❷they dance?

Emily: They dance to show their love to female birds.

Hojun: ❸That's interesting. Do you know any other animals that can dance?

Emily: Yes, some bees dance to show where to find food.

Hojun: That's cool! ❹In my opinion, dancing is a great way to communicate.

Emily: ❺I totally agree with you.

Emily: 호준아, 너는 일부 수컷 새들이 춤을 춘다는 것을 알고 있었니?
Hojun: 아니. 왜 춤을 추지?
Emily: 그들은 암컷 새들에게 그들의 사랑을 보여주기 위해 춤을 춰.
Hojun: 그거 흥미로운 걸. 춤을 출 수 있는 또 다른 동물들을 알고 있니?
Emily: 응, 일부 벌들은 먹이를 찾을 수 있는 곳을 보여주기 위해 춤을 춰.
Hojun: 멋지다! 내 의견으로는, 춤을 추는 것은 의사소통을 위한 굉장한 방법인 것 같아.
Emily: 전적으로 너에게 동의해.

❶ 'No, I didn't.'의 줄임말이다. ❷ they는 some male birds를 가리킨다.
❸ That's interesting. = Sounds interesting. = How interesting that is!
❹ In my opinion = In my view = In my eyes = To my mind = I would say that ~ 등의 표현을 사용하여 의견을 나타낼 수 있다.
❺ 동의하는 표현으로 'I'm with you on that.', 'I think so, too.' 또는 'I can't agree with you more.' 등으로 바꾸어 표현할 수 있다.

Check(√) True or False

(1) Some male birds dance to show their love to female birds.　　T ☐ F ☐

(2) Some bees dance to get some honey.　　T ☐ F ☐

Listen and Speak 2-B

Tom: What are you reading, Kelly?

Kelly: I'm reading a story about Michaela DePrince.

Tom: Michaela DePrince? Can you tell me more about ❶her?

Kelly: Sure. Michaela lost her parents when she was three. After that, she ❷had a lot of difficulties. But she never ❸gave up on her dream of becoming a dancer.

Tom: Wow, she worked very hard to be a good dancer. Kelly, you also have a dream to be a dancer, right?

Kelly: Yes. I will ❹try my best to be a great dancer like her.

Tom: ❺Keep up the good work. I'm sure you can make it.

Tom: 무엇을 읽고 있니, Kelly?
Kelly: Michaela DePrince에 대한 이야기를 읽고 있어.
Tom: Michaela DePrince? 그녀에 대해 좀 더 얘기해 줄 수 있니?
Kelly: 그래. Michaela는 그녀가 세 살일 때 부모를 잃었어. 그 후 그녀는 많은 역경을 겪었지. 그러나 그녀는 무용수가 되겠다는 꿈을 절대 포기하지 않았어.
Tom: 와, 그녀는 훌륭한 무용수가 되기 위해 굉장히 열심히 노력했구나. Kelly, 너도 무용수가 되려는 꿈이 있지, 그렇지?
Kelly: 응. 그녀처럼 멋진 무용수가 되기 위해 최선을 다할 거야.
Tom: 계속 노력해 봐. 난 네가 해낼 거라고 확신해.

❶ her는 Michaela DePrince를 가리킨다. ❷ have a lot of difficulties: 많은 역경을 겪다
❸ give up on: ~을 포기하다　　　❹ try one's best: 최선을 다하다
❺ keep up the good work: 계속 열심히 하다

Check(√) True or False

(3) Kelly wants to become a dancer in the future.　　T ☐ F ☐

(4) Michaela DePrince gave up on her dream because of her difficulties.　　T ☐ F ☐

Listen and Speak 1 – A-1

Jane: Minsu, ❶what do you think about that painting?

Minsu: Umm ... The people ❷look like they're ❸having fun.

Jane: I agree. In my opinion, the dancing boy really enjoys ❹dancing.

❶ 상대방에게 의견을 묻는 표현으로 'what's your opinion about that painting?'으로 물을 수 있다.
❷ look like: ~처럼 보이다 ❸ have fun: 즐거운 시간을 보내다
❹ enjoy는 동명사를 목적어로 취한다.

Listen and Speak 1 – A-2

Brian: Jimin, what do you think about this painting?

Jimin: In my opinion, it's interesting. I smiled when I first saw it.

Brian: ❶Me, too. The dancers in the painting ❷ look happy.

❶ 'Me, too.'는 'So did I.'로 바꾸어 쓸 수 있다.
❷ look+형용사: ~처럼 보이다

Listen and Speak 2 – A-1

Minji: I use my ❶voice to make music. Listen to my music. My voice is soft and cool. ❷I'm sure you will like ❸it.

Jimin: I move my body to express my feelings. Look at my movements. ❹Why don't you jump like me? I'm sure you'll feel great.

Sujin: I use my hands to ❺make sounds. Come and listen to my music. I'm sure you'll want to dance when you listen to it.

❶ voice: 목소리
❷ 확신을 나타내는 표현으로 'I'm certain ~'으로 바꾸어 쓸 수 있다.
❸ it은 my voice를 가리킨다.
❹ 'Why don't you ~?'는 제안하는 표현으로 'How about ~?', 'What about ~?', 'Let's ~.' 등으로 바꾸어 쓸 수 있다.
❺ make sounds: 소리를 내다

Real Life Communication

Junsu: You know what? The school dance contest will ❶be held soon.

Emily: That's right. I heard Jimin's class is going to perform a taekwondo dance and Tim's class is going to do a K-pop dance.

Brian: We should also decide ❷what to do.

Mina: How about a Buchaechum? In my opinion, it is easy to learn, and it's also beautiful.

Emily: That sounds like a good idea. But who will teach us?

Brian: Mina is good at traditional dances. Can you help us, Mina?

Mina: Of course, I will. I'm sure we'll have a lot of fun.

Junsu: Great. Let's ❸give it a try.

❶ be held: 개최되다, 열리다
❷ what to do: 무엇을 할지 = what we should do
❸ give it a try: 시도하다

Let's Check

Jenny: Look at the dancing girls, Dongjun. ❶ Aren't they amazing?

Dongjun: Girls? I can only see one dancer.

Jenny: Look more closely. Do you see many arms behind her?

Dongjun: Wow. I didn't know that there were other dancers behind her.

Jenny: That's right. I'm sure there are ❷more than 10 dancers.

❶ 부정의문문(=Are they not amazing?)
❷ more than: ~ 이상

● 다음 우리말과 일치하도록 빈칸에 알맞은 말을 쓰시오. (주어진 철자가 있으면 그 철자로 시작할 것)

Listen & Speak 1 A-1

Jane: Minsu, what do you think about that _____?

Minsu: Umm … The people look _____ they're _____ _____.

Jane: I agree. _____ _____ _____, the dancing boy really _____ _____.

Jane: 민수야, 저 그림에 대해 어떻게 생각해?
Minsu: 음… 사람들이 재미있게 노는 것처럼 보여.
Jane: 나도 동의해. 내 의견으로는, 춤추는 소년이 춤추는 것을 정말로 즐기는 것 같아.

Listen & Speak 1 A-2

Brian: Jimin, _____ do you think _____ _____ _____?

Jimin: In my opinion, it's _____. I _____ when I first saw it.

Brian: Me, too. The dancers in the painting _____ _____.

Brian: 지민아, 이 그림에 대해 어떻게 생각해?
Jimin: 내 의견으로는 흥미로워. 처음 이것을 봤을 때 난 미소 지었어.
Brian: 나도 그래. 그림 속 춤추는 사람들은 행복해 보여.

Listen & Speak 1 B

Emily: Hojun, did you know that _____ _____ _____?

Hojun: No. _____ do they dance?

Emily: They dance to show their _____ to _____ _____.

Hojun: That's interesting. Do you know _____ _____ _____ that can dance?

Emily: Yes, some _____ dance to show _____ _____ _____ _____.

Hojun: That's cool! In my opinion, dancing is a great way to _____.

Emily: I totally _____ _____ _____.

Emily: 호준아, 너는 일부 수컷 새들이 춤을 춘다는 것을 알고 있었니?
Hojun: 아니. 왜 춤을 추지?
Emily: 그들은 암컷 새들에게 그들의 사랑을 보여주기 위해 춤을 춰.
Hojun: 그거 흥미로운 걸. 춤을 출 수 있는 또 다른 동물들을 알고 있니?
Emily: 응, 일부 벌들은 먹이를 찾을 수 있는 곳을 보여주기 위해 춤을 춰.
Hojun: 멋지다! 내 의견으로는, 춤을 추는 것은 의사소통을 위한 굉장한 방법인 것 같아.
Emily: 전적으로 너에게 동의해.

Listen & Speak 2 A-1

Minji: I use _____ _____ to make music. Listen to my music. My voice is _____ and _____. I'm _____ you will like it.

Jimin: I move _____ _____ to express my feelings. Look at my _____. _____ _____ _____ you jump like me? I'm _____ you'll feel great.

Sujin: I use my hands to _____ _____. Come and listen to my music. I'm sure you'll want to _____ when you listen to it.

Minji: 나는 음악을 만들기 위해 내 목소리를 사용합니다. 내 음악을 들어보세요. 내 목소리는 부드럽고 멋지죠. 나는 당신이 그것을 좋아할 거라고 확신해요.
Jimin: 나는 내 감정을 표현하기 위해 내 몸을 움직입니다. 내 동작을 보세요. 나처럼 뛰어올라 보는 게 어때요? 나는 당신이 멋진 기분이 들 거라고 확신해요.
Sujin: 나는 소리를 만들기 위해 내 손을 사용합니다. 와서 내 음악을 들어보세요. 나는 당신이 이것을 들을 때 춤을 추고 싶을 거라고 확신해요.

Listen & Speak 2 B

Tom: _____ are you _____, Kelly?

Kelly: I'm reading a _____ _____ Michaela DePrince.

Tom: Michaela DePrince? Can you _____ me _____ about her?

Kelly: Sure. Michaela _____ her parents _____ she was three. _____ _____, she had a lot of difficulties. But she never _____ _____ _____ her dream of becoming a dancer.

Tom: Wow, she worked very hard _____ _____ a good dancer. Kelly, you also have a dream _____ _____ a dancer, _____?

Kelly: Yes. I will _____ _____ _____ to be a great dancer like her.

Tom: _____ _____ the good work. I'm sure you can _____ _____.

Real Life Communication

Junsu: You know _____? The school dance contest will be _____ soon.

Emily: That's right. I heard Jimin's class is going to _____ a taekwondo dance and Tim's class is going to do a K-pop dance.

Brian: We should also _____ _____ _____ _____.

Mina: _____ _____ a Buchaechum? In my _____, it is easy to learn, and it's also _____.

Emily: That _____ _____ a good idea. But who will teach us?

Brian: Mina _____ _____ _____ traditional dances. Can you help us, Mina?

Mina: Of course, I will. _____ _____ we'll have a lot of fun.

Junsu: Great. Let's _____ _____ _____ _____.

Let's Check

Jenny: Look at the _____ _____, Dongjun. Aren't they _____?

Dongjun: Girls? I can only see one dancer.

Jenny: _____ _____ closely. Do you see many arms _____ her?

Dongjun: Wow. I didn't know that there were _____ _____ _____ _____.

Jenny: That's _____. _____ _____ there are _____ than 10 dancers.

해석

Tom: 무엇을 읽고 있니, Kelly?
Kelly: Michaela DePrince에 대한 이야기를 읽고 있어.
Tom: Michaela DePrince? 그녀에 대해 좀 더 얘기해 줄 수 있니?
Kelly: 그래. Michaela는 세 살 때 부모를 잃었어. 그 후 그녀는 많은 역경을 겪었어. 그러나 그녀는 무용수가 되겠다는 꿈을 절대 포기하지 않았어.
Tom: 와, 그녀는 훌륭한 무용수가 되기 위해 굉장히 열심히 노력했구나. Kelly, 너도 무용수가 되려는 꿈이 있지, 그렇지?
Kelly: 응. 그녀처럼 멋진 무용수가 되기 위해 최선을 다할 거야.
Tom: 계속 노력해 봐. 난 네가 해낼 거라고 확신해.

Junsu: 있잖아. 학교 춤 경연 대회가 곧 열릴 거야.
Emily: 맞아. 지민이네 반은 태권도 춤을 공연하고, Tim네 반은 K-pop 춤을 출 거라고 들었어.
Brian: 우리도 무엇을 할지 결정해야 해.
Mina: 부채춤은 어때? 내 의견으로는, 그것은 배우기 쉽고 또한 아름다워.
Emily: 좋은 생각인 것 같아. 하지만 누가 우리를 가르치지?
Brian: 미나가 전통 춤을 잘 춰. 우리를 도울 수 있니, 미나야?
Mina: 물론, 그럴 거야. 우리는 매우 즐거울 거라고 확신해.
Junsu: 아주 좋아. 시도해 보자.

Jenny: 춤추는 여자들을 봐, 동준아. 대단하지 않니?
Donjun: 여자들? 난 단지 한 명의 무용수만 보이는 걸.
Jenny: 좀 더 가까이 봐. 그녀 뒤에 많은 팔들이 보이니?
Donjun: 와. 그녀 뒤에 다른 무용수들이 있는지 몰랐어.
Jenny: 맞아. 나는 10명 이상의 무용수들이 있다고 확신해.

[01~02] 다음 대화를 읽고 물음에 답하시오.

Jane: Minsu, what do you think about that painting?

Minsu: Umm ... The people look like they're having fun.

Jane: I agree. (A)_____, the dancing boy really enjoys (B)_____ (dance).

01 위 대화의 빈칸 (A)에 들어갈 말로 나머지와 의미가 <u>다른</u> 것은?

① To my mind

② In my opinion

③ In my view

④ In my eyes

⑤ To sum up

02 위 대화의 빈칸 (B)에 주어진 단어를 알맞은 형태로 쓰시오.

➡ _____

[03~04] 다음 대화를 읽고 물음에 답하시오.

Brian: Jimin, what do you think about this painting?

Jimin: In my opinion, it's (A)[interested / interesting]. I (B)[smiled / smiling] when I first saw it.

Brian: Me, too. The dancers in the painting look (C)[happy / happily].

03 위 대화의 (A)~(C)에 들어갈 말이 바르게 짝지어진 것은?

	(A)	(B)	(C)
①	interested	smiled	happy
②	interested	smiling	happily
③	interesting	smiled	happily
④	interesting	smiling	happily
⑤	interesting	smiled	happy

04 What does Brian think about the dancers in the painting?

➡ _____

[01~03] 다음 대화를 읽고 물음에 답하시오.

Emily: Hojun, did you know that some male birds dance?

Hojun: No. Why do they dance?

Emily: They dance to show their love to female birds.

Hojun: (A)_____ Do you know any other animals that can dance?

Emily: Yes, some bees dance to show where to find food.

Hojun: That's cool! In my opinion, dancing is a great way to communicate.

Emily: I totally agree with you.

01 위 대화의 빈칸 (A)에 들어갈 말로 나머지와 의미가 다른 것은?

① I'm interested in birds.
② What an interesting point!
③ Sounds interesting.
④ How interesting it is!
⑤ That's interesting.

서답형

02 위 대화에서 다음 영영풀이가 나타내는 말을 찾아 쓰시오.

> to give information about something to someone by speaking, writing, moving your hands, etc.

➡ _____

03 위 대화의 내용과 일치하지 않는 것은?

① 일부 수컷 새들이 춤을 춘다.
② 수컷 새들은 암컷 새들에게 그들의 사랑을 보여주기 위해 춤을 춘다.
③ 일부 벌들도 춤을 춘다.
④ 벌들은 먹이를 찾을 수 있는 곳을 보여주기 위해 춤을 춘다.
⑤ 호준은 동물들의 춤은 의사소통과는 관계가 없다고 생각한다.

[04~06] 다음 대화를 읽고 물음에 답하시오.

Minji: I use my voice to make music. Listen to my music. My voice is soft and cool. (A)I'm sure you will like it.

Jimin: I move my body to express my feelings. Look at my movements. (B)Why don't you jump like me? I'm sure you'll feel great.

Sujin: I use my hands to make sounds. Come and listen to my music. I'm sure you'll want to dance when you listen to it.

04 위 대화의 밑줄 친 (A)와 바꾸어 쓸 수 있는 것을 모두 고르시오.

① I'm certain you will like it.
② I want to know whether you like it.
③ I wonder if you like it or not.
④ I'm doubtful whether you like it.
⑤ I have no doubt that you will like it.

05 위 대화의 밑줄 친 (B)와 바꾸어 쓸 수 있는 것을 고르시오.

① I wonder how you jump like me.
② Let's jump like me.
③ Why did you jump like me?
④ How about jumping like me?
⑤ Do you know how to jump like me?

06 위 대화의 내용과 일치하지 않는 것은?

① 민지는 음악을 만들기 위해 목소리를 사용한다.
② 민지의 목소리는 부드럽고 멋지다.
③ 지민은 자신의 감정을 표현하기 위해 몸을 움직인다.
④ 지민은 자신처럼 뛰어 올라보면 멋진 기분이 들거라고 확신한다.
⑤ 수진은 춤을 추기 위해 그녀의 손을 사용한다.

[07~09] 다음 대화를 읽고 물음에 답하시오.

Tom: What are you reading, Kelly?

Kelly: I'm reading a story about Michaela DePrince.

Tom: Michaela DePrince? Can you tell me more about her?

Kelly: Sure. Michaela (A)[lost / losing] her parents when she was three. After that, she had a lot of difficulties. But she never gave up on her dream of becoming a dancer.

Tom: Wow, she worked very hard to be a good dancer. Kelly, you also have a dream to be a dancer, right?

Kelly: Yes. I will try my (B)[better / best] to be a great dancer like her.

Tom: (a)계속 노력해 봐. I'm sure you can (C)[make / have] it.

07 위 대화의 (A)~(C)에 들어갈 말로 바르게 짝지어진 것은?

	(A)	(B)	(C)
①	lost	better	make
②	lost	best	have
③	lost	best	make
④	losing	best	have
⑤	losing	better	make

서답형
08 위 대화의 밑줄 친 (a)의 우리말을 〈보기〉에 주어진 단어를 모두 배열하여 영작하시오.

┌─ 보기 ┐
the / work / keep / good / up

➡ _____

09 위 대화를 읽고 대답할 수 없는 것은?

① What is Kelly reading?

② When did Michaela's parents pass away?

③ What difficulties did Michaela have after becoming a dancer?

④ What did Michaela want to be?

⑤ What is Kelly going to do to be a great dancer?

[10~12] 다음 대화를 읽고 물음에 답하시오.

Tom: What are you reading, Kelly?

Kelly: I'm reading a story about Michaela DePrince.

Tom: Michaela DePrince? Can you tell me more about her?

Kelly: Sure. Michaela lost her parents when she was three. After that, she had a lot of difficulties. But she never gave up on her dream of becoming a dancer.

Tom: Wow, she worked very hard to be a good dancer. Kelly, you also have a dream to be a dancer, right?

Kelly: Yes. I will try my best to be a great dancer like her.

Tom: Keep up the good work. I'm sure you can make it.

10 What happened to Michaela when she was three?

➡ _____

11 What didn't Michaela give up on despite lots of difficulties?

➡ _____

12 What is Kelly going to do to realize her dream?

➡ _____

Conversation **서술형 시험대비**

01 다음 대화의 내용과 일치하도록 호준이의 일기를 완성하시오.

> Emily: Hojun, did you know that some male birds dance?
> Hojun: No. Why do they dance?
> Emily: They dance to show their love to female birds.
> Hojun: That's interesting. Do you know any other animals that can dance?
> Emily: Yes, some bees dance to show where to find food.
> Hojun: That's cool! In my opinion, dancing is a great way to communicate.
> Emily: I totally agree with you.

⬇

> Mon, Oct 7th, 2019
> Today, I learned about animals' dancing from Emily. She told me that some male birds dance because they want to (A)_____. Moreover, I heard that some bees also dance to (B)_____. It was so interesting. I thought that dancing is a great way to (C)_____ among the animals.

02 다음 대화의 내용과 일치하도록 주어진 표의 빈칸 (A)와 (B)를 완성하시오

> Junsu: You know what? The school dance contest will be held soon.
> Emily: That's right. I heard Jimin's class is going to perform a taekwondo dance and Tim's class is going to do a K-pop dance.
> Brian: We should also decide what to do.
> Mina: How about a Buchaechum? In my opinion, it is easy to learn, and it's also beautiful.

> Emily: That sounds like a good idea. But who will teach us?
> Brian: Mina is good at traditional dances. Can you help us, Mina?
> Mina: Of course, I will. I'm sure we'll have a lot of fun.
> Junsu: Great. Let's give it a try.

<What to Perform at the School Dance Contest>

	Type of dance	The reason
Jimin's class	a taekwondo dance	Taekwondo is a popular sport in the world.
Tim's class	a K-pop dance	It is exciting and popular in the world.
Brian's class	(A) _____	(B) _____ _____

03 다음 대화가 자연스럽게 이어지도록 순서대로 배열하시오.

> Tom: What are you reading, Kelly?
> Kelly: I'm reading a story about Michaela DePrince.
> (A) Yes. I will try my best to be a great dancer like her.
> (B) Michaela DePrince? Can you tell me more about her?
> (C) Keep up the good work. I'm sure you can make it.
> (D) Wow, she worked very hard to be a good dancer. Kelly, you also have a dream to be a dancer, right?
> (E) Sure. Michaela lost her parents when she was three. After that, she had a lot of difficulties. But she never gave up on her dream of becoming a dancer.

➡ _____

Grammar

교과서

① so ~ that ...

- She was **so** hungry **that** she ordered many dishes.
  그녀는 너무 배가 고파서 많은 요리를 주문했다.
- He is **so** happy **that** he wants to talk about it. 그는 너무 행복해서 그것에 관해 말하기를 원한다.

■ 'so ~ that ...'은 '너무 ~해서 …하다'는 뜻으로 that 이하에 결과가 나온다. 이때 that은 주어와 동사가 있는 절을 이끄는 것에 유의한다.

- She is **so** tired **that** she wants to go home. 그녀는 너무 피곤해서 집에 가고 싶다.
- There were **so** many children **that** it was noisy. 너무 많은 아이들이 있어서 시끄러웠다.

■ 'so+형용사/부사+that+주어+can't+동사원형'은 '너무 ~해서 …할 수 없다'는 의미로, 형용사나 부사가 that절의 원인이 되고, that절은 그 결과를 이끈다. 'too+형용사/부사+to부정사'로 바꾸어 쓸 수 있다.

- They are **so** nervous **that** they can't focus. 그들은 너무 초조해서 집중할 수 없다.
  = They are **too** nervous **to focus**.
- The boy was **so** short **that** he couldn't ride the bike. 그 소년은 키가 너무 작아서 자전거를 탈 수 없었다.
  = The boy was **too** short **to ride** the bike.

■ 반면에, '충분히 ~해서 …할 수 있다'는 의미를 나타낼 때에는 '형용사/부사+enough+to부정사'를 쓰고, 이는 'so+형용사/부사+that+주어+can+동사원형'과 같다.

- He is **so** generous **that** he can forgive you. 그는 아주 관대해서 너를 용서할 수 있다.
  = He is generous **enough to forgive** you.
- The candle is **so** bright **that** it can light the room. 그 초는 아주 밝아서 방을 밝힐 수 있다.
  = The candle is bright **enough to light** the room.

핵심 Check

1. 다음 우리말과 일치하도록 빈칸에 알맞은 말을 쓰시오.

(1) Clara는 아주 친절해서 모두가 그녀를 좋아한다.
→ Clara is _____ _____ _____ everyone likes her.

(2) 그 셔츠는 아주 커서 입을 수 없어.
→ The shirt is _____ _____ _____ I can't wear it.

(3) 그녀는 아주 부자여서 그 차를 살 수 있어.
→ She is _____ _____ _____ she can buy the car.

② 원급 비교

- Sally is **as** diligent **as** Kate. Sally는 Kate만큼 부지런해.
- They did the work **as** much **as** we did. 그들은 우리가 한 만큼 많이 그 일을 했어.

- 'as ~ as' 원급 비교는 두 개의 대상이 정도가 같을 때 사용할 수 있는 표현이다. 'as+형용사/부사의 원급+as'로 '~만큼 …한[하게]'라고 해석한다. 앞에 쓰인 as는 '그러한, 똑같은 정도로'라는 의미의 부사이며, 뒤에 쓰이고 있는 as는 '~와 같이'라는 의미로 접속사이다.
  - We enjoyed the party **as** much **as** you did. 우리도 너만큼 파티를 즐겼어.
  - That book is **as** cheap **as** this book. 저 책은 이 책만큼 값이 싸.

- 원급 비교의 부정인 'not as[so]+원급+as ~'는 '~만큼 …하지 않은[않게]'라는 의미로, 비교하는 두 대상의 정도가 같지 않을 때 쓸 수 있다.
  - You are **not as** honest **as** I am. 너는 나만큼 정직하지 않아.
  - This desk is **not as** big **as** my old one. 이 책상은 나의 예전 것만큼 크진 않아.

- 동등 비교를 이용하여 비교의 배수 표현이 가능하다. '배수사(twice, three times 등)+as+형용사/부사+as'의 형태이며 '~의 몇 배 만큼 …한[하게]'이라는 의미로 쓰인다.
  - This box is **two times as** heavy **as** that box. 이 상자는 저 상자보다 두 배 무겁다.
  - Your rope is **three times as** long **as** my rope. 너의 밧줄은 내 것보다 세 배 길다.

- 원급을 이용한 관용 표현
  'as+원급+as possible'은 '가능한 한 ~한[하게]'라고 해석되고 이는 'as+원급+as+주어+can[could]'와 같다. 그 외에도 'as quiet as a mouse(쥐 죽은 듯이 조용히)', 'as blind as a bat(시력이 매우 안 좋은)', 'as wise as an owl(매우 현명한)', 'as free as a bird(매우 자유로운)' 등이 있다.
  - Come here **as soon as possible**. 가능한 빨리 이곳으로 오렴.

- 원급을 이용한 최상급 표현
  'no other+단수 명사+동사+as[so] ~ as …'는 '어떠한 다른 명사도 …만큼 ~하지 않다'는 의미로 최상급을 나타낼 수 있다..
  - **No other** hero in Avengers is **as** brave **as** Iron Man. Avengers의 다른 어떤 영웅도 아이언맨만큼 용감하지 않다.
  = Iron Man is **the bravest** hero in Avengers.

핵심 Check

2. 다음 우리말과 일치하도록 빈칸에 알맞은 말을 쓰시오.
  (1) 작년만큼 덥지 않아요.
    ➡ It is _____ _____ _____ _____ it was last year.
  (2) 너는 Tom만큼 잘생겼어.
    ➡ You are _____ _____ _____ Tom.

01 다음 문장에서 어법상 <u>어색한</u> 부분을 바르게 고쳐 쓰시오.

(1) Kate was very tired that she went to bed early.

_____ ➡ _____

(2) Robert is as taller as Chuck.

_____ ➡ _____

(3) She was so upset to think clearly.

_____ ➡ _____

(4) This balloon is two time as big as that balloon.

_____ ➡ _____

02 괄호 안의 단어를 이용하여 알맞은 말을 빈칸에 쓰시오.

(1) The meat is _____ _____ _____ it is hard to chew. (tough)

(2) The paper is _____ _____ _____ be written. (thin)

(3) We were _____ _____ _____ we kept dancing. (happy)

(4) She is _____ _____ _____ lend me some money. (generous)

(5) He talks _____ _____ _____ be with. (much)

03 주어진 어구를 바르게 배열하여 다음 우리말을 영어로 쓰시오.

(1) 이 앨범에서 이 노래가 가장 아름다워. (this song / as / as / no / song / other / this album / beautiful / in / is)

➡ _____

(2) 너의 쿠키는 그의 쿠키만큼 맛있지 않아. (his / not / as / as / cookies / your / delicious / are)

➡ _____

(3) 이 산은 남산보다 세 배 높다. (Namsan / this mountain / three / as / as / is / times / high)

➡ _____

(4) 가능한 한 자주 전화하렴. (possible / as / as / me / call / often)

➡ _____

01 다음 빈칸에 들어갈 말로 가장 적절한 것은?

> Brian speaks _____ fast that I can't understand him.

① such   ② very   ③ so
④ too   ⑤ enough

02 다음 우리말을 영어로 바르게 옮긴 것은?

> 이것은 저것보다 두 배만큼 좋아.

① This is as good as that.
② This is as better as that.
③ This is better than that.
④ This is twice as good as that.
⑤ This is two time as good as that.

03 다음 중 문장의 의미가 서로 같지 <u>않은</u> 것은?

① Maya is so tall that she is good at playing basketball.
→ Maya is good at playing basketball because she is very tall.
② No other river in Korea is as long as this river.
→ This river is the longest river in Korea.
③ Kelly was so annoyed that she turned off her cellphone.
→ Because Kelly turned off her cellphone, she was annoyed.
④ You are too young to work.
→ You are so young that you can't work.
⑤ He is fast enough to win the race.
→ He is so fast that he can win the race.

서답형
04 주어진 단어를 이용하여 다음 우리말을 영어로 쓰시오.

> 그녀는 너무 바빠서 지금 우리와 함께 이야기할 수 없어요. (that / busy)

➡ _____

05 다음 빈칸에 들어갈 말로 가장 적절한 것은?

> We were going to meet here at 1 o'clock. You came here at 2 o'clock. Julia came here at 2 o'clock. Julia _____ you.

① came here as early as
② came here two times as late as
③ didn't come as late as
④ came here as late as
⑤ came earlier than

06 다음 빈칸에 들어갈 말로 가장 적절한 것은?

> He felt so miserable that he couldn't say a word.
> = He felt _____ say a word.

① very miserable to
② miserable enough to
③ so miserable that
④ too miserable to
⑤ too miserable that

서답형
07 다음 우리말을 영어로 쓰시오.

> 네 방은 내 방만큼 깨끗해.

➡ _____

08 다음 두 문장을 하나의 문장으로 바르게 표현한 것은?

> She felt very thirsty. So she drank a bottle of water.

① Although she felt very thirsty, she drank a bottle of water.
② She felt so thirsty that she couldn't drink a bottle of water.
③ She felt very thirsty because she drank a bottle of water.
④ She felt very thirsty although she drank a bottle of water.
⑤ She felt so thirsty that she drank a bottle of water.

09 다음 빈칸에 들어갈 말이 바르게 짝지어진 것은?

> • Olivia felt _____ cold that she couldn't fall asleep.
> • Tom is brave _____ to fight for us.
> • The lamp is not as _____ as my lamp.

① too – too – bright
② too – enough – brighter
③ so – enough – bright
④ so – too – bright
⑤ so – too – brighter

서답형
10 주어진 단어를 사용하여 다음 우리말을 지시에 맞게 영어로 쓰시오.

> 나는 너무 바빠서 숙제를 할 수 없었어. (do)

(1) to부정사를 사용하여

➡ _____

(2) that절을 사용하여

➡ _____

11 다음 중 어법상 틀린 문장은?

① The sun shines as bright as it did yesterday.
② No other planet in space is as beautiful as Earth.
③ The movie was exciting enough to watching two times.
④ She likes to walk so much that she walks every day.
⑤ The weather was so nice that we went to the zoo.

12 다음 주어진 문장과 같은 의미의 문장을 모두 고르시오.

> I can't play with you because I am very busy.

① Although I am very busy, I can play with you.
② I am too busy to play with you.
③ Because I can't play with you, I am very busy.
④ I am so busy that I can't play with you.
⑤ I am busy enough to play with you.

13 다음 빈칸에 들어갈 말로 적절하지 않은 것은?

> Melisa is _____ Betty.

① as lovely as   ② as pretty as
③ as friendly as   ④ not as taller as
⑤ not as smart as

서답형
14 주어진 문장과 같은 의미의 문장을 쓰시오.

> I was too young to see the movie.

➡ _____

서답형
15 아홉 개의 단어를 사용하여 다음 우리말을 영어로 쓸 때 세 번째와 일곱 번째로 오는 단어를 바르게 묶은 것은?

> 목걸이들이 너무 비싸서 우리는 그것들을 살 수 없었어.

① were – that ② so – we
③ expensive – buy ④ so – couldn't
⑤ were – couldn't

16 다음 중 우리말을 영어로 바르게 옮기지 <u>않은</u> 것은?

① 그는 Jason만큼 크게 말하지 않는다.
→ He doesn't talk as loudly as Jason.
② 나는 너무 열심히 일해서 피곤했다.
→ I worked so hard that I was tired.
③ 너의 다리는 내 다리만큼 길어.
→ Your legs are as long as my legs.
④ 내 친구들 중 Paul이 가장 친절해.
→ No other friend of mine is as kind as Paul.
⑤ 그녀는 책상을 옮기기에 충분히 힘이 세.
→ She is too strong to move the desk.

중요
17 다음 빈칸에 들어갈 말이 바르게 짝지은 것은?

> Julie was so happy that she could invite everyone to her party.
> = Julie was _____ invite everyone to her party.

① too happy to ② happy enough to
③ happy because ④ very happy to
⑤ enough happy to

서답형
18 주어진 단어를 활용하여 다음 우리말을 영어로 쓰시오. (8 words)

> 그들은 우리만큼 가난하지 않아. (poor)

➡ _____

19 다음 대화의 빈칸에 들어갈 말로 적절한 것을 <u>모두</u> 고르시오.

> A: Did you have your dinner?
> B: No, I _____ my dinner.

① was tired enough to have
② was too tired to have
③ was so tired that I could have
④ was tired that I had
⑤ was so tired that I couldn't have

중요
20 다음 우리말을 영어로 옮길 때 빈칸에 들어갈 말로 가장 적절한 것은?

> 사탕은 아이스크림만큼 달콤한 맛이 난다.
> Candies _____ ice cream.

① taste as sweetly as
② taste sweeter than
③ taste as sweet as
④ taste as bitter as
⑤ taste not as sweet as

서답형
21 주어진 단어를 바르게 배열하여 다음 우리말을 영어로 쓰시오. 필요하다면 어형을 바꾸시오.

> 그녀는 너무 화가 나서 일찍 집으로 갔다.
> (early / she / she / upset / went / was / that / home / so)

➡ _____

서답형
22 다음 빈칸에 알맞은 말을 쓰시오.

(1) James is 170cm tall. Parker is 178cm tall. So James is _____ Parker.
(2) Flowers are expensive these days. A rose is ten thousand won. A lily is also ten thousand won. A rose is _____ a lily.

01 다음 문장과 같은 의미의 문장을 쓰시오.

(1) She is so bright that she can solve all the puzzles.

➡ _____

(2) He runs fast enough to win the race.

➡ _____

(3) It was so hot that I couldn't go out.

➡ _____

(4) They were so poor that they couldn't buy books as much as they wanted.

➡ _____

_____

(5) They studied so hard that they could pass the test.

➡ _____

02 주어진 단어를 사용하여 다음 우리말을 영어로 쓰시오.

너는 네 여동생만큼 똑똑하니?
(clever)

➡ _____

03 다음 우리말을 영어로 옮길 때, 빈칸에 알맞은 말을 쓰시오.

그 책은 너무 어려워서 나는 그것을 읽기를 포기했어.
➡ The book was _____ _____
_____ I gave up reading it.

04 다음 세 학생에 관한 표를 읽고 문장을 완성하시오. 주어진 단어를 활용하시오.

	Kevin	Daisy	Peter
age	17	17	19
height	185	160	178
weight	71	50	71

(heavy / much / short / old)

(1) Kevin is _____ Daisy. But he is _____ Peter.

(2) No other student of them is _____ Daisy.

(3) Peter is _____ Kevin. But He weighs _____ Kevin.

(4) Daisy is _____ Kevin and Peter.

05 주어진 단어를 활용하여 다음 대화의 우리말을 영어로 쓰시오.

A: How was the food?
B: 음식이 너무 뜨거워서 나는 혀를 데었어요.
(burn one's tongue)

➡ _____

06 다음 문장을 읽고 두 사람의 기상 시간을 비교하는 문장을 쓰시오.

Emily gets up at seven o'clock in the morning. Judy gets up at seven o'clock in the morning. Both students get up early in the morning.

➡ _____

07 다음 두 문장을 조건에 맞게 하나의 문장으로 표현하시오.

> I woke up late. So I couldn't attend the meeting.

(1) to부정사를 사용하여

➡ _____

(2) that절을 사용하여

➡ _____

08 다음 그림을 참고하여 개와 고양이를 비교하는 문장을 쓰시오.

4kg   4kg

➡ _____

09 주어진 단어를 활용하여 다음 우리말을 영어로 쓰시오.

> 그녀는 운전을 너무 잘해서 항상 나를 데리러 와요.
> (that / pick up)

➡ _____

10 다음 우리말에 맞게 주어진 단어를 활용하여 빈칸에 알맞은 말을 쓰시오.

> Helen은 자유로운 시간이 결코 없어. 그녀는 매우 바빠.
> ➡ Helen never has any free time. She is
> _____. (bee)

11 다음 글을 읽고 주어진 단어를 활용하여 비교하는 문장을 완성하시오.

> The library is three kilometers away from here. The book store is also three kilometers away from here.

➡ The library is _____ the book store from here. (far)

 12 주어진 단어를 이용하여 다음 우리말에 맞게 빈칸을 완성하시오.

> 어제 너는 너무 무례해서 나는 너에게 실망했어.
> (rude / that / disappoint)

➡ Yesterday, _____

_____ .

13 주어진 단어를 활용하여 다음 대화의 빈칸에 알맞은 말을 쓰시오.

> **A:** _____ ?
>   (much / eat / pizza / Tom)
> **B:** Yes. He ate two pieces of pizza and I ate also two pieces of pizza.

14 다음 문장과 같은 의미의 문장을 쓰시오.

> I know June well enough to ask for help.

➡ _____

 15 주어진 단어를 활용하여 다음 우리말을 영어로 쓰시오.

> 그 책은 이 책보다 세 배 두꺼워.
> (thick / as)

➡ _____

Dance with a Story

Why do people dance? They dance to express feelings, give happiness to others, or enjoy themselves. Let's take a look at different kinds of dance around the world.

India: Kathakali

Kathakali tells a story. The dancers tell stories through their body movements. These stories are usually about a fight between good and evil. Dancers who are playing good characters paint their faces green. Those who are playing evil characters wear black make-up. Interestingly, in *Kathakali*, only men are allowed to dance. The body movements are so powerful that the dancers need to train for many years.

express: 표현하다
take a look: 살펴보다
movement: 움직임, 동작
fight 싸움
good and evil: 선과 악
character: 등장인물
make-up 화장, 분장
be allowed to: ~이 허용되다
train 훈련하다

📎 확인문제

• 다음 문장이 본문의 내용과 일치하면 T, 일치하지 않으면 F를 쓰시오.

1 People dance with one specific reason. ☐

2 By dancing, people enjoy themselves. ☐

3 There are various types of dance around the world. ☐

4 There is no story in the dance *Kathakali*. ☐

5 Dancers who are playing evil characters wear green make-up. ☐

6 Women aren't allowed to dance in *Kathakali*. ☐

New Zealand: *Haka*

When people visit New Zealand, they may meet a group of *haka*
시간의 부사절을 이끄는 접속사(~할 때) · 추측의 조동사
dancers. The dancers perform this traditional dance with scary faces.
Haka를 의미
This dance was originally performed by the Maori before a fight.
=The Maori originally performed this dance before a fight.
They wanted to show their strength to the enemy. The dancers looked
to부정사를 목적어로 취하는 동사
as scary as wild animals before fighting. Nowadays, in New Zealand,
as+형용사나 부사의 원급+as: ~만큼 …한 (동등비교) · = These days
rugby players usually perform a *haka* before a game to show their
빈도부사(일반동사 앞, be동사나 조동사 뒤에 위치) · to부정사의 부사적 용법 중 목적
strength to the other team.

Korea: *Buchaechum*

Buchaechum is a traditional Korean fan dance. The dancers wear
colorful *hanbok*. They dance with large fans that are painted in bright
주격 관계대명사
colors. The dancers move the fans gracefully to show different kinds
to부정사의 부사적 용법 중 목적
of beauty. Their movements look as beautiful as flowers or flying
as+형용사나 부사의 원급+as: ~만큼 …한 (동등비교)
birds. In Korea, *Buchaechum* is so popular that people can see it in
so+형용사/부사+that …: 너무 ~해서 …하다 (원인과 결과를 나타냄)
many traditional festivals.

perform: 공연하다, 연주하다
originally: 원래
strength: 힘
enemy: 적
wild: 야생의
colorful: 화려한, 다채로운
fan: 부채
bright: (색상이) 밝은
popular: 인기 있는

확인문제

● 다음 문장이 본문의 내용과 일치하면 T, 일치하지 않으면 F를 쓰시오.

1 The dancers perform a *haka* to show friendliness. ☐

2 By performing a *haka*, the Maori wanted to show they were scared. ☐

3 To show their strength, rugby players perform a *haka*. ☐

4 The fans used in *Buchaechum* are very simple. ☐

5 The *Buchaechum* dancers move their fans very fast. ☐

6 People are not interested in *Buchaechum* these days. ☐

• 우리말을 참고하여 빈칸에 알맞은 말을 쓰시오.

Dance with a Story

1 _____ do people _____?

2 They dance _____ _____ feelings, give happiness _____ others, or _____ _____.

3 Let's take a look at _____ _____ _____ _____ around the world

India: *Kathakali*

4 *Kathakali* _____ a story.

5 The dancers tell _____ _____ their _____ _____.

6 These stories are usually about _____ _____ _____ _____ _____ _____.

7 Dancers _____ _____ _____ good characters paint their faces _____.

8 Those _____ _____ _____ evil characters _____ _____ make-up.

9 _____, in *Kathakali*, only men _____ _____ dance.

10 The body movements are _____ _____ _____ the dancers need to train _____ many years.

New Zealand: *Haka*

11 When people visit New Zealand, they may _____ a group of _____ _____.

12 The dancers _____ this _____ dance with _____ _____.

이야기가 있는 춤

1 사람들은 왜 춤을 추는 걸까요?

2 사람들은 감정을 표현하고, 다른 사람들에게 행복감을 주거나 스스로 즐기기 위해 춤을 춥니다.

3 세계의 여러 가지 춤을 살펴봅시다.

인도: *Kathakali*

4 *Kathakali*에는 이야기가 있습니다.

5 춤꾼들은 몸동작을 통해 이야기합니다.

6 이러한 이야기들은 대개 선과 악의 싸움에 관한 것입니다.

7 선한 역할을 맡은 춤꾼들은 자신의 얼굴을 초록색으로 칠합니다.

8 악한 역할을 맡은 춤꾼들은 검은색 화장을 합니다.

9 재미있는 것은 *Kathakali* 춤에서 남자들만 춤추는 것이 허락된다는 사실입니다.

10 몸동작이 매우 힘이 넘쳐서 춤꾼들은 수년 동안 연습을 해야 합니다.

뉴질랜드: *Haka*

11 사람들이 뉴질랜드를 방문할 때, 그들은 *haka* 춤꾼들의 무리를 만날지도 모릅니다.

12 그 춤꾼들은 무서운 얼굴로 이 전통 춤을 춥니다.

13 This dance was _____ _____ _____ the Maori before a fight.

14 They wanted _____ _____ _____ _____ to the enemy.

15 The dancers looked _____ _____ _____ wild animals _____ fighting.

16 _____, in New Zealand, rugby players _____ _____ a *haka* before a game _____ _____ their strength to _____ _____ team.

Korea: *Buchaechum*

17 *Buchaechum* is a _____ Korean _____ dance.

18 The dancers _____ _____ _____.

19 They dance with large fans _____ _____ _____ in bright colors.

20 The dancers _____ the fans _____ to show _____ _____ _____ _____.

21 Their movements _____ _____ _____ _____ flowers or flying birds.

22 In Korea, *Buchaechum* is _____ _____ _____ people _____ _____ _____ in many traditional festivals.

13 이 춤은 원래 마오리족에 의해 싸움 전에 행해졌습니다.

14 그들은 적에게 그들의 힘을 보여 주고 싶었습니다.

15 춤꾼들은 싸움하기 전의 야생 동물들만큼 무섭게 보였습니다.

16 요즈음, 뉴질랜드에서는 럭비 선수들이 다른 팀에게 그들의 힘을 보여 주기 위해 게임 전에 주로 *haka*를 보여 줍니다.

한국: 부채춤

17 부채춤은 한국 전통 부채춤입니다.

18 춤꾼들은 다채로운 한복을 입습니다.

19 그들은 밝은 색으로 칠해진 커다란 부채를 가지고 춤을 춥니다.

20 그 춤꾼들은 다양한 종류의 미를 보여 주기 위해 부채를 우아하게 움직입니다.

21 그들의 움직임은 꽃 또는 날아다니는 새들처럼 우아하게 보입니다.

22 한국에서, 부채춤은 너무 인기가 있어서 사람들은 많은 전통 축제에서 그것을 볼 수 있습니다.

● 우리말을 참고하여 본문을 영작하시오.

Dance with a Story

1 사람들은 왜 춤을 추는 걸까요?

➡ _____

2 사람들은 감정을 표현하고, 다른 사람들에게 행복감을 주거나 스스로 즐기기 위해 춤을 춥니다.

➡ _____

3 세계의 여러 가지 춤을 살펴봅시다.

➡ _____

India: *Kathakali*

4 *Kathakali*에는 이야기가 있습니다.

➡ _____

5 춤꾼들은 몸동작을 통해 이야기합니다.

➡ _____

6 이러한 이야기들은 대개 선과 악의 싸움에 관한 것입니다.

➡ _____

7 선한 역할을 맡은 춤꾼들은 자신의 얼굴을 초록색으로 칠합니다.

➡ _____

8 악한 역할을 맡은 춤꾼들은 검은색 화장을 합니다.

➡ _____

9 재미있는 것은 *Kathakali* 춤에서 남자들만 춤추는 것이 허락된다는 사실입니다.

➡ _____

10 몸동작이 매우 힘이 넘쳐서 춤꾼들은 수년 동안 연습을 해야 합니다.

➡ _____

New Zealand: *Haka*

11 사람들이 뉴질랜드를 방문할 때, 그들은 *haka* 춤꾼들의 무리를 만날지도 모릅니다.

➡ _____

12 그 춤꾼들은 무서운 얼굴로 이 전통 춤을 춥니다.

➡ _____

13 이 춤은 원래 마오리족에 의해 싸움 전에 행해졌습니다.

➡ _____

14 그들은 적에게 그들의 힘을 보여 주고 싶었습니다.

➡ _____

15 그 춤꾼들은 싸움하기 전의 야생 동물들만큼 무섭게 보였습니다.

➡ _____

16 요즈음, 뉴질랜드에서는 럭비 선수들이 다른 팀에게 그들의 힘을 보여 주기 위해 게임 전에 주로 *haka*를 보여 줍니다.

➡ _____

_____

Korea: *Buchaechum*

17 부채춤은 한국 전통 부채춤입니다.

➡ _____

18 춤꾼들은 다채로운 한복을 입습니다.

➡ _____

19 그들은 밝은 색으로 칠해진 커다란 부채를 가지고 춤을 춥니다.

➡ _____

20 그 춤꾼들은 다양한 종류의 미를 보여 주기 위해 부채를 우아하게 움직입니다.

➡ _____

21 그들의 움직임은 꽃 또는 날아다니는 새들처럼 우아하게 보입니다.

➡ _____

22 한국에서, 부채춤은 너무 인기가 있어서 사람들은 많은 전통 축제에서 그것을 볼 수 있습니다.

➡ _____

[01~02] 다음 글을 읽고 물음에 답하시오.

(A)_____ They dance to express feelings, give happiness to others, or enjoy themselves. Let's take a look (B)_____ different kinds of dance around the world.

01 빈칸 (A)에 들어갈 말로 가장 적절한 것은?

① Why do people dance?

② Why do people express feelings?

③ When do people dance?

④ How do people dance?

⑤ How many kinds of dance are there?

02 다음 중 빈칸 (B)에 들어갈 말과 같은 말이 들어가는 것은?

① Minsu was taking care _____ his dog.

② I became interested _____ watching movies.

③ I don't agree _____ you.

④ Jason is good _____ playing the guitar and the piano.

⑤ The glass is full _____ orange juice.

[03~06] 다음 글을 읽고 물음에 답하시오.

India: *Kathakali*

Kathakali tells a story. The dancers tell stories through their body movements. These stories are usually about a fight between good and evil. Dancers (A)_____ are playing good characters paint their faces green. Those who are playing evil characters wear black make-up. Interestingly, in *Kathakali*, only men are allowed to dance. The body movements are so powerful that the dancers need to train for many years.

03 빈칸 (A)에 적절한 말을 <u>모두</u> 고르시오.

① who   ② which   ③ that

④ what   ⑤ whose

서답형

04 다음과 같이 풀이되는 말을 위 글에서 찾아 쓰시오.

> the act of moving your body or a part of your body

➡ _____

05 다음 중 위 글을 읽고 답할 수 있는 것은?

① When the dance started?

② Why are only men allowed to dance?

③ Through what do the dancers tell stories?

④ What do women do while men are dancing?

⑤ How long does the dance last?

서답형

06 According to the passage, what do dancers wear to express that they are playing evil characters? Answer in English with a full sentence.

➡ _____
_____

[07~09] 다음 글을 읽고 물음에 답하시오.

New Zealand: *Haka*

When people visit New Zealand, they may meet a group of *haka* dancers. The dancers perform this traditional dance with (A)_____. This dance was originally performed by the Maori before a fight. They wanted to show their strength to the enemy. The dancers looked as scary as wild animals before fighting. Nowadays, in New Zealand, rugby players usually perform a *haka* before a game to show their strength to the other team.

07 빈칸 (A)에 들어갈 말로 가장 적절한 것은?

① funny looks   ② beautiful clothes
③ wild animals   ④ friends and family
⑤ scary faces

08 다음 중 위 글을 읽고 답할 수 있는 것은?

① How many people are needed to perform a *haka*?
② What kind of clothes do dancers need to wear to perform a *haka*?
③ What is the reason why the Maori performed a *haka*?
④ Where is the most popular tourist attraction in New Zealand?
⑤ How many times was a *haka* performed by the Maori?

09 위 글의 내용에 맞게 빈칸에 알맞은 말을 쓰시오.

> In a way to _____ _____ _____, rugby players perform a *haka* before a game.

[10~12] 다음 글을 읽고 물음에 답하시오.

Korea: *Buchaechum*

   Buchaechum is a traditional Korean fan dance. The dancers wear colorful *hanbok*. They dance with large fans that are painted in bright colors. The dancers move the fans

gracefully to show different kinds of beauty. Their movements look as beautiful as flowers or (A)<u>flying</u> birds. In Korea, *Buchaechum* is so popular that people can see it in many traditional festivals.

10 다음 중 밑줄 친 (A)와 쓰임이 같은 것은?

① David and I enjoyed <u>having</u> conversation with each other.
② My dad was busy with <u>finding</u> the meaning of the word.
③ Your job is <u>keeping</u> this place as clean as possible.
④ Where is my <u>sleeping</u> bag?
⑤ We saw the bus <u>passing</u> by without stopping.

11 Where can people see *Buchaechum* in Korea? Answer in English with a full sentence.

➡ _____
_____

12 다음 중 위 글의 내용을 제대로 이해한 사람은?

① 민하: 나는 부채춤의 한복 색깔이 매우 단조로운 것에 놀랐어.
② 준영: 이젠 부채춤을 더 이상 볼 수 없다는 것이 참 안타까운 일이야.
③ 세호: 부채가 움직이는 모습이 꽃과 같다니 얼마나 아름다울까.
④ 은종: 부채춤의 격렬한 움직임에서 힘을 느낄 수 있겠어.
⑤ 대민: 한국에서 부채춤이 인기가 없어져서 사라지게 된 것이야.

[13~17] 다음 글을 읽고 물음에 답하시오.

Why do people dance? They dance to express feelings, give happiness to others, or enjoy ⓐ themselves. Let's take a look at different kinds of dance around the world.

India: *Kathakali*

Kathakali tells a story. The dancers tell stories through their body movements. These stories are usually about a fight between good and evil. Dancers who are playing good characters paint their faces green. Those who are playing (A)_____ characters wear black make-up. Interestingly, in *Kathakali*, only men are allowed to dance. The body movements are so powerful that the dancers need to train for many years.

13 다음 중 빈칸 (A)에 들어갈 말로 가장 적절한 것은?

① funny ② brave ③ boring
④ evil ⑤ mysterious

14 다음 중 밑줄 친 ⓐ와 쓰임이 <u>다른</u> 것은?

① Look at yourself! You look terrible.
② Please help yourself to the salad.
③ Did you make this cake yourself?
④ He cut himself on a knife yesterday.
⑤ Have you hurt yourself?

15 다음 중 위 글의 내용으로 보아 알 수 있는 것은?

① the origin of the dance
② the number of dancers
③ people who are allowed to dance
④ the popularity of the dance
⑤ when people dance *Kathakali*

16 다음은 *Kathakali* 춤꾼 중 한 명의 말이다. 글의 내용에 맞게 빈칸에 알맞은 말을 쓰시오.

In order to play a _____ _____, I paint my face green.

서답형

17 Write the reason why the dancers need to train for many years to dance *Kathakali*. Answer in English and use the phrase 'it's because.'

➡ _____
_____

[18~21] 다음 글을 읽고 물음에 답하시오.

New Zealand: *Haka*

When people visit New Zealand, they may meet a group of *haka* dancers.
[A] Nowadays, in New Zealand, rugby players usually perform a *haka* before a game to show their strength to the other team.
[B] They wanted to show their strength to the enemy. The dancers looked as scary as wild animals before fighting.
[C] The dancers perform this traditional dance with scary faces. This dance was originally performed ⓐ_____ the Maori before a fight.

서답형

18 빈칸 ⓐ에 알맞은 말을 쓰시오.

➡ _____

19 자연스러운 글이 되도록 [A]~[C]를 바르게 배열한 것은?

① [A] – [C] – [B] ② [B] – [A] – [C]
③ [B] – [C] – [A] ④ [C] – [A] – [B]
⑤ [C] – [B] – [A]

20 글의 내용에 맞게 빈칸에 알맞은 말을 쓰시오.

> A: Alex, do you know what a *haka* is?
>
> B: Yes, I do. It's _____
>
> _____.

21 다음 중 위 글의 내용과 일치하지 <u>않는</u> 것은?

① We may meet a group of people who perform a *haka* in New Zealand.

② The Maori used to perform a *haka* before a fight.

③ The dancers who perform a *haka* look scary.

④ People who perform a *haka* can't be seen nowadays.

⑤ Rugby players perform a *haka* in order to show the other team how strong they are.

[22~24] 다음 글을 읽고 물음에 답하시오.

Korea: *Buchaechum*

  Buchaechum is a traditional Korean fan dance. The dancers wear colorful *hanbok*. They dance with large fans that are painted in bright colors. The dancers move the fans gracefully (A)<u>to show</u> different kinds of beauty. Their movements look as beautiful as flowers or flying birds. In Korea, *Buchaechum* is so popular that people can see (B)<u>it</u> in many traditional festivals.

22 다음 중 밑줄 친 (A)와 쓰임이 같은 것은?

① It was nice <u>to see</u> you again.

② What I want is <u>to take</u> a rest.

③ They decided <u>to make</u> a plan.

④ I went to bed early <u>to wake</u> up early.

⑤ Is there anything <u>to sit</u> on?

23 밑줄 친 (B)가 가리키는 것을 우리말로 쓰시오.

➡ _____

24 다음 중 위 글의 내용과 일치하는 것은?

① People who dance *Buchaechum* wear normal clothes.

② *Hanbok* is painted in bright colors in *Buchaechum*.

③ Fans are used to catch a flying bird.

④ *Buchaechum* is popular enough to be seen in many traditional festivals.

⑤ Many flowers are used to decorate the stage of the show.

[25~26] 다음 글을 읽고 물음에 답하시오.

Come and Enjoy the Step Dance

  A step dance is a traditional dance in Ireland. The dancers wear colorful costumes. In my opinion, the dancers look as (A)_____ as dolls. The dancers move their feet so fast that they look like they're flying!

25 단어 cute을 어법에 맞게 (A)에 쓰시오.

➡ _____

26 다음 중 위 글을 읽고 답할 수 <u>없는</u> 것은?

① What is a step dance?

② What do the dancers of a step dance wear?

③ What do the dancers look like when they dance?

④ How do the dancers look in their costumes?

⑤ Why do the people in Ireland perform a step dance?

[01~05] 다음 글을 읽고 물음에 답하시오.

Why do people dance? They dance to express feelings, give happiness to others, or enjoy themselves. Let's take a look at different kinds of dance around the world.

India: *Kathakali*

Kathakali tells a story. The dancers tell stories through their body movements. These stories are usually about a fight between good and evil. Dancers who are playing good characters paint their faces green. Those who are playing evil characters wear black make-up. Interestingly, in *Kathakali*, only men are allowed to dance. (A)Because the body movements are very powerful, the dancers need to train for many years.

01 Write the reason why people dance. Answer in English with a full sentence.

➡ _____

_____

02 When we see people dance *Kathakali* with wearing green make-up, what can we think? Answer in English with the words below.

(think / play)

➡ _____

03 위 글의 내용에 맞게 빈칸에 알맞은 말을 쓰시오.

People _____ for many reasons. For example, in *Kathakali* from _____, dancers dance to express a _____ between _____.

04 How do the *Kathakali* dancers tell stories? Answer in English with a full sentence.

➡ _____

05 주어진 단어를 이용하여 밑줄 친 (A)와 같은 의미의 문장을 쓰시오.

(so / that)

➡ _____

[06~08] 다음 글을 읽고 물음에 답하시오.

New Zealand: *Haka*

When people visit New Zealand, they may meet a group of *haka* dancers. The dancers perform this traditional dance with scary faces. This dance was originally performed by the Maori before a fight. They wanted to show their strength to the enemy. The dancers looked as scary as wild animals before fighting. Nowadays, in New Zealand, rugby players usually perform a *haka* before a game to show their strength to the other team.

06 주어진 단어를 이용하여 다음 물음에 답하시오.

Q: How do dancers perform a *haka*?
(with)

➡ _____

07 글의 내용에 맞게 빈칸에 알맞은 말을 쓰시오.

> *Haka* is a traditional dance in New Zealand. The Maori performed the dance to show their strength _____ _____ _____. And now it is performed by rugby players in New Zealand to show _____ _____ _____ _____ _____ _____.

08 다음 중 위 글의 내용과 일치하지 <u>않는</u> 것을 한 군데 찾아 바르게 고쳐 쓰시오.

> If you want to see people perform a *haka*, go to New Zealand. This traditional dance looks scary. It is usually performed by a single person.

_____ ➡ _____

[09~11] 다음 글을 읽고 물음에 답하시오.

> **Korea:** *Buchaechum*
>
> *Buchaechum* is a traditional Korean fan dance. The dancers wear colorful *hanbok*. They dance with large fans that (A)_____ in bright colors. The dancers move the fans gracefully to show different kinds of beauty. Their movements look as beautiful as flowers or flying birds. In Korea, *Buchaechum* is so popular that people can see it in many traditional festivals.

09 단어 paint를 어법에 맞게 빈칸 (A)에 쓰시오.

➡ _____

10 According to the passage, what is *Buchaechum*?

➡ _____

11 Write the reason why the dancers move the fans gracefully. Use the phrase below.

> (It's because / want)

➡ _____
_____

[12~14] 다음 글을 읽고 물음에 답하시오.

> *Tarantella*, Italy
>
>   In the past, people danced the *tarantella* for sick people. Nowadays, it is a couple's dance. People dance the *tarantella* on happy days such as weddings.
>
> *Adumu*, Kenya
>
> This dance is performed before a fight. It is also called a jumping dance. Dancers jump high in the air. When a dancer jumps, other dancers cheer him on with loud noises.

12 Why did people dance the *tarantella* in the past? Answer in English with a full sentence.

➡ _____

13 According to the passage, what can we see when we attend an Italian friend's wedding?

➡ _____

14 When is the dance *Adumu* performed?

➡ _____

Listen and Speak 2 - C

A: I'm going to a culture event in our town next week. Do you want to join me?
_{to부정사의 명사적 용법}

B: Sounds interesting.

A: We can enjoy dancing from many countries. I'm sure we'll have a lot of
_{enjoy+동명사}   _{= certain}   _{= much}
fun.

구문해설 · have fun: 즐거운 시간을 보내다

A: 나는 다음 주말에 우리 마을에서 열리는 문화 행사에 갈 거야. 나와 같이 갈래?
B: 재미있겠다.
A: 우리는 많은 국가에서 온 춤들을 즐길 수 있어. 우리는 매우 즐거울 거라고 확신해.

Culture & Life

Tarantella, Italy

In the past, people danced the *tarantella* for sick people.
_{~을 위해}

Nowadays, it is a couple's dance. People dance the *tarantella* on happy days
_{*Tarantella* 지칭}   _{특정 날짜 앞에 전치사 on}
such as weddings.
_{=like}

구문해설 · past: 과거 · nowadays: 요즈음 · such as: ~와 같은

Tarantella – 이탈리아
과거에, 사람들은 아픈 사람들을 위해 **tarantella**를 추었다. 요즈음, 이 춤은 커플 춤이다. 사람들은 결혼식 같은 행복한 날에 **tarantella**를 춘다.

Culture & Life

Adumu, Kenya

This dance is performed before a fight. It is also called a jumping dance.
_{dance는 perform의 대상이므로 수동태}   _{People also call it a jumping dance.}
Dancers jump high in the air. When a dancer jumps, other dancers cheer him
_{높이}   _{타동사+대명사 목적어+부사}
on with loud noises.

구문해설 · perform: 행하다, 수행하다 · cheer ~ on: ~을 응원하다 · noise: 소음

Adumu – 케냐
이 춤은 전투하기 전에 춘다. 이것은 점핑 댄스라고도 불린다. 춤꾼들은 공중에 높이 뛰어오른다. 한 춤꾼이 점프하면, 다른 사람들은 큰 소리를 내며 그를 응원한다.

Words & Expressions

01 다음 짝지어진 단어의 관계가 같도록 빈칸에 알맞은 말을 쓰시오.

sure : unsure = comfortable : _____

02 다음 문장에 공통으로 들어갈 말을 고르시오.

- I don't want to give up _____ achieving my goal.
- I took a taxi to arrive at the meeting _____ time.

① to   ② from   ③ by
④ on   ⑤ of

03 다음 영영풀이가 가리키는 것을 고르시오.

a flat object that you wave with your hand which makes the air cooler

① field   ② pan
③ fight   ④ fan
⑤ uniform

04 다음 중 밑줄 친 부분의 뜻풀이가 바르지 않은 것은?

① Have you ever played rugby? 럭비
② What are you going to perform on the school dancing contest? 공연하다
③ Through dancing, you can communicate with people around the world. 의사소통하다
④ When Irene danced gracefully, I fell in love with her. 신나게
⑤ It's windy outside, so bring your sweater. 바람이 센

05 다음 문장의 빈칸에 들어갈 말을 〈보기〉에서 골라 쓰시오.

┌ 보기 ┐
bright / scared / wild / hide / popular

(1) It is not easy to tame _____ animals.
(2) I'll _____ this letter in a drawer.
(3) Picasso didn't use _____ colors.
(4) He is very _____ among students.
(5) I was so _____ that I hid under my bed.

06 다음 주어진 문장의 밑줄 친 express와 다른 의미로 쓰인 것은?

Teachers express their concerns about the changes in school.

① Singing is one of the ways to express my feelings.
② Her face expresses how happy she is.
③ I didn't have enough time, so I decided to travel by express.
④ I was so nervous that I couldn't express what I meant.
⑤ How can I express all my thoughts in one page?

07 다음 우리말을 주어진 단어를 이용하여 영작하시오.

(1) 그들은 적에게 그들의 힘을 보여 주고 싶었다. (show, strength)
➡ _____

(2) 다른 춤꾼들은 그를 큰 소리로 응원한다. (noises, up, other)
➡ _____

(3) 수진이는 사자만큼 용감하다. (as, is)
➡ _____

08 다음 대화가 자연스럽게 이어지도록 순서대로 배열하시오.

(A) In my opinion, it's interesting. I smiled when I first saw it.
(B) Me, too. The dancers in the painting look happy.
(C) Jimin, what do you think about this painting?

➡ _____

[09~11] 다음 대화를 읽고 물음에 답하시오.

Jenny: (A) Look at the dancing girls, Dongjun. Aren't they amazing?
Dongjun: (B) Girls? I can only see one dancer.
Jenny: (C) Do you see many arms behind her?
Dongjun: (D) Wow. I didn't know that there were other dancers behind her.
Jenny: (E) That's right. I'm sure there are more than 10 dancers.

09 위 대화의 (A)~(E) 중 주어진 문장이 들어가기에 적절한 곳은?

Look more closely.

① (A)　② (B)　③ (C)　④ (D)　⑤ (E)

10 위 대화를 읽고 동준이의 감정으로 적절한 것은?

① nervous
② disappointed
③ lonely
④ surprised
⑤ terrible

11 위 대화의 내용과 일치하지 <u>않는</u> 것은?

① Jenny와 동준이는 춤추는 여자들을 보고 있다.
② 동준이는 처음에 한 명의 무용수만 발견했다.
③ 많은 팔을 가진 한 명의 무용수를 발견할 수 있다.
④ 동준은 한 명의 무용수 뒤에 다른 무용수들이 있다는 것을 몰랐었다.
⑤ Jenny는 10명 이상의 무용수들이 있다는 것을 확신한다.

12 다음 대화에서 (A)~(E)가 자연스럽게 이어지도록 순서대로 배열하시오.

Junsu: You know what? The school dance contest will be held soon.
Emily: That's right. I heard Jimin's class is going to perform a taekwondo dance and Tim's class is going to do a K-pop dance.
(A) How about a *Buchaechum*? In my opinion, it is easy to learn, and it's also beautiful.
(B) Of course, I will. I'm sure we'll have a lot of fun.
(C) That sounds like a good idea. But who will teach us?
(D) We should also decide what to do.
(E) Mina is good at traditional dances. Can you help us, Mina?

➡ _____

[13~15] 다음 대화를 읽고 물음에 답하시오.

Emily: Hojun, did you know that some male birds dance?
Hojun: No. Why do they dance?
Emily: They dance to show their love to female birds.
Hojun: That's interesting. Do you know any other animals that can dance?
Emily: Yes, some bees dance to show (A)_____ _____.
Hojun: That's cool! In my opinion, dancing is a great way to communicate.
Emily: (B)I'm with you on that. (agree)

13 위 대화의 빈칸 (A)에 '먹이를 찾을 수 있는 곳'을 뜻하도록 〈보기〉에 주어진 단어들 중 필요한 4단어만을 사용하여 완성하시오.

┌─ 보기 ├─
find / to / of / where / how / them / food
└─────────────────┘

➡ _____

14 위 대화의 밑줄 친 (B)와 의미가 같도록 주어진 단어를 사용하여 다시 쓰시오.

➡ _____

15 위 대화를 읽고 대답할 수 없는 것은?

① Why do some male birds dance?
② What do some male birds want to show to female birds by dancing?
③ Why do some bees dance?
④ What does Hojun think about animals' dancing?
⑤ How do some animals communicate while dancing?

Grammar

16 다음 빈칸에 들어갈 말로 가장 적절한 것은?

The earrings are so precious _____ she always wears them.

① what   ② which   ③ too
④ that   ⑤ if

17 다음 문장과 같은 의미의 문장으로 가장 적절한 것은?

This river is the longest river in the world.

① No other river in the world is as short as this river.
② This river is not as long as the other rivers in the world.
③ No other river in the world is as long as this river.
④ This river is shorter than any other river in the world.
⑤ This river is not as short as the other rivers in the world.

18 주어진 단어를 활용하여 다음 우리말을 영어로 쓰시오.

그녀는 매우 현명해. (as / owl)

➡ _____

19 다음 우리말을 영어로 바르게 옮긴 것을 모두 고르시오.

그는 너무 어려서 그 책을 이해할 수 없었다.

① He is very young that he can't understand the book.
② He was so young that he couldn't understand the book.
③ He was young enough to understand the book.
④ He was so young that he could understand the book.
⑤ He was too young to understand the book.

20 다음 중 어법상 바르지 않은 것은?

① She reads as many books as I do.
② The boy is smart enough to speak five languages.
③ The train runs two times as fast as this train.
④ These shoes are too tight that I can't wear them.
⑤ I was happy enough to hold a party.

21 다음 중 빈칸에 들어갈 말로 가장 적절한 것은?

> The room is _____ that it can hold a hundred people.

① very big   ② too big

③ so big   ④ big enough

⑤ bigger than

22 다음 두 문장의 의미가 같도록 빈칸에 알맞은 말을 쓰시오.

> Tom is the tallest basketball player in America.
>
> = _____ _____ _____ _____
>
>   in America _____ _____ _____
>
> _____ Tom.

23 다음 대화의 빈칸에 들어갈 말로 가장 적절한 것은?

> A: Did you drink the water?
> B: No, _____.
> A: Oh, let me warm up the water.

① it was too dangerous to eat

② it was so cold that I couldn't drink it

③ it was cold enough to drink

④ it was as cold as mine

⑤ it was too hot to drink

24 다음 표의 내용과 일치하지 <u>않는</u> 것은?

Rope A	Rope B	Rope C	Rope D
100cm	200cm	100cm	210cm

① Rope A is not as long as Rope B.

② Rope C is not as long as Rope D.

③ No other rope is as long as Rope B.

④ Rope A is as long as Rope C.

⑤ Rope B is not as long as Rope D.

25 주어진 단어를 활용하여 다음 우리말을 영어로 쓰시오.

> 나는 너무 행복해서 하루 종일 노래를 불렀어. (that / all day)

➡ _____

26 주어진 단어를 활용하여 다음 대화의 빈칸에 알맞은 말을 쓰시오.

> A: Is Sumin brave?
> B: Sure, she _____.
>   (as / a lion)

27 주어진 문장과 같은 의미의 문장을 쓰시오.

> He is too talkative to listen to others.

➡ _____

Reading

[28~32] 다음 글을 읽고 물음에 답하시오.

Why do people dance? They dance to express feelings, give happiness (A)_____ others, or enjoy themselves. Let's take a look at different (B)kinds of dance around the world.

India: *Kathakali*

Kathakali tells a story. The dancers tell stories through their body movements. These stories are usually about a fight between good and evil. Dancers who are playing good characters paint their faces green. Those who are playing evil characters wear black make-up. Interestingly, in *Kathakali*, only men are allowed to dance. The body movements are so powerful that the dancers need to train for many years.

28 다음 중 빈칸 (A)에 들어갈 말로 가장 적절한 것은?

① in   ② to   ③ at

④ on   ⑤ for

29 다음 중 밑줄 친 (B)와 쓰임이 같은 것은?

① James is very kind to animals.

② Exercises of this kind are very well known.

③ The weather was very kind to us.

④ Would you be kind enough to turn off the radio?

⑤ It's very kind of you to say so!

30 다음 중 위 글의 내용과 일치하지 않는 것은?

① By dancing, people can express their feelings.

② There are many types of dance around the world.

③ If you see someone wear black make-up in *Kathakali*, it means he is playing an evil character.

④ Performing *Kathakali* is limited to only men.

⑤ There is no need to train hard to perform a *Kathakali*.

31 What kind of story does *Kathakali* try to tell? Answer in English with a full sentence.

➡ _____

_____

32 According to the passage, how do the body movements of the dancers look? Answer in English with a full sentence.

➡ _____

[33~35] 다음 글을 읽고 물음에 답하시오.

> **Korea:** *Buchaechum*
>
> *Buchaechum* is a traditional Korean fan dance. The dancers wear colorful *hanbok*. They dance with large fans that are painted in bright colors. The dancers move the fans gracefully to show different kinds of beauty. Their movements look as beautiful as flowers or flying birds. In Korea, *Buchaechum* is so popular that people can see it in many traditional festivals.

33 다음 중 부채춤 공연에서 찾아볼 수 없는 것은?

① dancers wearing *hanbok*

② dancers moving gracefully

③ flowers and flying birds

④ fans painted in bright colors

⑤ beautiful movements of fans

34 다음 중 위 글을 읽고 답할 수 있는 것은?

① Who made *Buchaechum*?

② When was *Buchaechum* performed first?

③ How many fans are there in *Buchaechum*?

④ Why do the dancers move the fans gracefully?

⑤ How many people are needed to perform *Buchaechum*?

35 Write the reason why people can see *Buchaechum* in many traditional festivals in Korea. Use the word 'because.'

➡ _____

[01~02] 다음 대화를 읽고 물음에 답하시오.

> Jane: Minsu, (a)저 그림에 대해 어떻게 생각해?
> Minsu: Umm ... The people look like they're having fun.
> Jane: (A)_____ In my opinion, the dancing boy really enjoys dancing.

🖉 출제율 90%

01 위 대화의 빈칸 (A)에 들어갈 말로 나머지와 의미가 <u>다른</u> 것은?

① I think so, too.
② I agree with you.
③ I believe so, too.
④ I disagree with you.
⑤ I see it that way, too.

🖉 출제율 100%

02 위 대화의 밑줄 친 (a)의 우리말을 〈보기〉에 주어진 단어를 배열하여 영작하시오.

> ┤ 보기 ├
> about / painting / what / that / do / think / you

➡ _____

[03~05] 다음 대화를 읽고 물음에 답하시오.

> Emily: Hojun, did you know that some male birds dance?
> Hojun: No. Why do they dance?
> Emily: They dance to show their love to female birds.
> Hojun: That's interesting. Do you know any other animals that can dance?
> Emily: Yes, some bees dance to show where to find food.
> Hojun: That's cool! (A)_____, dancing is a great way to communicate.
> Emily: I totally agree with you.

🖉 출제율 90%

03 위 대화의 빈칸 (A)에 '내 의견으로는'을 의미하도록 3단어로 영작하시오.

➡ _____

🖉 출제율 95%

04 What do some male birds show by dancing?

➡ _____

🖉 출제율 90%

05 What information do some bees show by dancing?

➡ _____

[06~07] 다음 대화를 읽고 물음에 답하시오.

> Jenny: Look at the dancing girls, Dongjun. Aren't they (A)[amazed / amazing]?
> Dongjun: Girls? I can only see one dancer.
> Jenny: Look more closely. Do you see many arms behind her?
> Dongjun: Wow. I didn't know (B)[that / which] there were other dancers behind her.
> Jenny: That's right. I'm sure there (C)[is / are] more than 10 dancers.

🖉 출제율 95%

06 위 대화의 (A)~(C)에 들어갈 말이 바르게 짝지어진 것은?

	(A)	(B)	(C)
①	amazed	that	is
②	amazed	which	are
③	amazing	that	are
④	amazing	which	is
⑤	amazing	that	is

07 위 대화의 내용과 일치하도록 빈칸을 완성하시오.

> Dongjun: When I saw the dancing girls at first, I thought there was only one dancer. However, looking more closely again, I found that (A)_____ behind her. Because of many arms, I could guess that (B)_____.

[08~10] 다음 대화를 읽고 물음에 답하시오.

> Junsu: You know what? The school dance contest will ⓐ<u>hold</u> soon.
> Emily: That's right. I heard Jimin's class is going to perform a taekwondo dance and Tim's class is going to do a K-pop dance.
> Brian: We should also decide ⓑ<u>what to do</u>.
> Mina: How about a *Buchaechum*? In my opinion, it is easy to learn, and it's also beautiful.
> Emily: That ⓒ<u>sounds like</u> a good idea. But who will teach us?
> Brian: Mina ⓓ<u>is good at</u> traditional dances. (A) Can you help us, Mina?
> Mina: Of course, I will. I'm sure we'll have a lot of fun.
> Junsu: Great. Let's ⓔ<u>give it a try</u>.

출제율 95%

08 위 대화의 밑줄 친 ⓐ~ⓔ 중 어법상 어색한 것을 찾아 바르게 고치시오.

➡ _____

출제율 90%

09 위 대화의 밑줄 친 (A)와 바꾸어 쓸 수 있는 것은?

① What can I do for you, Mina?
② Can you give us a hand, Mina?
③ How can I help you, Mina?
④ Do you need my help, Mina?
⑤ May I help you, Mina?

출제율 100%

10 위 대화의 내용과 일치하지 <u>않는</u> 것은?

① 곧 학교 춤 대회가 열릴 것이다.
② 지민이네 반은 태권도 춤을 공연할 것이다.
③ Tim네 반은 K-pop 춤을 선보일 것이다.
④ 미나는 전통 춤을 잘 춘다.
⑤ 부채춤은 아름답지만 배우기가 어렵다.

출제율 90%

11 주어진 단어를 사용하여 다음 문장과 같은 의미의 문장을 쓰시오.

> He is so funny that he can be a comedian.
> (to)

➡ _____

출제율 95%

12 다음 중 의미하는 것이 <u>다른</u> 하나는?

① She is beautiful enough to be a movie star.
② She is so beautiful that she can be a movie star.
③ She can be a movie star because she is very beautiful.
④ She is very beautiful, so she can be a movie star.
⑤ She can be a movie star although she is beautiful.

출제율 90%

13 다음 빈칸에 알맞은 말을 쓰시오.

> A: I heard that Leo has red hair, right?
> B: Yes. His hair is _____ _____ _____ a tomato.

출제율 100%

14 다음 중 어법상 옳은 문장은?

① He is strong enough to moving it.
② She is too sad that she said nothing.
③ Your kite is as colorful as mine.
④ Ann was is as lighter as air when he danced with her.
⑤ This pond is too dangerous swim in.

출제율 90%

15 주어진 단어를 이용하여 다음 두 문장을 하나의 문장으로 쓰시오.

The dancer is so beautiful. I can't take my eyes off her. (that)

➡ _____

출제율 95%

16 다음 중 빈칸에 들어갈 말로 가장 적절한 것은?

I am so sick _____.

① because I want to go to school
② that I can't get up
③ so I enjoy my holiday
④ that I play with my friends
⑤ that I am excited

출제율 100%

17 다음 우리말을 영어로 바르게 옮기지 <u>않은</u> 것은?

① 너는 나보다 두 배만큼 많이 잔다.
→ You sleep two times as much as I do.
② 그 도서관은 쥐 죽은 듯이 조용해.
→ The library is as quiet as a mouse.
③ 나는 가능한 한 빨리 네가 이곳에 도착하길 바란다.
→ I hope you arrive here as soon as possible.
④ 그 자동차는 그 나라에서 가장 빠르다.
→ No other cars in the country is as fast as the car.
⑤ 네 방은 내 방만큼 지저분하지 않아.
→ Your room is not as messy as my room.

[18~21] 다음 글을 읽고 물음에 답하시오.

New Zealand: *Haka*

When people visit New Zealand, they may meet a group of *haka* dancers. The dancers ①<u>perform</u> this traditional dance with ②<u>scared</u> faces. This dance was ③<u>originally</u> performed by the Maori before a fight. They wanted to show ④<u>their strength</u> to the enemy. The dancers looked as scary as ⑤<u>wild animals</u> before fighting. (A)Nowadays, in New Zealand, rugby players usually perform a *haka* before a game to show their strength to the other team.

출제율 90%

18 밑줄 친 (A)를 대신하여 쓰일 수 있는 것으로 가장 적절한 것은?

① At last   ② Suddenly
③ These days   ④ All at once
⑤ Fortunately

출제율 100%

19 ①~⑤ 중 글의 흐름상 어색한 것은?

①   ②   ③   ④   ⑤

출제율 95%

20 다음 중 글의 내용과 일치하는 것은?

① It is hard to see people perform a *haka* in New Zealand.
② The Maori learned how to perform a *haka* from other tribes.
③ Before performing a *haka*, the Maori fought the enemy.
④ You can see the *haka* at rugby matches nowadays.
⑤ The Maori performed the *haka* to find better mates.

21 출제율 90%

What did the Maori want to do by performing a *haka*?

➡ _____

[22~23] 다음 글을 읽고 물음에 답하시오.

Tarantella, Italy

In the past, people danced the *tarantella* for sick people. Nowadays, it is a couple's dance. People dance the *tarantella* (A)_____ happy days such as weddings.

Adumu, Kenya

This dance is performed before a fight. It is also called a jumping dance. Dancers jump high in the air. When a dancer jumps, other dancers cheer him on with loud noises.

22 출제율 95%

빈칸 (A)에 들어갈 말로 가장 적절한 것은?

① in   ② about   ③ at
④ to   ⑤ on

23 출제율 100%

다음 중 위 글을 읽고 답할 수 <u>없는</u> 것은?

① Why did people dance the *tarantella* in the past?
② Who dances the *tarantella* these days?
③ Where can we see people dance the *tarantella*?
④ What do other dancers do when dancers jump high while dancing *Adumu*?
⑤ What do dancers need to perform the *adumu*?

[24~25] 다음 글을 읽고 물음에 답하시오.

Korea: *Buchaechum*

Buchaechum is a traditional Korean fan dance. The dancers wear colorful *hanbok*. They dance with large fans that are painted in bright colors. The dancers move the fans gracefully to show different kinds of beauty. Their movements look as beautiful as flowers or flying birds. In Korea, *Buchaechum* is so popular that people can see it in many traditional festivals.

24 출제율 90%

What do the dancers' movements look like? Answer in English with a full sentence.

➡ _____

25 출제율 95%

위 글의 내용에 맞게 빈칸에 알맞은 말을 쓰시오.

According to the passage, we need _____ _____ and _____ _____ _____ _____ bright colors to dance *Buchaechum*.

서술형 실전문제

[01~03] 다음 대화를 읽고 물음에 답하시오.

> Junsu: You know what? The school dance contest will be held soon.
>
> Emily: That's right. I heard Jimin's class is going to perform a taekwondo dance and Tim's class is going to do a K-pop dance.
>
> Brian: We should also decide what to do.
>
> Mina: How about a *Buchaechum*? In my opinion, it is easy to learn, and it's also beautiful.
>
> Emily: That sounds like a good idea. But who will teach us?
>
> Brian: Mina is good at traditional dances. Can you help us, Mina?
>
> Mina: Of course, I will. I'm sure we'll have a lot of fun.
>
> Junsu: Great. Let's give it a try.

01 What is Jimin's class going to perform at the school dance contest?

➡ _____

02 What is Mina good at?

➡ _____

03 What does Mina think about a *Buchaechum*?

➡ _____

_____

04 다음 주어진 문장과 같은 의미의 문장을 쓰시오.

> I can't dance in front of many people because I am too shy.

(1) to부정사를 사용하여

➡ _____

(2) that절을 사용하여

➡ _____

05 다음 대화를 읽고 빈칸에 알맞은 말을 쓰시오.

> A: I'm planning to buy a bike. How about you, Brian?
>
> B: I don't need one. It's because my bike still works well.

➡ Brian's bike _____ he doesn't want to buy another one.

06 다음 글을 하나의 문장으로 표현하시오.

> The diamond ring is 20,000 dollars. It is expensive. The car is the same price.

➡ _____

07 다음 주어진 단어를 이용해 우리말을 영어로 쓰시오.

> 그녀는 거북이만큼 느려. (turtle)

➡ _____

08 주어진 어구를 바르게 배열하여 다음 우리말을 영어로 쓰시오.

> 그 파티는 너무 즐거워서 누구도 떠나길 원치 않았다.
> (leave / the party / so / enjoyable / was / to / nobody / that / wanted)

➡ _____

_____

[09~10] 다음 글을 읽고 물음에 답하시오.

India: *Kathakali*

  Kathakali tells a story. The dancers tell stories through their body movements. These stories are usually about a fight between good and evil. Dancers who are playing good characters paint their faces green. Those who are playing evil characters wear black make-up. Interestingly, in *Kathakali*, only men are allowed to dance. The body movements are so powerful that the dancers need to train for many years.

09 다음은 카타할리 공연을 보고 있는 친구들의 대화이다. 빈칸에 알맞은 말을 쓰시오.

> A: I don't understand what the dance tries to say.
> B: Let me explain. Do you see the man whose face is _____? He is playing a good character.
> A: Really? That's interesting. Then, what about the man who is _____ _____ _____?
> B: He is playing an _____ _____.

10 위 글의 내용을 바탕으로 *Kathakali*를 소개하는 홍보 글을 완성하시오.

> *Kathakali* is a traditional dance in _____. The dancers tell _____ about a fight between _____. Interestingly, only _____ are allowed to dance. The body movements are so _____ that the dancers need to train for many years.

[11~12] 다음 글을 읽고 물음에 답하시오.

Come and Enjoy the Step Dance

  A step dance is a traditional dance in Ireland. The dancers wear colorful costumes. In my opinion, (A)_____. The dancers move their feet so fast that they look like they're flying!

11 원급 비교 표현을 이용하여 다음 두 문장을 하나의 문장으로 빈칸 (A)에 쓰시오.

> The dancers look cute. They are like dolls.

➡ _____

12 위 글의 내용에 맞게 빈칸에 알맞은 말을 쓰시오.

> The dancers who do a step dance move their feet _____ _____ _____ it is hard to see their feet!

창의사고력 서술형 문제

01 다음 대화의 내용과 일치하도록 Kelly의 일기를 완성하시오.

> **Tom:** What are you reading, Kelly?
> **Kelly:** I'm reading a story about Michaela DePrince.
> **Tom:** Michaela DePrince? Can you tell me more about her?
> **Kelly:** Sure. Michaela lost her parents when she was three. After that, she had a lot of difficulties. But she never gave up on her dream of becoming a dancer.
> **Tom:** Wow, she worked very hard to be a good dancer. Kelly, you also have a dream to be a dancer, right?
> **Kelly:** Yes. I will try my best to be a great dancer like her.
> **Tom:** Keep up the good work. I'm sure you can make it.

Mon, Oct 7th, 2019

Today, I read a story about Michaela DePrince. The reason why I chose this book is that I want to be (A)_____ like her. The story was so impressive that I shared it with Tom. I explained Michaela's story to Tom including her difficulties and her great efforts to become (B)_____. After reading her story, I decided to (C)_____. Tom also encouraged me a lot, so I appreciated him.

02 'so ~ that' 구문을 이용하여 두 문장을 의미에 맞게 연결하시오.

> The wind was very strong.　　It blew my hat off my head.
> The soup was very hot.　　I couldn't eat it.
> She is very friendly.　　She will throw a party for us.

(1) _____

(2) _____

(3) _____

03 다음은 아일랜드 전통 춤에 관한 사실과 의견이다. 이를 참고하여 아일랜드 전통 춤을 소개하는 글을 완성하시오.

> Step Dance, Ireland
> Fact 1 – wear colorful costumes
> Opinion 1 – look like cute dolls
> Fact 2 – move their feet fast
> Opinion 2 – look like they're flying

A step dance is a traditional dance in _____. The dancers _____. In my opinion, the dancers look _____. The dancers _____ that they look _____!

단원별 모의고사

01 다음 영영풀이가 가리키는 것을 고르시오.

> a particular type of clothing worn by all the members of a group or organization such as the police, the army, etc.

① dress
② uniform
③ movement
④ culture
⑤ costume

02 다음 문장의 빈칸에 들어갈 말을 〈보기〉에서 골라 쓰시오.
(필요하면 변형할 것.)

> ┤ 보기 ├
> be good at / good and evil / have fun / take a look / give up on

(1) Why don't you go out and _____ at the festival?

(2) Let's _____ at some traditional games in Scotland.

(3) It's the story of a fight between _____.

(4) She _____ dancing.

(5) Don't _____ your dream.

[03~04] 다음 대화를 읽고 물음에 답하시오.

Junsu: You know what? The school dance contest will be held soon.

Emily: That's right. I heard Jimin's class is going to perform a taekwondo dance and Tim's class is going to do a K-pop dance.

Brian: We should also decide what to do.

Mina: How about a *Buchaechum*? In my opinion, it is easy to learn, and it's also beautiful.

Emily: That sounds like a good idea. But who will teach us?

Brian: Mina is good at traditional dances. Can you help us, Mina?

Mina: Of course, I will. (A)_____

Junsu: Great. Let's give it a try.

03 위 대화의 빈칸 (A)에 들어갈 말을 〈보기〉에 주어진 단어들을 모두 배열하여 완성하시오.

> ┤ 보기 ├
> we'll / I'm / of / have / fun / sure / lot / a

➡ _____

04 위 대화를 읽고 대답할 수 없는 것은?

① What is Jimin's class going to perform?
② What does Mina think about a *Buchaechum*?
③ What kind of dance is Tim's class going to perform?
④ What is Mina good at?
⑤ Why did Jimin's class choose a taekwondo dance?

[05~07] 다음 대화를 읽고 물음에 답하시오.

Tom: What are you reading, Kelly?

Kelly: (A) I'm reading a story about Michaela DePrince.

Tom: (B) Michaela DePrince? Can you tell me more about her?

Kelly: (C) After that, she had a lot of difficulties. But she never gave up on her dream of becoming a dancer.

Tom: (D) Wow, she worked very hard to be a good dancer. Kelly, you also have a dream to be a dancer, right?

Kelly: (E) Yes. I will ⓐtry my best to be a great dancer like her.

Tom: Keep up the good work. I'm sure you can make it.

05 위 대화의 (A)~(E) 중 주어진 문장이 들어가기에 적절한 곳은?

> Sure. Michaela lost her parents when she was three.

① (A) ② (B) ③ (C) ④ (D) ⑤ (E)

06 위 대화의 밑줄 친 ⓐ와 바꾸어 쓸 수 있는 것은?

① do ② work ③ take
④ make ⑤ have

07 위 대화의 내용과 일치하지 <u>않는</u> 것은?

① Michaela는 3살 때 부모님을 잃었다.
② Michaela는 부모님을 잃은 후 많은 역경을 겪었다.
③ Michaela는 무용수가 되겠다는 꿈을 절대 포기하지 않았다.
④ Michaela는 훌륭한 무용수가 되기 위해 굉장히 열심히 노력했다.
⑤ Michaela는 무용수로 계속 좋은 일들을 하고 있다.

08 다음 대화의 (A)~(C)에 들어갈 말이 바르게 짝지어진 것은?

> Minji: I use my voice to make music. Listen to my music. My voice is soft and cool. I'm sure you will like it.
> Jimin: I move my body to (A)[impress / express] my feelings. Look at my movements. Why don't you jump like me? I'm (B)[certain / unsure] you'll feel great.
> Sujin: I use my hands to make sounds. Come and listen to my music. I'm sure you'll want to dance (C)[what / when] you listen to it.

	(A)	(B)	(C)
①	impress	certain	what
②	impress	unsure	when
③	express	certain	when
④	express	unsure	when
⑤	express	certain	what

09 다음 대화가 자연스럽게 이어지도록 순서대로 배열하시오.

> Emily: Hojun, did you know that some male birds dance?
> Hojun: No. Why do they dance?
> (A) Yes, some bees dance to show where to find food.
> (B) They dance to show their love to female birds.
> (C) I totally agree with you.
> (D) That's interesting. Do you know any other animals that can dance?
> (E) That's cool! In my opinion, dancing is a great way to communicate.

➡ _____

[10~11] 다음 대화를 읽고 물음에 답하시오.

> Minji: I use my voice to make music. Listen to my music. My voice is soft and cool. I'm sure you will like it.
> Jimin: I move my body to express my feelings. Look at my movements. Why don't you jump like me? I'm sure you'll feel great.
> Sujin: I use my hands to make sounds. Come and listen to my music. I'm sure you'll want to dance when you listen to it.

10 What does Minji use to make music?

➡ _____

11 Why does Jimin move her body?

➡ _____

12 다음 중 어법상 바르지 <u>않은</u> 것은?

① She was not as lazy as my sister.
② The coffee tastes so great that I will have another cup.
③ No other city in Korea is as big as Seoul.
④ Mina and Sujin is the same age. Mina is as old as Sujin.
⑤ Your nail is twice longer as mine.

13 다음 우리말을 영어로 바르게 옮긴 것은?

나는 그녀만큼 빠르게 달릴 수 없어.

① I can run not as fast as she.
② I can't run as faster as she.
③ I can't run as fast as she.
④ I can run as fast as she.
⑤ She can run as fast as I.

14 다음 문장과 같은 의미의 문장으로 가장 적절한 것은?

It was raining heavily. So we canceled the field trip.

① It was raining heavily enough to cancel the field trip.
② It was raining too heavily that we canceled the field trip.
③ We canceled the field trip although it was raining heavily.
④ It was raining so heavily that we canceled the field trip.
⑤ It was raining heavily because we canceled the field trip.

15 주어진 단어를 활용하여 다음 우리말을 영어로 쓰시오.

그녀는 매우 바빠. (as / bee)

➡ _____

16 주어진 단어를 활용하여 다음 우리말을 영어로 쓰시오.

그 영화는 너무 감동적이어서 나는 많이 울었어. (moving / a lot)

➡ _____

[17~18] 다음 글을 읽고 물음에 답하시오.

Why do people dance? ①They dance ②to express feelings, give happiness ③to others, or ④enjoying themselves. Let's take a look ⑤at different kinds of dance around the world.

17 위 글에 이어질 내용으로 가장 적절한 것은?

① various kinds of feelings
② why people like to dance
③ various kinds of dance around the world
④ what people do when they are happy
⑤ some reasons why people enjoy watching dances

18 ①~⑤ 중 어법상 바르지 <u>않은</u> 것은?

①   ②   ③   ④   ⑤

[19~20] 다음 글을 읽고 물음에 답하시오.

Korea: *Buchaechum*

Buchaechum is a traditional Korean fan dance. The dancers wear colorful *hanbok*. They dance with large fans that are painted in bright colors. The dancers move the fans gracefully to show different kinds of beauty. Their movements look as (A)_____ as flowers or flying birds. In Korea, *Buchaechum* is so popular that people can see it in many traditional festivals.

19 빈칸 (A)에 들어갈 말로 가장 적절한 것은?

① difficult
② beautiful
③ boring
④ annoying
⑤ embarrassing

20 위 글의 제목으로 가장 적절한 것은?

① Come and Dance *Buchaechum* with Us
② *Buchaechum*, Most Loved Dance in Korea
③ Korean Traditional Dance, *Buchaechum*
④ Useful Tool, A Korean Fan
⑤ Enjoy the Beauty of Korea with Flowers

[21~24] 다음 글을 읽고 물음에 답하시오.

New Zealand: *Haka*

When people visit New Zealand, they may meet a group of *haka* dancers. The dancers ① perform this traditional dance with ②scary faces. This dance was originally performed by the Maori before a fight. (A)They wanted to show their ③strength to the ④enemy. The dancers looked as scary as ⑤wild animals before fighting. Nowadays, in New Zealand, rugby players usually perform a *haka* before a game to show (B)their strength to the other team.

21 밑줄 친 (A)와 (B)가 가리키는 것을 각각 쓰시오.

➡ (A) _____ (B) _____

22 Why do rugby players in New Zealand usually perform a *haka* before a game? Answer in English with a full sentence.

➡ _____

_____

23 위 글의 내용에 맞게 다음 물음에 완전한 문장의 영어로 답하시오.

> **Q:** When did the Maori originally perform a *haka*?

➡ _____

24 다음 중 ①~⑤의 풀이로 적절하지 않은 것은?

① to entertain an audience by singing or acting
② rather frightening
③ the state of being weak
④ someone who attacks or tries to harm another
⑤ living in nature without human control or care

Lesson 7

Magic or Science?

 의사소통 기능

- 질문하기
  Which sport do you want to learn?

- 희망 · 기대 표현하기
  I can't wait to see the difference.

 언어 형식

- 가주어 It
  It is exciting **to watch** a magic show.

- How come ...?
  How come the water rose into the glass?

Words & Expressions

교과서

Key Words

- **abracadabra** [æbrəkədǽbrə] 명 수리수리마수리 (주문)
- **absorb** [æbsɔ́ːrb] 동 흡수하다
- **balloon** [bəlúːn] 명 풍선
- **behind** [biháind] 전 ~ 뒤에
- **candle** [kǽndl] 명 양초
- **coin** [kɔin] 명 동전
- **compare** [kəmpɛ́ər] 동 비교하다
- **confuse** [kənfjúːz] 동 혼동하게 하다
- **contract** [kəntrǽkt] 동 수축하다
- **difference** [dífərəns] 명 차이, 차이점
- **disappear** [dìsəpíər] 동 사라지다
- **dry** [drai] 형 마른, 비가 오지 않는
- **escape** [iskéip] 동 탈출하다, (액체, 가스가) 새다
- **expand** [ikspǽnd] 동 팽창하다
- **experiment** [ikspérəmənt] 명 실험
- **fill** [fil] 동 채우다
- **flame** [fleim] 명 불꽃
- **flavor** [fléivər] 명 맛
- **float** [flout] 동 뜨다
- **freezer** [fríːzər] 명 냉동고
- **hold** [hould] 동 잡다, 쥐다
- **instead** [instéd] 부 대신에
- **lightning** [láitniŋ] 명 번개
- **magic** [mǽdʒik] 명 마술, 마법
- **material** [mətíəriəl] 명 재료, 물질
- **mix** [miks] 동 섞다
- **move** [muːv] 동 움직이다
- **necessary** [nésəsèri] 형 필요한
- **ocean** [óuʃən] 명 대양, 바다
- **practice** [prǽktis] 명 연습
- **prepare** [pripɛ́ər] 동 준비하다
- **pressure** [préʃər] 명 압력
- **push** [puʃ] 동 밀다
- **rise** [raiz] 동 오르다, 올라가다
- **rose** [rouz] 명 장미
- **safe** [seif] 형 안전한
- **secret** [síːkrit] 명 비밀
- **sink** [siŋk] 동 가라앉다
- **sunburn** [sʌ́nbərn] 명 볕에 탐
- **sunscreen** [sʌ́nskriːn] 명 자외선 차단제
- **trick** [trik] 명 마술, 속임수
- **weigh** [wei] 동 무게를 재다

Key Expressions

- **a glass of** 한 잔의
- **burn out** 타 버리다
- **cool down** 차가워지다
- **dry season** 건기
- **for a long time** 오랫동안
- **give it a try** 시도해 보다
- **pick out** 골라내다
- **see through** 속을 들여다 보다
- **sign up for** ~을 신청하다
- **some day** 언젠가, 머지않아
- **stick to** ~을 (바꾸지 않고) 고수하다
- **turn A into B** A가 B로 변하다

Word Power

※ 서로 반대되는 뜻을 가진 어휘

- □ **contract** 수축하다 ↔ **expand** 팽창하다
- □ **dry** 건조한 ↔ **wet** 젖은
- □ **behind** ~ 뒤에 ↔ **in front of** ~ 앞에
- □ **necessary** 필요한 ↔ **unnecessary** 불필요한
- □ **safe** 안전한 ↔ **dangerous** 위험한
- □ **sink** 가라앉다 ↔ **float** 뜨다

- □ **fill** 채우다 ↔ **empty** 비우다
- □ **mix** 섞다 ↔ **separate** 분리하다
- □ **appear** 나타나다 ↔ **disappear** 사라지다
- □ **rise** 올라가다 ↔ **drop** 떨어지다
- □ **careful** 주의 깊은 ↔ **careless** 부주의한
- □ **absorb** 흡수하다 ↔ **release** 방출하다

English Dictionary

- □ **absorb** 흡수하다
  → to take in something in a natural or gradual way
  자연스럽거나 점차적인 방식으로 무언가를 받아들이다

- □ **confuse** 혼동하다
  → to mistake one person or thing for another
  누군가 또는 어떤 것을 다른 것으로 잘못 알다

- □ **contract** 수축하다
  → to become smaller
  더 작아지다

- □ **expand** 팽창하다
  → to increase in size, range, or amount
  크기, 범위, 또는 양에서 증가하다

- □ **float** 뜨다
  → to rest on top of a liquid or in the air
  액체 맨 윗부분에 또는 공기 중에 있다

- □ **freezer** 냉동고
  → a device or room for freezing food or keeping it frozen
  음식을 얼리거나 언 채로 유지되도록 하기 위한 장치 또는 공간

- □ **magic** 마술의
  → having the power to make impossible things happen
  불가능한 일들이 일어나게 만드는 힘을 가진

- □ **material** 물질, 재료
  → a substance that things can be made from
  무언가가 그로부터 만들 수 있는 재료

- □ **mix** 섞다
  → to combine two or more substances so that they become a single substance
  두 개 이상의 물질을 결합하여 하나의 물질이 되게 하다

- □ **practice** 연습
  → the activity of doing something again and again in order to become better at it
  더 잘하기 위해 무언가를 계속해서 하는 활동

- □ **secret** 비밀
  → a piece of information that is kept hidden from other people 다른 사람들에게 숨겨진 정보

- □ **sink** 가라앉다
  → to go down below the surface of water
  물의 표면 아래로 내려가다

- □ **trick** 속임수, 마술
  → something done to surprise or confuse someone
  누군가를 놀라게 하거나 혼란시키기 위해 행해지는 것

- □ **weigh** 무게를 재다
  → to find how heavy someone or something is
  누군가 또는 무언가가 얼마나 무거운지 알아내다

서답형

01 다음 짝지어진 단어의 관계가 같도록 빈칸에 알맞은 말을 쓰시오.

> increase : decrease = appear : _____

02 다음 영영풀이가 가리키는 것을 고르시오.

> to increase in size, range, or amount

① expand ② sink
③ float ④ weigh
⑤ hold

중요

03 다음 중 밑줄 친 부분의 뜻풀이가 바르지 <u>않은</u> 것은?

① The material doesn't <u>absorb</u> the water. 흡수하다
② Which things will Ms. Jeong <u>weigh</u> for the test? 무게를 재다
③ I want to learn how to hold a <u>flame</u> without burning my hands. 불꽃
④ I always <u>confuse</u> your bag and mine. 비교하다
⑤ Can you tell me the <u>secret</u> of success? 비밀

04 다음 문장에 공통으로 들어갈 말을 고르시오.

> • It is _____ to prepare something for a dry season.
> • This machine is _____ for treating disease.
> • Exercise is _____ to keep your health.

① safe ② necessary
③ confusing ④ amazing
⑤ dry

중요

05 다음 주어진 문장의 밑줄 친 rose와 같은 의미로 쓰인 것은?

> The sales <u>rose</u> by 20 percent last week.

① The cloud of smoke <u>rose</u> suddenly.
② She drew a <u>rose</u> on her note.
③ Some flowers, like <u>roses</u>, need special care.
④ The prince was looking for a <u>rose</u>.
⑤ When I smelled the <u>rose</u>, I felt so happy.

서답형

06 다음 우리말에 맞게 빈칸에 알맞은 말을 쓰시오.

(1) 우리는 경비원들을 속이고 지나가기 위해 속임수를 생각해 내야 했다.
➡ We had to think of _____ to get past the guards.

(2) 나는 특별한 물질을 컵 하나에 넣어 두었다.
➡ I put a special _____ into one of the cups.

(3) 우리 아빠는 나를 위해 매일 아침을 준비하신다.
➡ My father always _____ breakfast for me every day.

(4) 당신은 속을 들여다볼 수 없는 컵을 사용하는 것이 필요하다.
➡ It's _____ to use cups that you can't see through.

(5) 공기는 더 높은 압력을 생성한다.
➡ Air creates higher _____.

(6) 회사의 확장 계획에 대해 어떻게 생각하세요?
➡ What do you think of the company's plans to _____?

01 다음 짝지어진 단어의 관계가 같도록 빈칸에 알맞은 말을 쓰시오.

contract : expand = sink : _____

02 다음 문장의 빈칸에 들어갈 말을 〈보기〉에서 골라 쓰시오.

┌─ 보기 ─┐
stick to / cooled down / see through /
turn ~ into / burned out

(1) I can't _____ _____ the window.
(2) The magician can _____ rain _____ snow.
(3) After an hour, the candle _____ _____.
(4) The weather has _____ _____ a little.
(5) I _____ _____ what I think I am good at.

03 다음 우리말을 주어진 단어를 이용하여 영작하시오.

(1) 우리는 물고기 대신에 손가락을 사용할 수 있다.
➡ We can use a finger _____ of a fish.
(2) 달걀이 물에 뜰 때, 그것들은 신선하지 않다.
➡ When eggs _____ in water, they're not fresh.
(3) 마술 공연을 보는 것은 흥미롭다.
➡ It's exciting to watch a _____ show.
(4) 그것이 물을 유리컵 속으로 밀었다.
➡ It _____ the water into the glass.

04 다음 우리말과 일치하도록 주어진 어구를 모두 배열하여 영작하시오.

(1) 네가 싫어하는 채소들을 골라내는 것은 좋지 않다.
(that / good / to / it / don't / is / pick out / not / you / like / vegetables)
➡ _____
_____

(2) 내가 시도해 볼게.
(it / I'll / a / give / try)
➡ _____

(3) 졸리면, 차가운 물 한 잔을 마셔라.
(drink / if / sleepy / are / you / water / cold / a glass / of)
➡ _____

(4) 나는 배드민턴 수업을 신청했다.
(the / class / badminton / signed / for / up / I)
➡ _____

05 다음 문장의 빈칸에 들어갈 말을 〈보기〉에서 골라 쓰시오.

┌─ 보기 ─┐
hold / coin / sunburn / expands /
escape / contract

(1) It is necessary to wear sunscreen to prevent _____.
(2) _____ the bottle in your hands for a while.
(3) As the air gets warm, it _____.
(4) You can see how a _____ dances in a bottle.
(5) The expanding air tries to _____ from the bottle.
(6) When you bend your arms, your muscles _____.

Conteneur 교과서
Conversation

① 질문하기

> **Which sport do you want to learn?** 너는 어느 운동을 배우고 싶니?

- 'Which …?'는 '어느[어떤] …?'라는 뜻으로, 어떤 것을 선택하고자 하는지 묻는 표현이다. Which 뒤에는 sport, flavor, activity 등의 표현이 온다.

질문하기

- Which sport do you like? Badminton or soccer? 너는 어느 운동을 좋아하니? 배드민턴 또는 축구?
- What's your favorite color? 가장 좋아하는 색이 무엇이니?

선호 말하기

- I like soccer most[best]. 나는 축구를 가장 좋아한다.
- I love playing basketball. 나는 농구하기를 매우 좋아한다.
- I'm fond of ~. 나는 ~을 좋아한다.
- My favorite sport is dodge ball. 내가 가장 좋아하는 운동은 피구이다.
- I enjoy playing baseball (very much). 나는 야구하기를 (매우) 즐긴다.

핵심 Check

1. 다음 우리말과 일치하도록 빈칸에 알맞은 말을 쓰시오.

(1) **A:** _____ _____ do you want to visit the most? (너는 어느 나라를 가장 방문하고 싶니?)

B: I want to visit Indonesia. (나는 인도네시아를 방문하고 싶어.)

(2) **A:** _____ _____ does Sejun want to play? (세준이는 어느 운동을 하고 싶어 하니?)

B: He wants to play basketball. (그는 농구를 하고 싶어 해.)

(3) **A:** _____ _____ _____ _____, a straw or a potato?

(짚과 감자 중 어느 것이 더 강하니?)

B: It's a potato, isn't it? (감자야. 그렇지 않니?)

② 희망·기대 표현하기

I can't wait to see the difference. 나는 빨리 그 차이를 보고 싶어.

■ "I can't wait to …'는 '나는 …이 무척 기다려져.'라는 뜻으로, 희망이나 기대를 말할 때 쓰는 표현이다. to 뒤에는 동사원형이 온다. 이 표현은 'I'm looking forward to -ing'로 바꿔 쓸 수 있다.

바라거나 기대하는 일 표현하기

• I can't wait for the cooking class. 나는 요리 수업이 매우 기대가 된다.

• I can't wait to go on a picnic. 나는 소풍가는 것이 매우 기대된다.

• I'm looking forward to meeting my friend. 나는 내 친구를 만나기를 기대하고 있다.

• I really want to visit the museum. 나는 정말로 박물관에 가고 싶다.

핵심 Check

2. 다음 우리말과 일치하도록 빈칸에 알맞은 말을 쓰시오.

(1) **A:** We are going to visit the science museum. (우리는 과학 박물관에 방문할 거야.)

B: I _____ _____ to go there. (나는 빨리 그곳에 가고 싶어.)

(2) **A:** What are you going to do this Sunday? (이번 주 일요일에 무엇을 할 예정이니?)

B: I'm going to visit my grandparents. I'm _____ _____ _____ _____ them. (나는 그들을 만나기를 무척 기대하고 있어.)

(3) **A:** I _____ _____ _____ _____ _____ _____.
(나는 너를 다시 빨리 보고 싶어.)

B: Me too.

Listen and Speak 1 A

W: Today we'll make ice cream. ❶Which ❷flavor do you want to make? ❸How about strawberry? First, mix two cups of milk, two cups of heavy cream, and half a cup of sugar. ❹Next, cut five strawberries into small pieces. Then, mix everything together and put it in the freezer. That's it. It's easy to make, isn't it? Why don't you ❺try making it at home?

W: 오늘 우리는 아이스크림을 만들 거예요. 여러분은 어느 맛을 만들고 싶은가요? 딸기는 어때요? 첫째로, 우유 2컵, 헤비 크림 2컵, 설탕 1/2컵을 섞으세요. 다음, 딸기 5개를 작은 조각으로 자르세요. 그 다음에, 모든 것을 섞어서 냉동실에 넣으세요. 이게 다예요. 만들기 쉽죠, 그렇지 않나요? 집에서 아이스크림을 만들어 보는 게 어때요?

❶ 'Which ~?'는 '어느[어떤] ~?'라는 뜻으로 어느 것을 선택하고자 하는지 묻는 표현이다.
❷ flavor: 맛
❸ How about ~? = What about ~?: '~는 어때?'라는 제안을 나타낸다.
❹ Next = Second
❺ try -ing: ~해 보다, cf. try to ~: ~하려고 노력하다

Check(√) True or False

(1) The woman explains how to make strawberry ice cream.　　T ☐ F ☐

(2) The woman needs a cup of sugar to make ice cream.　　T ☐ F ☐

 Listen and Speak 2 A

B: Ms. Jeong, does ❶a glass of water ❷weigh more when there's a fish in it?

W: Yes, it does. We can test it now.

B: But how? We don't have a fish.

W: We can use a finger ❸instead of a fish.

B: How will that work?

W: I'll weigh a glass of water first. Then I will put my finger in the water and weigh it to ❹compare.

B: Oh, ❺I can't wait to see the difference.

B: 정 선생님, 물속에 물고기가 있을 때 물 1잔의 무게가 더 무겁나요?
W: 응, 그렇단다. 우리는 지금 실험해 볼 수 있어.
B: 하지만 어떻게요? 물고기가 없는데요.
W: 우리는 물고기 대신 손가락을 사용할 수 있단다.
B: 어떻게 할 수 있어요?
W: 먼저 물 1잔의 무게를 잴 거야. 그 다음에 비교하기 위해 물속에 손가락을 넣고 무게를 잴 거란다.
B: 아, 차이를 빨리 알고 싶어요.

❶ a glass of: 한 잔의
❷ weigh: 무게를 재다, cf. weight: 무게
❸ instead of: ~ 대신에
❹ compare: 비교하다
❺ I can't wait to ~ = I'm looking forward to -ing: 매우 ~하고 싶다, ~을 기대하다

Check(√) True or False

(3) They don't have a fish now.　　T ☐ F ☐

(4) The finger will be used to do an experiment.　　T ☐ F ☐

Listen and Speak 1 B

B: Yujin, why did you ❶put the eggs in water?

G: I'm ❷picking out the bad eggs.

B: Which eggs are fresh, and which ❸ones are not?

G: Eggs ❹that ❺sink in water are fresh. When eggs ❻float in water, they're not fresh. You shouldn't eat them.

B: That's interesting. Why do the bad eggs float?

G: Because they have gas inside. The gas acts like the air in a balloon.

B: Oh, I see.

❶ put A in B: A를 B에 넣다
❷ pick out: 골라내다
❸ ones = eggs
❹ 주격 관계대명사로 which로 바꾸어 쓸 수 있다.
❺ sink: 가라앉다
❻ float: 뜨다

Listen and Speak 2 B

King Sejong: It ❶hasn't rained ❷for a long time.

Jang Yeongsil: Yes. The ❸dry season is ❹lasting too long. The farmers are very worried.

King Sejong: We should do something to help ❺them.

Jang Yeongsil: How about making a special clock?

King Sejong: A clock? How will that help?

Jang Yeongsil: The clock will show the time and the seasons. We can use ❻it to prepare for the dry season.

King Sejong: That sounds like a good idea. But who's going to make it?

Jang Yeongsil: I'll ❼give it a try. I know a lot about time and the seasons.

King Sejong: Okay, I can't wait to see your clock.

❶ 현재완료 시제가 쓰였다.
❷ for a long time: 오랫동안
❸ dry season 건기
❹ last: 지속되다
❺ them = farmers
❻ it = the clock
❼ give it a try: 시도해 보다

Real Life Communication A

Brian: Mina, will you join our tennis club?

Mina: It sounds interesting, but I ❶signed up for a special class this fall.

Brian: Which class did you sign up for?

Mina: I signed up for a magic class. ❷I can't wait to learn new magic ❸tricks there.

Brian: That sounds cool! ❹Have you learned magic tricks before?

Mina: Yes, I learned some before, but I need more practice.

Brian: I hope I can see your magic tricks some day.

❶ sign up for: ~을 신청하다
❷ 'I'm looking forward to learning new magic tricks there.'로 바꾸어 쓸 수 있다.
❸ trick: 마술, 속임수
❹ 현재완료 시제로 경험을 묻고 있다.

Let's Check

B: What are you reading, Jiwon?

G: I'm reading a book about magic and science.

B: That sounds interesting.

G: Yes. This book ❶introduces 100 magic tricks ❷that use science. I've learned about half of them.

B: That's cool. Can you show me some of the tricks?

G: Sure. I can show you a ❸balloon trick now.

B: Great! I can't wait to see ❹it.

❶ introduce: 소개하다
❷ 관계대명사로 which로 바꾸어 쓸 수 있다.
❸ ballon: 풍선
❹ it = a balloon trick

● 다음 우리말과 일치하도록 빈칸에 알맞은 말을 쓰시오.

Listen & Speak 1 A

W: Today we'll make ice cream. _____ _____ do you want to make? How about strawberry? _____, mix two cups of milk, two cups of heavy cream, and _____ _____ _____ of sugar. _____, cut five strawberries into small pieces. Then, _____ everything together and put it in the _____. That's it. It's easy to make, isn't it? Why don't you _____ _____ it at home?

해석

W: 오늘 우리는 아이스크림을 만들 거예요. 여러분은 어느 맛을 만들고 싶은가요? 딸기는 어때요? 첫째로, 우유 2컵, 헤비 크림 2컵, 설탕 1/2컵을 섞으세요. 다음, 딸기 5개를 작은 조각으로 자르세요. 그 다음에, 모든 것을 섞어서 냉동실에 넣으세요. 이게 다예요. 만들기 쉽죠, 그렇지 않나요? 집에서 아이스크림을 만들어 보는 게 어때요?

Listen & Speak 1 B

B: Yujin, why did you _____ the eggs in water?

G: I'm _____ _____ the bad eggs.

B: _____ eggs are fresh, and _____ ones are not?

G: Eggs _____ _____ _____ _____ are fresh. When eggs _____ in water, they're not fresh. You shouldn't eat them.

B: That's _____. Why do the bad eggs _____?

G: Because they have gas _____. The gas acts _____ the air in a _____.

B: Oh, I see.

B: 유진아, 왜 달걀을 물속에 넣었니?
G: 나는 상한 달걀을 골라내는 중이야.
B: 어느 달걀이 신선하고 어느 것이 신선하지 않은 거야?
G: 물에 가라앉는 달걀은 신선해. 달걀이 물에 뜨면, 그건 신선하지 않아. 그것들을 먹으면 안 돼.
B: 그거 재미있다. 상한 달걀은 왜 물에 뜨는 거니?
G: 상한 달걀은 속에 가스가 차기 때문이야. 가스가 풍선 속의 공기 같은 역할을 하거든.
B: 아, 이제 이해했다.

Listen & Speak 2 A

B: Ms. Jeong, does _____ _____ _____ water _____ more when there's a fish in it?

W: Yes, it does. We can _____ it now.

B: But how? We don't have a fish.

W: We can use a finger _____ _____ a fish.

B: How will that work?

W: I'll _____ a glass of water first. Then I will _____ my finger in the water and weigh it to _____.

B: Oh, I _____ _____ _____ see the difference.

B: 정 선생님, 물속에 물고기가 있을 때 물 1잔의 무게가 더 무겁나요?
W: 응, 그렇단다. 우리는 지금 실험해 볼 수 있어.
B: 하지만 어떻게요? 물고기가 없는데요.
W: 우리는 물고기 대신 손가락을 사용할 수 있단다.
B: 어떻게 할 수 있어요?
W: 먼저 물 1잔의 무게를 잴 거야. 그 다음에 비교하기 위해 물속에 손가락을 넣고 무게를 잴 거란다.
B: 아, 차이를 빨리 알고 싶어요.

Listen & Speak 2 B

King Sejong: It _____ _____ for a long time.

Jang Yeongsil: Yes. The dry season is _____ too long. The farmers are very _____.

King Sejong: We _____ do something to help them.

Jang Yeongsil: How about making a special _____?

King Sejong: A clock? How will that help?

Jang Yeongsil: The clock will show the time and the _____. We can use it _____ _____ _____ the _____ _____.

King Sejong: That sounds _____ a good idea. But who's going to make it?

Jang Yeongsil: I'll _____ _____ _____ _____. I know a lot about time and the seasons.

King Sejong: Okay, I _____ _____ _____ _____ _____.

Real Life Communication A

Brian: Mina, will you _____ our tennis club?

Mina: It sounds interesting, but I _____ _____ _____ a special class this _____.

Brian: Which class did you sign up for?

Mina: I signed up for a magic class. I can't _____ _____ learn new magic _____ there.

Brian: That sounds _____! _____ _____ _____ magic tricks before?

Mina: Yes, I learned some before, but I need more _____.

Brian: I hope I can see your magic tricks _____ _____.

Let's Check

B: What are you reading, Jiwon?

G: I'm reading a book about _____ and _____.

B: That sounds _____.

G: Yes. This book _____ 100 magic tricks that _____ _____. I've learned about _____ of them.

B: That's _____. Can you show me _____ of the tricks?

G: Sure. I can show you a _____ trick now.

B: Great! I can't _____ _____ see it.

해석

King Sejong: 오랫동안 비가 오지 않는구나.

Jang Yeongsil: 그렇습니다. 건기가 너무 오래 계속되고 있습니다. 농부들이 아주 걱정하고 있습니다.

King Sejong: 그들을 돕기 위해 뭐든 해야 한다.

Jang Yeongsil: 특별한 시계를 만드는 것은 어떨까요?

King Sejong: 시계? 그것이 어떻게 도움이 되겠느냐?

Jang Yeongsil: 시계는 시간과 계절을 알려줄 겁니다. 건기를 준비하기 위해 시계를 사용할 수 있습니다.

King Sejong: 그거 좋은 생각 같구나. 하지만 누가 시계를 만들겠느냐?

Jang Yeongsil: 제가 한번 해 보겠습니다. 저는 시간과 계절에 대해 많이 알고 있습니다.

King Sejong: 좋다, 네 시계를 빨리 보고 싶구나.

Brian: 미나야, 우리 테니스 동아리에 가입할래?

Mina: 재미있겠다. 하지만 나는 이번 가을에 특별 수업에 등록했어.

Brian: 무슨 수업에 등록했니?

Mina: 마술 수업에 등록했어. 거기서 새로운 마술 묘기를 빨리 배우고 싶어.

Brian: 그거 재미있겠다! 전에 마술 묘기를 배운 적이 있니?

Mina: 응, 전에 몇 가지 배웠어. 하지만 더 연습을 해야 해.

Brian: 언젠가 네 마술 묘기를 볼 수 있길 바라.

B: 지원아, 뭘 읽고 있니?

G: 마술과 과학에 관한 책을 읽고 있어.

B: 그거 재미있겠다.

G: 응. 이 책은 과학을 사용하는 100가지 마술을 소개하고 있어. 나는 그 중에 절반 정도를 익혔어.

B: 멋지다. 마술 중 몇 가지를 보여줄 수 있니?

G: 물론이지. 지금 풍선 마술을 보여줄 수 있어.

B: 멋지다! 빨리 보고 싶어.

[01~02] 다음 대화를 읽고 물음에 답하시오.

> Jaemin: Ms. Jeong, does a glass of water ⓐweigh more when there's a fish in it?
>
> Ms. Jeong: Yes, it ⓑdoes. We can test it now.
>
> Jaemin: But how? We don't have a fish.
>
> Ms. Jeong: We can use a finger ⓒinstead of a fish.
>
> Jaemin: How will that work?
>
> Ms. Jeong: I'll weigh a glass of water first. Then I will put my finger in the water and weigh it ⓓto compare.
>
> Jaemin: Oh, I can't wait to ⓔseeing the difference.

01 위 대화의 밑줄 친 ⓐ~ⓔ 중 어법상 어색한 것을 찾아 바르게 고치시오.

➡ _____

02 위 대화의 내용과 일치하지 않는 것은?

① 물속에 물고기가 있을 때 물 한 잔의 무게는 더 무겁다.

② 정 선생님과 재민이는 물고기 대신 손가락으로 실험하려고 한다.

③ 정 선생님은 물 한 잔의 무게를 잴 것이다.

④ 물 한 잔의 무게를 잰 후 물속에 손가락을 넣고 무게를 잴 것이다.

⑤ 재민이는 그 실험의 결과를 이미 알고 있다.

[03~04] 다음 대화를 읽고 물음에 답하시오.

> Brian: Mina, will you join our tennis club?
>
> Mina: It sounds interesting, but I signed up for a special class this fall.
>
> Brian: (A)무슨 수업에 등록했니? (for, which)
>
> Mina: I signed up for a magic class. I can't wait to learn new magic tricks there.
>
> Brian: That sounds cool! Have you learned magic tricks before?
>
> Mina: Yes, I learned some before, but I need more practice.
>
> Brian: I hope I can see your magic tricks some day.

03 위 대화의 밑줄 친 (A)의 우리말을 주어진 단어를 사용하여 영작하시오.

➡ _____

04 위 대화에서 알 수 있는 Mina의 심경으로 적절한 것은?

① excited　　② worried　　③ lonely

④ upset　　⑤ depressed

[01~03] 다음 글을 읽고 물음에 답하시오.

> Jane: Today we'll make ice cream. Which flavor do you want to make? How about strawberry? First, mix two cups of milk, two cups of heavy cream, and half a cup of sugar. Next, cut five strawberries into small pieces. Then, mix everything together and put it in the freezer. That's it. It's easy to make, (A)그렇지 않나요? Why don't you try making it at home?

서답형

01 위 글의 밑줄 친 (A)의 우리말을 두 단어를 사용하여 영작하시오.

➡ _____

서답형

02 위 글에서 언급한 아이스크림을 만들기 위한 준비물로서 바르지 <u>않은</u> 것은?

중요

03 위 글의 내용과 일치하지 <u>않는</u> 것은?

① Jane은 딸기 아이스크림 만드는 법을 설명하고 있다.
② 아이스크림을 만들기 위해 우유, 헤비 크림, 설탕, 딸기가 필요하다.
③ 딸기 5개를 작은 조각으로 잘라야 한다.
④ 모든 재료를 섞어서 냉동실에 넣어야 한다.
⑤ Jane은 집에서는 아이스크림을 만들지 않는다.

[04~06] 다음 대화를 읽고 물음에 답하시오.

> Brian: Yujin, why did you put the eggs in water?
> Yujin: I'm picking out the bad eggs.
> Brian: Which eggs are fresh, and (A)[which / what] ones are not?
> Yujin: Eggs that sink in water (B)[is / are] fresh. When eggs float in water, they're not fresh. You shouldn't eat (D)them.
> Brian: That's interesting. Why do the bad eggs float?
> Yujin: (C)[Because / Because of] they have gas inside. The gas acts like the air in a balloon.
> Brian: Oh, I see.

04 위 대화의 괄호 (A)~(C)에 들어갈 말로 바르게 짝지어진 것은?

① which – is – Because
② which – are – Because of
③ which – are – Because
④ what – are – Because of
⑤ what – is – Because

서답형

05 위 대화의 밑줄 친 (D)them이 가리키는 것을 우리말로 쓰시오.

➡ _____

중요

06 위 대화의 내용과 일치하지 <u>않는</u> 것은?

① 유진이는 상한 달걀을 골라내는 중이다.
② 물에 가라앉는 달걀은 신선한 것이다.
③ 달걀이 물에 뜨면 신선하지 않은 것이다.
④ 상한 달걀은 가스를 내뿜는다.
⑤ 가스가 풍선 속의 공기 같은 역할을 한다.

[07~08] 다음 대화를 읽고 물음에 답하시오.

> King Sejong: It hasn't rained for a long time.
>
> Jang Yeongsil: Yes. The dry season is lasting too long. The farmers are very worried.
>
> King Sejong: (A) We should do something to help them.
>
> Jang Yeongsil: (B) How about making a special clock?
>
> King Sejong: (C) A clock? How will that help?
>
> Jang Yeongsil: (D) We can use it to prepare for the dry season.
>
> King Sejong: (E) That sounds like a good idea. But who's going to make it?
>
> Jang Yeongsil: I'll give it a try. I know a lot about time and the seasons.
>
> King Sejong: Okay, I can't wait to see your clock.

07 위 대화의 (A)~(E) 중 주어진 문장이 들어가기에 적절한 곳은?

> The clock will show the time and the seasons.

① (A)   ② (B)   ③ (C)   ④ (D)   ⑤ (E)

08 위 대화를 읽고 대답할 수 없는 것은?

① What's the matter?

② What does Jang Yeongsil suggest?

③ Why does Jang Yeongsil want to make a special clock?

④ What does Jang Yeongsil know about a lot?

⑤ What does King Sejong do to finish the dry season?

[09~10] 다음 대화를 읽고 물음에 답하시오.

> Brian: Mina, will you join our tennis club?
>
> Mina: It sounds interesting, but I signed up for a special class this fall.
>
> Brian: Which class did you sign up for?
>
> Mina: I signed up for a magic class. I can't wait to learn new magic tricks there.
>
> Brian: _____(A)_____ Have you learned magic tricks before?
>
> Mina: Yes, I learned some before, but I need more practice.
>
> Brian: I hope I can see your magic tricks some day.

09 위 대화의 빈칸 (A)에 들어갈 말로 적절한 것은?

① I'm sorry to hear that.

② That sounds cool!

③ Take it easy.

④ I don't think so.

⑤ It's not your fault.

10 위 대화를 읽고 대답할 수 없는 것은?

① Which class did Mina sign up for this fall?

② Why couldn't Mina join the tennis club?

③ What does Mina want to learn in the magic class?

④ Has Mina learned magic tricks before?

⑤ How long has Mina practiced magic tricks?

[01~03] 다음 대화를 읽고 물음에 답하시오.

Jaemin: Ms. Jeong, does a glass of water weigh more when there's a fish in it?

Ms. Jeong: Yes, it does. We can test it now.

Jaemin: But how? We don't have a fish.

Ms. Jeong: We can use a finger instead of a fish.

Jaemin: How will that work?

Ms. Jeong: I'll weigh a glass of water first. Then I will put my finger in the water and weigh it to compare.

Jaemin: Oh, (A)<u>차이를 빨리 알고 싶어요</u>.

01 위 대화의 밑줄 친 (A)의 우리말을 <보기>에 주어진 모든 단어들을 배열하여 영작하시오.

┌─ 보기 ┐
to / I / difference / wait / can't / see / the
└──────────┘

➡ _____

02 What will Ms. Jeong use instead of a fish?

➡ _____

03 What do Ms. Jeong and Jaemin want to see through the experiment?

A: They want to see whether _____
_____ .

04 다음 대화에서 (A)~(E)를 자연스럽게 이어지도록 순서대로 배열하시오.

King Sejong: It hasn't rained for a long time.

Jang Yeongsil: Yes. The dry season is lasting too long. The farmers are very worried.

King Sejong: We should do something to help them.

(A) I'll give it a try. I know a lot about time and the seasons.
(B) A clock? How will that help?
(C) That sounds like a good idea. But who's going to make it?
(D) How about making a special clock?
(E) The clock will show the time and the seasons. We can use it to prepare for the dry season.

King Sejong: Okay, I can't wait to see your clock.

➡ _____

[05~06] 다음 글을 읽고 물음에 답하시오.

Jane: Today we'll make ice cream. Which flavor do you want to make? How about strawberry? First, mix two cups of milk, two cups of heavy cream, and half a cup of sugar. Next, cut five strawberries into small pieces. Then, mix everything together and put it in the freezer. That's it. It's easy to make, isn't it? Why don't you try making it at home?

05 According to Jane, what do you need to prepare for making strawberry ice cream?

➡ _____
_____

06 What should you do after cutting the strawberries into small pieces?

➡ _____
_____

Grammar

교과서

① 가주어 It

> - **It** is good **to meet** him. 그를 만나는 것은 좋다.
> - **It** is wrong **to speak** ill of your friends. 친구에 관해 나쁘게 말하는 것은 옳지 않다.

■ to부정사구가 주어로 쓰여 주어가 길어진 경우, 주어부를 문장의 맨 뒤로 보내고 이 자리에 It을 쓰는 것이 가주어 It이다. 명사절 접속사가 이끄는 that절 역시 이에 해당한다.

- **To keep** your promise is important.
  = **It** is important **to keep** your promise. 너의 약속을 지키는 것은 중요하다.
- **That he broke his leg** was surprising.
  = **It** was surprising **that** he broke his leg. 그의 다리가 부러졌다는 것은 놀라웠어.

■ 가주어 It은 따로 해석하지 않으며 to부정사구를 주어로 해석해야 한다. to부정사구의 부정은 'not+to V'로 표기한다.

- **It** is good **not to make** noises in the library. 도서관에서는 소음을 내지 않는 것이 좋다.
- **It** is bad **not to say** sorry when you do wrong. 네가 잘못을 했을 때 미안하다고 말하지 않는 것은 나빠.

■ 진주어 to부정사의 행위 주체를 명시하고 싶은 경우, 의미상의 주어로 'for/of+목적격'을 사용한다. 'for+목적격'은 '상황에 대한 의견'을 나타내는 형용사 뒤에서, 'of+목적격'은 '사람의 성격'을 나타내는 형용사 뒤에서 쓰인다.

- **It** is kind **of** her **to help** you. 그녀가 너를 도와주는 것은 친절해.
- **It** is not safe **for** you **to go** outside alone. 네가 혼자 밖으로 나가는 것은 안전하지 않아.

핵심 Check

1. 다음 우리말과 일치하도록 빈칸에 알맞은 말을 쓰시오.

(1) 식물을 돌보는 것은 쉽지 않다.
  ➡ It is not easy _____ _____ _____ of plants.

(2) 너를 매일 만나는 것은 좋아.
  ➡ It is nice _____ _____ you every day.

(3) 우리가 침착함을 유지하는 것은 중요해.
  ➡ It is important _____ _____ _____ _____ calm.

2 How come ...?

- **How come** you are angry with me? 도대체 너는 왜 내게 화가 났니?
- **How come** she came late? 그녀는 도대체 왜 늦었니?

■ 의문사 why와 how come은 의미는 비슷하지만 어순상의 차이를 보인다. 'How come+주어+동사 …?'로 쓰여 '도대체 왜 …?'라는 의미이지만, why는 'Why+동사+주어 …?'의 어순으로 쓰인다.

- **How come** you bought this? 도대체 이걸 왜 산 거야?

  Why did you buy this? 이것을 왜 산 거니?

  How come he made this cake? 도대체 왜 그가 이 케이크를 만든 거야?

  Why did he make this cake? 그는 왜 이 케이크를 만든 거야?

  How come she looked disappointed? 그녀는 도대체 왜 실망한 것처럼 보였니?

  Why did she look disappointed? 그녀는 왜 실망한 것처럼 보였니?

  How come you are here? 도대체 네가 왜 여기에 있는 거야?

  Why are you here? 너는 왜 여기에 있니?

  How come you sent the message like that? 도대체 너는 왜 그런 메시지를 보낸 거야?

  Why did you send the message like that? 왜 너는 그런 메시지를 보냈니?

핵심 Check

2. 다음 우리말을 영어로 쓰시오.

(1) 도대체 왜 내게 거짓말을 했니?

➡ _____ _____ you lied to me?

(2) 왜 그 소년이 울고 있니?

➡ _____ is the boy crying?

(3) 도대체 왜 그가 그런 말을 했니?

➡ _____ _____ he said things like that?

(4) 도대체 왜 그를 초대했니?

➡ _____ _____ you invited him?

Grammar 시험대비 기본평가

01 다음 문장에서 어법상 어색한 부분을 바르게 고쳐 쓰시오.

(1) It was difficult stop my bad habit.

_____ ➡ _____

(2) It is impossible of you to finish the project.

_____ ➡ _____

(3) How come did you meet her?

_____ ➡ _____

(4) How came he was with you?

_____ ➡ _____

02 다음 우리말과 일치하도록 빈칸에 알맞은 말을 쓰시오.

(1) 도대체 왜 그는 물을 그렇게 많이 마시는 거야?
➡ How come _____ _____ so much water?

(2) 왜 너는 운동을 열심히 하니?
➡ Why _____ _____ _____ hard?

(3) 도대체 왜 그녀가 슬퍼 보이는 거지?
➡ How come _____ _____ sad?

(4) 왜 너는 그렇게 빨리 달렸니?
➡ Why _____ _____ _____ so fast?

03 주어진 단어를 바르게 배열하여 다음 우리말을 영어로 쓰시오. 필요하다면 단어를 추가하시오.

(1) 운동을 규칙적으로 하는 것은 매우 중요해.

(exercise / regularly / important / is / it / very)

➡ _____

(2) 놀이공원에 가는 것은 신난다.

(it / the amusement park / exciting / to / go / is)

➡ _____

(3) 친구들에게 정직한 것은 중요해.

(your friends / important / honest / be / is / it / with)

➡ _____

(4) 그것을 설명하는 것은 나의 일이야. (it / it / explain / my job / is)

➡ _____

01 다음 빈칸에 들어갈 말로 가장 적절한 것은?

> It is good _____ early in the morning.

① wake up
② to wake up
③ woke up
④ to waking up
⑤ woken up

02 다음 우리말을 영어로 바르게 옮긴 것은?

> 도대체 왜 그녀는 우리에게 다시 돌아온 거야?

① Why is she coming back to us?
② Why is she returning to us?
③ How come she came back to us?
④ How come did she come back to us?
⑤ How came she came back to us?

03 다음 중 빈칸에 들어갈 말이 다른 하나는?

① It was wise _____ him to say sorry.
② It is generous _____ her to lend us money.
③ It is rude _____ you to talk like that to your elders.
④ It is easy _____ me to solve this problem.
⑤ It was careful _____ them to keep their valuables in the safe.

04 주어진 단어를 활용하여 다음 우리말을 영어로 쓰시오.

> 외국어를 배우는 것은 재미있다.
> (fun / it)

➡ _____

05 다음 주어진 문장의 밑줄 친 부분과 쓰임이 같은 것은?

> It is exciting to ride a bike with friends.

① The dog was barking at us to protect his house.
② It is surprising to see you here.
③ Is there anything to wear?
④ The man went into his room to take a rest.
⑤ We want you to do your best.

06 다음 빈칸에 들어갈 말이 바르게 짝지어진 것은?

> • It is amazing _____ the plants grow in our garden.
> • _____ he jogs every morning?

① see – Why
② to see – Why
③ saw – Why
④ to see – How come
⑤ to seeing – How come

07 다음 중 빈칸에 들어갈 말이 다른 하나는?

① _____ she took him to the store?
② _____ he broke his promise?
③ _____ we didn't take a bus?
④ _____ they didn't come?
⑤ _____ are we going to visit them?

08 다음 빈칸에 알맞은 말을 쓰시오.

> To read books is very fun.
> ➡ It is very fun _____ _____ _____.

09 주어진 단어를 바르게 배열하여 다음 우리말을 영어로 쓸 때 다섯 번째로 오는 단어는?

> 인사하는 방법을 아는 것은 좋다.
> (hello / nice / how / it / to / is / say / to / know)

① to ② nice ③ say
④ know ⑤ hello

10 다음 중 밑줄 친 부분의 쓰임이 다른 하나는?

① It is true that he succeeded in climbing the mountain.
② It was good to hear the news from her.
③ It is cloudy and windy.
④ It is fun to see movies.
⑤ It was wrong to make fun of your friend.

11 다음 중 어법상 바르지 않은 것은?

① How come you woke up so late?
② It is true that he made the robot.
③ That is surprising to see you play the piano.
④ It will be difficult for you to understand the book.
⑤ It was not easy to talk with her.

12 다음 중 어법상 바르지 않은 것은?

> ①It was ②careless ③for them ④to tell their children something ⑤like that.

① ② ③ ④ ⑤

13 주어진 단어를 활용하여 다음 우리말을 영어로 쓰시오.

> 도대체 그녀는 왜 그 재킷을 산 거야?
> (how / the jacket)

➡ _____

14 다음 중 우리말로 옮긴 것이 바르지 않은 것은?

① 도대체 왜 너는 내 말을 안 들은 거니?
→ How come you didn't listen to me?
② 네가 그 음악을 듣는 것은 놀랍다.
→ It is surprising for you to hear the music.
③ 그 단어들의 의미를 찾는 것은 도움이 될 거야.
→ It will be helpful to find the meanings of the words.
④ 그 일에 너를 추천하는 것은 나의 생각이 아니었어.
→ To recommend you for the job was not my idea.
⑤ 내가 너를 막는 것은 불가능했어.
→ It was impossible of me to stop you.

15 다음 빈칸에 들어갈 말로 가장 적절한 것은?

> _____ he broke into someone's house?

① Why ② What ③ When
④ How come ⑤ Where

16 주어진 단어를 바르게 배열하여 다음 우리말을 영어로 쓰시오. 필요하다면 단어를 추가하시오.

> 걷는 동안 휴대 전화기를 사용하지 않는 것이 중요하다.
> (important / your phone / walking / to / it / use / is / while)

➡ _____

17 다음 빈칸에 알맞은 말을 쓰시오.

> 도대체 그녀는 왜 어제 떠난 거야?
> ➡ How come _____ _____ yesterday?

18 다음 중 빈칸에 들어갈 말이 바르게 짝지어진 것은?

> • It is wise _____ her to go with you to the hospital.
> • It is necessary _____ they come here on time.

① to – to
② for – to
③ of – that
④ of – to
⑤ for – that

19 다음 우리말을 영어로 바르게 옮긴 것을 모두 고르시오.

> 부주의하게 운전하는 것은 위험하다.

① It is careless to drive dangerously.
② It is dangerous drive carelessly.
③ To drive carelessly is dangerous.
④ It is dangerous to drive carelessly.
⑤ It is careless drive dangerously.

20 다음 괄호 안의 단어를 어법에 맞게 쓸 때 형태가 다른 하나는?

① It is kind of him (help) you.
② It is rude of you (say) such words.
③ It is good at (build) nests on trees.
④ It is bad for you (use) someone's stuff without asking.
⑤ It is necessary for me (do) my homework.

21 다음 문장과 같은 의미의 문장을 쓰시오.

> To tell a stranger where you live is dangerous.

➡ _____

22 다음 중 빈칸에 들어갈 말이 바르게 짝지어진 것은?

> A: Your room is so messy. _____ you didn't clean your room?
> B: It's because I was too busy. It was impossible _____ me to clean the room.

① Why – that
② Why – of
③ How come – for
④ How come – of
⑤ How come – that

23 다음 중 어법상 옳은 것은?

① It is fun hear him talking about interesting stories.
② How come did you lose your weight?
③ It is brave for you to make the decision.
④ Why you weren't doing the laundry?
⑤ It is stupid of her to behave like that in front of so many people.

24 다음 주어진 단어를 활용하여 다음 문장과 같은 의미의 문장을 쓰시오.

> Why did you call me? (how)

➡ _____

01 주어진 단어를 활용하여 다음 우리말을 영어로 쓰시오.

> 헬멧을 쓰지 않는 것은 위험하다.
> (it / your / wear)

➡ _____

02 다음 빈칸에 알맞은 말을 쓰시오.

(1) 왜 그녀는 지금 너를 쳐다보고 있는 거야?
   ➡ How come _____ _____ _____
      at you now?
(2) 왜 너는 그 아이들을 초대한 거니?
   ➡ Why _____ _____ _____ the
      children?
(3) 도대체 왜 그 선생님은 우리에게 할 일을 그렇
   게 많이 주시는 거야?
   ➡ How come _____ _____ _____
      us so many things to do?
(4) 왜 우리는 그 식당으로 가고 있는 거야?
   ➡ How come _____ _____ _____
      to the restaurant?
(5) 왜 너는 모자를 쓰고 있는 거니?
   ➡ Why _____ _____ _____ a hat?

03 다음 문장과 같은 의미의 문장을 완성하시오.

(1) To travel abroad is exciting.
   ➡ It _____.
(2) To read this novel is not easy.
   ➡ It _____.
(3) It is useful to know how to use this
   machine.
   ➡ To _____.

04 주어진 단어를 바르게 배열하여 다음 우리말을 영어로 쓰시
오. 필요하다면 단어를 추가하시오.

> 네가 그렇게 말한 것은 어리석었어.
> (you / it / say / stupid / was / so / to)

➡ _____

05 주어진 단어를 활용하여 다음 문장과 같은 의미의 문장을
쓰시오.

> Why did you put your wallet on the table?
> (how)

➡ _____

06 다음 빈칸에 알맞은 말을 쓰시오.

> 내가 그 산을 오르는 것이 가능해?
> ➡ Is it possible _____ _____ _____
>   _____ up the mountain?

07 주어진 단어를 활용하여 다음 대화를 영어로 쓰시오.

> A: _____ (how / today)
> B: I am going to meet her today because
>   I don't have any free time tomorrow.

➡ _____

08 다음 빈칸에 알맞은 말을 쓰시오.

> It is surprising _____ he didn't call
> you.

09 다음 빈칸에 적절한 말을 쓰시오. 중요

_____ _____ you made her do the dishes?

= _____ did you make her do the dishes?

10 다음 대화의 빈칸에 알맞은 말을 쓰시오.

A: Is it easy _____?

B: I don't think so. To form good habits is not easy.

➡ _____

11 주어진 단어를 활용하여 다음 대화를 영어로 쓰시오. 고난이도

A: 도대체 왜 그녀는 나에게 사과하지 않는 거야? (how / say sorry)

B: 그녀가 너에게 미안하다고 말하는 것은 쉽지 않다고 생각해. (it / think)

A: _____

B: _____

12 다음 빈칸에 들어갈 알맞은 말을 쓰시오.

It was nice _____ you to send me a birthday card.

13 다음 문장에서 어법상 틀린 것을 바르게 고쳐 문장을 다시 쓰시오.

How come did you forget to bring the book?

➡ _____

14 주어진 단어를 바르게 배열하여 다음 우리말을 영어로 쓰시오. 필요하다면 단어를 추가하시오.

그가 너에게 자기의 옷을 빌려준 것은 정말 관대했어.

(his clothes / him / lend / generous / was / to / it / you)

➡ _____

15 주어진 단어를 활용하여 다음 문장과 같은 의미의 문장을 쓰시오.

Why did you book the restaurant? (how)

➡ _____

16 다음 빈칸에 알맞은 말을 쓰시오. 중요

A: Was it fun to watch the movie?

B: Yes. _____ was really fun.

➡ _____

17 다음 빈칸에 알맞은 말을 쓰시오.

너는 왜 John을 돕지 않았니?

= _____ _____ you didn't help John?

= _____ _____ _____ help John?

18 주어진 단어를 활용하여 다음 대화의 우리말을 영어로 쓰시오. 중요

A: 너는 왜 공부를 열심히 하는 거야? (how)

B: 공부를 열심히 하는 것은 나를 행복하게 해. (make me happy / it)

A: _____

B: _____

Reading

교과서

The Super Science Magic Show

Jina: Welcome to the Super Science Magic Show! It's always exciting
to see magic tricks. And it's more exciting to find out the secrets
behind them. Some people think the secret of magic is science.
Today, Ken, a member of the School Magic Club, will use science
to perform his tricks. Which tricks will he show us? I can't wait to
see them.

The Amazing Rising Water

Ken: Hello, everyone. Today, I'm going to show you something
amazing. Here's a dish with water in it. Now, I'll put a candle in
the middle of the dish. Next, I'll light the candle and cover it with
a glass. "Abracadabra!"

Jina: Look at the water! How come it rose into the glass?

Ken: Air expands when it gets hot and creates higher pressure. When it
gets cold, air contracts and creates lower pressure. When the flame
burnt out, the air inside the glass cooled down. As the air cooled
down, the air pressure dropped. So the air outside the glass was at
a higher pressure. It pushed the water into the glass.

magic 마술의
trick 속임수, 마술, 묘기
secret 비밀
candle 초, 양초
abracadabra 아브라카다브라 (주문)
expand 팽창하다
pressure 압력
contract 수축하다
flame 불꽃
burn out 타 버리다
cool down 식다, 차가워지다

확인문제

● 다음 문장이 본문의 내용과 일치하면 T, 일치하지 <u>않으면</u> F를 쓰시오.

1 Ken belongs to the School Magic Club. ☐

2 Ken will show students some tricks without using science. ☐

3 Air expands when it gets hot and creates lower pressure. ☐

4 As the air cooled down, the air pressure rose. ☐

5 The air inside the glass cooled down because the flame burnt out. ☐

The Secret of the Disappearing Water

현재분사(사라지는)

Ken: Now, I'm going to fill one of these cups with water. I will move
fill A with B: A를 B로 채우다

them around to confuse you. Jina, which cup has the water in it?
cups   to부정사의 부사적 용법 중 목적(~하기 위해서)

Jina: That's easy! It's the middle one.

Ken: Okay, let's check. See? No water.
= There is no water

Jina: Show me the other cups.
4형식 (show+사람+사물)

Ken: See? There's no water.

Jina: Wow! How come the water disappeared?
How come+주어+동사 ~?

Ken: Before the trick, I put a special material into one of the cups. The
put A into B: A를 B 안에 넣다

material absorbed the water and turned it into jelly. Then the jelly
the water

stuck to the bottom. If you want to try this trick, it's necessary to
stick(들러붙다)의 과거   진주어 to부정사

use cups that you can't see through.
목적격 관계대명사

Jina: Thank you for your great performance. It was really amazing!
현재분사(놀라움을 유발하는)

confuse 혼동하게 하다

material 물질, 재료

absorb 흡수하다

turn A into B A를 B로 바꾸다

bottom 바닥

necessary 필요한, 필연적인

see through 속을 들여다보다, 꿰뚫어

보다

📎 **확인문제**

● 다음 문장이 본문의 내용과 일치하면 T, 일치하지 않으면 F를 쓰시오.

1 Ken moved cups around including the one which had water in it. ☐

2 Jina thought that the cup which was in the middle had water. ☐

3 There was no water in all of the cups. ☐

4 The jelly didn't stick to the bottom of the cup. ☐

5 You need cups that can't be seen through to do the trick. ☐

6 Jina thought the performance that Ken showed was amazing. ☐

● 우리말을 참고하여 빈칸에 알맞은 말을 쓰시오.

1 Jina: _____ _____ the Super Science Magic Show!

2 _____ always _____ _____ _____ magic tricks.

3 And it's more exciting _____ _____ _____ the secrets _____ them.

4 Some people think the secret of magic _____ _____.

5 Today, Ken, a member of the School Magic Club, _____ _____ _____ _____ his tricks.

6 Which tricks _____ he _____ _____? I can't wait _____ _____ _____.

7 Ken: Hello, everyone. Today, I'm going _____ _____ _____ something amazing.

8 Here's a dish _____ _____ _____ _____.

9 Now, I'll _____ _____ _____ in the middle of the dish.

10 Next, I'll _____ the candle and _____ _____ _____ a glass. "Abracadabra!"

11 Jina: Look _____ the water! _____ _____ it _____ _____ the glass?

12 Ken: Air _____ when it gets _____ and creates _____ _____.

13 When it _____ _____, air _____ and creates _____ _____.

14 When the flame _____ _____, the air inside the glass _____ _____.

15 As the air _____ _____, the air pressure _____.

1 지나: 특별 과학 마술 쇼에 오신 것을 환영합니다!

2 마술을 보는 것은 항상 신나는 일입니다.

3 그리고 마술 뒤에 숨겨진 비밀을 알아내는 것은 더 신나는 일입니다.

4 어떤 사람들은 마술의 비밀이 과학이라고 생각합니다.

5 오늘 학교 마술 동아리 회원인 Ken은 마술을 수행하기 위해 과학을 사용할 것입니다.

6 그는 우리에게 어떤 마술을 보여 줄까요? 무척 기다려지는군요.

7 Ken: 안녕하세요, 여러분. 오늘, 저는 여러분에게 놀라운 무언가를 보여 주려고 합니다.

8 여기에 물이 담긴 접시가 있습니다.

9 이제, 저는 접시 한가운데에 초를 놓을 것입니다.

10 그다음에 초를 켜고 유리컵으로 초를 덮어 보겠습니다. "아브라카다브라!"

11 지나: 물을 보세요! 어째서 물이 유리컵 속으로 올라간 거지요?

12 Ken: 공기가 뜨거워지면 팽창해서, 더 높은 압력을 만듭니다.

13 공기가 차가워지면 수축해서, 더 낮은 압력을 만듭니다.

14 불꽃이 다 타 버렸을 때, 유리컵 속의 공기는 식어 버렸습니다.

15 공기가 식었으므로, 기압이 낮아졌습니다.

16 So the air outside the glass _____ _____ _____ _____.

17 It _____ the water _____ the glass.

18 Ken: Now, I'm going _____ _____ _____ _____ _____ _____ with water.

19 I will move _____ _____ _____ _____ you.

20 Jina, _____ _____ has the water in it?

21 Jina: That's easy! _____ the middle _____.

22 Ken: Okay, _____ _____. See? No water.

23 Jina: Show _____ _____ _____ _____.

24 Ken: See? There's _____ _____.

25 Jina: Wow! _____ _____ the water _____?

26 Ken: _____ the trick, I _____ a special material _____ one of _____ _____.

27 The material _____ the water and _____ _____ _____ jelly.

28 Then the jelly _____ _____ _____ _____.

29 If you want to try this trick, it's _____ _____ _____ cups _____ you can't see through.

30 Jina: Thank you _____ your great _____. It was really _____!

16 그래서 유리컵 밖의 공기 압력이 더 높아졌습니다.

17 높아진 압력의 공기가 물을 밀어서 유리컵으로 들어가게 된 것입니다.

18 Ken: 이제, 이 컵들 중 하나를 물로 채워 보겠습니다.

19 여러분을 헷갈리게 하려고 이 컵들을 섞어 보겠습니다.

20 지나, 어떤 컵에 물이 있을까요?

21 지나: 쉽네요! 가운데 컵이에요.

22 Ken: 좋습니다, 확인해 봅시다. 보셨죠? 물이 없군요.

23 지나: 다른 컵들도 보여 주세요.

24 Ken: 보셨죠? 물이 없네요.

25 지나: 왜! 어째서 물이 사라진 거죠?

26 Ken: 마술 전에, 저는 특별한 물질을 컵 하나에 넣어 두었습니다.

27 그 물질은 물을 흡수하고, 그것을 젤리로 변하게 했습니다.

28 그리고 나서 젤리는 컵 바닥에 달라붙었습니다.

29 여러분이 이 마술을 해 보고자 한다면, 속을 들여다볼 수 없는 컵을 사용해야 합니다.

30 지나: 멋진 공연 고맙습니다. 정말 놀라웠어요!

● 우리말을 참고하여 본문을 영작하시오.

1 지나: 특별 과학 마술 쇼에 오신 것을 환영합니다!

➡ _____

2 마술을 보는 것은 항상 신나는 일입니다.

➡ _____

3 그리고 마술 뒤에 숨겨진 비밀을 알아내는 것은 더 신나는 일입니다.

➡ _____

4 어떤 사람들은 마술의 비밀이 과학이라고 생각합니다.

➡ _____

5 오늘 학교 마술 동아리 회원인 Ken은 마술을 수행하기 위해 과학을 사용할 것입니다.

➡ _____

6 그는 우리에게 어떤 마술을 보여 줄까요? 무척 기다려지는군요.

➡ _____

7 Ken: 안녕하세요, 여러분. 오늘, 저는 여러분에게 놀라운 무언가를 보여 주려고 합니다.

➡ _____

8 여기에 물이 담긴 접시가 있습니다.

➡ _____

9 이제, 저는 접시 한가운데에 초를 놓을 것입니다.

➡ _____

10 그다음에 초를 켜고 유리컵으로 초를 덮어 보겠습니다. "아브라카다브라!"

➡ _____

11 지나: 물을 보세요! 어째서 물이 유리컵 속으로 올라간 거지요?

➡ _____

12 Ken: 공기가 뜨거워지면 팽창해서, 더 높은 압력을 만듭니다.

➡ _____

13 공기가 차가워지면 수축해서, 더 낮은 압력을 만듭니다.

➡ _____

14 불꽃이 다 타 버렸을 때, 유리컵 속의 공기는 식어 버렸습니다.

➡ _____

15 공기가 식었으므로, 기압이 낮아졌습니다.

➡ _____

16 그래서 유리컵 밖의 공기 압력이 더 높아졌습니다.

➡ _____

17 높아진 압력의 공기가 물을 밀어서 유리컵으로 들어가게 된 것입니다.

➡ _____

18 Ken: 이제, 이 컵들 중 하나를 물로 채워 보겠습니다.

➡ _____

19 여러분을 헷갈리게 하려고 이 컵들을 섞어 보겠습니다.

➡ _____

20 지나, 어떤 컵에 물이 있을까요?

➡ _____

21 지나: 쉽네요! 가운데 컵이에요.

➡ _____

22 Ken: 좋습니다, 확인해 봅시다. 보셨죠? 물이 없군요.

➡ _____

23 지나: 다른 컵들도 보여 주세요.

➡ _____

24 Ken: 보셨죠? 물이 없네요.

➡ _____

25 지나: 와! 어째서 물이 사라진 거죠?

➡ _____

26 Ken: 마술 전에, 저는 특별한 물질을 컵 하나에 넣어 두었습니다.

➡ _____

27 그 물질은 물을 흡수하고, 그것을 젤리로 변하게 했습니다.

➡ _____

28 그리고 나서 젤리는 컵 바닥에 달라붙었습니다.

➡ _____

29 여러분이 이 마술을 해 보고자 한다면, 속을 들여다볼 수 없는 컵을 사용해야 합니다.

➡ _____

30 지나: 멋진 공연 고맙습니다. 정말 놀라웠어요!

➡ _____

[01~03] 다음 글을 읽고 물음에 답하시오.

Jina: Welcome (A)_____ the Super Science Magic Show! It's always exciting to see magic tricks. And it's more exciting to find out the secrets behind them. Some people think the secret of magic is science. Today, Ken, a member of the School Magic Club, will use science to perform his tricks. Which tricks will he show us? I can't wait to see them.

01 다음 중 빈칸 (A)에 들어갈 말로 가장 적절한 것은?

① for ② to ③ in
④ at ⑤ about

02 What does Jina want to talk about?

① Science that uses magic.
② Magic used by scientists.
③ Magic using science.
④ Magical things around us.
⑤ The most surprising thing in the world.

서답형

03 Who is Ken? Answer in English with a full sentence.

➡ _____

[04~09] 다음 글을 읽고 물음에 답하시오.

Ken: Hello, everyone. Today, I'm going to show you something amazing. Here's a dish with water in it. Now, I'll put a candle in the middle of the dish. Next, I'll light the candle and cover it with a glass. "Abracadabra!"

Jina: Look at the water! How come it ①rose into the glass?

Ken: Air expands when it gets hot and creates higher pressure. When it gets cold, air contracts and creates ___(A)___ pressure. When the flame burnt out, the air inside the glass ②heated up. As the air ③cooled down, the air pressure ④dropped. So the air ⑤outside the glass was at a higher pressure. It pushed the water into the glass.

04 다음 중 빈칸 (A)에 들어갈 말로 가장 적절한 것은?

① higher ② the same ③ lower
④ no ⑤ strong

05 다음 ①~⑤ 중 글의 흐름상 어색한 것은?

① ② ③ ④ ⑤

06 다음 중 위 글에서 찾아볼 수 없는 것은?

① a boy who is showing a magic
② a girl watching a magic show
③ a dish which has water in it
④ a candle covered with a towel
⑤ water pushed into the glass from outside of the dish

서답형

07 What happened when Kevin covered the candle with a glass? Answer in English with a full sentence.

➡ _____

08 다음 중 위 글을 읽고 답할 수 있는 것은?

① How much water is there in the dish?
② What does Ken want to show?
③ How did Ken learn the magic?
④ Where did Ken show the magic?
⑤ When did Ken show the magic?

09 위 글의 내용에 맞게 빈칸에 알맞은 말을 쓰시오.

Pressure _____ causes the water to move into the glass.

[10~15] 다음 글을 읽고 물음에 답하시오.

Ken: Now, I'm going to fill one of these cups with water. I will move them around to confuse you. Jina, which cup has the water in it?
Jina: That's easy! It's the middle one.
Ken: Okay, let's check. See? No water.
Jina: Show me   (A)   cups.
Ken: See? There's no water.
Jina: Wow! How come the water disappeared?
Ken: ① Before the trick, I put a special material into one of the cups. ② The material absorbed the water and turned it into jelly. ③ If you want to try this trick, it's necessary to use cups that you can't see through. ④
Jina: ⑤ Thank you for your great performance. It was really amazing!

10 다음 중 빈칸 (A)에 들어갈 말로 가장 적절한 것은?

① the others   ② another
③ other   ④ the other
⑤ others

11 다음 ①~⑤ 중 주어진 문장이 들어가기에 가장 적절한 곳은?

Then the jelly stuck to the bottom.

①   ②   ③   ④   ⑤

서답형
12 다음과 같이 풀이되는 단어를 위 글에서 찾아 쓰시오.

to take in something in a natural or gradual way

➡ _____

서답형
13 What did Ken do after he filled one of cups with water? Answer in English with four words.

➡ _____

서답형
14 According to Ken, what is necessary if we want to try the trick?

➡ _____
_____

15 다음 중 위 글의 내용을 바르게 이해한 사람은?

① Teo: If there is no mysterious power, we can't perform the magic.
② Jenny: I will need only two cups to try the magic.
③ Chris: Ken made the water disappear by drinking it when no one saw him.
④ Paul: To try the magic, I will buy the special material which can take in water and turn it into jelly.
⑤ Nick: I need to buy a special material and some glasses which people can see through.

[16~18] 다음 글을 읽고 물음에 답하시오.

Jina: Welcome to the Super Science Magic Show! (A)It's always exciting to see magic tricks. And it's more exciting to find out the secrets behind (B)them. Some people think the secret of magic is science. Today, Ken, a member of the School Magic Club, will use science to perform his tricks. Which tricks will he show us? I can't wait to see them.

16 다음 중 밑줄 친 (A)와 쓰임이 같은 것은?

① It is rainy and windy.
② It is not what I said.
③ It is clear that you can't drive.
④ It is dark outside.
⑤ It is flowing under the bridge.

17 다음 밑줄 친 (B)가 가리키는 것을 위 글에서 찾아 쓰시오.

➡ _____

다음 중 위 글에 이어질 내용으로 가장 적절한 것은?

① Ken의 자기소개
② Ken의 과학을 이용한 발명품
③ Jina의 과학 동아리 소개
④ Ken의 과학을 이용한 마술 쇼
⑤ 마술에 숨겨진 비밀

[19~23] 다음 글을 읽고 물음에 답하시오.

Jina: Hello, everyone. Today, I'm going to show you ①amazing something.
(A) Next, I'll light the candle and cover it with a glass. "Abracadabra!"
(B) Now, I'll put a candle ②in the middle of the dish.
(C) Here's a dish with water in it.

Jina: Look at the water! _____ ⓐ

Ken: Air expands when it gets hot and creates higher pressure. When it ③gets cold, air contracts and creates lower pressure. When the flame ④burnt out, the air inside the glass cooled down. As the air cooled down, the air pressure dropped. So the air outside the glass was at a higher pressure. It pushed the water ⑤into the glass.

19 다음 중 빈칸 ⓐ에 들어갈 말로 가장 적절한 것은?

① Why did you cover it with a glass?
② How come you pour more water?
③ How come there is no water?
④ Why did you light the candle?
⑤ How come it rose into the glass?

20 자연스러운 글이 되도록 (A)~(C)를 바르게 배열한 것은?

① (A) – (C) – (B) ② (B) – (A) – (C)
③ (B) – (C) – (A) ④ (C) – (B) – (A)
⑤ (C) – (A) – (B)

서답형
21 According to the passage, which side of the air is at a higher pressure while the candle is still burning? Answer in English with a full sentence.

➡ _____

22 다음 ①~⑤ 중 어법상 바르지 않은 것은?

①   ②   ③   ④   ⑤

23 주어진 단어를 활용하여 Ken의 마술 쇼 제목을 쓰시오.

> The _____ Water (amaze, rise)

➡ _____

[24~27] 다음 글을 읽고 물음에 답하시오.

> **Ken:** Now, I'm going to fill one of these cups with water. I will move them around to confuse you. Jina, which cup has the water in it?
>
> **Jina:** That's easy! It's the middle one.
>
> **Ken:** Okay, let's check. See? No water.
>
> **Jina:** Show me the other cups.
>
> **Ken:** See? There's no water.
>
> **Jina:** Wow! (A)어째서 물이 사라진 거죠?
>
> **Ken:** Before the trick, I put (B)a special material into one of the cups. The material absorbed the water and turned it into jelly. Then the jelly stuck to the bottom. If you want to try this trick, it's necessary to use cups (C)that you can't see through.
>
> **Jina:** Thank you for your great performance. It was really amazing!

24 주어진 단어를 활용하여 밑줄 친 우리말 (A)를 영어로 쓰시오.

> (how)

➡ _____

25 다음 중 밑줄 친 (B)에 관한 설명으로 옳은 것은?

① Ken put it into one of the cups after the show.
② It can't take in water.
③ It turns water into jelly after absorbing water.
④ It is easy to remove it from the cup.
⑤ You should put it into all of the cups when trying the magic.

26 다음 중 밑줄 친 (C)와 쓰임이 같은 것은?

① I thought that we were lost.
② It was surprising that he accepted their apology.
③ The fact that he spread the news shocked everyone.
④ Did he say that he didn't serve the table?
⑤ The boy that you shook hands with is my cousin, Alan.

27 Write the reason why Ken moved around the cups after filling one of them with water. Answer in English with a full sentence.

➡ _____

[28~29] 다음 글을 읽고 물음에 답하시오.

> USA – The moving rocks in Death Valley
> How come the rocks move ___(A)___ their own? They weigh up to 300 kilograms each. Some scientists have watched their movements closely for a long time. Now we know that ice and wind move the rocks.

28 다음 중 빈칸 (A)에 들어갈 말로 가장 적절한 것은?

① in   ② about   ③ at
④ on   ⑤ out

29 위 글의 내용에 맞게 빈칸에 알맞은 말을 쓰시오.

> According to the research of the scientists, _____ make the rocks look like they move by themselves.

[01~03] 다음 글을 읽고 물음에 답하시오.

Jina: Welcome to the Super Science Magic Show! (A)It's always exciting to see magic tricks. And it's more exciting to find out the secrets behind them. Some people think the secret of magic is science. Today, Ken, a member of the School Magic Club, will use science to perform his tricks. Which tricks will he show us? I can't wait to see them.

01 According to Jina, what is more exciting about magic tricks? Answer in English with a full sentence.

➡ _____

_____

02 What will Ken perform? Answer in English with seven words.

➡ _____

03 밑줄 친 (A)가 의미하는 것을 위 글에서 찾아 쓰시오.

➡ _____

[04~08] 다음 글을 읽고 물음에 답하시오.

Ken: Hello, everyone. Today, I'm going to show you something amazing. Here's a dish with water in it. Now, I'll put a candle in the middle of the dish. Next, I'll light the candle and cover it with a glass. "Abracadabra!"

Jina: Look at the water! ___(A)___ it rose into the glass?

Ken: Air expands when it gets hot and creates higher pressure. When it gets cold, air contracts and creates lower pressure.

When the flame burnt out, the air inside the glass cooled down. As the air cooled down, the air pressure dropped. So the air outside the glass was at a higher pressure. It pushed the water into the glass.

04 빈칸 (A)에 알맞은 말을 쓰시오.

➡ _____

05 Where did Ken put the candle? Answer in English with a full sentence.

➡ _____

06 When air gets hot, what happens? Answer in English with a full sentence.

➡ _____

07 위 글의 내용에 맞게 빈칸에 알맞은 말을 쓰시오.

When air gets cold, it becomes smaller in size and creates _____ _____.

08 위 글의 내용에 맞게 빈칸에 알맞은 말을 쓰시오.

_____ Water Trick
When the flame _____ _____, the air inside the glass _____ down and the air pressure _____. The _____ air pressure _____ the glass _____ the water into the glass.

[09~12] 다음 글을 읽고 물음에 답하시오.

Ken: Now, I'm going to fill one of these cups with water. I will move them around to confuse you. Jina, which cup has the water in it?

Jina: That's easy! It's the middle one.

Ken: Okay, let's check. See? No water.

Jina: Show me the other cups.

Ken: See? There's no water.

Jina: Wow! How come the water disappeared?

Ken: Before the trick, I put a special material into one of the cups. The material absorbed the water and turned it into jelly. Then the jelly stuck to the bottom. If you want to try this trick, (A)to use cups that you can't see through is necessary.

Jina: Thank you for your great performance. (B)It was really amazing!

09 위 글의 내용에 맞게 다음 빈칸에 알맞은 말을 쓰시오.

Jina thought that the cup _____ _____ _____ _____ _____ _____ is the middle one.

10 What happens when the special material turns water into jelly? Answer in English and use the phrase 'of the cup.'

➡ _____

11 밑줄 친 (A)와 같은 의미의 문장을 쓰시오.

➡ _____

12 밑줄 친 (B)가 가리키는 것을 위 글에서 찾아 쓰시오.

➡ _____

[13~15] 다음 글을 읽고 물음에 답하시오.

A Dancing Coin

Can a coin dance? Let's test it. You need a coin and a bottle. Before you start, (A)병을 차갑게 하는 것이 중요합니다.(it)

Q: How do you do it?

A: First, put a coin on the mouth of the bottle. Then, hold the bottle in your hands for a while.

Q: What happens?

A: The coin moves up and down

Q: How come the coin moves?

A: Your hands warm the cold air inside the bottle. As the air gets warm, it expands. The expanding air tries to escape from the bottle.

13 What do we need to prepare to try the trick? Answer in English with a full sentence.

➡ _____

14 주어진 단어를 활용하여 밑줄 친 우리말 (A)를 영어로 쓰시오.

➡ _____

15 다음은 위 글을 요약한 것이다. 글의 내용과 일치하지 않는 것을 두 개 찾아 바르게 고쳐 쓰시오.

There is a simple trick you can do if you have a coin and a bottle. First, prepare a cool bottle. Second, put a coin on the bottom of the bottle. Third, hold the bottle with your hands for some time. Then, the coin will spin.

➡ _____

➡ _____

Real Life Communication B

A: Which class do you want to sign up for?

B: I want to take the badminton class. I like playing badminton. How about you?
= What about you?

A: I want to take the computer class. I can't wait to make a computer program there.
= look forward to making
= at the computer class

B: That sounds cool!

해석
A: 무슨 수업을 등록하고 싶니?
B: 난 배드민턴 수업을 듣고 싶어. 나는 배드민턴 치는 것을 좋아하거든. 너는?
A: 난 컴퓨터 수업을 듣고 싶어. 나는 빨리 거기에서 컴퓨터 프로그램을 만들고 싶어.
B: 멋진 것 같다!

구문해설 • sign up for: ~을 신청하다, 등록하다

Culture & Life

North Atlantic Ocean – The Bermuda Triangle

A number of airplanes and ships have disappeared in the Bermuda Triangle.
a number of+복수명사   자동사 (수동태 불가)
How come? It's still a mystery.
= Why?

구문해설 • a number of: 많은 • disappear: 사라지다 • still: 여전히

북대서양 – 버뮤다 삼각 지대
많은 비행기와 선박이 버뮤다 삼각 지대에서 사라졌다. 이 유가 무엇일까? 그것은 여전히 미스터리이다.

Culture & Life

Egypt – The pyramids

Some of the rocks that were used to build the pyramids weigh about 70 tons.
주격 관계대명사 be used to V: V 하는 데 사용되다   대략(전치사)
How was it possible to move such heavy rocks back then? It's still a mystery.
가주어   진주어 to부정사

구문해설 • rock: 바위 • build: 짓다 • weigh: 무게가 나가다 • possible: 가능한

이집트 – 피라미드
피라미드를 만드는 데 사용된 몇몇 바위들은 무게가 70톤 정도인 것들이 있다. 어떻게 그 시대에 그렇게 무거운 바위를 옮기는 것이 가능했을까? 그것은 여전히 미스터리이다.

Words & Expressions

01 다음 영영풀이가 가리키는 것을 고르시오.

having the power to make impossible things happen

① necessary ② magic
③ instead ④ dry
⑤ safe

02 다음 중 밑줄 친 부분의 뜻풀이가 바르지 않은 것은?

① Would you push the window up? 밀다
② There is a huge difference between them. 차이
③ Mix some water with the flour. 섞다
④ Don't forget to put the ice cream back in the freezer. 냉동실
⑤ The boat was beginning to sink fast. 세면대

03 다음 우리말에 맞게 빈칸에 알맞은 말을 쓰시오.

(1) 타 버리고 꽃으로 변해라!
➡ Burn out and _____ _____ a flower!

(2) 유리컵 속의 공기는 차가워졌다.
➡ The air inside the glass _____ _____.

(3) 어째서 Ken은 당신이 속을 들여다 볼 수 없는 컵을 사용했는가?
➡ How come Ken used cups that you can't _____ _____.

(4) 그 물질은 물을 흡수하고 그것을 젤리로 변화시켰다.
➡ The material absorbed the water and _____ it _____ jelly.

04 다음 주어진 문장의 밑줄 친 sink와 다른 의미로 쓰인 것은?

Don't leave your dirty plates in the sink.

① He is washing cups in the sink.
② The boat began to sink like a stone.
③ The sink is filled with water.
④ The sponge absorbed water from the sink.
⑤ The sink should be fixed to be used again.

05 다음 문장에 공통으로 들어갈 말을 고르시오.

• Would you _____ the milk with the flour?
• The cook is adding something to the _____.
• Water and oil do not _____.

① practice ② mix ③ move
④ contract ⑤ absorb

06 우리말과 일치하도록 주어진 어구를 모두 배열하여 영작하시오.

(1) 어느 불꽃이 먼저 꺼질까요?
(out / first / which / will / flame / burn)
➡ _____

(2) 나의 딸이 케이크 위에 촛불을 불었다.
(her / on / cake / my / blew / daughter / the candles / out)
➡ _____

(3) 물은 기온의 변화에 따라 팽창하고 수축한다.
(and / with / changes / temperature / in / expands / water / contracts)
➡ _____
_____

Conversation

07 다음 짝지어진 대화가 어색한 것은?

① A: Which trick do you want to learn?
   B: The ballon trick looks interesting. I want to learn how to move a can without touching it.

② A: Look at that girl. She's driving a robot.
   B: That looks really fun. I can't wait to try it.

③ A: Which eggs are fresh, and which ones are not?
   B: I can't wait to tell the difference.

④ A: Which program do you want to do at the science museum, Mira?
   B: I want to make lightning.

⑤ A: Which movie do you want to see?
   B: I want to see a 4D movie.

[08~10] 다음 대화를 읽고 물음에 답하시오.

King Sejong: It ⓐhasn't rained for a long time.
Jang Yeongsil: Yes. The dry season is lasting too long. The farmers are very worried.
King Sejong: We should do something ⓑto help them.
Jang Yeongsil: How about making a special clock?
King Sejong: A clock? How will that help?
Jang Yeongsil: The clock will show the time and the seasons. We can use it ⓒ to prepare for the dry season.
King Sejong: That ⓓsound like a good idea. But who's going to make it?
Jang Yeongsil: I'll give it a try. I know a lot about time and the seasons.
King Sejong: Okay, I can't wait ⓔto see your clock.

08 위 대화의 밑줄 친 ⓐ~ⓔ 중 어법상 어색한 것을 찾아 바르게 고치시오.

➡ _____

09 위 대화에서 나타난 세종대왕의 기분 변화로 적절한 것은?

① worried → disappointed
② worried → pleased
③ disappointed → nervous
④ disappointed → worried
⑤ pleased → worried

10 위 대화의 내용과 일치하지 <u>않는</u> 것은?

① 비가 오랫동안 내리지 않았다.
② 건기가 너무 오래 계속 되고 있어 농부들이 매우 걱정하고 있다.
③ 장영실은 농부들을 돕기 위해 특별한 시계를 만들 것을 제안하였다.
④ 장영실은 시간과 계절에 대해 많이 알고 있다.
⑤ 장영실은 비가 내리게 하기 위해 시계를 만들고자 한다.

[11~12] 다음 대화를 읽고 물음에 답하시오.

Brian: Yujin, why did you put the eggs in water?
Yujin: I'm picking out the bad eggs.
Brian: Which eggs are fresh, and which ones are not?
Yujin: Eggs that sink in water are fresh. When eggs float in water, they're not fresh. You shouldn't eat them.
Brian: That's interesting. Why do the bad eggs float?
Yujin: Because they have gas inside. The gas acts like the air in a balloon.
Brian: Oh, I see.

11 위 대화에서 다음의 영영풀이가 가리키는 것을 찾아 쓰시오.

> to go down below the surface of water

➡ _____

12 위 대화를 읽고 대답할 수 <u>없는</u> 것은?

① What is Yujin doing with the eggs?
② How can Yujin tell the fresh eggs from the bad ones?
③ What do the bad eggs have inside?
④ What does the gas act like?
⑤ What is Yujin going to do with a balloon?

13 〈보기〉에 주어진 단어를 다음 글의 빈칸에 알맞게 쓰시오.

> ┌─── 보기 ───
> strawberry / try / put / mix / cut / flavor

> **Jane:** Today we'll make ice cream. Which (A)_____ do you want to make? How about (B)_____? First, (C)_____ two cups of milk, two cups of heavy cream, and half a cup of sugar. Next, (D)_____ five strawberries into small pieces. Then, mix everything together and (E)_____ it in the freezer. That's it. It's easy to make, isn't it? Why don't you (F)_____ making it at home?

14 다음 우리말을 영어로 바르게 옮긴 것은?

> 네가 우리를 위해 나서 준 것은 정말 용감했어.

① It was brave you to step forward for us.
② It was brave for you to step forward for you.
③ It was brave of you step forward for us.
④ It was brave of you to step forward for us.
⑤ It was brave with you to step forward for us.

15 다음 빈칸에 들어갈 말로 적절하지 <u>않은</u> 것은?

> It is _____ for me to share my room with her.

① difficult   ② wise   ③ easy
④ hard   ⑤ necessary

16 다음 중 어법상 바르지 <u>않은</u> 것은?

① It is important to listen to others.
② It is foolish of you to behave like that.
③ How come you didn't take the umbrella?
④ Is it possible of her to stop biting her nail?
⑤ To see is to believe.

17 다음 중 밑줄 친 부분의 쓰임이 <u>다른</u> 하나는?

① It is okay for you <u>to wear</u> my clothes.
② <u>To keep</u> this place safe is important.
③ The bird is building a nest <u>to lay</u> eggs.
④ It is good <u>to go</u> out with you tonight.
⑤ <u>To meet</u> him in person is amazing.

18 주어진 단어를 활용하여 다음 우리말을 영어로 쓰시오.

> 그녀가 그 상자들을 옮기는 것은 쉽지 않아요.
> (it / move)

➡ _____

19 다음 빈칸에 들어갈 말이 바르게 짝지어진 것은?

> _____ is boring _____ he keeps saying the same thing over and over.

① That – that
② It – to
③ It – that
④ To – to
⑤ That – to

20 다음 중 빈칸에 들어갈 말이 다른 하나는?

① _____ she told you to go?
② _____ they didn't make it?
③ _____ he didn't want to see us?
④ _____ was there no one in the room?
⑤ _____ you didn't have your dinner?

21 다음 빈칸에 들어갈 말로 가장 적절한 것은?

> 왜 그는 매번 우리를 비난하는 거야?
> ➡ _____ he blames us every time?

① Why
② What
③ When
④ Who
⑤ How come

22 다음 중 어법상 옳은 문장은?

① That is necessary to tell the truth.
② It is kind for her to read a book to us.
③ Why do you look unsatisfied?
④ It is fun play tennis with friends.
⑤ How come did he drink the coffee?

23 주어진 단어를 활용하여 다음 문장과 같은 의미의 문장을 쓰시오.

> Why did she make an appointment?
> (come)

➡ _____

24 다음 빈칸에 알맞은 말을 쓰시오.

> Was it strange that he said so?
> ➡ Was it strange _____ _____ to say so?

Reading

[25~27] 다음 글을 읽고 물음에 답하시오.

> Ken: Hello, everyone. Today, I'm going to show you something amazing. Here's a dish with water in it. Now, I'll put a candle in the middle of the dish. Next, I'll (A)light the candle and cover it with a glass. "Abracadabra!"
> Jina: Look at the water! How come it rose into the glass?

25 다음 중 밑줄 친 (A)와 같은 의미로 쓰인 것은?

① This is a room with natural light.
② Did you turn the light on?
③ Julia has light blue eyes.
④ I need to buy light summer clothes.
⑤ She wanted to light a cooking stove.

26 위 글에 이어질 내용으로 가장 적절한 것은?

① the reason why Ken likes to do magic

② the time when Ken first started to do magic

③ the next magic that Ken prepared

④ the reason why the water rose into the glass

⑤ how Ken made the water disappear

27 위 마술의 원리를 바르게 배열하시오.

Air expands when it gets hot and creates higher pressure. And when it gets cold, air contracts and creates lower pressure.

ⓐ So the air outside the glass was at a higher pressure.

ⓑ It pushed the water into the glass.

ⓒ As the air cooled down, the air pressure dropped.

ⓓ When the flame burnt out, the air inside the glass cooled down.

➡ _____

[28~30] 다음 글을 읽고 물음에 답하시오.

Ken: Air expands when it gets hot and creates ①higher pressure. When it gets cold, air ②contracts and creates lower pressure. When the flame burnt out, the air inside the glass cooled down. As the air ③cooled down, the air pressure ④dropped. So the air outside the glass was at a higher pressure. (A)It ⑤pulled the water into the glass.

28 다음 밑줄 친 (A)가 가리키는 말을 위 글에서 찾아 쓰시오.

➡ _____

29 위 글의 ①~⑤ 중 글의 흐름상 어색한 것은?

①　②　③　④　⑤

30 다음과 같이 풀이할 수 있는 말을 위 글에서 찾아 쓰시오.

---

to increase in size, range, or amount

➡ _____

[31~32] 다음 대화를 읽고 물음에 답하시오.

Ken: Now, I'm going to fill one of these cups ____(A)____. I will move them around to confuse you. Jina, which cup has the water in it?

Jina: That's easy! It's the middle one.

Ken: Okay, let's check. See? No water.

Jina: Show me the other cups.

Ken: See? There's no water.

Jina: Wow! How come the water disappeared?

31 다음 중 빈칸 (A)에 들어갈 말로 가장 적절한 것은?

① with sand　　② with water

③ with oil　　④ with another cup

⑤ with balls

32 다음 중 위 대화의 제목으로 가장 적절한 것은?

① The Magic of a Disappearing Cup

② The Amazing Science Experiment

③ The Secret of the Special Material

④ The Man Who Disappeared

⑤ The Secret of the Disappearing Water

[01~02] 다음 글을 읽고 물음에 답하시오.

> Jane: Today we'll make ice cream. (A)여러분은 어떤 맛을 만들고 싶은가요? How about strawberry? First, mix two cups of milk, two cups of heavy cream, and half a cup of sugar. Next, cut five strawberries into small pieces. Then, mix everything together and put it in the freezer. That's it. It's easy to make, isn't it? Why don't you try making it at home?

출제율 90%

01 위 글의 밑줄 친 (A)의 우리말을 주어진 단어를 이용하여 영작하시오. (which, flavor, make)

➡ _____

출제율 85%

02 위 글에서 다음 영영풀이가 나타내는 말을 찾아 쓰시오.

> to combine two or more substances so that they become a single substance

➡ _____

[03~04] 다음 대화를 읽고 물음에 답하시오.

> Brian: Yujin, why did you put the eggs in water?
> Yujin: (A) I'm picking out the bad eggs.
> Brian: (B) Which eggs are fresh, and which ones are not?
> Yujin: (C) When eggs float in water, they're not fresh. You shouldn't eat them.
> Brian: (D) That's interesting. Why do the bad eggs float?
> Yujin: (E) Because they have gas inside. The gas acts like the air in a balloon.
> Brian: Oh, I see.

출제율 100%

03 위 대화의 (A)~(E) 중 주어진 문장이 들어가기에 적절한 곳은?

> Eggs that sink in water are fresh.

① (A)　② (B)　③ (C)　④ (D)　⑤ (E)

출제율 85%

04 위 대화의 내용과 일치하도록 빈칸에 알맞은 말을 쓰시오.

> When eggs _____ in water, they're fresh. On the other hand, the eggs that _____ in water are not fresh. Bad eggs have _____ inside. It acts like the _____ in a balloon.

[05~06] 다음 대화를 읽고 물음에 답하시오.

> Minsu: What are you reading, Jiwon?
> Jiwon: I'm reading a book ⓐabout magic and science.
> Minsu: That sounds ⓑinteresting.
> Jiwon: Yes. This book introduces 100 magic tricks that ⓒuses science. I've ⓓlearned about half of them.
> Minsu: That's cool. Can you show me some of the tricks?
> Jiwon: Sure. I can show you a balloon trick now.
> Minsu: Great! I can't wait ⓔto see it.

출제율 90%

05 위 대화의 밑줄 친 ⓐ~ⓔ 중 어법상 어색한 것을 찾아 바르게 고치시오.

➡ _____

출제율 95%

06 위 대화를 읽고 대답할 수 없는 것은?

① What is Jiwon reading?
② What does the book introduce?
③ How many tricks has Jiwon learned from the book?
④ Which trick can Jiwon show to Minsu?
⑤ How long has Jiwon practiced a balloon trick?

Brian: Mina, will you join our tennis club?
Mina: It sounds interesting, but I signed up for a special class this fall.
Brian: Which class did you sign up for?
Mina: I signed up for a magic class. I can't wait to learn new magic tricks there.
Brian: That sounds cool! Have you learned magic tricks before?
Mina: Yes, I learned some before, but I need more practice.
Brian: I hope I can see your magic tricks some day.

07 출제율 90%

Which class did Mina sign up for this fall?

➡ _____

08 출제율 95%

What is Mina looking forward to?

➡ _____

[09~10] 다음 대화를 읽고 물음에 답하시오.

Jaemin: Ms. Jeong, does a glass of water weigh more when there's a fish in it?
Ms. Jeong: (A) Yes, it does. We can test it now.
Jaemin: (B) But how? We don't have a fish.
Ms. Jeong: (C) We can use a finger instead of a fish.
Jaemin: (D) How will that work?
Ms. Jeong: (E) Then I will put my finger in the water and weigh it to compare.
Jaemin: Oh, (F)I can't wait to see the difference. (to, looking)

09 출제율 100%

위 대화의 (A)~(E) 중 주어진 문장이 들어가기에 적절한 곳은?

I'll weigh a glass of water first.

① (A)　② (B)　③ (C)　④ (D)　⑤ (E)

10 출제율 85%

위 대화의 밑줄 친 (F)와 의미가 같도록 주어진 단어들을 사용하여 다시 쓰시오.

➡ _____

11 출제율 90%

다음 빈칸에 들어갈 말로 가장 적절한 것은?

How come _____ the flower?

① did she send　② does he cut
③ she brought　④ did you bring
⑤ did I send

12 출제율 100%

다음 빈칸에 들어갈 말이 나머지와 다른 하나는?

① It is difficult _____ us to know who wrote the letter.
② Is it hard _____ you to focus on what you are doing?
③ It is necessary _____ him to drink eight glasses of water every day.
④ It is careful _____ her to bring her purse all the time.
⑤ Is it important _____ them to be on time here?

13 출제율 80%

다음 우리말을 영어로 옮길 때 빈칸에 알맞은 말을 쓰시오.

네가 그러한 결정을 내린 것은 정말 현명했어.
➡ _____ _____ _____ _____

_____ make such a decision.

14 다음 중 어법상 옳은 문장은? *출제율 95%*

① Is it possible to finding something meaningful in your life?
② How come is she complaining about it?
③ It is rude of you to not follow the advice.
④ Why he is sitting over there?
⑤ It is dangerous for us to swim in the river.

15 다음 중 어법상 옳은 것끼리 바르게 짝지은 것은? *출제율 90%*

(A) [That / It] is impossible to meet Ann on Sunday afternoon.
(B) It is important [to / that] he takes part in the race.
(C) [Why / How come] you lost the cap?

① That – to – Why
② That – that – How come
③ That – to – How come
④ It – that – How come
⑤ It – to – Why

16 주어진 어구를 활용하여 다음 우리말을 영어로 쓰시오. *출제율 95%*

그가 그 대회에서 우승했다는 것은 놀랍다.
(surprising / the competition / that / it)

➡ _____

17 일곱 개의 단어를 사용하여 다음 문장과 같은 의미의 문장을 쓰시오. *출제율 85%*

Why are you home so early?

➡ _____

[18~21] 다음 글을 읽고 물음에 답하시오.

Ken: Now, I'm going to fill one of these cups with water. I will move them around (A) to confuse you. Jina, which cup has the water in it?
Jina: That's easy! It's the middle one.
Ken: Okay, let's check. See? No water.
Jina: Show me the other cups.
Ken: See? There's no water.
Jina: Wow! How come the water disappeared?
Ken: Before the trick, I put a special material into one of the cups. The material absorbed the water and turned it into jelly. Then the jelly stuck to the bottom. If you want to try this trick, (B)it's necessary to use cups that you can't see through.
Jina: Thank you for your great performance. It was really amazing!

18 다음 중 밑줄 친 (A)와 쓰임이 같은 것은? *출제율 90%*

① I want you to tidy your room.
② He tried hard to succeed.
③ Is there any chance to win the race?
④ It is nice to hear it from you.
⑤ She planned to open a new office.

19 다음 중 위 글의 내용과 일치하는 것은? *출제율 100%*

① Ken prepared two cups.
② Jina thought it was difficult to find which cup had the water in it.
③ Ken moved around the cups to make Jina confused.
④ Jina didn't want to see if the other cups had the water in it.
⑤ Jina wasn't interested in the reason why the water disappeared.

20 출제율90%

Ken이 밑줄 친 (B)와 같이 말한 이유를 우리말로 쓰시오.

➡ _____

21 출제율95%

다음 중 Ken이 마술을 보여 주기 위하여 가장 먼저 한 일은?

① moving around the cups to confuse people

② pouring water into one of the cups

③ putting a special material into one of the cups

④ buying some jelly to treat people

⑤ preparing a cup which has a hole

[22~25] 다음 글을 읽고 물음에 답하시오.

A Dancing Coin

　Can a coin dance? Let's test it. You need a coin and a bottle. Before you start, it is important to cool the bottle.

Q: _____ ⓐ _____

A: First, put a coin on the mouth of the bottle. Then, hold the bottle in your hands for a while.

Q: _____ ⓑ _____

A: The coin moves up and down.

Q: _____ ⓒ _____

A: Your hands warm the cold air inside the bottle. As the air gets warm, it expands. The (A)　　　 air tries to escape from the bottle.

22 출제율95%

다음 빈칸 ⓐ~ⓒ에 주어진 문장을 내용에 맞게 쓰시오.

> • What happens?
> • How come the coin moves?
> • How do you do it?

ⓐ _____

ⓑ _____

ⓒ _____

23 출제율90%

위 글의 단어를 활용하여 빈칸 (A)에 알맞은 말을 쓰시오.

➡ _____

24 출제율100%

What is important to do before we do the magic?

① We should prepare an empty bottle.

② We need to prepare as many coins as possible.

③ Cooling the bottle is important.

④ It is important to keep the bottle open.

⑤ We should prepare a clean bottle.

25 출제율85%

글의 내용에 맞게 빈칸에 알맞은 말을 쓰시오.

> Because of the air ___ ___ ___
> ___ ___ ___, the coin on the mouth of the bottle moves up and down.

[01~03] 다음 대화를 읽고 물음에 답하시오.

Jang Yeongsil: Yes. The dry season is lasting too long. The farmers are very worried.

King Sejong: We should do something to help them.

Jang Yeongsil: How about making a special clock?

King Sejong: A clock? How will that help?

Jang Yeongsil: The clock will show the time and the seasons. We can use it to prepare for the dry season.

King Sejong: That sounds like a good idea. But who's going to make it?

Jang Yeongsil: I'll give it a try. I know a lot about time and the seasons.

King Sejong: Okay, I can't wait to see your clock.

01 What's the problem with King Sejong and Jang Yeongsil?

➡ _____

02 What does Jang Yeongsil suggest doing?

➡ _____

03 Why does Jang Yeongsil think the clock will help the farmers?

➡ _____

_____

04 주어진 어구를 바르게 배열하여 다음 우리말을 영어로 쓰시오. 두 개의 단어를 추가하시오.

그녀의 허락 없이 그녀의 사진을 찍다니 그는 무례해.
(her permission / it / without / rude / her / is / him / take / of / pictures)

➡ _____

_____

05 다음 빈칸에 알맞은 말을 쓰시오.

It is amazing that he exercises regularly.
= It is amazing _____ _____ _____ exercise regularly.

06 다음 대화의 빈칸에 들어갈 말을 일곱 단어로 쓰시오.

A: _____
B: I couldn't catch the bus because he woke up late.

07 다음 주어진 문장과 같은 의미의 문장을 쓰시오.

To keep a diary is important.
= _____ a diary.

08 주어진 단어를 활용하여 다음 우리말을 영어로 쓰시오.

도대체 왜 그들은 피곤한 거야? (how)

➡ _____

Jina: Wow! (A)How come the water disappeared?

Ken: Before the trick, I put a special material into one of the cups. The material absorbed the water and turned it into jelly. Then the jelly stuck to the bottom. If you want to try this trick, it's necessary to use cups that you can't see through.

Jina: Thank you for your great performance. It was really amazing!

09 What did Ken put into one of the cups? Answer in English with a full sentence.

➡ _____

10 How come the water in the cup turned into jelly? Answer in English with a full sentence.

➡ _____

_____

11 주어진 단어를 활용하여 문장 (A)와 같은 의미의 문장을 쓰시오.

(why)

➡ _____

[12~13] 다음 글을 읽고 물음에 답하시오.

A Dancing Coin

Can a coin dance? Let's test it. You need a coin and a bottle. Before you start, it is important to cool the bottle.

Q: How do you do it?

A: First, put a coin on the mouth of the bottle. Then, hold the bottle in your hands for a while.

Q: What happens?

A: The coin moves up and down.

Q: How come the coin moves?

A: Your hands ___(A)___ the cold air inside the bottle. As the air ___(B)___ warm, it ___(C)___. The expanding air tries to ___(D)___ from the bottle.

12 주어진 단어를 내용에 맞게 빈칸 (A)~(D)에 쓰시오. 필요하다면 어형을 바꾸시오.

escape / warm / expand / get

(A) _____ (B) _____

(C) _____ (D) _____

13 위 마술의 순서를 바르게 배열하시오.

ⓐ Hold the bottle in your hands. ⓑ Cool a bottle. ⓒ After a while, the coin will move. ⓓ Put a coin on the mouth of the bottle.

➡ _____

01 다음 대화의 내용과 일치하도록 빈칸을 완성하시오.

> **King Sejong:** It hasn't rained for a long time.
>
> **Jang Yeongsil:** Yes. The dry season is lasting too long. The farmers are very worried.
>
> **King Sejong:** We should do something to help them.
>
> **Jang Yeongsil:** How about making a special clock?
>
> **King Sejong:** A clock? How will that help?
>
> **Jang Yeongsil:** The clock will show the time and the seasons. We can use it to prepare for the dry season.
>
> **King Sejong:** That sounds like a good idea. But who's going to make it?
>
> **Jang Yeongsil:** I'll give it a try. I know a lot about time and the seasons.
>
> **King Sejong:** Okay, I can't wait to see your clock.

> King Sejong was worried about farmers because (A)_____ was lasting too long. When he looked for the way to help them, Jang Yeonsil suggested making (B)_____. King Sejong wondered how that clock could help farmers. Jang Yeonsil explained that the clock would show (C)_____, so it could be used (D)_____. Fortunately, Jang Yeongsli knew a lot about (E)_____, so he tried to invent it.

02 가주어 it과 주어진 to부정사구를 활용하여 여러 가지 문장을 쓰시오.

> to make many friends / to love your pet / to save your allowance / to think others first

(1) _____

(2) _____

(3) _____

(4) _____

단원별 모의고사

01 다음 영영풀이가 가리키는 것을 고르시오.

> a device or room for freezing food or keeping it frozen

① coin　　　② balloon
③ freezer　　④ candle
⑤ pressure

02 다음 우리말에 맞게 빈칸에 알맞은 말을 쓰시오.

(1) 가스는 풍선 안의 공기처럼 작용한다.
　➡ The gas acts like the air in a _____.

(2) 나는 접시 한 가운데에 양초를 놓을 것이다.
　➡ I'll put a _____ in the middle of the dish.

(3) 나는 비교하기 위해서 물속에 내 손가락을 넣을 것이다.
　➡ I will put my finger in the water to _____.

03 다음 문장의 빈칸에 들어갈 말을 〈보기〉에서 골라 쓰시오.

> ─┤ 보기 ├─
> flames / material / absorbs / pressure / experiment

(1) Apply _____ to the wound to stop the bleeding.
(2) They tried to put out the fire, but the _____ grew higher.
(3) The sponge _____ water.
(4) Steel is an essential _____ in building.
(5) Students are doing a science _____ with a candle.

[04~05] 다음 대화를 읽고 물음에 답하시오.

Minsu: What are you reading, Jiwon?
Jiwon: I'm reading a book about magic and science.
Minsu: That sounds interesting.
Jiwon: Yes. This book introduces 100 magic tricks that use science. I've learned about half of (A)them.
Minsu: That's cool. Can you show me some of the tricks?
Jiwon: Sure. I can show you a balloon trick now.
Minsu: Great! I can't wait to see it.

04 위 대화의 밑줄 친 (A)them이 가리키는 것을 찾아 쓰시오.

➡ _____

05 위 대화의 내용과 일치하지 <u>않는</u> 것은?

① 지원이는 마술과 과학에 관한 책을 읽고 있다.
② 책은 과학을 사용하는 100가지 마술을 소개하고 있다.
③ 지원이는 책에서 소개한 마술 중 절반 정도를 익혔다.
④ 지원이는 풍선 마술을 보여 줄 수 있다.
⑤ 민수는 지원이가 소개한 책을 빨리 읽고 싶다.

[06~07] 다음 대화를 읽고 물음에 답하시오.

Brian: Mina, will you join our tennis club?
Mina: It sounds interesting, but I signed up for a special class this fall.
Brian: Which class did you sign up for?
Mina: I signed up for a magic class. ____(A)____
Brian: That sounds cool! Have you learned magic tricks before?
Mina: Yes, I learned some before, but I need more practice.
Brian: I hope I can see your magic tricks some day.

06 〈보기〉에 주어진 단어들을 모두 배열하여 위 대화의 빈칸 (A)에 쓰시오.

보기
tricks / new / there / can't / to / I / wait / learn / magic

➡ _____

07 위 대화의 내용과 일치하지 <u>않는</u> 것은?

① 미나는 이번 가을에 특별 수업에 등록했다.
② 미나는 마술 수업에 등록했다.
③ 미나는 새로운 마술 묘기를 빨리 배우고 싶어 한다.
④ 미나는 전에 마술 묘기를 배운 적이 없다.
⑤ Brian은 언젠가 미나의 마술 묘기를 볼 수 있기를 바란다.

08 다음 대화의 밑줄 친 (A)와 바꾸어 쓸 수 있는 것은?

> Jaemin: Ms. Jeong, does a glass of water weigh more when there's a fish in it?
> Ms. Jeong: Yes, it does. We can test it now.
> Jaemin: But how? We don't have a fish.
> Ms. Jeong: We can use a finger instead of a fish.
> Jaemin: How will that work?
> Ms. Jeong: I'll weigh a glass of water first. Then I will put my finger in the water and weigh it to compare.
> Jaemin: Oh, (A)<u>I can't wait to see the difference.</u>

① I don't have time to wait to see the difference.
② I'm not able to see the difference.
③ I'm looking forward to seeing the difference.
④ I'm doubtful if there is the difference.
⑤ I don't know how to tell the difference.

[09~10] 다음 글을 읽고 물음에 답하시오.

> Jane: Today we'll make ice cream. ⓐ<u>Which</u> flavor do you want to make? How about strawberry? First, ⓑ<u>mix</u> two cups of milk, two cups of heavy cream, and half a cup of sugar. Next, cut five strawberries into small pieces. Then, mix everything together and ⓒ<u>putting</u> it in the freezer. That's it. It's easy ⓓ<u>to make</u>, isn't it? Why don't you try ⓔ<u>making</u> it at home?

09 위 대화의 밑줄 친 ⓐ~ⓔ 중 어법상 어색한 것을 찾아 바르게 고치시오.

➡ _____

10 위 글을 읽고 대답할 수 <u>없는</u> 것은?

① Which flavor ice cream is Jane going to make?
② What should Jane prepare to make the ice cream?
③ How much milk does Jane need to make the ice cream?
④ What should Jane do after cutting five strawberries into small pieces?
⑤ How long should Jane keep the mix in the freezer?

[11~12] 다음 대화를 읽고 물음에 답하시오.

> Brian: Yujin, why did you put the eggs in water?
> Yujin: I'm picking out the bad eggs.
> Brian: Which eggs are fresh, and which ones are not?
> Yujin: Eggs that sink in water are fresh. When eggs float in water, they're not fresh. You shouldn't eat them.
> Brian: That's interesting. Why do the bad eggs float?
> Yujin: Because they have gas inside. The gas acts like the air in a balloon.
> Brian: Oh, I see.

11 Which eggs are not fresh?

➡ _____

12 What makes the bad eggs float in the water?

➡ _____

13 다음 빈칸에 들어갈 말이 바르게 짝지어진 것은?

> (A) _____ it is so cold here?
> (B) It is clever _____ her to know the answer.

① Why – to
② Why – for
③ How come – in
④ How come – of
⑤ How come – to

14 다음 중 어법상 바르지 않은 것은?

① It is nice of her to give you a candy.
② How come you are so busy these days?
③ It is considerate of her to do the volunteer work.
④ Why did you throw away the paper?
⑤ It is possible of him to ride a bike alone.

15 다음 중 밑줄 친 부분의 쓰임이 다른 하나는?

① It is dangerous for you to be alone in the playground.
② It is foolish of her to believe such a thing.
③ It is my duty to protect you.
④ It is a great idea to invent something to make your life comfortable.
⑤ It was very dark in the forest and the girl couldn't find the way.

16 다음 빈칸에 알맞은 말을 쓰시오.

> 그가 너의 생일에 축하하지 않은 것은 인색했어.
> ➡ It was mean _____ _____ _____
> _____ say congratulations on your birthday.

17 주어진 단어를 활용하여 다음 우리말을 영어로 쓰시오.

> 도대체 왜 그는 파티에 오지 않는 거야?
> (how / to the party)

➡ _____

[18~19] 다음 글을 읽고 물음에 답하시오.

> Jina: Wow! How come the water disappeared?
> Ken: (A) Then the jelly stuck to the bottom.
> (B) Before the trick, I put a special material into one of the cups.
> (C) Therefore, if you want to try this trick, it's necessary to use cups that you can't see through.
> (D) The material absorbed the water and turned it into jelly.
> Jina: Thank you for your great performance. It was really amazing!

18 자연스러운 글이 되도록 (A)~(D)를 바르게 배열하시오.

➡ _____

19 다음은 위 마술의 원리를 요약한 것이다. 빈칸에 알맞은 말을 쓰시오.

> The special material in the cup _____ the water and turned it into jelly. Then the jelly _____ to _____ _____.

[20~21] 다음 글을 읽고 물음에 답하시오.

Jina: Welcome to the Super Science Magic Show! It's always exciting to see magic tricks. And it's more exciting to find out the secrets behind them. Some people think the secret of magic is science. Today, Ken, a member of the School Magic Club, will use science to perform his tricks. Which tricks will he show us? (A)I can't wait to see them.

20 According to Jina, what will Ken use to perform his tricks? Answer in English with a full sentence.

➡ _____

21 다음 중 밑줄 친 (A)가 의미하는 것으로 가장 적절한 것은?

① I have been waiting for Ken for a long time.
② I don't have any interest in seeing a magic show.
③ I am really looking forward to seeing them.
④ I want Ken to show us many tricks more often.
⑤ I can't help seeing the show as soon as possible.

[22~25] 다음 글을 읽고 물음에 답하시오.

Ken: Hello, everyone. Today, I'm going to ① show you something amazing. ②Here's a dish with water in it. Now, I'll put a candle in the middle of the dish. Next, I'll light the candle and cover ③it with a glass. "Abracadabra!"
Jina: Look at the water! ④Why it rose into the glass?
Ken: Air expands when it gets hot and creates ⑤higher pressure. When it gets cold, air contracts and creates lower pressure. When the flame burnt out, the air inside the glass cooled down. As the air cooled down, the air pressure dropped. So the air outside the glass was at a higher pressure. It pushed the water into the glass.

22 위 글의 ①~⑤ 중 어법상 바르지 않은 것은?

①　　　②　　　③　　　④　　　⑤

23 What happened to the water after the flame in the glass burnt out?

➡ _____

24 위 글을 읽고 답할 수 없는 것은?

① What happens when air gets cold?
② What should we do if we want air to contract?
③ When does air expand?
④ Why did the air pressure inside the glass drop?
⑤ How long did the candle burn?

25 What did Ken do after lighting the candle? Answer in English with a full sentence.

➡ _____

Lesson 8

Call It Courage

 의사소통 기능

- 알고 있는지 묻기
  Have you heard of the Gobi Desert?
  Have you heard about the soccer match on Saturday?

- 격려하기
  Don't give up!

언어 형식

- 사역동사
  My mom **made** me **clean** my room.

- Although
  Although it was raining, I played soccer.

Words & Expressions

Key Words

- **achievement** [ətʃíːvmənt] 명 성과
- **against** [əgénst] 전 ~에 맞서
- **although** [ɔːlðóu] 접 비록 ~일지라도
- **amazing** [əméiziŋ] 형 놀라운
- **bare** [bɛər] 형 벌거벗은, 맨 ~
- **bat** [bæt] 명 배트
- **care** [kɛər] 동 걱정하다, 관심을 갖다
- **completely** [kəmplíːtli] 부 완전히
- **courage** [kə́ːridʒ] 명 용기
- **cross** [krɔːs] 동 건너다, 가로지르다, 횡단하다
- **decide** [disáid] 동 결정하다, 결심하다
- **desert** [dézərt] 명 사막
- **discouraged** [diskə́ːridʒd] 형 낙담한
- **everywhere** [évriwer] 부 모든 곳에, 어디나
- **excellent** [éksələnt] 형 훌륭한
- **exercise** [éksərsàiz] 동 운동하다
- **experience** [ikspíəriəns] 동 경험하다
- **floating** [flóutiŋ] 형 떠 있는
- **gather** [gǽðər] 동 모으다, 모이다
- **healthy** [hélθi] 형 건강한
- **ice hockey** 아이스하키

- **impossible** [impásəbl] 형 불가능한
- **lose** [luːz] 동 지다, 잃다
- **match** [mætʃ] 명 경기
- **meal** [miːl] 명 식사, 끼니
- **nail** [neil] 동 못질하다 명 못
- **proud** [praud] 형 자랑스러워하는
- **semi-final** [sèmifáinl] 명 준결승전
- **shaky** [ʃéiki] 형 흔들리는, 휘청거리는
- **shoot** [ʃuːt] 동 슛하다
- **shout** [ʃaut] 동 소리 지르다, 소리치다
- **slippery** [slípəri] 형 미끄러운
- **still** [stil] 부 그럼에도, 하지만, 여전히
- **sweater** [swétər] 명 스웨터
- **tournament** [túərnəmənt] 명 토너먼트
- **ugly** [ʌ́gli] 형 못생긴, 추한
- **village** [vílidʒ] 명 마을
- **villager** [vílidʒər] 명 마을 사람
- **wash** [wɑʃ] 동 씻다
- **weak** [wiːk] 형 약한
- **wide** [waid] 형 넓은
- **windy** [wíndi] 형 바람이 센

Key Expressions

- **be about to** 막 ~하려고 하다
- **be good at** ~을 잘하다
- **fall into** ~에 빠지다
- **give it a try** 시도해 보다
- **give up** 포기하다
- **in fact** 사실은

- **in front of** ~의 앞에
- **laugh at** ~을 비웃다
- **on foot** 걸어서, 도보로
- **take off** ~을 벗다
- **try[do] one's best** 최선을 다하다
- **try out for** ~을 지원하다

Word Power

※ 서로 반대되는 뜻을 가진 어휘

- **encouraged** 용기를 북돋운 ↔ **discouraged** 낙담한
- **healthy** 건강한 ↔ **unhealthy** 건강하지 않은
- **weak** 약한 ↔ **strong** 강한
- **ugly** 못생긴 ↔ **handsome** 잘생긴
- **wide** 넓은 ↔ **narrow** 좁은

- **possible** 가능한 ↔ **impossible** 불가능한
- **win** 이기다 ↔ **lose** 지다
- **gather** 모이다, 모으다 ↔ **spread** 퍼지다
- **inside** 안에 ↔ **outside** 밖에
- **in front of** ~의 앞에 ↔ **behind** ~ 뒤에

English Dictionary

- **achievement** 성과
  → a thing done successfully, typically by effort, courage, or skill
  일반적으로 노력, 용기 또는 기술에 의해 성공적으로 이루어진 것

- **bare** 벌거벗은
  → not covered by clothes
  옷에 의해 덮여지지 않은

- **courage** 용기
  → the quality of being brave when you are facing a difficult or dangerous situation, or when you are very ill
  당신이 어려움 또는 위험한 상황을 마주하고 있을 때 또는 당신이 매우 아플 때 용감해 지는 자질

- **discouraged** 낙담한
  → no longer having the confidence you need to continue doing something
  무언가를 계속하기 위해 당신이 필요한 자신감을 더 이상 갖고 있지 않은

- **gather** 모으다
  → to get things from different places and put them together in one place
  다른 장소들에서 물건을 구해서 그것들을 한 장소에 함께 놓다

- **impossible** 불가능한
  → unable to be done or to happen
  이루어지거나 일어날 수 없는

- **lose** 지다
  → to fail to win a game
  경기에서 이기지 못하다

- **match** 경기
  → a contest between two or more players or teams
  둘 또는 그 이상의 선수들이나 팀들 간의 경쟁

- **nail** 못질하다
  → to fasten something to something else with nails
  못으로 어떤 것을 다른 어떤 것에 고정시키다

- **proud** 자랑스러워하는
  → feeling pleased about something that you have done or something that you own
  당신이 한 것 또는 당신이 소유한 것에 대해 즐거움을 느끼는

- **shaky** 흔들리는, 휘청거리는
  → not firm or steady
  확고하거나 꾸준하지 않은

- **shoot** 슛하다
  → to kick or throw a ball in a sport such as football or basketball towards the place where you can get a point
  축구 또는 농구 같은 운동에서 당신이 득점할 수 있는 곳을 향해 공을 차거나 던지다

- **villager** 마을 사람
  → someone who lives in a village
  마을에 사는 사람

- **weak** 약한
  → not physically strong
  신체적으로 강하지 않은

서답형

01 다음 짝지어진 단어의 관계가 같도록 빈칸에 알맞은 말을 쓰시오.

> wide : narrow = strong : _____

02 다음 영영풀이가 가리키는 것을 고르시오.

> not covered by clothes

① bear   ② bare   ③ still
④ proud   ⑤ care

03 다음 중 밑줄 친 부분의 뜻풀이가 바르지 <u>않은</u> 것은?

① I was <u>completely</u> surprised by the news. 완전히

② My brother <u>gathered</u> more wood while I prepared a fire. 모았다

③ Can you <u>nail</u> this sign to a tree? 손톱

④ The board was <u>shaky</u> when I went up to dive. 흔들리는

⑤ I looked <u>everywhere</u> for my key but I couldn't find it. 모든 곳에

서답형

04 다음 문장의 빈칸에 들어갈 말을 〈보기〉에서 골라 쓰시오.

> ┌─ 보기 ─┐
> exercise / deserts / experience /
> cross / healthy

(1) Not much water can be found in _____.
(2) You should _____ the street at a green light.
(3) I don't want to _____ riding that roller coaster.
(4) I want to live a _____ life.
(5) I try to _____ at least three times a week.

서답형

05 다음 우리말에 맞게 빈칸에 알맞은 말을 쓰시오.

(1) Jane은 시험에서 최선을 다했다.
➡ Jane _____ _____ _____ at the test.

(2) 사실 그들은 훌륭한 기술을 쌓았다.
➡ _____ _____, they built excellent skills.

(3) 사람들은 그들의 생각을 비웃었다.
➡ People _____ _____ their idea.

(4) 그들은 시도해 보기로 결심했다.
➡ They decided to _____ _____
_____ _____.

(5) 그들이 막 떠나려고 했을 때, 마을 사람들이 그들에게 새 신발을 주었다.
➡ When they _____ _____ _____
leave, the villagers gave them new shoes.

06 다음 주어진 문장의 밑줄 친 cross와 다른 의미로 쓰인 것은?

> I don't want to <u>cross</u> the desert on foot.

① We <u>crossed</u> the road and joined Jack.
② Waving her hand, she <u>crossed</u> the bridge.
③ Don't <u>cross</u> the street here.
④ Jack finally <u>crossed</u> the finishing line.
⑤ I'm always wearing my <u>cross</u> necklace.

01 다음 짝지어진 단어의 관계가 같도록 빈칸에 알맞은 말을 쓰시오.

> inside : outside = encouraged : _____

02 다음 우리말에 맞게 빈칸에 알맞은 말을 쓰시오.

(1) 후반전에 그들은 신발을 벗었다.
➡ They _____ _____ their shoes during the second half.

(2) 나는 도서관 앞에서 Tom을 기다렸다.
➡ I waited for Tom _____ _____ _____ the library.

(3) 그는 걸어서 학교에 간다.
➡ He goes to school _____ _____ .

(4) 공과 소년들은 종종 바다에 빠지곤 했다.
➡ The ball and the boys would often _____ _____ the sea.

03 다음 문장의 빈칸에 들어갈 말을 〈보기〉에서 골라 쓰시오.

> ┤ 보기 ├
> weak / meals / lose / match / against

(1) Did you see the soccer _____ last night?

(2) We'll play _____ the other team in the afternoon.

(3) My legs felt _____ after running for an hour.

(4) We might _____ if we don't play as a team.

(5) My pet eats five _____ a day.

04 다음 우리말과 일치하도록 주어진 어구를 모두 배열하여 영작하시오.

(1) 길을 따라 걷는 동안 나는 구멍에 빠졌다.
(hole / I / the / a / along / into / road / while / fell / walking)
➡ _____

(2) 열심히 노력하고 절대 포기해서는 안 된다.
(never / and / hard / you / up / should / try / give)
➡ _____

(3) 외투를 벗지 마세요.
(off / don't / coat / your / take)
➡ _____

05 다음 문장의 빈칸에 들어갈 말을 〈보기〉에서 골라 쓰시오.

> ┤ 보기 ├
> laughed at / tried out for / give up / is good at / in fact

(1) Sarah _____ _____ _____ the cheerleading squad.

(2) You shouldn't _____ _____ no matter how difficult it is.

(3) People _____ _____ my painting but I was proud of myself for completing it.

(4) We thought the questions were hard. _____ _____ , they were easy.

(5) Brian _____ _____ _____ drawing pictures.

Conversation

① 알고 있는지 묻기

> • Have you heard of the Gobi Desert? 고비 사막에 대해 들어 봤니?
> • Have you heard about the soccer match on Saturday? 토요일 축구 경기에 대해 들어 봤니?

■ 'Have you heard of / about …?'은 '너는 …에 대해 들어 봤니?'라는 뜻으로, 상대방이 어떤 것을 알고 있는지 묻는 표현이다. 'Have you heard' 다음에 of가 오는 경우는 어떤 사실, 사물, 사람의 존재 자체를 아는지 물을 때 사용한다. about의 경우는 어떤 행사나 사람이 한 일을 구체적으로 아는지 물을 때 사용한다. 이에 대한 대답으로 긍정일 때는 'Yes, I have.', 부정일 때는 'No, I haven't.'로 대답한다.

알고 있는지 묻기

> • Have you heard about Thomas Edison? Thomas Edison에 대해 들어 봤니?
> • Do you know how to keep your health? 건강을 지키는 법을 아니?

알고 있는지 대답하기

> • I've been told about my new English teacher. 나는 나의 새 영어 선생님에 대해 들었다.
> • I'm aware of what's going on. 나는 무슨 일이 일어나고 있는지 알고 있다.

핵심 Check

1. 다음 우리말과 일치하도록 빈칸에 알맞은 말을 쓰시오.

   (1) A: _____ _____ _____ of cricket? (cricket에 대해 들어 본 적이 있나요?)
       B: No, I haven't. (아니요, 들어 본 적 없어요.)

   (2) A: Have you heard of Beethoven? (베토벤에 대해 들어 본 적이 있나요?)
       B: _____, _____ _____. (예, 들어 보았어요.)

   (3) A: Have you heard of Anthony Webb? (Anthony Webb에 대해 들어 본 적이 있나요?)
       B: _____, _____ _____. Who is he? (아니요, 들어 본 적 없어요. 그가 누구인데요?)

② 격려하기

Don't give up! 포기하지 마!

■ 어떤 사람을 격려할 때 'Don't give up!'이라는 표현을 쓰는데 이것 이외에도, 'You can do it!', 'You'll do better next time.' 등의 표현을 사용할 수 있다.

격려하기

- There's always a next time. 항상 다음 기회가 있어.
- Cheer up! 기운 내!
- You can do it! 너는 할 수 있어!
- Don't give up! 포기하지 마!
- Don't be so hard on yourself. 너무 자책하지 마.
- Don't take it too hard. 너무 상심하지 마.
- You are a great player. 너는 훌륭한 선수야.

핵심 Check

2. 다음 우리말과 일치하도록 빈칸에 알맞은 말을 쓰시오.

(1) **A:** I'd like to play soccer well, but it's not easy. (나는 축구를 잘하고 싶어, 근데 쉽지 않아.)

   B: _____ _____ _____ _____ _____. You are a great player.

   (너무 상심하지 마. 너는 훌륭한 선수야.)

(2) **A:** I didn't do well in the match. My shoot was so weak.

   (나는 시합에서 잘하지 못했어. 내 슛은 너무 약했어.)

   B: _____ _____ _____ _____ _____ _____. (너무 자책하지 마.)

(3) **A:** We are a weak team, so everyone thinks that we are going to lose.

   (우리는 약한 팀이야. 그래서 모든 사람들이 우리가 질 거라고 생각해.)

   B: _____ _____! _____ _____ _____ _____! (기운 내! 너는 할 수 있어!)

Conversation 교과서 대화문 익히기

Listen & Speak 1 A

G: Tim, ❶have you heard of the Gobi Desert?

B: Yes, I have. Isn't it in Mongolia and China?

G: Yes, it is. Yesterday, I saw a TV show about people ❷who crossed the desert ❸on foot.

B: Only on foot?

G: Yes, it took them about 51 days.

B: Wow, that's amazing. I want to experience life in the desert but I don't want to cross ❹it on foot.

G: Well, I want to try and cross the Gobi Desert in 50 days.

G: Tim, 너는 고비 사막에 대해 들어 봤니?

B: 응, 들어 봤어. 그것은 몽골과 중국에 있지 않니?

G: 응, 맞아. 어제 나는 걸어서 그 사막을 건넌 사람들에 관한 TV 쇼를 봤어.

B: 단지 걸어서만?

G: 응, 51일 정도 걸렸어.

B: 와, 놀랍다. 나는 사막에서의 삶을 경험하고 싶지만 그곳을 걸어서 건너고 싶지는 않아.

G: 음, 나는 시도해 보고 싶고 고비 사막을 50일 내로 건너고 싶어.

❶ 'Have you heard of / about ...?'은 '너는 ...을 들어 봤니?'라는 뜻으로, 상대방이 어떤 것을 알고 있는지 묻는 표현이다.
❷ who는 선행사 people에 대한 주격 관계대명사이다.
❸ on foot: 걸어서, 도보로
❹ it은 the desert, 즉 고비 사막을 가리킨다.

Check(√) True or False

(1) The Gobi Desert is in Mongolia and China.   T ☐ F ☐

(2) The girl crossed the desert on foot in 51 days.   T ☐ F ☐

Listen & Speak 2 A

W: What can you do to be healthy? First, ❶try to exercise every day. Second, try to eat healthy food. Don't eat too much fast food. Third, wash your hands before ❷meals. Do ❸these tips sound hard to do? Well, take one step ❹at a time and don't ❺give up. Then you'll live a healthy life.

W: 당신은 건강해지기 위해 무엇을 할 수 있는가? 먼저, 매일 운동하도록 해라. 둘째, 건강에 좋은 음식을 먹도록 해라. 패스트푸드를 너무 많이 먹지 마라. 셋째, 식사 전에 손을 씻어라. 이 조언들이 실천하기에 어렵게 들리는가? 음, 한 번에 하나씩 행하고 포기하지 마라. 그러면 당신은 건강한 삶을 살 것이다.

❶ try to ~: ~하려고 노력하다, 애쓰다
❷ meal: 식사
❸ these tips는 앞에서 언급한 3가지 조언들을 가리킨다.
❹ at a time: 한번에
❺ give up: 포기하다

Check(√) True or False

(3) The woman explains how to be healthy.   T ☐ F ☐

(4) It is not good for your health to eat too much fast food.   T ☐ F ☐

Listen & Speak 1 B

G: Alex, have you heard about this year's "Ugly Sweater Party?"

B: ❶Of course, I have. It's on December 5th, right?

G: That's right. Are you going to go?

B: I want to, but I don't have an ugly sweater.

G: I have ❷one ❸that I don't wear at home. You can have it if you want.

B: Thanks. That would be great.

G: Let's meet ❹in front of the Student Center and go inside together.

B: Sure. See you then.

❶ 알고 있음을 대답하는 것으로 'Yes, I have.'로 바꾸어 쓸 수 있다.
❷ one은 an ugly sweater를 가리킨다.
❸ 목적격 관계대명사로 which로 바꾸어 쓸 수 있다.
❹ in front of: ~ 앞에

Real Life Communication A

Father: Emily, are you excited about your match on Saturday?

Emily: Not really. We're playing ❶against a strong team. I think we'll lose.

Father: Don't say that. Have you heard about the Greek team in the 2004 Euro Cup?

Emily: ❷No, I haven't. What about them?

Father: They were a weak team, so everyone thought that they would ❸lose.

Emily: What happened?

Father: They played as a team and ❹worked hard. Finally, they won the Euro Cup. So, don't give up.

Emily: Thanks, Dad. We'll ❺try our best.

❶ against: ~에 맞서
❷ 들어 본 적이 없음을 가리킨다.
❸ lose 지다 ↔ win 이기다
❹ played와 병렬 구조이다.
❺ try[do] one's best: 최선을 다하다

Listen & Speak 2 B

G: Hojun, are you going to ❶try out for the school ice hockey team? The new season ❷ is about to start.

B: ❸I'm not sure.

G: Why not?

B: I heard that Tony and Brad are also trying out for the team. They're so good.

G: Well, you're also good at ice hockey, so ❹ don't give up!

B: Okay, I'll try my best. ❺Thanks a lot.

❶ try out for: ~에 지원하다
❷ be about to ~: 막 ~하려고 하다
❸ I'm not sure.: 잘 모르겠어. (확신이 없음을 나타내는 표현)
❹ 격려하는 표현으로 'Cheer up!' 등으로 바꾸어 쓸 수 있다.
❺ Thanks a lot. = Thank you very much.

Let's Check ❶

B: Have you heard of Thomas Edison? When he was young, he couldn't read well. Also, he lost all of the ❶hearing in his left ear. ❷Still, he became a great scientist. Although you may have difficulties, be ❸like Edison and don't give up.

❶ hearing: 청각, 청력
❷ still은 '그럼에도'를 의미하며 'Nevertheless'로 바꾸어 쓸 수 있다.
❸ like: ~처럼

● 다음 우리말과 일치하도록 빈칸에 알맞은 말을 쓰시오.

Listen & Speak 1 A

G: Tim, _____ _____ _____ of the Gobi Desert?

B: Yes, I _____. Isn't it in Mongolia and China?

G: Yes, it is. Yesterday, I saw a TV show about people _____ _____ the desert _____ _____.

B: Only on foot?

G: Yes, it _____ them _____ 51 days.

B: Wow, that's amazing. I want to _____ life in the _____ but I don't want to _____ it on foot.

G: Well, I want to _____ and cross the Gobi Desert _____ 50 days.

G: Tim, 너는 고비 사막에 대해 들어 봤니?

B: 응, 들어 봤어. 그것은 몽골과 중국에 있지 않니?

G: 응, 맞아. 어제 나는 걸어서 그 사막을 건넌 사람들에 관한 TV 쇼를 봤어.

B: 단지 걸어서만?

G: 응, 51일 정도 걸렸어.

B: 와, 놀랍다. 나는 사막에서의 삶을 경험하고 싶지만 그곳을 걸어서 건너고 싶지는 않아.

G: 음, 나는 시도해 보고 싶고 고비 사막을 50일 내로 건너고 싶어.

Listen & Speak 1 B

G: Alex, _____ _____ _____ _____ _____ this year's "Ugly Sweater Party?"

B: Of course, I _____. It's _____ December 5th, right?

G: That's _____. Are you going to go?

B: I _____ _____, but I don't have an ugly sweater.

G: I have one that _____ _____ _____ _____ _____. You can have it _____ _____ _____.

B: Thanks. That would be great.

G: Let's meet _____ _____ _____ the Student Center and _____ _____ together.

B: Sure. _____ you then.

G: Alex, 너는 올해의 "못생긴 스웨터 파티"에 대해 들어 봤니?

B: 물론 들어 봤어. 그것은 12월 5일에 열려, 맞지?

G: 맞아. 너 갈 거니?

B: 가고 싶지만 나는 못생긴 스웨터가 없어.

G: 집에 내가 입지 않는 스웨터가 한 벌 있어. 네가 원하면 그걸 가져도 좋아.

B: 고마워. 그래주면 좋겠어.

G: 학생회관 앞에서 만나서 같이 들어가자.

B: 그래. 그때 보자.

Listen & Speak 2 A

W: What can you do to be _____? First, try to _____ every day. Second, _____ _____ eat healthy food. _____ _____ too much fast food. Third, _____ your hands before _____. Do these tips _____ _____ to do? Well, _____ one _____ at a time and don't _____ _____. Then you'll _____ a healthy _____.

W: 당신은 건강해지기 위해 무엇을 할 수 있는가? 먼저, 매일 운동하도록 해라. 둘째, 건강에 좋은 음식을 먹도록 해라. 패스트푸드를 너무 많이 먹지 마라. 셋째, 식사 전에 손을 씻어라. 이 조언들이 실천하기에 어렵게 들리는가? 음, 한 번에 하나씩 행하고 포기하지 마라. 그러면 당신은 건강한 삶을 살 것이다.

Listen & Speak 2 B

G: Hojun, are you going to _____ _____ _____ the school ice hockey team? The new season is _____ to start.

B: I'm not _____.

G: _____ _____?

B: I heard that Tony and Brad are also _____ _____ _____ the team. They're so good.

G: Well, you're also _____ _____ ice hockey, so _____ _____ _____!

B: Okay, I'll _____ _____ _____. Thanks a lot.

Real Life Communication

Father: Emily, are you _____ about your _____ on Saturday?

Emily: Not really. We're playing _____ a strong team. I think we'll _____.

Father: Don't say that. _____ _____ _____ about the Greek team in the 2004 Euro Cup?

Emily: _____, I _____. What _____ them?

Father: They were a weak team, _____ everyone thought that they would _____.

Emily: _____ _____?

Father: They played as a team and _____ _____. Finally, they _____ the Euro Cup. So, don't _____ _____.

Emily: Thanks, Dad. We'll _____ _____ _____.

Let's Check ❶

B: _____ _____ _____ _____ Thomas Edison? When he was young, he couldn't _____ _____. Also, he _____ all of the _____ _____ his left ear. _____, he became a great scientist. Although you may have _____, _____ _____ Edison and _____ _____ _____.

G: 호준아, 너 학교 아이스하키 팀에 지원할 예정이니? 새 시즌이 곧 시작돼.
B: 잘 모르겠어.
G: 왜 몰라?
B: Tony와 Brad도 그 팀에 지원할 거라고 들었어. 그들은 굉장히 잘해.
G: 음, 너 또한 아이스하키를 잘하잖아, 그러니 포기하지 마!
B: 알았어, 최선을 다할게. 정말 고마워.

Father: Emily, 토요일에 있을 경기에 대해 설레니?
Emily: 그렇진 않아요. 우리는 강한 팀에 맞서 시합할 거예요. 우리가 질 것 같아요.
Father: 그렇게 말하지 마. 너는 2004 유로컵에서 그리스 팀에 대해 들어 봤니?
Emily: 아니요, 들어본 적 없어요. 그들이 어땠는데요?
Father: 그들은 약한 팀이었어, 그래서 모두가 그들이 질 거라고 생각했지.
Emily: 무슨 일이 일어났는데요?
Father: 그들은 한 팀으로 경기하며 열심히 노력했어. 결국 그들은 유로컵에서 우승했단다. 그러니 포기하지 마.
Emily: 감사해요, 아빠. 우리도 최선을 다할게요.

B: 당신은 Thomas Edison에 대해 들어 봤나요? 어렸을 때 그는 글을 잘 읽지 못했습니다. 또한 그는 왼쪽 귀가 전혀 들리지 않았습니다. 그럼에도 그는 위대한 과학자가 되었습니다. 당신이 어려움을 갖고 있을지라도, Edison처럼 되고 포기하지 마세요.

[01~02] 다음 글을 읽고 물음에 답하시오.

> B: (A)당신은 Thomas Edison에 대해 들어 봤나요?(of, have) When he was young, he couldn't read well. Also, he lost all of the hearing in his left ear. (B)Still, he became a great scientist. Although you may have difficulties, be like Edison and don't give up.

01 위 글의 밑줄 친 (A)의 우리말을 주어진 단어를 사용하여 영작하시오.

➡ _____

02 위 글의 밑줄 친 (B)Still과 같은 뜻으로 쓰인 것은?

① Even though I had some bread, I'm still hungry.
② The weather was cold and wet. Still, we had a great time together.
③ Do you still live in the same city?
④ I'm still waiting for his reply.
⑤ Are you still using this old pen?

[03~04] 다음 글을 읽고 물음에 답하시오.

> W: What can you do to be healthy? First, try to exercise every day. (A) Second, try to eat healthy food. (B) Don't eat too much fast food. (C) Third, wash your hands before meals. (D) Well, take one step at a time and don't give up. (E) Then you'll live a healthy life.

03 위 글의 (A)~(E) 중 주어진 문장이 들어가기에 적절한 곳은?

> Do these tips sound hard to do?

① (A)　　② (B)　　③ (C)　　④ (D)　　⑤ (E)

04 위 글의 내용과 일치하지 <u>않는</u> 것은?

① 여자는 건강해지는 법에 대해 설명하고 있다.
② 여자는 매일 운동을 할 것을 조언하였다.
③ 여자는 건강에 좋은 음식을 먹도록 조언하였다.
④ 여자는 식사 전에 손을 씻을 것을 조언하였다.
⑤ 여자의 조언들은 실천하기가 어렵지 않다.

[01~03] 다음 대화를 읽고 물음에 답하시오.

Mina: Tim, have you heard of the Gobi Desert?
Tim: Yes, I (A)[did / have]. Isn't it in Mongolia and China?
Mina: Yes, it is. Yesterday, I saw a TV show about people (B)[which / who] crossed the desert on foot.
Tim: Only on foot?
Mina: Yes, it took them about 51 days.
Tim: Wow, that's amazing. I want to experience life in the desert (C)[but / and] I don't want to cross it on foot.
Mina: Well, I want to try and cross the Gobi Desert in 50 days.

서답형

01 위 대화에서 다음의 영영풀이가 가리키는 것을 찾아 쓰시오.

> an area of very dry land that is usually covered with sand and is very hot

➡ _____

02 위 대화의 괄호 (A)~(C)에 들어갈 말이 바르게 짝지어진 것은?

① did – which – but
② did – who – and
③ have – who – but
④ have – who – and
⑤ have – which – but

중요

03 위 글의 내용과 일치하지 <u>않는</u> 것은?

① Tim은 고비 사막에 대해 들어 봤다.
② 고비 사막은 몽골과 중국에 있다.
③ 미나는 어제 걸어서 사막을 건넌 사람들에 관한 TV 쇼를 봤다.
④ 사람들이 걸어서 고비 사막을 건너는 데 약 51일 정도 걸렸다.
⑤ Tim은 사막에서의 삶을 경험하고 걸어서 고비 사막을 건너고 싶어 한다.

서답형

04 다음 대화에서 (A)~(E)가 자연스럽게 이어지도록 순서대로 배열하시오.

Father: Emily, are you excited about your match on Saturday?
Emily: Not really. We're playing against a strong team. I think we'll lose.

(A) What happened?
(B) No, I haven't. What about them?
(C) They played as a team and worked hard. Finally, they won the Euro Cup. So, don't give up.
(D) They were a weak team, so everyone thought that they would lose.
(E) Don't say that. Have you heard about the Greek team in the 2004 Euro Cup?

Emily: Thanks, Dad. We'll try our best.

➡ _____

[05~06] 다음 글을 읽고 물음에 답하시오.

W: What can you do to be ⓐhealthy? First, try to exercise every day. Second, try to eat healthy food. Don't eat too much ⓑ fast food. Third, wash your hands ⓒ before meals. Do these tips sound ⓓhard to do? Well, take one step at a time and ⓔ give up. Then you'll live a healthy life.

서답형

05 위 글의 밑줄 친 ⓐ~ⓔ 중 내용의 흐름상 어색한 것을 찾아 바르게 고치시오.

➡ _____

서답형

06 위 글에서 제시한 건강한 삶을 살기 위한 조언 3가지를 찾아 우리말로 간단하게 설명하시오.

➡ _____

_____

[07~08] 다음 대화를 읽고 물음에 답하시오.

Suji: Hojun, are you going to try out for the school ice hockey team? The new season is about to start.

Hojun: I'm not sure.

Suji: Why not?

Hojun: I heard that Tony and Brad are also trying out for the team. They're so good.

Suji: Well, you're also good at ice hockey, so _____!

Hojun: Okay, I'll try my best. Thanks a lot.

07 위 대화의 빈칸에 들어갈 말로 적절한 것은?

① don't give up
② don't try out for it
③ that's a relief
④ please forgive me
⑤ forget it

08 위 대화의 내용과 일치하지 <u>않는</u> 것은?

① Tony와 Brad가 학교 아이스하키 팀에 지원한다.
② 아이스하키 팀의 새로운 시즌이 곧 시작된다.
③ 호준이는 학교 아이스하키 팀에 지원할지 고민 중이다.
④ Tony와 Brad는 아이스하키를 아주 잘한다.
⑤ 호준이는 아이스하키 경기에 최선을 다할 것이다.

[09~10] 다음 대화를 읽고 물음에 답하시오.

Sora: Alex, have you heard about this year's "Ugly Sweater Party?"

Alex: Of course, I have. It's on December 5th, right?

Sora: That's right. Are you going to go?

Alex: I want to, but I don't have an ugly sweater.

Sora: I have one that I don't wear at home. You can have it if you want.

Alex: Thanks. That would be great.

Sora: Let's meet in front of the Student Center and go inside together.

Alex: Sure. See you then.

중요

09 위 대화에서 나타난 Alex의 심경 변화로 적절한 것은?

① depressed → worried
② depressed → pleased
③ pleased → worried
④ pleased → satisfied
⑤ satisfied → dissatisfied

서답형

10 위 대화의 내용과 일치하도록 빈칸을 완성하시오.

Although Alex didn't have his own (A)_____ _____, he could go to "Ugly Sweater Party" because of (B)_____ help. He borrowed her sweater that (C)_____ _____ _____. He really appreciated her.

[01~02] 다음 대화를 읽고 물음에 답하시오.

> Sora: Alex, have you ⓐheard about this year's "Ugly Sweater Party?"
>
> Alex: Of course, I ⓑhave. It's ⓒon December 5th, right?
>
> Sora: That's right. Are you going to go?
>
> Alex: I want to, but I don't have an ugly sweater.
>
> Sora: I have one ⓓwho I don't wear at home. You can have it if you want.
>
> Alex: Thanks. That would be great.
>
> Sora: Let's meet ⓔin front of the Student Center and go inside together.
>
> Alex: Sure. See you then.

01 위 대화의 밑줄 친 ⓐ~ⓔ 중 어법상 어색한 것을 찾아 바르게 고치시오.

➡ _____

02 위 대화의 내용과 일치하도록 빈칸을 완성하시오.

> <Ugly Sweater Party>
> Date: _____ _____
> Time: 4pm – 6pm
> Place: _____ _____
> Notice: You should wear _____ _____.

03 다음 〈보기〉에 주어진 단어들을 골라 빈칸의 알맞은 곳에 써서 대화를 완성하시오.

> ┌─ 보기 ─
> tips / fast / take / exercise / meals / healthy / wash

> W: What can you do to be (1)_____? First, try to (2)_____ every day. Second, try to eat healthy food. Don't eat too much (3)_____ food. Third, (4)_____ your hands before (5)_____. Do these (6)_____ sound hard to do? Well, (7)_____ one step at a time and don't give up. Then you'll live a healthy life.

[04~06] 다음 글을 읽고 물음에 답하시오.

> B: ⓐHave you heard of Thomas Edison? When he was young, he couldn't read well. Also, he lost all of the ⓑhearing in his left ear. ⓒStill, he became a great scientist. ⓓDespite you may have difficulties, be ⓔlike Edison and 포기하지 마.

04 위 글의 밑줄 친 우리말을 세 단어로 영작하시오.

➡ _____

05 위 글의 밑줄 친 ⓐ~ⓔ 중 어법상 어색한 것을 찾아 바르게 고쳐 쓰시오.

➡ _____

06 What difficulties did Edison have?

➡ _____
_____

Grammar

교과서

① 사역동사

> • Patrick **makes** me **ride** the bike. Patrick은 내가 그 자전거를 타게 한다.
> • Olando **had** us **watch** his show. Olando는 우리가 그의 쇼를 관람하게 했다.

- 사역동사는 문장의 주어가 목적어에게 어떠한 행동을 하도록 시키는 동사로 make, have, let 등이 이에 속한다.
  - Kevin **made** us **come** to his party. Kevin은 우리가 그의 파티에 오게 했다.
  - They **had** me **tell** about the information. 그들은 내가 그 정보에 관해 말하게 했다.
  - She **let** us **play** with her toy. 그녀는 우리가 그녀의 장난감을 가지고 놀게 했다.

- 사역동사는 5형식에 속하여 목적격 보어를 갖는데, 사역동사의 목적격 보어는 동사원형의 형태를 취하며, '~에게 …을 하게 하다'라고 해석하는 것에 유의한다.
  - Molly **made** me **feel** frustrated. Molly는 내가 좌절감을 느끼게 했다.
  - Jason **had** us **walk** his dog. Jason은 우리가 그의 개를 산책시키게 하였다.
  - Mom **let** me **wear** her blouse. 엄마는 내가 그녀의 블라우스를 입게 하셨다.

- 준사역동사인 help는 목적격 보어로 to부정사나 동사원형 형태를 취한다.
  - Jason **helped** us **(to) solve** the problem. Jason은 우리가 그 문제를 풀게 도와주었다.

- 목적어와 목적격 보어의 관계가 수동인 경우 사역동사 make, have는 목적격 보어로 과거분사를 쓰며, let은 목적격 보어로 'let+be p.p.' 형태를 쓴다.
  - June **had** her bike **repaired** by Karl. June은 그녀의 자전거가 Karl에 의해 수리되게 했다.
  - Paul **let** the wall **be painted**. Paul은 그 벽이 칠해지도록 하였다.

핵심 Check

1. 다음 우리말과 일치하도록 빈칸에 알맞은 말을 쓰시오.

   (1) 선생님은 우리가 서로를 돕게 하셨다.

   ➡ The teacher had _____ _____ each other.

   (2) 나는 그가 내 스마트폰을 사용하게 했다.

   ➡ I let _____ _____ my smartphone.

   (3) 그들이 요청하는 대로 되게 하여라.

   ➡ Let it be _____ as they ask.

② Although

> • **Although** I like skiing, I hate winter. 비록 내가 스키 타는 것을 좋아한다 해도, 나는 겨울이 싫어.
> • **Though** I was not welcomed, I was happy. 비록 내가 환영받지는 못했다 해도, 나는 행복했다.

■ '비록 ~이지만[~일지라도]'라는 의미로 쓰이는 although는 양보의 부사절을 이끄는 접속사이다. 이에 해당하는 접속사로는 though, even though, while 등이 있다.

- **Although** you are in trouble, you have to stay cool. 비록 곤경에 처한다 해도, 너는 평정을 유지해야 한다.
- **While** I bought the car, I didn't drive it often. 내가 그 차를 샀다 해도, 나는 그것을 잘 몰고 다니지 않았다.
- **Though** she was my friend, she spoke ill of me.
  비록 그녀가 내 친구였다 해도, 그녀는 나에 관해 좋지 않게 말했다.

■ 양보의 부사절을 이끄는 접속사는 주절의 앞뒤에 모두 위치할 수 있으며, 주절 앞에 올 경우 콤마를 쓴다. 단, while이 양보의 의미를 나타낼 때는 주절의 앞에 위치한다.

- He pretended to be dead **though** he wasn't. 그는 죽지 않았지만 죽은 척했다.
- She followed the rule **although** she didn't think that it was a good one.
  그녀는 그것이 좋은 규칙이라고 생각하지 않았지만 그 규칙을 따랐다.
- **Although** they came late, they had dinner with us. 비록 그들이 늦게 왔다 해도, 우리와 함께 저녁을 먹었다.

■ despite(= in spite of)와 혼동하지 않도록 주의한다. despite도 '~일지라도'라는 의미를 갖지만, 전치사로 명사구를 이끈다.

- **Despite** being tired, I did what I had to do.
  = **Although** I was tired, I did what I had to do.

핵심 Check

2. 다음 우리말을 영어로 쓰시오.
(1) 비록 내가 그를 참아냈다 해도, 우리는 결국 헤어졌다.
➡ _____ I put up with him, we broke up in the end.
(2) 나는 목이 말랐지만, 물을 마시지 않았다.
➡ I didn't drink water _____ I was thirsty.
(3) 비록 그녀가 집에 일찍 왔다 해도, 우리는 그녀를 볼 수 없었다.
➡ _____ _____ she came home early, we couldn't see her.

01 다음 문장에서 어법상 <u>어색한</u> 부분을 바르게 고쳐 쓰시오.

(1) He made his sister doing the dishes.

_____ ➡ _____

(2) Paul made his wife thought about the problem carefully.

_____ ➡ _____

(3) Despite I drank lots of water, I felt thirsty.

_____ ➡ _____

(4) Even she didn't invite me, I went to her party.

_____ ➡ _____

02 주어진 단어를 어법에 맞게 빈칸에 쓰시오.

(1) Gloria _____ together yesterday. (us / have / sing)
(2) Alicia _____ her car key the other day. (find / me / make)
(3) Mom _____ ramyeon for Dad last night. (cook / me / let)
(4) Mr. Park _____ by five. (finish / the project / have)

03 주어진 어구를 바르게 배열하여 다음 우리말을 영어로 쓰시오. ((1), (2), (4)는 접속사로 시작할 것.)

(1) 나는 그 집을 좋아하지만, 학교에서 너무 멀다.

(my school / it's / the house / like / too / far from / although / I)

➡ _____

(2) 나는 피곤했지만, 숙제를 했다.

(my homework / I / I / tired / was / did / though)

➡ _____

(3) 졸렸지만 Julia는 공부했다.

(sleepy / studied / Julia / was / she / although)

➡ _____

(4) 그가 나이가 많다 할지라도, 아주 힘이 세다.

(old / though / quite / he / is / he / is / strong)

➡ _____

01 다음 빈칸에 들어갈 말로 가장 적절한 것은?

> Jim had his sister _____ a documentary about protecting animals.

① watching
② to watch
③ watch
④ to watching
⑤ watched

02 다음 중 빈칸에 들어갈 말이 <u>다른</u> 하나는?

① _____ we woke up late, we couldn't attend the meeting.
② _____ I was listening to music, I couldn't hear what she said.
③ _____ someone stole my bag, I had to buy another one.
④ _____ she was busy, she came to visit us.
⑤ _____ she was not interested in the movie, she didn't watch it.

03 다음 빈칸에 들어갈 말로 적절하지 <u>않은</u> 것은?

> _____ they dropped by the hospital many times, they couldn't see the patient.

① Although
② Though
③ Even though
④ While
⑤ Despite

서답형
04 주어진 단어를 활용하여 다음 우리말을 영어로 쓰시오.

> 나는 내 차가 수리되게 했다.
> (have / fix)

➡ _____

05 다음 중 어법상 옳은 문장은? (2개)

① Minsu kept talking though he was told not to do so.
② She had her brother brought his note.
③ Who let you go outside?
④ Jason had the room clean.
⑤ Despite she was sad, she had to smile.

06 다음 빈칸에 공통으로 들어갈 말로 가장 적절한 것은?

> • She _____ me help her finish her homework.
> • They _____ us very happy.
> • I _____ them some delicious cookies.

① took
② had
③ made
④ let
⑤ got

07 다음 주어진 문장의 밑줄 친 부분과 같은 의미로 쓰인 것은?

> <u>While</u> I am willing to help him, he doesn't want my help.

① <u>While</u> I was talking with you, he called me.
② <u>While</u> you were having lunch, they visited your office.
③ <u>While</u> she was watering the plants, I ironed out my pants.
④ <u>While</u> you were out there, someone came to meet you in person.
⑤ <u>While</u> the sun was shining, it wasn't very warm.

서답형

08 적절한 접속사와 주어진 단어를 이용하여 다음 우리말을 영어로 쓰시오.

> 내가 강에서 수영하는 것을 좋아한다 해도, 나는 여름이 싫어. (in the river / hate)

➡ _____

09 다음 우리말을 영어로 바르게 옮기지 <u>않은</u> 것은?

① 그들은 내가 저녁을 차리게 했다.
  → They made me fix dinner.
② 비록 중요한 것은 아니었지만, 나는 그것에 관해 말하려고 노력했다.
  → I tried to talk about it although it was not important.
③ 그녀는 그가 그 의자들을 옮기게 했다.
  → She had him move the chairs.
④ 비록 우리 팀은 경기에 졌지만, 우리는 그들을 자랑스러워했다.
  → Even though our team lost the game, we were proud of our team.
⑤ 그는 건물이 파란 색으로 칠해지게 했다.
  → He had the building paint in blue.

10 다음 중 어법상 바르지 <u>않은</u> 것은?

> ①Even though what I ②heard yesterday, I will do ③what I want to do. My courage ④lets me ⑤follow my voice.

①   ②   ③   ④   ⑤

서답형

11 적절한 부사절 접속사를 사용하여 다음 두 문장을 하나의 문장으로 쓰시오.

> He wasn't hungry. He had dinner with her.

➡ _____

12 다음 빈칸에 들어갈 말로 적절하지 <u>않은</u> 것은?

> They _____ us play the game one more time.

① let   ② made   ③ had
④ helped   ⑤ wanted

13 다음 중 빈칸에 들어갈 말이 바르게 짝지어진 것은?

> • _____ her efforts, she failed.
> • Kevin had me _____ his job instead of him.

① Despite – do   ② Despite – done
③ Though – do   ④ Even though – do
⑤ In spite of – to do

14 다음 중 주어진 문장의 빈칸에 들어갈 말과 같은 말이 들어가는 것은?

> _____ Judy is the tallest girl in the class, she is not good at playing basketball.

① _____ I first met her, she was reading something.
② _____ he came home, he took a shower.
③ _____ I'm broke, I don't want your help any more.
④ _____ she felt sick, she went home early to take a rest.
⑤ _____ you want to succeed, do your best all the time.

서답형

15 주어진 단어를 어법에 맞게 빈칸에 쓰시오.

> Mom had the tree _____ by him. (plant)

16 다음 문장과 같은 의미의 문장은?

> In spite of being late, he was allowed to enter the room.

① Because of being late, he was allowed to enter the room.

② Although he was allowed to enter the room, he was late.

③ When he was late, he was allowed to enter the room.

④ He was allowed to enter the room though he was late.

⑤ Unless he was late, he was allowed to enter the room.

17 다음 중 빈칸에 들어갈 동사의 형태가 <u>다른</u> 하나는?

① Jacob didn't let me _____ his computer.

② The teacher had us _____ each other.

③ She let her son _____ the car.

④ I allowed them _____ soccer after school.

⑤ Who made you _____ the windows?

18 주어진 어구를 바르게 배열하여 다음 우리말을 영어로 쓰시오.

> 제발 답이 무엇인지 알려 주세요.
> (know / is / let / what / please / me / the answer)

➡ _____

19 다음 빈칸에 들어갈 말로 가장 적절한 것은?

> She made her son _____ the bus.

① taking   ② took   ③ take
④ to taking   ⑤ taken

20 다음 중 빈칸에 들어갈 말로 알맞지 <u>않은</u> 것은?

> _____ I was very tired, I had to finish all the work.

① Though   ② Even though
③ Although   ④ Despite
⑤ While

21 다음 우리말을 영어로 바르게 옮긴 것은?

> 우리는 그들이 정원에서 놀게 했다.

① We had them played in the garden.

② We help them playing in the garden.

③ We made them to play in the garden.

④ We let them play in the garden.

⑤ We let them be played in the garden.

22 주어진 어구를 활용하여 다음 우리말을 영어로 쓰시오.

> 그들은 내게 그 이야기 전체를 반복하게 만들었다.
> (make / repeat / the whole)

➡ _____

23 다음 빈칸에 알맞은 말을 쓰시오.

> _____ they are so poor, they seem happy.

24 다음 우리말 의미에 맞게 빈칸에 알맞은 말을 쓰시오.

> 나는 머리카락을 잘랐다.
> ➡ I had my hair _____.

Grammar **181**

01 적절한 부사절 접속사를 이용하여 다음 문장과 같은 의미의 문장을 쓰시오. (접속사로 시작할 것.)

> I got up early, but I was late for school.

➡ _____

02 다음 빈칸에 알맞은 말을 쓰시오.

Mom made me do	
take care of my baby sister	○
water the flowers	×
brush my teeth after dinner	○

(1) Mom made me _____ _____ _____ _____ _____ , and I did it.

(2) Mom made me _____ _____ _____ , but I didn't do it.

(3) Mom made me _____ _____ _____ _____ _____ , and I did it.

03 주어진 단어를 어법에 맞게 빈칸에 쓰시오.

(1) David helped the woman _____ the road. (cross)

(2) My mother had her wallet _____ yesterday. (steal)

(3) Who had the cheese _____? (slice)

04 적절한 접속사를 이용하여 다음 두 문장을 하나의 자연스러운 문장으로 쓰시오. (접속사로 시작할 것.)

> • The man hurt his leg.
> • It rained a lot.
> • Clara brought her umbrella.

> • She was wet.
> • He could walk.
> • We went to the zoo.

➡ _____

➡ _____

➡ _____

05 다음 대화의 빈칸에 알맞은 말을 쓰시오.

> A: What was so funny? I heard you laugh.
> B: Oh, the movie I saw was really funny. It made me _____.

06 주어진 말을 빈칸에 어법에 맞게 쓰시오.

> ┤ 보기 ├
> despite   although   even though

(1) The waiters at the restaurant were polite _____ the service was slow.

(2) _____ the great success, there is a small problem.

(3) _____ the deer ate food, they began to lose weight.

07 괄호 안의 단어를 어법에 맞게 바르게 배열하여 다음 시를 완성하시오.

One Fine Day
We (shout / people / had) "Go, Go, Tigers!"
That (feel / made / our team / strong).
We didn't (the other team / let / win).
It was a fine day.

➡ _____

_____

08 주어진 단어를 활용하여 다음 우리말을 영어로 쓰시오.

비록 바람이 불었지만, 나는 축구를 하러 나갔다.
(even though / windy / play)

➡ _____

09 다음 대화의 빈칸에 알맞은 말을 쓰시오.

A: Why do you exercise in the evening?
B: It's because my parents have _____
_____ in the evening.

10 다음 문장에서 어법상 틀린 것을 바르게 고쳐 쓰시오.

Jenny let her dog running around.

➡ _____

11 적절한 접속사를 이용하여 다음 두 문장을 하나의 문장으로 쓰시오. (접속사로 시작할 것.)

(1) There was a heavy storm. People were safe inside.

➡ _____

_____

(2) His throat was sore. He sang beautifully.

➡ _____

(3) She was upset. She smiled at him.

➡ _____

12 주어진 단어를 활용하여 다음 상황을 하나의 문장으로 요약하시오. (Peter로 시작할 것.)

Peter wanted me to sing in front of people. But I didn't want to do it. He kept saying that I should do it, so I sang in front of people. (make)

➡ _____

_____

13 주어진 단어를 어법에 맞게 빈칸에 쓰시오.

(1) I had my clothes _____ by him. (wash)
(2) My mom made my little sister _____ care of by my brother. (take)
(3) We let the book _____ _____ by other students. (read)
(4) I had my report _____ by my best friend. (review)

Playing Soccer on the Water

Koh Panyee was a small floating village in the middle of the sea. Although the boys in the village never played soccer before, they loved watching it on TV. One day, the boys decided to make their own soccer team. However, people laughed at their idea.

"That's impossible."

"What makes you say so?"

"Look around. Where are you going to play soccer?"

The villagers were right. The boys had no place to play soccer. They were discouraged.

"Don't give up! We can still play soccer."

"How?"

"Let's make our own soccer field."

The boys gathered old boats and pieces of wood. They put the boats together and nailed the wood to them. After much hard work, they finally had a floating field. It was shaky and had nails everywhere. The ball and the boys would often fall into the sea, so the field was always wet and slippery.

---

floating 떠 있는
village 마을
middle 중앙, 가운데
although 비록 ~일지라도
decide 결정하다
own 자신의
laugh at 비웃다
impossible 불가능한
villager 마을 사람
discouraged 낙담한
give up 포기하다
field 운동장, 들판
gather 모으다
nail 못을 박다
shaky 흔들거리는, 휘청거리는
everywhere 어디에나

📎 **확인문제**

● 다음 문장이 본문의 내용과 일치하면 T, 일치하지 <u>않으면</u> F를 쓰시오.

1 Koh Panyee was a small village floating on the water. ☐

2 The boys in Koh Panyee played often soccer on the ground. ☐

3 A soccer team was made by the boys. ☐

4 People thought that the boys could make their own soccer team. ☐

5 The boys made their own soccer field out of old boats and pieces of wood. ☐

They had no shoes so they had to play in <u>bare feet</u>. <u>Still</u>, they didn't
　　　　　　　　　　　　　　　　　　맨발　　그럼에도 불구하고
care. In fact, they built excellent skills and <u>enjoyed playing soccer</u>
　　　　　　　　　　　　　　　　　　　　동명사를 목적어로 취하는 동사
more.

　<u>One day</u>, a boy brought a poster about a soccer tournament. They
　어느 날
decided to <u>give it a try</u>. When they <u>were about to leave</u>, the villagers
　　　　시도해 보다　　　　　　be about to V: 막 V하려고 하다
gave them new shoes and uniforms. <u>Some</u> even came to watch the
4형식 동사(give+사람+사물)　　　　　　= Some villagers
game. <u>This</u> made the boys <u>feel</u> better. <u>At first</u>, people saw them <u>as</u> the
몇몇 마을 사람들이 경기를 보러 온 것　동사 원형　　처음에　　　　　　～으로(자격)
weakest team. However, when the tournament started, the soccer team

surprised everyone.

　<u>On</u> the day of the semi-final, <u>it</u> was raining hard. They were losing <u>by</u>
특정한 날 앞에 전치사 on　　　　　비인칭 주어　　　　　　차이를 나타내는 전치사 (두 골 차이로)
two goals and <u>it</u> looked impossible <u>to win</u>.
　　　　　　가주어　　　　　　진주어
"The other team is so strong," they thought.

　But the boys didn't give up. They took off their shoes <u>during</u> the
　　　　　　　　　　　　　　　　　　　　　　　　　～ 동안
second half and the game changed completely. They played better in

the rain <u>thanks to</u> the slippery field at home. Although they lost by a
　　　～ 덕분에
score of <u>three to two</u>, still, they felt proud of <u>themselves</u>. They didn't
　　　　3대 2　　　　　　　　　주어와 목적어가 같으므로 재귀대명사 (재귀적 용법)
give up when they were losing. They <u>tried their best</u> <u>until the end</u>.
　　　　　　　　　　　　　　　　try one's best: 최선을 다하다　　끝까지

fall into ~에 빠지다
slippery 미끄러운
bare 벌거벗은, 맨 ~
in fact 사실상
tournament 토너먼트
semi-final 준결승
take off 벗다
completely 완전히
proud 자랑스러운
until ~까지

📎 **확인문제**

● 다음 문장이 본문의 내용과 일치하면 T, 일치하지 <u>않으면</u> F를 쓰시오.

1　Although boys played in bare feet, they enjoyed playing soccer. ☐

2　One of adults in the village brought a poster about a soccer tournament. ☐

3　The villagers didn't care that the boys took part in the soccer game. ☐

4　The boys didn't wear their shoes during the second half. ☐

5　The boys did their best. ☐

● 우리말을 참고하여 빈칸에 알맞은 말을 쓰시오.

1 Koh Panyee was a small _____ _____ in the _____ of the sea.

2 _____ the boys in the village _____ _____ _____ before, they loved _____ _____ on TV.

3 One day, the boys _____ _____ _____ their own soccer team.

4 _____, people _____ _____ their idea.

5 "That's _____."

6 "What _____ you _____ _____?"

7 "_____ _____. Where are you going _____ _____ soccer?"

8 The villagers _____ _____. The boys had no place _____ _____ _____.

9 They were _____.

10 "Don't _____ _____! We can _____ _____ _____."

11 "_____?"

12 "Let's _____ _____ _____ soccer field."

13 The boys _____ old boats and _____ _____ wood.

14 They _____ the boats _____ and _____ the wood _____ them.

15 _____ _____ hard work, they finally _____ _____ _____ _____.

16 It was _____ and had _____ everywhere.

1 Koh Panyee는 바다 가운데 떠 있는 작은 수상 마을이었다.

2 비록 그 마을의 소년들은 이전에 축구를 해 본 적이 없었지만, 그들은 그것을 TV로 보는 것을 정말 좋아했다.

3 어느 날, 그 소년들은 그들만의 축구팀을 만들기로 하였다.

4 그러나 사람들은 그들의 생각을 비웃었다.

5 "그것은 불가능해."

6 "왜 그렇게 말하는 거죠?"

7 "주위를 둘러봐. 너희는 어디서 축구를 할 거니?"

8 마을 사람들이 옳았다. 소년들은 축구를 할 장소가 없었다.

9 그들은 낙담했다.

10 "포기하지 마! 우리는 여전히 축구를 할 수 있어."

11 "어떻게?"

12 "우리만의 축구장을 만들자."

13 소년들은 낡은 배와 나뭇조각들을 모았다.

14 그들은 배를 합치고 그것들 위에 나무를 못으로 박았다.

15 매우 열심히 일한 후, 그들은 마침내 떠 있는 축구장을 가지게 되었다.

16 그것은 흔들리고 곳곳에 못이 있었다.

17 The ball and the boys _____ _____ _____ _____ the sea, so the field was always _____ and _____.

18 They had _____ _____ so they had to play in _____ _____.

19 Still, _____ didn't _____.

20 _____ _____, they built _____ skills and _____ playing soccer more.

21 One day, a boy _____ _____ _____ about a soccer tournament.

22 They _____ _____ give _____ a try.

23 _____ they _____ _____ _____ _____, the villagers gave _____ new shoes and uniforms.

24 Some even came to watch the game. This _____ the boys _____ better.

25 At first, people _____ them _____ the _____ team.

26 _____, when the tournament _____, the soccer team _____ everyone.

27 _____ the day of the semi-final, it _____ _____ _____.

28 They were _____ _____ _____ _____ and it looked _____ _____ _____.

29 "_____ team is _____ _____," they thought.

30 But the boys didn't _____ _____.

31 They _____ _____ their shoes _____ the second half and the game _____ _____.

32 They _____ _____ in the rain thanks to the slippery field at home.

33 Although they _____ _____ a score of three _____ two, still, they felt _____ _____ _____.

34 They didn't give up _____ _____ _____ _____. They _____ _____ _____ until the end.

---

17 공과 소년들은 종종 바다에 빠졌고, 축구장은 항상 젖어 있고 미끄러웠다.

18 그들은 신발이 없어서 맨발로 축구를 해야 했다.

19 그런데도 그들은 상관하지 않았다.

20 실제로 그들은 훌륭한 기술을 쌓았고 더욱 더 축구를 즐겼다.

21 어느 날, 한 소년이 축구 토너먼트에 관한 포스터를 가지고 왔다.

22 그들은 한번 해 보기로 결정했다.

23 그들이 떠나려고 할 때, 마을 사람들은 그들에게 새 신발과 축구복을 주었다.

24 몇몇은 심지어 경기를 보러 왔다. 이것은 소년들의 기분을 더 좋게 만들었다.

25 처음에, 사람들은 그들을 가장 약한 팀으로 보았다.

26 그러나 토너먼트가 시작되었을 때, 그 축구팀은 모든 사람들을 놀라게 했다.

27 준결승전 날, 비가 심하게 오고 있었다.

28 그들은 두 골 차로 지고 있었고, 이기는 것은 불가능해 보였다.

29 "다른 팀이 아주 강해."라고 그들은 생각했다.

30 그러나 소년들은 포기하지 않았다.

31 그들은 후반전에 그들의 신발을 벗었고 경기는 완전히 바뀌었다.

32 고향의 미끄러운 축구장 덕분에 그들은 빗속에서 더 잘하였다.

33 비록 그들은 3대 2로 졌지만, 그들은 그들 자신이 자랑스러웠다.

34 그들은 그들이 지고 있을 때 포기하지 않았다. 그들은 끝까지 최선을 다하였다.

● 우리말을 참고하여 본문을 영작하시오.

1 ▸ Koh Panyee는 바다 가운데 떠 있는 작은 수상 마을이었다.

➡ _____

2 ▸ 비록 그 마을의 소년들은 이전에 축구를 해 본 적이 없었지만, 그들은 그것을 TV로 보는 것을 정말 좋아했다.

➡ _____

3 ▸ 어느 날, 그 소년들은 그들만의 축구팀을 만들기로 하였다.

➡ _____

4 ▸ 그러나 사람들은 그들의 생각을 비웃었다.

➡ _____

5 ▸ "그것은 불가능해."

➡ _____

6 ▸ "왜 그렇게 말하는 거죠?"

➡ _____

7 ▸ "주위를 둘러봐. 너희는 어디서 축구를 할 거니?"

➡ _____

8 ▸ 마을 사람들이 옳았다. 소년들은 축구를 할 장소가 없었다.

➡ _____

9 ▸ 그들은 낙담했다.

➡ _____

10 ▸ "포기하지 마! 우리는 여전히 축구를 할 수 있어."

➡ _____

11 ▸ "어떻게?"

➡ _____

12 ▸ "우리만의 축구장을 만들자."

➡ _____

13 ▸ 소년들은 낡은 배와 나뭇조각들을 모았다.

➡ _____

14 ▸ 그들은 배를 합치고 그것들 위에 나무를 못으로 박았다.

➡ _____

15 ▸ 매우 열심히 일한 후, 그들은 마침내 떠 있는 축구장을 가지게 되었다.

➡ _____

16 ▸ 그것은 흔들리고 곳곳에 못이 있었다.

➡ _____

17 공과 소년들은 종종 바다에 빠졌고, 축구장은 항상 젖어 있고 미끄러웠다.

➡ _____

18 그들은 신발이 없어서 맨발로 축구를 해야 했다.

➡ _____

19 그런데도 그들은 상관하지 않았다.

➡ _____

20 실제로 그들은 훌륭한 기술을 쌓았고 더욱 더 축구를 즐겼다.

➡ _____

21 어느 날, 한 소년이 축구 토너먼트에 관한 포스터를 가지고 왔다.

➡ _____

22 그들은 한번 해 보기로 결정했다.

➡ _____

23 그들이 떠나려고 할 때, 마을 사람들은 그들에게 새 신발과 축구복을 주었다.

➡ _____

24 몇몇은 심지어 경기를 보러 왔다. 이것은 소년들의 기분을 더 좋게 만들었다.

➡ _____

25 처음에, 사람들은 그들을 가장 약한 팀으로 보았다.

➡ _____

26 그러나 토너먼트가 시작되었을 때, 그 축구팀은 모든 사람들을 놀라게 했다.

➡ _____

27 준결승전 날, 비가 심하게 오고 있었다.

➡ _____

28 그들은 두 골 차로 지고 있었고, 이기는 것은 불가능해 보였다.

➡ _____

29 "다른 팀이 아주 강해."라고 그들은 생각했다.

➡ _____

30 그러나 소년들은 포기하지 않았다.

➡ _____

31 그들은 후반전에 그들의 신발을 벗었고 경기는 완전히 바뀌었다.

➡ _____

32 고향의 미끄러운 축구장 덕분에 그들은 빗속에서 더 잘하였다.

➡ _____

33 비록 그들은 3대 2로 졌지만, 그들은 그들 자신이 자랑스러웠다.

➡ _____

34 그들은 그들이 지고 있을 때 포기하지 않았다. 그들은 끝까지 최선을 다하였다.

➡ _____

[01~03] 다음 글을 읽고 물음에 답하시오.

Koh Panyee was a small _____(A)_____ village in the middle of the sea. Although the boys in the village never played soccer before, they loved watching it on TV. One day, the boys decided to make their own soccer team. _____(B)_____, people laughed at their idea.
"That's impossible."
"What makes you say so?"
"Look around. Where are you going to play soccer?"
The villagers were right. The boys had no place to play soccer. They were discouraged.
"Don't give up! We can still play soccer."
"How?"
"Let's make our own soccer field."

서답형

01 단어 float을 어법에 맞게 빈칸 (A)에 쓰시오.

➡ _____

02 다음 중 빈칸 (B)에 들어갈 말로 적절한 것은?

① In addition   ② Besides
③ However   ④ As a result
⑤ For example

03 다음 중 위 글의 내용과 일치하는 것은?

① Koh Panyee is located in the middle of the island.
② The boys in the village often played soccer.
③ People in the village thought it was possible to make a soccer team.
④ The boys gave up making their own soccer team.
⑤ The boys enjoyed watching soccer on TV.

[04~07] 다음 글을 읽고 물음에 답하시오.

The boys gathered old boats and pieces of wood. ①They put the boats together and nailed the wood to ②them. After much hard work, they finally had (A)a floating field. It was shaky and had nails everywhere. The ball and the boys would often fall into the sea, so the field was always wet and slippery. ③They had no shoes so ④they had to play in bare feet. Still, they didn't care. In fact, ⑤ they built excellent skills and enjoyed (B) play soccer more.

04 다음 ①~⑤ 중 지칭하는 것이 다른 하나는?

①   ②   ③   ④   ⑤

05 다음 중 밑줄 친 (A)에 대한 설명으로 바르지 <u>않은</u> 것은?

① It was made by the boys who wanted to play soccer on it.
② It was made up of old boats and pieces of wood.
③ It had so many nails everywhere.
④ It was not stable.
⑤ It was floating in the air.

서답형

06 다음과 같이 풀이되는 말을 위 글에서 찾아 쓰시오.

difficult to stand on, move on, or hold because of being smooth, wet, icy, etc.

➡ _____

서답형

07 밑줄 친 (B)를 어법에 맞게 고쳐 쓰시오.

➡ _____

[08~12] 다음 글을 읽고 물음에 답하시오.

One day, a boy brought a poster about a soccer tournament. ① They decided to give it a try. When they were about to leave, the villagers gave them new shoes and uniforms. Some even came to watch the game. ② At first, people saw them as the weakest team. ③ However, when the tournament started, the soccer team surprised everyone.

On the day of the semi-final, it was raining (A)hard. ④ They were losing by two goals and it looked impossible to win. ⑤ "The other team is so strong," they thought. But the boys didn't give up. They took off their shoes during the second half and the game changed completely. They played better in the rain (B)thanks to the slippery field at home. Although they lost by a score of three to two, still, they felt proud of themselves. They didn't give up when they were losing. They tried their best until the end.

08 ①~⑤ 중 다음 주어진 문장이 들어가기에 가장 적절한 곳은?

> This made the boys feel better.

①   ②   ③   ④   ⑤

09 다음 중 밑줄 친 (A)와 같은 의미로 쓰인 것은?

① It's hard to learn a foreign language.
② I've had a long hard day.
③ The bread is hard to chew.
④ It was snowing hard then.
⑤ She is a very hard worker.

10 다음 중 밑줄 친 (B)를 대신하여 쓸 수 있는 것은?

① despite   ② beside
③ due to   ④ according to
⑤ as well as

11 다음 중 위 글을 읽고 답할 수 없는 것은?

① What was the poster about?
② Who gave the boys new shoes and uniforms?
③ What did the boys do during the second half?
④ Why did the boys play better in the rain?
⑤ How many games did the boys play?

서답형

12 위 글의 내용에 맞게 빈칸에 알맞은 말을 쓰시오.

> _____ the boys thought the other team was very strong, they didn't _____ _____.

[13~15] 다음 글을 읽고 물음에 답하시오.

My ①favorite sport is basketball. However, I wasn't really good at it ②at first. I couldn't shoot well unlike other players. Although I felt ③encouraged, I didn't ④give up. I practiced shooting for an hour every day. (A) This made me (B)to shoot well. Now, I'm ⑤ the best player on our team.

13 다음 ①~⑤ 중 글의 흐름상 어색한 것은?

①   ②   ③   ④   ⑤

14 밑줄 친 (A)가 의미하는 것을 우리말로 쓰시오.

➡ _____

15 밑줄 친 (B)를 어법에 맞게 고쳐 쓰시오.

➡ _____

[16~19] 다음 글을 읽고 물음에 답하시오.

Koh Panyee was a small floating village in the middle of the sea. Although the boys in the village never played soccer before, they loved watching it on TV. One day, the boys decided to make their own soccer team. However, people laughed ___(A)___ their idea.
"That's impossible."
"What makes you say so?"
"Look around. Where are you going to play soccer?"
The villagers were right. The boys had no place to play soccer. They were ___(B)___.

16 다음 중 빈칸 (A)에 들어갈 말과 같은 말이 들어가는 것은?

① Please take good care _____ your baby brother, Tommy.
② They are not interested _____ making something from clay.
③ I don't want you to give _____ your dream.
④ They are looking forward _____ visiting the museum.
⑤ Simon jumped up and down because he was pleased _____ the news.

17 다음 중 빈칸 (B)에 들어갈 말로 가장 적절한 것은?

① thankful   ② delighted   ③ bored
④ surprised   ⑤ discouraged

18 What did the boys decide to do? Answer in English with a full sentence.

➡ _____

19 다음 중 위 글의 내용과 일치하는 것은?

① People in the village supported the boys' idea.
② There was a soccer field in Koh Panyee.
③ There was no TV in the village.
④ The boys had much experience of playing soccer.
⑤ The village was in the middle of the sea.

[20~22] 다음 글을 읽고 물음에 답하시오.

"Don't give up! We can still play soccer."
"How?"
"Let's make our own soccer field."
The boys gathered old boats and pieces of wood. They put the boats together and nailed the wood to them. After much hard work, they finally had a floating field. It was shaky and had nails everywhere. The ball and the boys would often fall into the sea, so the field was always wet and slippery. They had no shoes so they had to play in bare feet. Still, they didn't care. In fact, they built excellent skills and enjoyed playing soccer more.

20 다음 중 위 글의 내용을 잘못 이해한 사람은?

① James: It must be really hard to make a floating field.

② Kevin: I really respect the boy's will.

③ Jim: I can't imagine playing soccer without wearing shoes. It must be really difficult.

④ Penny: I think their floating field was not safe enough to play soccer because of the nails.

⑤ Peter: The soccer field must be very steady and stable.

서답형

21 위 글의 내용에 맞게 다음 빈칸에 알맞은 말을 쓰시오.

_____ there were many difficulties, the boys didn't care and _____ _____ _____, enjoying playing soccer more.

중요

22 다음 중 위 글을 읽고 답할 수 있는 것은?

① How many boats were needed to make the soccer field?

② From where did the boys bring the boats and pieces of wood?

③ When did the boys usually play soccer?

④ How many boys gathered to make the soccer field?

⑤ Who nailed the wood to the old boats?

[23~26] 다음 글을 읽고 물음에 답하시오.

One day, a boy brought a poster about a soccer tournament. They decided (A)to give it a try. When they were about ①to leave, the villagers gave them new shoes and uniforms. Some even came ②to watch the game. This

made the boys ③feel better. At first, people saw them as the weakest team. However, when the tournament started, the soccer team surprised everyone.

On the day of the semi-final, it was raining hard. They were losing by two goals and it looked impossible ④to win.

"The other team is so strong," they thought.

But the boys didn't give up. They took off their shoes during the second half and the game changed completely. They played better in the rain thanks to the slippery field at home. Although they lost by a score of three to two, still, they felt proud of ⑤them. They didn't give up when they were losing. They tried their best until the end.

23 밑줄 친 (A)의 의미로 가장 적절한 것은?

① to make a poster about the soccer team

② to take part in the tournament

③ to use it for making a soccer field

④ to try hard to take part in the show

⑤ to gather more boys to play soccer with

서답형

24 What did the villagers give to the boys? Answer in English with a full sentence.

➡ _____

서답형

25 How was the weather on the day of the semi-final?

➡ _____

26 ①~⑤ 중 어법상 바르지 않은 것은?

①   ②   ③   ④   ⑤

[01~03] 다음 글을 읽고 물음에 답하시오.

Koh Panyee was a small floating village in the middle of the sea. Although the boys in the village never played soccer before, they loved watching it on TV. One day, the boys decided to make their own soccer team. However, people laughed at their idea.

"(A)That's impossible."

"What makes you say so?"

"Look around. Where are you going to play soccer?"

The villagers were right. The boys had no place to play soccer. They were discouraged.

"Don't give up! We can still play soccer."

"How?"

"Let's make our own soccer field."

01 밑줄 친 (A)가 의미하는 것을 위 글에서 찾아 영어로 쓰시오.

➡ _____

02 Where is Koh Panyee? Answer in English with a full sentence.

➡ _____

03 위 글의 내용에 맞게 빈칸에 알맞은 말을 쓰시오.

The boys living in a small village called _____ _____ loved to watch soccer but they had no experience of _____ _____. So, they decided to _____ _____ _____ soccer team _____ difficult conditions.

[04~07] 다음 글을 읽고 물음에 답하시오.

The boys gathered old boats and pieces of wood. They put the boats together and nailed the wood to them. After much hard work, they finally had a floating field. (A)It was shaky and had nails everywhere. The ball and the boys would often fall into the sea, so the field was always wet and slippery. They had no shoes so they had to play in bare feet. Still, they didn't care. In fact, they built excellent skills and enjoyed playing soccer more.

04 Write the reason why the field was always wet and slippery. Use the phrase 'It's because.'

➡ _____
_____

05 What did the boys gather to make their own soccer field? Answer in English with a full sentence.

➡ _____

06 밑줄 친 (A)가 가리키는 것을 위 글에서 찾아 쓰시오.

➡ _____

07 위 글의 표현을 이용하여 다음 우리말을 영어로 쓰시오.

비록 신발이 없다 할지라도, 우리는 신경 쓰지 않았어.

➡ _____

[08~12] 다음 글을 읽고 물음에 답하시오.

One day, a boy brought a poster about a soccer tournament. They decided to give it a try. When they were about to leave, the villagers gave them new shoes and uniforms. Some even came to watch the game. This made the boys feel better. At first, people saw them as the weakest team. However, when the tournament started, the soccer team surprised everyone.

On the day of the semi-final, it was raining hard. They were losing by two goals and (A) 이기는 것은 불가능해 보였다.

"The other team is so strong," they thought.

But the boys didn't give up. They took off their shoes during the second half and the game changed completely. They played better in the rain thanks to the slippery field at home.   ⓐ   they lost by a score of three to two, still, they felt proud of themselves. They didn't give up when they were losing. They tried their best until the end.

08 빈칸 ⓐ에 알맞은 접속사를 쓰시오.

➡ _____

09 What did a boy bring? Answer in English with a full sentence.

➡ _____

10 주어진 단어를 활용하여 밑줄 친 우리말 (A)를 영어로 쓰시오.

(it / look)

➡ _____

11 What did the boys do during the second half?

➡ _____

12 위 글의 내용에 맞게 빈칸에 알맞은 말을 쓰시오.

Because of the slippery field at home, they _____ _____ _____ _____
_____.

[13~15] 다음 글을 읽고 물음에 답하시오.

Dear Koh Panyee Soccer Team
  Hello, I became ①your fan after watching one of your matches. Everyone thought you ②would lose because the other team was ③ weak. But you didn't give up. During the second half, I was surprised to see you play in bare feet. You were playing ④better than before! I guess playing soccer on a field in the sea helped you a lot. Although you ⑤lost by a score of three to two, I became a fan of your team. Hope to see you soon.

Yours,
Fern Yahtie

13 ①~⑤ 중 글의 흐름상 어색한 것을 바르게 고쳐 쓰시오.

_____ ➡ _____

14 What made Fern surprised? Answer in English with a full sentence.

➡ _____

15 글의 내용에 맞게 빈칸에 알맞은 말을 쓰시오.

Watching one of Koh Panyee soccer team's matches made Fern Yahtie _____ _____ _____.

교과서

구석구석

Real Life Communication - Step 2

A: I want to be a basketball player but I'm too short. Should I give up?
　to부정사의 명사적 용법(목적어)　　　　　　너무
B: No, don't give up! Have you heard of Anthony Webb?
　　격려하기　　　　have+p.p: 현재 완료
A: No, I haven't. Who is he?
　　don't(x)
B: He was a basketball player. He was short, but he won the 1986 Slam Dunk

Contest.

구문해설 • give up: 포기하다

Culture & Life

The women's field hockey team from Zimbabwe surprised the whole world.
　　　　　　　　　　　　　출신을 나타내는 전치사
Although they had only a month to prepare, they won the gold medal at the
양보의 부사절 접속사　　　　　　　　　to부정사의 형용사적 용법
1980 Olympic Games.

구문해설 • surprise: ~을 놀라게 하다　• whole: 전체의　• although: 비록 ~일지라도
• prepare: 준비하다

Let's Write

My favorite sport is basketball. However, I wasn't really good at it at first. I
　　　　　　　　　　　　　　　　　　　　　　　basketball 지칭
couldn't shoot well unlike other players. Although I felt discouraged, I didn't
　　　　　　전치사(~와 달리)　　　　　　　　감정을 느낄 때 쓰는 과거분사
give up. I practiced shooting for an hour every day. This made me shoot well.
　　동명사를 목적어로 취하는 동사　　　　　　　　　　사역동사+목적어+동사원형
Now, I'm the best player on our team.

구문해설 • favorite: 가장 좋아하는　• unlike: ~와 달리　• discouraged: 낙담한
• practice: 연습하다

해석

A: 나는 농구 선수가 되고 싶어. 근데 나는 키가 너무 작아. 내가 포기해야 할까?
B: 아니, 포기하지 매 Anthony Webb에 대해 들어 봤니?
A: 아니. 그가 누군데?
B: 그는 농구선수였어. 그는 키가 작았지만, 1986 Slam Dunk Contest에서 우승했어.

짐바브웨 여자 필드하키 팀은 전 세계를 놀라게 했다. 비록 그들은 준비할 시간이 한 달 밖에 없었지만, 그들은 1980년 올림픽 게임에서 금메달을 땄다.

내가 가장 좋아하는 운동은 농구이다. 그러나 처음에 나는 농구를 잘하지 못했다. 나는 다른 선수들과 달리 슛을 잘하지 못했다. 나는 낙담했지만, 포기하지 않았다. 나는 매일 한 시간 동안 슛 연습을 했다. 이것이 내가 슛을 잘하게 했다. 이제, 나는 우리 팀에서 가장 잘하는 선수이다.

01 다음 짝지어진 단어의 관계가 같도록 빈칸에 알맞은 말을 쓰시오.

> patient : impatient = possible : _____

02 다음 영영풀이가 가리키는 것을 고르시오.

> to kick or throw a ball in a sport such as football or basketball towards the place where you can get a point

① shoot ② shout ③ gather
④ decide ⑤ match

03 다음 중 밑줄 친 부분의 뜻풀이가 바르지 않은 것은?

① The floor was slippery, so be careful. 미끄러운
② The rugby field was wet after the rain. ...장
③ It's impossible to get back home in time for dinner. 불가능한
④ All the villagers got together to celebrate the New Year. 마을
⑤ I want to have my own room. 자신의

04 다음 우리말에 맞게 빈칸을 완성하시오.

(1) 오늘 우리는 강한 팀에 맞서 큰 경기를 했다.
➡ Today, we had a big match _____ a strong team.
(2) 비록 비가 내리고 있었지만, 나는 축구를 했다.
➡ _____ it was raining, I played soccer.
(3) 그들은 맨발로 뛰지만 행복하다.
➡ They play in _____ feet but they're happy.
(4) 그럼에도 그들은 그들 자신이 자랑스러웠다.
➡ _____, they felt proud of themselves.

05 다음 주어진 문장의 밑줄 친 match와 같은 의미로 쓰인 것은?

> Are you looking forward to your tennis match tomorrow?

① The match ended in a victory for my team.
② The curtains and carpet are a good match.
③ Jimmy and Emma are a perfect match for each other.
④ Would you give me a box of matches?
⑤ The little girl stroke the last match.

06 다음 문장에 공통으로 들어갈 말을 고르시오.

> • Stop biting your _____s. It's not good for your health.
> • She caught her sweater on a _____.
> • Would you _____ up the door for me?

① nail ② shoot
③ bat ④ match
⑤ meal

07 다음 우리말과 일치하도록 주어진 단어를 모두 배열하여 영작하시오.

(1) 나는 마라톤 경주 후에 내 자신이 자랑스러웠다.
(proud / the / marathon / after / race / felt / I / of / myself)
➡ _____
(2) 그녀는 맨발로 숲을 걸었다.
(bare / she / the / in / woods / feet / walked / in)
➡ _____
(3) 지더라도 낙담하지 마라.
(be / you / even / lose / if / don't / discouraged)
➡ _____

Conversation

[08~10] 다음 대화를 읽고 물음에 답하시오.

> Father: Emily, are you ⓐexcited about your match on Saturday?
>
> Emily: Not really. We're playing against a strong team. I think we'll lose.
>
> Father: Don't say ⓑthat. Have you heard about the Greek team in the 2004 Euro Cup?
>
> Emily: No, I ⓒdidn't. What about them?
>
> Father: They were a weak team, so everyone thought ⓓthat they would lose.
>
> Emily: What happened?
>
> Father: They played as a team and ⓔworked hard. Finally, they won the Euro Cup. So, _____(A)_____.
>
> Emily: Thanks, Dad. We'll try our best.

08 위 대화의 밑줄 친 ⓐ~ⓔ 중 어법상 어색한 것을 찾아 바르게 고치시오.

➡ _____

09 위 대화의 빈칸 (A)에 들어갈 말로 어색한 것은?

① don't give up
② cheer up
③ believe you can do it
④ try your best
⑤ try next time

10 위 대화의 내용과 일치하지 않는 것은?

① Emily는 토요일에 경기가 있다.
② Emily는 강한 팀에 맞서 시합을 할 것이다.
③ 2004 유로컵에서 그리스 팀은 약한 팀이었다.
④ 2004 유로컵에서 그리스 팀은 한 팀으로 경기하며 열심히 노력하였다.
⑤ 2004 유로컵에서 그리스 팀은 준우승하였다.

[11~12] 다음 대화를 읽고 물음에 답하시오.

> Sora: Alex, have you heard about this year's "Ugly Sweater Party?"
>
> Alex: Of course, I have. It's on December 5th, right?
>
> Sora: That's right. Are you going to go?
>
> Alex: I want to, but I don't have an ugly sweater.
>
> Sora: I have one that I don't wear at home. You can have it if you want.
>
> Alex: Thanks. That would be great.
>
> Sora: Let's meet in front of the Student Center and go inside together.
>
> Alex: Sure. See you then.

11 When will this year's "Ugly Sweater Party" be held?

➡ _____

12 Where will Sora and Alex meet?

➡ _____

13 다음 대화가 자연스럽게 이어지도록 순서대로 배열하시오.

> Suji: Hojun, are you going to try out for the school ice hockey team? The new season is about to start.

> (A) Okay, I'll try my best. Thanks a lot.
> (B) Why not?
> (C) I'm not sure.
> (D) Well, you're also good at ice hockey, so don't give up!
> (E) I heard that Tony and Brad are also trying out for the team. They're so good.

➡ _____

14 다음 짝지어진 대화가 어색한 것은?

① A: Have you heard of Sepak Takraw?
　B: No, I haven't. What is it?

② A: Have you heard of cricket?
　B: Of course I have.

③ A: I'd like to play soccer well, but it's not easy.
　B: Don't give up. Why don't you practice every day after school?

④ A: I want to be a basketball player but I'm too short. Should I give up?
　B: No, don't give up!

⑤ A: I want to be a baseball player but I'm not good at it. What should I do?
　B: I'll do my best to be a good player.

Grammar

15 다음 빈칸에 들어갈 말로 가장 적절한 것은?

> She didn't make me _____ out late at night.

① staying　② to stay　③ stay
④ to staying　⑤ stayed

16 다음 중 빈칸에 들어갈 말이 <u>다른</u> 하나는?

① I did it _____ he told me to.

② We didn't tell you _____ we knew that it would hurt you.

③ _____ we are here, we are going to visit the most famous museum in this area.

④ Anne was fond of Tom _____ he often annoyed her.

⑤ Orlando ordered much food _____ he was hungry.

17 주어진 문장과 같은 의미의 문장은?

> I had him carry my heavy bag.

① I made him to carry my heavy bag.
② I let him carrying my heavy bag.
③ I wanted him carry my heavy bag.
④ I had my heavy bag carried by him.
⑤ I helped him to carry my heavy bag.

18 적절한 접속사로 시작하여 다음 두 문장을 하나의 문장으로 쓰시오.

> I was tired. I studied hard in class.

➡ _____

19 다음 중 어법상 올바른 문장은?

① She got Jim walk the dog.
② I made her to wash dishes.
③ Despite she didn't like it, she pretended to like it.
④ Who let you play the guitar?
⑤ In spite the rain, he went to school by bicycle.

20 다음 중 빈칸에 들어갈 말로 알맞지 <u>않은</u> 것은?

> My mom _____ me clean the floor.

① had　② made　③ helped
④ let　⑤ got

21 다음 우리말에 맞게 빈칸에 알맞은 말을 쓰시오.

> 비록 그는 일찍 떠났지만, 비행기를 놓쳤다.
>
> ➡ _____ _____ _____ _____
>
>   though _____ _____ _____.

22 다음 빈칸에 들어갈 말로 적절한 것을 모두 고르시오.

> My cousin helped me _____ into my new apartment.

① move
② moving
③ to move
④ to moving
⑤ moved

23 다음 중 빈칸에 들어갈 말이 바르게 짝지어진 것은?

> • _____ the weather was cold, I went swimming.
> • _____ me go shopping with my friends.

① Despite – Let
② Even though – Let's
③ Although – Allow
④ Even though – Let
⑤ Although – Get

24 다음 빈칸에 알맞은 말을 쓰시오.

> 비록 네가 말을 물가로 끌고 갈 수는 있더라도, 말이 물을 마시게 할 수는 없다.
>
> ➡ _____ you can lead a horse to water, you can't make him _____ it.

25 주어진 단어를 활용하여 다음 우리말을 8단어로 이루어진 한 문장의 영어로 쓰시오.

> 나의 부모님은 내가 폭력적인 영화를 보게 하지 않으신다.
>
> (let / violent movies)

➡ _____

Reading

[26~28] 다음 글을 읽고 물음에 답하시오.

> Koh Panyee was a small floating village in the middle of the sea. Although the boys in the village never played soccer before, they loved watching it on TV. One day, the boys decided to make their own soccer team. However, people laughed at their idea.
> "That's impossible."
> "ⓐWhat makes you to say so?"
> "Look around. _____(A)_____"
> The villagers were right. The boys had no place to play soccer. They were discouraged.
> "Don't give up! We can still play soccer."
> "How?"
> "Let's make our own soccer field."

26 다음 중 빈칸 (A)에 들어갈 말로 가장 적절한 것은?

① Who are you going to play with?
② What do you want to do?
③ Why do you want to do that?
④ Where are you going to play soccer?
⑤ Who is going to teach you how to play soccer?

27 밑줄 친 ⓐ에서 어법상 틀린 것을 바르게 고쳐 문장을 다시 쓰시오.

➡ _____

28 위 글에 이어질 내용으로 적절한 것은?

① the boys who are trying to see soccer on TV

② the reason why the boys live in the village

③ the boys who are trying to make their soccer field

④ how to play soccer in the water

⑤ the reason why people laughed at the boys

[29~30] 다음 글을 읽고 물음에 답하시오.

My favorite sport is basketball. However, I wasn't really good at it at first. I couldn't shoot well unlike other players. Although I felt discouraged, I didn't give up. I practiced ___(A)___ for an hour every day. This made me ___(B)___ well. Now, I'm the best player on our team.

29 단어 shoot을 어법에 맞게 빈칸 (A)와 (B)에 각각 쓰시오.

(A) _____ (B) _____

30 다음 중 위 글의 내용과 일치하는 것은?

① The writer doesn't like basketball that much.

② The writer was very good at playing basketball from the beginning.

③ The writer shot as well as other players.

④ The writer tried hard to be good at basketball.

⑤ No other player in his team is as bad as the writer.

[31~33] 다음 글을 읽고 물음에 답하시오.

The boys gathered old boats and pieces of wood.
(A) Still, they didn't care. ___@___, they built excellent skills and enjoyed playing soccer more.
(B) It was shaky and had nails everywhere. The ball and the boys would often fall into the sea, so the field was always wet and slippery. They had no shoes so they had to play in bare feet.
(C) They put the boats together and nailed the wood to them. After much hard work, they finally had a floating field.

31 다음 빈칸 @에 들어갈 말로 적절한 것을 <u>모두</u> 고르시오.

① On the other hand ② Actually

③ In fact ④ Probably

⑤ Unfortunately

32 자연스러운 글이 되도록 (A)~(C)를 바르게 배열한 것은?

① (A) – (C) – (B) ② (B) – (A) – (C)

③ (B) – (C) – (A) ④ (C) – (A) – (B)

⑤ (C) – (B) – (A)

33 Write the reason why the boys had to play soccer in bare feet. Use the phrase 'It's because.'

➡ _____

[01~02] 다음 대화를 읽고 물음에 답하시오.

Mina: Tim, have you heard of the Gobi Desert?
Tim: Yes, I have. Isn't it in Mongolia and China?
Mina: Yes, it is. Yesterday, I saw a TV show about people who crossed the desert on foot.
Tim: Only on foot?
Mina: Yes, it took them about 51 days.
Tim: Wow, that's amazing. I want to experience life in the desert but I don't want to cross it on foot.
Mina: Well, I want to try and cross the Gobi Desert in 50 days.

출제율 90%

01 위 대화의 내용과 일치하도록 빈칸을 완성하시오.

Mina saw a TV show about people crossing the Gobi desert on (A)_____. It took them about (B)_____ days. She felt interesting and told it to Tim. When she explained about it, Tim also surprised and said that he wanted (C)_____ _____ _____ _____ _____. However, Tim didn't want to (D)_____ _____ _____ _____ _____. On the other hand, Mina, who had a brave heart, wanted to (E)_____ _____ _____ _____ _____ _____ _____.

출제율 100%

02 위 대화에서 나타난 Mina의 성격으로 적절한 것은?

① brave
② polite
③ shy
④ thoughtful
⑤ honest

[03~05] 다음 대화를 읽고 물음에 답하시오.

Father: Emily, are you excited about your match on Saturday?
Emily: Not really. We're playing against a strong team. I think we'll lose.
Father: (A) Don't say that. Have you heard about the Greek team in the 2004 Euro Cup?
Emily: (B) What about them?
Father: (C) They were a weak team, so everyone thought that they would lose.
Emily: (D) What happened?
Father: (E) They played as a team and worked hard. Finally, they won the Euro Cup. So, don't give up.
Emily: Thanks, Dad. We'll try our best.

출제율 100%

03 위 대화의 (A)~(E) 중 주어진 문장이 들어가기에 적절한 곳은?

No, I haven't.

① (A)   ② (B)   ③ (C)   ④ (D)   ⑤ (E)

출제율 90%

04 위 대화에서 다음의 영영풀이가 가리키는 것을 찾아 쓰시오.

a contest between two or more players or teams

➡ _____

출제율 95%

05 위 대화를 읽고 대답할 수 없는 것은?

① What is Emily going to do on Saturday?
② Which team won the 2004 Euro Cup?
③ How could the Greek team win the 2004 Euro Cup?
④ Has Emily heard about the Greek team in the 2004 Euro Cup?
⑤ What did Emily do to win the game?

[06~08] 다음 대화를 읽고 물음에 답하시오.

Mina: Tim, have you heard of the Gobi Desert?
Tim: _____(A)_____ Isn't ⓐit in Mongolia and China?
Mina: Yes, ⓑit is. Yesterday, I saw a TV show about people who crossed the desert on foot.
Tim: Only on foot?
Mina: Yes, ⓒit took them about 51 days.
Tim: Wow, that's amazing. I want to experience life in the desert but I don't want to cross ⓓit on foot.
Mina: Well, I want to try and cross ⓔit in 50 days.

06 위 대화의 빈칸 (A)에 들어갈 말로 적절한 것은?

① Yes, I do. ② Yes, I have.
③ Yes, I did. ④ No, I didn't.
⑤ No, I don't.

07 위 대화의 밑줄 친 ⓐ~ⓔ 중 가리키는 대상이 나머지와 다른 것은?

① ⓐ ② ⓑ ③ ⓒ ④ ⓓ ⑤ ⓔ

08 위 대화를 읽고 대답할 수 없는 것은?

① When did Mina see a TV show about people crossing the Gobi Desert?
② How long did it take people to cross the Gobi Desert on foot on a TV show?
③ Where is the Gobi Desert located?
④ What does Mina want to do in the Gobi Desert?
⑤ Why doesn't Tim want to cross the Goby Desert on foot?

[09~10] 다음 대화를 읽고 물음에 답하시오.

Suji: Hojun, are you going to try out for the school ice hockey team? The new season is about to start.
Hojun: I'm not sure.
Suji: Why not?
Hojun: I heard that Tony and Brad are also trying out for the team. They're so good.
Suji: Well, you're also good at ice hockey, so don't give up!
Hojun: Okay, I'll try my best. Thanks a lot.

09 Which team did Tony and Brad try out for?

➡ _____

10 What did Hojun promise to do?

➡ _____

11 다음 빈칸에 들어갈 말이 바르게 짝지어진 것은?

_____ Mina needed a passport photo, she had her picture _____ by her little brother who didn't know how to take pictures well.

① Because – taking ② Although – take
③ Since – take ④ Although – took
⑤ Even though – taken

12 다음 중 어법상 바르지 않은 것은?

Yesterday, I ①asked my roommate ②to let ③me ④to use her shoe polish and she allowed me ⑤to use it.

① ② ③ ④ ⑤

13 알맞은 부사절 접속사로 시작하여 다음 두 문장을 하나의 문장으로 쓰시오.

> The weather was very cold. She went out for a walk.

➡ _____

_____

14 다음 빈칸에 적절하지 <u>않은</u> 것은?

> Mrs. Wilson _____ the children wash their hands before dinner.

① helps　　② makes　　③ lets
④ has　　⑤ gets

15 다음 중 우리말을 영어로 바르게 옮긴 것은? (2개)

① 비록 그는 몸이 아팠지만, 수업에 출석했다.
　→ He attended class although he was sick.
② 알람이 울렸지만, 나는 일어나지 않았다.
　→ Despite the alarm rang, I didn't get up.
③ 비록 그가 영국에서 태어났을지라도, 그는 한국 소년이다.
　→ He is a Korean boy because he was born in England.
④ Jane은 웨이터에게 그녀의 차를 가지고 오라고 하였다.
　→ Jane had the waiter brought her tea.
⑤ 그 경찰관은 그가 차에서 내리게 했다.
　→ The police officer had him get out of his car.

16 단어 take를 어법에 맞게 빈칸에 쓰시오.

> We had a professional photographer _____ pictures of everyone at the wedding. We had over 50 pictures _____.

[17~18] 다음 글을 읽고 물음에 답하시오.

> One day, a boy brought a poster about a soccer tournament.
>
> (A) Some even came to watch the game. This made the boys feel better. At first, people saw them as the weakest team.
> (B) They decided to give it a try. When they were about to leave, the villagers gave them new shoes and uniforms.
> (C) However, when the tournament started, the soccer team surprised everyone.

17 자연스러운 글이 되도록 (A)~(C)를 바르게 배열하시오.

➡ _____

18 위 글의 내용에 맞게 빈칸에 알맞은 말을 쓰시오.

> _____ people thought the team was the weakest team, they were _____ by the team when the tournament started.

[19~21] 다음 글을 읽고 물음에 답하시오.

On the day of the semi-final, it was raining hard. They were losing ___(A)___ two goals and it looked impossible to win.

"The other team is so strong," they thought.

But the boys didn't give up. They took off their shoes during the second half and the game changed completely. They played better in the rain thanks to the slippery field at home. Although they lost by a score of three to two, still, they felt proud of themselves. They didn't give up when they were losing. They tried their best until the end.

19 다음 중 빈칸 (A)에 들어갈 말로 가장 적절한 것은?

① in ② on ③ to ④ by ⑤ at

20 다음 중 위 글의 내용과 일치하는 것은?

① 결승전 날에 비가 심하게 내렸다.
② 소년들의 팀은 처음에 두 골 차이로 이기고 있었다.
③ 소년들은 전반전에 신발을 벗었다.
④ 소년들은 빗속에서 경기를 더 잘하였다.
⑤ 소년들은 3대 2로 경기를 이겼다.

21 How did the boys feel about themselves after the game? Answer in English with a full sentence.

➡ _____

[22~24] 다음 글을 읽고 물음에 답하시오.

Dear Koh Panyee Soccer Team
Hello, I became your fan after ①watching one of your matches. Everyone thought you would lose because the other team ②was strong. But you didn't give up. During the second half, I was surprised ③to see you play in bare feet. You were playing better than before! I guess ④playing soccer on a field in the sea helped you a lot. ⑤Despite you lost by a score of three to two, I became a fan of your team. Hope to see you soon.

Yours,
Fern Yahtie

22 위 글의 ①~⑤ 중 어법상 바르지 <u>않은</u> 것은?

① ② ③ ④ ⑤

23 위 글의 내용에 맞게 빈칸에 알맞은 말을 쓰시오.

Fern thought playing in bare feet made the players _____ _____ _____ _____.

24 다음 중 위 글의 내용과 일치하는 것은?

① Fern Yahtie is not interested in soccer at all.
② Koh Panyee Soccer Team looked as strong as all the other teams.
③ Koh Panyee Soccer Team members played the game without any shoes on during the second half.
④ Koh Panyee Soccer Team won the game in the end.
⑤ Koh Panyee Soccer Team lost the game because they played in bare feet.

[01~03] 다음 대화를 읽고 물음에 답하시오.

Mina: Tim, (A)고비 사막에 대해 들어 보았니? (of, Gobi Desert)

Tim: Yes, I have. Isn't it in Mongolia and China?

Mina: Yes, it is. Yesterday, I saw a TV show about people who crossed the desert on foot.

Tim: Only on foot?

Mina: Yes, it took them about 51 days.

Tim: Wow, that's amazing. I want to experience life in the desert but I don't want to cross it on foot.

Mina: Well, I want to try and cross the Gobi Desert in 50 days.

01 위 대화의 밑줄 친 (A)의 우리말을 주어진 단어를 사용하여 영작하시오.

➡ _____

02 How long did it take people to cross the Gobi Desert on foot on a TV show?

➡ _____

03 What does Mina want to try?

➡ _____
_____

04 적절한 부사절 접속사로 시작하여 다음 두 문장을 하나의 문장으로 표현하시오.

He doesn't have time. He tries to exercise every day.

➡ _____
_____

05 주어진 단어를 바르게 배열하여 다음 일기를 완성하시오. 필요할 경우 어형을 바꾸시오.

Today we had my mother's birthday party. My dad baked a cake. He (write / have / me) letters on the cake with chocolate cream. Then, we made some cookies. Lastly, he (me / clean / make) the table.

➡ _____

06 주어진 어구를 활용하여 다음 우리말을 영어로 쓰시오. (접속사로 시작할 것)

비록 나는 매우 피곤했지만, 늦게까지 깨어 있었다. (stay up late)

➡ _____

07 주어진 단어를 어법에 맞게 빈칸에 쓰시오.

When Scott went shopping, he found a jacket that he really liked. After he had the sleeves _____(shorten), it fit him perfectly.

08 다음 우리말에 맞게 빈칸에 알맞은 말을 네 단어로 쓰시오.

그의 얼굴에 나타난 슬픈 표정은 내게 그를 향해 미안함을 느끼게 했다.
➡ The sad expression on his face _____ _____ _____ _____ for him.

[09~12] 다음 글을 읽고 물음에 답하시오.

(A)

Who? Boys in Koh Panyee
What?
The boys make a soccer team but there is no place to play soccer.   (B) , they aren't discouraged. They make a floating field. It's shaky and they play in bare feet but they're happy. One day, (C)그들은 토너먼트에 참가한다. Will they make it to the finals?

09 주어진 단어를 바르게 배열하여 빈칸 (A)에 들어갈 위 글의 제목을 완성하시오.

(courage / team / with / soccer / a)

➡ _____

10 다음 글을 참고하여 빈칸 (B)에 들어갈 알맞은 말을 쓰시오.

You use this word when you are adding a comment which is surprising or which contrasts with what has just been said.

➡ _____

11 위 글의 내용에 맞게 빈칸에 알맞은 말을 쓰시오.

After making their own soccer field, the boys are happy even though _____ _____ _____ _____ _____ _____ _____ _____ .

12 주어진 단어를 활용하여 밑줄 친 우리말 (C)를 영어로 쓰시오.

(take)

➡ _____

[13~16] 다음 글을 읽고 물음에 답하시오.

On the day of the semi-final, it was raining hardly. They were losing by two goals and it looked impossible to win.
"The other team is so strong," they thought.
But the boys didn't give up. They took off their shoes during the second half and the game changed completely. They played better in the rain thanks to the slippery field at home. Although they lost by a score of three to two, still, they felt proud of themselves. (A)They didn't give up when they were losing. They tried their best until the end.

13 How many goals did the team get in the end? Answer in English with a full sentence.

➡ _____

14 위 글에서 문맥상 어색한 어휘 하나를 찾아 바르게 고치시오.

_____ ➡ _____

15 빈칸에 알맞은 말을 써서 밑줄 친 문장 (A)와 같은 의미의 문장을 완성하시오.

They didn't give up _____ they were losing.

16 위 글의 내용에 맞게 빈칸에 알맞은 말을 쓰시오.

The slippery field at home made them _____ _____ _____ _____ .

01 다음 대화의 내용과 일치하도록 호준이의 일기를 완성하시오.

> **Suji:** Hojun, are you going to try out for the school ice hockey team? The new season is about to start.
>
> **Hojun:** I'm not sure.
>
> **Suji:** Why not?
>
> **Hojun:** I heard that Tony and Brad are also trying out for the team. They're so good.
>
> **Suji:** Well, you're also good at ice hockey, so don't give up!
>
> **Hojun:** Okay, I'll try my best. Thanks a lot.

> Mon, Dec 9th, 2019
>
> I was thinking about whether I would try out for (A)_____. Actually, I was not confident because I heard that (B)_____ tried out for the team. I knew they're so good players. When I talked with Suji, she encouraged me not to (C)_____. She said I'm also good at ice hockey. I promised her to (D)_____.

02 사역동사와 주어진 단어를 활용하여 여러 가지 문장을 쓰시오.

> clean   go out   do   take

(1) _____

(2) _____

(3) _____

(4) _____

01 다음 영영풀이가 가리키는 것을 고르시오.

> a thing done successfully, typically by effort, courage, or skill

① tournament
② project
③ courage
④ experience
⑤ achievement

02 다음 우리말에 맞게 빈칸에 알맞은 말을 쓰시오.

(1) 준결승전 날, 비가 심하게 내리고 있었다.
➡ On the day of the _____, it was raining hard.

(2) 그것은 흔들리고 그들은 맨발로 뛴다.
➡ It's _____ and they play in bare feet.

(3) 나는 다른 선수들과 달리 슛을 잘할 수 없었다.
➡ I couldn't _____ well unlike other players.

03 다음 문장의 빈칸에 들어갈 말이 순서대로 짝지어진 것은?

> (A) I decided to _____ out for the math contest.
> (B) Even though there are many difficulties, don't _____ up.
> (C) In Korea, people usually _____ off their shoes when they enter the rooms.

① try – take – give
② try – give – take
③ give – try – take
④ give – take – try
⑤ take – give – try

[04~05] 다음 대화를 읽고 물음에 답하시오.

Sora: Alex, have you heard about this year's "Ugly Sweater Party?"
Alex: Of course, I have. It's on December 5th, right?
Sora: (A) That's right. Are you going to go?
Alex: (B) I want to, but I don't have an ugly sweater.
Sora: (C) You can have it if you want.
Alex: (D) Thanks. That would be great.
Sora: (E) Let's meet in front of the Student Center and go inside together.
Alex: Sure. See you then.

04 위 대화의 (A)~(E) 중 다음 주어진 문장이 들어가기에 적절한 곳은?

> I have one that I don't wear at home.

① (A) ② (B) ③ (C) ④ (D) ⑤ (E)

05 위 대화의 내용과 일치하지 <u>않는</u> 것은?

① 소라와 Alex는 올해의 "못생긴 스웨터 파티"에 대해 알고 있다.
② 올해의 "못생긴 스웨터 파티"는 12월 5일에 열린다.
③ Alex는 못생긴 스웨터가 없어서 새로 살 것이다.
④ 소라는 입지 않는 못생긴 스웨터 한 벌을 갖고 있다.
⑤ 소라와 Alex는 학생회관 앞에서 만나서 같이 들어갈 것이다.

06 다음 글을 읽고 대답할 수 <u>없는</u> 것은?

> W: What can you do to be healthy? First, try to exercise every day. Second, try to eat healthy food. Don't eat too much fast food. Third, wash your hands before meals. Do these tips sound hard to do? Well, take one step at a time and don't give up. Then you'll live a healthy life.

① What is the woman talking about?
② What should we eat to be healthy?
③ What should we do every day to live a healthy life?
④ What should we do before meals?
⑤ Which tip is the most important to be healthy?

07 다음 우리말과 일치하도록 주어진 어구를 사용하여 영작하시오.

(1) 그것은 흔들렸고 어디나 못이 있었다.
  (had, everywhere)
  ➡ _____

(2) 소년들은 낡은 배와 나뭇조각들을 모았다.
  (pieces, boats)
  ➡ _____

[08~09] 다음 대화를 읽고 물음에 답하시오.

> Suji: Hojun, are you going to try out for the school ice hockey team? The new season is about to start.
> Hojun: I'm not (A)[sure / doubtful].
> Suji: Why not?
> Hojun: I heard that _____ⓐ_____ . They're so good.
> Suji: Well, you're also good at ice hockey, so don't (B)[cheer / give] up!
> Hojun: Okay, I'll try my (C)[better / best]. Thanks a lot.

08 위 대화의 빈칸 ⓐ에 들어갈 말을 주어진 단어를 모두 배열하여 영작하시오.

> ┤ 보기 ├
> also / the / trying / Tony and Brad / for / team / are / out

➡ _____

09 위 대화의 빈칸 (A)~(C)에 들어갈 말이 바르게 짝지어진 것은?

① sure – cheer – better
② sure – give – best
③ sure – give – better
④ doubtful – give – best
⑤ doubtful – cheer – better

[10~12] 다음 대화를 읽고 물음에 답하시오.

> Father: Emily, are you excited about your match on Saturday?
> Emily: Not really. We're playing against a strong team. I think we'll lose.
> Father: Don't say that. Have you heard about the Greek team in the 2004 Euro Cup?
> Emily: No, I haven't. What about ⓐthem?
> Father: ⓑThey were a weak team, so ⓒeveryone thought that they would lose.
> Emily: What happened?
> Father: ⓓThey played as a team and worked hard. Finally, ⓔthey won the Euro Cup. So, don't give up.
> Emily: Thanks, Dad. We'll try our best.

10 위 대화의 밑줄 친 ⓐ~ⓔ 중 가리키는 대상이 나머지와 다른 것은?

① ⓐ   ② ⓑ   ③ ⓒ   ④ ⓓ   ⑤ ⓔ

11 Although the Greek team was a weak team, how could they win the 2004 Euro Cup?

➡ _____

12 위 대화의 내용과 일치하도록 빈칸을 완성하시오.

Emily's father told Emily how (A)_____ _____ _____ won the 2004 Euro Cup because her father didn't want her to (B)_____ _____ her match on (C)_____. After talking with her father, Emily decided to (D)_____ _____ _____.

13 주어진 문장과 같은 의미의 문장을 쓰시오.

I had Tom repair my shoes.
= I had my shoes _____ _____ _____.

14 다음 중 어법상 바른 문장은?

① Peeling onions always makes me crying.
② Despite she felt scared, she had to stay cool.
③ The man had the restaurant ran by his wife.
④ Although you didn't invite me to the party I didn't care.
⑤ I had my computer fixed by Ann.

15 다음 빈칸에 들어갈 말이 바르게 짝지어진 것은?

Candace had her children _____ them _____ out their garage.

① to help – to clean   ② helped – cleaned
③ help – to clean   ④ help – to cleaning
⑤ helping – cleaning

[16~18] 다음 글을 읽고 물음에 답하시오.

The boys ①gathered old boats and pieces of wood. They put the boats together and ②nailed the wood to them. After much hard work, they finally had a ③floating field. It was shaky and had nails everywhere. The ball and the boys would often fall into the sea, so the field was always ④dry and slippery. They had no shoes so they had to play in bare feet. Still, they ⑤didn't care. In fact, they built excellent skills and enjoyed playing soccer more.

16 위 글의 ①~⑤ 중 글의 흐름상 어색한 것은?

①   ②   ③   ④   ⑤

17 다음 중 위 글의 내용과 일치하는 것은?

① The boys put apart the boats.
② The boys wanted someone to make their soccer field.
③ There were no nails on the field.
④ The boys hammered the nails by themselves.
⑤ The boys fenced the field in order not to fall into the sea.

18 다음과 같이 풀이되는 말을 위 글에서 찾아 쓰시오.

> not covered by clothing, shoes, a hat, etc.

➡ _____

[19~20] 다음 글을 읽고 물음에 답하시오.

> Koh Panyee was a small floating village in the middle of the sea. Although the boys in the village never played soccer before, they loved watching it on TV. One day, the boys decided to make their own soccer team. However, people laughed at their idea.
> "That's impossible."
> "What makes you say so?"
> "Look around. Where are you going to play soccer?"
> The villagers were right. The boys had no place (A)to play soccer. They were discouraged.
> "Don't give up! We can still play soccer."
> "How?"
> "Let's make our own soccer field."

19 위 글의 내용과 일치하지 <u>않는</u> 것은?

① Koh Panyee was floating on the sea.
② The boys in the village made up their mind to make their own soccer team.
③ What people said about the boys' idea had a point because there was no place to play soccer.
④ The boys decided to make their own soccer field so that they could play soccer.
⑤ People in the village encouraged the boys to make their soccer team.

20 다음 중 밑줄 친 (A)와 쓰임이 같은 것은?

① It enables us <u>to live</u> our lives comfortably.
② It is not a great idea <u>to tell</u> him the truth.
③ Is there any chance <u>to see</u> him again?
④ They tried hard <u>to make</u> the machine work.
⑤ We hope <u>to see</u> you soon.

[21~23] 다음 글을 읽고 물음에 답하시오.

> One day, a boy brought a poster about a soccer tournament. ①They decided to give it a try. When ②they were about to leave, the villagers gave ③them new shoes and uniforms. Some of ④them even came to watch the game. This made the boys feel better. At first, people saw ⑤them as the weakest team. However, when the tournament started, the soccer team surprised everyone.
> On the day of the semi-final, it was raining hard. They were losing by two goals and it looked impossible to win.
> "The other team is so strong," they thought.
> But the boys didn't give up.

21 위 글의 ①~⑤ 중 지칭하는 것이 <u>다른</u> 하나는?

①   ②   ③   ④   ⑤

22 What did the boys decided to do after seeing a poster? Answer in English with a full sentence.

➡ _____

23 다음은 경기에 참가한 소년의 말이다. 위 글의 표현을 활용하여 영어로 쓰시오.

> 비록 이기는 것이 불가능해 보였지만, 우리는 포기하지 않았습니다.

➡ _____

_____

Middle School 2-2
학교시험 완벽 대비

2학기 전과정

적중100 plus

영어 기출문제집

영어 중 2

지학 | 민찬규

Best Collection

내용문의 중등영어발전소 적중100 편집부 TEL 070-4416-3636

INSIGHT
on the textbook

교과서 파헤치기

영어 기출 문제집

적중100 plus
2학기 전과정

영어 중 2

지학 | 민찬규

Insight
on the textbook

교과서 파헤치기

※ 다음 영어를 우리말로 쓰시오.

01 block _____

02 half _____

03 delete _____

04 accident _____

05 throw _____

06 somewhere _____

07 dragon _____

08 bottom _____

09 suspect _____

10 lie _____

11 escape _____

12 outside _____

13 clue _____

14 hide _____

15 detective _____

16 luckily _____

17 bean _____

18 twice _____

19 space _____

20 inside _____

21 congratulation _____

22 scene _____

23 strange _____

24 thief _____

25 prize _____

26 safely _____

27 explain _____

28 straight _____

29 finally _____

30 disappear _____

31 fold _____

32 none _____

33 solve _____

34 riddle _____

35 button _____

36 help yourself _____

37 write down _____

38 turn over _____

39 catch a thief _____

40 fill A with B _____

41 for free _____

42 at the time of _____

43 make it to ~ _____

※ 다음 우리말을 영어로 쓰시오.

01	단추	
02	장면	
03	단서, 실마리	
04	던지다	
05	맨 아래 (부분)	
06	이상한	
07	설명하다	
08	접다	
09	건너다	
10	반, 절반	
11	어딘가에	
12	삭제하다	
13	두 번	
14	마침내	
15	숨기다, 숨다	
16	거짓말하다	
17	똑바로, 일직선으로	
18	사고	
19	해결하다	
20	사라지다	
21	콩	

22	용의자	
23	탈출하다	
24	다행히	
25	축하	
26	공간	
27	~ 밖에, 밖으로	
28	상	
29	수수께끼	
30	안전하게	
31	탐정, 형사	
32	양초	
33	도둑	
34	우표	
35	용	
36	A를 B로 채우다	
37	뒤집다	
38	~에 이르는데 성공하다	
39	공짜로	
40	~이 일어나던 때에	
41	적다	
42	도둑을 잡다	
43	마음껏 드세요	

※ 다음 영영풀이에 알맞은 단어를 <보기>에서 골라 쓴 후, 우리말 뜻을 쓰시오.

1 _____ : to go or come into a place: _____

2 _____ : someone who is thought to be guilty of a crime: _____

3 _____ : a seed or a pod that comes from a climbing plant and is cooked as food: _____

4 _____ : the flat surface on the lowest side of an object: _____

5 _____ : someone who steals things from another person or place: _____

6 _____ : exactly or about 50% of an amount, time, distance, number etc.: _____

7 _____ : an object or piece of information that helps someone solve a crime or mystery: _____

8 _____ : to go from one side of something such as a road, river, room, etc. to the other: _____

9 _____ : to remove something that has been written down or stored in a computer: _____

10 _____ : a long wooden stick with a special shape that is used in some sports and games: _____

11 _____ : an event in which a car, train, plane, etc. is damaged and often someone is hurt: _____

12 _____ : someone who is paid to discover information about someone or something: _____

13 _____ : a question that is deliberately very confusing and has a humorous or clever answer: _____

14 _____ : to leave a place when someone is trying to catch you or stop you, or when there is a dangerous situation: _____

15 _____ : to put or keep someone or something in a place where they/it cannot be seen or found: _____

16 _____ : a small piece of paper with a design on it that you buy and stick on an envelope or a package before you post it: _____

보기			
riddle	suspect	detective	delete
bean	escape	hide	clue
accident	thief	bat	cross
enter	bottom	stamp	half

※ 다음 우리말과 일치하도록 빈칸에 알맞은 말을 쓰시오.

Listen & Speak 1-A

Jimin: Do you _____ _____ _____ the new game _____ I _____?

Brian: Sure, _____ is _____, Jimin?

Jimin: It's _____ a soccer game but the players are _____ and _____. You _____ _____ _____ these buttons _____.

Brian: That _____ _____. _____ _____ _____ _____ _____ _____ the buttons?

Jimin: Sure.

Jimin: 내가 산 새로운 게임을 하고 싶니?
Brian: 물론이야. 그게 뭐니, 지민아?
Jimin: 축구 시합 같은 것인데 선수들이 용과 해야야. 게임을 하려면 이 버튼들을 사용해야 해.
Brian: 재밌을 거 같아. 버튼 사용법을 설명해 줄 수 있니?
Jimin: 물론이지.

Listen & Speak 1-B

Jack: Kelly, here's a _____. You can see this _____ _____ _____, _____ in a year, but _____ _____ _____. What is this?

Kelly: _____ _____ _____ _____ _____.

Jack: It's the letter "E."

Kelly: I don't _____ _____. _____ _____ _____ _____ _____ _____?

Jack: Well, there are two "E"s in the word "week," one "E" in the word "_____" but _____ "E"s in the word "_____."

Kelly: Aha! Now I _____ _____.

Jack: Kelly, 수수께끼가 있어. 넌 이것을 1주에 두 번, 1년에 한 번 볼 수 있어, 하지만 1일에는 전혀 볼 수가 없어. 이게 뭐게?
Kelly: 전혀 모르겠어.
Jack: 알파벳 'E'야.
Kelly: 이해가 안 가. 이유를 설명해 줄 수 있니?
Jack: 음, 단어 week에는 'E'가 2개 있고, 단어 year에는 'E'가 1개 있고, 단어 day에는 'E'가 없잖아.
Kelly: 아! 이제 이해했다.

Listen & Speak 2-A

Tom: Yujin, _____ _____ my paper fox.

Yujin: That's cute. _____ _____ _____ _____ _____ _____ _____?

Tom: _____, fold a paper _____ _____ to _____ _____ _____. _____, _____ _____ _____ of the triangle to the _____ _____. _____, fold _____ of the bottom line to the top _____ _____ _____. _____, _____ it _____ and draw a face.

Yujin: That _____ _____.

Tom: 유진아, 내 종이 여우를 봐.
Yujin: 귀엽다. 어떻게 만들었니?
Tom: 먼저, 종이를 반으로 접어서 세모를 만들어. 두 번째로, 세모의 꼭대기를 맨 아랫선 쪽으로 접어. 세 번째로, 맨 아랫선 양쪽 끝을 위로 접어서 귀를 만들어. 그러고 나서, 그것을 뒤집어서 얼굴을 그려.
Yujin: 쉽구나.

Listen & Speak 2-B

Jane: Minsu, do you know the TV show about the student _____?

Minsu: Yes. I love that show, but I _____ _____ it _____ _____. What was it _____?

Jane: Well, _____ _____ the bikes at school _____.

Minsu: So, what _____ he _____?

Jane: _____, he _____ _____ the school. _____, he met some _____ and asked questions. _____, he _____ the _____. The thief was ....

Minsu: No, _____ _____ me! I'll _____ it _____.

Real Life Communication

Emily: Junsu, do you want to _____ a riddle?

Junsu: Sure, what is it?

Emily: There is a farmer. _____, the farmer buys a fox, a duck, and _____ _____ _____ _____. Then, the farmer _____ _____ _____ _____ _____.

Junsu: What's the problem?

Emily: The boat _____ _____ _____ the farmer and _____ _____ thing.

Junsu: _____ _____ _____ that the farmer can _____ only one thing _____ _____ _____?

Emily: Yes. Also, the fox will eat the duck or the duck will eat the beans if the farmer isn't there. _____ _____ _____ _____ _____ _____ _____ _____ the river _____?

Junsu: Hmm ....

Let's Check

Minjun: Wow! Something _____ really _____, Mom. What is it?

Mom: We're _____ _____ have tacos _____ _____. _____ _____.

Minjun: _____ _____ _____ _____ _____ _____ _____ _____ a taco?

Mom: _____, _____ your tortilla _____ vegetables and meat. _____, _____ some sauce _____ _____ _____.

Minjun: Sounds _____!

Mom: _____ you _____ some cheese?

Minjun: No, _____.

Jane: 민수야, 학생 탐정이 나오는 TV 쇼를 아니?

Minsu: 응, 나는 그 쇼를 아주 좋아하지만 이번 주에는 못 봤어. 무슨 내용이었어?

Jane: 음, 학교의 모든 자전거들이 사라졌어.

Minsu: 그래서 그가 무엇을 했어?

Jane: 첫째로, 그는 학교를 둘러 봤어. 그리고 나서, 몇몇의 용의자를 만나서 질문을 했지. 마침내, 그는 도둑을 찾았어. 도둑은....

Minsu: 안 돼, 말하지 마! 내가 나중에 볼 거야.

Emily: 준수야, 수수께끼 하나 풀어볼래?

Junsu: 물론이지, 뭔데?

Emily: 한 농부가 있어. 먼저 농부는 여우, 오리, 콩 자루를 하나씩 사. 그리고 나서, 농부는 강을 건너야 해.

Junsu: 뭐가 문제인데?

Emily: 보트는 단지 농부와 한 가지만 더 옮길 수 있어.

Junsu: 농부가 한 번에 오직 한 가지만 옮길 수 있다는 말이니?

Emily: 응. 또한 만약 농부가 없다면 여우가 오리를 먹거나, 오리가 콩을 먹을 거야. 전부를 강 건너로 안전하게 옮길 방법을 설명할 수 있겠니?

Junsu: 음....

Minjun: 와! 뭔가 정말 좋은 냄새가 나요, 엄마. 뭐예요?

Mom: 우리는 저녁 식사로 타코를 먹을 거야. 맘껏 먹으렴.

Minjun: 타코 만드는 법을 설명해 주실 수 있어요?

Mom: 먼저, 토르티야를 채소와 코기로 채워. 그 다음, 위에 약간의 소스를 추가하렴.

Minjun: 맛있을 것 같아요!

Mom: 치즈 좀 줄까?

Minjun: 아뇨, 괜찮아요.

※ 다음 우리말에 맞도록 대화를 영어로 쓰시오.

Listen & Speak 1-A

Jimin: _____

Brian: _____

Jimin: _____

_____

Brian: _____

Jimin: _____

Listen & Speak 1-B

Jack: _____

_____

Kelly: _____

Jack: _____

Kelly: _____

Jack: _____

_____

Kelly: _____

Listen & Speak 2-A

Tom: _____

Yujin: _____

Tom: _____

_____

_____

Yujin: _____

해석

Jimin: 내가 산 새로운 게임을 하고 싶니?
Brian: 물론이야. 그게 뭐니, 지민아?
Jimin: 축구 시합 같은 것인데 선수들이 용과 해마야. 게임을 하려면 이 버튼들을 사용해야 해.
Brian: 재밌을 거 같아. 버튼 사용법을 설명해 줄 수 있니?
Jimin: 물론이지.

Jack: Kelly, 수수께끼가 있어. 넌 이것을 1주에 두 번, 1년에 한 번 볼 수 있어, 하지만 1일에는 전혀 볼 수가 없어. 이게 뭐게?
Kelly: 전혀 모르겠어.
Jack: 알파벳 'E'야.
Kelly: 이해가 안 가. 이유를 설명해 줄 수 있니?
Jack: 음, 단어 week에는 'E'가 2개 있고, 단어 year에는 'E'가 1개 있고, 단어 day에는 'E'가 없잖아.
Kelly: 아! 이제 이해했다.

Tom: 유진아, 내 종이 여우를 봐.
Yujin: 귀엽다. 어떻게 만들었니?
Tom: 먼저, 종이를 반으로 접어서 세모를 만들어. 두 번째로, 세모의 꼭대기를 맨 아랫선 쪽으로 접어. 세 번째로, 맨 아랫선 양쪽 끝을 위로 접어서 귀를 만들어. 그러고 나서, 그것을 뒤집어서 얼굴을 그려.
Yujin: 쉽구나.

Listen & Speak 2-B

Jane: _____

Minsu: _____

Jane: _____

Minsu: _____

Jane: _____

_____

Minsu: _____

Real Life Communication

Emily: _____

Junsu: _____

Emily: _____

_____

Junsu: _____

Emily: _____

Junsu: _____

Emily: _____

_____

_____

Junsu: _____

Let's Check

Minjun: _____

Mom: _____

Minjun: _____

Mom: _____

_____

Minjun: _____

Mom: _____

Minjun: _____

Jane: 민수야, 학생 탐정이 나오는 TV 쇼를 아니?

Minsu: 응, 나는 그 쇼를 아주 좋아하지만 이번 주에는 못 봤어. 무슨 내용이었어?

Jane: 음, 학교의 모든 자전거들이 사라졌어.

Minsu: 그래서 그가 무엇을 했어?

Jane: 첫째로, 그는 학교를 둘러 봤어. 그러고 나서, 몇몇의 용의자를 만나서 질문을 했지. 마침내, 그는 도둑을 찾았어. 도둑은....

Minsu: 안 돼, 말하지 마! 내가 나중에 볼 거야.

Emily: 준수야, 수수께끼 하나 풀어볼래?

Junsu: 물론이지, 뭔데?

Emily: 한 농부가 있어. 먼저 농부는 여우, 오리, 콩 자루를 하나씩 사. 그러고 나서, 농부는 강을 건너야 해.

Junsu: 뭐가 문제인데?

Emily: 보트는 단지 농부와 한 가지만 더 옮길 수 있어.

Junsu: 농부가 한 번에 오직 한 가지만 옮길 수 있다는 말이니?

Emily: 응. 또한 만약 농부가 없다면 여우가 오리를 먹거나, 오리가 콩을 먹을 거야. 전부를 강 건너로 안전하게 옮길 방법을 설명할 수 있겠니?

Junsu: 음....

Minjun: 와! 뭔가 정말 좋은 냄새가 나요, 엄마. 뭐예요?

Mom: 우리는 저녁 식사로 타코를 먹을 거야. 맘껏 먹으렴.

Minjun: 타코 만드는 법을 설명해 주실 수 있어요?

Mom: 먼저, 토르티야를 채소와 코기로 채워. 그 다음, 위에 약간의 소스를 추가하렴.

Minjun: 맛있을 것 같아요!

Mom: 치즈 좀 줄까?

Minjun: 아뇨, 괜찮아요.

※ 다음 우리말과 일치하도록 빈칸에 알맞은 것을 골라 쓰시오.

The Great Escape

1 _____ _____ the _____ Tower.
　　A. Escape　　　B. to　　　　C. Welcome

2 You will _____ the _____ room in _____ tower.
　　A. first　　　　B. our　　　　C. enter

3 You need to _____ some _____ to _____.
　　A. riddles　　　B. solve　　　C. escape

4 Clues can _____ _____ somewhere _____ the room.
　　A. inside　　　B. found　　　C. be

5 So, _____ you _____ to _____ like Sherlock Holmes?
　　A. think　　　　B. are　　　　C. ready

Room # 1

6 Mr. Doodle was _____ _____ a car _____ Sunday afternoon.
　　A. by　　　　　B. on　　　　　C. hit

7 _____, he wasn't _____ _____, but he didn't _____ the driver.
　　A. see　　　　B. badly　　　C. hurt　　　D. luckily

8 Three _____ were _____ _____ a police officer.
　　A. by　　　　　B. suspects　　C. questioned

9 Ms. A said she was _____ a book at the _____ of the _____.
　　A. accident　　B. time　　　C. reading

10 Mr. B _____ he _____ _____ his dog.
　　A. was　　　　B. said　　　　C. walking

11 Ms. C said she _____ _____ _____.
　　A. making　　　B. breakfast　　C. was

12 _____ _____ Mr. Doodle? Can you _____ why?
　　A. hit　　　　B. explain　　　C. who

13 Do you _____ the answer? _____ it _____.
　　A. have　　　　B. down　　　C. write

14 Then you can _____ _____ the _____ room.
　　A. next　　　　B. to　　　　C. move

15 **Clue** The _____ _____ the afternoon.
　　A. in　　　　　B. happened　　C. accident

16 Congratulations! You _____ _____ _____ the second room.
　　A. to　　　　　B. made　　　　C. it

대탈출

1 '탈출탑'에 오신 것을 환영합니다.

2 당신은 저희 탑의 첫 번째 방에 들어갈 것입니다.

3 당신은 탈출하기 위하여 몇 개의 수수께끼를 풀어야 합니다.

4 단서들은 방 어딘가에서 발견될 수 있습니다.

5 그러면 당신은 셜록 홈스처럼 생각할 준비가 되었나요?

방 # 1

6 Doodle씨는 일요일 오후에 차에 치였습니다.

7 다행히 그는 심하게 다치지 않았으나 그는 운전자를 보지 못했습니다.

8 세 명의 용의자들이 경찰에게 심문을 받았습니다.

9 A씨는 사고가 일어난 시간에 책을 읽고 있었다고 말했습니다.

10 B씨는 그의 개를 산책시키고 있었다고 말했습니다.

11 C씨는 아침을 만들고 있었다고 말했습니다.

12 누가 Doodle씨를 치었을까요? 왜 그런지 설명할 수 있나요?

13 답을 가지고 있나요? 적어 보세요.

14 그런 다음, 당신은 다음 방으로 갈 수 있습니다.

15 단서: 사건은 오후에 일어났습니다.

16 축하합니다! 당신은 두 번째 방에 오는 데 성공하셨습니다.

17 However, the second room is _____ _____ to _____ than the first one. Good luck!

    A. escape   B. harder   C. much

Room #2

18 Jay _____ an email _____ his favorite _____ store.

    A. clothing   B. from   C. gets

19 The title _____ "You _____ our Lucky Day _____!"

    A. won   B. reads   C. event

20 Jay is _____ . He _____ _____ it.

    A. quickly   B. surprised   C. opens

21 JayJr@kmail.com

You _____ _____ 'Lucky Day' _____!

    A. our   B. event   C. won

22 Congratulations! You _____ _____ a special _____.

    A. prize   B. won   C. have

23 _____ our Lucky Day event, you can _____ any seven _____ from our store for _____!

    A. free   B. choose   C. items   D. during

24 Come _____ our store _____ November 31.

    A. on   B. to

25 We _____ _____ _____ see you.

    A. wait   B. to   C. can't

26 _____ _____, Kay Brown

    A. yours   B. truly

27 _____, Jay thinks that the event isn't _____ and _____ the email.

    A. deletes   B. real   C. however

28 _____ you _____ _____?

    A. explain   B. why   C. can

29 **Clue** _____ are _____ 30 or 31 _____ in a month.

    A. usually   B. days   C. there

30 Do you _____ the _____?

    A. answer   B. have

31 _____ it _____ and then you are _____ to go!

    A. down   B. free   C. write

---

17 그러나 두 번째 방은 첫 번째 방보다 탈출하기 훨씬 더 어렵습니다. 행운을 빕니다!

방 # 2

18 Jay는 그가 가장 좋아하는 옷 가게로부터 이메일을 받습니다.

19 제목은 "당신은 '행운의 날' 행사에 당첨되었습니다!"라고 적혀 있습니다.

20 Jay는 놀랍니다. 그는 재빨리 그것을 엽니다.

21 JayJr@kmail.com
당신은 우리의 '행운의 날' 행사에 당첨되었습니다!

22 축하합니다! 당신은 특별한 상품을 받게 되었습니다.

23 '행운의 날' 행사 동안, 당신은 우리 가게에서 일곱 가지 상품을 아무거나 무료로 선택할 수 있습니다!

24 11월 31일에 우리 가게로 오세요.

25 우리는 몹시 당신을 보기를 기대합니다.

26 안녕히 계십시오, Kay Brown

27 그러나 Jay는 그 행사가 사실이 아니라고 생각하고 이메일을 삭제합니다.

28 왜 그런지 설명할 수 있나요?

29 단서: 한 달은 주로 30일 또는 31일이 있습니다.

30 답을 가지고 계신가요?

31 그것을 적으면, 당신은 자유롭게 가실 수 있습니다!

※ 다음 우리말과 일치하도록 빈칸에 알맞은 말을 쓰시오.

The Great Escape

1 _____ _____ the Escape Tower.

2 You will _____ _____ _____ _____ in our tower.

3 You _____ _____ _____ _____ _____ to escape.

4 Clues can _____ _____ somewhere _____ the room.

5 So, _____ you _____ _____ _____ _____ Sherlock Holmes?

Room # 1

6 Mr. Doodle _____ _____ _____ a car _____ Sunday afternoon.

7 _____, he _____ _____ _____, but he _____ _____ the driver.

8 Three suspects _____ _____ _____ a police officer.

9 Ms. A said she was _____ _____ _____ _____ _____ _____ _____ _____.

10 Mr. B _____ he _____ _____ his dog.

11 Ms. C said she _____ _____ _____.

12 _____ _____ Mr. Doodle? Can you _____ _____?

13 Do you have the answer? _____ _____.

14 Then you _____ _____ _____ the next room.

15 **Clue** The _____ _____ _____ the afternoon.

16 Congratulations! You _____ _____ _____ the second room.

대탈출

1 '탈출탑'에 오신 것을 환영합니다.

2 당신은 저희 탑의 첫 번째 방에 들어갈 것입니다.

3 당신은 탈출하기 위하여 몇 개의 수수께끼를 풀어야 합니다.

4 단서들은 방 어딘가에서 발견될 수 있습니다.

5 그러면 당신은 셜록 홈스처럼 생각할 준비가 되었나요?

방 # 1

6 Doodle씨는 일요일 오후에 차에 치였습니다.

7 다행히 그는 심하게 다치지 않았으나 그는 운전자를 보지 못했습니다.

8 세 명의 용의자들이 경찰에게 심문을 받았습니다.

9 A씨는 사고가 일어난 시간에 책을 읽고 있었다고 말했습니다.

10 B씨는 그의 개를 산책시키고 있었다고 말했습니다.

11 C씨는 아침을 만들고 있었다고 말했습니다.

12 누가 Doodle씨를 치었을까요? 왜 그런지 설명할 수 있나요?

13 답을 가지고 있나요? 적어 보세요.

14 그런 다음, 당신은 다음 방으로 갈 수 있습니다.

15 단서: 사건은 오후에 일어났습니다.

16 축하합니다! 당신은 두 번째 방에 오는 데 성공하셨습니다.

17 _____, the second room is _____ _____ _____ _____ _____ the first one. Good luck!

Room #2

18 Jay _____ an email _____ his favorite _____ _____.

19 The title _____ "You _____ our Lucky Day event!"

20 Jay is _____. He _____ _____ it.

21 JayJr@kmail.com

You _____ _____ 'Lucky Day' event!

22 _____! You _____ a special _____.

23 _____ our Lucky Day event, you can _____ any seven items _____ our store _____ _____!

24 _____ _____ our store _____ November 31.

25 We _____ _____ _____ _____ you.

26 _____ _____, Kay Brown

27 _____, Jay _____ _____ the event _____ _____ and _____ the email.

28 _____ you _____ _____?

29 **Clue** _____ _____ 30 or 31 _____ in a month.

30 Do you _____ _____ _____?

31 _____ _____ _____ and then you _____ _____ _____!

17 그러나 두 번째 방은 첫 번째 방보다 탈출하기 훨씬 더 어렵습니다. 행운을 빕니다!

방 # 2

18 Jay는 그가 가장 좋아하는 옷 가게로부터 이메일을 받습니다.

19 제목은 "당신은 '행운의 날' 행사에 당첨되었습니다!"라고 적혀 있습니다.

20 Jay는 놀랍니다. 그는 재빨리 그것을 엽니다.

21 JayJr@kmail.com
당신은 우리의 '행운의 날' 행사에 당첨되었습니다!

22 축하합니다! 당신은 특별한 상품을 받게 되었습니다.

23 '행운의 날' 행사 동안, 당신은 우리 가게에서 일곱 가지 상품을 아무거나 무료로 선택할 수 있습니다!

24 11월 31일에 우리 가게로 오세요.

25 우리는 몹시 당신을 보기를 기대합니다.

26 안녕히 계십시오, Kay Brown

27 그러나 Jay는 그 행사가 사실이 아니라고 생각하고 이메일을 삭제합니다.

28 왜 그런지 설명할 수 있나요?

29 단서: 한 달은 주로 30일 또는 31일이 있습니다.

30 답을 가지고 계신가요?

31 그것을 적으면, 당신은 자유롭게 가실 수 있습니다!

※ 다음 문장을 우리말로 쓰시오.

The Great Escape

1 Welcome to the Escape Tower.

➡ _____

2 You will enter the first room in our tower.

➡ _____

3 You need to solve some riddles to escape.

➡ _____

4 Clues can be found somewhere inside the room.

➡ _____

5 So, are you ready to think like Sherlock Holmes?

➡ _____

Room #1

6 Mr. Doodle was hit by a car on Sunday afternoon.

➡ _____

7 Luckily, he wasn't badly hurt, but he didn't see the driver.

➡ _____

8 Three suspects were questioned by a police officer.

➡ _____

9 Ms. A said she was reading a book at the time of the accident.

➡ _____

10 Mr. B said he was walking his dog.

➡ _____

11 Ms. C said she was making breakfast.

➡ _____

12 Who hit Mr. Doodle? Can you explain why?

➡ _____

13 Do you have the answer? Write it down.

➡ _____

14 Then you can move to the next room.

➡ _____

15 Clue The accident happened in the afternoon.

➡ _____

16 Congratulations! You made it to the second room.

➡ _____

17 However, the second room is much harder to escape than the first one. Good luck!

➡ _____

Room #2

18 Jay gets an email from his favorite clothing store.

➡ _____

19 The title reads "You won our Lucky Day event!"

➡ _____

20 Jay is surprised. He quickly opens it.

➡ _____

21 JayJr@kmail.com
You won our 'Lucky Day' event!

➡ _____

22 Congratulations! You have won a special prize.

➡ _____

23 During our Lucky Day event, you can choose any seven items from our store for free!

➡ _____

24 Come to our store on November 31.

➡ _____

25 We can't wait to see you.

➡ _____

26 Truly yours, Kay Brown

➡ _____

27 However, Jay thinks that the event isn't real and deletes the email.

➡ _____

28 Can you explain why?

➡ _____

29 Clue There are usually 30 or 31 days in a month.

➡ _____

30 Do you have the answer?

➡ _____

31 Write it down and then you are free to go!

➡ _____

※ 다음 괄호 안의 단어들을 우리말에 맞도록 바르게 배열하시오.

The Great Escape

1 (to / Welcome / Tower. / Escape / the)
➡ _____

2 (will / you / the / enter / room / first / tower. / our / in)
➡ _____

3 (need / you / solve / to / riddles / some / escape. / to)
➡ _____

4 (can / clues / found / be / inside / somewhere / room. / the)
➡ _____

5 (are / so, / ready / you / think / to / Sherlock / like / Holmes?)
➡ _____

Room #1

6 (Doodle / Mr. / hit / was / a / by / car / afternoon. / Sunday / on)
➡ _____

7 (he / luckily, / wasn't / hurt, / badly / but / didn't / he / driver. / the / see)
➡ _____

8 (suspects / three / questioned / were / a / by / officer. / police)
➡ _____

9 (A / Ms. / she / said / redaing / was / book / a / the / at / time / accident. / the / of)
➡ _____

10 (B / Mr. / he / said / walking / was / dog. / his)
➡ _____

11 (C / Ms. / she / said / making / was / breakfast.)
➡ _____

12 (hit / who / Doodle? / Mr. // you / can / why? / explain)
➡ _____

13 (you / do / have / answer? / the // down. / it / write)
➡ _____

14 (you / then / move / can / the / to / room. / next)
➡ _____

15 (clue // accident / the / in / happened / afternoon. / the)
➡ _____

16 (congratulations! // made / you / to / it / room. / second / the)
➡ _____

대탈출

1 '탈출탑'에 오신 것을 환영합니다.

2 당신은 저희 탑의 첫 번째 방에 들어갈 것입니다.

3 당신은 탈출하기 위하여 몇 개의 수수께끼를 풀어야 합니다.

4 단서들은 방 어딘가에서 발견될 수 있습니다.

5 그러면 당신은 셜록 홈스처럼 생각할 준비가 되었나요?

방 # 1

6 Doodle씨는 일요일 오후에 차에 치였습니다.

7 다행히 그는 심하게 다치지 않았으나 그는 운전자를 보지 못했습니다.

8 세 명의 용의자들이 경찰에게 심문을 받았습니다.

9 A씨는 사고가 일어난 시간에 책을 읽고 있었다고 말했습니다.

10 B씨는 그의 개를 산책시키고 있었다고 말했습니다.

11 C씨는 아침을 만들고 있었다고 말했습니다.

12 누가 Doodle씨를 치었을까요? 왜 그런지 설명할 수 있나요?

13 답을 가지고 있나요? 적어 보세요.

14 그런 다음, 당신은 다음 방으로 갈 수 있습니다.

15 단서: 사건은 오후에 일어났습니다.

16 축하합니다! 당신은 두 번째 방에 오는 데 성공하셨습니다.

17 (however, / second / the / is / room / harder / much / escape / to / than / first / the / one. // luck! / good)
➡ _____
_____

Room #2

18 (gets / Jay / email / an / his / from / store. / clothing / favorite)
➡ _____

19 (title / the / reads / "you / our / won / Day / event!" / Lucky)
➡ _____

20 (is / Jay / surprised. // he / quickly / it. / opens)
➡ _____

21 JayJr@kmail.com
(won / you / event! / our / Day' / 'Lucky)
➡ JayJr@kmail.com _____

22 (congratulations! // have / you / a / prize. / special / won)
➡ _____

23 (our / during / event, / Day / Lucky / can / you / any / choose / items / seven / from / store / our / free! / for)
➡ _____
_____

24 (to / come / store / our / 31. / November / on)
➡ _____

25 (can't / we / see / wait / you. / to)
➡ _____

26 (yours, / truly / Brown / Kay)
➡ _____

27 (however, / thinks / Jay / the / that / isn't / event / deletes / and / real / email. / the)
➡ _____
_____

28 (you / can / why? / explain)
➡ _____

29 (clue // are / there / 30 / usually / 31 / or / month. / a / in / days)
➡ _____

30 (you / do / have / answer? / the)
➡ _____

31 (down / it / write / then / and / are / you / go! / to / free)
➡ _____

17 그러나 두 번째 방은 첫 번째 방보다 탈출하기 훨씬 더 어렵습니다. 행운을 빕니다!

방 # 2

18 Jay는 그가 가장 좋아하는 옷 가게로부터 이메일을 받습니다.

19 제목은 "당신은 '행운의 날' 행사에 당첨되었습니다!"라고 적혀 있습니다.

20 Jay는 놀랍니다. 그는 재빨리 그것을 엽니다.

21 JayJr@kmail.com
당신은 우리의 '행운의 날' 행사에 당첨되었습니다!

22 축하합니다! 당신은 특별한 상품을 받게 되었습니다.

23 '행운의 날' 행사 동안, 당신은 우리 가게에서 일곱 가지 상품을 아무거나 무료로 선택할 수 있습니다!

24 11월 31일에 우리 가게로 오세요.

25 우리는 몹시 당신을 보기를 기대합니다.

26 안녕히 계십시오, Kay Brown

27 그러나 Jay는 그 행사가 사실이 아니라고 생각하고 이메일을 삭제합니다.

28 왜 그런지 설명할 수 있나요?

29 단서: 한 달은 주로 30일 또는 31일이 있습니다.

30 답을 가지고 계신가요?

31 그것을 적으면, 당신은 자유롭게 가실 수 있습니다!

※ 다음 우리말을 영어로 쓰시오.

The Great Escape

1 '탈출 탑'에 오신 것을 환영합니다.

➡ _____

2 당신은 저희 탑의 첫 번째 방에 들어갈 것입니다.

➡ _____

3 당신은 탈출하기 위하여 몇 개의 수수께끼를 풀어야 합니다.

➡ _____

4 단서들은 방 어딘가에서 발견될 수 있습니다.

➡ _____

5 그러면 당신은 셜록 홈스처럼 생각할 준비가 되었나요?

➡ _____

Room #1

6 Doodle씨는 일요일 오후에 차에 치였습니다.

➡ _____

7 다행히 그는 심하게 다치지 않았으나 그는 운전자를 보지 못했습니다.

➡ _____

8 세 명의 용의자들이 경찰에게 심문을 받았습니다.

➡ _____

9 A씨는 사고가 일어난 시간에 책을 읽고 있었다고 말했습니다.

➡ _____

10 B씨는 그의 개를 산책시키고 있었다고 말했습니다.

➡ _____

11 C씨는 아침을 만들고 있었다고 말했습니다.

➡ _____

12 누가 Doodle씨를 치었을까요? 왜 그런지 설명할 수 있나요?

➡ _____

13 답을 가지고 있나요? 적어 보세요.

➡ _____

14 그런 다음, 당신은 다음 방으로 갈 수 있습니다.

➡ _____

15 단서: 사건은 오후에 일어났습니다.

➡ _____

16 축하합니다! 당신은 두 번째 방에 오는 데 성공하셨습니다.

➡ _____

17 그러나 두 번째 방은 첫 번째 방보다 탈출하기 훨씬 더 어렵습니다. 행운을 빕니다!

➡ _____

Room #2

18 Jay는 그가 가장 좋아하는 옷 가게로부터 이메일을 받습니다.

➡ _____

19 제목은 "당신은 '행운의 날' 행사에 당첨되었습니다!"라고 적혀 있습니다.

➡ _____

20 Jay는 놀랍니다. 그는 재빨리 그것을 엽니다.

➡ _____

21 JayJr@kmail.com
당신은 우리의 '행운의 날' 행사에 당첨되었습니다!

➡ JayJr@kmail.com _____

22 축하합니다! 당신은 특별한 상품을 받게 되었습니다.

➡ _____

23 '행운의 날' 행사 동안, 당신은 우리 가게에서 일곱 가지 상품을 아무거나 공짜로 선택할 수 있습니다!

➡ _____

24 11월 31일에 우리 가게로 오세요.

➡ _____

25 우리는 몹시 당신을 보기를 기대합니다.

➡ _____

26 안녕히 계십시오, Kay Brown

➡ _____

27 그러나 Jay는 그 행사가 사실이 아니라고 생각하고 이메일을 삭제합니다.

➡ _____

28 왜 그런지 설명할 수 있나요?

➡ _____

29 단서: 한 달은 주로 30일 또는 31일이 있습니다.

➡ _____

30 답을 가지고 계신가요?

➡ _____

31 그것을 적으면, 당신은 자유롭게 가실 수 있습니다!

➡ _____

※ 다음 우리말과 일치하도록 빈칸에 알맞은 말을 쓰시오.

Listen and Speak 1-C

1. A: _____ _____ _____ this riddle.

2. B: Sure.

3. A: Four people _____ _____ one umbrella, but nobody _____ _____. Can you _____ _____?

4. B: Yes! It's _____ it's _____ _____ _____!

1. A: 이 수수께끼를 풀어봐.
2. B: 그래.
3. A: 4명의 사람들이 하나의 우산 아래 있는데 아무도 젖지 않아. 이유를 설명할 수 있겠니?
4. B: 응! 왜냐하면 맑은 날이기 때문이야.

Let's Write

1. _____ was _____ Sunday.

2. Dohun was _____ _____.

3. _____, he _____ _____ _____ in the next room.

4. When he _____ _____ the room, the window _____ _____.

5. When he _____ _____, Sujin _____ _____ a baseball bat and Ted _____ _____ a ball to his dog.

6. Who _____ the window?

7. How _____ it be _____?

1. 지난 일요일이었다.
2. 도훈이는 집에 있었다.
3. 갑자기, 그는 옆방에서 나는 어떤 소리를 들었다.
4. 그가 그 방으로 갔을 때, 창문이 깨져 있었다.
5. 도훈이가 밖을 보았을 때, 수진이는 야구 방망이를 들고 있었고 Ted는 그의 개에게 공을 던지고 있었다.
6. 누가 창문을 깼을까?
7. 그것은 어떻게 설명될 수 있을까?

Culture & Life

1. This is the _____ _____ of the Sphinx.

2. Oedipus _____ _____ _____ it to _____ _____ Thebes.

3. This is the question _____ the Sphinx _____ _____.

4. _____ creature _____ _____ _____ _____ _____ in the morning, two legs in the afternoon, and three legs in the evening?

1. 이것은 스핑크스의 유명한 수수께끼이다.
2. 오이디푸스는 Thebes에 들어가기 위해 그것을 풀어야 한다.
3. 이것은 스핑크스가 그에게 묻는 질문이다.
4. 어느 생명체가 아침에는 네 다리로 걷고, 오후에는 두 다리로 걷고, 저녁에는 세 다리로 걷는가?

※ 다음 우리말을 영어로 쓰시오.

Listen and Speak 1-C

1. A: 이 수수께끼를 풀어봐.

    ➡ _____

2. B: 그래.

    ➡ _____

3. A: 4명의 사람들이 하나의 우산 아래 있는데 아무도 젖지 않아. 이유를 설명할 수 있겠니?

    ➡ _____

4. B: 응! 왜냐하면 맑은 날이기 때문이야.

    ➡ _____

Let's Write

1. 지난 일요일이었다.

    ➡ _____

2. 도훈이는 집에 있었다.

    ➡ _____

3. 갑자기, 그는 옆방에서 나는 어떤 소리를 들었다.

    ➡ _____

4. 그가 그 방으로 갔을 때, 창문이 깨져 있었다.

    ➡ _____

5. 도훈가 밖을 보았을 때, 수진이는 야구 방망이를 들고 있었고 Ted는 그의 개에게 공을 던지고 있었다.

    ➡ _____

6. 누가 창문을 깼을까?

    ➡ _____

7. 그것은 어떻게 설명될 수 있을까?

    ➡ _____

Culture & Life

1. 이것은 스핑크스의 유명한 수수께끼이다.

    ➡ _____

2. 오이디푸스는 Thebes에 들어가기 위해 그것을 풀어야 한다.

    ➡ _____

3. 이것은 스핑크스가 그에게 묻는 질문이다.

    ➡ _____

4. 어느 생명체가 아침에는 네 다리로 걷고, 오후에는 두 다리로 걷고, 저녁에는 세 다리로 걷는가?

    ➡ _____

    _____

※ 다음 영어를 우리말로 쓰시오.

01 between _____

02 character _____

03 strength _____

04 brave _____

05 through _____

06 bright _____

07 powerful _____

08 enemy _____

09 express _____

10 fight _____

11 fan _____

12 hide _____

13 cheer _____

14 scared _____

15 communicate _____

16 behind _____

17 scary _____

18 hold _____

19 popular _____

20 costume _____

21 interestingly _____

22 female _____

23 windy _____

24 traditional _____

25 nowadays _____

26 opinion _____

27 originally _____

28 male _____

29 perform _____

30 comfortable _____

31 totally _____

32 wild _____

33 couple _____

34 gracefully _____

35 in my opinion _____

36 be allowed to _____

37 take a look _____

38 give up on _____

39 on time _____

40 try one's best _____

41 look like _____

42 make a sound _____

43 keep up the good work _____

※ 다음 우리말을 영어로 쓰시오.

01 등장인물 _____

02 암컷의, 여성의 _____

03 인기 있는 _____

04 용감한 _____

05 의사소통하다 _____

06 (색상이) 밝은 _____

07 적 _____

08 표현하다 _____

09 부채 _____

10 확실한 _____

11 야생의 _____

12 두 사람, 남녀 _____

13 전통적인 _____

14 ～ 사이에 _____

15 바람이 많이 부는 _____

16 우아하게 _____

17 의상, 복장 _____

18 ～ 뒤에 _____

19 흥미 있게도 _____

20 ～을 통해 _____

21 수컷의, 남성의 _____

22 완전히 _____

23 오늘날에는 _____

24 무서운 _____

25 의견 _____

26 숨다 _____

27 원래, 본래 _____

28 움직임, 동작 _____

29 공연하다 _____

30 싸움, 다툼 _____

31 강한, 힘 있는 _____

32 응원하다 _____

33 편안한 _____

34 힘 _____

35 살펴보다 _____

36 최선을 다하다 _____

37 내 의견으로는 _____

38 ～을 포기하다 _____

39 정시에 _____

40 소리를 내다 _____

41 ～처럼 들리다, ～일 것 같다 _____

42 ～을 잘하다 _____

43 ～이 허용되다 _____

※ 다음 영영풀이에 알맞은 단어를 <보기>에서 골라 쓴 후, 우리말 뜻을 쓰시오.

1 _____ : liked by a lot of people: _____

2 _____ : at or towards the back of a thing or person: _____

3 _____ : an act of moving: _____

4 _____ : to stop holding or carrying something so that it falls: _____

5 _____ : living in a natural state, not changed or controlled by people: _____

6 _____ : the physical power and energy that makes someone strong: _____

7 _____ : dealing with danger, pain, or difficult situations with courage and
    confidence: _____

8 _____ : a flat object that you wave with your hand which makes the air cooler:
    _____

9 _____ : in the beginning, before other things happened or before things changed:
    _____

10 _____ : to put or keep someone or something in a place where they/it cannot be
    seen or found: _____

11 _____ : to tell or show what you are feeling or thinking by using words, looks, or
    action: _____

12 _____ : an area of land in the country, especially one where crops are grown or
    animals feed on grass: _____

13 _____ : to do something to entertain people, for example by acting a play or
    playing a piece of music: _____

14 _____ : a particular type of clothing worn by all the members of a group or
    organization such as the police, the army, etc.: _____

15 _____ : to shout as a way of showing happiness, praise, approval, or support of
    someone or something: _____

16 _____ : making you feel physically relaxed, without any pain or without being
    too hot, cold, etc.: _____

보기			
cheer	comfortable	popular	strength
originally	behind	express	field
drop	wild	brave	hide
uniform	fan	movement	perform

※ 다음 우리말과 일치하도록 빈칸에 알맞은 말을 쓰시오.

Listen & Speak 1 A-1

Jane: Minsu, _____ do you _____ _____ that _____?

Minsu: Umm … The people _____ _____ they're _____.

Jane: I agree. _____ _____ _____, the dancing boy really

_____ _____.

Listen & Speak 1 A-2

Brian: Jimin, _____ do you think _____ _____ _____?

Jimin: In my opinion, it's _____. I _____ _____ I _____

_____ it.

Brian: _____, _____. The dancers in the painting _____ _____.

Listen & Speak 1 B

Emily: Hojun, did you know that _____ _____ _____ _____?

Hojun: No. _____ do they _____?

Emily: They dance _____ _____ their _____ to _____

_____.

Hojun: That's interesting. Do you know _____ _____ _____

that can dance?

Emily: Yes, some _____ dance to show _____ _____ _____

_____.

Hojun: That's cool! In my opinion, dancing is a great _____

_____ _____.

Emily: I _____ _____ _____ _____.

Listen & Speak 2 A-1

Minji: I use _____ _____ to make music. _____ _____ my

music. My voice is _____ and _____. I'm _____ you will

like it.

Jimin: I move _____ _____ _____ _____ _____ my feelings. Look

at my _____. _____ you jump _____ me? I'm

_____ you'll _____ _____.

Sujin: I use my hands to _____ _____. Come and listen to my

music. I'm sure you'll want to _____ when you listen to it.

해석

Jane: 민수야, 저 그림에 대해 어떻게 생각해?

Minsu: 음… 사람들이 재미있게 노는 것처럼 보여.

Jane: 나도 동의해. 내 의견으로는, 춤추는 소년이 춤추는 것을 정말로 즐기는 것 같아.

Brian: 지민아, 이 그림에 대해 어떻게 생각해?

Jimin: 내 의견으로는 흥미로워. 처음 이것을 봤을 때 난 미소 지었어.

Brian: 나도 그래. 그림 속 춤추는 사람들은 행복해 보여.

Emily: 호준아, 너는 일부 수컷 새들이 춤을 춘다는 것을 알고 있었니?

Hojun: 아니. 왜 춤을 추지?

Emily: 그들은 암컷 새들에게 그들의 사랑을 보여주기 위해 춤을 춰.

Hojun: 그거 흥미로운 걸. 춤을 출 수 있는 또 다른 동물들을 알고 있니?

Emily: 응, 일부 벌들은 먹이를 찾을 수 있는 곳을 보여주기 위해 춤을 춰.

Hojun: 멋지다! 내 의견으로는, 춤을 추는 것은 의사소통을 위한 굉장한 방법인 것 같아.

Emily: 전적으로 너에게 동의해.

Minji: 나는 음악을 만들기 위해 내 목소리를 사용합니다. 내 음악을 들어보세요. 내 목소리는 부드럽고 멋지죠. 나는 당신이 그것을 좋아할 거라고 확신해요.

Jimin: 나는 내 감정을 표현하기 위해 내 몸을 움직입니다. 내 동작을 보세요. 나처럼 뛰어올라 보는 게 어때요? 나는 당신이 멋진 기분이 들 거라고 확신해요.

Sujin: 나는 소리를 만들기 위해 내 손을 사용합니다. 와서 내 음악을 들어 보세요. 나는 당신이 이것을 들을 때 춤을 추고 싶을 거라고 확신해요

Listen & Speak 2 B

Tom: _____ are you _____, Kelly?

Kelly: I'm reading a _____ _____ Michaela DePrince.

Tom: Michaela DePrince? Can you _____ me _____ about her?

Kelly: Sure. Michaela _____ her parents _____ she was three. _____ _____, she had a lot of _____. But she never _____ _____ _____ her dream of becoming a dancer.

Tom: Wow, she _____ very _____ _____ _____ a good dancer. Kelly, you also have a dream _____ _____ a dancer, _____?

Kelly: Yes. I will _____ _____ _____ to be a great dancer like her.

Tom: _____ _____ the good _____. I'm _____ you can _____ _____.

Real Life Communication

Junsu: You know _____? The school dance contest _____ _____ _____ soon.

Emily: That's right. I heard Jimin's class is going to _____ a taekwondo dance and Tim's class is going to do a K-pop dance.

Brian: We should also _____ _____ _____ _____.

Mina: _____ _____ a Buchaechum? In my _____, it is _____ _____ _____, and it's also _____.

Emily: That _____ _____ a good idea. But who will teach us?

Brian: Mina _____ _____ _____ traditional dances. Can you help us, Mina?

Mina: Of course, I will. _____ _____ we'll have a lot of fun.

Junsu: Great. Let's _____ _____ _____ _____.

Let's Check

Jenny: Look at the _____ _____, Dongjun. Aren't they _____?

Dongjun: Girls? I can _____ _____ one dancer.

Jenny: _____ _____ _____. Do you see many arms _____ her?

Dongjun: Wow. I _____ _____ that there were _____ _____ _____.

Jenny: That's _____. _____ _____ there are _____ 10 dancers.

Tom: 무엇을 읽고 있니, Kelly?

Kelly: Michaela DePrince에 대한 이야기를 읽고 있어.

Tom: Michaela DePrince? 그녀에 대해 좀 더 얘기해 줄 수 있니?

Kelly: 그래. Michaela는 세 살 때 부모를 잃었어. 그 후 그녀는 많은 역경을 겪었지. 그러나 그녀는 무용수가 되겠다는 꿈을 절대 포기하지 않았어.

Tom: 와, 그녀는 훌륭한 무용수가 되기 위해 굉장히 열심히 노력했구나. Kelly, 너도 무용수가 되려는 꿈이 있지, 그렇지?

Kelly: 응. 그녀처럼 멋진 무용수가 되기 위해 최선을 다할 거야.

Tom: 계속 노력해 봐. 난 네가 해낼 거라고 확신해.

Junsu: 있잖아. 학교 춤 경연 대회가 곧 열릴 거야.

Emily: 맞아. 지민이네 반은 태권도 춤을 공연하고, Tim네 반은 K-pop 춤을 출 거라고 들었어.

Brian: 우리도 무엇을 할지 결정해야 해.

Mina: 부채춤은 어때? 내 의견으로는, 그것은 배우기 쉽고 또한 아름다워.

Emily: 좋은 생각인 것 같아. 하지만 누가 우리를 가르치지?

Brian: 미나가 전통 춤을 잘 춰. 우리를 도울 수 있니, 미나야?

Mina: 물론, 그럴 거야. 우리는 매우 즐거울 거라고 확신해.

Junsu: 아주 좋아. 시도해 보자.

Jenny: 춤추는 여자들을 봐, 동준아. 대단하지 않니?

Donjun: 여자들? 난 단지 한 명의 무용수만 보이는 걸.

Jenny: 좀 더 가까이 봐. 그녀 뒤에 많은 팔들이 보이니?

Donjun: 와. 그녀 뒤에 다른 무용수들이 있는지 몰랐어.

Jenny: 맞아. 나는 10명 이상의 무용수들이 있다고 확신해.

※ 다음 우리말에 맞도록 대화를 영어로 쓰시오.

Listen & Speak 1 A-1

Jane: _____

Minsu: _____

Jane: _____

Listen & Speak 1 A-2

Brian: _____

Jimin: _____

Brian: _____

Listen & Speak 1 B

Emily: _____

Hojun: _____

Emily: _____

Hojun: _____

Emily: _____

Hojun: _____

Emily: _____

Listen & Speak 2 A-1

Minji: _____

_____

Jimin: _____

_____

Sujin: _____

_____

해석

Jane: 민수야, 저 그림에 대해 어떻게 생각해?
Minsu: 음… 사람들이 재미있게 노는 것처럼 보여.
Jane: 나도 동의해. 내 의견으로는, 춤추는 소년이 춤추는 것을 정말로 즐기는 것 같아.

Brian: 지민아, 이 그림에 대해 어떻게 생각해?
Jimin: 내 의견으로는 흥미로워. 처음 이것을 봤을 때 난 미소 지었어.
Brian: 나도 그래. 그림 속 춤추는 사람들은 행복해 보여.

Emily: 호준아, 너는 일부 수컷 새들이 춤을 춘다는 것을 알고 있었니?
Hojun: 아니. 왜 춤을 추지?
Emily: 그들은 암컷 새들에게 그들의 사랑을 보여주기 위해 춤을 춰.
Hojun: 그거 흥미로운 걸. 춤을 출 수 있는 또 다른 동물들을 알고 있니?
Emily: 응, 일부 벌들은 먹이를 찾을 수 있는 곳을 보여주기 위해 춤을 춰.
Hojun: 멋지다! 내 의견으로는, 춤을 추는 것은 의사소통을 위한 굉장한 방법인 것 같아.
Emily: 전적으로 너에게 동의해.

Minji: 나는 음악을 만들기 위해 내 목소리를 사용합니다. 내 음악을 들어보세요. 내 목소리는 부드럽고 멋지죠. 나는 당신이 그것을 좋아할 거라고 확신해요.
Jimin: 나는 내 감정을 표현하기 위해 내 몸을 움직입니다. 내 동작을 보세요. 나처럼 뛰어올라 보는 게 어때요? 나는 당신이 멋진 기분이 들 거라고 확신해요.
Sujin: 나는 소리를 만들기 위해 내 손을 사용합니다. 와서 내 음악을 들어 보세요. 나는 당신이 이것을 들을 때 춤을 추고 싶을 거라고 확신해요.

Listen & Speak 2 B

Tom: _____

Kelly: _____

Tom: _____

Kelly: _____

_____

Tom: _____

_____

Kelly: _____

Tom: _____

Real Life Communication

Junsu: _____

Emily: _____

_____

Brian: _____

Mina _____

Emily: _____

Brian: _____

Mina: _____

Junsu: _____

Let's Check

Jenny: _____

Dongjun: _____

Jenny: _____

Dongjun: _____

Jenny: _____

Tom: 무엇을 읽고 있니, Kelly?

Kelly: Michaela DePrince에 대한 이 야기를 읽고 있어.

Tom: Michaela DePrince? 그녀에 대 해 좀 더 얘기해 줄 수 있니?

Kelly: 그래. Michaela는 세 살 때 부모 를 잃었어. 그 후 그녀는 많은 역 경을 겪었지. 그러나 그녀는 무용 수가 되겠다는 꿈을 절대 포기하 지 않았어.

Tom: 와, 그녀는 훌륭한 무용수가 되기 위해 굉장히 열심히 노력했구나. Kelly, 너도 무용수가 되려는 꿈이 있지, 그렇지?

Kelly: 응. 그녀처럼 멋진 무용수가 되 기 위해 최선을 다할 거야.

Tom: 계속 노력해 봐. 난 네가 해낼 거 라고 확신해.

Junsu: 있잖아. 학교 춤 경연 대회가 곧 열릴 거야.

Emily: 맞아. 지민이네 반은 태권도 춤 을 공연하고, Tim네 반은 K-pop 춤을 출 거라고 들었어.

Brian: 우리도 무엇을 할지 결정해야 해.

Mina: 부채춤은 어때? 내 의견으로는, 그것은 배우기 쉽고 또한 아름다 워.

Emily: 좋은 생각인 것 같아. 하지만 누 가 우리를 가르치지?

Brian: 미나가 전통 춤을 잘 춰. 우리를 도울 수 있니, 미나야?

Mina: 물론, 그럴 거야. 우리는 매우 즐 거울 거라고 확신해.

Junsu: 아주 좋아. 시도해 보자.

Jenny: 춤추는 여자들을 봐, 동준아. 대 단하지 않니?

Donjun: 여자들? 난 단지 한 명의 무용 수만 보이는 걸.

Jenny: 좀 더 가까이 봐. 그녀 뒤에 많 은 팔들이 보이니?

Donjun: 와. 그녀 뒤에 다른 무용수들 이 있는지 몰랐어.

Jenny: 맞아. 나는 10명 이상의 무용수 들이 있다고 확신해.

※ 다음 우리말과 일치하도록 빈칸에 알맞은 것을 골라 쓰시오.

Dance with a Story

1 _____ do people _____?
A. dance   B. why

2 They dance to _____ feelings, give _____ to others, or
_____ _____.
A. enjoy   B. express   C. themselves   D. happiness

3 Let's _____ a look at _____ _____ of dance _____
the world.
A. kinds   B. take   C. around   D. different

India: *Kathakali*

4 *Kathakali* _____ a _____.
A. story   B. tells

5 The dancers tell _____ _____ their _____ _____.
A. body   B. stories   C. movements   D. through

6 These stories are usually about a _____ between _____
and _____.
A. good   B. fight   C. evil

7 Dancers who are _____ good _____ paint their faces
_____.
A. green   B. playing   C. characters

8 Those who are playing _____ characters _____ black
_____.
A. wear   B. evil   C. make-up

9 _____, in *Kathakali*, only men are _____ _____ dance.
A. allowed   B. interestingly   C. to

10 The body _____ are so _____ that the dancers need to
_____ for many years.
A. train   B. powerful   C. movements

New Zealand: *Haka*

11 _____ people _____ New Zealand, they _____ _____
a group of *haka* dancers.
A. may   B. visit   C. when   D. meet

12 The dancers _____ this _____ dance with _____ faces.
A. traditional   B. perform   C. scary

이야기가 있는 춤

1 사람들은 왜 춤을 추는 걸까요?

2 사람들은 감정을 표현하고, 다른 사람들에게 행복감을 주거나 스스로 즐기기 위해 춤을 춥니다.

3 세계의 여러 가지 춤을 살펴봅시다.

인도: *Kathakali*

4 *Kathakali*에는 이야기가 있습니다.

5 춤꾼들은 몸동작을 통해 이야기합니다.

6 이러한 이야기들은 대개 선과 악의 싸움에 관한 것입니다.

7 선한 역할을 맡은 춤꾼들은 자신의 얼굴을 초록색으로 칠합니다.

8 악한 역할을 맡은 춤꾼들은 검은색 화장을 합니다.

9 재미있는 것은 *Kathakali* 춤에서 남자들만 춤추는 것이 허락된다는 사실입니다.

10 몸동작이 매우 힘이 넘쳐서 춤꾼들은 수년 동안 연습을 해야 합니다.

뉴질랜드: *Haka*

11 사람들이 뉴질랜드를 방문할 때, 그들은 *haka* 춤꾼들의 무리를 만날지도 모릅니다.

12 그 춤꾼들은 무서운 얼굴로 이 전통 춤을 춥니다.

13 This dance was _____ _____ by the Maori before a _____.

    A. performed   B. fight   C. originally

14 They wanted to _____ their _____ to the _____.

    A. enemy   B. show   C. strength

15 The dancers _____ as _____ _____ wild animals _____ fighting.

    A. before   B. scary   C. looked   D. as

16 _____, in New Zealand, rugby players usually _____ a *haka* before a game to _____ their strength to the _____ team.

    A. perform   B. nowadays   C. other   D. show

Korea: *Buchaechum*

17 *Buchaechum* is a _____ Korean _____ _____.

    A. fan   B. traditional   C. dance

18 The dancers _____ _____ *hanbok*.

    A. colorful   B. wear

19 They dance _____ large fans that are _____ in _____ colors.

    A. bright   B. with   C. painted

20 The dancers _____ the fans _____ to show _____ kinds of _____.

    A. gracefully   B. beauty   C. move   D. different

21 Their _____ look _____ _____ as flowers or _____ birds.

    A. as   B. flying   C. beautiful   D. movements

22 In Korea, *Buchaechum* is _____ _____ _____ people can see it in many _____ festivals.

    A. that   B. popular   C. so   D. traditional

13 이 춤은 원래 마오리족에 의해 싸움 전에 행해졌습니다.

14 그들은 적에게 그들의 힘을 보여 주고 싶었습니다.

15 춤꾼들은 싸움하기 전의 야생 동물들만큼 무섭게 보였습니다.

16 요즈음, 뉴질랜드에서는 럭비 선수들이 다른 팀에게 그들의 힘을 보여 주기 위해 게임 전에 주로 *haka*를 보여 줍니다.

한국: 부채춤

17 부채춤은 한국 전통 부채춤입니다.

18 춤꾼들은 다채로운 한복을 입습니다.

19 그들은 밝은 색으로 칠해진 커다란 부채를 가지고 춤을 춥니다.

20 그 춤꾼들은 다양한 종류의 미를 보여 주기 위해 부채를 우아하게 움직입니다.

21 그들의 움직임은 꽃 또는 날아다니는 새들처럼 우아하게 보입니다.

22 한국에서, 부채춤은 너무 인기가 있어서 사람들은 많은 전통 축제에서 그것을 볼 수 있습니다.

※ 다음 우리말과 일치하도록 빈칸에 알맞은 말을 쓰시오.

Dance with a Story

1 _____ do people _____?

2 They dance _____ _____ _____, give happiness _____ _____, or _____ _____.

3 _____ _____ a look at _____ _____ _____ around the world

India: *Kathakali*

4 *Kathakali* _____ a _____.

5 The dancers tell _____ _____ their _____ _____.

6 These stories are usually about _____ _____ _____ _____ _____ _____.

7 Dancers _____ _____ _____ _____ _____ paint their faces _____.

8 Those _____ _____ _____ evil characters _____ _____ _____.

9 _____, in *Kathakali*, only men _____ _____ _____ _____.

10 The body movements are _____ _____ _____ the dancers _____ _____ train _____ many years.

New Zealand: *Haka*

11 When people visit New Zealand, they _____ a group of _____ _____.

12 The dancers _____ this _____ dance _____ _____.

이야기가 있는 춤

1 사람들은 왜 춤을 추는 걸까요?

2 사람들은 감정을 표현하고, 다른 사람들에게 행복감을 주거나 스스로 즐기기 위해 춤을 춥니다.

3 세계의 여러 가지 춤을 살펴봅시다.

인도: *Kathakali*

4 *Kathakali*에는 이야기가 있습니다.

5 춤꾼들은 몸동작을 통해 이야기합니다.

6 이러한 이야기들은 대개 선과 악의 싸움에 관한 것입니다.

7 선한 역할을 맡은 춤꾼들은 자신의 얼굴을 초록색으로 칠합니다.

8 악한 역할을 맡은 춤꾼들은 검은색 화장을 합니다.

9 재미있는 것은 *Kathakali* 춤에서 남자들만 춤추는 것이 허락된다는 사실입니다.

10 몸동작이 매우 힘이 넘쳐서 춤꾼들은 수년 동안 연습을 해야 합니다.

뉴질랜드: *Haka*

11 사람들이 뉴질랜드를 방문할 때, 그들은 *haka* 춤꾼들의 무리를 만날지도 모릅니다.

12 그 춤꾼들은 무서운 얼굴로 이 전통 춤을 춥니다.

13 This dance was _____ _____ _____ the Maori before a _____.

14 They wanted _____ _____ _____ _____ to the _____.

15 The dancers _____ _____ _____ _____ wild animals _____ _____.

16 _____, in New Zealand, rugby players _____ _____ a *haka* before a game _____ _____ their strength _____ _____ _____ _____.

Korea: *Buchaechum*

17 *Buchaechum* is a _____ _____ _____ _____.

18 The dancers _____ _____ _____.

19 They dance _____ large fans _____ _____ _____ in bright colors.

20 The dancers _____ the fans _____ to show _____ _____ _____ _____.

21 Their movements _____ _____ _____ _____ flowers or _____ _____.

22 In Korea, *Buchaechum* is _____ _____ _____ people _____ _____ _____ in many traditional festivals.

13 이 춤은 원래 마오리족에 의해 싸움 전에 행해졌습니다.

14 그들은 적에게 그들의 힘을 보여 주고 싶었습니다.

15 춤꾼들은 싸움하기 전의 야생 동물들만큼 무섭게 보였습니다.

16 요즈음, 뉴질랜드에서는 럭비 선수들이 다른 팀에게 그들의 힘을 보여 주기 위해 게임 전에 주로 *haka*를 보여 줍니다.

한국: 부채춤

17 부채춤은 한국 전통 부채춤입니다.

18 춤꾼들은 다채로운 한복을 입습니다.

19 그들은 밝은 색으로 칠해진 커다란 부채를 가지고 춤을 춥니다.

20 그 춤꾼들은 다양한 종류의 미를 보여 주기 위해 부채를 우아하게 움직입니다.

21 그들의 움직임은 꽃 또는 날아다니는 새들처럼 우아하게 보입니다.

22 한국에서, 부채춤은 너무 인기가 있어서 사람들은 많은 전통 축제에서 그것을 볼 수 있습니다.

※ 다음 문장을 우리말로 쓰시오.

Dance with a Story

1 Why do people dance?

➡ _____

2 They dance to express feelings, give happiness to others, or enjoy themselves.

➡ _____

3 Let's take a look at different kinds of dance around the world.

➡ _____

India: *Kathakali*

4 *Kathakali* tells a story.

➡ _____

5 The dancers tell stories through their body movements.

➡ _____

6 These stories are usually about a fight between good and evil.

➡ _____

7 Dancers who are playing good characters paint their faces green.

➡ _____

8 Those who are playing evil characters wear black make-up.

➡ _____

9 Interestingly, in *Kathakali*, only men are allowed to dance.

➡ _____

10 The body movements are so powerful that the dancers need to train for many years.

➡ _____

New Zealand: *Haka*

11 When people visit New Zealand, they may meet a group of haka dancers.

➡ _____

12 The dancers perform this traditional dance with scary faces.

➡ _____

13 This dance was originally performed by the Maori before a fight.

➡ _____

14 They wanted to show their strength to the enemy.

➡ _____

15 The dancers looked as scary as wild animals before fighting.

➡ _____

16 Nowadays, in New Zealand, rugby players usually perform a *haka* before a game to show their strength to the other team.

➡ _____

Korea: *Buchaechum*

17 *Buchaechum* is a traditional Korean fan dance.

➡ _____

18 The dancers wear colorful *hanbok*.

➡ _____

19 They dance with large fans that are painted in bright colors.

➡ _____

20 The dancers move the fans gracefully to show different kinds of beauty.

➡ _____

21 Their movements look as beautiful as flowers or flying birds.

➡ _____

22 In Korea, *Buchaechum* is so popular that people can see it in many traditional festivals.

➡ _____

※ 다음 괄호 안의 단어들을 우리말에 맞도록 바르게 배열하시오.

Dance with a Story

1 (do / why / dance? / people)
➡ _____

2 (dance / they / express / to / feelings, / happiness / give / others, / to / or / themselves. / enjoy)
➡ _____
_____

3 (take / let's / look / a / different / at / kinds / dance / of / around / world. / the)
➡ _____

India: *Kathakali*

4 (tells / *Kathakali* / story. / a)
➡ _____

5 (dancers / the / stories / tell / through / body / their / movements.)
➡ _____

6 (stories / these / are / about / usually / fight / a / between / evil. / and / good)
➡ _____

7 (who / dancers / are / good / playing / characters / their / paint / green. / faces)
➡ _____

8 (those / are / who / playing / evil / wear / characters / make-up. / black)
➡ _____

9 (in / interestingly, / *Kathakali*, / men / only / allowed / are / dance. / to)
➡ _____

10 (body / the / are / movements / so / that / powerful / dancers / the / to / need / train / many / for / years.)
➡ _____
_____

New Zealand: *Haka*

11 (people / when / New / visit / Zealand, / may / they / meet / a / *haka* / of / group / dancers.)
➡ _____

12 (dancers / the / this / perform / traditional / with / dance / faces. / scary)
➡ _____

이야기가 있는 춤

1 사람들은 왜 춤을 추는 걸까요?

2 사람들은 감정을 표현하고, 다른 사람들에게 행복감을 주거나 스스로 즐기기 위해 춤을 춥니다.

3 세계의 여러 가지 춤을 살펴봅시다.

인도: *Kathakali*

4 *Kathakali*에는 이야기가 있습니다.

5 춤꾼들은 몸동작을 통해 이야기합니다.

6 이러한 이야기들은 대개 선과 악의 싸움에 관한 것입니다.

7 선한 역할을 맡은 춤꾼들은 자신의 얼굴을 초록색으로 칠합니다.

8 악한 역할을 맡은 춤꾼들은 검은색 화장을 합니다.

9 재미있는 것은 *Kathakali* 춤에서 남자들만 춤추는 것이 허락된다는 사실입니다.

10 몸동작이 매우 힘이 넘쳐서 춤꾼들은 수년 동안 연습을 해야 합니다.

뉴질랜드: *Haka*

11 사람들이 뉴질랜드를 방문할 때, 그들은 *haka* 춤꾼들의 무리를 만날지도 모릅니다.

12 그 춤꾼들은 무서운 얼굴로 이 전통 춤을 춥니다.

13 (dance / this / originally / was / by / performed / the / before / Maori / fight. / a)

➡ _____

14 (wanted / they / show / to / strength / their / to / enemy. / the)

➡ _____

15 (dancers / the / as / looked / scary / as / animals / wild / fighting. / before)

➡ _____

16 (in / nowadays, / Zealand, / New / players / rugby / perform / usually / *haka* / a / before / game / a / show / to / strength / their / the / to / team. / other)

➡ _____

Korea: *Buchaechum*

17 (is / *Buchaechum* / a / Korean / traditional / dance. / fan)

➡ _____

18 (dancers / the / colorful / wear / *hanbok*.)

➡ _____

19 (dance / they / large / with / that / fans / are / in / printed / colors. / bright)

➡ _____

20 (dancers / the / move / fans / the / to / gracefully / show / kinds / different / beauty. / of)

➡ _____

21 (movements / their / as / look / beautiful / flowers / as / birds. / or / flying)

➡ _____

22 (Korea, / in / *Buchaechum* / so / is / popular / people / that / see / can / in / many / it / festivals. / traditional)

➡ _____

13 이 춤은 원래 마오리족에 의해 싸움 전에 행해졌습니다.

14 그들은 적에게 그들의 힘을 보여 주고 싶었습니다.

15 춤꾼들은 싸움하기 전의 야생 동물들만큼 무섭게 보였습니다.

16 요즘, 뉴질랜드에서는 럭비 선수들이 다른 팀에게 그들의 힘을 보여 주기 위해 게임 전에 주로 *haka*를 보여 줍니다.

한국: 부채춤

17 부채춤은 한국 전통 부채춤입니다.

18 춤꾼들은 다채로운 한복을 입습니다.

19 그들은 밝은 색으로 칠해진 커다란 부채를 가지고 춤을 춥니다.

20 그 춤꾼들은 다양한 종류의 미를 보여 주기 위해 부채를 우아하게 움직입니다.

21 그들의 움직임은 꽃 또는 날아다니는 새들처럼 우아하게 보입니다.

22 한국에서, 부채춤은 너무 인기가 있어서 사람들은 많은 전통 축제에서 그것을 볼 수 있습니다.

※ 다음 우리말을 영어로 쓰시오.

Dance with a Story

1 ▶ 사람들은 왜 춤을 추는 걸까요?

➡ _____

2 ▶ 사람들은 감정을 표현하고, 다른 사람들에게 행복감을 주거나 스스로 즐기기 위해 춤을 춥니다.

➡ _____

3 ▶ 세계의 여러 가지 춤을 살펴봅시다.

➡ _____

India: _Kathakali_

4 ▶ _Kathakali_에는 이야기가 있습니다.

➡ _____

5 ▶ 춤꾼들은 몸동작을 통해 이야기합니다.

➡ _____

6 ▶ 이러한 이야기들은 대개 선과 악의 싸움에 관한 것입니다.

➡ _____

7 ▶ 선한 역할을 맡은 춤꾼들은 자신의 얼굴을 초록색으로 칠합니다.

➡ _____

8 ▶ 악한 역할을 맡은 춤꾼들은 검은색 화장을 합니다.

➡ _____

9 ▶ 재미있는 것은 _Kathakali_ 춤에서 남자들만 춤추는 것이 허락된다는 사실입니다.

➡ _____

10 ▶ 몸동작이 매우 힘이 넘쳐서 춤꾼들은 수년 동안 연습을 해야 합니다.

➡ _____

New Zealand: _Haka_

11 ▶ 사람들이 뉴질랜드를 방문할 때, 그들은 _haka_ 춤꾼들의 무리를 만날지도 모릅니다.

➡ _____

12 ▶ 그 춤꾼들은 무서운 얼굴로 이 전통 춤을 춥니다.

➡ _____

13 이 춤은 원래 마오리족에 의해 싸움 전에 행해졌습니다.

➡ _____

14 그들은 적에게 그들의 힘을 보여 주고 싶었습니다.

➡ _____

15 그 춤꾼들은 싸움하기 전의 야생 동물들만큼 무섭게 보였습니다.

➡ _____

16 요즈음, 뉴질랜드에서는 럭비 선수들이 다른 팀에게 그들의 힘을 보여 주기 위해 게임 전에 주로 *haka*를 보여 줍니다.

➡ _____
_____

Korea: *Buchaechum*

17 부채춤은 한국 전통 부채춤입니다.

➡ _____

18 춤꾼들은 다채로운 한복을 입습니다.

➡ _____

19 그들은 밝은 색으로 칠해진 커다란 부채를 가지고 춤을 춥니다.

➡ _____

20 그 춤꾼들은 다양한 종류의 미를 보여 주기 위해 부채를 우아하게 움직입니다.

➡ _____

21 그들의 움직임은 꽃 또는 날아다니는 새들처럼 우아하게 보입니다.

➡ _____

22 한국에서, 부채춤은 너무 인기가 있어서 사람들은 많은 전통 축제에서 그것을 볼 수 있습니다.

➡ _____

※ 다음 우리말과 일치하도록 빈칸에 알맞은 말을 쓰시오.

Listen and Speak 2 - C

1. A: I'm _____ _____ a _____ _____ in our town next week. Do you _____ _____ _____ me?

2. B: _____ interesting.

3. A: We can _____ _____ from many countries. I'm _____ we'll have _____ _____ _____ _____.

1. A: 나는 다음 주말에 우리 마을에서 열리는 문화 행사에 갈 거야. 나와 같이 갈래?
2. B: 재미있겠다.
3. A: 우리는 많은 국가에서 온 춤들을 즐길 수 있어. 우리는 매우 즐거울 거라고 확신해.

Culture & Life

1. *Tarantella*, _____

2. _____ _____ _____, people danced the *tarantella* for _____ _____.

3. _____, it is a _____ _____.

4. People dance the *tarantella* _____ happy days _____ _____ _____.

1. Tarantella – 이탈리아
2. 과거에, 사람들은 아픈 사람들을 위해 tarantella를 추었다.
3. 요즈음, 이 춤은 커플 춤이다.
4. 사람들은 결혼식 같은 행복한 날에 tarantella를 춘다.

Culture & Life

1. *Adumu*, _____

2. This dance _____ _____ before a _____.

3. It _____ _____ _____ a jumping dance.

4. Dancers _____ _____ in the air.

5. _____ a dancer jumps, other dancers _____ him _____ with _____ _____.

1. Adumu – 케냐
2. 이 춤은 전투하기 전에 춘다.
3. 이것은 점핑 댄스라고도 불린다.
4. 춤꾼들은 공중에 높이 뛰어오른다.
5. 한 춤꾼이 점프하면, 다른 사람들은 큰 소리를 내며 그를 응원한다.

※ **다음 우리말을 영어로 쓰시오.**

Listen and Speak 2 - C

1. A: 나는 다음 주말에 우리 마을에서 열리는 문화 행사에 갈 거야. 나와 같이 갈래?
   ➡ _____

2. B: 재미있겠다.
   ➡ _____

3. A: 우리는 많은 국가에서 온 춤들을 즐길 수 있어. 우리는 매우 즐거울 거라고 확신해.
   ➡ _____

Culture & Life

1. Tarantella – 이탈리아
   ➡ _____

2. 과거에, 사람들은 아픈 사람들을 위해 tarantella를 추었다.
   ➡ _____

3. 요즈음, 이 춤은 커플 춤이다.
   ➡ _____

4. 사람들은 결혼식 같은 행복한 날에 tarantella를 춘다.
   ➡ _____

Culture & Life

1. Adumu – 케냐
   ➡ _____

2. 이 춤은 전투하기 전에 춘다.
   ➡ _____

3. 이것은 점핑 댄스라고도 불린다.
   ➡ _____

4. 춤꾼들은 공중에 높이 뛰어오른다.
   ➡ _____

5. 한 춤꾼이 점프하면, 다른 사람들은 큰 소리를 내며 그를 응원한다.
   ➡ _____

※ 다음 영어를 우리말로 쓰시오.

01 flavor

02 safe

03 difference

04 escape

05 fill

06 freezer

07 instead

08 sink

09 float

10 lightning

11 pressure

12 secret

13 behind

14 prepare

15 sunburn

16 expand

17 trick

18 material

19 compare

20 absorb

21 flame

22 contract

23 disappear

24 experiment

25 dry

26 confuse

27 rise

28 weigh

29 magic

30 sunscreen

31 hold

32 candle

33 practice

34 necessary

35 for a long time

36 cool down

37 sign up for

38 give it a try

39 stick to

40 burn out

41 pick out

42 see through

43 turn A into B

※ 다음 우리말을 영어로 쓰시오.

01	동전	_____
02	채우다	_____
03	연습	_____
04	마술, 마법	_____
05	사라지다	_____
06	마른, 비가 오지 않는	_____
07	팽창하다	_____
08	양초	_____
09	볕에 탐	_____
10	맛	_____
11	가라앉다	_____
12	흡수하다	_____
13	비밀	_____
14	대신에	_____
15	번개	_____
16	재료, 물질	_____
17	자외선 차단제	_____
18	차이, 차이점	_____
19	수축하다	_____
20	섞다	_____
21	실험	_____

22	필요한	_____
23	안전한	_____
24	마술, 속임수	_____
25	불꽃	_____
26	준비하다	_____
27	혼동하게 하다	_____
28	뜨다	_____
29	탈출하다, (액체, 가스가) 새다	_____
30	비교하다	_____
31	압력	_____
32	무게를 재다	_____
33	오르다, 올라가다	_____
34	냉동고	_____
35	골라내다	_____
36	타 버리다	_____
37	~을 (바꾸지 않고) 고수하다	_____
38	오랫동안	_____
39	차가워지다	_____
40	A가 B로 변하다	_____
41	~을 신청하다	_____
42	시도해 보다	_____
43	속을 들여다 보다	_____

※ 다음 영영풀이에 알맞은 단어를 <보기>에서 골라 쓴 후, 우리말 뜻을 쓰시오.

1 _____ : to become impossible to see: _____

2 _____ : to become smaller: _____

3 _____ : to combine two or more substances so that they become a single substance: _____

4 _____ : to go down below the surface of water: _____

5 _____ : to increase in size, range, or amount: _____

6 _____ : to rest on top of a liquid or in the air: _____

7 _____ : to mistake one person or thing for another: _____

8 _____ : a substance that things can be made from: _____

9 _____ : something done to surprise or confuse someone: _____

10 _____ : a device or room for freezing food or keeping it frozen: _____

11 _____ : to find how heavy someone or something is: _____

12 _____ : to take in something in a natural or gradual way: _____

13 _____ : having the power to make impossible things happen: _____

14 _____ : a scientific test that is done in order to study what happens and to gain new knowledge: _____

15 _____ : a piece of information that is kept hidden from other people: _____

16 _____ : the activity of doing something again and again in order to become better at it: _____

보기			
secret	expand	contract	absorb
trick	magic	weigh	confuse
practice	float	sink	experiment
freezer	disappear	material	mix

42 Lesson 7. Magic or Science?

※ 다음 우리말과 일치하도록 빈칸에 알맞은 말을 쓰시오.

Listen & Speak 1 A

W: Today we'll make ice cream. _____ _____ do you want to make? _____ _____ strawberry? _____, mix two cups of milk, two cups of heavy cream, and _____ _____ _____ of sugar. _____, _____ five strawberries _____ small pieces. Then, _____ everything together and put it in the _____. That's it. It's _____ _____ _____, _____ it? _____ _____ you _____ _____ it at home?

W: 오늘 우리는 아이스크림을 만들 거예요. 여러분은 어느 맛을 만들고 싶은가요? 딸기는 어때요? 첫째로, 우유 2컵, 헤비 크림 2컵, 설탕 1/2컵을 섞으세요. 다음, 딸기 5개를 작은 조각으로 자르세요. 그 다음에, 모든 것을 섞어서 냉동실에 넣으세요. 이게 다예요. 만들기 쉽죠, 그렇지 않나요? 집에서 아이스크림을 만들어 보는 게 어때요?

Listen & Speak 1 B

B: Yujin, _____ did you _____ the eggs in water?

G: I'm _____ _____ the bad eggs.

B: _____ _____ are fresh, and _____ ones are not?

G: Eggs _____ _____ _____ _____ are fresh. When eggs _____ in water, they're not fresh. You _____ _____ them.

B: That's _____. Why do the bad eggs _____?

G: _____ they have gas _____. The gas _____ _____ the air in a _____.

B: Oh, I see.

B: 유진아, 왜 달걀을 물속에 넣었니?
G: 나는 상한 달걀을 골라내는 중이야.
B: 어느 달걀이 신선하고 어느 것이 신선하지 않은 거야?
G: 물에 가라앉는 달걀은 신선해. 달걀이 물에 뜨면, 그건 신선하지 않아. 그것들을 먹으면 안 돼.
B: 그거 재미있다. 상한 달걀은 왜 물에 뜨는 거니?
G: 상한 달걀은 속에 가스가 차기 때문이야. 가스가 풍선 속의 공기 같은 역할을 하거든.
B: 아, 이제 이해했다.

Listen & Speak 2 A

B: Ms. Jeong, does _____ _____ _____ water _____ more when there's a fish in it?

W: Yes, it does. We _____ _____ it now.

B: But how? We don't have a _____.

W: We _____ _____ a finger _____ _____ a fish.

B: _____ will that _____?

W: I'll _____ a glass of water first. Then I will _____ my finger in the water and _____ it to _____.

B: Oh, I _____ _____ _____ see the _____.

B: 정 선생님, 물속에 물고기가 있을 때 물 1잔의 무게가 더 무겁나요?
W: 응, 그렇단다. 우리는 지금 실험해 볼 수 있어.
B: 하지만 어떻게요? 물고기가 없는데요.
W: 우리는 물고기 대신 손가락을 사용할 수 있단다.
B: 어떻게 할 수 있어요?
W: 먼저 물 1잔의 무게를 잴 거야. 그 다음에 비교하기 위해 물속에 손가락을 넣고 무게를 잴 거란다.
B: 아, 차이를 빨리 알고 싶어요.

Listen & Speak 2 B

King Sejong: It _____ _____ _____ a long time.

Jang Yeongsil: Yes. The _____ _____ is _____ too long. The farmers are very _____.

King Sejong: We _____ do something _____ _____ them.

Jang Yeongsil: How about making a _____ _____?

King Sejong: A clock? _____ will that _____?

Jang Yeongsil: The clock will show the time and the _____. We can use it _____ _____ _____ the _____ _____.

King Sejong: That _____ _____ a good idea. But who's _____ _____ make it?

Jang Yeongsil: I'll _____ _____ _____ _____. I know _____ _____ about time and the seasons.

King Sejong: Okay, I _____ _____ _____ _____ _____ _____.

Real Life Communication A

Brian: Mina, will you _____ our tennis club?

Mina: It _____ _____, but I _____ _____ _____ a special class this _____.

Brian: _____ _____ did you sign up for?

Mina: I signed up for a _____ _____. I _____ _____ _____ learn new magic _____ there.

Brian: That sounds _____! _____ _____ _____ magic tricks before?

Mina: Yes, I learned some before, but I need _____ _____.

Brian: I hope I can see your magic tricks _____ _____.

Let's Check

B: What _____ you _____, Jiwon?

G: I'm reading a book about _____ and _____.

B: That _____ _____.

G: Yes. This book _____ 100 magic tricks that _____ _____. I've _____ _____ _____ of them.

B: That's _____. Can you show me _____ of the tricks?

G: Sure. I can show you a _____ _____ now.

B: Great! I _____ _____ _____ it.

King Sejong: 오랫동안 비가 오지 않는구나.

Jang Yeongsil: 그렇습니다. 건기가 너무 오래 계속되고 있습니다. 농부들이 아주 걱정하고 있습니다.

King Sejong: 그들을 돕기 위해 뭔가 해야 한다.

Jang Yeongsil: 특별한 시계를 만드는 것은 어떨까요?

King Sejong: 시계? 그것이 어떻게 도움이 되겠느냐?

Jang Yeongsil: 시계는 시간과 계절을 알려줄 겁니다. 건기를 준비하기 위해 시계를 사용할 수 있습니다.

King Sejong: 그거 좋은 생각 같구나. 하지만 누가 시계를 만들겠느냐?

Jang Yeongsil: 제가 한번 해 보겠습니다. 저는 시간과 계절에 대해 많이 알고 있습니다.

King Sejong: 좋다, 네 시계를 빨리 보고 싶구나.

Brian: 미나야, 우리 테니스 동아리에 가입할래?

Mina: 재미있겠다. 하지만 나는 이번 가을에 특별 수업에 등록했어.

Brian: 무슨 수업에 등록했니?

Mina: 마술 수업에 등록했어. 거기서 새로운 마술 묘기를 빨리 배우고 싶어.

Brian: 그거 재미있겠다! 전에 마술 묘기를 배운 적이 있니?

Mina: 응, 전에 몇 가지 배웠어, 하지만 더 연습을 해야 해.

Brian: 언젠가 네 마술 묘기를 볼 수 있길 바라.

B: 지원아, 뭘 읽고 있니?

G: 마술과 과학에 관한 책을 읽고 있어.

B: 그거 재미있겠다.

G: 응. 이 책은 과학을 사용하는 100가지 마술을 소개하고 있어. 나는 그 중에 절반 정도를 익혔어.

B: 멋지다. 마술 중 몇 가지를 보여줄 수 있니?

G: 물론이지. 지금 풍선 마술을 보여줄 수 있어.

B: 멋지다! 빨리 보고 싶어.

※ 다음 우리말에 맞도록 대화를 영어로 쓰시오.

해석

Listen & Speak 1 A

W: _____

_____

_____

_____

W: 오늘 우리는 아이스크림을 만들 거예요. 여러분은 어느 맛을 만들고 싶은가요? 딸기는 어때요? 첫째로, 우유 2컵, 헤비 크림 2컵, 설탕 1/2컵을 섞으세요. 다음, 딸기 5개를 작은 조각으로 자르세요. 그 다음에, 모든 것을 섞어서 냉동실에 넣으세요. 이게 다예요. 만들기 쉽죠, 그렇지 않나요? 집에서 아이스크림을 만들어 보는 게 어때요?

Listen & Speak 1 B

B: _____

G: _____

B: _____

G: _____

_____

B: _____

G: _____

B: _____

B: 유진아, 왜 달걀을 물속에 넣었니?
G: 나는 상한 달걀을 골라내는 중이야.
B: 어느 달걀이 신선하고 어느 것이 신선하지 않은 거야?
G: 물에 가라앉는 달걀은 신선해. 달걀이 물에 뜨면, 그건 신선하지 않아. 그것들을 먹으면 안 돼.
B: 그거 재미있다. 상한 달걀은 왜 물에 뜨는 거니?
G: 상한 달걀은 속에 가스가 차기 때문이야. 가스가 풍선 속의 공기 같은 역할을 하거든.
B: 아, 이제 이해했다.

Listen & Speak 2 A

B: _____

W: _____

B: _____

W: _____

B: _____

W: _____

B: _____

B: 정 선생님, 물속에 물고기가 있을 때 물 1잔의 무게가 더 무겁나요?
W: 응, 그렇단다. 우리는 지금 실험해 볼 수 있어.
B: 하지만 어떻게요? 물고기가 없는데요.
W: 우리는 물고기 대신 손가락을 사용할 수 있단다.
B: 어떻게 할 수 있어요?
W: 먼저 물 1잔의 무게를 잴 거야. 그 다음에 비교하기 위해 물속에 손가락을 넣고 무게를 잴 거란다.
B: 아, 차이를 빨리 알고 싶어요.

Listen & Speak 2 B

King Sejong: _____

Jang Yeongsil: _____

King Sejong: _____

Jang Yeongsil: _____

King Sejong: _____

Jang Yeongsil: _____

_____

King Sejong: _____

Jang Yeongsil: _____

King Sejong: _____

King Sejong: 오랫동안 비가 오지 않는구나.

Jang Yeongsil: 그렇습니다. 건기가 너무 오래 계속되고 있습니다. 농부들이 아주 걱정하고 있습니다.

King Sejong: 그들을 돕기 위해 뭐든 해야 한다.

Jang Yeongsil: 특별한 시계를 만드는 것은 어떨까요?

King Sejong: 시계? 그것이 어떻게 도움이 되겠느냐?

Jang Yeongsil: 시계는 시간과 계절을 알려줄 겁니다. 건기를 준비하기 위해 시계를 사용할 수 있습니다.

King Sejong: 그거 좋은 생각 같구나. 하지만 누가 시계를 만들겠느냐?

Jang Yeongsil: 제가 한번 해 보겠습니다. 저는 시간과 계절에 대해 많이 알고 있습니다.

King Sejong: 좋다, 네 시계를 빨리 보고 싶구나.

Real Life Communication A

Brian: _____

Mina: _____

Brian: _____

Mina: _____

Brian: _____

Mina: _____

Brian: _____

Brian: 미나야, 우리 테니스 동아리에 가입할래?

Mina: 재미있겠다. 하지만 나는 이번 가을에 특별 수업에 등록했어.

Brian: 무슨 수업에 등록했니?

Mina: 마술 수업에 등록했어. 거기서 새로운 마술 묘기를 빨리 배우고 싶어.

Brian: 그거 재미있겠다! 전에 마술 묘기를 배운 적이 있니?

Mina: 응, 전에 몇 가지 배웠어, 하지만 더 연습을 해야 해.

Brian: 언젠가 네 마술 묘기를 볼 수 있길 바라.

Let's Check

B: _____

G: _____

B: _____

G: _____

B: _____

G: _____

B: _____

B: 지원아, 뭘 읽고 있니?

G: 마술과 과학에 관한 책을 읽고 있어.

B: 그거 재미있겠다.

G: 응. 이 책은 과학을 사용하는 100가지 마술을 소개하고 있어. 나는 그 중에 절반 정도를 익혔어.

B: 멋지다. 마술 중 몇 가지를 보여줄 수 있니?

G: 물론이지. 지금 풍선 마술을 보여줄 수 있어.

B: 멋지다! 빨리 보고 싶어.

※ 다음 우리말과 일치하도록 빈칸에 알맞은 것을 골라 쓰시오.

1 Jina: _____ _____ the _____ Science _____ Show!

A. Magic   B. to   C. welcome   D. Super

2 _____ always _____ to _____ magic _____ .

A. exciting   B. tricks   C. see   D. it's

3 And it's _____ exciting to _____ _____ the secrets _____ them.

A. find   B. behind   C. out   D. more

4 Some people think the _____ of _____ is _____ .

A. magic   B. science   C. secret

5 Today, Ken, a _____ of the School Magic Club, will use _____ to _____ his _____ .

A. perform   B. member   C. tricks   D. science

6 Which tricks will he _____ us? I _____ to see them.

A. wait   B. show   C. can't

7 Ken: Hello, everyone. Today, I'm going to _____ you _____ _____ .

A. something   B. show   C. amazing

8 Here's a _____ _____ in it.

A. with   B. dish   C. water

9 Now, I'll _____ a candle in the _____ of the _____ .

A. middle   B. put   C. dish

10 Next, I'll _____ the candle and _____ it _____ a glass. "Abracadabra!"

A. cover   B. light   C. with

11 Jina: Look at the water! _____ _____ it _____ the glass?

A. come   B. into   C. how   D. rose

12 Ken: Air _____ when it gets _____ and creates _____ _____ .

A. hot   B. pressure   C. expands   D. higher

13 When it _____ cold, air _____ and creates _____ _____ .

A. contracts   B. pressure   C. gets   D. lower

14 When the flame _____ _____ , the air inside the glass _____ _____ .

A. pressure   B. out   C. lower   D. burnt

15 As the air _____ down, the air _____ _____ .

A. pressure   B. cooled   C. dropped

1 지나: 특별 과학 마술 쇼에 오신 것을 환영합니다!

2 마술을 보는 것은 항상 신나는 일입니다.

3 그리고 마술 뒤에 숨겨진 비밀을 알아내는 것은 더 신나는 일입니다.

4 어떤 사람들은 마술의 비밀이 과학이라고 생각합니다.

5 오늘 학교 마술 동아리 회원인 Ken은 마술을 수행하기 위해 과학을 사용할 것입니다.

6 그는 우리에게 어떤 마술을 보여 줄까요? 무척 기다려지는군요.

7 Ken: 안녕하세요, 여러분. 오늘, 저는 여러분에게 놀라운 무언가를 보여 주려고 합니다.

8 여기에 물이 담긴 접시가 있습니다.

9 이제, 저는 접시 한가운데에 초를 놓을 것입니다.

10 그다음에 초를 켜고 유리컵으로 초를 덮어 보겠습니다. "아브라카다브라!"

11 지나: 물을 보세요! 어째서 물이 유리컵 속으로 올라간 거지요?

12 Ken: 공기가 뜨거워지면 팽창해서, 더 높은 압력을 만듭니다.

13 공기가 차가워지면 수축해서, 더 낮은 압력을 만듭니다.

14 불꽃이 다 타 버렸을 때, 유리컵 속의 공기는 식어 버렸습니다.

15 공기가 식었으므로, 기압이 낮아졌습니다.

16 So the air _____ the glass was at a _____ _____ .

    A. higher   B. outside   C. pressure

17 It _____ the _____ into the _____ .

    A. water   B. pushed   C. glass

18 Ken: Now, I'm going to _____ _____ of these cups _____ _____ .

    A. fill   B. water   C. with   D. one

19 I will _____ them _____ to _____ you.

    A. around   B. move   C. confuse

20 Jina, _____ _____ has the _____ in it?

    A. cup   B. which   C. water

21 Jina: That's _____ ! It's the _____ _____ .

    A. one   B. easy   C. middle

22 Ken: Okay, _____ _____ . See? No water.

    A. check   B. let's

23 Jina: Show _____ _____ _____ _____ .

    A. other   B. me   C. cups   D. the

24 Ken: See? _____ _____ _____ .

    A. no   B. there's   C. water

25 Jina: Wow! _____ _____ the water _____ ?

    A. come   B. how   C. disappeared

26 Ken: _____ the trick, I _____ a special material _____ one of the _____ .

    A. put   B. into   C. before   D. cups

27 The material _____ the water and _____ it _____ jelly.

    A. turned   B. absorbed   C. into

28 Then the jelly _____ _____ the _____ .

    A. bottom   B. to   C. stuck

29 If you want to _____ this trick, it's _____ to _____ cups that you can't see _____ .

    A. necessary   B. try   C. through   D. use

30 Jina: Thank you _____ your great _____ . It was really _____ !

    A. performance   B. for   C. amazing

Step1

16 그래서 유리컵 밖의 공기 압력이 더 높아졌습니다.

17 높아진 압력의 공기가 물을 밀어서 유리컵으로 들어가게 된 것입니다.

18 Ken: 이제, 이 컵들 중 하나를 물로 채워 보겠습니다.

19 여러분을 헷갈리게 하려고 이 컵들을 섞어 보겠습니다.

20 지나, 어떤 컵에 물이 있을까요?

21 지나: 쉽네요! 가운데 컵이에요.

22 Ken: 좋습니다, 확인해 봅시다. 보셨죠? 물이 없군요.

23 지나: 다른 컵들도 보여 주세요.

24 Ken: 보셨죠? 물이 없네요.

25 지나: 왜 어째서 물이 사라진 거죠?

26 Ken: 마술 전에, 저는 특별한 물질을 컵 하나에 넣어 두었습니다.

27 그 물질은 물을 흡수하고, 그것을 젤리로 변하게 했습니다.

28 그러고 나서 젤리는 컵 바닥에 달라붙었습니다.

29 여러분이 이 마술을 해 보고자 한다면, 속을 들여다볼 수 없는 컵을 사용해야 합니다.

30 지나: 멋진 공연 고맙습니다. 정말 놀라웠어요!

※ 다음 우리말과 일치하도록 빈칸에 알맞은 말을 쓰시오.

1 Jina: _____ _____ the Super _____ _____ Show!

2 _____ always _____ _____ _____ magic tricks.

3 And it's more exciting _____ _____ _____ the secrets _____ them.

4 Some people think the _____ of magic _____ _____.

5 Today, Ken, a member of the School Magic Club, _____ _____ _____ _____ _____ his _____.

6 Which tricks _____ he _____ _____? I can't _____ _____ _____ _____.

7 Ken: Hello, everyone. Today, I'm going _____ _____ _____ _____ _____.

8 Here's a dish _____ _____ _____ _____.

9 Now, I'll _____ _____ _____ in the _____ of the dish.

10 Next, I'll _____ the candle and _____ _____ _____ a glass. "Abracadabra!"

11 Jina: _____ _____ the water! _____ _____ it _____ _____ the glass?

12 Ken: Air _____ when it _____ _____ and _____ _____ _____.

13 When it _____ _____, air _____ and _____ _____ _____.

14 When the flame _____ _____, the air inside the glass _____ _____.

15 As the air _____ _____, the air pressure _____.

1 지나: 특별 과학 마술 쇼에 오신 것을 환영합니다!

2 마술을 보는 것은 항상 신나는 일입니다.

3 그리고 마술 뒤에 숨겨진 비밀을 알아내는 것은 더 신나는 일입니다.

4 어떤 사람들은 마술의 비밀이 과학이라고 생각합니다.

5 오늘 학교 마술 동아리 회원인 Ken은 마술을 수행하기 위해 과학을 사용할 것입니다.

6 그는 우리에게 어떤 마술을 보여 줄까요? 무척 기다려지는군요.

7 Ken: 안녕하세요, 여러분. 오늘, 저는 여러분에게 놀라운 무언가를 보여 주려고 합니다.

8 여기에 물이 담긴 접시가 있습니다.

9 이제, 저는 접시 한가운데에 초를 놓을 것입니다.

10 그다음에 초를 켜고 유리컵으로 초를 덮어 보겠습니다. "아브라카다브라!"

11 지나: 물을 보세요! 어째서 물이 유리컵 속으로 올라간 거지요?

12 Ken: 공기가 뜨거워지면 팽창해서, 더 높은 압력을 만듭니다.

13 공기가 차가워지면 수축해서, 더 낮은 압력을 만듭니다.

14 불꽃이 다 타 버렸을 때, 유리컵 속의 공기는 식어 버렸습니다.

15 공기가 식었으므로, 기압이 낮아졌습니다.

16 So the air _____ the glass _____ _____ _____ _____ _____.

17 It _____ the water _____ the glass.

18 Ken: Now, I'm _____ _____ _____ _____ _____ _____ _____ _____ water.

19 I will move _____ _____ _____ _____ you.

20 Jina, _____ _____ has the water in it?

21 Jina: That's easy! _____ the _____ _____.

22 Ken: Okay, _____ _____. See? No water.

23 Jina: Show _____ _____ _____ _____.

24 Ken: See? There's _____ _____.

25 Jina: Wow! _____ _____ the water _____?

26 Ken: _____ the trick, I _____ a special material _____ _____ _____ _____ _____.

27 The material _____ the water and _____ _____ _____ _____ jelly.

28 Then the jelly _____ _____ _____ _____.

29 If you _____ _____ _____ this trick, it's _____ _____ _____ cups _____ you can't _____ _____.

30 Jina: Thank you _____ your great _____. It was really _____!

16 그래서 유리컵 밖의 공기 압력이 더 높아졌습니다.

17 높아진 압력의 공기가 물을 밀어서 유리컵으로 들어가게 된 것입니다.

18 Ken: 이제, 이 컵들 중 하나를 물로 채워 보겠습니다.

19 여러분을 헷갈리게 하려고 이 컵들을 섞어 보겠습니다.

20 지나, 어떤 컵에 물이 있을까요?

21 지나: 쉬워요! 가운데 컵이에요.

22 Ken: 좋습니다. 확인해 봅시다. 보셨죠? 물이 없군요.

23 지나: 다른 컵들도 보여 주세요.

24 Ken: 보셨죠? 물이 없네요.

25 지나: 왜! 어째서 물이 사라진 거죠?

26 Ken: 마술 전에, 저는 특별한 물질을 컵 하나에 넣어 두었습니다.

27 그 물질은 물을 흡수하고, 그것을 젤리로 변하게 했습니다.

28 그러고 나서 젤리는 컵 바닥에 달라붙었습니다.

29 여러분이 이 마술을 해 보고자 한다면, 속을 들여다볼 수 없는 컵을 사용해야 합니다.

30 지나: 멋진 공연 고맙습니다. 정말 놀라웠어요!

※ 다음 문장을 우리말로 쓰시오.

1 ▶ Jina: Welcome to the Super Science Magic Show!

➡ _____

2 ▶ It's always exciting to see magic tricks.

➡ _____

3 ▶ And it's more exciting to find out the secrets behind them.

➡ _____

4 ▶ Some people think the secret of magic is science.

➡ _____

5 ▶ Today, Ken, a member of the School Magic Club, will use science to perform his tricks.

➡ _____

6 ▶ Which tricks will he show us? I can't wait to see them.

➡ _____

7 ▶ Ken: Hello, everyone. Today, I'm going to show you something amazing.

➡ _____

8 ▶ Here's a dish with water in it.

➡ _____

9 ▶ Now, I'll put a candle in the middle of the dish.

➡ _____

10 ▶ Next, I'll light the candle and cover it with a glass. "Abracadabra!"

➡ _____

11 ▶ Jina: Look at the water! How come it rose into the glass?

➡ _____

12 ▶ Ken: Air expands when it gets hot and creates higher pressure.

➡ _____

13 ▶ When it gets cold, air contracts and creates lower pressure.

➡ _____

14 ▶ When the flame burnt out, the air inside the glass cooled down.

➡ _____

15 ▶ As the air cooled down, the air pressure dropped.

➡ _____

16 ▸ So the air outside the glass was at a higher pressure.

➡ _____

17 ▸ It pushed the water into the glass.

➡ _____

18 ▸ Ken: Now, I'm going to fill one of these cups with water.

➡ _____

19 ▸ I will move them around to confuse you.

➡ _____

20 ▸ Jina, which cup has the water in it?

➡ _____

21 ▸ Jina: That's easy! It's the middle one.

➡ _____

22 ▸ Ken: Okay, let's check. See? No water.

➡ _____

23 ▸ Jina: Show me the other cups.

➡ _____

24 ▸ Ken: See? There's no water.

➡ _____

25 ▸ Jina: Wow! How come the water disappeared?

➡ _____

26 ▸ Ken: Before the trick, I put a special material into one of the cups.

➡ _____

27 ▸ The material absorbed the water and turned it into jelly.

➡ _____

28 ▸ Then the jelly stuck to the bottom.

➡ _____

29 ▸ If you want to try this trick, it's necessary to use cups that you can't see through.

➡ _____

30 ▸ Jina: Thank you for your great performance. It was really amazing!

➡ _____

※ 다음 괄호 안의 단어들을 우리말에 맞도록 바르게 배열하시오.

1 (Jina: / to / welcome / the / Science / Super / Show! / Magic)
➡ _____

2 (always / it's / to / exciting / see / tricks. / magic)
➡ _____

3 (it's / and / exciting / more / find / to / out / secrets / the / them. / behind)
➡ _____

4 (people / some / the / think / of / secret / is / magic / science.)
➡ _____

5 (Ken, / today, / member / a / of / School / the / Club, / Magic / use / will / to / science / perform / tricks. / his)
➡ _____

6 (tricks / which / he / will / us? / show // I / wait / can't / see / them. / to)
➡ _____

7 (Ken: / everyone. / hello, // today, / going / I'm / show / to / something / you / amazing.)
➡ _____

8 (a / here's / with / dish / in / water / it.)
➡ _____

9 (now, / put / I'll / candle / a / the / in / of / middle / dish. / the)
➡ _____

10 (next, / light / I'll / candle / the / and / it / cover / with / glass. / a // "Abracadabra!")
➡ _____

11 (Jina: / at / look / water! / the // come / how / rose / it / the / into / glass?)
➡ _____

12 (Ken: / expands / air / it / when / gets / and / hot / higher / creates / pressure.)
➡ _____

13 (it / when / cold, / gets / contracts / air / and / lower / creates / pressure.)
➡ _____

14 (the / when / burnt / flame / out, / air / the / inside / glass / the / down. / cooled)
➡ _____

15 (the / as / cooled / air / down, / air / the / dropped. / pressure)
➡ _____

1 지나: 특별 과학 마술 쇼에 오신 것을 환영합니다!

2 마술을 보는 것은 항상 신나는 일입니다.

3 그리고 마술 뒤에 숨겨진 비밀을 알아내는 것은 더 신나는 일입니다.

4 어떤 사람들은 마술의 비밀이 과학이라고 생각합니다.

5 오늘 학교 마술 동아리 회원인 Ken은 마술을 수행하기 위해 과학을 사용할 것입니다.

6 그는 우리에게 어떤 마술을 보여 줄까요? 무척 기다려지는군요.

7 Ken: 안녕하세요, 여러분. 오늘, 저는 여러분에게 놀라운 무언가를 보여 주려고 합니다.

8 여기에 물이 담긴 접시가 있습니다.

9 이제, 저는 접시 한가운데에 초를 놓을 것입니다.

10 그다음에 초를 켜고 유리컵으로 초를 덮어 보겠습니다. "아브라카다브라!"

11 지나: 물을 보세요! 어째서 물이 유리컵 속으로 올라간 거지요?

12 Ken: 공기가 뜨거워지면 팽창해서, 더 높은 압력을 만듭니다.

13 공기가 차가워지면 수축해서, 더 낮은 압력을 만듭니다.

14 불꽃이 다 타 버렸을 때, 유리컵 속의 공기는 식어 버렸습니다.

15 공기가 식었으므로, 기압이 낮아졌습니다.

16 (the / so / outside / air / glass / the / at / was / a / pressure. / higher)

➡ _____

17 (pushed / it / water / the / the / glass. / into)

➡ _____

18 (Ken: / now, / going / I'm / fill / to / of / one / cups / these / water. / with)

➡ _____

19 (I / move / will / around / them / confuse / you. / to)

➡ _____

20 (Jina, / cup / which / the / has / in / it? / water)

➡ _____

21 (Jina: / easy! / that's // the / it's / one. / middle)

➡ _____

22 (Ken: / okay, / check. / let's // see? // water. / no)

➡ _____

23 (Jina: / me / show / other / the / cups.)

➡ _____

24 (Ken: / see? // no / there's / water.)

➡ _____

25 (Jina: / wow! // come / how / water / the / disappeared?)

➡ _____

26 (Ken: / the / before / trick, / put / I / a / material / special / one / into / cups. / the / of)

➡ _____

27 (material / the / absorbed / water / the / and / it / turned / jelly. / into)

➡ _____

28 (the / then / stuck / jelly / to / bottom. / the)

➡ _____

29 (you / if / to / want / try / trick, / this / necessary / it's / use / to / cups / you / that / see / can't / through.)

➡ _____

➡ _____

30 (Jina: / you / thank / your / for / performance. / great // was / it / amazing! / really)

➡ _____

16 그래서 유리컵 밖의 공기 압력이 더 높아졌습니다.

17 높아진 압력의 공기가 물을 밀어서 유리컵으로 들어가게 된 것입니다.

18 Ken: 이제, 이 컵들 중 하나를 물로 채워 보겠습니다.

19 여러분을 헷갈리게 하려고 이 컵들을 섞어 보겠습니다.

20 지나, 어떤 컵에 물이 있을까요?

21 지나: 쉽네요! 가운데 컵이에요.

22 Ken: 좋습니다. 확인해 봅시다. 보셨죠? 물이 없군요.

23 지나: 다른 컵들도 보여 주세요.

24 Ken: 보셨죠? 물이 없네요.

25 지나: 왜! 어째서 물이 사라진 거죠?

26 Ken: 마술 전에, 저는 특별한 물질을 컵 하나에 넣어 두었습니다.

27 그 물질은 물을 흡수하고, 그것을 젤리로 변하게 했습니다.

28 그리고 나서 젤리는 컵 바닥에 달라붙었습니다.

29 여러분이 이 마술을 해 보고자 한다면, 속을 들여다볼 수 없는 컵을 사용해야 합니다.

30 지나: 멋진 공연 고맙습니다. 정말 놀라웠어요!

※ 다음 우리말을 영어로 쓰시오.

1. 지나: 특별 과학 마술 쇼에 오신 것을 환영합니다!

   ➡ _____

2. 마술을 보는 것은 항상 신나는 일입니다.

   ➡ _____

3. 그리고 마술 뒤에 숨겨진 비밀을 알아내는 것은 더 신나는 일입니다.

   ➡ _____

4. 어떤 사람들은 마술의 비밀이 과학이라고 생각합니다.

   ➡ _____

5. 오늘 학교 마술 동아리 회원인 Ken은 마술을 수행하기 위해 과학을 사용할 것입니다.

   ➡ _____

6. 그는 우리에게 어떤 마술을 보여 줄까요? 무척 기다려지는군요.

   ➡ _____

7. Ken: 안녕하세요, 여러분. 오늘, 저는 여러분에게 놀라운 무언가를 보여 주려고 합니다.

   ➡ _____

8. 여기에 물이 담긴 접시가 있습니다.

   ➡ _____

9. 이제, 저는 접시 한가운데에 초를 놓을 것입니다.

   ➡ _____

10. 그다음에 초를 켜고 유리컵으로 초를 덮어 보겠습니다. "아브라카다브라!"

    ➡ _____

11. 지나: 물을 보세요! 어째서 물이 유리컵 속으로 올라간 거지요?

    ➡ _____

12. Ken: 공기가 뜨거워지면 팽창해서, 더 높은 압력을 만듭니다.

    ➡ _____

13. 공기가 차가워지면 수축해서, 더 낮은 압력을 만듭니다.

    ➡ _____

14. 불꽃이 다 타 버렸을 때, 유리컵 속의 공기는 식어 버렸습니다.

    ➡ _____

15. 공기가 식었으므로, 기압이 낮아졌습니다.

    ➡ _____

16 그래서 유리컵 밖의 공기 압력이 더 높아졌습니다.

➡ _____

17 높아진 압력의 공기가 물을 밀어서 유리컵으로 들어가게 된 것입니다.

➡ _____

18 Ken: 이제, 이 컵들 중 하나를 물로 채워 보겠습니다.

➡ _____

19 여러분을 헷갈리게 하려고 이 컵들을 섞어 보겠습니다.

➡ _____

20 지나, 어떤 컵에 물이 있을까요?

➡ _____

21 지나: 쉽네요! 가운데 컵이에요.

➡ _____

22 Ken: 좋습니다, 확인해 봅시다. 보셨죠? 물이 없군요.

➡ _____

23 지나: 다른 컵들도 보여 주세요.

➡ _____

24 Ken: 보셨죠? 물이 없네요.

➡ _____

25 지나: 와! 어째서 물이 사라진 거죠?

➡ _____

26 Ken: 마술 전에, 저는 특별한 물질을 컵 하나에 넣어 두었습니다.

➡ _____

27 그 물질은 물을 흡수하고, 그것을 젤리로 변하게 했습니다.

➡ _____

28 그러고 나서 젤리는 컵 바닥에 달라붙었습니다.

➡ _____

29 여러분이 이 마술을 해 보고자 한다면, 속을 들여다볼 수 없는 컵을 사용해야 합니다.

➡ _____

30 지나: 멋진 공연 고맙습니다. 정말 놀라웠어요!

➡ _____

※ 다음 우리말과 일치하도록 빈칸에 알맞은 말을 쓰시오.

Real Life Communication B

1. A: _____ _____ do you want to _____ _____ _____?

2. B: I want to _____ the badminton _____. I _____ _____ badminton. How _____ you?

3. A: I want to _____ _____ _____ _____. I _____ _____ make a computer program there.

4. B: That _____ cool!

1. A: 무슨 수업을 등록하고 싶니?
2. B: 난 배드민턴 수업을 듣고 싶어. 나는 배드민턴 치는 것을 좋아하거든. 너는?
3. A: 난 컴퓨터 수업을 듣고 싶어. 나는 빨리 거기에서 컴퓨터 프로그램을 만들고 싶어.
4. B: 맛진 것 같다!

Culture & Life

1. North _____ _____ – The Bermuda _____

2. _____ _____ _____ airplanes and ships _____ _____ in the Bermuda Triangle.

3. How _____?

4. It's _____ a mystery.

1. 북대서양 – 버뮤다 삼각 지대
2. 많은 비행기와 선박이 버뮤다 삼각 지대에서 사라졌다.
3. 이유가 무엇일까?
4. 그것은 여전히 미스터리이다.

Culture & Life

1. _____ – The pyramids

2. Some of the rocks _____ _____ _____ _____ the pyramids _____ _____ 70 tons.

3. How was _____ _____ _____ _____ such heavy rocks back then?

4. It's _____ _____ _____.

1. 이집트 – 피라미드
2. 피라미드를 만드는 데 사용된 몇몇 바위들은 무게가 70톤 정도인 것들이 있다.
3. 어떻게 그 시대에 그렇게 무거운 바위를 옮기는 것이 가능했을까?
4. 그것은 여전히 미스터리이다.

※ 다음 우리말을 영어로 쓰시오.

Real Life Communication B

1. A: 무슨 수업을 등록하고 싶니?

➡ _____

2. B: 난 배드민턴 수업을 듣고 싶어. 나는 배드민턴 치는 것을 좋아하거든. 너는?

➡ _____

3. A: 난 컴퓨터 수업을 듣고 싶어. 나는 빨리 거기에서 컴퓨터 프로그램을 만들고 싶어.

➡ _____

4. B: 멋진 것 같다!

➡ _____

Culture & Life

1. 북대서양 – 버뮤다 삼각 지대

➡ _____

2. 많은 비행기와 선박이 버뮤다 삼각 지대에서 사라졌다.

➡ _____

3. 이유가 무엇일까?

➡ _____

4. 그것은 여전히 미스터리이다.

➡ _____

Culture & Life

1. 이집트 – 피라미드

➡ _____

2. 피라미드를 만드는 데 사용된 몇몇 바위들은 무게가 70톤 정도인 것들이 있다.

➡ _____

3. 어떻게 그 시대에 그렇게 무거운 바위를 옮기는 것이 가능했을까?

➡ _____

4. 그것은 여전히 미스터리이다.

➡ _____

※ 다음 영어를 우리말로 쓰시오.

01 slippery _____

02 wide _____

03 bare _____

04 everywhere _____

05 village _____

06 shaky _____

07 ugly _____

08 excellent _____

09 experience _____

10 care _____

11 floating _____

12 gather _____

13 healthy _____

14 against _____

15 impossible _____

16 courage _____

17 match _____

18 meal _____

19 achievement _____

20 nail _____

21 exercise _____

22 proud _____

23 semi-final _____

24 discouraged _____

25 weak _____

26 amazing _____

27 shout _____

28 although _____

29 tournament _____

30 villager _____

31 completely _____

32 lose _____

33 decide _____

34 windy _____

35 fall into _____

36 try[do] one's best _____

37 on foot _____

38 try out for _____

39 give it a try _____

40 in fact _____

41 be about to _____

42 give up _____

43 laugh at _____

※ 다음 우리말을 영어로 쓰시오.

01 소리 지르다 _____

02 비록 ~일지라도 _____

03 걱정하다, 관심을 갖다 _____

04 흔들리는, 휘청거리는 _____

05 완전히 _____

06 낙담한 _____

07 미끄러운 _____

08 결정하다 _____

09 못질하다; 못 _____

10 모든 곳에, 어디나 _____

11 넓은 _____

12 경험하다 _____

13 떠 있는 _____

14 성과 _____

15 훌륭한 _____

16 ~에 맞서 _____

17 모으다, 모이다 _____

18 경기 _____

19 건강한 _____

20 슛하다 _____

21 약한 _____

22 벌거벗은, 맨 ~ _____

23 불가능한 _____

24 마을 사람 _____

25 지다, 잃다 _____

26 용기 _____

27 놀라운 _____

28 바람이 센 _____

29 식사, 끼니 _____

30 못생긴, 추한 _____

31 자랑스러워하는 _____

32 준결승전 _____

33 운동하다 _____

34 씻다 _____

35 사실은 _____

36 걸어서, 도보로 _____

37 시도해 보다 _____

38 ~을 비웃다 _____

39 최선을 다하다 _____

40 포기하다 _____

41 막 ~하려고 하다 _____

42 ~에 빠지다 _____

43 ~을 잘하다 _____

※ 다음 영영풀이에 알맞은 단어를 <보기>에서 골라 쓴 후, 우리말 뜻을 쓰시오.

1 _____ : extremely good: _____

2 _____ : not physically strong: _____

3 _____ : to fail to win a game: _____

4 _____ : not covered by clothes: _____

5 _____ : to say something very loudly: _____

6 _____ : someone who lives in a village: _____

7 _____ : not firm or steady: _____

8 _____ : a contest between two or more players or teams: _____

9 _____ : to fasten something to something else with nails: _____

10 _____ : a thing done successfully, typically by effort, courage, or skill:
_____

11 _____ : to get things from different places and put them together in one place:
_____

12 _____ : no longer having the confidence you need to continue doing something:
_____

13 _____ : feeling pleased about something that you have done or something that you
own: _____

14 _____ : difficult to hold or to stand or move on, because it is smooth, wet or
polished: _____

15 _____ : the quality of being brave when you are facing a difficult or dangerous
situation, or when you are very ill: _____

16 _____ : to kick or throw a ball in a sport such as football or basketball towards
the place where you can get a point: _____

보기			
shoot	gather	achievement	discouraged
nail	lose	match	villager
weak	excellent	slippery	shout
courage	bare	shaky	proud

※ 다음 우리말과 일치하도록 빈칸에 알맞은 말을 쓰시오.

해석

Listen & Speak 1 A

G: Tim, _____ _____ _____ _____ the Gobi Desert?

B: Yes, I _____. _____ it _____ Mongolia and China?

G: Yes, it is. Yesterday, I _____ a TV show about people _____ _____ the desert _____ _____.

B: _____ on foot?

G: Yes, it _____ them _____ 51 days.

B: Wow, that's amazing. I want _____ _____ _____ in the _____ but I don't want to _____ it _____ _____.

G: Well, I want to _____ and _____ the Gobi Desert _____ 50 days.

G: Tim, 너는 고비 사막에 대해 들어 봤니?

B: 응, 들어 봤어. 그것은 몽골과 중국에 있지 않니?

G: 응, 맞아. 어제 나는 걸어서 그 사막을 건넌 사람들에 관한 TV 쇼를 봤어.

B: 단지 걸어서만?

G: 응, 51일 정도 걸렸어.

B: 와, 놀랍다. 나는 사막에서의 삶을 경험하고 싶지만 그곳을 걸어서 건너고 싶지는 않아.

G: 음, 나는 시도해 보고 싶고 고비 사막을 50일 내로 건너고 싶어.

Listen & Speak 1 B

G: Alex, _____ _____ _____ _____ this year's "Ugly Sweater Party?"

B: Of _____, I _____. It's _____ December 5th, _____?

G: That's _____. Are you _____ _____ go?

B: I _____ _____, but I don't have an ugly sweater.

G: I have one that _____ _____ _____ _____ _____ _____. You can have it _____ _____ _____.

B: Thanks. That _____ be great.

G: _____ _____ _____ _____ _____ the Student Center and _____ _____ together.

B: _____. _____ you then.

G: Alex, 너는 올해의 "못생긴 스웨터 파티"에 대해 들어 봤니?

B: 물론 들어 봤어. 그것은 12월 5일에 열려, 맞지?

G: 맞아. 너 갈 거니?

B: 가고 싶지만 나는 못생긴 스웨터가 없어.

G: 집에 내가 입지 않는 스웨터가 한 벌 있어. 네가 원하면 그걸 가져도 좋아.

B: 고마워. 그래주면 좋겠어.

G: 학생회관 앞에서 만나서 같이 들어가자.

B: 그래. 그때 보자.

Listen & Speak 2 A

W: What can you do to be _____? First, try to _____ every day. Second, _____ _____ _____ _____ _____ _____. _____ _____ too much fast food. Third, _____ your hands before _____. Do these tips _____ _____ to do? Well, _____ one _____ _____ _____ _____ and don't _____ _____. Then you'll _____ a healthy _____.

W: 당신은 건강해지기 위해 무엇을 할 수 있는가? 먼저, 매일 운동하도록 해라. 둘째, 건강에 좋은 음식을 먹도록 해라. 패스트푸드를 너무 많이 먹지 마라. 셋째, 식사 전에 손을 씻어라. 이 조언들이 실천하기에 어렵게 들리는가? 음, 한 번에 하나씩 행하고 포기하지 마라. 그러면 당신은 건강한 삶을 살 것이다.

Listen & Speak 2 B

G: Hojun, are you going to _____ _____ _____ the school ice hockey team? The new season _____ _____ _____ start.

B: I'm not _____.

G: _____ _____?

B: I _____ that Tony and Brad are also _____ _____ _____ the team. They're so good.

G: Well, you're also _____ _____ ice hockey, so _____ _____ _____!

B: Okay, I'll _____ _____ _____. Thanks _____ _____.

G: 호준아, 너 학교 아이스하키 팀에 지원할 예정이니? 새 시즌이 곧 시작돼.
B: 잘 모르겠어.
G: 왜 몰라?
B: Tony와 Brad도 그 팀에 지원할 거라고 들었어. 그들은 굉장히 잘해.
G: 음, 너 또한 아이스하키를 잘하잖아, 그러니 포기하지 마!
B: 알았어, 최선을 다할게. 정말 고마워.

Real Life Communication

Father: Emily, are you _____ about your _____ on Saturday?

Emily: Not really. We're playing _____ a strong team. I think we'll _____.

Father: _____ _____ that. _____ _____ _____ _____ the Greek team in the 2004 Euro Cup?

Emily: _____, I _____. What _____ them?

Father: They were a weak team, _____ everyone _____ that they would _____.

Emily: _____ _____?

Father: They played _____ a team and _____ _____. Finally, they _____ the Euro Cup. So, don't _____ _____.

Emily: Thanks, Dad. We'll _____ _____ _____.

Father: Emily, 토요일에 있을 경기에 대해 설레니?
Emily: 그렇진 않아요. 우리는 강한 팀에 맞서 시합할 거예요. 우리가 질 것 같아요.
Father: 그렇게 말하지 마. 너는 2004 유로컵에서 그리스 팀에 대해 들어 봤니?
Emily: 아니요, 들어본 적 없어요. 그들이 어땠는데요?
Father: 그들은 약한 팀이었어, 그래서 모두가 그들이 질 거라고 생각했지.
Emily: 무슨 일이 일어났는데요?
Father: 그들은 한 팀으로 경기하며 열심히 노력했어. 결국 그들은 유로컵에서 우승했단다. 그러니 포기하지 마.
Emily: 감사해요, 아빠. 우리도 최선을 다할게요.

Let's Check ❶

B: _____ _____ _____ _____ Thomas Edison? _____ he was young, he _____ _____. Also, he _____ all of the _____ _____ his left ear. _____, he became a great scientist. _____ you may have _____, _____ _____ Edison and _____ _____.

B: 당신은 Thomas Edison에 대해 들어 봤나요? 어렸을 때 그는 글을 잘 읽지 못했습니다. 또한 그는 왼쪽 귀가 전혀 들리지 않았습니다. 그럼에도 그는 위대한 과학자가 되었습니다. 당신이 어려움을 갖고 있을지라도, Edison처럼 되고 포기하지 마세요.

※ 다음 우리말에 맞도록 대화를 영어로 쓰시오.

해석

Listen & Speak 1 A

G: _____

B: _____

G: _____

_____

B: _____

G: _____

B: _____

_____

G: _____

Listen & Speak 1 B

G: _____

B: _____

G: _____

B: _____

G: _____

B: _____

G: _____

B: _____

Listen & Speak 2 A

W: _____

_____

_____

_____

G: Tim, 너는 고비 사막에 대해 들어 봤니?

B: 응, 들어 봤어. 그것은 몽골과 중국에 있지 않니?

G: 응, 맞아. 어제 나는 걸어서 그 사막을 건넌 사람들에 관한 TV 쇼를 봤어.

B: 단지 걸어서만?

G: 응, 51일 정도 걸렸어.

B: 와, 놀랍다. 나는 사막에서의 삶을 경험하고 싶지만 그곳을 걸어서 건너고 싶지는 않아.

G: 음, 나는 시도해 보고 싶고 고비 사막을 50일 내로 건너고 싶어.

G: Alex, 너는 올해의 "못생긴 스웨터 파티"에 대해 들어 봤니?

B: 물론 들어 봤어. 그것은 12월 5일에 열려, 맞지?

G: 맞아. 너 갈 거니?

B: 가고 싶지만 나는 못생긴 스웨터가 없어.

G: 집에 내가 입지 않는 스웨터가 한 벌 있어. 네가 원하면 그걸 가져도 좋아.

B: 고마워. 그래주면 좋겠어.

G: 학생회관 앞에서 만나서 같이 들어가자.

B: 그래. 그때 보자.

W: 당신은 건강해지기 위해 무엇을 할 수 있는가? 먼저, 매일 운동하도록 해라. 둘째, 건강에 좋은 음식을 먹도록 해라. 패스트푸드를 너무 많이 먹지 마라. 셋째, 식사 전에 손을 씻어라. 이 조언들이 실천하기에 어렵게 들리는가? 음, 한 번에 하나씩 행하고 포기하지 마라. 그러면 당신은 건강한 삶을 살 것이다.

Listen & Speak 2 B

G: _____

_____

B: _____

G: _____

B: _____

G: _____

B: _____

G: 호준아, 너 학교 아이스하키 팀에 지원할 예정이니? 새 시즌이 곧 시작돼.
B: 잘 모르겠어.
G: 왜 몰라?
B: Tony와 Brad도 그 팀에 지원할 거라고 들었어. 그들은 굉장히 잘해.
G: 음, 너 또한 아이스하키를 잘하잖아, 그러니 포기하지 마!
B: 알았어, 최선을 다할게. 정말 고마워.

Real Life Communication

Father: _____

Emily: _____

Father: _____

Emily: _____

Father: _____

Emily: _____

Father: _____

_____

Emily: _____

Father: Emily, 토요일에 있을 경기에 대해 설레니?
Emily: 그렇진 않아요. 우리는 강한 팀에 맞서 시합할 거예요. 우리가 질 것 같아요.
Father: 그렇게 말하지 마. 너는 2004 유로컵에서 그리스 팀에 대해 들어 봤니?
Emily: 아니요, 들어본 적 없어요. 그들이 어땠는데요?
Father: 그들은 약한 팀이었어, 그래서 모두가 그들이 질 거라고 생각했지.
Emily: 무슨 일이 일어났는데요?
Father: 그들은 한 팀으로 경기하며 열심히 노력했어. 결국 그들은 유로컵에서 우승했단다. 그러니 포기하지 마.
Emily: 감사해요, 아빠. 우리도 최선을 다할게요.

Let's Check ❶

B: _____

_____

_____

_____

B: 당신은 Thomas Edison에 대해 들어 봤나요? 어렸을 때 그는 글을 잘 읽지 못했습니다. 또한 그는 왼쪽 귀가 전혀 들리지 않았습니다. 그럼에도 그는 위대한 과학자가 되었습니다. 당신이 어려움을 갖고 있을지라도, Edison처럼 되고 포기하지 마세요.

※ 다음 우리말과 일치하도록 빈칸에 알맞은 것을 골라 쓰시오.

1 Koh Panyee was a small _____ _____ in the _____ of the sea.
   A. village   B. floating   C. middle

2 _____ the boys in the village _____ _____ soccer before, they loved _____ it on TV.
   A. never   B. watching   C. played   D. although

3 One day, the boys _____ _____ _____ their _____ soccer team.
   A. own   B. decided   C. make   D. to

4 _____, people _____ _____ their idea.
   A. laughed   B. at   C. however

5 "_____ _____."
   A. impossible   B. that's

6 "What _____ you _____ _____?"
   A. say   B. makes   C. so

7 "_____ _____. Where are you _____ to _____ soccer?"
   A. going   B. around   C. look   D. play

8 The _____ were _____. The boys had no _____ _____ play soccer.
   A. right   B. place   C. to   D. villagers

9 They _____ _____.
   A. discouraged   B. were

10 "Don't _____ _____! We can _____ _____ soccer."
   A. up   B. still   C. give   D. play

11 "How?"

12 "_____ make our _____ soccer _____."
   A. field   B. own   C. let's

13 The boys _____ old boats and _____ _____ wood.
   A. pieces   B. gathered   C. of

14 They _____ the boats _____ and _____ the wood _____ them.
   A. together   B. to   C. put   D. nailed

15 _____ much hard _____, they _____ had a _____ field.
   A. work   B. after   C. floating   D. finally

16 It was _____ and had _____ _____.
   A. nails   B. shaky   C. everywhere

---

1 Koh Panyee는 바다 가운데 떠 있는 작은 수상 마을이었다.

2 비록 그 마을의 소년들은 이전에 축구를 해 본 적이 없었지만, 그들은 그것을 TV로 보는 것을 정말 좋아했다.

3 어느 날, 그 소년들은 그들만의 축구팀을 만들기로 하였다.

4 그러나 사람들은 그들의 생각을 비웃었다.

5 "그것은 불가능해."

6 "왜 그렇게 말하는 거죠?"

7 "주위를 둘러봐. 너희는 어디서 축구를 할 거니?"

8 마을 사람들이 옳았다. 소년들은 축구를 할 장소가 없었다.

9 그들은 낙담했다.

10 "포기하지 마! 우리는 여전히 축구를 할 수 있어."

11 "어떻게?"

12 "우리만의 축구장을 만들자."

13 소년들은 낡은 배와 나뭇조각들을 모았다.

14 그들은 배를 합치고 그것들 위에 나무를 못으로 박았다.

15 매우 열심히 일한 후, 그들은 마침내 떠 있는 축구장을 가지게 되었다.

16 그것은 흔들리고 곳곳에 못이 있었다.

17 The ball and the boys would often _____ _____ the sea, so the field was always _____ and _____.

A. into   B. slippery   C. wet   D. fall

18 They had _____ _____ so they had to play in _____ _____.

A. bare   B. shoes   C. no   D. feet

19 _____, they didn't _____.

A. care   B. still

20 _____ _____, they built _____ skills and _____ playing soccer more.

A. fact   B. enjoyed   C. excellent   D. in

21 _____ day, a boy _____ a _____ about a soccer _____.

A. brought   B. one   C. tournament   D. poster

22 They _____ _____ give _____ a _____.

A. decided   B. to   C. try   D. it

23 _____ they were _____ to _____, the villagers gave them new _____ and uniforms.

A. leave   B. about   C. when   D. shoes

24 Some _____ came to watch the game. This _____ the boys _____ _____.

A. made   B. better   C. feel   D. even

25 _____ first, people _____ them _____ the _____ team.

A. weakest   B. at   C. as   D. saw

26 _____, when the tournament _____, the soccer team _____ everyone.

A. surprised   B. however   C. started

27 _____ the day of the _____, it was _____ _____.

A. raining   B. on   C. hard   D. semi-final

28 They were _____ _____ two goals and it looked _____ to _____.

A. by   B. win   C. impossible   D. losing

29 "The _____ team is so _____," they _____.

A. strong   B. other   C. thought

30 But the boys _____ _____ _____.

A. up   B. give   C. didn't

31 They _____ _____ their shoes _____ the second half and the game changed _____.

A. during   B. off   C. completely   D. took

32 They played _____ in the rain _____ _____ the _____ field at home.

A. to   B. slippery   C. thanks   D. better

33 Although they lost _____ a score of three _____ two, still, they felt _____ _____ themselves.

A. of   B. by   C. to   D. proud

34 They didn't _____ up when they were _____. They _____ their best _____ the end.

A. tried   B. give   C. until   D. losing

※ 다음 우리말과 일치하도록 빈칸에 알맞은 말을 쓰시오.

1 Koh Panyee was _____ _____ _____ _____ in the _____ of the sea.

2 _____ the boys in the village _____ _____ _____ before, they loved _____ _____ _____ _____.

3 _____ _____, the boys _____ _____ _____ their own soccer team.

4 _____, people _____ _____ _____ _____.

5 "That's _____."

6 "What _____ you _____ _____?"

7 "_____ _____. Where _____ you _____ _____ _____ soccer?"

8 The villagers _____ _____. The boys had _____ _____ _____ _____ _____.

9 They _____ _____.

10 "Don't _____ _____! We can _____ _____ _____ _____."

11 "_____?"

12 "_____ _____ _____ _____ soccer field."

13 The boys _____ old boats and _____ _____ _____.

14 They _____ the boats _____ and _____ the wood _____ them.

15 _____ _____ hard work, they _____ _____ _____ _____ _____.

16 It was _____ and _____ _____ _____.

---

1 Koh Panyee는 바다 가운데 떠 있는 작은 수상 마을이었다.

2 비록 그 마을의 소년들은 이전에 축구를 해 본 적이 없었지만, 그들은 그것을 TV로 보는 것을 정말 좋아했다.

3 어느 날, 그 소년들은 그들만의 축구팀을 만들기로 하였다.

4 그러나 사람들은 그들의 생각을 비웃었다.

5 "그것은 불가능해."

6 "왜 그렇게 말하는 거죠?"

7 "주위를 둘러봐. 너희는 어디서 축구를 할 거니?"

8 마을 사람들이 옳았다. 소년들은 축구를 할 장소가 없었다.

9 그들은 낙담했다.

10 "포기하지 마! 우리는 여전히 축구를 할 수 있어."

11 "어떻게?"

12 "우리만의 축구장을 만들자."

13 소년들은 낡은 배와 나뭇조각들을 모았다.

14 그들은 배를 합치고 그것들 위에 나무를 못으로 박았다.

15 매우 열심히 일한 후, 그들은 마침내 떠 있는 축구장을 가지게 되었다.

16 그것은 흔들리고 곳곳에 못이 있었다.

17 The ball and the boys _____ _____ _____ _____ the sea, so the field was _____ _____ and _____.

18 They had _____ _____ so they _____ _____ play in _____ _____.

19 _____, _____ didn't _____.

20 _____ _____, they built _____ skills and _____ _____ soccer more.

21 One day, a boy _____ _____ _____ about a soccer tournament.

22 They _____ _____ give _____ a _____.

23 _____ they _____ _____ _____ _____, the villagers gave _____ _____ _____ and uniforms.

24 Some even came to watch the game. This _____ the boys _____ _____.

25 At first, people _____ them _____ the _____ team.

26 _____, _____ the tournament _____, the soccer team _____ _____.

27 _____ the day of the semi-final, it _____ _____ _____ _____.

28 They were _____ _____ _____ _____ and it looked _____ _____ _____.

29 "_____ _____ team is _____ _____," they thought.

30 _____ the boys didn't _____ _____.

31 They _____ _____ their shoes _____ the _____ _____ and the game _____ _____.

32 They _____ _____ in the rain _____ _____ the slippery field at home.

33 _____ they _____ _____ a score of three _____ two, still, they felt _____ _____.

34 They didn't _____ _____ _____ _____ _____ _____. They _____ _____ _____ _____ until the end.

17 공과 소년들은 종종 바다에 빠졌고, 축구장은 항상 젖어 있고 미끄러웠다.

18 그들은 신발이 없어서 맨발로 축구를 해야 했다.

19 그런데도 그들은 상관하지 않았다.

20 실제로 그들은 훌륭한 기술을 쌓았고 더욱 더 축구를 즐겼다.

21 어느 날, 한 소년이 축구 토너먼트에 관한 포스터를 가지고 왔다.

22 그들은 한번 해 보기로 결정했다.

23 그들이 떠나려고 할 때, 마을 사람들은 그들에게 새 신발과 축구복을 주었다.

24 몇몇은 심지어 경기를 보러 왔다. 이것은 소년들의 기분을 더 좋게 만들었다.

25 처음에, 사람들은 그들을 가장 약한 팀으로 보았다.

26 그러나 토너먼트가 시작되었을 때, 그 축구팀은 모든 사람들을 놀라게 했다.

27 준결승전 날, 비가 심하게 오고 있었다.

28 그들은 두 골 차로 지고 있었고, 이기는 것은 불가능해 보였다.

29 "다른 팀이 아주 강해."라고 그들은 생각했다.

30 그러나 소년들은 포기하지 않았다.

31 그들은 후반전에 그들의 신발을 벗었고 경기는 완전히 바뀌었다.

32 고향의 미끄러운 축구장 덕분에 그들은 빗속에서 더 잘하였다.

33 비록 그들은 3대 2로 졌지만, 그들은 그들 자신이 자랑스러웠다.

34 그들은 그들이 지고 있을 때 포기하지 않았다. 그들은 끝까지 최선을 다하였다.

※ 다음 문장을 우리말로 쓰시오.

1 Koh Panyee was a small floating village in the middle of the sea.

➡ _____

2 Although the boys in the village never played soccer before, they loved watching it on TV.

➡ _____

3 One day, the boys decided to make their own soccer team.

➡ _____

4 However, people laughed at their idea.

➡ _____

5 "That's impossible."

➡ _____

6 "What makes you say so?"

➡ _____

7 "Look around. Where are you going to play soccer?"

➡ _____

8 The villagers were right. The boys had no place to play soccer.

➡ _____

9 They were discouraged.

➡ _____

10 "Don't give up! We can still play soccer."

➡ _____

11 "How?"

➡ _____

12 "Let's make our own soccer field."

➡ _____

13 The boys gathered old boats and pieces of wood.

➡ _____

14 They put the boats together and nailed the wood to them.

➡ _____

15 After much hard work, they finally had a floating field.

➡ _____

16 It was shaky and had nails everywhere.

➡ _____

17 The ball and the boys would often fall into the sea, so the field was always wet and slippery.

➡ _____

18 They had no shoes so they had to play in bare feet.

➡ _____

19 Still, they didn't care.

➡ _____

20 In fact, they built excellent skills and enjoyed playing soccer more.

➡ _____

21 One day, a boy brought a poster about a soccer tournament.

➡ _____

22 They decided to give it a try.

➡ _____

23 When they were about to leave, the villagers gave them new shoes and uniforms.

➡ _____

24 Some even came to watch the game. This made the boys feel better.

➡ _____

25 At first, people saw them as the weakest team.

➡ _____

26 However, when the tournament started, the soccer team surprised everyone.

➡ _____

27 On the day of the semi-final, it was raining hard.

➡ _____

28 They were losing by two goals and it looked impossible to win.

➡ _____

29 "The other team is so strong," they thought.

➡ _____

30 But the boys didn't give up.

➡ _____

31 They took off their shoes during the second half and the game changed completely.

➡ _____

32 They played better in the rain thanks to the slippery field at home.

➡ _____

33 Although they lost by a score of three to two, still, they felt proud of themselves.

➡ _____

34 They didn't give up when they were losing. They tried their best until the end.

➡ _____

※ 다음 괄호 안의 단어들을 우리말에 맞도록 바르게 배열하시오.

1 (Panyee / Koh / was / small / a / floating / village / the / in / middle / the / of / sea.)
➡ _____

2 (the / although / boys / in / village / the / played / never / before, / soccer / loved / they / it / watching / TV. / on)
➡ _____

3 (day, / one / boys / the / to / decided / make / own / their / team. / soccer)
➡ _____

4 (people / however, / at / laughed / idea. / their)
➡ _____

5 (impossible." / "that's)
➡ _____

6 (makes / "what / say / you / so?")
➡ _____

7 (around. / "look // are / where / going / you / soccer?" / play / to)
➡ _____

8 (villagers / the / right. / were // boys / the / no / had / to / place / soccer. / play)
➡ _____

9 (discouraged. / were / they)
➡ _____

10 (give / "don't / up! // can / we / play / still / soccer.")
➡ _____

11 ("how?")
➡ _____

12 (make / "let's / own / our / field." / soccer)
➡ _____

13 (boys / the / gathered / boats / old / and / wood. / of / pieces)
➡ _____

14 (put / they / boats / the / together / and / the / nailed / wood / them. / to)
➡ _____

15 (much / after / work, / hard / they / had / finally / a / field. / floating)
➡ _____

16 (was / it / shaky / and / nails / had / everywhere.)
➡ _____

1 Koh Panyee는 바다 가운데 떠 있는 작은 수상 마을이었다.

2 비록 그 마을의 소년들은 이전에 축구를 해 본 적이 없었지만, 그들은 그것을 TV로 보는 것을 정말 좋아했다.

3 어느 날, 그 소년들은 그들만의 축구팀을 만들기로 하였다.

4 그러나 사람들은 그들의 생각을 비웃었다.

5 "그것은 불가능해."

6 "왜 그렇게 말하는 거죠?"

7 "주위를 둘러봐. 너희는 어디서 축구를 할 거니?"

8 마을 사람들이 옳았다. 소년들은 축구를 할 장소가 없었다.

9 그들은 낙담했다.

10 "포기하지 마! 우리는 여전히 축구를 할 수 있어."

11 "어떻게?"

12 "우리만의 축구장을 만들자."

13 소년들은 낡은 배와 나뭇조각들을 모았다.

14 그들은 배를 합치고 그것들 위에 나무를 못으로 박았다.

15 매우 열심히 일한 후, 그들은 마침내 떠 있는 축구장을 가지게 되었다.

16 그것은 흔들리고 곳곳에 못이 있었다.

17 (ball / the / and / boys / the / often / would / fall / into / sea, / the / so / field / the / always / was / slippery. / and / wet)
➡ _____

18 (had / no / they / shoes / they / so / had / play / to / in / feet. / bare)
➡ _____

19 (they / still, / care. / didn't)
➡ _____

20 (fact, / in / built / they / skills / excellent / and / playing / enjoyed / more. / soccer)
➡ _____

21 (day, / one / boy / a / brought / poster / a / about / soccer / a / tournament.)
➡ _____

22 (decided / they / give / to / try. / a / it)
➡ _____

23 (they / when / about / were / leave, / to / villagers / the / them / gave / shoes / new / uniforms. / and)
➡ _____

24 (even / some / to / came / watch / game. / the // this / the / made / boys / better. / feel)
➡ _____

25 (first, / at / saw / people / them / the / as / team. / weakest)
➡ _____

26 (however, / the / when / started, / tournament / soccer / the / team / everyone. / surprised)
➡ _____

27 (the / on / day / the / of / semi-final, / was / it / hard. / raining)
➡ _____

28 (they / losing / were / two / by / goals / and / looked / it / to / impossible / win.)
➡ _____

29 ("the / team / other / so / is / strong" / thought. / they)
➡ _____

30 (But / boys / the / give / didn't / up.)
➡ _____

31 (took / they / off / shoes / their / the / during / half / second / and / game / changed / the / completely.)
➡ _____

32 (played / they / better / the / in / thanks / rain / to / field / the / slippery / home. / at)
➡ _____

33 (they / although / by / lost / score / a / three / of / two, / to / still, / felt / they / proud / themselves. / of)
➡ _____

34 (didn't / they / up / give / they / when / losing. / were // tried / they / best / their / until / end. / the)
➡ _____

17 공과 소년들은 종종 바다에 빠졌고, 축구장은 항상 젖어 있고 미끄러웠다.

18 그들은 신발이 없어서 맨발로 축구를 해야 했다.

19 그런데도 그들은 상관하지 않았다.

20 실제로 그들은 훌륭한 기술을 쌓았고 더욱 더 축구를 즐겼다.

21 어느 날, 한 소년이 축구 토너먼트에 관한 포스터를 가지고 왔다.

22 그들은 한번 해 보기로 결정했다.

23 그들이 떠나려고 할 때, 마을 사람들은 그들에게 새 신발과 축구복을 주었다.

24 몇몇은 심지어 경기를 보러 왔다. 이것은 소년들의 기분을 더 좋게 만들었다.

25 처음에, 사람들은 그들을 가장 약한 팀으로 보았다.

26 그러나 토너먼트가 시작되었을 때, 그 축구팀은 모든 사람들을 놀라게 했다.

27 준결승전 날, 비가 심하게 오고 있었다.

28 그들은 두 골 차로 지고 있었고, 이기는 것은 불가능해 보였다.

29 "다른 팀이 아주 강해."라고 그들은 생각했다.

30 그러나 소년들은 포기하지 않았다.

31 그들은 후반전에 그들의 신발을 벗었고 경기는 완전히 바뀌었다.

32 고향의 미끄러운 축구장 덕분에 그들은 빗속에서 더 잘하였다.

33 비록 그들은 3대 2로 졌지만, 그들은 그들 자신이 자랑스러웠다.

34 그들은 그들이 지고 있을 때 포기하지 않았다. 그들은 끝까지 최선을 다하였다.

※ 다음 우리말을 영어로 쓰시오.

1 Koh Panyee는 바다 가운데 떠 있는 작은 수상 마을이었다.

➡ _____

2 비록 그 마을의 소년들은 이전에 축구를 해 본 적이 없었지만, 그들은 그것을 TV로 보는 것을 정말 좋아했다.

➡ _____

3 어느 날, 그 소년들은 그들만의 축구팀을 만들기로 하였다.

➡ _____

4 그러나 사람들은 그들의 생각을 비웃었다.

➡ _____

5 "그것은 불가능해."

➡ _____

6 "왜 그렇게 말하는 거죠?"

➡ _____

7 "주위를 둘러봐. 너희는 어디서 축구를 할 거니?"

➡ _____

8 마을 사람들이 옳았다. 소년들은 축구를 할 장소가 없었다.

➡ _____

9 그들은 낙담했다.

➡ _____

10 "포기하지 마! 우리는 여전히 축구를 할 수 있어."

➡ _____

11 "어떻게?"

➡ _____

12 "우리만의 축구장을 만들자."

➡ _____

13 소년들은 낡은 배와 나뭇조각들을 모았다.

➡ _____

14 그들은 배를 합치고 그것들 위에 나무를 못으로 박았다.

➡ _____

15 매우 열심히 일한 후, 그들은 마침내 떠 있는 축구장을 가지게 되었다.

➡ _____

16 그것은 흔들리고 곳곳에 못이 있었다.

➡ _____

17 공과 소년들은 종종 바다에 빠졌고, 축구장은 항상 젖어 있고 미끄러웠다.
➡ _____

18 그들은 신발이 없어서 맨발로 축구를 해야 했다.
➡ _____

19 그런데도 그들은 상관하지 않았다.
➡ _____

20 실제로 그들은 훌륭한 기술을 쌓았고 더욱 더 축구를 즐겼다.
➡ _____

21 어느 날, 한 소년이 축구 토너먼트에 관한 포스터를 가지고 왔다.
➡ _____

22 그들은 한번 해 보기로 결정했다.
➡ _____

23 그들이 떠나려고 할 때, 마을 사람들은 그들에게 새 신발과 축구복을 주었다.
➡ _____

24 몇몇은 심지어 경기를 보러 왔다. 이것은 소년들의 기분을 더 좋게 만들었다.
➡ _____

25 처음에, 사람들은 그들을 가장 약한 팀으로 보았다.
➡ _____

26 그러나 토너먼트가 시작되었을 때, 그 축구팀은 모든 사람들을 놀라게 했다.
➡ _____

27 준결승전 날, 비가 심하게 오고 있었다.
➡ _____

28 그들은 두 골 차로 지고 있었고, 이기는 것은 불가능해 보였다.
➡ _____

29 "다른 팀이 아주 강해."라고 그들은 생각했다.
➡ _____

30 그러나 소년들은 포기하지 않았다.
➡ _____

31 그들은 후반전에 그들의 신발을 벗었고 경기는 완전히 바뀌었다.
➡ _____

32 고향의 미끄러운 축구장 덕분에 그들은 빗속에서 더 잘하였다.
➡ _____

33 비록 그들은 3대 2로 졌지만, 그들은 그들 자신이 자랑스러웠다.
➡ _____

34 그들은 그들이 지고 있을 때 포기하지 않았다. 그들은 끝까지 최선을 다하였다.
➡ _____

※ 다음 우리말과 일치하도록 빈칸에 알맞은 말을 쓰시오.

Real Life Communication - Step 2

1. A: I _____ _____ _____ a basketball player _____ I'm
   _____ _____. Should I _____ _____?

2. B: No, _____ _____ _____! _____ you _____ _____
   of Anthony Webb?

3. A: No, I _____. Who is he?

4. B: He was a _____ _____. He was _____, but he _____
   the 1986 Slam Dunk Contest.

1. A: 나는 농구 선수가 되고 싶어. 근데 나는 키가 너무 작아. 내가 포기해야 할까?
2. B: 아니, 포기하지 마! Anthony Webb 에 대해 들어 봤니?
3. A: 아니, 그가 누군데?
4. B: 그는 농구선수였어. 그는 키가 작았지만, 1986 Slam Dunk Contest에서 우승했어.

Culture & Life

1. The women's field hockey team _____ Zimbabwe _____ the
   _____ _____.

2. _____ they had _____ _____ _____ _____,
   they _____ the gold medal _____ the 1980 Olympic Games.

1. 짐바브웨 여자 필드하키 팀은 전 세계를 놀라게 했다.
2. 비록 그들은 준비할 시간이 한 달밖에 없었지만, 그들은 1980년 올림픽 게임에서 금메달을 땄다.

Let's Write

1. _____ _____ _____ is basketball.

2. _____, I _____ really _____ _____ it at first.

3. I couldn't shoot well _____ _____ _____.

4. Although I _____ _____, I didn't _____ _____.

5. I _____ shooting _____ _____ _____ _____ _____.

6. This _____ _____ _____ well. Now, I'm _____ _____
   _____ on our team.

1. 내가 가장 좋아하는 운동은 농구이다.
2. 그러나 처음에 나는 농구를 잘하지 못했다.
3. 나는 다른 선수들과 달리 슛을 잘하지 못했다.
4. 나는 낙담했지만, 포기하지 않았다.
5. 나는 매일 한 시간 동안 슛 연습을 했다.
6. 이것이 내가 슛을 잘하게 했다. 이제, 나는 우리 팀에서 가장 잘하는 선수이다.

※ 다음 우리말을 영어로 쓰시오.

Real Life Communication - Step 2

1. A: 나는 농구 선수가 되고 싶어. 근데 나는 키가 너무 작아. 내가 포기해야 할까?

   ➡ _____

2. B: 아니, 포기하지 마! Anthony Webb에 대해 들어 봤니?

   ➡ _____

3. A: 아니, 그가 누군데?

   ➡ _____

4. B: 그는 농구선수였어. 그는 키가 작았지만, 1986 Slam Dunk Contest에서 우승했어.

   ➡ _____

Culture & Life

1. 짐바브웨 여자 필드하키 팀은 전 세계를 놀라게 했다.

   ➡ _____

2. 비록 그들은 준비할 시간이 한 달밖에 없었지만, 그들은 1980년 올림픽 게임에서 금메달을 땄다.

   ➡ _____

Let's Write

1. 내가 가장 좋아하는 운동은 농구이다.

   ➡ _____

2. 그러나 처음에 나는 농구를 잘하지 못했다.

   ➡ _____

3. 나는 다른 선수들과 달리 슛을 잘하지 못했다.

   ➡ _____

4. 나는 낙담했지만, 포기하지 않았다.

   ➡ _____

5. 나는 매일 한 시간 동안 슛 연습을 했다.

   ➡ _____

6. 이것이 내가 슛을 잘하게 했다. 이제, 나는 우리 팀에서 가장 잘하는 선수이다.

   ➡ _____

MEMO

MEMO

MEMO

영어 기출 문제집

2학기
정답 및 해설

지학 | 민찬규

중2

Lesson 5

I Don't Have a Clue

시험대비 실력평가   p.08

01 disappear   02 ②   03 ④

04 (1) detectives (2) Fold, half (3) solved

05 (1) made it to (2) for free (3) turn over (4) Help yourself

06 ②   07 ⑤

01 주어진 단어의 관계는 반의어 관계이다. appear: 나타나다, disappear: 사라지다

02 '적어 놓았거나 컴퓨터에 저장해 놓은 무언가를 제거하다'를 나타내는 것은 delete(삭제하다)이다.

03 hide는 '숨기다'를 뜻한다.

04 detective: 탐정, fold: 접다, solve: 해결하다

05 make it to: ~에 이르는 데 성공하다, for free: 무료로, turn over: 뒤집다, help yourself: 마음껏 드세요

06 주어진 문장에서 suspect는 '용의자'를 뜻하며 이와 같은 의미로 쓰인 것은 ②번이다. 나머지는 모두 '의심하다'라는 의미로 사용되었다. food poisoning: 식중독

07 첫 번째 문장에서 lie는 '눕다'를 뜻하지만 두 번째, 세 번째 문장에서는 '거짓말하다'를 의미한다.

서술형 시험대비   p.09

01 outside

02 (1) twice (2) at the time (3) for free

03 (1) Can you explain the story to me?

    (2) You should take the pills twice a day.

    (3) I cut the bread into triangles.

04 (1) accident (2) hurt (3) question (4) delete

05 (1) The police were sure (that) they could catch the thief.

    (2) Turn over the page and look at the picture.

    (3) Would you fill this bottle with water?

06 table

01 주어진 단어의 관계는 반의어 관계이다. inside: ~ 안에, outside: ~ 밖에

02 twice: 두 번, at the time of: ~이 일어나던 때에, for free: 무료로

03 explain A to B: A를 B에게 설명하다 ('explain A B'의 형식으로 쓰이지 않음에 유의한다.) pill: 환약, 알약 triangle: 삼각형

06 세 개 또는 네 개의 다리가 있지만 걸을 수 없는 것은 table을 가리킨다.

교과서 Conversation

핵심 Check   p.10~11

1 (1) explain

    (2) Let me know

    (3) Can you tell me what happened yesterday

2 (1) First / Then (2) First / Then (3) First / Second / Third / Then

교과서 대화문 익히기

Check(√) True or False   p.12

1 T   2 T   3 T   4 F

교과서 확인학습   p.14~15

Listen & Speak 1 - A

that, bought / like, dragons, seahorses / need to use, to play / sounds, Can you explain how to use

Listen & Speak 1 - B

riddle, twice, once, never in a day / I have no idea / get it, Can you explain why / get it

Listen & Speak 2 - A

look at / How did you make it / First, in half / Second, bottom line / Third, both ends / Then, turn, over / easy

Listen & Talk 2 - B

detective / didn't see, this week, about / all of, disappeared / did, do / First, looked around / Then, suspects / Finally, thief / don't tell, watch, later

Real Life Communication

solve / First, a bag of beans / needs to cross a river / hold, one more / take, at a time / Can you explain how to move everything across

Let's Check

smells, good / going to, for dinner / Help yourself /

Can you explain how to make / First, fill, with / Then, on the top / delicious / Would, like / thanks

시험대비 기본평가 p.16

01 (D) → (A) → (C) → (B) 02 triangle
03 (A) Second (B) Third 04 ③

01 (D) 제안 → (A) 수용 및 질문 → (C) 게임 설명 → (B) 반응
02 3개의 선과 3개의 각으로 구성된 모양을 가리키는 말은 triangle(삼각형)이다.
04 ③ 두 번째 단계에서 세모의 꼭대기를 맨 아랫선 쪽으로 접어야 한다.

시험대비 실력평가 p.17~18

01 ②, ⑤ 02 ② 03 E 04 ②
05 the paper fox 06 She should fold the top of the triangle to the bottom line.
07 She should make the ears first. 08 ④
09 ③ 10 맘껏 먹으렴.
11 Can you explain how to make a taco? 12 ①
13 (a) with (b) delicious

01 (A)는 설명을 요청하는 표현이다. ②번은 상대방의 이해를 점 검하는 표현이며 ⑤번은 제안을 나타낸다.
02 ② Brian이 Jimin과 운동장에서 축구하고 싶어한다는 설명은 대 화의 내용과 일치하지 않는다.
03 'week'이라는 단어에는 'E'가 2번, 'year'라는 단어에는 한 번 나오지만 'day'라는 단어에는 한 번도 나오지 않는다.
06 유진은 종이를 반으로 접어 삼각형을 만든 후에 세모의 꼭대기 를 맨 아랫선 쪽으로 접어야 한다.
07 유진은 얼굴을 그리기 전에 귀를 먼저 만들어야 한다.
08 이어지는 대화에서 Then ~ 그리고 Finally로 절차를 열거하고 있으므로 (D)가 적절하다.
09 대화를 통해 학교에서 모든 자전거를 훔친 도둑이 누구인지는 알 수 없다.
10 Help yourself.: 마음껏 드세요.
11 explain: 설명하다
12 (C)는 음식을 권유하는 표현으로 ①번과 바꾸어 쓸 수 있다.
13 (a) fill A with B: A를 B로 채우다, (b) sound+형용사 보어: ~일 것 같다

서술형 시험대비 p.19

01 He bought a fox, a duck, and a bag of beans.
02 He could load only one thing at a time.
03 The fox will eat the duck.
04 how to move
05 (D) → (B) → (A) → (C)
06 (A) Fold the top of the triangle to the bottom line.
   (B) Fold both ends of the bottom line to the top to make ears.
   (C) Turn it over and draw a face.

01 농부는 강을 건너기 전에 여우, 오리, 한 자루의 콩을 샀다.
02 농부는 한 번에 하나씩만 배에 실을 수 있다.
03 농부가 없다면 여우가 오리를 먹을 것이다.
04 how to+동사원형: ~하는 방법
05 (D) 좋은 냄새가 무엇인지 질문 → (B) 저녁 메뉴 설명 → (A) 만드는 법 질문 → (C) 만드는 과정 설명

교과서
Grammar

핵심 Check p.20~21

1 (1) was painted by (2) was taught
2 (1) will clean the room / will be cleaned by me
  (2) must do our homework / must be done by us
  (3) will help her / will be helped by him

시험대비 기본평가 p.22

01 (1) made → was made
  (2) will complete → will be completed
  (3) is caused → causes
  (4) can't open → can't be opened
02 (1) was stolen (2) be sent (3) visit (4) are held
  (5) is looked up to (6) play (7) be played
03 (1) The classroom is cleaned every day.
  (2) When was this building built?
  (3) We were not given tickets by him.
  (4) This must be done before tonight.
  (5) The door will be closed in 10 minutes.

01 (1), (2) 스웨터는 만들어지는 것이고, 건물 역시 완공되어지는 것이므로 수동태를 쓰는 것이 옳다. (3) 부주의한 운전이 사고를 유발하는 것이므로 능동태를 써야 한다. (4) 창문은 스스로 여는 것이 아니므로 수동태를 쓰는 것이 옳다.

02 주어가 동사의 행위의 주체가 될 수 있으면 능동태를, 동사의 행위의 대상이 될 경우 수동태를 쓴다.

03 동사의 행위의 주체가 될 수 없는 주어들이므로 수동태를 쓰는 것이 옳다. 수동태의 형태는 'be 동사+p.p.' 형태임에 유의한다.

01 ⑤   02 ④   03 ③
04 was not woken up   05 ④   06 ③
07 ⑤   08 The fish will be cooked by her.
09 ③
10 Will the letter be sent to the right address?
11 ②
12 You will be punished by the teacher.   13 ④
14 ③   15 ⑤   16 ③
17 are taken care of by   18 ⑤
19 Stamps are sold in a post office (by them).
20 seen   21 (1) He was seen dancing by me.
   (2) The cake will be bought by Jack.
   (3) Was the juice drunk by you?   22 ②
23 ⑤   24 ①
25 will be taken care of by me
26 This bridge must be repaired.

01 사고 발생이 과거이며 주어가 복수이므로 ⑤번이 옳다.

02 고기는 '보관되는 것'이므로 수동태를 쓰는 것이 옳다.

03 목적어가 these books이므로 이를 주어로 하고 동사 should return을 수동태로 만든 ③번이 같은 의미의 문장이다.

04 능동태에서 일반동사의 부정형이 쓰였으므로 수동태 역시 부정문으로 쓰는 것에 유의한다.

05 ④ '노래'가 주어이므로 수동태를 써서 was sung이라고 쓰는 것이 옳다.

06 모든 시점이 과거이며 주어가 동사의 행위의 대상이므로 수동태를 쓰는 것이 옳다. find(찾다)-found-found

07 동작의 주체가 일반인이거나 막연한 사람일 때, 그리고 명확하지 않을 때 'by+행위자'를 생략한다.

08 목적어가 the fish이므로 이를 주어로 하고 조동사의 수동태는 '조동사+be+p.p.'를 쓰는 것에 유의하여 문장을 만든다.

09 shut은 3단 변화가 동일한 형태인 shut-shut-shut임에 유의한다. shut down: 문을 닫다

10 편지는 '보내지는' 것이므로 will be sent를 쓰되 의문문임에 유의하여 will the letter be sent의 어순으로 쓴다.

11 모두 동사의 행위의 대상이 되어 played가 들어가지만 ②번은 행위의 주체이므로 playing이 들어간다.

12 너희들이 벌을 받는 대상이 되므로 수동태를 쓰는 것이 옳다.

13 speak well of: ~에 대해 좋게 말하다

14 바깥이 추웠으므로 히터를 틀었다고 보는 것이 옳으며, 'by+행위자'를 써야 한다. 구동사의 수동태의 경우 동사만 p,p형으로 변화시켜 수동태를 만들 수 있다.

15 by 이외의 다른 전치사를 쓰는 수동태에 유의하자. be interested in: ~에 흥미가 있다

16 run의 3단 변화는 run-ran-run이다.

17 take care of의 수동태는 be taken care of를 써야 하며 주어가 복수 명사이므로 are taken care of를 쓴다. 'by+행위자'를 쓰는 것을 잊지 않는다.

18 be crowded with: ~으로 붐비다, be satisfied with: ~에 만족하다

19 sell–sold–sold: ~을 팔다, 팔리다

20 주어진 우리말을 수동태를 활용하여 영어로 쓰면 'This performance will be seen by many people.'이다.

21 (1) 5형식 동사의 수동태에서 목적격 보어가 원형부정사가 아닌 경우 그대로 쓸 수 있다. (2) 조동사가 있는 수동태는 '조동사+be+p.p.'를 쓴다. (3) 의문문이므로 수동태 의문문을 쓴다.

22 ② happen은 자동사이므로 수동태로 쓸 수 없다.

23 'Your brothers help you.'를 수동태로 고쳐 'You are helped by your brothers.'를 쓰고 의문문을 만들기 위하여 주어와 동사 자리를 바꾸면 된다.

24 buy와 make는 4형식 동사로, 직접목적어를 주어로 한 수동태에서 간접목적어에 전치사 for를 쓴다.

25 조동사의 수동태는 '조동사+be+p.p.' 형태임에 유의한다.

26 의무를 나타내는 조동사 must를 대신하여 should를 써도 무방하다. 다리는 수리되는 대상이므로 수동태를 쓰는 것에 유의하자.

01 The project will not be given up by us.
02 My parents will use the treadmill.
03 will be offered   04 were put on by David
05 be made, be bought, be invited
06 (1) was laughed at (2) be arrested (3) ate (4) be cut
   (5) serves
07 will be written
08 When was this house built?
09 should be told the news
10 (1) Chris may be offered a job by the company. /
    A job may be offered to Chris by the company.
   (2) This letter must be sent by you before June 1.
   (3) Thomas Edison invented the electric light bulb
     in 1879.
   (4) The class will be divided into two sections by
     me.
   (5) People grow rice in many countries.

11 must be worn

12 should be finished

13 is married

14 originated, are grown, were introduced

15 are required to wear uniforms

16 was dropped by Timmy after dinner last night

17 (1) Food must not be brought into the lab (by you).

   (2) Cell phones should be turned off (by you).

   (3) UFO sightings cannot be explained (by us).

01 조동사가 있는 문장의 수동태는 '조동사+be+p.p.' 형태를 쓰며 부정어는 조동사 뒤에 위치시킨다.

02 주어가 동사의 행위의 주체가 되므로 능동태를 쓰는 것이 옳다. The treadmill will be used by my parents.로 고칠 수도 있다. treadmill: 러닝머신

03 주어가 행위의 대상이 되는 사물이므로 수동태를 쓰는 것이 옳다.

04 3인칭 단수 주어에서 동사 put이 쓰인 것으로 보아 과거시제임을 알 수 있다. 따라서 수동태로 바꿀 경우 복수 주어 The pants에 맞추어 were put on을 쓴다.

05 케이크가 만들어지고, 풍선이 구매되며, 친구들이 초대되는 것이므로 모두 수동태를 쓰는 것이 옳다.

06 (1) Julia는 반 친구들에 의해 웃음거리가 되었다. 그녀는 매우 당황했다. (2) 걱정 마. 그 용의자는 경찰에 의해 반드시 체포될 거야. (3) 내 개가 어젯밤에 탁자 위에 있던 모든 피자를 먹었다. (4) 등록금이 절반으로 삭감될 것이라는 소식은 나를 행복하게 한다. (5) 주방장은 직접 고객을 응대한다. 그래서 고객들은 만족을 느낀다.

07 주어인 '대본(a script)'은 행위의 대상이므로 수동태를 쓰는 것이 옳다.

08 집이 지어지는 것이므로 수동태를 쓰고, 시점은 과거이므로 was를 쓰는 것이 옳다.

09 4형식 동사의 간접목적어가 주어로 쓰인 수동태에서, 직접목적어에는 전치사를 쓰지 않는다.

10 (1) 4형식 동사는 목적어가 두 개이므로 두 개의 수동태를 만들 수 있다. 직접목적어가 주어로 쓰인 경우 간접목적어에 전치사를 붙이는 것에 유의하자. (2), (4) 조동사의 수동태는 '조동사+be+p.p.' 형태이다. (3) 과거에 발생한 일이므로 과거시제를 쓰는 것에 유의한다. (5) 능동태의 주어가 복수이므로 동사의 수를 일치시키는 것에 유의한다.

11 능동태의 목적어가 주어 자리에 있으므로 수동태로 쓰인 문장임을 알 수 있다.

12 주어가 동사의 행위의 대상이 되므로 수동태를 쓰는 것이 옳다. chore: 허드렛일, 하기 싫은 일

13 결혼한 상태임을 말할 때에는 'be married'를 쓴다.

14 바나나는 아시아에서 유래했지만 지금은 전 세계 사람들에 의해 재배되고 있다. 바나나는 1516년에 미국에 소개되었다.

originate은 '비롯되다, 유래하다'는 의미로 쓰일 경우 자동사로 수동태로 쓰이지 않는다.

15 교복을 입도록 요구받는다는 의미가 자연스럽다. 따라서 수동태를 활용하여 문장을 완성할 수 있다.

16 능동태의 목적어가 주어로 쓰이고 있으므로 수동태를 쓰는 것이 옳다.

17 조동사가 있는 수동태는 '조동사+be+p.p.'이다.

교과서
Reading

확인문제   p.28

1 T 2 F 3 T 4 F

확인문제   p.29

1 F 2 T 3 F 4 F 5 T 6 F

교과서 확인학습 A   p.30~31

01 to   02 enter the first room

03 to solve some riddles

04 be found, inside   05 are, to think

06 was hit by, on

07 Luckily, badly hurt, see

08 were questioned by

09 reading a book, the accident   10 was walking

11 was making breakfast

12 Who hit, explain   13 Write it down

14 move to   15 happened in

16 made it to

17 much harder to escape than

18 gets, from   19 reads, won   20 surprised

21 won   22 Congratulations, have won

23 During, choose, from, for free

24 to, on   25 wait to see   26 Truly yours

27 However, isn't real, deletes

28 Can, why   29 There are usually, days

30 have the answer

31 it, are free to go

1 Welcome to the Escape Tower.

2 You will enter the first room in our tower.

3 You need to solve some riddles to escape.

4 Clues can be found somewhere inside the room.

5 So, are you ready to think like Sherlock Holmes?

6 Mr. Doodle was hit by a car on Sunday afternoon.

7 Luckily, he wasn't badly hurt, but he didn't see the driver.

8 Three suspects were questioned by a police officer.

9 Ms. A said she was reading a book at the time of the accident.

10 Mr. B said he was walking his dog.

11 Ms. C said she was making breakfast.

12 Who hit Mr. Doodle? Can you explain why?

13 Do you have the answer? Write it down.

14 Then you can move to the next room.

15 Clue The accident happened in the afternoon.

16 Congratulations! You made it to the second room.

17 However, the second room is much harder to escape than the first one. Good luck!

18 Jay gets an email from his favorite clothing store.

19 The title reads "You won our Lucky Day event!"

20 Jay is surprised. He quickly opens it.

21 You won our 'Lucky Day' event!

22 Congratulations! You have won a special prize.

23 During our Lucky Day event, you can choose any seven items from our store for free!

24 Come to our store on November 31.

25 We can't wait to see you.

26 Truly yours, Kay Brown

27 However, Jay thinks that the event isn't real and deletes the email.

28 Can you explain why?

29 Clue There are usually 30 or 31 days in a month.

30 Do you have the answer?

31 Write it down and then you are free to go!

01 clue   02 ⑤   03 ②   04 ④

05 ②   06 ①

07 There are three suspects.

08 We have to go to the second room.

09 is surprised   10 the email   11 ③

12 ④

---

13 He can choose any seven items from their store for free.   14 ②

15 can find clues somewhere inside the room

16 ②   17 ①   18 was not seen by

19 She was reading a book (when Mr. Doodle was hit by a car).   20 ③

21 is written down   22 accident   23 ③

24 ④   25 ③   26 you are free to go

27 is deleted by Jay   28 ⑤

29 on November 31, 30 days

30 easy to escape

01 무언가를 발견하고, 이해하고 또는 미스터리나 수수께끼를 풀도록 돕는 것은 '단서(clue)'이다.

02 ⑤ 셜록 홈즈처럼 생각할 준비가 되었느냐고 물었을 뿐 그가 이 타워에서 많은 것을 생각하곤 했다는 말은 없다.

03 밑줄 친 (A)는 동사 need의 목적어로 쓰인 to부정사이다. ① anything을 수식하는 형용사 ② hopes의 목적어 ③ 부사적 용법 중 목적 ④ 부사적 용법 중 감정의 원인 ⑤ 부사적 용법 중 판단의 근거

04 과거에 발생한 일이며 차에 치였다는 의미이므로 ④번이 옳다.

05 ② Mr. Doodle이 운전자를 보지 못한 이유는 위 글에 나와 있지 않다.

06 심하게 다치지 않았다고 하였으므로 Luckily라고 쓰는 것이 옳다.

07 용의자는 세 명이라고 하였다.

08 첫 번째 방에서 탈출하고 나면 두 번째 방으로 가야 한다.

09 시점은 현재이며, 이메일 제목이 Jay를 놀라게 한 것이다. Jay가 주어로 쓰였으므로 수동태로 빈칸을 채워야 한다.

10 옷 가게에서 온 이메일을 가리키는 인칭대명사이다.

11 특정 날짜 앞에는 전치사 on을 쓴다.

12 밑줄 친 (D)는 명사절 접속사로 완전한 문장을 이끈다. ④번은 불완전한 문장을 이끄는 관계대명사이다.

13 행운의 날 행사 동안 그들의 가게에서 아무거나 일곱 가지 상품을 공짜로 선택할 수 있다고 하였다.

14 이메일의 제목은 'You won our Lucky Day event!'였다.

15 수동태를 능동태로 바꾸는 문제이다. 수동태에 쓰인 주어를 능동태의 목적어로 만든다.

16 특정한 순간이나 시각 앞에 쓰이는 전치사는 at이다.

17 (A) 주어가 동사의 행위의 주체가 되므로 수동태를 쓸 수 없다. (B) 지칭하는 것이 the answer이므로 단수 명사를 지칭하는 it이 알맞다. (C) happen은 자동사이므로 수동태로 쓰일 수 없다.

18 Mr. Doodle은 운전자를 보지 못했다고 하였다. 운전자가 주어이므로 수동태를 쓰는 것이 옳다.

19 Ms. A는 Mr. Doodle이 차에 치였을 때 책을 읽고 있었다고

하였다.

20 hardly는 '거의 ~하지 않은'이란 의미의 부사이다. Mr. Doodle이 거의 다치지 않았다는 것은 글의 내용과 일치하지 않는다.

21 답을 쓰면 다음 방으로 갈 수 있다고 하였다. 사물이 주어이므로 수동태를 쓰는 것이 옳다.

22 예고되지 않고 피해나 부상을 유발하는 갑작스러운 사건은 '사고(accident)'이다.

23 두 번째 방으로 온 것을 축하하지만 두 번째 방은 첫 번째 방보다 탈출하기 더 어렵다고 하였으므로 '그러나'가 가장 적절하다.

24 '~로부터'라는 의미의 전치사 from이 들어가는 것이 옳다.

25 for free는 '무료로'라는 의미이다. 따라서 ③번이 옳다.

26 free: 자유로운, 자유의

27 Jay가 이메일을 지운다고 하였다. 주어가 사물이며 시점은 현재이므로 is deleted를 쓴다.

28 Jay가 이메일을 언제 받았는지는 위 글을 읽고 알 수 없다.

29 Jay가 이메일을 믿지 않은 이유는, 11월은 30일까지 있는데 행사 날짜가 11월 31일이라고 표기되어 있었기 때문이다.

30 두 번째 방은 첫 번째 방보다 탈출하기 훨씬 더 어렵다고 하였으므로, 두 번째 방은 첫 번째 방만큼 탈출하기 쉽지 않다는 말을 쓸 수 있다.

서술형 시험대비 p.38~39

01 We need to solve some riddles.

02 You will enter the first room in our tower.

03 escape, like Sherlock Holmes

04 A car hit Mr. Doodle on Sunday afternoon.

05 wasn't seen by him

06 He was walking his dog.

07 He was hit by a car (on Sunday afternoon).

08 The second room is much harder to escape than the first one.

09 is opened quickly by Jay

10 There are usually 30 or 31 days in a month.

11 He won their 'Lucky Day' event.

12 He thinks that the event isn't real and deletes the email.

13 is surprised at[by]

14 a sound in the next room was heard by him.

15 It was broken last Sunday.

16 was the window broken

17 Sujin was holding a baseball bat.

01 방을 탈출하기 위하여 몇 개의 수수께끼를 풀어야 한다고 하였다.

02 enter는 타동사이므로 목적어 앞에 전치사 into가 불필요하다.

03 해석: 방을 탈출하기 위해서는 셜록 홈즈처럼 생각해야 한다.

04 by a car가 쓰인 것으로 보아 행위의 주체가 a car임을 알 수 있다. 과거시제이므로 hit을 쓴다.

05 목적어가 주어로 쓰였으므로 능동태를 수동태로 전환하는 문제이다.

06 두 번째 용의자인 Mr. B는 개를 산책시키던 중이라고 하였다.

07 Mr. Doodle은 일요일 오후에 차에 치였다고 하였다.

08 much는 비교급을 강조하는 부사로 '훨씬'이라고 해석된다.

09 목적어를 주어 자리에 배치하였으므로 능동태를 수동태로 전환하는 문제임을 알 수 있다.

10 '~이 있다'는 표현은 There is/are로 쓴다. 빈도부사 usually의 위치는 be동사 뒤이다.

11 이메일에 따르면 Jay는 옷가게의 '행운의 날' 행사에 당첨되었다고 하였다.

12 이메일을 읽은 후 Jay는 그 행사가 사실이 아니라고 생각하고 이메일을 삭제한다고 하였다.

13 Jay는 이메일 제목을 읽고 놀란다고 하였다. surprise는 수동태로 쓰일 때 by 대신에 at을 주로 쓴다. by를 써도 좋다.

14 과거동사이므로 수동태로 전환할 때 was heard로 쓴다.

15 지난 일요일에 창문이 깨졌다고 하였다.

16 의문문이 있는 문장의 수동태이다. 우선 'The window was broken by whom.'을 쓴 후 전치사와 의문사를 문두에 배치하면 된다.

17 수진이는 야구 방망이를 들고 있었다고 하였다.

영역별 핵심문제 p.41~45

01 ③　　　　02 ⑤

03 (1) Frist, draw a circle.

(2) Second, put a star inside the circle.

(3) Then, put a triangle on top of the circle.

04 (1) escaped　(2) suspect　(3) clues　(4) Delete

05 (1) ready to　(2) at the time of　(3) Write down

06 ①　　07 ⓐ → that (또는 which)　　08 ⑤

09 riddle　　10 ③　　11 ⓔ → draw　12 ①

13 ③　　14 ⑤　　15 ④　　16 ⑤

17 ⑤　　　　18 When will the food be delivered?

19 ③　　20 ④　　21 ②

22 We are interested in studying English.　23 ②, ④

24 ②　　　　25 ④

26 (1) Trash must be picked up by us.

(2) Peter looks down on Kelly.　　27 ①

28 ②　　　　29 It happened in the afternoon.

30 a bike → a car / dinner → breakfast　31 title

32 Our Lucky Day event was won by you.

33 ⑤　　　　34 ③

7

01 '다른 사람이나 장소로부터 물건들을 훔치는 사람'을 가리키는 말은 thief(도둑)이다.

02 hold: 잡다, 쥐다, by oneself: 도움을 받지 않고, 혼자서, detective: 탐정

03 circle: 원, inside: ~의 안에, on top of: ~의 위에, triangle: 삼각형

04 escape: 탈출하다, suspect: 용의자, clue: 단서, delete: 삭제하다

06 주어진 문장에서 cross는 '건너다'를 뜻하며 이와 같은 의미로 쓰인 것은 ①번이다. 나머지는 모두 '십자가, X표'를 의미한다.

07 the new game을 수식하는 목적격 관계대명사 that이나 which가 적절하다.

09 '게임으로 질문하고 놀랍거나 재미있는 대답을 갖는 질문'을 가리키는 말은 riddle(수수께끼)이다.

10 이어지는 문장에서 이해되지 않은 답에 대해 설명을 요청하고 있으므로 (C)가 적절하다.

11 명령문의 동사 turn과 병렬 구조로 draw가 적절하다.

12 열거를 나타내고 있으므로 next 등으로 열거를 이어나갈 수 있다.

13 주어진 문장은 타코를 만드는 과정의 일부를 Then으로 이어서 설명하고 있으므로 (C)가 적절하다.

15 by 이외에 다른 전치사를 쓰는 수동태 문제이다. 모두 전치사 with를 쓰지만 surprised는 전치사 at을 쓴다.

16 die는 자동사이므로 수동태로 쓸 수 없다.

17 make를 p.p.로 바꾸고 나머지는 그대로 쓴다. 행위자 앞에 전치사 by를 쓰는 것을 기억하자.

18 음식이 배달되는 것이므로 수동태를 쓴다. 미래의 일이므로 will을 쓰고 의문사는 문장 맨 앞에 놓는다.

19 ③ 4형식 동사 ask가 직접목적어를 수동태의 주어로 사용할 경우 간접목적어에 전치사 of를 쓴다.

20 be located: ~에 위치해 있다, '존재하다'는 의미의 exist는 자동사로 수동태가 불가능하다.

21 작문이 쓰여지는 것이므로 should be written이라고 써야 한다. composition: 작문, 작곡

22 interest는 by 이외의 전치사를 쓰는 수동태이다.

23 4형식 동사의 수동태에서 직접목적어가 주어로 쓰인 경우 간접목적어에 특정 전치사를 부여한다. teach는 to를 쓰는 동사이다.

24 ⓐ will be sharpened ⓑ Were the flowers picked up? ⓔ is played

25 *Romeo and Juliet*은 책 이름으로 단수 취급하며 시점이 과거이므로 was written by를 쓰는 것이 옳다.

26 (1) 조동사의 수동태는 '조동사+be+p.p.' 형태이다. (2) look down on: 무시하다, 경멸하다

27 많이 다치지는 않았지만 운전자를 보지 못했다는 내용이 가장

자연스럽다. 따라서 ①번에 들어가는 것이 옳다.

28 (A)는 to부정사의 부사적 용법 중 '목적'으로 쓰였다. ① 명사적 용법(목적격 보어) ② 부사적 용법 '목적' ③ 형용사적 용법 ④ 명사적 용법(진주어) ⑤ 부사적 용법 '감정의 원인'

29 그 사건은 오후에 발생하였다.

30 Mr. Doodle은 자전거가 아닌 차에 치였으며, Ms. C는 아침을 만들고 있었다고 하였다.

31 책, 노래, 혹은 영화 같은 것에 식별하거나 묘사하기 위해서 주어지는 이름은 '제목'이다.

32 능동태의 목적어인 our Lucky Day event가 주어가 되고 시제는 과거이므로 was won으로 쓰는 것에 유의한다.

33 답을 알면 적으라고 하였다. 따라서 ⑤번은 답할 수 있다.

34 ③ Jay가 이메일을 지운 이유는 행사가 사실이 아니라고 생각해서이다.

단원별 예상문제 p.46~49

01 ①	02 ④	03 ②	04 ②, ④

05 Can you explain why? 　06 ③

07 Help yourself. 　08 (A) tacos (B) I should fill my tortilla with vegetables and meat (C) add some sauce on the top

09 (B) → (C) → (D) → (A)

10 'E'는 'week'이라는 단어에는 2번, 'year'라는 단어에는 한 번 나오지만, 'day'라는 단어에는 한 번도 나오지 않기 때문이다.

11 ③ 　12 ④

13 The table was set and the candles were lit.

14 ⑤ 　15 ①, ⑤ 　16 will be delivered

17 (1) The kids were told to leave.
　(2) I was heard singing in my room by Thomas.

18 ⑤ 　19 ③

20 You made it to the second room.

21 three suspects / questioned them

22 ⑤ 　23 ⑤

24 He was throwing a ball to his dog. 　25 ③

01 (A)는 자신의 이해를 점검하는 표현이므로 이해를 점검하는 ①번과 바꾸어 쓸 수 있다.

03 '어떤 범죄의 죄가 있다고 생각되는 사람'을 가리키는 말은 suspect(용의자)이다.

04 Finally는 '마침내'를 뜻하며 이와 바꾸어 쓸 수 있는 표현은 'Eventually(결국), At last(마침내)'이다. Though: 비록 ~일지라도, Nevertheless: 그럼에도 불구하고, Initially: 처음에는

06 Kelly는 처음에 답을 이해하지 못했다는 설명이 대화의 내용과 일치한다.

08 나는 엄마와 저녁식사로 타코를 먹었다. 매우 맛있었다. 나는 타코를 어떻게 만드는지 궁금했다. 엄마는 내게 먼저 토르티야에 야채와 고기를 넣고 그 다음에 위에 소스를 추가해야 한다고 말해 주셨다. 다음에 나는 그것을 혼자 만들어볼 것이다.

09 (B) 관심 끌기 → (C) 만드는 방법 질문 → (D) 만드는 방법 설명 → (A) 반응

11 행위자가 불분명하거나 일반 사람들일 때 'by+행위자'를 생략할 수 있다.

12 disappoint는 수동태로 쓰일 때 by 대신에 전치사 with를 쓰는 동사이다.

13 식탁이 차려지고 양초들에 불이 켜지는 것은 모두 수동태를 쓰는 것이 옳다.

14 건물은 손상을 입는 것이므로 수동태로 쓰는 것이 옳으며, disappear는 자동사이므로 수동태로 쓰일 수 없다.

15 그 소녀가 공에 맞았다는 것은 공이 그 소녀를 쳤다는 의미이다. 따라서 ①, ⑤번이 옳다.

16 조동사가 있는 수동태의 형태는 '조동사+be+p.p.'이다.

17 5형식 동사의 수동태에서 목적격 보어가 원형부정사가 아닌 경우는 그대로 쓰일 수 있다.

18 Mr. Doodle이 일요일 오후에 차에 치임 - (C) 다행히도 많이 다치지 않았지만 운전자를 보지 못하고 경찰은 용의자 세 명을 심문함 - (B) 용의자 셋을 심문한 이야기가 나오고 - (A) 누가 범인인지 답을 쓰면 다음 방으로 갈 수 있다는 순서가 가장 자연스럽다.

19 (A)는 '다행히도'라는 의미이다. 따라서 ③번이 옳다. ① 특히 ② 최근에 ④ 갑자기 ⑤ 특히

20 make it to: ~에 이르다

21 용의자는 세 명이라고 하였으며, 경찰이 그들을 심문했다고 하였다. 경찰이 주어로 있으므로 능동태를 써서 표현한다.

22 두 번째 방은 첫 번째 방보다 탈출하기 훨씬 더 어렵다고 하였다. 따라서 ⑤번은 옳지 않다.

23 주어가 동사의 행위의 주체가 되는지 유무를 판단하여 답을 고를 수 있다.

24 도훈이 창밖을 보았을 때 Ted는 개에게 공을 던지는 중이었다.

25 ③ 도훈이가 있던 옆방의 창문이 깨졌다.

🦊 서술형 실전문제   p.50~51

01 Can you explain how to use the buttons?

02 They are going to play the new game that Jimin bought.

03 They can play the game by using the buttons.

04 all of the bikes at school disappeared

05 He looked around the school. Then, he met some suspects and asked questions.

06 (1) The coffee was already made.
   (2) Was the book returned by you?
   (3) My friends will be invited by me.

07 were attacked by

08 will be made by

09 The missing girl was found by the police yesterday.

10 is expected

11 Luckily

12 were questioned by a police officer

13 I[We] can find them inside the room.

14 broke the window

15 He was at home last Sunday.

16 explain

01 how to+동사원형: ~하는 방법

02 Jimin과 Brain은 Jimin이 산 새로운 게임을 함께 할 것이다.

03 Jimin과 Brian은 버튼을 사용해서 게임을 할 수 있다.

04 민수가 놓친 TV쇼는 학교에 있던 모든 자전거가 사라진 사건에 대한 것이다. case: 사건

05 학생 탐정은 도둑을 찾기 위해 학교를 둘러보았다. 그러고 나서 그는 몇 명의 용의자들을 만나 질문을 하였다.

06 (1) 행위의 주체가 불분명할 때에는 'by+행위자'를 생략할 수 있다. (3) 조동사가 있는 문장의 수동태는 '조동사+be+p.p.' 형태를 쓰는 것에 유의한다.

07 attack: ~을 공격하다

08 사물이 주어이므로 수동태를 써서 문장을 완성할 수 있다.

09 발견된 것이므로 수동태를 써야 하며, 어제 일어난 일이므로 과거시제를 쓴다.

10 정시에 올 것으로 예상된다는 의미가 적절하므로 수동태를 써야 한다.

11 문맥상 문장을 수식하는 부사로 바꾼다.

12 목적어 three suspects가 주어로 쓰이고 있으므로 수동태 문장을 완성하는 문제임을 알 수 있다.

14 행위의 주체가 불분명할 때에는 'by+행위자'를 생략하여 수동태를 만들며 문장 (A)는 이에 해당한다. 불분명한 주어로 시작하는 문장이므로 능동태를 쓰는 것이 옳다.

15 도훈이는 지난주 일요일에 집에 있었다.

16 수동태 문장을 능동태로 전환한 것이다. 주어가 동사의 행위의 주체가 될 수 있으므로 explain을 쓰는 것이 옳다.

01 (A) all of the bikes at school disappeared
(B) had missed[hadn't seen]
(C) the student detective
(D) the thief
02 (A) was the book read
(B) were not[weren't] seen
(C) was made by

|모범답안|

03 (1) The flowers will be sent to her on Monday
(2) The mountain can be seen from here.
(3) The performance was shown last month.
(4) The food can't be eaten inside the building.
(5) Only three books can be borrowed by a person at a time.

01 나는 학생 탐정이 나오는 TV 쇼에 매료되었다. 나는 민수 또한 그 TV 쇼를 아주 좋아한다는 이야기를 듣고 기뻤다. 이번 주, 방송분은 매우 흥미로웠다. 쇼는 학교의 모든 자전거들이 사라진 범죄에 관한 것이었다. 나 또한 자전거를 잃어버린 경험이 있었기 때문에 그것은 더 재미있었다. 내가 이것에 대해 민수에게 이야기했을 때, 그는 이 방송분을 보지 못했다고 이야기했다. 나는 그에게 범인을 잡기 위해 학생 탐정이 한 것에 대해 이야기했다. 나는 누가 범인인지 알지만 민수는 알고 싶어 하지 않았다. 그는 나중에 그것을 볼 것이라고 말했다.

02 경찰이 용의자 A에게 책을 어디에서 읽었느냐고 묻는 말이다. by you가 있으므로 수동태를 쓸 수 있다. (B) 누구도 용의자 B가 개를 산책시키는 것을 보지 못했다고 하였고, 이것은 누구에 의해서도 목격되지 않았다는 의미이므로 마찬가지로 수동태를 쓸 수 있다. (C) 대답으로 미루어 보아 무엇이 만들어졌는지를 묻는 말이 들어가는 것이 옳다.

01 (s)afe   02 ①
03 (1) hide   (2) case   (3) candle   (4) triangle
04 ②   05 detective   06 ⑤   07 ⑤
08 Can you explain how to move everything across the river safely?
09 ③
10 (A) the fox (B) the duck (C) the beans (D) the duck
11 (E) → (B) → (A) → (C) → (D)   12 ⑤
13 ⑤   14 ②
15 The rock star was surrounded by hundreds of fans outside the theater.
16 ④   17 was caused by lightning
18 당신은 우리 가게에서 일곱 가지 상품을 아무거나 무료로

선택할 수 있습니다.   19 ④   20 ④
21 November 31 / deleted his email
22 Seven items are free during the event.   23 ③
24 ③   25 How can it be explained?

01 주어진 단어의 관계는 반의어 관계이다. safe: 안전한, dangerous: 위험한
02 '누군가가 범죄나 미스터리를 풀도록 도와주는 물체나 정보'를 가리키는 말은 clue(단서)이다.
03 case: 사건 opposite: 맞은편의, 반대쪽의
04 scene은 '현장, 장면, 풍경' 등을 뜻한다.
05 범죄를 조사하고 범죄자를 잡는 경찰을 가리키는 말은 detective(형사)이다. detective: 탐정, 형사
06 appear: 나타나다, disappear: 사라지다, suspect: 용의자, suspend: 매달다, thief: 도둑, chief: 장(長), 우두머리
07 Minsu는 Jane에게 도둑이 누구인지 이야기하지 말라고 했으므로 ⑤번 설명은 대화의 내용과 일치하지 않는다. deal with: 다루다 investigate: 조사하다
09 ③ 농부가 왜 강을 건너야 하는지는 알 수 없다.
11 (E) 수수께끼 제시 → (B) 모르겠다고 말함 → (A) 정답 제시 → (C) 설명 요청 → (D) 정답에 대한 이유 설명
13 조동사 부정형의 수동태이므로 '조동사+not+be+p.p.' 형태를 써야 한다.
14 belong to는 상태를 나타내는 동사이므로 수동태로 쓰일 수 없다. symptom: 증상
15 목적어가 the rock star이므로 이를 주어로 하여 수동태를 만들 수 있다.
16 annoy는 수동태로 쓰일 경우 전치사 with, about, at과 주로 함께 쓰인다.
17 '불은 번개에 의해 야기되었다'는 문장을 완성하는 것이 적절하다.
18 any는 긍정문에서 '무엇이든, 아무것이든'의 뜻이다.
19 thinks와 병렬 관계에 있으므로 deletes라고 쓰는 것이 옳다.
20 Jay는 이메일 제목을 보고 놀라 빠르게 그것을 열어보았다고 하였으므로 ④번이 글의 내용과 일치한다.
21 행사 날짜는 11월 31일이라고 하였고, Jay는 이메일 내용이 사실이 아니라고 생각하여 메일을 지운다고 하였다.
22 행사 동안 일곱 가지 상품을 무료로 선택할 수 있다고 하였다.
23 Jay 외에 몇 명의 사람들이 이메일을 받았는지는 위 글을 읽고 알 수 없다.
24 도훈이네 집으로 던져진 공은 위 글에서 찾아볼 수 없다.
25 주어로 쓸 수 있는 것은 it밖에 없으므로 행위의 대상으로 보아 수동태를 써서 나타내는 것이 옳다.

We're Here to Dance

시험대비 실력평가 p.60

01 female　　02 ①　　03 ⑤

04 (1) behind　(2) strength　(3) graceful　(4) traditional

05 ③　　　　06 ①

01 주어진 관계는 반의어 관계를 나타낸다. male 수컷의, 남성의, female 암컷의, 여성의

02 '용기와 자신감을 갖고 위험, 고통 또는 어려운 상황을 다루는'을 뜻하는 말은 brave(용감한)이다.

03 opinion: 의견

04 graceful: 우아한, strength: 힘, behind: ~ 뒤에, traditional:전통적인

05 주어진 문장에서 character는 '등장인물'을 뜻하며 이와 같은 의미로 쓰인 것은 ③번이다. 나머지는 모두 '성격, 기질'을 뜻한다.

06 good and evil: 선과 악, be good at: ~을 잘하다

서술형 시험대비 p.61

01 enemy

02 (1) expressed　(2) perform　(3) originally

　　(4) strength　(5) enemy

03 (1) are allowed to　(2) make sounds

　　(3) try(또는 do) your best

04 (1) In my opinion, dancers look as cute as dolls.

　　(2) The boy's shoes are so comfortable that he can wear them all day.

　　(3) Do you see many people behind the actors?

05 (1) The dance is so popular that everybody learns it.

　　(2) Don't miss this great show which was originally performed in Hungary.

　　(3) I move my body to express my feelings.

01 주어진 관계는 반의어 관계를 나타낸다. enemy: 적, friend: 친구

02 enemy: 적, express: 표현하다, originally: 원래, 본래, strength: 힘, perform: 공연하다

03 be allowed to: ~이 허용되다, make sounds: 소리를 내다, try[do] one's best: 최선을 다하다

04 in my opinion: 내 의견으로는, comfortable: 편안한, behind: ~ 뒤에

05 popular: 인기 있는, originally: 원래, 본래, express: 표현하다

교과서 Conversation

핵심 Check p.62~63

1 (1) What do you think about / In my opinion

　(2) wearing a school uniform / I think that, should not wear a school uniform

2 (1) culture event / interesting / I'm sure

　(2) I'm certain

교과서 대화문 익히기

Check(√) True or False p.64

1 T　2 F　3 T　4 F

교과서 확인학습 p.66~67

Listen & Speak 1 A-1

painting / like, having fun / In my opinion, enjoys dancing

Listen & Speak 1 A-2

what, about this painting / interesting, smiled / look happy

Listen & Speak 1 B

some male birds dance / Why / love, female birds / any other animals / bees, where to find food / communicate / agree with you

Listen & Speak 2 A-1

my voice, soft, cool, sure / my body, movements, Why don't, sure / make sounds, dance

Listen & Speak 2 B

What, reading / story about / tell, more / lost, when , After that, gave up on / to be, to be, right / try my best / Keep up, make it

Real Life Communication

what, held / perform / decide what to do / How about,

Let's Check

dancing girls, amazing / Look more, behind / other dancers behind her / right, I'm sure, more

10 Michaela는 3살 때 그녀의 부모님을 잃었다.

11 Michaela는 많은 어려움에도 불구하고 무용수가 되고자 하는 꿈을 포기 하지 않았다.

12 Kelly는 그녀의 꿈을 이루기 위해 최선을 다할 것이다.

시험대비 기본평가   p.68

01 ⑤   02 dancing   03 ⑤

04 He thinks that the dancers in the painting look happy.

01 나머지는 모두 '내 의견으로는'이라는 뜻으로 쓰였지만 ⑤번은 '요약해서 말하면'을 나타낸다.

02 enjoy는 동명사를 목적어로 취한다.

03 (A)에는 '흥미로운'을 뜻하는 interesting, (B)는 동사 smiled, (C)는 'look+형용사= ~처럼 보이다'를 나타내므로 happy가 적절하다.

04 Brian은 그림에서 춤추는 사람들이 행복해 보인다고 생각한다.

시험대비 실력평가   p.69~70

01 ①   02 communicate   03 ⑤

04 ①, ⑤   05 ④   06 ⑤   07 ③

08 Keep up the good work. 09 ③

10 She lost her parents.

11 She didn't give up on her dream of becoming a dancer.

12 She is going to try her best.

01 나머지는 모두 상대방의 설명에 흥미를 나타내지만 ①번은 '나는 새들에 흥미를 갖고 있다.'를 나타낸다.

02 '말하기, 글쓰기, 손 움직이기 등에 의해 누군가에게 무언가에 대해 정보를 주다'를 뜻하는 말은 communicate(의사소통하다)이다.

04 (A)는 확신을 나타내는 표현으로 ①, ⑤번과 바꾸어 쓸 수 있다.

05 (A)는 본인처럼 뛰어 올라볼 것을 권유하는 표현이므로 ④번과 바꾸어 쓸 수 있다.

06 수진은 소리를 만들기 위해 손을 사용한다.

07 (A)는 동사 lost, (B)는 try one's best(최선을 다하다)이므로 best, (C)는 make it(해내다)이므로 ③번이 적절하다.

08 keep up the good work: 계속 열심히 하다

09 Michaela가 무용수가 된 후 어떤 어려움을 겪었는지는 대화를

통해 알 수 없다.

10 Michaela는 3살 때 그녀의 부모님을 잃었다.

11 Michaela는 많은 어려움에도 불구하고 무용수가 되고자 하는 꿈을 포기 하지 않았다.

12 Kelly는 그녀의 꿈을 이루기 위해 최선을 다할 것이다.

서술형 시험대비   p.71

01 (A) show their love to female birds

   (B) show where to find food

   (C) communicate

02 (A) a Buchaechum

   (B) It is easy to learn, and it's also beautiful

03 (B) → (E) → (D) → (A) → (C)

01 오늘 나는 Emily로부터 동물들의 춤에 대해 배웠다. 그녀는 내게 몇몇 수컷 새들이 암컷 새들에게 그들의 사랑을 보여주기 위해 춤을 춘다고 말했다. 게다가 일부 벌들이 먹이를 찾을 수 있는 곳을 보여주기 위해 춤을 춘다고 들었다. 이것은 매우 흥미로웠다. 나는 춤이 동물들 사이에 의사소통을 위한 굉장한 방법이라고 생각했다.

03 (B) Michaela DePrince에 대한 설명 요청 → (E) Michaela DePrince에 대한 설명 → (D) 반응 및 Kelly의 장래 희망 확인 → (A) 대답 및 다짐 나타내기 → (C) 격려

교과서

Grammar

핵심 Check   p.72~73

1 (1) so nice[kind] that   (2) so big[large] that

   (3) so rich that

2 (1) not as[so] hot as   (2) as handsome as

시험대비 기본평가   p.74

01 (1) very → so   (2) taller → tall   (3) so → too

   (4) two time → two times

02 (1) so tough that   (2) too thin to   (3) so happy that   (4) generous enough to   (5) too much to

03 (1) No other song in this album is as beautiful as this song.

   (2) Your cookies are not as delicious as his.

   (3) This mountain is three times as high as Namsan.

   (4) Call me as often as possible.

01 (1) 원인과 결과를 나타내는 어구는 so ~ that이다. (2) as ~ as 사이에는 형용사나 부사의 원급이 온다. (3) '너무 ~해서 … 할 수 없는'은 'too ~ to V' 혹은 'so ~ that 주어 can't'로 표현한다. (4) 비교급을 이용하여 배수 표현을 나타낼 때에는 times를 쓰는 것에 유의한다.

02 'so ~ that 주어 동사'는 원인과 결과를 나타내는 어구이다. that절에서 can't가 쓰이면 '너무 ~해서 … 할 수 없는'이란 의미로 쓰이며, 이는 'too ~ to V'와 같다. that절에서 can이 쓰이면 '~하기에 충분히 …한'이란 의미가 되어 'so ~ that 주어 can' 혹은 '~ enough to V'로 표현할 수 있다.

03 (1) 원급을 이용하여 최상급을 표현할 수 있다. (2) 원급 비교의 부정인 'not as[so]+원급+as ~'는 '~만큼 …하지 않은[않게]'라는 의미로, 비교하는 두 대상의 정도가 같지 않을 때 쓸 수 있다. (3) 원급으로 나타낼 수 있는 비교 표현은 '배수사+as+원급+as'이다. (4) as ~ as possible: 가능한 한 ~하게

시험대비 실력평가 p.75~77

01 ③　　　02 ④　　　03 ③
04 She is so busy that she can't talk with us now.
05 ④　　　06 ④　　　07 Your room is as clean as mine.　08 ⑤　　　09 ③
10 (1) I was too busy to do my homework.
　　(2) I was so busy that I couldn't do my homework.
11 ③　　　12 ②, ④　　　13 ④
14 I was so young that I couldn't see the movie.
15 ④　　　16 ⑤　　　17 ②
18 They are not as[so] poor as we are.　　19 ②, ⑤
20 ③
21 She was so upset that she went home early.
22 (1) not as[so] tall as　(2) as expensive as

---

01 원인과 결과를 이끄는 구문은 'so ~ that 주어 동사'이다.

02 배수사(twice, two times)를 사용하여 비교급을 나타낼 때에는 '배수사 as 원급 as'로 표현한다.

03 ③ 원인은 Kelly가 성가신 것이고 그 결과 휴대전화기를 끈 것이다.

04 'so ~ that 주어 동사'는 원인과 결과를 나타내는 어구이다. that절에서 can't가 쓰이면 '너무 ~해서 … 할 수 없는'이란 의미로 쓰인다.

05 약속은 1시였지만 you와 Julia 모두 2시에 왔으므로 동등비교 표현을 쓰는 것이 적절하다.

06 'so ~ that 주어 can't'와 같은 표현은 'too ~ to V'이다.

07 mine을 대신하여 my room을 써도 좋다. 동등비교 표현이므로 'as 원급 as'를 사용한다.

08 목이 마른 것이 원인이고 생수 한 병을 모두 마신 것이 결과이므

로 'so ~ that' 구문을 이용하는 것이 적절하다.

09 원인과 결과를 나타내는 것은 'so ~ that' 구문이고, '그는 우리를 위해 싸워줄 만큼 충분히 용감하다.'는 의미이므로 enough가 적절하다. 동등 비교는 'as 형용사나 부사의 원급 as'를 사용한다.

10 너무 ~해서 …할 수 없는'은 'too ~ to V' 혹은 'so ~ that 주어 can't 동사원형'으로 표현할 수 있다.

11 ③ '~ enough to V'이다.

12 '내가 매우 바쁘기 때문에 너와 함께 놀 수 없다.'는 의미이므로 'too ~ to V' 혹은 'so ~ that 주어 can't 동사원형'으로 나타낼 수 있다.

13 동등비교 표현인 'as ~ as' 사이에는 형용사나 부사의 원급이 오는 것이 적절하다.

14 'too ~ to V'는 'so ~ that 주어 can't 동사원형'과 같다.

15 Necklaces were so expensive that we couldn't buy them.

16 '~하기에 충분히 …한'이라고 하였으므로 'strong enough to move the desk'라고 쓰는 것이 적절하다.

17 'so ~ that 주어 can 동사원형'은 '~ enough to V'와 같다.

18 동등비교의 부정이므로 'not as[so] ~ as'를 쓴다.

19 '너무 ~해서 …할 수 없는'은 'too ~ to V' 혹은 'so ~ that 주어 can't 동사원형'으로 표현할 수 있다.

20 동등비교이므로 'as ~ as'를 써서 나타낸다. taste: ~한 맛이 나다

21 원인과 결과를 나타내는 어구는 'so ~ that'이다.

22 James는 Parker만큼 크지 않으며, 장미와 백합은 한 송이에 만 원이므로 장미는 백합만큼 비싸다고 말할 수 있다.

서술형 시험대비 p.78~79

01 (1) She is bright enough to solve all the puzzles.
　　(2) He runs so fast that he can win the race.
　　(3) It was too hot for me to go out.
　　(4) They were too poor to buy books as much as they wanted.
　　(5) They studied hard enough to pass the test.
02 Are you as clever as your sister?
03 so difficult that
04 (1) as old as, not as[so] old as
　　(2) as[so] short as
　　(3) not as[so] tall as, as much as
　　(4) not as[so] heavy as
05 The food was so hot that I burned my tongue.
06 Emily gets up as early as Judy.

07 (1) I woke up too late to attend the meeting.

   (2) I woke up so late that I couldn't attend the meeting.

08 The dog is as heavy as the cat.

09 She drives so well that she always picks me up.

10 as busy as a bee

11 as far as

12 you were so rude that I was disappointed with you

13 Did you eat pizza as much as Tom

14 I know June so well that I can ask for help.

15 The book is three times as thick as this book.

01 '너무 ~해서 …할 수 없는'이란 의미의 'so ~ that 주어 can't 동사원형'은 'too ~ to V'와 같다. that절에서 can이 쓰이면 '~하기에 충분히 …한'이란 의미가 되며 'so ~ that 주어 can' 혹은 '~ enough to V'로 표현할 수 있다.

02 '~만큼 …한'은 동등비교 표현을 사용하여 나타낼 수 있다.

03 어려운 것이 원인이고 책 읽기를 포기한 것이 결과이므로 'so ~ that' 구문을 활용하여 문장을 완성한다.

04 Kevin은 Daisy와 나이가 같지만 Peter만큼 나이가 들지 않았다. 세 학생 중 Daisy가 가장 키가 작으며, 가장 가볍다. Peter는 Kevin만큼 크지 않지만 Kevin과 체중이 같다.

05 너무 뜨거운 것이 원인이 되어 혀를 데인 것이 결과이므로 'so ~ that' 구문을 활용하여 문장을 쓸 수 있다.

06 두 사람은 모두 오전 7시에 일어나며, 두 학생 모두 아침 일찍 일어난다고 하였으므로 동등비교 표현을 사용하여 나타낼 수 있다.

07 늦게 일어난 것이 원인이 되어 회의에 참석할 수 없는 결과를 낳았으므로 '너무 ~해서 …할 수 없는'이란 의미의 'too ~ to V' 혹은 'so ~ that 주어 can't 동사원형'으로 표현할 수 있다.

08 개와 고양이의 무게가 같으므로 동등비교 표현을 활용한다.

09 운전을 잘하는 것이 원인이고 나를 데리러 오는 것이 결과이므로 'so ~ that' 구문으로 나타낼 수 있다.

10 as busy as a bee: 매우 바쁜

11 서점과 도서관이 이곳에서 모두 3킬로미터 떨어진 곳에 있으므로, 도서관은 서점만큼 멀다고 말할 수 있다.

12 was를 대신하여 felt를 써도 좋다.

13 얼마나 먹었는지를 답하고 있으므로 '너는 피자를 Tom만큼 많이 먹었니?'라는 질문을 할 수 있다.

14 '~할 만큼 충분히 …한'이란 의미의 '~ enough to V'는 'so ~ that 주어 can 동사원형'과 같다.

15 원급으로 비교 표현을 할 때에는 '배수사+as 원급 as'를 사용한다.

확인문제   p.80

1 F   2 T   3 T   4 F   5 F   6 T

확인문제   p.81

1 F   2 F   3 T   4 F   5 F   6 F

교과서 확인학습 A   p.82~83

01 Why, dance   02 to express, to, enjoy themselves

03 different kinds of dance

04 tells

05 stories through, body movements

06 a fight between good and evil

07 who are playing, green

08 who are playing, wear black

09 Interestingly, are allowed to

10 so powerful that, for

11 meet, *haka* dancers

12 perform, traditional, scary faces

13 originally performed by

14 to show their strength

15 as scary as, before

16 Nowadays, usually perform, to show, the other

17 traditional, fan

18 wear colorful *hanbok*

19 that are painted

20 move, gracefully, different kinds of beauty

21 look as beautiful as

22 so popular that, can see it

교과서 확인학습 B   p.84~85

1 Why do people dance?

2 They dance to express feelings, give happiness to others, or enjoy themselves.

3 Let's take a look at different kinds of dance around the world.

4 *Kathakali* tells a story.

5 The dancers tell stories through their body movements.

6 These stories are usually about a fight between good and evil.

7 Dancers who are playing good characters paint their faces green.

8 Those who are playing evil characters wear black make–up.

9 Interestingly, in *Kathakali*, only men are allowed to dance.

10 The body movements are so powerful that the dancers need to train for many years.

11 When people visit New Zealand, they may meet a group of *haka* dancers.

12 The dancers perform this traditional dance with scary faces.

13 This dance was originally performed by the Maori before a fight.

14 They wanted to show their strength to the enemy.

15 The dancers looked as scary as wild animals before fighting.

16 Nowadays, in New Zealand, rugby players usually perform a haka before a game to show their strength to the other team.

17 *Buchaechum* is a traditional Korean fan dance.

18 The dancers wear colorful *hanbok*.

19 They dance with large fans that are painted in bright colors.

20 The dancers move the fans gracefully to show different kinds of beauty.

21 Their movements look as beautiful as flowers or flying birds.

22 In Korea, *Buchaechum* is so popular that people can see it in many traditional festivals.

시험대비 실력평가   p.86~89

01 ①　　02 ④　　03 ①, ③

04 movement　05 ③

06 They wear black make–up to express that they are playing evil characters.

07 ⑤　　08 ③　　09 show their strength

10 ⑤

11 People can see Buchaechum in many traditional festivals in Korea.　12 ③　　13 ④

14 ③　　15 ③　　16 good character

17 It's because the body movements are so powerful that the dancers need to train for many years.

18 by　　19 ⑤

20 the traditional dance in New Zealand　21 ④

22 ④　　23 부채춤　　24 ④　　25 cute

26 ⑤

01 이어지는 말로 보아 사람들이 왜 춤을 추는지를 묻는 말이 들어가는 것이 적절하다.

02 빈칸 (B)에는 전치사 at이 들어간다. ① take care of: ~을 돌보다 ② become interested in: ~에 흥미를 갖게 되다 ③ agree with: ~에 동의하다 ④ be good at: ~을 잘하다 ⑤ be full of: ~으로 가득 차다

03 사람을 선행사로 받는 주격 관계대명사가 쓰인다. 따라서 who 또는 that이 적절하다.

04 몸을 움직이는 행위나 몸의 일부를 움직이는 행위는 '움직임, 동작(movement)'이다.

05 ③ 춤꾼들은 몸동작을 통해 이야기한다고 하였다.

06 춤꾼들은 악한 역할을 맡은 것을 표현하기 위해 검은색 화장을 한다고 하였다.

07 적에게 힘을 보여 주고자 춘 춤에서 기인한 것이라고 하였으므로 scary faces가 가장 적절하다.

08 ③ 마오리족이 haka 춤을 춘 이유는 적들에게 그들의 힘을 보여주고 싶어서라고 하였다. attraction: 관광지, 관광명소

09 럭비 선수들이 다른 팀에게 그들의 힘을 보여주기 위해 게임 전에 haka를 보여준다고 하였다.

10 (A)는 birds를 수식하는 현재분사로 쓰이고 있다. 모두 동명사이지만 ⑤번은 현재분사이다.

11 한국의 많은 전통 축제에서 부채춤을 볼 수 있다고 하였다.

12 부채춤을 추는 춤꾼들은 다채로운 한복을 입고 우아하게 부채를 움직인다고 하였다. 부채춤은 너무 인기가 있어서 많은 전통 축제에서 그것을 볼 수 있다.

13 선과 악에 관한 이야기를 들려주고자 하는 춤이고 앞 문장에서는 선한 역할을 맡은 춤꾼들이 얼굴을 무슨 색으로 칠하는지가 나와 있으므로 evil이 가장 적절하다.

14 재귀대명사의 재귀적 용법으로 주어와 목적어가 같을 때 쓰인 재귀대명사이다. ③번은 강조 용법으로 쓰였으며 생략해도 무방하다.

15 ③ 오직 남성만이 춤을 추도록 허용되었다고 하였다.

16 선한 역할을 맡은 춤꾼들은 얼굴을 초록색으로 칠한다고 하였다.

17 춤꾼들이 수 년 동안 연습을 해야 하는 이유는 몸동작이 매우 힘이 넘쳐서이다.

18 수동태의 행위 주체를 표현하는 by가 적절하다.

19 뉴질랜드에서 만날 수 있는 haka 춤꾼 무리들 - [C] 이들은 전통 춤을 추는 것으로 원래 마오리 족에 의해 행해지던 것임 -

[B] 마오리족들은 적에게 그들의 힘을 보여주고 싶어서 춤을 춤 - [A] 요즘에는 럭비 선수들이 이 춤을 춤

20 *haka*는 뉴질랜드의 전통 춤이라고 하였다.

21 요즘에는 럭비선수들이 *haka* 춤을 춘다고 하였다.

22 (A)는 부사적 용법 중 '목적'으로 쓰인 to부정사이다. ①, ②, ③ 명사적 용법 ④ 부사적 용법 중 목적 ⑤ 형용사적 용법

23 부채춤을 가리키는 말이다.

24 부채춤은 한국에서 매우 인기가 있어서 많은 전통 축제에서 볼 수 있다고 하였다.

25 원급 비교이므로 형용사의 원래 형태를 쓴다.

26 아일랜드 사람들이 왜 스텝 댄스를 추는지는 위 글에 나와 있지 않다.

서술형 시험대비
p.90~91

01 People dance to express feelings, give happiness to others, or enjoy themselves.
02 We can think that they are playing good characters.
03 dance, India, fight, good and evil
04 They tell stories through their body movements.
05 The body movements are so powerful that the dancers need to train for many years.
06 They perform a haka with scary faces.
07 to the enemy, their strength to the other team
08 a single person → a group of people
09 are painted
10 It is a traditional Korean fan dance.
11 It's because they want to show different kinds of beauty.
12 They danced the *tarantella* for sick people.
13 We can see people dance the *tarantella*.
14 It is performed before a fight.

01 사람들은 감정을 표현하거나, 다른 사람들에게 행복감을 주거나, 스스로 즐기기 위해 춤을 춘다고 하였다.

02 선한 역할을 맡은 사람은 얼굴을 녹색으로 칠한다.

03 사람들은 많은 이유로 춤을 춘다. 예를 들어서, 인도 춤 카타칼리에서는 사람들이 선과 악 사이의 싸움을 표현하기 위해 춤꾼들이 춤을 춘다.

04 카타칼리 춤꾼들은 몸동작을 통하여 이야기한다고 하였다.

05 동작이 매우 힘이 넘쳐서 춤꾼들은 수년 동안 연습을 해야 한다고 하였다. 'so ~ that'은 원인과 결과를 나타내는 어구이므로 춤동작이 매우 힘이 넘치는 것을 원인으로 하여 문장을 만들 수

있다.

06 하카 춤꾼들은 무서운 얼굴을 하고 이 춤을 춘다고 하였다.

07 마오리족은 적에게 자신들의 힘을 보여 주고자 하카를 추었고, 지금은 럭비 선수들이 상대 팀에게 자신들의 힘을 보여 주기 위하여 하카를 춘다고 하였다.

08 적이나 상대에게 강함을 보여주기 위하여 추는 하카 춤은 전쟁 전에 부족 사람들에 의해서, 혹은 경기 전에 선수들에 의해서 행해지므로 여러 사람이 추는 춤임을 알 수 있다.

09 fans는 색칠되는 대상이므로 수동태를 쓴다.

10 부채춤은 한국 전통 부채춤이라고 하였다.

11 다양한 종류의 미를 보여 주기 위해서 부채를 우아하게 움직인다고 하였다.

12 과거에 사람들이 타란텔라를 춘 이유는 아픈 사람들을 위해서라고 하였다.

13 요즘에는 결혼식과 같은 행복한 날에 추는 춤이라고 하였으므로 사람들이 타란텔라를 추는 것을 보는 것이 가능하다.

14 아두무 춤은 전투하기 전에 춘다고 하였다.

영역별 핵심문제
p.93~97

01 uncomfortable   02 ④   03 ④
04 ④
05 (1) wild (2) hide (3) bright (4) popular (5) scared
06 ③
07 (1) They wanted to show their strength to the enemy.
   (2) Other dancers cheer him up with loud noises.
   (3) Sujin is as brave as a lion.
08 (C) → (A) → (B)   09 ③   10 ④
11 ③   12 (D) → (A) → (C) → (E) → (B)
13 where to find food   14 I agree with you.
15 ⑤   16 ④   17 ③
18 She is as wise as an owl.   19 ②, ⑤
20 ④   21 ③
22 No other basketball player, is as[so] tall as
23 ②   24 ③
25 I was so happy that I sang all day.
26 is as brave as a lion
27 He is so talkative that he can't listen to others.
28 ②   29 ②   30 ⑤
31 *Kathakali* tries to tell a story about a fight between good and evil.
32 The body movements look very powerful.
33 ③   34 ④
35 Because it is so popular.

01 주어진 관계는 반의어 관계이다. comfortable: 편안한, uncomfortable: 불편한

02 give up on ~을 포기하다, on time 정시에

03 '당신이 손을 움직여 공기를 더 시원하게 만드는 평평한 물체'를 가리키는 말은 fan(부채)이다.

04 gracefully: 우아하게

05 bright: 밝은, scared: 겁먹은, wild: 야생의, hide: 숨다, 숨기다 popular: 인기 있는 tame: 길들이다

06 주어진 문장과 나머지 문장에서 express는 모두 '표현하다'를 나타내지만 ③번은 '급행'을 나타낸다.

07 strength: 힘, cheer: 응원하다, brave: 용감한

08 (C) 그림에 대한 의견 묻기 → (A) 의견 말하기 → (B) 동의 및 추가 설명

09 주어진 문장은 좀 더 가까이 볼 것을 권유하는 문장으로 (C)가 적절하다.

10 nervous: 긴장한, disappointed: 실망한, lonely: 외로운, surprised: 놀란, terrible: 무서운

11 한 명의 무용수 뒤에 많은 팔들을 볼 수 있다.

12 (D) 결정의 필요성 언급 → (A) 제안 및 의견 설명 → (C) 반응 및 질문 → (E) 질문에 대한 대답 → (B) 반응 및 확신 표현

15 위 대화를 통해 몇몇 동물들이 춤을 추며 어떻게 의사소통을 하는지는 알 수 없다.

16 원인과 결과를 나타내는 문장이므로 'so ~ that' 구문을 쓰는 것이 적절하다.

17 'No other 단수 명사+동사+ as 원급 as'로 최상급을 나타낼 수 있다.

18 as wise as owl: 매우 현명한

19 '너무 ~해서 …할 수 없는'이란 의미의 'so ~ that 주어 can't 동사원형'은 'too ~ to V'과 같다.

20 'too ~ to V' 혹은 'so ~ that 주어 can't 동사원형'을 쓰는 것이 적절하다.

21 원인과 결과를 이끄는 문장이므로 'so ~ that' 구문을 쓰는 것이 적절하다.

22 원급으로 최상급의 의미를 나타내려면 'no other+단수 명사+동사+as[so] ~ as …'로 쓰는 것이 적절하다.

23 이어지는 말로 보아 물이 너무 차서 마실 수 없었다는 말이 들어가는 것이 적절하다.

24 가장 긴 밧줄은 D이다.

25 행복한 것이 원인이고 노래를 부른 것이 결과이므로 'so ~ that' 구문을 쓴다.

26 원급 비교를 이용하여 사자처럼 용감하다는 말을 쓸 수 있다.

27 해석: 그는 너무 말이 많아서 다른 사람의 말을 들을 수 없다.

28 give는 4형식 동사이다. 3형식으로 전환할 때 간접목적어에 to를 부여한다..

29 밑줄 친 (B)는 '종류'라는 의미의 명사이다. 따라서 ②번이 적절하다. 나머지는 모두 형용사로 '친절한, 다정한'이란 의미이다.

30 카타칼리 춤동작은 매우 힘이 넘쳐서 춤꾼들은 몇 년 동안 연습을 해야 한다고 하였다.

31 카타칼리를 추는 춤꾼들은 선과 악의 싸움에 관한 이야기를 한다.

32 춤동작은 매우 힘이 넘쳐 보인다고 하였다.

33 꽃과 날아가는 새는 부채춤의 우아함을 빗댄 표현이다.

34 다양한 종류의 미를 보여 주기 위해 부채를 우아하게 움직이는 것이라고 하였다.

35 부채춤을 한국 전통 축제 장소에서 볼 수 있는 이유는 매우 인기 있어서이다.

단원별 예상문제　　　　　　　p.98~101

01 ④
02 what do you think about that painting?
03 In my opinion[view]
04 They show their love to female birds.
05 They show where to find food.
06 ③
07 (A) there were other dancers
　　(B) there were more than 10 dancers
08 ⓐ → be held
09 ②　　　　　　10 ⑤
11 He is funny enough to be a comedian.
12 ⑤　　　　13 as red as　14 ③
15 The dancer is so beautiful that I can't take my eyes off her.
16 ②　　　17 ④　　　18 ③　　　19 ②
20 ④
21 They wanted to show their strength to the enemy.
22 ⑤　　　　　23 ⑤
24 They look like flowers or flying birds.
25 colorful *hanbok*, large fans painted in

01 나머지는 모두 상대방의 의견에 동의를 나타내지만 ④번은 이의를 나타낸다.

04 수컷 새들은 암컷 새들에게 그들의 사랑을 보여준다.

05 일부 벌들은 춤을 추며 먹이를 찾을 수 있는 곳을 보여준다.

06 (A) amazed: 깜짝 놀란, amazing: 굉장한, (B) know의 목적절을 이끄는 접속사 that, (C) there is+단수 명사, there are+복수 명사

07 처음 무용수를 보았을 때, 나는 오직 한 명의 무용수만 있다고 생각했다. 그러나 다시 좀 더 자세히 보며, 나는 그녀 뒤에 다른 무용수들이 있다는 것을 알았다. 많은 팔들 때문에 나는 10명 이상의 무용수가 있었다는 것을 추측할 수 있었다.

08 학교 춤 대회가 곧 열릴 것이라는 수동태가 되어야 하므로 be held가 적절하다.

09 (A)는 도움을 요청하는 표현으로 ②번과 바꾸어 쓸 수 있다.

10 부채춤은 배우기가 쉽고 아름답다.

11 'so ~ that 주어 can 동사원형'은 '~ enough to V'와 같다.

12 모두 원인과 결과를 나타내는 문장이지만 ⑤번은 그렇지 않다.

13 토마토만큼 머리 색깔이 붉다는 의미이다.

14 각각 ① to move ② so sad ④ as light as ⑤ to swim이라고 쓰는 것이 옳다.

15 take one's eyes off: ~에서 눈을 떼다

16 원인과 결과를 나타내는 말로 가장 적절한 것은 ②번이다.

17 원급으로 최상급의 의미를 나타내기 위해서는 'no other 단수 명사'로 쓰는 것이 적절하다.

18 nowadays는 '요즘에'라는 의미이다. 따라서 these days가 가장 적절하다.

19 적들에게 그들의 힘을 보여 주기 위해서 추는 춤이므로 '겁에 질린(scared)' 표정은 어색하다. scary가 적절하다.

20 요즘에는 뉴질랜드 럭비 선수들이 시합 전에 주로 하카를 춘다고 하였다.

21 하카 춤을 춤으로써 마오리 부족들은 적에게 자신의 힘을 보여 주기를 원했다.

22 특정한 날짜 앞에는 전치사 on이 쓰인다.

23 아두무를 추기 위해서 무엇이 필요한지는 위 글에 나와 있지 않다.

24 춤꾼들의 움직임은 꽃이나 날아다니는 새들처럼 아름다워 보인다고 하였다.

25 부채춤을 추기 위해서는 다채로운 한복과 밝게 색칠된 큰 부채가 필요하다.

서술형 실전문제 p.102~103

01 Jimin's class is going to perform a taekwondo dance.

02 She is good at traditional dances.

03 She thinks that it is easy to learn and it's also beautiful.

04 (1) I am too shy to dance in front of many people.
   (2) I am so shy that I can't dance in front of many people.

05 works so well that

06 The diamond ring is as expensive as the car.

07 She is as slow as a turtle.

08 The party was so enjoyable that nobody wanted to leave.

09 green / wearing black make-up / evil character

10 India, stories, good and evil, men, powerful

11 the dancers look as cute as dolls

12 so fast that

01 지민이네 반은 태권도 춤을 공연할 것이다.

02 미나는 전통 춤을 잘 춘다.

03 미나는 부채춤이 배우기 쉽고 또한 아름답다고 생각한다.

04 '너무 ~해서 …할 수 없는'은 'too ~ to V' 혹은 'so ~ that 주어 can't 동사원형'으로 나타낼 수 있다.

05 Brian이 자전거를 또 사지 않으려는 이유는 지금 자전거가 작동이 너무 잘 되어서이다.

06 자동차와 다이아몬드 반지의 가격이 동일하므로 원급 비교를 사용하여 나타낼 수 있다.

07 거북이와 동등 비교를 하고 있으므로 'as 원급 as'를 사용하여 문장을 만든다.

08 enjoyable: 즐거운

09 카타할리에서 얼굴을 초록색으로 칠한 춤꾼들은 선한 역할을 맡은 것이고, 악한 역할을 맡은 춤꾼은 검은색 화장을 한다고 하였다.

10 카타할리는 인도 전통 춤이고 이야기가 있는 춤이다. 이야기들은 선과 악의 싸움에 관한 것이며 춤 동작이 매우 힘이 넘친다고 하였다.

11 춤꾼들은 인형과 같이 귀엽게 보인다고 하였으므로 '춤꾼들은 인형만큼 귀여워 보인다.'고 말할 수 있다.

12 발을 너무 빨리 움직여서 그들의 발을 보기 힘들다는 말이 적절하다.

창의사고력 서술형 문제 p.104

|모범답안|

01 (A) a great dancer   (B) a dancer
   (C) try my best to be a great dancer like her

02 (1) |모범답안| The wind was so strong that it blew my hat off my head.
   (2) |모범답안| The soup was so hot that I couldn't eat it.
   (3) |모범답안| She is so friendly that she will throw a party for us.

03 Ireland / wear colorful costumes / as cute as dolls / move their feet so fast / like they're flying

01 오늘 나는 Michaela DePrince에 관한 이야기를 읽었다. 이 책을 고른 이유는 나는 그녀처럼 훌륭한 무용수가 되고 싶기 때문이다. 이야기는 매우 인상 깊어서 나는 Tom과 그것을 나누었다. 나는 Tom에게 그녀의 어려움과 무용수가 되기 위한 그녀의 많은 노력들을 포함하여 Michaela의 이야기를 설명하였다. 그녀의 이야기를 읽은 후 나는 그녀처럼 훌륭한 무용수가 되기 위해 최선을 다할 것을 다짐하였다. Tom 또한 나를 많이 격려하여서 나는 그가 매우 고마웠다.

01 ②   02 (1) have fun   (2) take a look
    (3) good and evil   (4) is good at   (5) give up on
03 I'm sure we'll have a lot of fun.
04 ⑤   05 ③   06 ①   07 ⑤
08 ③   09 (B) → (D) → (A) → (E) → (C)
10 She uses her voice to make music.
11 She moves her body to express her feelings.
12 ⑤   13 ③   14 ④
15 She is as busy as a bee.
16 The movie was so moving that I cried a lot.
17 ③   18 ④   19 ②   20 ③
21 (A) The Maori   (B) rugby players
22 They perform a haka to show their strength to the
   other team.
23 They performed a *haka* before a fight.   24 ③

01 '경찰, 군인 등과 같이 집단 또는 조직의 모든 구성원들이 입는
   옷의 특별한 종류'를 가리키는 말은 uniform(제복)이다.

02 have fun 즐거운 시간을 보내다, take a look 살펴보다, good
   and evil 선과 악, be good at ~을 잘하다, give up on ~을
   포기하다

04 위 대화를 통해 왜 지민이네 반이 태권도 춤을 선택했는지 알 수
   없다.

05 주어진 문장은 Michaela에 대해 이야기해 달라는 Tom의 부탁
   에 대한 대답으로 적절하므로 (C)가 적절하다.

06 try one's best = do one's best = 최선을 다하다

07 위 대화를 통해 Michaela DePrince가 무용수로 계속 좋은 일
   들을 하고 있는지는 알 수 없다.

08 (A) impress: 감명을 주다, express: 표현하다, (B) certain:
   확실한, unsure: 불확실한, (C) 의미상 '당신이 이것을 들을 때'
   가 적절하므로 접속사 when이 적절하다.

09 (B) 춤을 추는 이유 설명 → (D) 춤을 추는 다른 동물들이 있는
   지 질문 → (A) 대답 및 설명 → (E) 춤에 대한 의견 표현하기
   → (C) 동의 표현

10 민지는 음악을 만들기 위해 그녀의 목소리를 사용한다.

11 지민은 그녀의 감정을 표현하기 위해 몸을 움직인다.

12 twice as long as mine이라고 쓰는 것이 적절하다.

13 '~만큼 …할 수 없는'은 동등비교의 부정으로 표현할 수 있다.

14 폭우가 원인이 되어 학교 현장 학습을 취소한 것이 결과이므로
   ④번이 적절하다.

15 '벌만큼 바쁜'이라는 동등 비교 표현으로 나타낼 수 있다.

16 원인과 결과를 나타내고 있으므로 'so ~ that' 구문을 활용하여
   답할 수 있다.

17 세계의 여러 가지 춤을 살펴보자고 하였으므로 ③번이 가장 적
   절하다.

18 to부정사에 병렬로 연결되어 있으므로 enjoy라고 쓰는 것이 적
   절하다.

19 비교 대상으로 미루어 보아 '아름다운'이 적절하다.

20 위 글은 한국 전통 춤인 부채춤에 관하여 정보를 제공하는 글이
   므로 ③번이 가장 적절하다.

21 각각 마오리 부족과 오늘날의 럭비 선수들을 가리키는 말이다.

22 뉴질랜드 럭비 선수들은 그들의 힘을 보여주기 위해 시합 전에 주
   로 하카를 춘다고 하였다.

23 마오리족은 싸움 전에 하카를 추었다.

24 strength는 '힘'이라는 의미이므로 the state of being strong
   이라고 풀이하는 것이 적절하다.

Magic or Science?

시험대비 실력평가
p.112

01 disappear
02 ①
03 ④
04 ②
05 ①
06 (1) trick (2) material (3) prepares (4) necessary (5) pressure (6) expand

01 주어진 관계는 반의어 관계를 나타낸다. disappear: 사라지다
02 '크기, 범위, 또는 양에서 증가하다'를 가리키는 말은 expand(팽창하다)이다.
03 confuse: 혼동하다
04 necessary: 필요한
05 주어진 문장에서 rose는 rise(오르다, 올라가다)의 과거형으로 이와 같은 의미를 가진 것은 ①번이다. 나머지는 모두 '장미'를 뜻한다.
06 trick: 마술, 속임수, material: 재료, 물질, prepare: 준비하다, necessary: 필요한, pressure: 압력, expand: 팽창하다, 확장하다

서술형 시험대비
p.113

01 float
02 (1) see through (2) turn, into (3) burned out
   (4) cooled down (5) stick to
03 (1) instead (2) float (3) magic (4) pushed
04 (1) It is not good to pick out vegetables that you don't like.
   (2) I'll give it a try.
   (3) If you are sleepy, drink a glass of cold water.
   (4) I signed up for the badminton class.
05 (1) sunburn (2) Hold (3) expands
   (4) coin (5) escape (6) contract

01 주어진 관계는 반의어 관계를 나타낸다. sink: 가라앉다, float: 뜨다
02 tick to: ~을 고수하다, cool down: 차가워지다, see through: 속을 들여다보다, turn A into B: A를 B로 바꾸다, burn out: 타 버리다
03 instead of: ~ 대신에, float: 뜨다, magic: 마술의, push: 밀다
04 pick out 골라내다, give it a try 시도해 보다, a glass of 한 잔의, sign up for ~을 신청하다
05 hold: 잡다, coin: 동전, sunburn: 볕에 탐, expand: 팽창하다, escape: 탈출하다, 새다 contract: 수축하다

핵심 Check
p.114~115

1 (1) Which country (2) Which sport
  (3) Which one is stronger
2 (1) can't wait (2) looking forward to meeting
  (3) can't wait to see you again

교과서 대화문 익히기

Check(√) True or False
p.116

1 T   2 F   3 T   4 T

교과서 확인학습
p.118~119

Listen & Speak 1 A
Which flavor, First, half a cup, Next, mix, freezer, try making

Listen & Speak 1 B
put / picking out / Which, which / that sink in water, float / interesting, float / inside, like, balloon

Listen & Speak 2 A
a glass of, weigh / test / instead of / weigh, put / compare / can't wait to

Listen & Speak 2 B
hasn't rained / lasting, worried / should / clock / seasons, to prepare for, dry season / like / give it a try / can't wait to see your clock

Real Life Communication A
join / signed up for, fall / wait to, tricks / cool, Have you learned / practice / some day

Let's Check
magic, science / interesting / introduces, use science / half / cool, some / balloon / wait to

시험대비 기본평가
p.120

01 ⓔ → see   02 ⑤
03 Which class did you sign up for?   04 ①

01 I can't wait to 동사원형: 나는 ~이 무척 기다려져.

04 Mina는 새로운 마술 묘기를 배우게 돼서 신이 나 있다.

06 딸기를 작게 자른 다음 모든 것을 섞어서 냉동실에 넣어야 한다.

시험대비 실력평가
p.121~122

01 isn't it?	02 Sugar	03 ⑤	04 ③
05 물 위에 뜨는 달걀		06 ③	07 ④
08 ⑤	09 ②	10 ⑤	

01 부가의문문으로 앞의 문장의 주어가 it이며 긍정문이므로 'isn't it?'이 적절하다.

02 설탕은 반 컵이 필요하다.

03 집에서 아이스크림을 만들어 볼 것을 제안한다.

04 (A)는 둘 중에서 선택하는 것이므로 which, (B)는 주어가 Eggs이므로 동사는 are, (C)는 주어와 동사가 있는 절이 이어지므로 because가 적절하다.

06 상한 달걀 속에 가스가 찬다.

07 주어진 문장은 시계가 어떻게 도움이 되는지에 대한 대답이므로 (D)가 적절하다.

08 세종대왕이 걷기를 끝내기 위해 무엇을 하는지 알 수 없다.

09 마술 수업에 등록한 상대방에게 '멋지다'라고 호응해 주는 표현이 적절하다.

10 얼마나 오랫동안 미나가 마술 묘기를 연습해 왔었는지는 알 수 없다.

서술형 시험대비
p.123

01 I can't wait to see the difference.
02 She will use a finger.
03 a glass of water weighs more when there's a fish in it
04 (D) → (B) → (E) → (C) → (A)
05 We need to prepare two cups of milk, two cups of heavy cream, half a cup of sugar, and five strawberries.
06 We should mix everything together and put it in the freezer.

02 정 선생님은 물고기 대신 손가락을 사용할 것이다.

03 정 선생님은 재민이와 실험을 통해 물 한 잔이 물속에 물고기가 있을 때 무게가 더 나가는지 아닌지 확인하고 싶어 한다.

04 (D) 시계를 만들 것을 제안 → (B) 어떻게 도움이 될지 질문 → (E) 도움이 되는 이유 설명 → (C) 관심 표현 및 질문 → (A) 대답 및 이유 설명

05 Jane에 따르면 딸기 아이스크림을 만들기 위해 두 컵의 우유, 두 컵의 헤비 크림, 반 컵의 설탕, 그리고 5개의 딸기를 준비해야 한다.

Grammar
교과서

핵심 Check
p.124~125

1 (1) to take care　(2) to meet　(3) for us to stay
2 (1) How come　(2) Why　(3) How come　(4) How come

시험대비 기본평가
p.126

01 (1) stop → to stop
(2) of you → for you
(3) did you meet → you meet
(4) came → come
02 (1) he drinks (2) do you exercise
(3) she looks (4) did you run
03 (1) It is very important to exercise regularly.
(2) It is exciting to go to the amusement park.
(3) It is important to be honest with your friends.
(4) It is my job to explain it.

01 (1) 진주어로 쓰이는 것은 to부정사이다. (2) 상황에 대한 의견을 나타내는 형용사가 나오므로 의미상 주어로 'for+목적격'을 쓴다. (3) How come을 Why로 바꾸어도 좋다. (4) '도대체 왜 …?' 라고 쓰이는 것은 'How come'이다.

02 'How come+주어+동사 …?'로 쓰여 '도대체 왜 …?'라는 의미이고, 'Why+동사+주어 …?' 어 순임에 유의한다.

03 가주어 it을 대신하여 진주어 to부정사를 사용하여 문장을 쓸 수 있다.

시험대비 실력평가
p.127~129

01 ②	02 ③	03 ④	04 It is fun to learn a foreign language.
			05 ②
06 ④			
07 ⑤	08 to read books		09 ④
10 ③	11 ③	12 ③	13 How come she bought the jacket?
			14 ⑤
15 ④	16 It is important not to use your phone while walking.		17 she left
			18 ③
19 ③, ④	20 ③	21 It is dangerous to tell a stranger where you live.	22 ③
			23 ⑤
24 How come you called me?			

01 진주어이므로 to부정사를 쓰는 것이 적절하다.

02 'How come+주어+동사' 어순에 유의한다.

03 easy는 사람의 성질을 나타내는 형용사가 아니므로 의미상의 주어로 'for+목적격'을 쓴다. 나머지는 모두 of를 사용한다.

04 '외국어를 배우는 것'이 주어이므로 to learn a foreign language라고 쓴다.

05 주어진 문장의 밑줄 친 부분은 진주어로 쓰인 to부정사이다. ①, ④ 부사적 용법 중 목적 ② 진주어 ③ 형용사적 용법 ⑤ 명사적 용법(목적격 보어)

06 진주어로 쓰일 수 있는 것은 to부정사이며, 의문문에서 '주어+동사' 어순을 이끄는 것은 How come이다.

07 '주어+동사'의 어순을 이끄는 것은 'How come'이고, '동사+주어'의 어순을 이끄는 것은 'Why'이다.

08 진주어로 to부정사를 쓰는 것이 적절하다.

09 It is nice to know how to say hello.

10 모두 가주어 It이지만, ③번의 It은 날짜, 날씨, 거리, 명암 등을 나타내는 비인칭 주어이다.

11 진주어로 쓰일 수 있는 것은 It이다.

12 careless는 '부주의한'이란 의미로 사람의 성격을 나타내는 형용사이므로 의미상의 주어로 'of+목적격'을 써야 한다.

13 'How come+주어+동사' 어순에 유의한다.

14 impossible은 사람의 성격과 관련된 형용사가 아니므로 의미상의 주어로 'for+목적격'을 쓴다.

15 '주어+동사' 어순의 의문문이므로 How come이 적절하다.

16 휴대 전화기를 사용하지 않는 것이라고 하였으므로 to부정사의 부정으로 'not to V'를 쓰는 것에 유의한다.

17 How come이 이끄는 문장의 어순은 '주어+동사'임에 유의한다.

18 wise는 사람의 성격을 나타내는 형용사이므로 의미상의 주어로 'of+목적격'을 쓴다. 절이 이어지고 있으므로 두 번째 빈칸에는 진주어절을 이끄는 that을 쓴다.

19 '부주의하게 운전하는 것'이 주어이므로 주어를 to drive carelessly라고 쓰는 것이 적절하다.

20 모두 가주어 it에 진주어 to부정사가 쓰이지만, ③번에는 전치사 at의 목적어로 동명사 building이 쓰인다.

21 가주어 it을 이용하여 진주어 구문을 문장 맨 뒤로 보내어 같은 의미의 문장을 쓸 수 있다.

22 어순으로 보아 How come이 적절하며, impossible은 사람의 성격을 나타내는 형용사가 아니므로 의미상의 주어로 'for+목적격'을 쓰는 것이 적절하다.

23 ① hear → to hear ② did you lose → you lost ③ for you → of you ④ you weren't → weren't you

24 How come은 'How come+주어+동사 ~?' 어순임에 유의한다.

01 It is dangerous not to wear your helmet.

02 (1) she is looking (2) did you invite
    (3) the teacher gives (4) we are going
    (5) are you wearing

03 (1) is exciting to travel abroad
    (2) is not easy to read this novel
    (3) know how to use this machine is useful

04 It was stupid of you to say so.

05 How come you put your wallet on the table?

06 for me to climb

07 How come you are going to meet her today?

08 that

09 How come / Why

10 to form good habits

11 A: How come she doesn't say sorry to me?
    B: I think (that) it is not easy for her to say sorry to you.

12 of

13 How come you forgot to bring the book?

14 It was generous of him to lend you his clothes.

15 How come you booked the restaurant?

16 To watch the movie

17 How come / Why didn't you

18 A: How come you study hard?
    B: It makes me happy to study hard.

01 '헬멧을 쓰지 않는 것'이 주어이므로 to부정사 진주어 앞에 부정어 not을 쓰는 것에 유의한다.

02 의문사 why와 how come은 의미는 비슷하지만 어순상의 차이를 보인다. 'How come+주어+동사 …?'로 쓰여 '도대체 왜 …?'라는 의미이지만, 'Why+동사+주어 …?' 어순으로 쓰인다.

03 to부정사구가 주어로 올 경우 주어가 길어지므로 가주어 it을 쓰고 to부정사구는 진주어로 만들어 문장 뒤로 보낸다.

04 '그렇게 말한 것'의 주체가 '너'이며, 사람의 성격을 나타내는 형용사가 쓰이고 있으므로 의미상의 주어로 'of you'를 쓰는 것이 적절하다.

05 'How come+주어+동사' 어순에 유의하여 답을 쓴다.

06 '산을 오르는 것'이 진주어이고 주체는 '나'이므로 for me to climb이라고 쓰는 것이 적절하다.

07 이어지는 답변에서 내가 그녀를 오늘 만나려는 이유를 설명하고 있으므로 '왜 오늘 그녀를 만나려고 하는 거야?'라고 질문했음을 알 수 있다.

08 절을 이끌고 있으므로 진주어 절을 이끄는 that이 오는 것이 적절하다.

09 비슷한 의미를 가졌지만 How come은 '주어+동사' 어순을 이끌고 Why는 '동사+주어' 어순을 이끈다.

10 이어지는 답변으로 보아 '좋은 습관을 형성하는 것은 쉬운가요?'라고 질문했음을 알 수 있다.

11 '너에게 미안하다고 말하는 것'의 주체가 '그녀'이며 easy는 사람의 성격을 나타내는 형용사가 아니므로 의미상의 주어 로 'for her'를 쓰는 것에 유의한다.

12 사람의 성격과 관련된 형용사가 나와 있으므로 의미상의 주어로 'of+목적격'을 쓴다.

13 'How come+주어+동사' 어순임에 유의한다.

14 generous는 사람의 성격을 나타내는 형용사이므로 의미상의 주어로 'of+목적격'을 쓰는 것에 유의한다.

15 How come은 '주어+동사' 어순을 이끈다.

16 '그 영화를 보는 것'이라는 주어를 쓰는 것이 적절하다.

17 'How come+주어+동사'로 쓰이고 'Why+동사+ 주어' 어순임에 유의한다.

18 A: 'How come+주어+동사' 어순이며, '공부를 열심히 하는 것'이 주어이므로 to study hard를 진주어로, it을 가주어로 써서 문장을 완성할 수 있다.

Reading

확인문제
p.132

1 T 2 F 3 F 4 F 5 T

확인문제
p.133

1 T 2 T 3 T 4 F 5 T 6 T

교과서 확인학습 A
p.134~135

01 Welcome to   02 It's, exciting to see
03 to find out, behind   04 is science
05 will use science to perform
06 will, show us, to see them
07 to show you   08 with water in it
09 put a candle   10 light, cover it with
11 at, How come, rose into
12 expands, hot, higher pressure
13 gets cold, contracts, lower pressure
14 burnt out, lower pressure
15 cooled down, dropped
16 was at a higher pressure   17 pushed, into
18 to fill one of these cups
19 them around to confuse   20 which cup

21 It's, one   22 let's check
23 me the other cups   24 no water
25 How come, disappeared
26 Before, put, into, the cups
27 absorbed, turned it into
28 stuck to the bottom
29 necessary to us, that
30 for, performance, amazing

교과서 확인학습 B
p.136~137

1 Jina: Welcome to the Super Science Magic Show!

2 It's always exciting to see magic tricks.

3 And it's more exciting to find out the secrets behind them.

4 Some people think the secret of magic is science.

5 Today, Ken, a member of the School Magic Club, will use science to perform his tricks.

6 Which tricks will he show us? I can't wait to see them.

7 Ken: Hello, everyone. Today, I'm going to show you something amazing.

8 Here's a dish with water in it.

9 Now, I'll put a candle in the middle of the dish.

10 Next, I'll light the candle and cover it with a glass. "Abracadabra!"

11 Jina: Look at the water! How come it rose into the glass?

12 Ken: Air expands when it gets hot and creates higher pressure.

13 When it gets cold, air contracts and creates lower pressure.

14 When the flame burnt out, the air inside the glass cooled down.

15 As the air cooled down, the air pressure dropped.

16 So the air outside the glass was at a higher pressure.

17 It pushed the water into the glass.

18 Ken: Now, I'm going to fill one of these cups with water.

19 I will move them around to confuse you.

20 Jina, which cup has the water in it?

21 Jina: That's easy! It's the middle one.

22 Ken: Okay, let's check. See? No water.

23 Jina: Show me the other cups.

24 Ken: See? There's no water.

25 Jina: Wow! How come the water disappeared?

26 Ken: Before the trick, I put a special material into one of the cups.

27 The material absorbed the water and turned it into jelly.

28 Then the jelly stuck to the bottom.

29 If you want to try this trick, it's necessary to use cups that you can't see through.

30 Jina: Thank you for your great performance. It was really amazing!

시험대비 실력평가
p.138~141

01 ②　　02 ③　　03 Ken is a member of the School Magic Club.　　04 ③　　05 ②
06 ④　　07 The water outside the glass rose into the glass.　　08 ②　　09 change
10 ④　　11 ③　　12 absorb　　13 He moved them around.　　14 It is necessary for us to use cups that we can't see through.　　15 ④
16 ③　　17 magic tricks　　18 ④
19 ⑤　　20 ④　　21 The air inside the glass is at a higher pressure. 22 ①　　23 The Amazing Rising Water　　24 How come the water disappeared? 25 ③　　26 ⑤　　27 He moved them around to confuse us.　　28 ④
29 ice and wind

01 Welcome to ~.: ~에 오신 것을 환영합니다.

02 과학을 이용한 마술에 관한 이야기를 하려고 한다.

03 Kevin은 학교 마술 동아리 회원이라고 하였다.

04 공기가 뜨거워질 때 팽창한다면, 반대로 공기가 차가워질 경우 수축하면서 더 낮은 압력을 만드는 것을 유추할 수 있다.

05 불꽃이 다 타버리면 컵 속의 공기는 식어버리므로 'cooled down'이 적절하다.

06 Ken은 물이 든 접시 위의 초를 유리컵으로 덮었다고 하였다. 따라서 ④번은 찾아볼 수 없다.

07 Ken이 유리컵으로 초를 덮었을 때, 유리컵 밖에 있던 물이 유리컵 속으로 올라갔다.

08 Ken은 놀라운 어떤 것을 보여주기를 원하였고, 이는 과학을 적용한 마술이다.

09 글의 내용으로 보아 유리컵의 내부와 외부의 압력 변화로 인하여 물이 움직이게 되는 것을 알 수 있다. difference라고 써도 좋다.

10 이어지는 대화 내용으로 보아 나머지 모든 컵을 보여 달라고 했음을 유추할 수 있다.

11 the jelly는 물을 흡수한 특별한 물질이 변화하여 만들어진 것이다. 따라서 ③번이 가장 적절하다.

12 자연스럽거나 점진적인 방식으로 무언가를 받아들이는 것은 '흡수하다(absorb)'이다.

13 Ken은 컵들 중 하나에 물을 채운 후 컵들을 섞었다.

14 마술을 해 보고자 한다면, 속을 들여다볼 수 없는 컵을 사용해야 한다고 하였다.

15 Ken의 마술은 과학을 이용한 것이며 투명한 유리컵이 아니라 불투명한 컵을 이용해야 한다.

16 밑줄 친 (A)는 가주어 It이다. ①, ④ 비인칭 주어 ②, ⑤ 인칭 대명사 ③ 가주어

17 마술을 가리키는 대명사이다.

18 마술 동아리 회원인 Ken은 마술을 수행하기 위해 과학을 사용할 것이라고 하며 그를 소개하고 있으므로 ④번이 가장 적절하다.

19 이어지는 Ken의 설명으로 보아 왜 물이 유리컵 속으로 올라간 것인지를 묻는 말이 적절하다.

20 (C)에서 물이 담긴 접시가 처음으로 등장하고 (B) 그 접시 한가운데에 초를 놓고 (A) 그 초를 켜는 순서가 적절하다.

21 초가 타는 동안은 뜨거운 공기의 팽창으로 인하여 높은 압력이 만들어지므로 유리컵 내부의 공기가 더 높은 압력을 가진다.

22 '-thing, -body, -one'으로 끝나는 부정대명사는 형용사의 수식을 뒤에서 받는다. 따라서 something amazing 이라고 쓰는 것이 적절하다.

23 '신비한 솟아오르는 물'이 적절하다.

24 How come은 '주어+동사' 어순을 이끄는 것에 유의한다.

25 물을 흡수하면 그것을 젤리로 변하게 한다고 하였다.

26 (C)는 관계대명사 that으로 불완전한 문장을 이끈다. 모두 완전한 문장을 이끄는 명사절 접속사이지만 ⑤번은 관계대명사이다.

27 헷갈리게 하기 위해서 컵을 이리저리 섞는 것이라고 하였다.

28 on one's own: 혼자서, 혼자 힘으로

29 과학자들의 연구에 따르면 얼음과 바람이 바위가 혼자 움직이는 것처럼 보이게 만든다.

서술형 시험대비
p.142~143

01 It is more exciting to find out the secrets behind magic tricks.

02 He will perform his magic tricks.

03 to see magic tricks

04 How come

05 He put the candle in the middle of the dish.

06 It expands.

07 lower pressure

08 Rising, burnt out, cooled, dropped, higher, outside, pushed

09 which has the water in it

10 It sticks to the bottom of the cup.

11 it is necessary to use cups that you can't see through

12 your performance

13 We need to prepare a coin and a bottle.

14 it is important to cool the bottle

15 on the bottom → on the mouth /
   spin → move up and down

01 마술 뒤에 숨겨진 비밀에 관하여 알아내는 것이 더 신나는 일이라고 하였다.

02 Ken은 자신의 마술을 보여줄 것이라고 하였다.

03 가주어 It이므로 진주어를 의미하는 것이다.

04 이어지는 말에서 물이 솟아오르는 원리를 설명하고 있다.

05 Ken은 접시 한가운데에 초를 놓았다.

06 공기가 뜨거워지면 팽창한다고 하였다.

07 공기가 차가워지면 수축하면서 낮은 압력을 만들어 낸다고 하였다.

08 솟아오르는 물 마술이다. 불꽃이 다 타 버렸을 때 유리컵 안의 공기는 차가워지고 압력은 떨어졌다. 유리컵 밖의 높은 압력이 물을 유리컵 안으로 밀어 올렸다.

09 지나는 물이 있는 컵이 가운데 컵이라고 생각하였다.

10 젤리로 변한 물은 컵 바닥에 달라붙는다고 하였다.

11 가주어 it을 활용하여 같은 의미의 문장을 쓸 수 있다.

12 Ken이 한 공연을 가리키는 말이다.

13 마술을 하기 위해서는 동전과 병이 필요하다고 하였다.

14 가주어 it을 활용하여 문장을 쓸 수 있다. '병을 차갑게 하는 것'이 주어이므로 to cool the bottle을 주어로 문장을 만든다.

15 동전을 병 입구에 올려놓는 것이고, 손으로 잠시 병을 쥐고 있으면 동전이 위아래로 움직인다고 하였다. spin: 돌다

영역별 핵심문제

01 ②   02 ⑤

03 (1) turn into   (2) cooled down
   (3) see through   (4) turned, into

04 ②   05 ②

06 (1) Which flame will burn out first?
   (2) My daughter blew out the candles on her cake.
   (3) Water expands and contracts with changes in temperature.

07 ③   08 ⓓ → sounds   09 ②

10 ⑤   11 sink   12 ⑤

13 (A) flavor   (B) strawberry   (C) mix
   (D) cut   (E) put   (F) try

14 ④   15 ②   16 ④   17 ③

18 It is not easy for her to move the boxes.

19 ③   20 ④   21 ⑤   22 ③

23 How come she made an appointment?

24 for him   25 ⑤   26 ④

---

27 ⓓ-ⓒ-ⓐ-ⓑ

28 the air outside the glass   29 ⑤   30 expand

31 ②   32 ⑤

---

01 '불가능한 일들이 일어나게 만드는 힘을 가진' 것을 가리키는 것은 magic(마법의, 마술의)이다.

02 sink: 가라앉다

03 turn A into B A를 B로 바꾸다, cool down 차가워지다, see through 속을 들여다 보다

04 주어진 문장에서 sink(싱크대)를 가리킨다. ②번의 sink는 '가라앉다'를 가리킨다.

05 mix: 섞다; 혼합물, flour: 밀가루

06 flame: 불꽃, candle: 양초, expand: 팽창하다, contract: 수축하다

07 어느 계란들이 신선한지 묻는 질문에 차이를 구별하고 싶다는 대답은 어색하다.

08 주어가 3인칭 That이므로 단수 동사 sounds가 적절하다.

09 세종대왕은 비가 오랫동안 내리지 않아 걱정했지만 장영실이 시계를 만들어 건기를 대비하기 위해 사용할 수 있도록 한다는 이야기를 듣고 기뻐함을 알 수 있다.

11 '물의 표면 아래로 내려가다'를 가리키는 말은 sink(가라앉다)이다.

12 유진이가 풍선을 갖고 무엇을 하려고 하는지는 알 수 없다.

13 strawberry: 딸기, put A in B: A를 B에 놓다, mix: 섞다, cut: 자르다, flavor: 맛

14 '우리를 위해 나서 준 것'이 주어이며 이것의 주체가 '너'이고 사람의 성격을 나타내는 brave가 있으므로 의미상의 주어로 of you를 쓰는 것이 적절하다.

15 wise는 사람의 성격을 나타내는 형용사이므로 의미상의 주어로 'of+목적격'을 쓰는 것이 적절하다.

16 possible은 사람의 성격을 나타내는 형용사가 아니므로 의미상의 주어로 'for+목적격'을 쓴다.

17 모두 주어로 쓰인 to부정사이지만, ③번은 부사적 용법 중 '목적'으로 쓰여 '~하기 위해서'라고 해석된다. lay: (알을) 낳다

18 '그 상자들을 옮기는 것'이 주어이며 행위의 주체는 '그녀'이므로 'for her to move the boxes'라고 쓴다.

19 절을 이끌고 있으므로 두 번째 빈칸에는 that이 들어가야 하며, 첫 번째 빈칸에는 가주어 It이 적절하다.

20 모두 '주어+동사' 어순이므로 How come이 사용되지만 ④번은 '동사+주어' 어순이므로 Why가 쓰인다.

21 '주어+동사' 어순이므로 How come을 쓴다.

22 ① That → It ② for her → of her ④ play → to play ⑤ did he drink → he drank

23 How come은 '주어+동사' 어순을 이끄는 것에 유의한다.

24 strange는 의미상의 주어로 'for+목적격'을 쓴다.

25 (A)는 '불을 붙이다'는 의미로 쓰인 light이다. ① 빛 ② 전등

25

(전깃)불 ③ (색깔이) 연한, 옅은 ④ 가벼운 ⑤ 불을 붙이다

26 Jina가 왜 물이 유리컵 속으로 올라간 것인지를 묻고 있으므로 이에 대한 답변이 이어진다고 보는 것이 적절하다.

27 ⓓ 초가 다 탔을 때 유리컵 내부의 공기가 식었음 ⓒ 공기가 식으면서 공기 압력이 떨어짐 ⓐ 그래서 유리컵 밖의 공기 압력이 더 높아짐 ⓑ 압력이 높아진 바깥 공기가 물을 밀어서 유리컵 안으로 들어가게 함

28 유리컵 밖의 공기를 가리키는 말이다.

29 유리컵 밖의 공기 압력이 더 높아지면서 높아진 압력의 공기가 물을 밀어서 유리컵 안으로 들어가는 것이 적절하다. 따라서 pushed라고 써야 한다. pull: 당기다

30 크기, 범위, 혹은 양에 있어서의 증가는 '팽창하다 (expand)'이다.

31 이어지는 대화 내용으로 보아 컵에 물을 채운 것임을 알 수 있다.

32 사라지는 물의 비밀이 가장 적절하다.

단원별 예상문제   p.150~153

01 Which flavor do you want to make?   02 mix
03 ③   04 sink, float, gas, air   05 ⓒ → use   06 ⑤   07 She signed up for a magic class.   08 She is looking forward to learning new magic tricks.   09 ⑤   10 I'm looking forward to seeing the differences.   11 ③
12 ④   13 It was wise of you to   14 ⑤
15 ④   16 It is surprising that he won the competition.   17 How come you are home so early?
18 ②   19 ③   **20 특별한 물질을 숨기기 위해서**   21 ③   22 ⓐ How do you do it?
ⓑ What happens? ⓒ How come the coin moves?
23 expanding 24 ③   25 trying to escape from the bottle

02 '두 개 이상의 물질을 결합하여 하나의 물질이 되게 하다'는 mix(섞다)이다.

03 주어진 문장은 어느 달걀들이 신선한지, 신선하지 않은지에 대한 대답이므로 (C)가 적절하다.

04 달걀이 물에 가라앉을 때, 그것들은 신선하다. 반면에 물에 뜨는 달걀은 신선하지 않다. 상한 달걀은 속에 가스가 찬다. 그것은 풍선 속의 공기처럼 활동한다.

05 that의 선행사는 100 magic tricks이므로 동사는 use가 적절하다.

06 얼마나 오랫동안 지원이가 풍선 마술을 연습했는지는 알 수 없다.

07 미나는 이번 겨울에 마술 수업에 등록했다.

08 미나는 새로운 마술 묘기를 배우는 것을 기대하고 있다.

09 주어진 문장은 How will that work?에 대한 대답으로 적절하므로 (E)에 들어가는 것이 적절하다.

11 I can't wait to ~ = I'm looking forward to -ing: 나는 ~이 무척 기다려져

11 How come은 '주어+동사' 어순임에 유의한다.

12 모두 의미상의 주어로 'for+목적격'을 쓰는 형용사이지만, careful은 사람의 성격에 관련한 형용사이므로 의미상의 주어로 'of+목적격'을 쓴다.

13 wise는 사람의 성격에 관련된 형용사이므로 의미상의 주어로 'of+목적격'을 써서 문장을 완성한다.

14 ① to finding → to find ② is she → she is ③ to not follow → not to follow ④ he is → is he

15 (A) 가주어는 It이 쓰인다. (B) 절을 이끌고 있으므로 that을 쓴다. (C) '주어+동사' 어순이므로 How come을 쓴다.

16 '그가 그 대회에서 우승했다'는 것을 진주어절로 만들어 문장을 완성한다.

17 'How come+주어+동사' 어순에 유의한다.

18 (A)는 '~하기 위해서'라고 해석되는 to부정사의 부사적 용법이다. ① 명사적 용법 중 목적격 보어 ② 부사적 용법 중 목적 ③ 형용사적 용법 ④ 진주어 ⑤ 명사적 용법 중 목적어

19 Ken은 Jina가 혼란을 느끼도록 하기 위하여 컵들을 섞었다.

20 Ken은 마술의 비밀이 특별한 물질 때문이라고 밝혔다. 이를 숨기기 위해서는 속을 들여다볼 수 없는 컵을 사용해야 한다.

21 Ken은 마술 전에 특별한 물질을 컵 하나에 넣었다고 하였으므로 ③번이 가장 적절하다.

22 ⓐ 이어지는 문장이 방법을 설명하고 있으므로 어떻게 하는 것인지 묻는 말이 적절하며, ⓑ 동전이 위아래로 움직인다고 말하고 있으므로 무슨 일이 발생하는지 묻는 말이 들어가는 것이 적절하며, ⓒ 그 원리를 설명하고 있으므로 왜 움직이는지 묻는 말이 자연스럽다.

23 손이 병 안의 찬 공기를 데우면 공기가 따뜻해져서 팽창한다. 팽창하는 공기가 병에서 나가려고 하는 것이므로 'expanding'을 쓴다.

24 병을 차갑게 하는 것이 중요하다고 하였다.

25 병을 탈출하려는 공기 때문에 병 입구에 놓인 동전이 위아래로 움직이는 것이다.

서술형 실전문제   p.154~155

01 It hasn't rained for a long time.
02 He suggests making a special clock.
03 It's because the clock will show the time and the seasons, so they can use it to prepare for the dry season.
04 It is rude of him to take pictures of her without her permission.
05 for him to
06 How come you couldn't catch the bus?
07 It is important to keep
08 How come they are tired?

09 He put a special material into one of the cups.

10 Ken put a special material into the cup and it absorbed the water and turned it into jelly.

11 Why did the water disappear?

12 (A) warm (B) gets (C) expands (D) escape

13 ⓑ-ⓓ-ⓐ-ⓒ

01 오랫동안 비가 내리지 않았다.

02 장영실은 특별한 시계를 만들 것을 제안한다.

03 시계는 시간과 계절을 알려줘 건기를 준비하기 위해 사용할 수 있기 때문에 장영실은 시계가 농부들을 도와줄 것이라고 생각한다.

04 of와 to를 추가한다. rude는 사람의 성격을 나타내는 형용사이므로 의미상의 주어로 'of+목적격'을 쓴다.

05 that절에서 운동하는 주체가 'he'이므로 to부정사 구문으로 바꿀 때 의미상의 주어를 'for him'으로 쓸 수 있다.

06 답변에서 버스를 타지 못한 이유를 설명하고 있으므로 '왜 버스를 타지 못했니?'라는 질문을 쓰는 것이 적절하다.

07 진주로 to부정사를, 가주어로 It을 써서 나타낼 수 있다.

08 'How come+주어+동사' 어순임에 유의한다.

09 Ken은 컵들 중 하나에 특별한 물질을 넣었다고 하였다.

10 컵 안에 있는 물이 젤리로 변한 이유는, Ken이 넣어둔 특별한 물질이 물을 흡수하여 그것을 젤리로 변하게 만들었기 때문이다.

11 'How come+주어+동사' 어순이고, 'Why+동사+주어' 어순임에 유의한다.

12 차가운 병 속의 공기를 따뜻하게 하기 위해서 손으로 병을 쥐는 것이고, 병 속의 공기가 따뜻해지면서 공기가 팽창한다. 이 팽창하는 공기가 병에서 나가려고 하는 것이다.

13 ⓑ 병을 차갑게 하고 ⓓ 병 입구에 동전 하나를 올려둔 후 ⓐ 병을 두 손으로 잡고 ⓒ 얼마간의 시간이 지나면 동전이 움직일 것이다.

창의사고력 서술형 문제
p.156

01 (A) the dry season

(B) a special clock

(C) the time and seasons

(D) to prepare for the dry season

(E) time and the seasons

|모범답안|

02 (1) It is easy to make many friends.

(2) It is important to love your pet.

(3) It is necessary to save your allowance.

(4) It is hard to think others first.

01 세종대왕은 건기가 너무 오래 지속되고 있었기 때문에 농부들을 걱정했다. 그가 농부들을 도울 방법을 찾을 때 장영실은 특별한 시계를 만들 것을 제안하였다. 세종대왕은 어떻게 그 시계가 농부들을 도와줄 수 있을지 궁금했다. 장영실은 시계가 시간과 계절을 보여주므로 건기를 준비하는데 사용될 수 있다고 설명했다. 다행히도, 장영실은 시간과 계절에 대해 많이 알고 있어서 그는 이것을 발명하기 위해 노력했다.

단원별 모의고사
p.157~160

01 ③ 02 (1) balloon (2) candle (3) compare
03 (1) pressure (2) flames (3) absorbs (4) material
(5) experiment 04 100 magic tricks 05 ⑤
06 I can't wait to learn new magic tricks there.
07 ④ 08 ③ 09 ⓒ → put 10 ⑤
11 The eggs that[which] float in the water are not fresh. 12 The gas inside the eggs makes them float in the water. 13 ④ 14 ⑤
15 ⑤ 16 of him not to 17 How come he isn't coming to the party?
18 (B)–(D)–(A)–(C) 19 absorbed, stuck, the bottom 20 He will use science to perform his tricks. 21 ③ 22 ④ 23 The water rose into the glass. 24 ⑤ 25 He covered the candle with a glass.

01 '음식을 얼리거나 언채로 유지되도록 하기 위한 장치 또는 공간'을 가리키는 것은 freezer(냉동고)이다.

02 balloon: 풍선, candle: 양초, compare: 비교하다

03 flame: 불꽃, material: 재료, 물질, absorb: 흡수하다, pressure: 압력, experiment: 실험, bleed: 피흘리다

07 미나는 전에 마술 묘기를 배운 적이 있다.

07 I can't wait to ~: 나는 ~이 무척 기다려져. = I'm looking forward to ~ing

09 mix와 병렬구조를 이루는 동사로 put이 적절하다.

10 Jane은 섞은 것을 얼마나 오래 냉동실에 두어야 하는지 알 수 없다.

11 물에 뜨는 달걀들은 신선하지 않다.

12 달걀 안에 있는 가스가 그 달걀들을 물 위에 뜨게 만든다.

13 '주어+동사' 어순이므로 How come, clever는 사람의 성격을 나타내는 형용사이므로 to부정사의 의미상 주어로 'of+목적격'을 쓴다.

14 possible은 사람의 성격을 나타내는 형용사가 아니므로 의미상의 주어로 for him을 쓰는 것이 적절하다.

15 모두 가주어 It으로 쓰였지만 ⑤번은 명암을 나타내는 비인칭 용법이다.

16 to부정사의 부정은 'not to V' 형태이며, mean은 사람의 성격을 나타내는 형용사이므로 'of him'을 쓰는 것에 유의한다.

17 'How come+주어+동사' 어순임에 유의한다.

18 (B) 마술 전에 미리 특별한 물질을 넣어 둠 - (D) 이 물질이 물을 흡수하고 물을 젤리로 만듦 - (A) 그 젤리는 컵 바닥에 들러

27

붙음 - (C) 그러므로 이 마술을 하기 위해서는 반드시 속이 들여다 보이지 않는 컵을 써야 함.

19 컵 안에 있는 특별한 물질이 물을 흡수하고 그것을 젤리로 변하게 했다. 그리고 그 젤리는 바닥에 달라붙었다.

20 Ken은 자신의 마술을 위해 과학을 이용할 것이라고 하였다.

21 'I can't wait to ~'는 '나는 ~이 무척 기다려진다.'라는 뜻으로 'I'm looking forward to -ing'로 바꾸어 쓸 수 있다.

22 'How come+주어+동사' 어순이므로 How come을 쓰는 것이 적절하다. 'Why+동사+주어' 어순임에 유의하자.

23 물은 유리컵 안으로 솟아올랐다.

24 초가 얼마나 탔는지는 위 글을 읽고 답할 수 없다.

25 Ken은 초에 불을 붙인 후 유리컵으로 초를 덮었다.

Lesson 8

Call It Courage

01 weak   02 ②   03 ③

04 (1) deserts (2) cross (3) experience (4) healthy

(5) exercise   05 (1) tried[did] her best (2) In fact

(3) laughed at (4) give it a try (5) were about to

06 ⑤

01 주어진 관계는 반의어 관계를 나타낸다.

02 '옷에 의해 덮여지지 않은'을 가리키는 말은 bare(벌거벗은)이다.

03 nail: 못질하다

04 exercise: 운동하다, desert: 사막, experience: 경험하다, cross: 건너다, healthy: 건강한

05 try[do] one's best: 최선을 다하다, in fact: 사실은, laugh at: 비웃다, give it a try: 시도해 보다, be about to: 막 ~하려고 하다

06 주어진 문장에서 cross는 '건너다'를 뜻한다. ⑤번은 '십자가'를 의미한다.

서술형 시험대비   p.165

01 discouraged

02 (1) took off (2) in front of (3) on foot (4) fall into

03 (1) match (2) against (3) weak (4) lose (5) meals

04 (1) I fell into a hole while walking along the road.

(2) You should try hard and never give up.

(3) Don't take off your coat.

05 (1) tried out for (2) give up (3) laughed at

(4) In fact (5) is good at

01 주어진 관계는 반의어 관계를 나타낸다. encouraged 용기를 북돋운, discouraged 낙담한

02 take off: 벗다, in front of: ~의 앞에, on foot: 걸어서, 도보로, fall into: ~에 빠지다

03 weak: 약한, meal: 식사, lose: 지다, match: 경기, against: ~에 맞서

04 fall into: ~에 빠지다, give up: 포기하다, take off: 벗다

05 laugh at: 비웃다, try out for: 지원하다, give up: 포기하다, be good at: ~을 잘하다, in fact: 사실 squad: 분대, 소집단, 일단(의 사람들), 한 조(組), 팀

Conversation

핵심 Check   p.166~167

1 (1) Have you heard (2) Yes, I have

(3) No, I haven't

2 (1) Don't take it too hard

(2) Don't be so hard on yourself

(3) Cheer up, You can do it

교과서 대화문 익히기

Check(√) True or False   p.168

1 T   2 F   3 T   4 T

교과서 확인학습   p.170~171

Listen & Speak 1 A

have you heard / have / who crossed, on foot / took, about / experience, desert, cross / try, in

Listen & Speak 1 B

have you heard about / have, on / right / want to / I don't wear at home, if you want / in front of, go inside / See

Listen & Speak 2 A

healthy, exercise, try to, Don't eat, wash, meals, sound hard, take, step, give up, live, life

Listen & Speak 2 B

try out for, about / sure / Why not / trying out for / good at, don't give up / try my best

Real Life Communication A

excited, match / against, lose / Have you heard / No, haven't, about / so, lose / What happened / worked hard, won, give up / try our best

Let's Check ①

Have you heard of, read well, lost, hearing in, Still, difficilties, be like, don't give up

시험대비 기본평가   p.172

01 Have you heard of Thomas Edison?   02 ②

03 ④   04 ⑤

02 밑줄 친 (B)는 '그럼에도, 그럼에도 불구하고'를 의미하며 이와 같은 의미를 나타내는 것은 ②번이다. 나머지는 모두 '여전히'를 의미한다.

03 주어진 문장의 이 조언들(these tips)을 (D) 앞에서 설명하고 있으므로 (D)가 적절하다.

시험대비 실력평가
p.173~174

01 desert   02 ③   03 ⑤   04 (E) →
(B) → (D) → (A) → (C)   05 ⓔ → don't give up
06 첫째, 매일 운동할 것. 둘째, 건강에 좋은 음식을 먹을 것.
셋째, 식사 전에 손을 씻을 것.   07 ①   08 ⑤
09 ②   10 (A) ugly sweater (B) Sora's (C) she
didn't wear

01 '보통 모래로 덮여 있고 아주 더운 매우 건조한 땅의 지역'을 가리키는 말은 desert(사막)이다.

02 (A) 알고 있는지 묻는 현재완료 시제의 질문에 대한 대답으로 'Yes, I have.'가 적절하다. (B) 선행사가 사람이므로 'who', (C) 내용의 흐름상 경험하고 싶지만 걸어서 사막을 건너고 싶지 않다는 역접의 접속사가 적절하므로 'but'이 적절하다.

03 Tim은 고비 사막을 걸어서 건너고 싶지 않다고 이야기하였다.

04 (E) 알고 있는지 질문 → (B) 모른다고 대답 → (D) 그리스 팀에 대한 설명 → (A) 구체적 설명 요청 → (C) 대답 및 격려하기

05 포기하지 말아야 건강한 삶을 살 것이라는 내용이 자연스러우므로 'don't give up'이 적절하다.

07 빈칸에 들어갈 말로 격려하는 표현이 적절하다.

08 호준이는 아이스하키 팀 지원에 최선을 다할 것이다.

09 Alex는 "못생긴 스웨터 파티"에 가고 싶은데 스웨터가 없어서 우울했지만(depressed) 소라의 옷을 입고 갈 수 있게 되었으므로 기분이 좋아졌다(pleased).

10 비록 Alex는 그의 못생긴 스웨터가 없었지만 그는 소라의 도움으로 "못생긴 스웨터 파티"에 갈 수 있었다. 그는 그녀가 입지 않는 스웨터를 빌렸다. 그는 정말로 그녀에게 고마워했다.

서술형 시험대비
p.175

01 ⓓ → that 또는 which
02 December 5th / Student Center / an ugly sweater
03 (1) healthy (2) exercise (3) fast (4) wash (5) meals
   (6) tips (7) take
04 don't give up
05 ⓓ → Although[Though]
06 He couldn't read well and lost all of the hearing in
   his left ear.

01 one이 가리키는 것은 an ugly sweater로 선행사가 사물이므로 that이나 which가 적절하다.

05 Despite은 전치사이므로 접속사 Although[Though]가 적절하다.

06 그는 어렸을 때 글을 잘 읽지 못했고 왼쪽 귀가 전혀 들리지 않았다.

[교과서]
Grammar

핵심 Check
p.176~177

1 (1) us help   (2) him use   (3) done
2 (1) Although[Though]   (2) though[although]
   (3) Even though

시험대비 기본평가
p.178

01 (1) doing → do
   (2) thought → think
   (3) Despite → Although[Though]
   (4) Even → Even though
02 (1) had us sing (2) made me find
   (3) let me cook (4) had the project finished
03 (1) Although I like the house, it's too far from my
     school.
   (2) Though I was tired, I did my homework.
   (3) Julia studied although she was sleepy.
   (4) Though he is old, he is quite strong.

01 (1) 사역동사의 목적격 보어는 동사원형의 형태이다. (2) 목적어와 목적격 보어의 관계가 수동일 경우 과거분사를 쓰며 his wife는 생각하는 주체가 되므로 think를 쓴다. (3) 절을 이끌고 있으므로 Although나 Though를 쓴다. Despite은 명사구를 이끈다. (4) Even은 형용사 혹은 부사로 쓰이므로 문장을 이끄는 Even though를 쓰는 것이 적절하다.

02 사역동사의 목적어와 목적격 보어의 관계가 능동인 경우, 목적격 보어로 동사원형을 쓴다. 단, 목적어와 목적격 보어의 관계가 수동인 경우 목적격 보어로 과거분사를 쓴다.

03 (1), (2) 사역동사의 목적어와 목적격 보어의 관계가 능동인 경우 목적격 보어로 동사원형을 쓴다. (3), (4) '비록 ~일지라도'로 해석되며 문장을 이어주는 부사절 접속사는 though 혹은 although이다. 주절 앞에 쓰는 경우 콤마를 쓰는 것에 유의한다.

01 ③　　02 ④　　03 ⑤　　04 I had
my car fixed. 05 ①, ③　　06 ③　　07 ⑤
08 Although I like to swim in the river, I hate summer.
09 ⑤　　10 ①　　11 Although[Though] he
wasn't hungry, he had dinner with her. 12 ⑤
13 ①　　14 ③　　15 planted　16 ④
17 ④　　18 Please let me know what the
answer is. 19 ③　　20 ④　　21 ④
22 They made me repeat the whole story.
23 Although　24 cut

01 사역동사 have의 목적어와 목적격 보어의 관계가 능동이므로 목적격 보어로 동사원형을 쓴다.

02 모두 인과 관계를 이끄는 Because가 쓰이지만 ④번에는 양보의 부사절 접속사 Although가 쓰인다.

03 despite은 명사구를 이끄는 전치사이다. 주어와 동사를 포함하는 절을 이끄는 것은 접속사이다.

04 차는 수리되는 것이므로 목적격 보어로 과거분사를 쓴다.

05 ② brought → bring ④ clean → cleaned ⑤ Despite → Although

06 사역동사로 쓰이면서 4, 5형식에 모두 쓰일 수 있는 동사는 make이다. get은 5형식에서 목적격 보어로 to부정사를 취한다.

07 주어진 문장의 밑줄 친 부분은 양보의 부사절을 이끄는 While로 쓰였다. While은 '~ 동안'이라는 의미도 가지고 있으며 ①~④번은 모두 그와 같은 의미이지만 ⑤번은 양보의 부사절을 이끄는 While로 쓰였다.

08 '비록 ~한다 할지라도'는 although 혹은 though 등으로 표현한다. to swim 대신에 swimming을 써도 좋다.

09 건물이 paint되는 것이므로 과거분사를 쓰는 것이 적절하다.

10 명사구를 이끌고 있으므로 접속사 Even though가 아닌 전치사 Despite을 쓰는 것이 적절하다.

11 비록 배가 고프지 않았지만, 그는 그녀와 함께 저녁을 먹었다는 의미로 쓰는 것이 적절하며 although절을 주절 뒤에 쓸 경우 콤마를 쓰지 않음에 유의한다.

12 목적격 보어로 동사원형이 쓰이고 있으므로 want는 빈칸에 적절하지 않다. want는 to부정사를 목적격 보어로 취하는 동사이다.

13 명사구를 이끌고 있으므로 전치사 despite 혹은 in spite of, 사역동사 have의 목적격 보어로 쓰이며 목적어와 능동 관계에 있으므로 동사원형 형태를 쓰는 것이 적절하다.

14 주어진 문장의 빈칸에는 양보의 부사절을 이끄는 접속사 although 등이 쓰인다. ① When ② After ③ Although ④ Because ⑤ If

15 나무는 심어지는 것이므로 과거분사를 쓴다.

16 '늦었음에도 불구하고, 그는 그 방으로 들어가는 것이 허락되었다'라는 의미이다. 따라서 ④번이 적절하다.

17 모두 동사원형을 목적격 보어로 취하는 동사이지만 allow는 to부정사를 목적격 보어로 취한다.

18 사역동사 let은 목적어와 목적격 보어의 관계가 능동인 경우 목적격 보어로 동사원형을 쓴다.

19 make는 사역동사이며 목적어와 목적격 보어의 관계가 능동이므로 take가 적절하다.

20 Despite은 전치사이므로 문장을 이끌 수 없다.

21 사역동사의 목적어와 목적격 보어의 관계가 능동일 경우 목적격 보어로 동사원형을 쓰는 것이 적절하다.

22 이야기를 반복하는 주체가 '나'이며 그들이 나에게 시킨 것이므로 사역동사를 사용하되 목적격 보어로 동사원형을 쓰는 것이 적절하다.

23 Though, While, Even though를 써도 좋다.

24 사역동사 have의 목적어와 목적격 보어의 관계가 수동일 경우 목적격 보어로 과거분사를 쓴다.

01 Though I got up early, I was late for school.
02 (1) take care of my baby sister
　(2) water the flowers
　(3) brush my teeth after dinner
03 (1) cross (2) stolen (3) sliced
04 Although the man hurt his leg, he could walk.
　Although it rained a lot, we went to the zoo.
　Although Clara brought her umbrella, she was wet.
05 laugh
06 (1) although[even though] (2) Despite
　(3) Even though[Although]
07 had people shout, made our team feel strong, let the other team win
08 Even though it was windy, I went out to play soccer.
09 me exercise
10 Jenny let her dog run around.
11 (1) Although there was a heavy storm, people were safe inside.
　(2) Although his throat was sore, he sang beautifully.
　(3) Although she was upset, she smiled at him.
12 Peter made me sing in front of people though [although] I didn't want to.
13 (1) washed (2) taken (3) be read (4) reviewed

01 Though를 대신하여 Although, Even though 등을 써도 좋다.

02 목적어와 목적격 보어의 관계가 능동이므로 사역동사의 목적격 보어로 동사원형을 쓰는 것이 적절하다.

03 사역동사의 목적어와 목적격 보어의 관계가 능동 관계에 있을 경우 목적격 보어로 동사원형을, 수동 관계에 있을 경우 목적격 보어

로 과거분사를 쓴다. (1)은 to cross라고 써도 무방하다.

04 Although를 대신하여 다른 양보의 부사절 접속사를 사용해도 좋으며, 부사절을 주절 뒤로 배치할 경우 콤마를 쓰지 않는 것에 유의한다.

05 영화가 자신을 웃게 만들었다는 의미이다.

06 although와 even though는 접속사로서 주어와 동사를 포함하는 절을 이끌지만, despite은 전치사로 명사구를 이끄는 것에 유의한다.

07 사역동사 have, make, let은 목적어와 목적격 보어의 관계가 능동인 경우 목적격 보어로 동사원형을 쓴다.

08 양보의 부사절을 주절 뒤에 쓸 경우 콤마를 쓰지 않는다.

09 부모님이 내게 저녁에 운동을 하라고 시켰기 때문이라는 답이 가장 적절하다.

10 사역동사의 목적어와 목적격 보어의 관계가 능동인 경우 목적격 보어로 동사원형을 쓴다.

11 Although를 대신하여 Even though, Though를 써도 무방하며, 양보의 부사절을 주절 뒤에 쓸 경우 콤마를 쓰지 않는 것에 유의한다.

12 Peter는 내가 원하지 않았는데도 사람들 앞에서 노래하게 했다는 문장으로 쓸 수 있다.

13 사역동사 make, have의 목적어와 목적격 보어의 관계가 수동인 경우 목적격 보어로 과거분사를 쓴다. let은 be p.p.를 쓴다.

교과서 Reading

확인문제   p.184

1 T   2 F   3 T   4 F   5 T

확인문제   p.185

1 T   2 F   3 F   4 T   5 T

교과서 확인학습 A   p.186~187

01 floating village, middle
02 Although, never played soccer, watching it
03 decided to make
04 However, laughed at   05 impossible
06 makes, say so
07 Look around, to play
08 were right, to play soccer
09 discouraged   10 give up, still play soccer
11 How   12 make our own

13 gathered, pieces of
14 put, together, nailed, to
15 After much, had a floating field   16 shaky, nails
17 would often fall into, wet, slippery
18 no shoes, bare feet   19 they, care
20 In fact, excellent, enjoyed
21 brought a poster   22 decided to, it
23 When, were about to leave, them
24 made, feel   25 saw, as, weakest
26 However, started, surprised
27 On, was raining hard
28 losing by two goals, impossible to win
29 The other, so strong   30 give up
31 took off, during, changed completely
32 played better   33 lost by, to, proud of themselves
34 when they were losing, tried their best

교과서 확인학습 B   p.188~189

1 Koh Panyee was a small floating village in the middle of the sea.
2 Although the boys in the village never played soccer before, they loved watching it on TV.
3 One day, the boys decided to make their own soccer team.
4 However, people laughed at their idea.
5 "That's impossible."
6 "What makes you say so?"
7 "Look around. Where are you going to play soccer?"
8 The villagers were right. The boys had no place to play soccer.
9 They were discouraged.
10 "Don't give up! We can still play soccer."
11 "How?"
12 "Let's make our own soccer field."
13 The boys gathered old boats and pieces of wood.
14 They put the boats together and nailed the wood to them.
15 After much hard work, they finally had a floating field.
16 It was shaky and had nails everywhere.
17 The ball and the boys would often fall into the sea, so the field was always wet and slippery.
18 They had no shoes so they had to play in bare feet.
19 Still, they didn't care.
20 In fact, they built excellent skills and enjoyed playing soccer more.

21 One day, a boy brought a poster about a soccer tournament.

22 They decided to give it a try.

23 When they were about to leave, the villagers gave them new shoes and uniforms.

24 Some even came to watch the game. This made the boys feel better.

25 At first, people saw them as the weakest team.

26 However, when the tournament started, the soccer team surprised everyone.

27 On the day of the semi-final, it was raining hard.

28 They were losing by two goals and it looked impossible to win.

29 "The other team is so strong," they thought.

30 But the boys didn't give up.

31 They took off their shoes during the second half and the game changed completely.

32 They played better in the rain thanks to the slippery field at home.

33 Although they lost by a score of three to two, still, they felt proud of themselves.

34 They didn't give up when they were losing. They tried their best until the end.

시험대비 실력평가 　　　　　　　　　p.190~193

01 floating　　02 ③　　03 ⑤　　04 ②
05 ⑤　　06 slippery　　07 playing　　08 ②
09 ④　　10 ③　　11 ⑤
12 Although, give up　　13 ③
14 매일 한 시간 동안 슛 연습을 한 것　　15 shoot
16 ⑤　　17 ⑤
18 They decided to make their own soccer team.
19 ⑤　　20 ⑤　　21 Though, built excellent skills　　22 ⑤　　23 ②
24 They gave shoes and uniforms to the boys.
25 It was raining hard on the day of the semi-final.
26 ⑤

01 '떠 있는'이라는 의미이므로 현재분사로 쓰는 것이 적절하다.

02 소년들이 축구팀을 만들기로 결심했지만 사람들이 그들의 생각을 비웃었다는 것이 적절하다.

03 소년들은 축구를 해 본 적은 없지만 TV로 축구를 보는 것은 정말 좋아했다고 하였다.

04 모두 소년들을 지칭하고 있지만 ②번은 boats를 가리키는 말이다.

05 소년들이 종종 바다에 빠졌고 축구장이 항상 젖어 있고 미끄럽다고 하였으므로 공중에 떠 있다는 설명은 적절하지 않다.

06 부드럽거나 젖어 있거나 얼음에 덮여 있어서, 움직이거나 혹은 붙잡고 있기 힘든 것은 'slippery(미끄러운)'이다.

07 enjoy는 동명사를 목적어로 취하는 동사이다.

08 This가 의미하는 것은 마을사람들이 소년들에게 새 신발과 축구복을 사주고 경기를 보러 온 것이다.

09 (A)는 '심하게, 많이'라는 의미의 부사로 쓰인 hard이다. ① 어려운, 힘든 ② (육체적, 정신적으로) 힘든 ③ 딱딱한 ④ 심하게, 많이 ⑤ 열심히 하는

10 due to = thanks to: ~ 덕분에, ~ 때문에

11 소년들이 몇 개의 경기를 했는지는 알 수 없다.

12 Although를 대신하여 Though 혹은 Even though를 써도 좋다. 소년들은 다른 팀이 매우 강하다고 생각했지만 포기하지 않았다.

13 다른 선수들과 달리 슛을 잘하지 못해 낙담했지만 포기하지 않았다는 의미가 자연스러우므로 discouraged가 적절하다.

14 앞 문장을 가리키고 있다.

15 사역동사 make의 목적어와 목적격 보어의 관계가 능동인 경우 목적격 보어로 동사원형을 쓴다.

16 (A)에는 전치사 at이 들어간다. laugh at: 비웃다 ① take care of: ~을 돌보다 ② be interested in: ~에 흥미가 있다 ③ give up: ~을 포기하다 ④ look forward to: ~을 고대하다 ⑤ be pleased at: ~에 기뻐하다

17 축구팀을 만들겠다는 결심을 비웃는 어른들의 말에 낙심했다는 것이 가장 자연스럽다. ① 고마워하는 ② 기쁜 ③ 지루한 ④ 놀란

18 소년들은 자신들의 축구팀을 만들기로 결심했다.

19 마을 사람들은 소년들의 의견을 지지해 주지 않았으며, 그 이유는 축구를 할 공간이 없었기 때문이었다. 소년들은 축구를 해 본 적은 없지만 텔레비전을 통해 축구를 보는 것을 즐겼다. 마을은 바다 한 가운데에 있었다.

20 축구장이 흔들린다고 하였으므로 '흔들림 없고 안정적인 (steady and stable)'이라고 생각한 Peter가 잘못 이해 했다.

21 양보의 부사절 접속사 Though를 대신하여 Although, Even though를 써도 좋다.

22 소년들이 낡은 배에 직접 못질을 하여 축구장을 만들었다.

23 축구 토너먼트에 참가해 보기로 한 것을 의미한다.

24 마을 사람들은 소년들에게 신발과 축구복을 주었다.

25 준결승전 날에 비가 심하게 오고 있었다고 하였다.

26 주어와 목적어가 같으므로 재귀대명사 themselves를 쓰는 것이 적절하다.

서술형 시험대비 　　　　　　　　　p.194~195

01 making their own soccer team

02 It is in the middle of the sea.

03 Koh Panyee, playing it, make their own, despite

04 It's because the ball and the boys would often fall into the sea.

05 They gathered old boats and pieces of wood.

06 The floating field

07 Although there were no shoes, we didn't care.

08 Although

09 He brought a poster about a soccer tournament.

10 it looked impossible to win

11 They took off their shoes during the second half.

12 played better in the rain

13 ③번 → strong

14 Seeing them play in bare feet made Fern surprised.

15 become their fan

12 They will meet in front of the Student Center.

13 (C) → (B) → (E) → (D) → (A)

14 ⑤ 15 ③ 16 ④ 17 ④

18 Although I was tired, I studied hard in class.

19 ④ 20 ⑤

21 He missed the plane, he left early 22 ①, ③

23 ④ 24 Although, drink

25 My parents don't let me watch violent movies.

26 ④ 27 What makes you say so?

28 ③ 29 (A) shooting (B) shoot 30 ④

31 ②, ③ 32 ⑤

33 It's because they did not have shoes.

01 아이들이 자신의 축구팀을 만드는 것을 의미한다.

02 Koh Panyee 마을은 바다 가운데 있다고 하였다.

03 difficult conditions는 명사구이므로 전치사 despite을 쓰는 것에 유의한다. 해석: Koh Panyee라고 불리는 작은 마을에 사는 소년들은 축구를 보는 것을 아주 좋아하지만 그것을 해 본 경험은 없었다. 그래서, 어려운 조건에도 불구하고 그들은 자신들만의 축구팀을 만들기로 결심했다.

04 공과 소년들이 종종 바다에 빠져서 축구장이 항상 젖어 있고 미끄러웠다고 하였다.

05 소년들은 축구장을 만들기 위하여 낡은 배와 나뭇조각을 모았다.

06 소년들이 만든 물에 떠 있는 축구장을 가리킨다.

07 Though 혹은 Even though를 써도 좋다.

08 Even though, Though, While 모두 가능하다.

09 소년은 축구 토너먼트에 관한 포스터를 가지고 왔다.

10 가주어 it과 진주어 to부정사를 활용하여 문장을 쓸 수 있다.

11 후반전에 그들의 신발을 벗었다고 하였다.

12 고향의 미끄러운 축구장 때문에 그들은 빗속에서 더 잘하였다.

13 상대팀이 강했기 때문에 Panyee Soccer Team이 질 것이라고 생각했지만 그들이 포기하지 않았다는 것이 적절하다.

14 Fern은 선수들이 맨발로 경기하는 것을 보고 놀랐다고 하였다.

15 Koh Panyee 축구팀의 경기 중 하나를 본 것이 Fern Yahtie가 그들의 팬이 되게 하였다. 사역동사 make의 목적어와 목적격 보어의 관계가 능동이므로 목적격 보어로 동사원형을 쓴다.

영역별 핵심문제 p.197~201

01 impossible 02 ① 03 ④

04 (1) against (2) Although[Though] (3) bare (4) Still

05 ① 06 ①

07 (1) I felt proud of myself after the marathon race.

(2) She walked in the woods in bare feet.

(3) Don't be discouraged even if you lose.

08 ⓒ → haven't 09 ⑤ 10 ⑤

11 It will be held on December 5th.

01 주어진 관계는 반의어 관계를 나타낸다. patient: 인내심이 있는, impatient: 참을성이 없는, impossible: 불가능한

02 축구 또는 농구 같은 운동에서 당신이 득점할 수 있는 곳을 향해 공을 차거나 던지다

03 villager: 마을 사람

04 against: ~에 맞서, although[though]: 비록 ~일지라도, bare: 맨..., 벌거벗은, proud: 자랑스러워하는

05 주어진 문장에서 match는 '경기, 시합'을 가리키며 이와 같은 의미로 쓰인 것은 ①번이다. ②, ③번은 '잘 어울리는 것 [사람]' ④, ⑤번은 '성냥'을 뜻한다.

06 주어진 문장에서 nail은 각각 '손톱', '못', '못을 박다'의 의미로 쓰였다.

07 proud 자랑스러워하는, bare 벌거벗은, 맨..., discouraged 낙담한

08 현재완료 시제로 알고 있는지 묻고 있으므로 'No, I haven't.'로 대답한다.

09 (A)에 들어갈 말로 격려하는 표현이 적절하다.

10 2004 유로컵에서 그리스 팀은 우승하였다.

11 "못생긴 스웨터 파티"는 12월 5일에 열릴 것이다.

12 소라와 Alex는 학생회관 앞에서 만날 것이다.

13 (C) 아이스하키 팀 지원에 확실하지 않음을 대답 → (B) 이유 질문 → (E) 이유 설명 → (D) 격려 및 응원하기 → (A) 대답 및 감사 표현

14 고민을 표현하고 조언을 구하는 질문에 '나는 최선을 다할 것이다'라는 대답은 어색하다.

15 사역동사 make의 목적어와 목적격 보어의 관계가 능동인 경우 목적격 보어로 동사원형을 쓴다.

16 모두 인과 관계를 연결하는 접속사 because나 as가 들어 가지만, ④번에는 양보의 부사절 접속사 although가 쓰인다.

17 '나는 그가 내 무거운 가방을 들게 했다.'이므로 '나는 내 무거운 가방이 그에 의해 들어지게 했다.'라고 쓸 수 있다.

18 Although를 대신하여 Even though, Though를 써도 좋다.

19 ① walk → to walk ② to wash → wash ③ Despite

→ Although[Though] ⑤ In spite → In spite of 혹은 Despite

20 get은 목적격 보어로 to부정사를 취하는 동사이다.

21 양보의 부사절 접속사가 이끄는 문장이 주절 뒤에 있을 때는 콤마를 쓰지 않는다.

22 help는 목적격 보어로 to부정사와 원형부정사를 모두 취할 수 있다.

23 날씨가 추웠지만 수영을 하러 갔다고 하였으므로 양보의 부사절 접속사가 적절하며, 목적격 보어로 동사원형을 취하고 있으므로 Let이 가장 적절하다.

24 Although를 대신하여 Though 혹은 Even though를 써도 좋다. 말이 물을 마시게 하는 것이므로 사역동사의 목적격 보어로 동사원형을 쓴다.

25 사역동사의 목적어와 목적격 보어의 관계가 능동이므로 목적격 보어로 동사원형을 쓴다.

26 축구를 할 장소가 없었다고 하였으므로 ④번이 가장 적절하다.

27 사역동사 make의 목적어와 목적격 보어의 관계가 능동일 경우 목적격 보어로 동사원형을 쓴다.

28 소년들은 자신들의 축구장을 만들자고 하였으므로 ③번이 가장 적절하다.

29 (A) practice는 동명사를 목적어로 취하는 동사이다. (B) 사역동사의 목적어와 목적격 보어의 관계가 능동인 경우 목적격 보어로 동사원형을 쓴다.

30 글쓴이는 매일 한 시간 동안 슛 연습을 했다. 따라서 농구를 잘하기 위해서 열심히 노력했다는 것이 내용과 일치한다.

31 소년들은 실제로 훌륭한 기술을 쌓고 더 축구를 즐겼다는 것이 적절하다. Actually = In fact: 실제로, 사실

32 낡은 배와 나뭇조각들을 모은 소년들은 (C) 그것들을 합쳐서 축구장을 만들었다. (B) 그 축구장은 흔들리고 곳곳에 못이 있었다. 뿐만 아니라 축구장이 미끄럽고 맨발로 축구를 해야 했지만 (A) 소년들은 상관하지 않고 축구를 즐겼다.

33 소년들에게는 신발이 없었기 때문에 맨발로 축구를 해야 했다.

단원별 예상문제
p.202~205

01 (A) foot (B) 51 (C) to experience life in the desert (D) cross the desert on foot (E) try and cross the Gobi Desert in 50 days

02 ①　　**03** ②　　**04** match　　**05** ⑤

06 ②　　**07** ③　　**08** ⑤

09 They tried out for the school ice hockey team.

10 He promised to try his best.

11 ⑤　　**12** ④

13 Although the weather was very cold, she went out for a walk.

14 ⑤　　**15** ①, ⑤　　**16** take, taken

17 (B)-(A)-(C) **18** Although, surprised　　**19** ④

20 ④　　　**21** They felt proud of themselves.

22 ⑤　　　**23** play better than before　　**24** ③

01 미나는 걸어서 고비 사막을 건너는 사람들에 대한 TV쇼를 보았다. 그것은 그들에게 약 51일 정도 걸렸다. 그녀는 흥미를 느꼈고 이것을 Tim에게 이야기했다. 그녀가 이것에 대해 설명했을 때, Tim도 또한 놀랐고 그는 사막에서의 삶을 경험해 보고 싶다고 이야기하였다. 하지만 Tim은 사막을 걸어서 건너고 싶지는 않았다. 반면에 용감한 마음을 지닌 미나는 시도해 보고 50일 안에 고비 사막을 건너고 싶어 했다.

02 미나는 사막 생활 경험을 시도해 보고 고비 사막을 50일 내로 건너고 싶어 하므로 용감한(brave)이 적절하다. thoughtful: 사려 깊은, polite: 예의바른, shy: 수줍어하는, honest: 정직한

03 주어진 문장은 알고 있는지 여부를 묻는 질문에 대한 대답으로 적절하므로 (B)가 알맞다.

04 '둘 또는 그 이상의 선수들이나 팀들 간의 경쟁'을 가리키는 말은 match(경기)이다.

05 위 대화를 통해 Emily가 게임에 이기기 위해 무엇을 했는지는 알 수 없다.

07 나머지는 모두 고비 사막을 가리키지만, ⓒ는 비인칭 용법이다.

08 Tim은 왜 걸어서 고비 사막을 건너고 싶지 않은지 대화를 통해 알 수 없다.

09 Tony와 Brad는 학교 아이스하키 팀에 지원했다.

10 호준은 최선을 다할 것을 약속했다.

11 여권 사진이 필요했지만 사진을 잘 찍는 방법을 모르는 남동생이 사진을 찍게 했다는 의미이다. 사역동사의 목적어와 목적격 보어의 관계가 수동이므로 taken이 적절하다.

12 사역동사 let의 목적격 보어로 동사원형을 쓰는 것이 적절하다. shoe polish: 구두 광택제

13 Although를 대신하여 Even though 혹은 Though를 써도 좋다.

14 get은 목적격 보어로 to부정사를 취하는 동사이다.

15 ② Despite → Although ③ because → though ④ brought → bring

16 사역동사 have의 목적어와 목적격 보어의 관계가 능동인 경우 목적격 보어로 동사원형을, 수동인 경우 과거분사를 쓴다.

17 한 소년이 축구 토너먼트에 관한 포스터를 가지고 왔고 (B) 소년들은 한번 해 보기로 결정함. 떠나려고 할 때 마을 사람들이 새 신발과 축구복을 주었고, (A) 몇몇 사람들은 경기를 보러 오기도 함. 사람들은 소년들을 가장 약한 팀으로 보았음. (C) 하지만 토너먼트가 시작되자 사람들은 놀람.

18 비록 사람들은 그 팀이 가장 약한 팀일 것이라고 생각했지만, 토너먼트가 시작되었을 때 그들은 그 팀에 놀랐다.

19 두 골 '차이'로 지고 있었다는 의미이다. 정도나 비율의 차이를 나타내며 '~만큼'이라는 의미로 쓰이는 전치사는 by이다.

20 고향의 미끄러운 축구장 덕분에 빗속에서 경기를 더 잘하였다. 준결승전 날에 비가 심하게 내렸고, 소년들은 두 골 차로 지고 있었으

21 소년들은 스스로를 자랑스럽게 여겼다.

22 주어와 동사를 포함하는 절을 이끌고 있으므로 Although를 쓰는 것이 적절하다. Despite은 명사구를 이끄는 전치사이다.

23 Fern은 선수들이 맨발로 경기를 한 것이 선수들이 경기를 더 잘하게 만들었다고 생각했다. 사역동사 make의 목적어와 목적격 보어의 관계가 능동이므로 목적격 보어로 play를 쓴다.

24 후반전 동안 선수들은 맨발로 경기를 하였다. 따라서 신발을 신지 않고 경기에 임했다는 ③번이 글의 내용과 일치한다.

10 앞에서 언급한 내용과 상반되는 내용을 추가할 때 쓰는 말로 However가 적절하다.

11 그들만의 축구장을 만든 후, 비록 축구장이 흔들리고 맨발로 축구를 해야 하지만 소년들은 행복하다.

12 take part in: ~에 참가하다

13 3대 2로 졌다고 하였으므로 그 팀은 결국 2점을 얻었다고 할 수 있다.

14 hardly는 부사로 '거의 … 아니다[않다]'라는 의미이고 hard는 부사로 '몹시, 심하게'라는 의미이다.

15 though, even though를 써도 무방하다.

16 고향에 있는 미끄러운 축구장이 그들을 빗속에서 더 잘하게 하였다.

서술형 실전문제   p.206~207

01 have you heard of the Gobi Desert?

02 It took them about 51 days.

03 She wants to try and cross the Gobi Desert in 50 days.

04 Although[Though] he doesn't have time, he tries to exercise every day.

05 had me write, made me clean

06 Though I was very tired, I stayed up late.

07 shortened

08 made me feel sorry

09 A Soccer Team with Courage

10 However

11 it is shaky and they play in bare feet

12 they take part in a tournament

13 The team got two goals in the end.

14 hardly → hard

15 although

16 play better in the rain

---

02 약 51일이 걸렸다.

03 미나는 시도해 보고 고비 사막을 50일 내로 건너고 싶어 한다.

04 양보의 부사절 Although가 이끄는 문장을 주절 뒤에 쓰면 콤마를 쓰지 않는 것에 유의한다.

05 사역동사의 목적어와 목적격 보어의 관계가 능동이므로 목적격 보어로 동사원형을 쓴다. 과거에 일어난 일이므로 모두 과거시제를 쓴다.

06 Though를 대신하여 Although 혹은 Even though를 써도 무방하다.

07 사역동사 have의 목적어와 목적격 보어의 관계가 수동이므로 과거분사를 목적격 보어로 쓴다. shorten: 짧게 하다

08 '내가 미안함을 느끼게 하는' 것이므로 사역동사의 목적격 보어로 동사원형을 쓴다.

09 포기하지 않고 도전하는 소년들에 관한 이야기이므로 '용기 있는 축구팀'이 가장 적절하다.

창의사고력 서술형 문제   p.208

01 (A) the school ice hockey team
   (B) Tony and Brad
   (C) give up
   (D) try my best

|모범답안|

02 (1) My brother made me clean his room.
   (2) My dad let me go out with my friends.
   (3) The teacher had us do the project together.
   (4) My friend made me take her umbrella.

01 나는 학교 아이스하키 팀에 지원할지 고민하고 있었다. 사실, 나는 자신감이 없었다. 왜냐하면 Tony와 Brad가 아이스하키 팀에 지원했다고 들었기 때문이다. 나는 그들이 굉장히 잘하는 선수들이라는 것을 알았다. 내가 수지와 이야기했을 때, 그녀는 내가 포기하지 않도록 격려해 주었다. 그녀는 나도 아이스하키를 잘한다고 말했다. 나는 그녀에게 최선을 다할 것을 약속했다.

단원별 모의고사   p.209~212

01 ⑤   02 (1) semi-final (2) shaky (3) shoot

03 ②   04 ③   05 ③   06 ⑤

07 (1) It was shaky and had nails everywhere.
   (2) The boys gathered old boats and pieces of wood.

08 Tony and Brad are also trying out for the team

09 ②   10 ③

11 They played as a team and worked hard.

12 (A) the Greek team (B) give up (C) Saturday (D) try her best

13 repaired by Tom   14 ⑤   15 ③

16 ④   17 ④   18 bare   19 ⑤

20 ③   21 ④

22 They decided to give it a try.

23 Although it looked impossible to win, we didn't give up.

01 '일반적으로 노력, 용기 또는 기술에 의해 성공적으로 이루어진 것'을 가리키는 말은 achievement(성취)이다.

02 semi-final: 준결승전, shaky: 흔들리는, shoot: 슛하다

03 (A) try out for 지원하다, (B) give up 포기하다, (C) take off 벗다

04 (C) 다음 문장의 it이 주어진 문장의 one을 가리키므로 (C)가 적절하다.

05 Alex는 소라가 입지 않는 스웨터를 입을 것이다.

06 위 대화를 통해 건강해지기 위해 어느 조언이 가장 중요한지는 알 수 없다.

07 everywhere: 모든 곳에, gather: 모으다

09 (A)는 확실하지 않다는 말이 자연스러우므로 sure, (B) '포기하다'는 give up, (C) '최선을 다하다'를 의미하는 try one's best가 적절하다.

10 ⓒ를 제외한 나머지는 모두 the Greek team을 가리킨다.

11 비록 그리스 팀은 약팀이었지만 한 팀으로 경기하며 열심히 했기 때문에 2004 유로컵에서 우승할 수 있었다.

12 Emily의 아빠는 Emily에게 어떻게 그리스 팀이 2004 유로컵에서 이겼는지 이야기했다. 왜냐하면 그녀의 아빠는 그녀가 토요일에 있는 경기를 포기하기를 원하지 않았기 때문이다. 아빠와 이야기한 후, Emily는 최선을 다할 것을 결심했다.

13 신발은 수리되는 것이므로 과거분사로 쓰는 것이 적절하다.

14 ① crying → cry ② Despite → Although ③ ran → run ④ 주절 앞에 콤마를 써야 함.

15 아이들이 도와주도록 시킨 것이므로 첫 번째 빈칸에는 help이며 help의 목적격 보어로 to부정사나 동사원형이 모두 올 수 있으므로 ③번이 적절하다.

16 공과 소년들이 종종 바다에 빠져서 축구장이 항상 젖어 있고 미끄러웠다고 하는 것이 자연스럽다.

17 소년들은 망치질을 직접 하였다.

18 옷, 신발, 모자 등에 의해서 덮이지 않은 것은 '벌거벗은, 맨-(bare)'이다.

19 소년들이 축구팀을 만들겠다는 말에 사람들이 비웃었다고 하였으므로, 소년들이 축구팀을 만들도록 장려했다는 ⑤번은 글의 내용과 일치하지 않는다.

20 (A)는 to부정사의 형용사적 용법으로 쓰였다. ① 명사적 용법 중 목적격 보어 ② 진주어 ③ 형용사적 용법 ④ 부사적 용법 중 목적 ⑤ 명사적 용법 중 목적어

21 모두 소년들을 지칭하고 있지만 ④번은 마을 사람들을 가리킨다.

22 소년들은 축구 토너먼트에 관한 포스터를 본 후 한번 해 보기로 결정했다.

23 Although 대신 Though, Even though를 써도 무방하며, 양보의 부사절을 주절 뒤에 쓸 경우 콤마를 쓰지 않는다.

교과서 파헤치기

Lesson 5

1 enter, 입장하다   2 suspect, 용의자   3 bean, 콩
4 bottom, 맨 아래 (부분)   5 thief, 도둑   6 half, 반, 절반
7 clue, 단서, 실마리   8 cross, 건너다   9 delete, 삭제하다
10 bat, 방망이, 배트   11 accident, 사고
12 detective, 탐정   13 riddle, 수수께끼
14 escape, 탈출하다   15 hide, 숨기다   16 stamp, 우표

01 구역, 블록	02 반, 절반	03 삭제하다
04 사고	05 던지다	06 어딘가에
07 용	08 맨 아래 (부분)	09 용의자
10 거짓말하다	11 탈출하다	
12 ~ 밖에, 밖으로, 밖에		13 단서, 실마리
14 숨기다, 숨다	15 탐정, 형사	16 다행히
17 콩	18 두 번, 두 배	19 공간
20 ~의 안에, ~의 내부에		21 축하
22 장면	23 이상한	24 도둑
25 상	26 안전하게	27 설명하다
28 똑바로, 일직선으로		29 마침내
30 사라지다	31 접다	32 하나도 ~ 않다
33 해결하다	34 수수께끼	35 단추
36 마음껏 드세요	37 ~을 적다	38 ~을 뒤집다
39 도둑을 잡다	40 A를 B로 채우다	41 공짜로
42 ~이 일어나던 때에		
43 ~에 이르는데 성공하다		

01 button	02 scene	03 clue
04 throw	05 bottom	06 strange
07 explain	08 fold	09 cross
10 half	11 somewhere	12 delete
13 twice	14 finally	15 hide
16 lie	17 straight	18 accident
19 solve	20 disappear	21 bean
22 suspect	23 escape	24 luckily
25 congratulation	26 space	27 outside
28 prize	29 riddle	30 safely
31 detective	32 candle	33 thief
34 stamp	35 dragon	36 fill A with B
37 turn over	38 make it to ~	39 for free
40 at the time of	41 write down	42 catch a thief
43 help yourself		

Listen & Speak 1 - A
want to play, that, bought / what, it / like, dragons, seahorses, need to use, to play / sounds fun, Can you explain how to use

Listen & Speak 1 - B
riddle, twice in a week, once, never in a day / I have no idea / get it, Can you explain why / year, no, day / get it

Listen & Speak 2 - A
look at / How did you make it / First, in half, make a triangle, Second, fold the top, bottom line, Third, both ends, to make ears, Then, turn, over / sounds easy

Listen & Talk 2 - B
detective / didn't see, this week, about / all of, disappeared / did, do / First, looked around, Then, suspects, Finally, found, thief / don't tell, watch, later

Real Life Communication
solve / First, a bag of beans, needs to cross a river / can only hold, one more / Are you saying, take, at a time / Can you explain how to move everything across, safely

Let's Check
smells, good / going to, for dinner, Help yourself / Can you explain how to make / First, fill, with, Then, add, on the top / delicious / Would, like / thanks

Listen & Speak 1 - A

Jimin: Do you want to play the new game that I bought?

Brian: Sure, what is it, Jimin?

Jimin: It's like a soccer game but the players are dragons and seahorses. You need to use these buttons to play.

Brian: That sounds fun. Can you explain how to use the buttons?

Jimin: Sure.

Listen & Speak 1 - B

Jack: Kelly, here's a riddle. You can see this twice in a week, once in a year, but never in a day. What is this?

Kelly: I have no idea.

Jack: It's the letter "E."

Kelly: I don't get it. Can you explain why?

Jack: Well, there are two "E"s in the word "week," one "E" in the word "year" but no "E"s in the word "day."

Kelly: Aha! Now I get it.

Listen & Speak 2 - A

Tom: Yujin, look at my paper fox.

Yujin: That's cute. How did you make it?

Tom: First, fold a paper in half to make a triangle. Second, fold the top of the triangle to the bottom line. Third, fold both ends of the bottom line to the top to make ears. Then, turn it over and draw a face.

Yujin: That sounds easy.

Listen & Talk 2 - B

Jane: Minsu, do you know the TV show about the student detective?

Minsu: Yes. I love that show, but I didn't see it this week. What was it about?

Jane: Well, all of the bikes at school disappeared.

Minsu: So, what did he do?

Jane: First, he looked around the school. Then, he met some suspects and asked questions. Finally, he found the thief. The thief was ....

Minsu: No, don't tell me! I'll watch it later.

Real Life Communication

Emily: Junsu, do you want to solve a riddle?

Junsu: Sure, what is it?

Emily: There is a farmer. First, the farmer buys a fox, a duck, and a bag of beans. Then, the farmer needs to cross a river.

Junsu: What's the problem?

Emily: The boat can only hold the farmer and one more thing.

Junsu: Are you saying that the farmer can take only one thing at a time?

Emily: Yes. Also, the fox will eat the duck or the duck will eat the beans if the farmer isn't there. Can you explain how to move everything across the river safely?

Junsu: Hmm ....

Let's Check

Minjun: Wow! Something smells really good, Mom. What is it?

Mom: We're going to have tacos for dinner. Help yourself.

Minjun: Can you explain how to make a taco?

Mom: First, fill your tortilla with vegetables and meat. Then, add some sauce on the top.

Minjun: Sounds delicious!

Mom: Would you like some cheese?

Minjun: No, thanks.

본문 TEST Step 1   p.09~10

01 Welcome to, Escape	02 enter, first our
03 solve, riddles, escape	
04 be found, inside	
05 are, ready, think	06 hit by, on
07 Luckily, badly hurt, see	
08 suspects, questioned by	
09 reading, time, accident	
10 said, was walking	
11 was making breakfast	
12 Who hit, explain	
13 have, Write, down	14 move to, next
15 accident happened in	16 made it to
17 much harder, escape	
18 gets, from, clothing	
19 reads, won, event	
20 surprised, quickly opens	
21 won our, event	
22 have won, prize	
23 During, choose, item, free	
24 to, on	25 can't wait to	26 Truly yours
27 However, real, deletes	
28 Can, explain why	
29 There, usually, days	30 have, answer
31 Write, down, free	

본문 TEST Step 2   p.11~12

01 Welcome to	02 enter the first room
03 need to solve some riddles	
04 be found, inside	
05 are, ready to think like	06 was hit by, on
07 Luckily, wasn't badly hurt, didn't see	
08 were questioned by	

09 reading a book at the time of the accident

10 said, was walking

11 was making breakfast

12 Who hit, explain why

13 Write it down   14 can move to

15 accident happened in   16 made it to

17 However, much harder to escape than

18 gets, from, clothing store   19 reads, won

20 surprised, quickly opens

21 won our   22 Congratulations, have won, prize

23 During, choose, from, for free

24 Come to, on   25 can't wait to see

26 Truly yours

27 However, thinks that, isn't real, deletes

28 Can, explain why

29 There are usually, days

30 have the answer

31 Write it down, are free to go

---

1 '탈출 탑'에 오신 것을 환영합니다.

2 당신은 저희 탑의 첫 번째 방에 들어갈 것입니다.

3 당신은 탈출하기 위하여 몇 개의 수수께끼를 풀어야 합니다.

4 단서들은 방 어딘가에서 발견될 수 있습니다.

5 그러면 당신은 셜록 홈스처럼 생각할 준비가 되었나요?

6 Doodle씨는 일요일 오후에 차에 치였습니다.

7 다행히 그는 심하게 다치지 않았으나 그는 운전자를 보지 못했습니다.

8 세 명의 용의자들이 경찰에게 심문을 받았습니다.

9 A씨는 사고가 일어난 시간에 책을 읽고 있었다고 말했습니다.

10 B씨는 그의 개를 산책시키고 있었다고 말했습니다.

11 C씨는 아침을 만들고 있었다고 말했습니다.

12 누가 Doodle씨를 치었을까요? 왜 그런지 설명할 수 있나요?

13 답을 가지고 있나요? 적어 보세요.

14 그런 다음, 당신은 다음 방으로 갈 수 있습니다.

15 단서: 사건은 오후에 일어났습니다.

16 축하합니다! 당신은 두 번째 방에 오는 데 성공하셨습니다.

17 그러나 두 번째 방은 첫 번째 방보다 탈출하기 훨씬 더 어렵습니다. 행운을 빕니다!

18 Jay는 그가 가장 좋아하는 옷 가게로부터 이메일을 받습니다.

19 제목은 "당신은 '행운의 날' 행사에 당첨되었습니다!"라고 적혀 있습니다.

20 Jay는 놀랍니다. 그는 재빨리 그것을 엽니다.

21 당신은 우리의 '행운의 날' 행사에 당첨되었습니다!

22 축하합니다! 당신은 특별한 상품을 받게 되었습니다.

23 '행운의 날' 행사 동안, 당신은 우리 가게에서 일곱 가지 상품을 아무거나 공짜로 선택할 수 있습니다!

---

24 11월 31일에 우리 가게로 오세요.

25 우리는 몹시 당신을 보기를 기대합니다.

26 안녕히 계십시오, Kay Brown

27 그러나 Jay는 그 행사가 사실이 아니라고 생각하고 이메일을 삭제합니다.

28 왜 그런지 설명할 수 있나요?

29 단서: 한 달은 주로 30일 또는 31일이 있습니다.

30 답을 가지고 계신가요?

31 그것을 적으면, 당신은 자유롭게 가실 수 있습니다!

---

1 Welcome to the Escape Tower.

2 You will enter the first room in our tower.

3 You need to solve some riddles to escape.

4 Clues can be found somewhere inside the room.

5 So, are you ready to think like Sherlock Holmes?

6 Mr. Doodle was hit by a car on Sunday afternoon.

7 Luckily, he wasn't badly hurt, but he didn't see the driver.

8 Three suspects were questioned by a police officer.

9 Ms. A said she was reading a book at the time of the accident.

10 Mr. B said he was walking his dog.

11 Ms. C said she was making breakfast.

12 Who hit Mr. Doodle? Can you explain why?

13 Do you have the answer? Write it down.

14 Then you can move to the next room.

15 Clue The accident happened in the afternoon.

16 Congratulations! You made it to the second room.

17 However, the second room is much harder to escape than the first one. Good luck!

18 Jay gets an email from his favorite clothing store.

19 The title reads "You won our Lucky Day event!"

20 Jay is surprised. He quickly opens it.

21 You won our 'Lucky Day' event!

22 Congratulations! You have won a special prize.

23 During our Lucky Day event, you can choose any seven items from our store for free!

24 Come to our store on November 31.

25 We can't wait to see you.

26 Truly yours, Kay Brown

27 However, Jay thinks that the event isn't real and deletes the email.

28 Can you explain why?

29 Clue There are usually 30 or 31 days in a month.

30 Do you have the answer?

31 Write it down and then you are free to go!

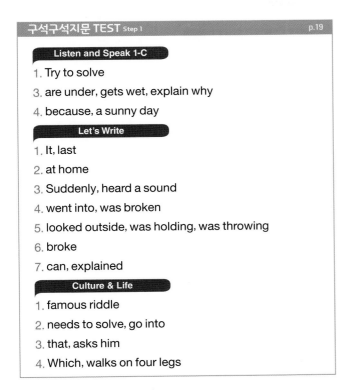

구석구석지문 TEST Step 1 p.19

Listen and Speak 1-C

1. Try to solve

3. are under, gets wet, explain why

4. because, a sunny day

Let's Write

1. It, last

2. at home

3. Suddenly, heard a sound

4. went into, was broken

5. looked outside, was holding, was throwing

6. broke

7. can, explained

Culture & Life

1. famous riddle

2. needs to solve, go into

3. that, asks him

4. Which, walks on four legs

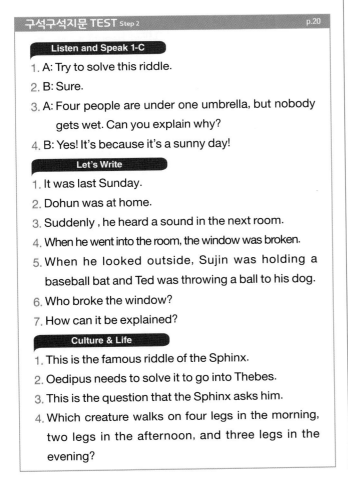

구석구석지문 TEST Step 2 p.20

Listen and Speak 1-C

1. A: Try to solve this riddle.

2. B: Sure.

3. A: Four people are under one umbrella, but nobody gets wet. Can you explain why?

4. B: Yes! It's because it's a sunny day!

Let's Write

1. It was last Sunday.

2. Dohun was at home.

3. Suddenly , he heard a sound in the next room.

4. When he went into the room, the window was broken.

5. When he looked outside, Sujin was holding a baseball bat and Ted was throwing a ball to his dog.

6. Who broke the window?

7. How can it be explained?

Culture & Life

1. This is the famous riddle of the Sphinx.

2. Oedipus needs to solve it to go into Thebes.

3. This is the question that the Sphinx asks him.

4. Which creature walks on four legs in the morning, two legs in the afternoon, and three legs in the evening?

단어 TEST Step 1   p.21

01 ~ 사이에	02 등장인물	03 힘
04 용감한	05 ~을 통해	06 (색상이) 밝은
07 강한, 힘 있는	08 적	09 표현하다
10 싸움, 다툼	11 부채	12 숨다
13 응원하다	14 겁먹은, 무서워하는	
15 의사소통하다	16 ~ 뒤에	17 무서운
18 열다, 개최하다	19 인기 있는	20 의상, 복장
21 흥미 있게도	22 암컷의, 여성의	23 바람이 많이 부는
24 전통적인	25 오늘날에는	26 의견
27 원래, 본래	28 수컷의, 남성의	29 공연하다
30 편안한	31 완전히	32 야생의
33 두 사람, 남녀	34 우아하게	35 내 의견으로는
36 ~이 허용되다	37 살펴보다	38 ~을 포기하다
39 정시에	40 최선을 다하다	41 ~처럼 보이다
42 소리를 내다	42 계속 열심히 하다	

단어 TEST Step 2   p.22

01 character	02 female	03 popular
04 brave	05 communicate	06 bright
07 enemy	08 express	09 fan
10 sure	11 wild	12 couple
13 traditional	14 between	15 windy
16 gracefully	17 costume	18 behind
19 interestingly	20 through	21 male
22 totally	23 nowadays	24 scary
25 opinion	26 hide	27 originally
28 movement	29 perform	30 fight
31 powerful	32 cheer	33 comfortable
34 strength	35 take a look	36 try one's best
37 in my opinion	38 give up on	39 on time
40 make a sound	41 sound like	42 be good at
43 be allowed to		

단어 TEST Step 3   p.23

1 popular, 인기 있는   2 behind, 뒤에

3 movement, 움직임   4 drop, 떨어뜨리다   5 wild, 야생의

6 strength, 힘   7 brave, 용감한   8 fan, 부채

9 originally, 원래, 본래   10 hide, 숨다

11 express, 표현하다   12 field, 들판

13 perform, 공연하다   14 uniform, 제복

---

15 cheer, 응원하다   16 comfortable, 편안한

대화문 TEST Step 1   p.24~25

Listen & Speak 1 A-1

what, think about, painting / look like, having fun / In my opinion, enjoys dancing

Listen & Speak 1 A-2

what, about this painting / interesting, smiled when, first saw / Me, too, look happy

Listen & Speak 1 B

some male birds dance / Why, dance / to show, love, female birds / any other animals / bees, where to find food / way to communicate / totally agree with you

Listen & Speak 2 A-1

my voice, Listen to, soft, cool, sure / my body to express, movements, Why don't, like, sure, feel great / make sounds, dance

Listen & Speak 2 B

What, reading / story about / tell, more / lost, when, After that, difficulties, gave up on / worked, hard to be, to be, right / try my best / Keep up, work, sure, make it

Real Life Communication

what, will be held / perform / decide what to do / How about, opinion, easy to learn, beautiful / sounds like / is good at / I'm sure / give it a try

Let's Check

dancing girls, amazing / only see / Look more closely, behind / didn't know, other dancers behind her / right, I'm sure, more than

대화문 TEST Step 2   p.26~27

Listen & Speak 1 A-1

Jane: Minsu, what do you think about that painting?

Minsu: Umm ... The people look like they're having fun.

Jane: I agree. In my opinion, the dancing boy really enjoys dancing.

Listen & Speak 1 A-2

Brian: Jimin, what do you think about this painting?

Jimin: In my opinion, it's interesting. I smiled when I first saw it.

Brian: Me, too. The dancers in the painting look happy.

Listen & Speak 1 B

Emily: Hojun, did you know that some male birds dance?

Hojun: No. Why do they dance?

Emily: They dance to show their love to female birds.

Hojun: That's interesting. Do you know any other animals that can dance?

Emily: Yes, some bees dance to show where to find food.

Hojun: That's cool! In my opinion, dancing is a great way to communicate.

Emily: I totally agree with you.

Listen & Speak 2 A-1

Minji: I use my voice to make music. Listen to my music. My voice is soft and cool. I'm sure you will like it.

Jimin: I move my body to express my feelings. Look at my movements. Why don't you jump like me? I'm sure you'll feel great.

Sujin: I use my hands to make sounds. Come and listen to my music. I'm sure you'll want to dance when you listen to it.

Listen & Speak 2 B

Tom: What are you reading, Kelly?

Kelly: I'm reading a story about Michaela DePrince.

Tom: Michaela DePrince? Can you tell me more about her?

Kelly: Sure. Michaela lost her parents when she was three. After that, she had a lot of difficulties. But she never gave up on her dream of becoming a dancer.

Tom: Wow, she worked very hard to be a good dancer. Kelly, you also have a dream to be a dancer, right?

Kelly: Yes. I will try my best to be a great dancer like her.

Tom: Keep up the good work. I'm sure you can make it.

Real Life Communication

Junsu: You know what? The school dance contest will be held soon.

Emily: That's right. I heard Jimin's class is going to perform a taekwondo dance and Tim's class is going to do a K-pop dance.

Brian: We should also decide what to do.

Mina How about a Buchaechum? In my opinion, it is easy to learn, and it's also beautiful.

Emily: That sounds like a good idea. But who will teach us?

Brian: Mina is good at traditional dances. Can you help us, Mina?

Mina: Of course, I will. I'm sure we'll have a lot of fun.

Junsu: Great. Let's give it a try.

Let's Check

Jenny: Look at the dancing girls, Dongjun. Aren't they amazing?

Dongjun: Girls? I can only see one dancer.

Jenny: Look more closely. Do you see many arms behind her?

Dongjun: Wow. I didn't know that there were other dancers behind her.

Jenny: That's right. I'm sure there are more than 10 dancers.

본문 TEST Step 1   p.28~29

01 Why, dance

02 express, happiness, enjoy themselves

03 take, different kinds, around

04 tells, story

05 stories through, body movements

06 fight, good, evil

07 playing, characters, green

08 eveil, wear, make-up

09 Interestingly, allowed to

10 movements, powerful, train

11 When, visit, may meet

12 perform, traditional, scary

13 originally performed, fight

14 show, strength, enemy

15 looked, scary as, before

16 Nowadays, perform, show, other

17 traditional, fan dance

18 wear colorful   19 with, painted, bright

20 move, gracefully, different, beauty

21 movements, as beautiful, flying

22 so popular that, traditional

본문 TEST Step 2   p.30~31

01 Why, dance

02 to express feelings, to others, enjoy themselves

03 Let's take, different kinds of dance

04 tells, story

05 stories through, body movements

06 a fight between good and evil

07 who are playing good characters, green

08 who are playing, wear black make-up

09 Interestingly, are allowed to dance

10 so powerful that, need to, for

11 may meet, *haka* dancers

12 perform, traditional, with scary faces

13 originally performed by, fight

14 to show their strength, enemy

15 looked as scary as, before fighting

16 Nowadays, usually perform, to show, to the other team

17 traditional Korean fan dance

18 wear colorful *hanbok*

19 with, that are painted

20 move, gracefully, different kinds of beauty

21 look as beautiful as, flying birds

22 so popular that, can see it

---

1 사람들은 왜 춤을 추는 걸까요?

2 사람들은 감정을 표현하고, 다른 사람들에게 행복감을 주거나 스스로 즐기기 위해 춤을 춥니다.

3 세계의 여러 가지 춤을 살펴봅시다.

4 Kathakali에는 이야기가 있습니다.

5 춤꾼들은 몸동작을 통해 이야기합니다.

6 이러한 이야기들은 대개 선과 악의 싸움에 관한 것입니다.

7 선한 역할을 맡은 춤꾼들은 자신의 얼굴을 초록색으로 칠합니다.

8 악한 역할을 맡은 춤꾼들은 검은색 화장을 합니다.

9 재미있는 것은 Kathakali 춤에서 남자들만 춤추는 것이 허락된다는 사실입니다.

10 몸동작이 매우 힘이 넘쳐서 춤꾼들은 수년 동안 연습을 해야 합니다.

11 사람들이 뉴질랜드를 방문할 때, 그들은 haka 춤꾼들의 무리를 만날지도 모릅니다.

12 그 춤꾼들은 무서운 얼굴로 이 전통 춤을 춥니다.

13 이 춤은 원래 마오리족에 의해 싸움 전에 행해졌습니다.

14 그들은 적에게 그들의 힘을 보여 주고 싶었습니다.

15 그 춤꾼들은 싸움하기 전의 야생 동물들만큼 무섭게 보였습니다.

16 요즈음, 뉴질랜드에서는 럭비 선수들이 다른 팀에게 그들의 힘을 보여 주기 위해 게임 전에 주로 haka 를 보여 줍니다.

17 부채춤은 한국 전통 부채춤입니다.

18 춤꾼들은 다채로운 한복을 입습니다.

19 그들은 밝은 색으로 칠해진 커다란 부채를 가지고 춤을 춥니다.

20 그 춤꾼들은 다양한 종류의 미를 보여 주기 위해 부채를 우아하게 움직입니다.

21 그들의 움직임은 꽃 또는 날아다니는 새들처럼 우아하게 보입니다.

---

22 한국에서, 부채춤은 너무 인기가 있어서 사람들은 많은 전통 축제에서 그것을 볼 수 있습니다.

---

1 Why do people dance?

2 They dance to express feelings, give happiness to others, or enjoy themselves.

3 Let's take a look at different kinds of dance around the world.

4 *Kathakali* tells a story.

5 The dancers tell stories through their body movements.

6 These stories are usually about a fight between good and evil.

7 Dancers who are playing good characters paint their faces green.

8 Those who are playing evil characters wear black make-up.

9 Interestingly, in *Kathakali*, only men are allowed to dance.

10 The body movements are so powerful that the dancers need to train for many years.

11 When people visit New Zealand, they may meet a group of *haka* dancers.

12 The dancers perform this traditional dance with scary faces.

13 This dance was originally performed by the Maori before a fight.

14 They wanted to show their strength to the enemy.

15 The dancers looked as scary as wild animals before fighting.

16 Nowadays, in New Zealand, rugby players usually perform a *haka* before a game to show their strength to the other team.

17 *Buchaechum* is a traditional Korean fan dance.

18 The dancers wear colorful *hanbok*.

19 They dance with large fans that are painted in bright colors.

20 The dancers move the fans gracefully to show different kinds of beauty.

21 Their movements look as beautiful as flowers or flying birds.

22 In Korea, *Buchaechum* is so popular that people can see it in many traditional festivals.

Listen and Speak 2 - C

1. going to, culture event, want to join
2. Sounds
3. enjoy dancing, sure, a lot of fun

Culture & Life

1. Italy
2. In the past, sick people
3. Nowadays, couple's dance
4. on, such as weddings

Culture & Life

1. Kenya
2. is performed, fight
3. is also called
4. jump high
5. When, cheer, on, loud noises

Listen and Speak 2 - C

1. A: I'm going to a culture event in our town next week. Do you want to join me?
2. B: Sounds interesting.
3. A: We can enjoy dancing from many countries. I'm sure we'll have a lot of fun.

Culture & Life

1. *Tarantella*, Italy
2. In the past, people danced the *tarantella* for sick people.
3. Nowadays, it is a couple's dance.
4. People dance the *tarantella* on happy days such as weddings.

Culture & Life

1. *Adumu*, Kenya
2. This dance is performed before a fight.
3. It is also called a jumping dance.
4. Dancers jump high in the air.
5. When a dancer jumps, other dancers cheer him on with loud noises.

Lesson 7

01 맛	02 안전한	03 차이, 차이점
04 탈출하다, (액체, 가스가) 새다		05 채우다
06 냉동고	07 대신에	08 가라앉다
09 뜨다	10 번개	11 압력
12 비밀	13 ~ 뒤에	14 준비하다
15 볕에 탐	16 팽창하다	17 마술, 속임수
18 재료, 물질	19 비교하다	20 흡수하다
21 불꽃	22 수축하다	23 사라지다
24 실험	25 마른, 비가 오지 않는	
26 혼동하게 하다	27 오르다, 올라가다	28 무게를 재다
29 마술, 마법	30 자외선 차단제	31 잡다, 쥐다
32 양초	33 연습	34 필요한
35 오랫동안	36 차가워지다	37 ~을 신청하다
38 시도해 보다	39 ~을 (바꾸지 않고) 고수하다	
40 타 버리다	41 골라내다	42 속을 들여다 보다
43 A가 B로 변하다		

01 coin	02 fill	03 practice
04 magic	05 disappear	06 dry
07 expand	08 candle	09 sunburn
10 flavor	11 sink	12 absorb
13 secret	14 instead	15 lightning
16 material	17 sunscreen	18 difference
19 contract	20 mix	21 experiment
22 necessary	23 safe	24 trick
25 flame	26 prepare	27 confuse
28 float	29 escape	30 compare
31 pressure	32 weigh	33 rise
34 freezer	35 pick out	36 burn out
37 stick to	38 for a long time	39 cool down
40 turn A into B	41 sign up for	42 give it a try
43 see through		

1 disappear, 사라지다   2 contract, 수축하다

3 mix, 섞다   4 sink, 가라앉다   5 expand, 팽창하다

6 float, 뜨다   7 confuse, 혼동하게 하다

8 material, 물질, 재료   9 trick, 속임수, 마술

10 freezer, 냉동고   11 weigh, 무게를 재다

12 absorb, 흡수하다   13 magic, 마술의
14 experiment, 실험   15 secret, 비밀
16 practice, 연습

대화문 TEST Step 1

Listen & Speak 1 A

Which flavor, How about, First, half a cup, Next, cut, into, mix, freezer, easy to make, isn't, Why don't, try making

Listen & Speak 1 B

why, put / picking out / Which eggs, which / that sink in water, float, shouldn't eat / interesting, float / Because, inside, acts like, balloon

Listen & Speak 2 A

a glass of, weigh / can test / fish / can use, instead of / How, work / weigh, put / weigh, compare / can't wait to, difference

Listen & Speak 2 B

hasn't rained for / dry season, lasting, worried / should, to help / special clock / How, help / seasons, to prepare for, dry season / sounds like, going to / give it a try, a lot / can't wait to see your clock

Real Life Communication A

join / sounds interesting, signed up for, fall / Which class / magic class, can't wait to, tricks / cool, Have you learned / more practice / some day

Let's Check

are, reading / magic, science / sounds, interesting / introduces, use science, learned about half / cool, some / balloon trick / can't wait to see

대화문 TEST Step 2

Listen & Speak 1 A

W: Today we'll make ice cream. Which flavor do you want to make? How about strawberry? First, mix two cups of milk, two cups of heavy cream, and half a cup of sugar. Next, cut five strawberries into small pieces. Then, mix everything together and put it in the freezer. That's it. It's easy to make, isn't it? Why don't you try making it at home?

Listen & Speak 1 B

B: Yujin, why did you put the eggs in water?
G: I'm picking out the bad eggs.
B: Which eggs are fresh, and which ones are not?

G: Eggs that sink in water are fresh. When eggs float in water, they're not fresh. You shouldn't eat them.
B: That's interesting. Why do the bad eggs float?
G: Because they have gas inside. The gas acts like the air in a balloon.
B: Oh, I see.

Listen & Speak 2 A

B: Ms. Jeong, does a glass of water weigh more when there's a fish in it?
W: Yes, it does. We can test it now.
B: But how? We don't have a fish.
W: We can use a finger instead of a fish.
B: How will that work?
W: I'll weigh a glass of water first. Then I will put my finger in the water and weigh it to compare.
B: Oh, I can't wait to see the difference.

Listen & Speak 2 B

King Sejong: It hasn't rained for a long time.
Jang Yeongsil: Yes. The dry season is lasting too long. The farmers are very worried.
King Sejong: We should do something to help them.
Jang Yeongsil: How about making a special clock?
King Sejong: A clock? How will that help?
Jang Yeongsil: The clock will show the time and the seasons. We can use it to prepare for the dry season.
King Sejong: That sounds like a good idea. But who's going to make it?
Jang Yeongsil: I'll give it a try. I know a lot about time and the seasons.
King Sejong: Okay, I can't wait to see your clock.

Real Life Communication A

Brian: Mina, will you join our tennis club?
Mina: It sounds interesting, but I signed up for a special class this fall.
Brian: Which class did you sign up for?
Mina: I signed up for a magic class. I can't wait to learn new magic tricks there.
Brian: That sounds cool! Have you learned magic tricks before?
Mina: Yes, I learned some before, but I need more practice.
Brian: I hope I can see your magic tricks some day.

Let's Check

B: What are you reading, Jiwon?
G: I'm reading a book about magic and science.
B: That sounds interesting.
G: Yes. This book introduces 100 magic tricks that

use science. I've learned about half of them.

B: That's cool. Can you show me some of the tricks?

G: Sure. I can show you a balloon trick now.

B: Great! I can't wait to see it.

본문 TEST Step 1
p.47~48

01 Welcome to, Super, Magic

02 It's, exciting, see, tricks

03 more, find out, behind

04 secret, magic, science

05 member, science, perform, tricks

06 show, can't wait

07 show, something amazing

08 dish with water

09 put, middle, dish

10 light, cover, with

11 How come, rose into

12 expands, hot, higher pressure

13 gets, contracts, lower pressure

14 burnt out, lower pressure

15 cooled, pressure dropped

16 outside, higher pressure

17 pushed, water, glass

18 fill one, with water

19 move, around, confuse

20 which cup, water

21 easy, middle one   22 let's check

23 me the other cups

24 There's no water

25 How come, disappeared

26 Before, put, into, cups

27 absorbed, turned, into

28 stuck to, bottom

29 try, necessary, use, through

30 for, performance, amazing

본문 TEST Step 2
p.49~50

01 Welcome to, Science Magic

02 It's, exciting to see

03 to find out, behind

04 secret, is science

05 will use science to perform, tricks

06 will, show us, wait to see them

07 to show you something amazing

08 with water in it

09 put a candle, middle

10 light, cover it with

11 Look at, How come, rose into

12 expands, gets hot, creates higher pressure

13 gets cold, contracts, creates lower pressure

14 burnt out, lower pressure

15 cooled down, dropped

16 outside, was at a higher pressure

17 pushed, into

18 going to fill one of these cups with

19 them around to confuse

20 which cup   21 It's, middle one

22 let's check   23 me the other cups

24 no water   25 How come, disappeared

26 Before, put, into one of the cups

27 absorbed, turned it into

28 stuck to the bottom

29 want to try, necessary to use, that, see through

30 for, performance, amazing

본문 TEST Step 3
p.51~52

1 지나: 특별 과학 마술 쇼에 오신 것을 환영합니다!

2 마술을 보는 것은 항상 신나는 일입니다.

3 그리고 마술 뒤에 숨겨진 비밀을 알아내는 것은 더 신나는 일입니다.

4 어떤 사람들은 마술의 비밀이 과학이라고 생각합니다.

5 오늘 학교 마술 동아리 회원인 Ken은 마술을 수행하기 위해 과학을 사용할 것입니다.

6 그는 우리에게 어떤 마술을 보여 줄까요? 무척 기다려지는군요.

7 Ken: 안녕하세요, 여러분. 오늘, 저는 여러분에게 놀라운 무언가를 보여 주려고 합니다.

8 여기에 물이 담긴 접시가 있습니다.

9 이제, 저는 접시 한가운데에 초를 놓을 것입니다.

10 그다음에 초를 켜고 유리컵으로 초를 덮어 보겠습니다. "아브라카다브라!"

11 지나: 물을 보세요! 어째서 물이 유리컵 속으로 올라간 거지요?

12 Ken: 공기가 뜨거워지면 팽창해서, 더 높은 압력을 만듭니다.

13 공기가 차가워지면 수축해서, 더 낮은 압력을 만듭니다.

14 불꽃이 다 타 버렸을 때, 유리컵 속의 공기는 식어 버렸습니다.

15 공기가 식었으므로, 기압이 낮아졌습니다.

16 그래서 유리컵 밖의 공기 압력이 더 높아졌습니다.

17 높아진 압력의 공기가 물을 밀어서 유리컵으로 들어가게 된 것입니다.

18 Ken: 이제, 이 컵들 중 하나를 물로 채워 보겠습니다.

19 여러분을 헷갈리게 하려고 이 컵들을 섞어 보겠습니다.

20 지나, 어떤 컵에 물이 있을까요?

21 지나: 쉽네요! 가운데 컵이에요.

22 Ken: 좋습니다. 확인해 봅시다. 보셨죠? 물이 없군요.

23 지나: 다른 컵들도 보여 주세요.

24 Ken: 보셨죠? 물이 없네요.

25 지나: 왜! 어째서 물이 사라진 거죠?

26 Ken: 마술 전에, 저는 특별한 물질을 컵 하나에 넣어 두었습니다.

27 그 물질은 물을 흡수하고, 그것을 젤리로 변하게 했습니다.

28 그러고 나서 젤리는 컵 바닥에 달라붙었습니다.

29 여러분이 이 마술을 해 보고자 한다면, 속을 들여다볼 수 없는 컵을 사용해야 합니다.

30 지나: 멋진 공연 고맙습니다. 정말 놀라웠어요!

21 Jina: That's easy! It's the middle one.

22 Ken: Okay, let's check. See? No water.

23 Jina: Show me the other cups.

24 Ken: See? There's no water.

25 Jina: Wow! How come the water disappeared?

26 Ken: Before the trick, I put a special material into one of the cups.

27 The material absorbed the water and turned it into jelly.

28 Then the jelly stuck to the bottom.

29 If you want to try this trick, it's necessary to use cups that you can't see through.

30 Jina: Thank you for your great performance. It was really amazing!

본문 TEST Step 4-Step 5   p.53~56

1 Jina: Welcome to the Super Science Magic Show!

2 It's always exciting to see magic tricks.

3 And it's more exciting to find out the secrets behind them.

4 Some people think the secret of magic is science.

5 Today, Ken, a member of the School Magic Club, will use science to perform his tricks.

6 Which tricks will he show us? I can't wait to see them.

7 Ken: Hello, everyone. Today, I'm going to show you something amazing.

8 Here's a dish with water in it.

9 Now, I'll put a candle in the middle of the dish.

10 Next, I'll light the candle and cover it with a glass. "Abracadabra!"

11 Jina: Look at the water! How come it rose into the glass?

12 Ken: Air expands when it gets hot and creates higher pressure.

13 When it gets cold, air contracts and creates lower pressure.

14 When the flame burnt out, the air inside the glass cooled down.

15 As the air cooled down, the air pressure dropped.

16 So the air outside the glass was at a higher pressure.

17 It pushed the water into the glass.

18 Ken: Now, I'm going to fill one of these cups with water.

19 I will move them around to confuse you.

20 Jina, which cup has the water in it?

구석구석지문 TEST Step 1   p.57

Real Life Communication B

1. Which class, sign up for

2. take, class, like playing, about

3. take the computer class, can't wait to

4. sounds

Culture & Life

1. Atlantic Ocean, Triangle

2. A number of, have disappeared

3. come

4. still

Culture & Life

1. Egypt

2. that were used to build, weigh about

3. it possible to move

4. still a mystery

구석구석지문 TEST Step 2   p.58

Real Life Communication B

1. A: Which class do you want to sign up for ?

2. B: I want to take the badminton class. I like playing badminton. How about you?

3. A: I want to take the computer class. I can't wait to make a computer program there.

4. B: That sounds cool!

Culture & Life

1. North Atlantic Ocean – The Bermuda Triangle

2. A number of airplanes and ships have disappeared in the Bermuda Triangle.

3. How come?

4. It's still a mystery.

1. Egypt – The pyramids
2. Some of the rocks that were used to build the pyramids weigh about 70 tons.
3. How was it possible to move such heavy rocks back then?
4. It's still a mystery.

49

13 proud, 자랑스러워하는   14 slippery, 미끄러운

15 courage, 용기   16 shoot, 슛하다

단어 TEST Step 1   p.59

01 미끄러운	02 넓은	03 벌거벗은, 맨 ~
04 모든 곳에, 어디나	05 마을	06 흔들리는, 휘청거리는
07 못생긴, 추한	08 훌륭한	09 경험하다
10 걱정하다, 관심을 갖다		11 떠 있는
12 모으다, 모이다	13 건강한	14 ~에 맞서
15 불가능한	16 용기	17 경기
18 식사, 끼니	19 성과	20 못하다; 못
21 운동하다	22 자랑스러워하는	23 준결승전
24 낙담한	25 약한	26 놀라운
27 소리 지르다, 소리치다		28 비록 ~일지라도
29 토너먼트	30 마을 사람	31 완전히
32 지다, 잃다	33 결정하다, 결심하다	
34 바람이 센	35 ~에 빠지다	36 최선을 다하다
37 걸어서, 도보로	38 ~을 지원하다	39 시도해 보다
40 사실은	41 막 ~하려고 하다	42 포기하다
43 ~을 비웃다		

단어 TEST Step 2   p.60

01 shout	02 although	03 care
04 shaky	05 completely	06 discouraged
07 slippery	08 decide	09 nail
10 everywhere	11 wide	12 experience
13 floating	14 achievement	15 excellent
16 against	17 gather	18 match
19 healthy	20 shoot	21 weak
22 bare	23 impossible	24 villager
25 lose	26 courage	27 amazing
28 windy	29 meal	30 ugly
31 proud	32 semi-final	33 exercise
34 wash	35 in fact	36 on foot
37 give it a try	38 laugh at	
39 try[do] one's best		40 give up
41 be about to	42 fall into	43 be good at

단어 TEST Step 3   p.61

1 excellent, 훌륭한   2 weak, 약한   3 lose, 지다

4 bare, 벌거벗은   5 shout, 소리치다   6 villager, 마을 사람

7 shaky, 흔들리는, 휘청거리는   8 match, 경기

9 nail, 못질하다   10 achievement, 성과

11 gather, 모으다   12 discouraged, 낙담한

대화문 TEST Step 1   p.62~63

Listen & Speak 1 A

have you heard of / have. Isn't, in / saw, who crossed. on foot / Only / took, about / to experience life. desert, cross, on foot / try, cross, in

Listen & Speak 1 B

have you heard about / course, have, on, right / right, going to / want to / I don't wear at home, if you want / would / Let's meet in front of, go inside / Sure, See

Listen & Speak 2 A

healthy, exercise, try to eat healthy food, Don't eat, wash, meals, sound hard, take, step at a time, give up, live, life

Listen & Speak 2 B

try out for, is about to / sure / Why not / heard, trying out for / good at, don't give up / try my best, a lot

Real Life Communication

excited, match / against, lost / Don't say, Have you heard about / No, haven't, about / so, thought, lose / What happened / as. worked hard, won, give up / try our best

Let's Check ❶

Have you heard of, When, couldn't read well, lost, hearing in, Still, Although, difficulties, be like, don't give up

대화문 TEST Step 2   p.64~65

Listen & Speak 1 A

G: Tim, have you heard of the Gobi Desert?

B: Yes, I have. Isn't it in Mongolia and China?

G: Yes, it is. Yesterday, I saw a TV show about people who crossed the desert on foot.

B: Only on foot?

G: Yes, it took them about 51 days.

B: Wow, that's amazing. I want to experience life in the desert but I don't want to cross it on foot.

G: Well, I want to try and cross the Gobi Desert in 50 days.

Listen & Speak 1 B

G: Alex, have you heard about this year's "Ugly Sweater Party?"

B: Of course, I have. It's on December 5th, right?

G: That's right. Are you going to go?

B: I want to, but I don't have an ugly sweater.

G: I have one that I don't wear at home. You can have it if you want.

B: Thanks. That would be great.

G: Let's meet in front of the Student Center and go inside together.

B: Sure. See you then.

Listen & Speak 2 A

W: What can you do to be healthy? First, try to exercise every day. Second, try to eat healthy food. Don't eat too much fast food. Third, wash your hands before meals. Do these tips sound hard to do? Well, take one step at a time and don't give up. Then you'll live a healthy life.

Listen & Speak 2 B

G: Hojun, are you going to try out for the school ice hockey team? The new season is about to start.

B: I'm not sure.

G: Why not?

B: I heard that Tony and Brad are also trying out for the team. They're so good.

G: Well, you're also good at ice hockey, so don't give up!

B: Okay, I'll try my best. Thanks a lot.

Real Life Communication

Father: Emily, are you excited about your match on Saturday?

Emily: Not really. We're playing against a strong team. I think we'll lose.

Father: Don't say that. Have you heard about the Greek team in the 2004 Euro Cup?

Emily: No, I haven't. What about them?

Father: They were a weak team, so everyone thought that they would lose.

Emily: What happened?

Father: They played as a team and worked hard. Finally, they won the Euro Cup. So, don't give up.

Emily: Thanks, Dad. We'll try our best.

Let's Check ❶

B: Have you heard of Thomas Edison? When he was young, he couldn't read well. Also, he lost all of the hearing in his left ear. Still, he became a great scientist. Although you may have difficulties, be like Edison and don't give up.

01 floating village, middle

02 Although, never played, watching

03 decided to make, own

04 However, laughed at

05 That's impossible   06 makes, say so

07 Look around, going, play

08 villagers, right, place to

09 were discouraged

10 give up, still play

12 Let's, own, field

13 gathered, pieces of

14 put, together, nailed, to

15 After, work, finally, floating

16 shaky, nails everywhere

17 fall into, wet, slippery

18 no shoes, bare feet   19 Still, care

20 In fact, excellent, enjoyed

21 One, brought, poster, tournament

22 decided to, it, try

23 When, about, leave, shoes

24 even, made, feel better

25 At, saw, as, weakest

26 However, started, surprised

27 On, semi-final, raining hard

28 losing by, impossible, win

29 other, strong, thought   30 didn't give up

31 took off, during, completely

32 better, thanks to, slippery

33 by, to, proud of

34 give, losing, tried, until

01 a small floating village, middle

02 Although, never played soccer, watching it on TV

03 One day, decided to make

04 However, laughed at their idea

05 impossible   06 makes, say so

07 Look around, are, going to play

08 were right, no place to play soccer

09 were discouraged

10 give up, still play soccer   11 How

12 Let's make our own

13 gathered, pieces of wood

14 put, together, nailed, to

15 After much, finally had a floating field

16 shaky, had nails everywhere
17 would often fall into, always wet, slippery
18 no shoes, had to, bare feet   19 Still, they, care
20 In fact, excellent, enjoyed playing
21 brought a poster
22 decided to, it, try
23 When, were about to leave, them new shoes
24 made, feel better
25 saw, as, weakest
26 However, when, started, surprised everyone
27 On, was raining hard
28 losing by two goals, impossible to win
29 The other, so strong   30 But, give up
31 took off, during, second half, changed completely
32 played better, thanks to
33 Although, lost by, to, proud of themselves
34 give up when they were losing, tried their best

24 몇몇은 심지어 경기를 보러 왔다. 이것은 소년들의 기분을 더 좋게 만들었다.
25 처음에, 사람들은 그들을 가장 약한 팀으로 보았다.
26 그러나 토너먼트가 시작되었을 때, 그 축구팀은 모든 사람들을 놀라게 했다.
27 준결승전 날, 비가 심하게 오고 있었다.
28 그들은 두 골 차로 지고 있었고, 이기는 것은 불가능해 보였다.
29 "다른 팀이 아주 강해."라고 그들은 생각했다.
30 그러나 소년들은 포기하지 않았다.
31 그들은 후반전에 그들의 신발을 벗었고 경기는 완전히 바뀌었다.
32 고향의 미끄러운 축구장 덕분에 그들은 빗속에서 더 잘하였다.
33 비록 그들은 3대 2로 졌지만, 그들은 그들 자신이 자랑스러웠다.
34 그들은 그들이 지고 있을 때 포기하지 않았다. 그들은 끝까지 최선을 다하였다.

본문 TEST Step 3
p.70~71

1 Koh Panyee는 바다 가운데 떠 있는 작은 수상 마을이었다.
2 비록 그 마을의 소년들은 이전에 축구를 해 본 적이 없었지만, 그들은 그것을 TV로 보는 것을 정말 좋아했다.
3 어느 날, 그 소년들은 그들만의 축구팀을 만들기로 하였다.
4 그러나 사람들은 그들의 생각을 비웃었다.
5 "그것은 불가능해."
6 "왜 그렇게 말하는 거죠?"
7 "주위를 둘러봐. 너희는 어디서 축구를 할 거니?"
8 마을 사람들이 옳았다. 소년들은 축구를 할 장소가 없었다.
9 그들은 낙담했다.
10 "포기하지 마! 우리는 여전히 축구를 할 수 있어."
11 "어떻게?"
12 "우리만의 축구장을 만들자."
13 소년들은 낡은 배와 나뭇조각들을 모았다.
14 그들은 배를 합치고 그것들 위에 나무를 못으로 박았다.
15 매우 열심히 일한 후, 그들은 마침내 떠 있는 축구장을 가지게 되었다.
16 그것은 흔들리고 곳곳에 못이 있었다.
17 공과 소년들은 종종 바다에 빠졌고, 축구장은 항상 젖어 있고 미끄러웠다.
18 그들은 신발이 없어서 맨발로 축구를 해야 했다.
19 그런데도 그들은 상관하지 않았다.
20 실제로 그들은 훌륭한 기술을 쌓았고 더욱 더 축구를 즐겼다.
21 어느 날, 한 소년이 축구 토너먼트에 관한 포스터를 가지고 왔다.
22 그들은 한번 해 보기로 결정했다.
23 그들이 떠나려고 할 때, 마을 사람들은 그들에게 새 신발과 축구복을 주었다.

본문 TEST Step 4 - Step 5
p.72~75

1 Koh Panyee was a small floating village in the middle of the sea.
2 Although the boys in the village never played soccer before, they loved watching it on TV.
3 One day, the boys decided to make their own soccer team.
4 However, people laughed at their idea.
5 "That's impossible."
6 "What makes you say so?"
7 "Look around. Where are you going to play soccer?"
8 The villagers were right. The boys had no place to play soccer.
9 They were discouraged.
10 "Don't give up! We can still play soccer."
11 "How?"
12 "Let's make our own soccer field."
13 The boys gathered old boats and pieces of wood.
14 They put the boats together and nailed the wood to them.
15 After much hard work, they finally had a floating field.
16 It was shaky and had nails everywhere.
17 The ball and the boys would often fall into the sea, so the field was always wet and slippery.
18 They had no shoes so they had to play in bare feet.
19 Still, they didn't care.
20 In fact, they built excellent skills and enjoyed playing soccer more.

21 One day, a boy brought a poster about a soccer tournament.

22 They decided to give it a try.

23 When they were about to leave, the villagers gave them new shoes and uniforms.

24 Some even came to watch the game. This made the boys feel better.

25 At first, people saw them as the weakest team.

26 However, when the tournament started, the soccer team surprised everyone.

27 On the day of the semi-final, it was raining hard.

28 They were losing by two goals and it looked impossible to win.

29 "The other team is so strong," they thought.

30 But the boys didn't give up.

31 They took off their shoes during the second half and the game changed completely.

32 They played better in the rain thanks to the slippery field at home.

33 Although they lost by a score of three to two, still, they felt proud of themselves.

34 They didn't give up when they were losing. They tried their best until the end.

2. B: No, don't give up! Have you heard of Anthony Webb?

3. A: No, I haven't. Who is he?

4. B: He was a basketball player. He was short, but he won the 1986 Slam Dunk Contest.

Culture & Life

1. The women's field hockey team from Zimbabwe surprised the whole world.

2. Although they had only a month to prepare, they won the gold medal at the 1980 Olympic Games.

Let's Write

1. My favorite sport is basketball.

2. However, I wasn't really good at it at first.

3. I couldn't shoot well unlike other players.

4. Although I felt discouraged, I didn't give up.

5. I practiced shooting for an hour every day.

6. This made me shoot well. Now, I'm the best player on our team.

구석구석지문 TEST Step 1   p.76

Real Life Communication - Step 2

1. want to be, but, too short, give up

2. don't give up, Have, heard of

3. haven't

4. basketball player, short, won

Culture & Life

1. from, surprised, whole world

2. Although, only a month to prepare, won, at

Let's Write

1. My favorite sport

2. However, wasn't, good at

3. unlike other players

4. felt discouraged, give up

5. practiced, for an hour every day

6. made me shoot, the best player

구석구석지문 TEST Step 2   p.77

Real Life Communication - Step 2

1. A: I want to be a basketball player but I'm too short. Should I give up?

MEMO

MEMO

적중 100 + 특별부록

Plan B

우리학교 최신기출

지학ㆍ민찬규 교과서를 배우는

학교 시험문제 분석ㆍ모음ㆍ해설집

전국단위 학교 시험문제 수집 및 분석
출제 빈도가 높은 문제 위주로 선별
문제 풀이에 필요한 상세한 해설

중2-2
영어

지학ㆍ민찬규

◎ 선택형 문항의 답안은 컴퓨터용 수정 싸인펜을 사용하여 OMR 답안지에 바르게 표기하시오.
◎ 서술형 문제는 답을 답안지에 반드시 검정 볼펜으로 쓰시오.
◎ 총 30문항 100점 만점입니다. 문항별 배점은 각 문항에 표시되어 있습니다.

[울산 ○○중]

01 다음 빈칸에 들어갈 말로 알맞은 것은? (3점)

'Delete' means 'to _____ something that has been written down or stored in a computer'.

① remove
② direct
③ detect
④ confuse
⑤ discover

[울산 ○○중]

02 다음 영영 풀이에 해당하는 단어가 <u>아닌</u> 것은? (4점)

- someone who is thought to be guilty of a crime
- someone who is paid to discover information about a crime
- an object or a piece of information that helps someone solve a crime or mystery
- an event in which a car, train, plane, etc. is damaged and often someone is hurt

① clue
② thief
③ suspect
④ accident
⑤ detective

[서울 영등포구 ○○중]

03 다음 중 단어와 영영 풀이가 맞지 <u>않는</u> 것은? (3점)

① bottom - a small, round thing that you can push to turn on a TV or a computer
② express - to talk or show what you are feeling
③ triangle - a shape that has three lines
④ detective - a person who finds information about a crime
⑤ riddle - a difficult question that often has a funny answer

[울산시 ○○중]

04 다음 주어진 우리말에 가장 알맞은 영어 문장은? (3점)

삼각형을 만들기 위해서 종이를 반으로 접어라.

① Put a piece of paper in half.
② Cut a piece of paper to make a circle.
③ Fold a piece of paper in half to make a circle.
④ Cut a piece of paper in half to make a triangle.
⑤ Fold a piece of paper in half to make a triangle.

[충북 ○○중]

05 다음 중 어법상 바른 것은? (3점)

① The box was found by under the table.
② The cake will be brought to us by 6 p.m.
③ Even a small voice can be hear at night.
④ The car must is washed by my father.
⑤ These pictures was taken in Paris by my grandfather.

06 다음 대화의 밑줄 친 우리말과 같은 의미가 되도록 영어 문장을 완성하시오. (4점)

> Jimin: You need to use these buttons to play the game.
>
> Mark: <u>버튼 사용하는 방법을 설명해 줄 수 있니?</u>
>
> Jimin: Sure.

→ _____ ?

07 다음 중 어법상 옳은 것만을 있는 대로 고른 것은? (4점)

> ⓐ Many books is read by him.
> ⓑ Thieves are caught by the police.
> ⓒ The book should not be put here.
> ⓓ Coffee beans are grew in Columbia.
> ⓔ The first plane was invented in 1903.
> ⓕ Stamps and coins are collected by she.
> ⓖ Was he beat up by the police on the street?
> ⓗ The show will be cancel if the weather is bad.

① ⓐ, ⓒ, ⓓ
② ⓑ, ⓒ, ⓔ
③ ⓔ, ⓕ, ⓖ
④ ⓓ, ⓔ, ⓕ, ⓗ
⑤ ⓑ, ⓓ, ⓖ, ⓗ

08 다음 중 어법상 <u>어색한</u> 문장 2개를 고른 것은? (3점)

① I was raised by my grandmother.
② The mountain can being seen from here.
③ A girl called Alice was invited to the party.
④ The flowers will be send to her on Monday.
⑤ The game will be canceled if the weather is bad.

09 다음 문장을 수동태 문장으로 바꿔 쓰시오. (5점)

(1) You can hear the sound from far away.

→ _____

(2) Does your father drive this car?

→ _____

10 다음 문장을 수동태로 바르게 옮긴 것은? (3점)

Henry wrote The Gift of the Magi.

① The Gift of the Magi is written by Henry.

② The Gift of the Magi was wrote by Henry.

③ The Gift of the Magi was written by Henry.

④ The Gift of the Magi was written with Henry.

⑤ The Gift of the Magi were written by Henry.

12 다음 대화의 내용과 일치하지 않는 것은? (3점)

B: Yujin, look at my paper fox.

G: That's cute. How did you make it?

B: First, fold a paper in half to make a triangle. Second, fold the top of the triangle to the bottom line. Third, fold both ends of the bottom line to the top of make ears. Then, turn it over and draw a face.

G: That sounds difficult for me.

① 총 4단계를 거쳐 종이여우를 만들 수 있다.

② 마지막 단계는 뒤집어서 얼굴을 그린다.

③ Boy는 종이여우를 만들어 Girl에게 보여주고 있다.

④ Girl은 종이여우 만드는 방법이 어렵다고 생각한다.

⑤ 종이여우를 만드는 첫 번째 단계는 종이를 반으로 접어 사각형 모양으로 만든다.

11 다음 글의 빈칸에 들어갈 말을 주어진 단어를 이용하여 알맞게 채운 것은? (3점)

It is very beautiful today. So my family is going to the park to enjoy the evening. Bright stars can (A)_____ at night. We've heard a movie (B)_____ at 9 p.m. in the park. And also, delicious food (C)_____ at the food truck at that time. Tonight will be great.

* 동사 see, show, buy 이용

	(A)	(B)	(C)
①	sees	how	buy
②	saw	showed	bought
③	are seen	will show	can buy
④	be saw	will be show	can be buy
⑤	be seen	will be shown	can be bought

13 다음 중 대화의 내용이 <u>어색한</u> 것은? (3점)

① A: You are good at traditional dances. Can you help us?

B: Of course, I will.

② A: We should also decide what to do for the school festival.

B: How about a Buchaechum? I think it is easy to learn.

③ A: Jimin, what do you think about this painting?

B: In my opinion, it's interesting.

④ A: Do you want to play the new game that I bought?

B: Sure, what is it?

⑤ A: Kelly, there's a riddle. You can see this twice in a week, once in a year, but never in a day. What is this?

B: I really like riddles.

[14~16] 다음 대화를 읽고 물음에 답하시오.

Emily: Junsu, do you want to solve a riddle?

Junsu: Sure, what is it?

Emily: There is a farmer. (A) Then, the farmer needs to cross a river. (B)

Junsu: What's the problem?

Emily: (C) The boat can only hold the farmer and one more thing. (D)

Junsu: Are you saying that the farmer can take only one thing at a time?

Emily: Yes. (E) Also, the fox will eat the duck or the duck will eat the beans if the farmer isn't there. (A)<u>모든 것을 어떻게 강 건너로 안전하게 옮기는지 설명해 줄 수 있니?</u>

Junsu: Hmm... Oh! I got it. First, the farmer crosses the river with the duck. Second, he comes back and takes the fox. Third, he leaves the fox and comes back with the duck. Then, he leaves the duck and takes the beans.

14 위 대화의 흐름으로 보아, 주어진 문장이 들어가기에 가장 적절한 곳은? (3점)

First, the farmer buys a fox, a duck, and a bag of beans.

① (A) ② (B) ③ (C)

④ (D) ⑤ (E)

15 위 대화의 내용과 일치하는 것 중 2개를 고른 것은? (3점)

① 농부가 없으면 여우는 콩을 먹는다.
② 농부는 여우와 오리만 한 곳에 남겨둬선 안 된다.
③ Junsu의 해결 방안은 오리를 여우보다 먼저 강 건너로 옮겨야 한다.
④ Junsu의 수수께끼 풀이로는 농부가 강을 3번만 건너도 문제를 해결 가능하다.
⑤ 농부는 한 번에 두 개(여우, 오리, 콩 중에서) 이상을 가지고 강을 건널 수 있다.

17 다음 주어진 말에 이어질 대화의 순서를 바르게 배열한 것은? (4점)

A: Minsu, do you know the TV show about the student detective?
ⓐ Well, all of the bikes at school disappeared.
ⓑ No, don't tell me! I'll watch it later.
ⓒ So, what did he do?
ⓓ Yes, I love that show, but I didn't see it this week. What was about it?
ⓔ First, he looked around the school. Then, he met some suspects and asked questions. Finally, he found the thief. The thief was....

① ⓑ-ⓐ-ⓒ-ⓓ-ⓔ
② ⓓ-ⓐ-ⓔ-ⓒ-ⓑ
③ ⓑ-ⓐ-ⓒ-ⓔ-ⓓ
④ ⓓ-ⓐ-ⓒ-ⓔ-ⓑ
⑤ ⓐ-ⓒ-ⓓ-ⓑ-ⓔ

16 위 대화의 밑줄 친 (A)문장을 우리말과 같도록 주어진 단어를 사용하여 영작하시오. (4점)

보기

explain / how / move / can / to / you / everything

조건

• <보기>의 단어를 모두 사용하시오.

(A) 모든 것을 어떻게 강 건너로 안전하게 옮기는지 설명해 줄 수 있니?

→ _____ across the river safely?

18 다음 글의 내용으로 보아 바로 이어서 해야 할 행동이 아닌 것은? (3점)

Welcome to the Escape Tower. You will enter the first room in our tower. You need to solve some riddles to escape. Clues can be found somewhere inside the room. So, are you ready to think like Sherlock Holmes?

① 탈출을 위해 몇 가지 문제를 푼다.
② 방 안에 있는 단서들을 찾는다.
③ 첫 번째 방으로 들어간다.
④ 셜록 홈즈를 만난다.
⑤ 탐정처럼 생각한다.

Welcome to the Escape Tower. You will enter the first room in our tower. You need ⓐto solve some riddles to escape. Clues can ⓑbe found somewhere inside the room. So, are you ready to think (A)like Sherlock Holmes?

Room #1

(B)A car hit Mr. Doodle on Sunday afternoon. Luckily, he wasn't badly hurt, but he didn't see the driver. Three suspects ⓒwas questioned by a police officer. Ms. A said she was reading a book at the time of the accident. Mr. B said he ⓓwas walking his dog. Ms. C said she was making breakfast. Who hit Mr. Doodle? Can you explain why? Do you have the answer? (가)Write ⓔit down. Then you can move to the next room.

19 다음 중 위 글의 (A)like와 밑줄 친 부분의 뜻이 <u>다른</u> 것은? (3점)

① She thinks I <u>like</u> her.

② Jane ran <u>like</u> the wind.

③ Don't look at me <u>like</u> that.

④ You must do this <u>like</u> that.

⑤ I've heard that I have to act <u>like</u> everyone else.

20 위 글의 밑줄 친 부분 중 어법상 올바르지 <u>않은</u> 것은? (3점)

① ⓐ ② ⓑ ③ ⓒ

④ ⓓ ⑤ ⓔ

21 위 글의 밑줄 친 (B)문장을 주어진 표현으로 시작하여 같은 의미가 되도록 영작하시오. (4점)

A car hit Mr. Doodle.
= Mr. Doodle _____.

→ _____

22 위 글의 내용으로 바르지 <u>않은</u> 것은? (3점)

① You should solve riddles to escape the tower.

② You need to find the person who hit Mr. Doodle.

③ The accident happened to Mr. Doodle on Sunday afternoon.

④ Mr. Doodle had a car accident but he wasn't hurt at all.

⑤ A police officer asked the suspects some questions.

23 위 글의 (가)의 요구대로 답을 썼을 때, 빈칸에 들어갈 말이 차례대로 배열된 것은? (3점)

> _____ hit Mr. Doodle because she/he said that he/she was _____ at the time of the accident, Sunday _____.

① Mr. B - walking his dog - afternoon

② Ms. A - reading a book - afternoon

③ Ms. C - making breakfast - afternoon

④ Ms. A - reading a book - morning

⑤ Ms. C - making breakfast - morning

24 위 글을 읽고 질문에 답할 수 없는 것은? (4점)

① When did the accident happen?

② Where was Mr. B at the time of accident?

③ Did Mr. Doodle see the driver who hit him?

④ What was Ms. A doing on Sunday afternoon?

⑤ How can we get out of the Escape Tower?

25 위 글을 읽고 난 반응으로 가장 적절한 것은? (3점)

① 현서: Mr. Doodle은 왜 토요일 오전에 밖에 나갔을까?

② 서진: 용의자 4명 중에서 Ms. C가 제일 의심스러워.

③ 효진: Mr. B는 왜 일요일에 개밥을 주지 않았는지 궁금해.

④ 서빈: Ms. A는 책을 읽었다는 엄청난 거짓말을 하고 있군.

⑤ 지민: 오후에 아침식사를 만든다고 한 Ms. C가 범인 같아.

[26~30] 다음 글을 읽고 물음에 답하시오.

> Congratulations! You made it to the second room. However, the second room is (A)_____ harder to escape than the first one. Good luck!
>
> **Room #2**
> Jay gets an email from his favorite clothing store. The title reads "You won our Lucky Day event!" Jay is (B)_____. He quickly opens it.
>
> JayJr@kmail.com
> You won our 'Lucky Day' event!
> Congratulations!
> You have won a special prize. During our Lucky Day event, you can choose any seven items from our store for free! Come to our store on November 31. We can't wait to see you.
>
> Truly yours,
> Kay Brown
>
> (가)_____, Jay thinks (나)that the event isn't real and deletes the email. Can you explain why?
> Do you have the answer? Write it down and then you are free to go!

26 위 글의 빈칸 (A), (B)에 들어갈 말이 맞게 짝지어진 것은? (3점)

	(A)	(B)
①	much	surprising
②	much	surprised
③	very	surprising
④	very	surprised
⑤	even	surprising

27 위 글의 빈칸 (가)에 들어갈 연결어로 가장 적절한 것은? (3점)

① Therefore
② However
③ Fortunately
④ Thus
⑤ In addition

29 위 글의 밑줄 친 (나)that의 쓰임과 같지 <u>않은</u> 것은? (3점)

① She says <u>that</u> Kelly lost her wallet.
② Jane believes <u>that</u> Tom will come to school.
③ I was told <u>that</u> English is a fun subject.
④ Eric thinks <u>that</u> Jinho can make cupcakes.
⑤ Junsu likes Kelly <u>that</u> everyone hates.

28 위 글은 방을 탈출하기 위해 풀어야 하는 수수께끼에 대한 글이다. 내용으로 알맞지 <u>않은</u> 것은? (4점)

① The email says Jay got a special prize.
② You can know the event is on November 31 from the email.
③ Jay's favorite clothing store sent an email to Jay in the riddle.
④ Jay can get any 7 items at the clothing store
⑤ Jay deleted the email because he didn't want to go shopping.

30 Why does Jay think that this event isn't real? (3점)

① Jay doesn't like the clothing store.
② Jay is very busy on November 31.
③ Jay couldn't open the email on his computer.
④ Jay is not interested in winning a special prize.
⑤ Jay knows that there are only 30 days in November.

반 이 름		점수

문항수 : 선택형(22문항)　서술형(8문항)　　20 ．　．　．

◎ 선택형 문항의 답안은 컴퓨터용 수정 싸인펜을 사용
하여 OMR 답안지에 바르게 표기하시오.
◎ 서술형 문제는 답을 답안지에 반드시 검정 볼펜으
로 쓰시오.
◎ 총 30문항 100점 만점입니다. 문항별 배점은 각
문항에 표시되어 있습니다.

[서울 영등포구 ○○중]

01 다음 단어의 설명이 옳은 것은?　　　　(3점)

① thief: someone who is paid to discover
information about someone or something

② detective: someone who steals things from
another person or place

③ suspect: someone who is thought to be guilty
of a crime

④ straight: without cost or payment

⑤ escape: to go or come into a place

[경북 ○○중]

02 다음 동사를 수동태의 형태로 쓴 것으로 올바르지 <u>않은</u> 것은?
　　　　(3점)

① find – be found

② make – be made

③ use – be used

④ hide – be hided

⑤ read – be read

[울산 ○○중]

03 다음 주어진 설명에 해당하는 단어로 가장 알맞은 것은?　(3점)

to remove something that has been written down or stored in a computer

① detect

② block

③ accident

④ delete

⑤ bottom

[울산 ○○중]

04 다음 두 문장의 빈칸에 공통으로 들어갈 단어는?　　(3점)

• I move my body _____ express my feelings. • I use my hands _____ make sounds.

① at　　　　② by　　　　③ to

④ in　　　　⑤ from

[경북 ○○중]

05 다음 중 어법상 <u>어색한</u> 문장은?　　　　(3점)

① When will the building be build?

② The room was cleaned by Sujin's father.

③ The package will be delivered by James.

④ The schedule can be changed anytime.

⑤ This event might be cancelled due to the
rain.

06 다음 질문에 대한 답을 주어진 표현으로 시작하는 영어 문장으로 작성하시오. (4점)

> (A) Who built these houses?
> → These houses _____ Jake.
>
> (B) Who sings the song in the show?
> → The song _____ the boy.

(A): _____

(B): _____

07 다음 주어진 어구를 활용하여 문장의 의미에 맞게 수동태 문장으로 완성하시오. (필요시 단어의 변형 및 추가) (5점)

> (1) 여름에 많은 파리가 음식 주변에서 보일 수 있다.
> (a lot of / the food / can / flies / see / around / be / in summer)

→ _____

> (2) 다음 주에 대통령에 의해 연설이 있을 것이다.
> (next / the president / give / be / week / a speech)

→ _____

08 다음 중 수동태 문장의 전환이 올바른 것은? (3점)

① I will not sing this song.
  → This song will not be sang by me.
② My mom will buy the coat.
  → The coat will been bought by my mom.
③ Did Mr. Collins make this card last week?
  → Was this card made by Mr. Collins last week?
④ In the Strange World, a little mouse leads the lion.
  → In the Strange World, the lion is lead by a little mouse.
⑤ Jake and his friends should take care of the sick people.
  → The sick people should be took care of by Jake and his friends.

09 다음 우리말에 해당하는 영어 문장을 완성하시오. (4점)

> 조건
> 1. hard / than / escape / one 필수 사용 (총 12 단어)
> 2. 우리말 내용과 어법, 시제에 맞게 쓸 것

> 두 번째 방은 첫 번째 방보다 탈출하기 훨씬 더 어렵습니다.

→ _____

10 다음 중 어법상 올바른 문장을 <u>모두</u> 고른 것은?   (3점)

ⓐ This room is cleaned every day.
ⓑ The movie was seen by many people.
ⓒ The flowers will send to her on Monday.
ⓓ The performance will be shown next week.
ⓔ My sister was planted these roses.
ⓕ He was invited some friends to his party.

① ⓐ, ⓑ, ⓓ
② ⓐ, ⓔ, ⓕ
③ ⓑ, ⓒ, ⓓ
④ ⓑ, ⓒ, ⓔ
⑤ ⓒ, ⓓ, ⓕ

11 다음 질문에 대한 답을 주어진 표현으로 시작하는 영어 문장으로 작성하시오.   (4점)

(1) Who wrote this book?

→ This book _____ J.K. Rowling.

(2) Who will wash this car?

→ This car _____ Henry.

[12~13] 다음 대화를 읽고 물음에 답하시오.

B: Kelly, here's a (가)_____. You can see this twice in a week, once in a year, but never in a day. What is this?
G: I have no idea.
B: It's the letter "E."
G: I don't get it. (A)_____
B: Well, there are two "E"s in the word "week," one "E" in the word "year" but no "E"s in the word "day."
G: Aha! Now I get it.

12 위 대화를 읽고 빈칸 (가)에 들어갈 단어로 가장 적절한 것은?   (3점)

① book
② riddle
③ painting
④ drama
⑤ movie

13 위 대화의 내용상 빈칸 (A)에 들어갈 가장 알맞은 것은?   (3점)

① Enjoy yourself.
② May I help you?
③ Good idea. Thanks.
④ Can you explain why?
⑤ Can you listen to me correctly?

14 다음 대화의 빈칸에 알맞은 문장은? (3점)

> G: Do you want to play the new game that I bought?
> B: Sure, what is it, Kelly?
> G: It's like a soccer game, but the players are dragons and seahorses. You need to use these buttons to play.
> B: That sounds fun. _____
> G: Sure.

① What was it about?

② Did you solve the riddle?

③ How did you make it?

④ It's because it's a sunny day.

⑤ Can you explain how to use these buttons?

15 다음 대화를 읽고, 민수가 이후에 할 행동으로 가장 적절한 것은? (3점)

> G: Minsu, do you know the TV show about the student detective?
> B: Yes. I love that show, but I didn't see it this week. What was it about?
> G: Well, all of the bikes at school disappeared.
> B: So, what did he do?
> G: First, he looked around the school. Then, he met some suspects and asked questions. Finally, he found the thief. The thief was ....
> B: No, don't tell me! I'll watch it later.

① 용의자 찾기

② 자전거 확인하기

③ 학교 주변 둘러보기

④ 학생 탐정 도전하기

⑤ 놓친 TV 프로그램 다시 보기

[16~20] 다음 글을 읽고 물음에 답하시오.

A man lives on the 12th floor of an apartment building. Every morning he wakes up, gets dressed, eats breakfast, goes to the elevator, takes it down to the first floor, and leaves the building for work. After work, if there is someone else in the elevator or if it is raining that day, he goes straight to his apartment on the 12th floor. (A)_____, if there is nobody else in the elevator and if it doesn't rain that day, he goes to the 10th floor and walks up the stairs. Can you explain why?

Well, (가)_____. (B)_____ he can ask people to push it for him. Or, (나)he can push it with his umbrella!

16 Which is true about the man? (3점)

① He lives on the 10th floor of an apartment building.

② He asks other people to push the button of the elevator when he can't push it.

③ He doesn't use the elevator on rainy days.

④ He walks up the stairs to exercise for his health on sunny days.

⑤ He doesn't use the elevator when he goes to work.

17 위 글의 제목으로 가장 적절한 것은? (3점)

① The man who loved rainy days

② The man who worked very hard

③ The man who was too short

④ The man who loved the elevator

⑤ The man who didn't have an umbrella

18 위 글의 빈칸 (가)를 주어진 〈보기〉의 단어를 모두 사용하여 완성하시오. (4점)

보기

the man / he / the / button / can't / reach / short / so / top / is

→ _____

19 위 글의 (A), (B)에 들어갈 말로 알맞게 연결된 것은? (3점)

	(A)	(B)
①	Also	However
②	But	Moreover
③	And	However
④	Nowadays	Also
⑤	However	But

20 위 글의 밑줄 친 (나)를 우리말로 옮기시오. (3점)

→ _____

[21~24] 다음 글을 읽고 물음에 답하시오.

Congratulations! (A) You made it to the second room. ⓐHowever, the second room is ⓑmuch harder to escape than the first one. (B) Good luck!

Room #2

(C) Jay gets an email from his favorite clothing store. The title reads "You won our Lucky Day event!" Jay is surprised. (D) He quickly opens ⓒit.

JayJr@kmail.com

You won our 'Lucky Day' event!
Congratulations!
You have won a special prize. During our Lucky Day event, you can choose any seven items from our store ⓓfor free! Come to our store on November 31. We ⓔcan't wait to see you.

Truly yours,
Kay Brown

(E) Can you explain why?
Clue: There are usually 30 or 31 days in a month.

Do you have the answer? Write it down and then you are free to go!
Riddle #2 Solved.

21 위 글의 흐름으로 보아, 주어진 문장이 들어가기에 가장 적절한 곳은? (3점)

However, Jay thinks that the event isn't real and deletes the email.

① (A)   ② (B)   ③ (C)

④ (D)   ⑤ (E)

22 위 글의 밑줄 친 @~ⓔ의 표현에 대한 설명으로 적절하지 않은 것은? (3점)

① ⓐ의 'However'는 '그러나'라는 뜻으로 앞의 내용과 반대되는 내용이 나올 때 쓰인다.

② ⓑ의 'much'는 '훨씬'이라는 뜻으로 'even'으로 바꿔쓸 수 있다.

③ ⓒ의 'it'이 가리키는 것은 'an email'이다.

④ ⓓ의 'for free'는 '공짜로'라는 뜻이다.

⑤ ⓔ의 'can't wait to'는 '~하기를 기대할 수 없다'라는 뜻이다.

23 다음 질문에 대한 답을 영어 문장으로 작성하시오. (4점)

> Q: Why does Jay think the email isn't real?
> A: Because _____.

→ _____

24 위 글의 내용과 일치하는 것은? (3점)

① Jay sends an email to his favorite clothing store.

② The email says Jay won a special prize.

③ The clothing store will open in December.

④ The email says, during the Lucky Day event, Jay can buy any seven items that he wants.

⑤ Jay keeps the email because it's a free coupon.

[25~30] 다음 글을 읽고 물음에 답하시오.

Welcome to the Escape Tower. You will enter the first room in our tower. You need to solve some riddles to escape. Clues can be found ⓐsomewhere inside the room. So, are you ready to think like Sherlock Holmes?

Room #1

Mr. Doodle was hit by a car on Sunday afternoon. ⓑFortunately, he wasn't badly hurt, but he didn't see the driver. (A) Three suspects were ⓒanswered by a police officer. (B) Ms. A said she was reading a book at the time of the accident. Mr. B said he was walking his dog. Ms. C said she was making breakfast. (C) Why do you think so? (D) Do you have the answer? (E) Write (가)it down. Then you can move to the next room.

Congratulations! You ⓓmade it to the second room. ⓔHowever, the second room is much harder to escape than the first one. Good luck!

25 위 글의 (A)~(E) 중 다음 문장이 들어갈 가장 알맞은 곳은? (3점)

> Who hit Mr. Doodle?

① (A)　　② (B)　　③ (C)

④ (D)　　⑤ (E)

26 위 글의 밑줄 친 ⓐ~ⓔ 중, 문맥상 낱말의 쓰임이 적절하지 않은 것은? (3점)

① ⓐ ② ⓑ ③ ⓒ

④ ⓓ ⑤ ⓔ

27 위 글의 밑줄 친 (가)it이 가리키는 것은? (3점)

① a riddle

② a book

③ the driver

④ breakfast

⑤ the answer

28 위 글의 내용으로 답할 수 있는 질문 2개는? (3점)

① When was Mr. Doodle hit by a car?

② How many suspects did the police officer meet?

③ What was Ms. A reading on Sunday morning?

④ Where was Mr. B walking his dog at the time of the accident?

⑤ What was Ms. C doing on Sunday evening?

29 위 글의 내용에 맞도록 다음 질문의 답을 영어로 완성하시오. (6점)

> Q: Who hit Mr. Doodle and why do you think so?
> A: (1)_____ hit Mr. Doodle. The accident happened in the (2)_____, not in the morning, but he/she said that (3)_____ _____ at the time of the accident.

(1)_____

(2)_____

(3)_____

30 위 글의 내용과 일치하는 것은? (3점)

① Mr. Doodle was hit by a car and hurt a lot.

② The police officer thought that Mr. Doodle was lying.

③ To escape the tower, you need help from Sherlock Holmes.

④ Mr. Doodle saw the driver and helped the police catch him.

⑤ The accident happened on Sunday afternoon when Mr. B was walking his dog.

◎ 선택형 문항의 답안은 컴퓨터용 수정 싸인펜을 사용하여 OMR 답안지에 바르게 표기하시오.
◎ 서술형 문제는 답을 답안지에 반드시 검정 볼펜으로 쓰시오.
◎ 총 30문항 100점 만점입니다. 문항별 배점은 각 문항에 표시되어 있습니다.

[경북 ○○중]

01 다음 문장의 빈칸에 공통으로 들어갈 단어로 가장 적절한 것은? (3점)

> I could learn valuable lessons _____ this experience. People can express their opinions _____ writing.

① across
② between
③ with
④ through
⑤ thorough

[울산 ○○중]

02 다음 문장의 빈칸에 들어갈 단어의 영영 풀이로 알맞은 것은? (3점)

> The car's engine is so _____ that it goes uphill easily.

① living in a natural state
② having great power or strength
③ holding or carrying something so that it may not fall
④ dealing with danger, pain or difficult situations with courage and confidence
⑤ making you feel physically relaxed, without any pain or without being too hot, cold.

[충북 ○○중]

03 다음 빈칸 어느 곳에도 들어가기에 적절하지 <u>않은</u> 단어는? (단, 중복 사용 불가) (3점)

> • I can't go to the concert. Mom didn't _____ me to go there.
> • Look at that girl! She is wearing a _____ Hanbok.
> • He never has any free time like bees. He is very _____.
> • The _____ questioned the thief.
> • When he gets _____, he becomes red like a lobster.

① allow
② lucky
③ detective
④ colorful
⑤ busy

[부산 ○○중]

04 다음 괄호 안에서 적절한 것을 골라 쓰시오. (3점)

> She never has any free time. She is [as / more] busy as a bee.

→ _____

05 다음 문장을 'as 원급 as' 구문을 사용하여 한 문장으로 바꾸어 쓰시오. (4점)

> The blue hat is 10,000 won. The red hat is 10,000 won. They are both cheap.

→ The blue hat _____.

06 다음 중 어법상 옳은 것은? (3점)

① The tea is so cold that I can't drink.

② It was so hot that we can't go on a picnic.

③ It was such big shirt that I couldn't wear it.

④ She was so that stupid she made the mistake.

⑤ The movie was so great that I watched it three times.

07 다음 〈보기〉의 두 문장을 한 문장으로 바꾼 것으로 가장 적절한 것은? (3점)

> **보기**
> Junho is 172cm. His father is 172cm, too.

① Junho is as tall his father.

② Junho is as tall as his father.

③ His father is as tall Junho.

④ Junho is tall as his father as.

⑤ His father as is tall as Junho.

08 다음 중 어법상 올바른 문장을 2개 고른 것은? (4점)

① My brother is not as cleverer as your brother.

② The dancers move their feet so fast that they look they're flying.

③ They dance with large fans that are painted in bright colors.

④ The Maori performed the haka to show their strength to the enemy.

⑤ Buchaechum is so popular that people can see in many traditional festivals.

09 다음 우리말과 일치하도록 so ～ that 구문으로 영작하시오. (추가 단어 있음, 단어 형태 변형 불가) (4점)

> 그 질문은 너무 어려워서 나는 그것을 풀 수 없었다.

> **조건**
> • 과거시제 사용

> **보기**
> hard / solve

→ _____

10 다음 두 문장을 의미가 같도록 한 문장으로 영작하시오. (5점)

(A)
- The dog is heavy.
- The cat is heavier than the dog.

(B)
- Kevin is slow.
- A turtle is slower than Kevin.

조건
- 'as ~ as'를 반드시 이용할 것

(A): _____

(B): _____

[12~13] 다음 대화를 읽고 물음에 답하시오.

G: Hojun, did you know that some male birds dance?
B: No. Why do they dance?
G: They dance to show their love to female birds.
B: That's interesting. Do you know any other animals that can dance?
G: Yes, some bees dance to show where to find food.
B: That's cool! In my opinion, dancing is a great way to communicate.
G: I totally agree with you.

12 Why do some male birds dance? (4점)

→ They _____.

11 다음 대화의 빈칸에 들어갈 말로 알맞지 <u>않은</u> 것은? (3점)

A: Minsu, what do you think about that painting?
B: Umm... The people look like they're having fun.
A: I agree. _____, the dancing boy really enjoys dancing.

① In my view
② In my eyes
③ To my mind
④ In the end
⑤ In my opinion

13 위 대화의 주제로 가장 알맞은 것은? (3점)

① 춤추는 동물들
② 먹이를 찾는 벌들
③ 의사소통의 어려움
④ 춤출 때 영향을 주는 요소들
⑤ 동물이 사랑을 표현하는 방법

14 다음 중 대화가 <u>어색한</u> 것을 고르면?

(3점)

① A: I use my voice to make music. Listen to my music.

B: Really? It's interesting!

A: My voice is soft and cool. I am sure you will like it.

② A: First, draw a circle. Second, put a star inside. Then, put a triangle on the top.

B: Did I draw it correctly?

A: No, you didn't.

③ A: Can you explain how to make cookies?

B: Sure. I think the cat ate the cookies.

④ A: What do you think about this painting?

B: In my view, it's interesting. I smiled when I first saw it.

⑤ A: Wow! Something smells really good. Mom, what is it?

B: We are going to have tacos for dinner. Help yourself.

A: Sounds good!

Junsu: You know what? The school dance contest will be held soon.
Emily: That's right. I heard Jimin's class is going to perform a taekwondo dance and Tim's class is going to do a K-pop dance.
Brian: We should also decide what to do.
Mina: How about a Buchaechum? (A)_____, and it's also beautiful.
Emily: That sounds like a good idea. But who will teach us?
Brian: Mina is good at traditional dances. Can you help us, Mina?
Mina: Of course, I will. (B)<u>나는 우리가 많이 재미있을 거라고 확신해</u>.
Junsu: Great. Let's give it a try.

15 위 대화의 빈칸 (A)에 가장 알맞은 표현은?

(3점)

① In my opinion, it's not easy to dance

② In my opinion, it is hard to teach

③ In my opinion, it is easy to learn

④ In my opinion, it is not good to see

⑤ In my opinion, it is easy to give up

16 위 대화의 밑줄 친 우리말 (B)에 맞는 문장을 영작하시오. (4점)

조건

• 'sure / have / fun'을 반드시 사용할 것
• 8단어를 사용할 것

→ _____

Korea: Buchaechum

Buchaechum is a traditional Korean fan dance. The dancers wear colorful hanbok. They dance with large fans that are painted in bright colors. The dancers move the fans gracefully to show different kinds of beauty. Their movements look as beautiful as flowers or flying birds. (A)Because Buchaechum is very popular in Korea, people can see it in many traditional festivals.

[울산 ○○중]

17 위 글에서 다음 영영 풀이에 해당하는 단어를 고르면? (3점)

> liked by a lot of people

① popular
② bright
③ colorful
④ different
⑤ traditional

[울산 ○○중]

18 위 글의 밑줄 친 문장 (A)를 'so ... that ~' 구문을 이용하여 바꾸어 쓰고 해석하시오. (5점)

(1) 바꾸어 쓰기

→ _____

(2) 해석하기

→ _____

The dragon dance is an important part of the New Year Festival in China. Many Chinese people believe that the dragon is so powerful that it can ⓐchase away evil ⓑspirits. (A)So at New Year, people wish for good luck by watching the dragon dance. (B)Different cultures have many difference events for New Year's day. (C)In the dragon dance, a team of dancers expresses a dragon costume. (D)The costume is colored gold, red, yellow and green. (E)Dragon costumes are usually heavy and long. Some are as heavy as 90 kilograms, and as long as 100 meters. Dancers stand under the dragon costume and hold it up high. They ⓒrise and lower the costume ⓓwhile they dance among the people. Its movements are so ⓔdynamic that it looks like a flying dragon. Now the dragon dance is one of the most popular dances in the world. People can enjoy it in many parts of the world.

[서울 영등포구 ○○중]

19 위 글의 (A)~(E) 중 흐름상 어색한 문장은? (3점)

① (A)   ② (B)   ③ (C)
④ (D)   ⑤ (E)

20 위 글의 밑줄 친 어휘의 쓰임이 <u>어색한</u> 것은? (3점)

① ⓐ   ② ⓑ   ③ ⓒ

④ ⓓ   ⑤ ⓔ

[22~24] 다음 글을 읽고 물음에 답하시오.

Why do people dance? They dance to express feelings, give ⓐ<u>happy</u> to others, or enjoy themselves. (가)<u>세계의 여러 다양한 종류의 춤을 살펴봅시다.</u>

India: Kathakali

Kathakali tells a story. The dancers tell stories ⓑ<u>though</u> their body movements. These stories are usually about a fight between good and evil. Dancers who are playing good characters paint their faces green. Those ⓒ<u>which</u> are playing evil characters wear black make-up. ⓓ<u>Interesting</u>, in Kathakali, only men are allowed to dance. The body movements are so ⓔ<u>powerful</u> that the dancers need to train for many years.

22 위 글의 밑줄 친 ⓐ~ⓔ의 쓰임이 바른 것은? (3점)

① ⓐ   ② ⓑ   ③ ⓒ

④ ⓓ   ⑤ ⓔ

21 위 글의 내용과 다음 홍보문 중 일치하는 것을 2개 고른 것은? (3점)

Come and enjoy Dragon Dance!

ⓐ<u>Don't miss this great show which was originally performed in Japan!</u> ⓑ<u>Come and wish for good luck for the New Year.</u> ⓒ<u>You can see the dancers wearing black and white costumes.</u> ⓓ<u>They jump over the costumes in front of the people.</u> ⓔ<u>The movements are very powerful just like flying dragons!</u> Come and enjoy the moment together!

① ⓐ   ② ⓑ   ③ ⓒ

④ ⓓ   ⑤ ⓔ

23 위 글을 읽고 답할 수 <u>없는</u> 질문은? (3점)

① How do Kathakali dancers tell stories?

② What do Kathakali stories tell about?

③ Do women dance in Kathakali with men?

④ What colors do Kathakali dancers paint their faces?

⑤ What kinds of clothing do Kathakali dancers wear?

24 위 글의 밑줄 친 우리말 (가)를 <보기>의 주어진 어구들을 재배열하여 영어 문장을 완성하시오. (4점)

> **보기**
>
> around / at / dance / different / let's / a look /
> kinds / of / take / the world

→ _____

25 위 글의 밑줄 친 (A) 부분의 단어를 올바른 순서대로 나열한 것은? (3점)

① The dancers as looked as scary wild animals

② The dancers looked scary as wild as animals

③ The dancers looked as scary as wild animals

④ Wild animals looked as scary as the dancers

⑤ Animals looked scary as wild as the dancers

[25~30] 다음 글을 읽고 물음에 답하시오.

When people visit New Zealand, they may meet a group of haka dancers. The dancers perform this traditional dance with scary faces. This dance was originally performed by the Maori before a fight. (B)They wanted to show their (D)_____ to the enemy. (A)[wild / animals / as / scary / the dancers / as / looked] before fighting. Nowadays, in New Zealand, rugby players usually perform a haka before a game to show their (D)_____ to the other team.

Buchaechum is a traditional Korean fan dance. The dancers wear colorful hanbok. They dance with large fans that are painted in bright colors. The dancers move the fans gracefully to show different kinds of beauty. Their movements look ⓐ꽃이나 나는 새처럼 매우 아름답게. In Korea, Buchaechum is so popular that people can see (C)it in many traditional festivals.

26 위 글의 빈칸 (D)에 공통으로 들어갈 단어로 가장 적절한 것은? (3점)

① kindness

② sympathy

③ strength

④ weakness

⑤ hospitality

27 위 글의 밑줄 친 (B), (C)가 의미하는 것을 순서대로 나열한 것으로 가장 적절한 것은? (3점)

	(B)	(C)
①	the Maori	Buchaechum
②	people	Buchaechum
③	faces	Korea
④	people	hanbok
⑤	the Maori	beauty

28 위 글의 밑줄 친 ⓐ의 우리말을 영어로 바르게 옮긴 것은? (3점)

① beautifully as flowers or flying birds
② flowers as beautiful as flying birds
③ flowers or flying birds as beautiful as
④ beautiful as flowers or flying birds as
⑤ as beautiful as flowers or flying birds

29 위 글의 내용과 일치하지 <u>않는</u> 것은? (3점)

① Haka 무용수들은 무서운 얼굴로 전통춤을 춘다.
② Haka는 원래 싸움 전에 마오리족에 의해 행해졌다.
③ 요즘에는 럭비 선수들이 힘을 보여주기 위해 Haka를 춘다.
④ 부채춤은 한복을 입고 추는 한국의 전통 춤이다.
⑤ 부채춤의 인기는 줄어들고 있어 전통 축제에서 보기 힘들다.

30 위 글을 요약한 내용 중 빈칸 ⓐ~ⓔ에 <u>어색한</u> 것은? (3점)

> Both Haka and Buchaechum are ⓐ_____ dances. The Maori dance Haka to express their ⓑ_____ to the ⓒ_____. Buchaechum dancers wear hanbok and hold ⓓ_____ in their hands. Buchaechum creates different kinds of ⓔ_____.

① ⓐ: traditional
② ⓑ: stories
③ ⓒ: enemy
④ ⓓ: fans
⑤ ⓔ: beauty

문항수 : 선택형(23문항) 서술형(7문항)

반 이름

점수

20 . . .

◎ 선택형 문항의 답안은 컴퓨터용 수정 싸인펜을 사용
하여 OMR 답안지에 바르게 표기하시오.

◎ 서술형 문제는 답을 답안지에 반드시 검정 볼펜으
로 쓰시오.

◎ 총 30문항 100점 만점입니다. 문항별 배점은 각
문항에 표시되어 있습니다.

[울산 ○○중]

01 다음 중 빈칸에 들어갈 말로 알맞지 <u>않은</u> 것은?   (3점)

- He walked across the _____.
- She danced _____ like a swan.
- This poem was _____ written in French.
- When the enemy attacked, we were _____ powerless against them.

① field
② originally
③ enemy
④ totally
⑤ gracefully

[서울 강동구 ○○중]

02 다음 각 단어들의 영영 풀이 중 옳은 것은?   (3점)

① originally: at or towards the back of a thing or person

② brave: showing unfriendly behavior towards people or ideas

③ comfortable: making you feel physically relaxed, without any pain or without being too hot, cold, etc.

④ express: to do something to entertain people, for example by acting a play or playing a piece of music

⑤ allow: to tell or show what you are feeling or thinking by using words, looks, or actions

[서울 영등포구 ○○중]

03 다음 중 밑줄 친 표현을 바르게 사용한 사람을 <u>모두</u> 고른 것은?   (3점)

(A) 현민: Dancing is a great way to <u>communicate</u>.
(B) 종원: I totally <u>agree of</u> your opinion.
(C) 하은: First, draw a circle. <u>Then</u>, put a star inside it.
(D) 해강: Some bees dance to show <u>what</u> to find food.
(E) 석준: People look like they're <u>doing</u> fun.

① 하은, 해강
② 종원, 석준
③ 현민, 하은
④ 종원, 해강
⑤ 현민, 석준

[부산 ○○중]

04 다음 주어진 단어를 활용하여 비교하는 문장을 완성하시오.   (3점)

Mina is 155cm tall and Jane is 160cm tall.
Mina is _____ _____ _____
_____ Jane.
(as / tall / not)

→ _____

05 다음 문장 중 어법상 올바른 문장은? (3점)

① The pizza was so big that seven people ate it together.

② The children were so excited that keeps yelling.

③ I was so happily that I could dance all day.

④ She was so sad and depressed that cry so much.

⑤ He is so wisely that everybody likes him.

07 다음 중 어법상 <u>어색한</u> 것은? (3점)

① Tom is as lighter as air.

② My cat is as white as snow.

③ He runs as fast as a rabbit.

④ It was so cold that I caught a cold.

⑤ The music was so loud that I couldn't sleep.

06 다음 우리말에 맞도록 문장을 영작하시오. (5점)

(A) 그녀는 너무 똑똑해서 그 퍼즐들을 풀 수 있다.
(B) 나는 너무 행복해서 하루 종일 노래를 불렀다.

┌─ 조건 ─
• 'so ~ that' 구문을 사용할 것
• smart, all day를 사용할 것
└

(A): _____

(B): _____

08 다음 각각의 문장을 지시대로 고쳐 쓰시오. (6점)

(1) 주어진 문장을 'enough to'를 사용하여 같은 의미로 고쳐 쓰시오.
She is so bright that she can solve all the puzzles.
→ _____

(2) 주어진 문장을 'too ~ to'를 사용하여 같은 의미로 고쳐 쓰시오.
He is so young that he can't read the book.
→ _____

(1) _____

(2) _____

09 다음 우리말과 일치하도록 so ~ that 구문으로 영작하시오. (추가 단어 있음, 단어 형태 변형 불가) (4점)

비가 심하게 와서 그 학교는 현장학습을 취소했다.

조건
• 과거시제 사용

보기
heavily / raining / canceled / the field trip

→ _____

10 다음 주어진 단어를 배열하여 빈칸에 알맞은 말을 쓰시오. (주어진 단어를 한 번씩 모두 사용할 것) (4점)

A: Jinsu always gets high scores on every test.
B: Yes, _____.
(an / is / owl / as / he / smart / as)

→ _____

11 다음 두 사람의 대화가 <u>어색한</u> 것은? (3점)

① A: What do you think about wearing a school uniform?
B: In my opinion, we should not wear a school uniform because it's not comfortable.

② A: How about Wendy's photo? In my opinion, her photo is very creative.
B: I agree with you. I'm sure she'll win the contest.

③ A: I'm going to a culture event in our town next weekend. Do you want to join me?
B: You know what? Keep up the good work.

④ A: We are going to do a K-pop dance. You are good at dances. Can you help us, Mina?
B: Of course, I will. I'm sure we'll have a lot of fun.

⑤ A: You know what? The school dance contest will be held soon. How about a Buchaechum? It is easy for us to learn.
B: Great. Let's give it a try.

[12~13] 다음 대화를 읽고 물음에 답하시오.

Junsu: You know what? (A)학교 춤 경연 대회가 곧 개최될 거야.

Emily: That's right. I heard Jimin's class is going to perform a taekwondo dance and Tim's class is going to do a K-pop dance.

Brian: We should also decide what to do.

Mina: How about a Buchaechum? In my opinion, it is easy to learn, and it's also beautiful.

Emily: That sounds like a good idea. But who will teach us?

Brian: Mina is good at traditional dances. Can you help us, Mina?

Mina: Of course. I will. I'm sure we'll have a lot of fun.

Junsu: Great. Let's give it a try.

[14~15] 다음 대화를 읽고 물음에 답하시오.

B: What are you reading, Kelly?

G: I'm reading a story about Michaela DePrince.

B: Michaela DePrince? (A) Can you tell me more about her?

G: Sure. Michaela lost her parents when she was three. (B) But she never gave up on her dream of becoming a dancer. (C)

B: (D) Wow, she worked very hard to be a good dancer. Kelly, you also have a dream to be a dancer, right? (E)

G: Yes. I will try my best to be a great dancer like her.

B: Keep up the good work. I'm sure you can make it.

*G: girl, B: boy

[경북 ○○중]

12 위 대화의 밑줄 친 (A)의 우리말을 영작한 것으로 가장 적절한 것은? (3점)

① Soon the school dance contest will be hold.

② The school dance contest will hold soon.

③ The soon school dance will be holded.

④ The school dance contest will be helded soon.

⑤ The school dance contest will be held soon.

[강원 ○○중]

14 위 대화에서 아래 문장이 들어갈 곳으로 가장 적절한 것은? (3점)

| After that, she had a lot of difficulties. |

① (A)   ② (B)   ③ (C)

④ (D)   ⑤ (E)

[경북 ○○중]

13 위 대화의 내용과 일치하지 <u>않는</u> 것은? (3점)

① 지민이네 반은 태권도 춤을 경연하기로 했다.

② Tim의 반은 K-pop 춤을 선보이기로 했다.

③ Mina는 전통춤을 잘 출 수 있다.

④ Junsu는 부채춤을 배우는 것을 도와주기로 했다.

⑤ Mina는 부채춤이 배우기 쉽고 아름답다고 생각했다.

[강원 ○○중]

15 위 대화의 내용과 일치하지 <u>않는</u> 것은? (3점)

① Michaela DePrince는 무용수이다.

② Kelly의 꿈은 무용수가 되는 것이다.

③ Michaela DePrince는 세 살 때 부모님을 잃었다.

④ Michaela DePrince는 무용수가 되는 꿈을 포기했다.

⑤ Kelly는 Michaela DePrince에 대한 이야기를 읽고 있다.

[16~17] 다음 대화를 읽고 물음에 답하시오.

G: Minsu, _____ that painting?

B: Umm... The people look like they're having fun.

G: I agree. In my opinion, the dancing boy really enjoys dancing.

B: Jimin, _____ this painting?

G: In my opinion, it's interesting. I smiled when I first saw it.

B: Me, too. The dancers in the painting look happy.

[충북 ○○중]

16 위 대화의 내용과 일치하지 <u>않는</u> 것은? (3점)

① A boy is dancing in the painting.

② Minsu and Jimin agree with each other.

③ The speakers are looking at some paintings.

④ Jimin smiled when she first saw the painting.

⑤ Minsu thinks that the people in the painting look tired.

[충북 ○○중]

17 위 대화의 빈칸에 공통으로 들어갈 가장 알맞은 표현은? (3점)

① where did you get

② how do you paint

③ what do you think about

④ can you tell me how to paint

⑤ what are you going to do with

[서울 강동구 ○○중]

18 다음 글의 내용으로 보아 답할 수 <u>없는</u> 질문은? (4점)

Tarantella, Italy

In the past, people danced the tarantella for sick people. Nowadays, it is a couple's dance. People dance the tarantella on happy days such as weddings.

Adumu, Kenya

This dance is performed before a fight. It is also called a jumping dance. Dancers jump high in the air. When a dancer jumps, other dancers cheer him on with loud noises.

Nongakmu, Korea

Nongakmu is performed by farmers. They dance it to thank each other for their hard work in the fields. They wear special hats and move their heads to the music they play.

① For whom was tarantella originally performed?

② Nowadays, when do Italian people perform tarantella?

③ Why did dancers in Adumu jump high and cheer with loud noises?

④ Where and why do the Korean farmers perform Nongakmu?

⑤ What do Korean farmers perform to thank each other for their hard work in the field?

(가)_____ do people dance? (A) They dance to express feelings, give happiness to others, or enjoy ⓐthemselves. (B) Let's take a look at different kinds of dance around the world.

Kathakali tells a story. (C) The dancers tell stories (나)_____ their body movements. These stories are ⓑusually (다)_____ a fight between good and evil. Dancers who are playing good characters ⓒpaints their faces green. (D) Interestingly, in Kathakali, only men ⓓare allowed to dance. (E) The body movements are so powerful ⓔthat the dancers need to train for many years.

[경북 ○○중]

19 위 글에서 주어진 문장이 들어갈 곳으로 가장 적절한 곳은? (3점)

Those who are playing evil characters wear black make-up.

① (A) ② (B) ③ (C)
④ (D) ⑤ (E)

[경북 ○○중]

20 위 글의 ⓐ~ⓔ 중 어법상 올바르지 않은 것은? (3점)

① ⓐ ② ⓑ ③ ⓒ
④ ⓓ ⑤ ⓔ

[서울 강동구 ○○중]

21 위 글의 빈칸 (가)~(다)에 알맞은 것은? (3점)

	(가)	(나)	(다)
①	Why	for	as
②	How	about	like
③	What	of	with
④	Why	through	about
⑤	How	in	to

[서울 강동구 ○○중]

22 다음 중 위 글의 내용과 일치하는 것은? (3점)

① Without dances, humans can't communicate with each other.
② Every Kathakali always has a story that tells a fight between good and evil.
③ Women are not allowed to dance in Kathakali because they can't fight for many years.
④ All the dances around the world can't express their feelings without their powerful body movements.
⑤ Kathakali dancers playing evil characters wear black make-up.

India: Kathakali

Kathakali tells a story. The dancers tell stories through their body movements. These stories are usually about a fight (A)_____ good and evil. Dancers (B)_____ are playing good characters paint their faces green. Those (C)_____ are playing evil characters wear black make-up. (D)_____, in Kathakali, (A)남자들만이 춤추도록 허용된다. The body movements are so powerful (E)_____ the dancers need to train for many years.

23 위 글의 빈칸 (A)~(E) 중 어법상 들어갈 말이 적절하지 <u>않은</u> 것은? (3점)

① (A): between

② (B): who

③ (C): which

④ (D): Interestingly

⑤ (E): that

24 위 글에서 밑줄 친 (A)의 우리말과 일치하도록 주어진 단어를 이용하여 영작하시오. (4점)

> **조건**
> • 반드시 주어진 단어를 사용할 것
> • 어법에 맞게 변형하여 사용할 것

> (A)남자들만이 춤추도록 허용된다.
>   men / allow

→ _____

25 위 글의 내용과 일치하는 것은? (3점)

① The dancers move their body to tell a story.

② Kathakali tries to tell a story about defeating the enemy.

③ Good characters in Kathakali paint their faces black.

④ In Kathakali, both women and men are allowed to dance.

⑤ The dancers take a short time to learn the body movements.

[26~30] 다음 글을 읽고 물음에 답하시오.

New Zealand: Haka

When people visit New Zealand, they may meet a group of haka dancers. (가)<u>They</u> perform this traditional dance with scary faces. This dance was originally ⓐ<u>performing</u> by the Maori before a fight. (나)<u>They</u> wanted to show their strength to the enemy. The dancers looked as ⓑ<u>scarily</u> as wild animals before fighting. Nowadays, in New Zealand, rugby players usually perform a haka before a game to show (다)<u>their</u> strength to the other team.

Korea: Buchaechum

Buchaechum is a ⓒ<u>traditionally</u> Korean fan dance. The dancers wear ⓓ<u>colorful</u> hanbok. (라)<u>They</u> dance with large fans that are ⓔ<u>painting</u> in bright colors. The dancers move the fans ⓕ<u>graceful</u> to show different kinds of beauty. (A)<u>그들의 움직임은 꽃들 또는 날아다니는 새들만큼 아름다워 보인다</u>. In Korea, Buchaechum is so popular that people can see (마)<u>it</u> in many traditional festivals.

26 위 글의 밑줄 친 ⓐ~ⓕ 중 어법상 적절한 것의 개수는? (3점)

① 1개　　　② 2개　　　③ 3개

④ 4개　　　⑤ 5개

29 위 글의 내용과 일치하는 것은? (3점)

① The Maori didn't start to dance haka for the first time.

② When the Maori won the fight, they danced haka.

③ The rugby players dance haka to show their strong powers against the other team.

④ The Buchaechum dancers wear one color's hanbok.

⑤ The Buchaechum dancers dance to show different kinds of beauty with many flowers.

27 위 글의 (가)~(마) 중 가리키는 대상이 알맞게 연결된 것은? (3점)

① (가): People

② (나): Haka dancers

③ (다): The Maori's

④ (라): Rugby players

⑤ (마): Buchaechum

28 위 글의 제목으로 가장 적절한 것은? (3점)

① Beautiful Nature of New Zealand and Korea

② Dances of New Zealand and Korea

③ Amazing Dance of Wild Animals

④ Different Kinds of Uniforms

⑤ Changing Old Traditions

30 위 글의 밑줄 친 (A)의 우리말과 일치하도록 〈보기〉의 어구를 모두 활용하여 영작하시오. (추가 단어 있음) (4점)

> 보기
> movements / as / their / or / flying birds

→ _____

◎ 선택형 문항의 답안은 컴퓨터용 수정 싸인펜을 사용하여 OMR 답안지에 바르게 표기하시오.
◎ 서술형 문제는 답을 답안지에 반드시 검정 볼펜으로 쓰시오.
◎ 총 30문항 100점 만점입니다. 문항별 배점은 각 문항에 표시되어 있습니다.

[울산 ○○중]

01 다음 중 짝지어진 두 단어의 관계가 나머지와 <u>다른</u> 것은? (3점)

① sink - float
② push - pull
③ put on - wear
④ expand - contract
⑤ appear - disappear

[서울 영등포구 ○○중]

02 다음 영영 풀이에 알맞은 단어는? (4점)

to become larger in size, number, or amount, or to make something become larger

① compare ② contract
③ float ④ expand
⑤ rise

[울산 ○○중]

03 다음 빈칸에 들어갈 가장 알맞은 말은? (3점)

_____ Safety Rules

• It is important to listen carefully to the teacher.
• It is necessary to wash your hands after experiments.

① Subway ② Library ③ Museum
④ Science ⑤ Cinema

[울산 ○○중]

04 다음 〈보기〉의 밑줄 친 It의 쓰임과 같은 것은? (3점)

보기

<u>It</u> is fun to do a science experiment.

① How far is <u>it</u> from here to Ulsan?
② <u>It</u> is a beautiful sunny day.
③ <u>It</u>'s snowing on the mountains.
④ <u>It</u> is 2km from the station to the amusement park.
⑤ <u>It</u> is not safe to play with fire at home.

[울산 ○○중]

05 다음 주어진 영어를 우리말에 맞도록 순서대로 배열할 때 세 번째로 오는 말은? (3점)

I / see / to / can't / wait / your clock
나는 너의 시계가 너무 보고 싶어.

① I
② see
③ can't
④ your clock
⑤ wait

[충북 ○○중]

06 다음 중 어법상 바른 문장은? (3점)

① It's kind for you to help me.
② It's not easy of me to study English.
③ It's boring of her to stay home all day.
④ It's important that we eat healthy food.
⑤ It's not safe of you to play with fire at home.

07 다음 중 어법상 올바른 것은? (3점)

① How come the eggs are floating in the water?

② Why flying fish jump out of the water?

③ Why was Sujin missed the bus again?

④ How come do they work on Sunday?

⑤ Why did Brad broke the window?

08 다음 빈칸 (A), (B), (C)에 들어갈 말이 바르게 짝지어진 것은? (4점)

1. It's important to (A)_____ the bottle.
2. (B)_____ a coin on the mouth of the bottle.
3. (C)_____ the bottle in your hands for a while.
4. The coin moves up and down.

	(A)	(B)	(C)
①	cool	Warm	Put
②	warm	Put	Hold
③	cool	Put	Hold
④	hold	Warm	Put
⑤	hold	Cool	Warm

09 다음 대화 중 흐름상 어색한 것은? (3점)

① A: Which movie do you want to see?

　B: I want to see The Frozen.

② A: Which sports do you want to learn?

　B: I want to learn how to play badminton.

③ A: Which food do you want to eat?

　B: I want to eat at the restaurant.

④ A: Which country do you want to visit?

　B: I want to visit England.

⑤ A: Which concert do you want to go to?

　B: I want to go to the BTS concert.

\

10 다음 대화의 빈칸에 가장 알맞은 표현은? (3점)

Brian: Mina, will you join our tennis club?

Mina: It sounds interesting, but I signed up for a special class this fall.

Brian: _____

Mina: I signed up for a magic class. I can't wait to learn new magic tricks there.

① How did you sign up for the class?

② Why did you sign up for the class?

③ Which class did you sign up for?

④ What did you want to do in the class?

⑤ Which trick did you like best?

11 다음 대화의 흐름상 빈칸에 알맞은 것은? (4점)

> Today we'll make ice cream. Which flavor do you want to make? How about strawberry? First, mix two cups of milk, two cups of heavy cream, and half a cup of sugar. Next, cut five strawberries into small pieces. Then, _____. That's it. It's easy to make, isn't it? Why don't you try making it at home?

① add some salt and put it in hot water

② mix everything together and fry it in a fan

③ add some sauce and mix everything together

④ mix everything together and put it in hot water

⑤ mix everything together and put it in the freezer

12 위 대화의 흐름상 빈칸 (가)에 들어갈 말로 가장 알맞은 것은? (3점)

① worried

② happy

③ bored

④ brave

⑤ excited

13 위 대화의 빈칸 ⓐ~ⓔ에 들어갈 말로 어색한 것은? (3점)

① ⓐ: didn't rain

② ⓑ: How about

③ ⓒ: sounds like

④ ⓓ: give it a try

⑤ ⓔ: can't wait to

[12~14] 다음 대화를 읽고 물음에 답하시오.

A: It ⓐ_____ for a long time.
B: Yes. The dry season is lasting too long. The farmers are very (가)_____.
A: We should do something to help them.
B: ⓑ_____ making a special clock?
A: A clock? How will that help?
B: The clock will show the time and the seasons. We can use it to prepare for the dry season.
A: That ⓒ_____ a good idea. But who's going to make it?
B: I'll ⓓ_____. I know a lot about time and the seasons.
A: Okay, I ⓔ_____ see your clock.
　　　　　　　　*A: King Sejong, B: Jang Yeongsil

14 위 대화를 읽고 질문에 대답할 수 없는 것은? (3점)

① Who is going to make the clock?

② What can the clock be used for?

③ How will the clock help the farmers?

④ What do farmers do during dry season?

⑤ What's the problem with the farmers?

[15~16] 다음 대화를 읽고 물음에 답하시오.

B: Yujin, why did you put the eggs in water?
G: I'm picking out the bad eggs. (A)
B: Which eggs are fresh, and which ones are not? (B)
G: Eggs that sink in water are fresh. (C) You shouldn't eat them.
B: That's interesting. Why do the bad eggs float? (D)
G: Because they have gas inside. The gas acts like the air in a balloon. (E)
B: Oh, I see.

[울산 ○○중]

15 위 대화의 (A)~(E) 중 주어진 문장이 들어갈 알맞은 위치는?

(4점)

When eggs float in water, they are not fresh.

① (A)   ② (B)   ③ (C)

④ (D)   ⑤ (E)

[울산 ○○중]

16 위 대화의 내용과 일치하지 <u>않는</u> 것은?   (3점)

① Yujin can explain why the bad eggs float.

② If eggs float in water, it's good to eat them.

③ If eggs are not fresh, they will float in water.

④ Fresh eggs will sink to the bottom in water.

⑤ Bad eggs float in water because they have gas inside.

[17~19] 다음 글을 읽고 물음에 답하시오.

Jina: Welcome to the Super Science Magic Show! ⓐIt's always exciting to see magic tricks. And it's more exciting to find out the secrets behind ⓑthem. Some people think the secret of magic is science. Today, Ken, a member of the School Magic Club, will use science to perform his tricks. Which tricks will ⓒhe show us? I can't wait to see ⓓthem.

[서울 영등포구 ○○중]

17 위 글의 ⓐ~ⓓ가 가리키는 것이 옳은 것끼리 짝지어진 것은?

(4점)

ⓐ: to find out the secrets behind them
ⓑ: magic tricks
ⓒ: Ken
ⓓ: Ken's tricks

① ⓐ,ⓑ,ⓒ

② ⓑ,ⓒ,ⓓ

③ ⓐ,ⓑ,ⓓ

④ ⓐ,ⓒ,ⓓ

⑤ ⓐ,ⓑ,ⓒ,ⓓ

[충북 ○○중]

18 위 글의 내용으로 바르지 <u>않은</u> 것은?   (3점)

① Jina is introducing the magic show.

② Ken belongs to the School Magic Club.

③ Jina really wants to see the magic tricks.

④ People think science can be the secret of magic.

⑤ Ken and a member of the School Magic Club will perform the magic.

19 위 글 뒤에 이어질 내용은? (3점)

① 마술에 담긴 과학적 비밀이 소개된다.

② Jina가 마술을 하게 된 이유를 설명한다.

③ Jina의 마술 속임수 설명이 계속된다.

④ 학교 마술 동아리 회원이 소개된다.

⑤ Ken의 마술쇼가 이어진다.

[21~24] 다음 글을 읽고 물음에 답하시오.

> Ken: Now, I'm going to fill one of these cups with water. (A)I will move them around to confuse you. Jina, which cup has the water in it?
>
> Jina: (B)That's easy! It's the middle one.
>
> Ken: Okay, let's check. See? No water.
>
> Jina: Show me the other cups.
>
> Ken: See? There's no water.
>
> Jina: Wow! (C)How come the water disappeared?
>
> Ken: Before the trick, I put a special material into one of the cups. The material absorbed the water and turned it into jelly. Then the jelly stuck to the bottom. If you want to try this trick, (D)@it's necessary to use cups that you can see through.
>
> Jina: Thank you for your great performance. (E)It was really amazing!

21 위 글의 흐름상 어색한 문장은? (3점)

① (A)   ② (B)   ③ (C)
④ (D)   ⑤ (E)

20 다음 글의 제목으로 가장 알맞은 것은? (4점)

> How come the rocks in Death Valley move on their own? They weigh up to 300 kilograms each. Some scientists have watched their movements closely for a long time. Now we know that ice and wind move the rocks.

① The Pyramids

② The Dancing Coin

③ The Bermuda Triangle

④ The Amazing Rising Water

⑤ The Moving Rocks in Death Valley

22 위 글의 밑줄 친 @it과 쓰임이 같은 것은? (3점)

① It is getting colder nowadays.

② Isn't it important to eat breakfast?

③ How far is it from here to the subway station?

④ I know it sounds crazy but it may work.

⑤ It is so easy that even a 3-year old boy can solve it.

23 위 글의 제목으로 가장 어울리는 것은? (3점)

① How to Confuse People

② The Importance of the Trick

③ Jina, a Magician

④ An Importance of a Performance Skill

⑤ The Secret of the Disappearing Water

[25~30] 다음 글을 읽고 물음에 답하시오.

Jina: Welcome to the Super Science Magic Show! It's always exciting to see magic tricks. And it's more exciting to find out the secrets behind them. Some people think the secret of magic is science. Today, Ken, a member of the School Magic Club, will use science to perform his tricks. Which tricks will he show us? I can't wait to see them.

Ken: Hello, everyone. Today, I'm going to show you something amazing. Here's a dish with water in (A)it. Now, I'll put a candle in the middle of the dish. Next, I'll (가)light the candle and cover it with a glass. "Abracadabra!"

Jina: Look at the water! (나)How come (B)it rose into the glass?

Ken: Air expands when it gets hot and creates higher pressure. When it gets cold, air contracts and creates (C)_____. When the flame burnt out, the air inside the glass cooled down. As the air cooled down, the air pressure (D)_____. So the air outside the glass was at a (E)_____. It pushed the water into the glass.

24 위 글의 내용과 일치하는 것은? (4점)

① Ken said nothing while performing his trick.

② Jina already knew why the water disappeared.

③ Ken put a special material into one of the cups after the trick.

④ Ken showed the magic show of the disappearing water.

⑤ You need to prepare some cups you can see inside for this trick.

25 위 글의 밑줄 친 (가)light와 같은 의미로 쓰인 것은? (3점)

① A light rain began to fall.

② All plants need light and water.

③ Sound travels more slowly than light.

④ I just want something light for lunch.

⑤ I tried to light the fire, but the wood was wet.

26 위 글의 밑줄 친 (나)와 의미가 같은 것은? (3점)

① Where did it rise?

② What is in the glass?

③ When did it get into the glass?

④ How about getting into the glass?

⑤ Why did the water rise into the glass?

29 위 글을 읽고, 다음 질문에 대한 답을 본문의 내용에 근거해서 쓰시오. (4점)

> Q: What happened in the glass right after Ken said "Abracadabra!"?
> A: The water _____.

> <Directions>
> • 문법에 맞도록 쓸 것

→ _____

27 위 글의 밑줄 친 (A), (B)가 가리키는 것으로 알맞은 것은? (3점)

	(A)	(B)
①	a dish	the water
②	a candle	a dish
③	a glass	the candle
④	the water	a dish
⑤	air	a glass

28 위 글의 흐름상 빈칸 (C), (D), (E)에 알맞은 것은? (4점)

	(C)	(D)	(E)
①	higher pressure	rose	higher pressure
②	higher pressure	dropped	lower pressure
③	lower pressure	dropped	lower pressure
④	lower pressure	dropped	higher pressure
⑤	lower pressure	rose	higher pressure

30 위 글의 내용과 일치하는 것은? (4점)

① 유리컵 속의 물이 없어지는 마술이다.

② Jina는 사람들 앞에서 마술쇼를 할 것이다.

③ 공기가 뜨거워지면 팽창해서 더 높은 압력을 만든다.

④ 유리컵 속의 촛불이 꺼지면 기압이 높아진다.

⑤ 마술의 비밀이 과학이라고 생각하는 사람은 아무도 없다.

◎ 선택형 문항의 답안은 컴퓨터용 수정 싸인펜을 사용하여 OMR 답안지에 바르게 표기하시오.
◎ 서술형 문제는 답을 답안지에 반드시 검정 볼펜으로 쓰시오.
◎ 총 30문항 100점 만점입니다. 문항별 배점은 각 문항에 표시되어 있습니다.

[부산 ○○중]

01 다음 중 뜻풀이가 <u>어색한</u> 것은? (3점)

① take off: 벗다
② in fact: 사실은
③ laugh at: 비웃다
④ thanks to: ~ 덕분에
⑤ give it a try: 건네주다

[서울 영등포구 ○○중]

02 다음 빈칸에 들어갈 말이 <u>아닌</u> 것은? (3점)

- The air _____ moves from high to low.
- This room is made of a special material that _____s sound.
- Students are doing a science _____ with a candle.
- The _____s grew higher because of the strong wind.

① absorb
② flame
③ pressure
④ experiment
⑤ burn

[울산 ○○중]

03 다음 영영 풀이에 해당하는 단어는? (3점)

to become smaller or narrower

① absorb
② expand
③ float
④ contract
⑤ pressure

[서울 영등포구 ○○중]

04 다음 중 빈칸에 가장 알맞은 말은? (3점)

It is important _____ many problems to get a good grade on the math test.

① solve
② solves
③ solved
④ solving
⑤ to solve

[울산 ○○중]

05 다음 밑줄 친 부분의 용법이 나머지 넷과 <u>다른</u> 것은? (3점)

① <u>To talk</u> with her is interesting.
② I want something hot <u>to drink</u>.
③ My hobby is <u>to draw</u> a picture.
④ It is fun <u>to do</u> a science experiment.
⑤ They decided <u>to sign</u> up for the magic club.

06 다음 중 어법이 어색한 것은? (3점)

① It was careless for him to do so.

② It is surprising that he has won the game.

③ Do you think it's difficult to learn a foreign language?

④ I think it's necessary for us to drink milk every day.

⑤ Isn't it dangerous for them to play with fire at home?

08 다음 대화의 내용으로 어색한 것은? (3점)

① A: She is driving a robot.

  B: That looks fun. I can't wait to try it.

② A: Have you heard of cricket?

  B: Yes, I have. People use a wide bat in cricket.

③ A: Which trick do you want to learn?

  B: I signed up for a magic class.

④ A: I want to play soccer well, but it's not easy.

  B: Don't give up. Why don't you practice hard?

⑤ A: Which season do you like best?

  B: I like winter best.

07 다음 우리말을 〈조건〉에 맞게 영작하시오. (6점)

조건
- It과 to 동사원형을 이용할 것.
- 주어진 단어를 반드시 사용할 것.

(1) K-pop 춤을 배우는 것은 재미있다. (fun)

→ _____.

(2) 100미터를 15초 안에 달리는 것은 어렵다. (difficult)

→ _____.

(3) 집에 하루 종일 머무르는 것은 지루하다. (boring)

→ _____.

A: Kyuwon, ⓐ_____ did you put the eggs in water?

B: I'm picking out the bad eggs.

A: ⓑ_____ eggs are fresh, and ⓒ_____ ones are not?

B: Eggs that sink in water are fresh. ⓓ_____ eggs float in water, they're not fresh. You shouldn't eat them.

A: That's interesting. ⓔ_____ do the bad eggs float?

B: Because they have gas inside. The gas acts like the air in a balloon.

A: Oh, I see.

*A: Nojun , B: Kyuwon

[서울 영등포구 ○○중]

09 위 대화의 ⓐ~ⓔ에 들어갈 말이 같은 것으로 짝지어진 것은? (3점)

① ⓐ, ⓑ

② ⓑ, ⓓ

③ ⓐ, ⓔ

④ ⓑ, ⓒ, ⓓ

⑤ ⓐ, ⓒ, ⓔ

[강원 ○○중]

10 위 대화의 내용과 일치하지 <u>않는</u> 것은? (3점)

① 물에 가라앉는 계란은 신선하다.

② Nojun은 상한 계란을 골라내고 있다.

③ 물에 뜨는 계란은 신선하지 않은 것이다.

④ 계란이 뜨는 이유는 안에 가스가 생겨서이다.

⑤ 계란 속 가스는 풍선 속의 공기와 같은 역할을 한다.

King Sejong: It hasn't rained ⓐ<u>for a long time</u>.

Jang Yeongsil: Yes. The dry season is ⓑ<u>lasting</u> too long. The farmers are very worried.

King Sejong: We should do something to help (A)<u>them</u>.

Jang Yeongsil: How about making a special clock?

King Sejong: A clock? How will (B)<u>that</u> help?

Jang Yeongsil: The clock will show the time and the seasons. We can use it ⓒ<u>to prepare</u> for the dry season.

King Sejong: That sounds like a good idea. But who's going to make it?

Jang Yeongsil: I'll ⓓ<u>give it a try</u>. I know a lot about time and the seasons.

King Sejong: Okay. I ⓔ<u>can't wait to</u> see your clock.

[충북 ○○중]

11 위 대화의 ⓐ~ⓔ의 설명으로 옳지 <u>않은</u> 것은? (3점)

① ⓐ for a long time: 오랫동안

② ⓑ last: 마지막의

③ ⓒ to prepare: 대비하기 위해서

④ ⓓ give it a try: 시도해 보다

⑤ ⓔ can't wait to: 무척 ~하기를 기다리다

12 위 대화의 (A), (B)가 가리키는 것으로 바른 것은? (3점)

	(A)	(B)
①	the farmers	the season
②	the farmers	the clock
③	the clocks	the clock
④	the seasons	the clock
⑤	the farmers	the rain

13 위 대화의 내용을 잘못 이해한 학생은? (3점)

① Hanjun: 세종대왕은 농부를 도와줘야 한다고 생각해.

② Jihun: 오랫동안 비가 오지 않아 농부들이 걱정하고 있어.

③ Heechan: 세종대왕은 농부를 위한 특별한 농기구를 발명하려고 해.

④ Hyuckjun: 장영실은 시간과 계절에 대해 많이 알고 있다고 했어.

⑤ Seongyun: 그 특별한 시계는 건조한 계절을 대비할 때 사용할 수 있어.

14 위 대화의 내용으로 답할 수 있는 것 2개는? (3점)

① Why are the farmers worried?

② What does the clock look like?

③ What can people do by using the clock?

④ What does King Sejong know about time?

⑤ What material will Yeongsil use to make the clock?

[15~16] 다음 대화를 읽고 물음에 답하시오.

B: Ms. Jeong, does a glass of water weigh more when there's a fish in it?

W: Yes, it does. We can test it now.

B: But how? We don't have a fish.

W: We can use a finger instead of a fish.

B: How will that work?

W: I'll weigh a glass of water first. Then I will put my finger in the water and weigh it to compare.

B: Oh, (A)I can't wait to see the difference.

*W: Woman, B: Boy

15 위 대화의 밑줄 친 (A)의 의도는? (3점)

① 기대 표현하기

② 감탄하기

③ 충고하기

④ 약속하기

⑤ 유감 표현하기

16 위 대화의 내용과 일치하지 않는 것은? (3점)

① 두 사람은 실험에 쓸 물고기가 없다.

② 두 사람은 손가락을 이용해서 실험할 것이다.

③ 위 실험의 과정에서 무게는 총 한 번만 재면 된다.

④ 한 잔의 물에 물고기가 들어가면 물컵의 무게는 증가한다.

⑤ 실험에서 먼저 할 일은 물 한 컵의 무게를 재는 것이다.

Jina: Welcome to the Super Science Magic Show! It's always exciting (가)to see magic tricks. And (A)(당신이 그 비밀들을 찾아내는 것은 더 흥미롭다) behind ⓐthem. Some people think the secret of magic is science. Today, ⓑKen, a member of the School Magic Club, will use science to perform his tricks. Which tricks will he show us? I ⓒcan't wait to see them.

The Amazing Rising Water

Ken: Hello, everyone. Today, I'm going to show you something amazing. Here's a dish with water in it. Now, I'll put a candle in the middle of the dish. Next, I'll light the candle and cover it with ⓓa glass. "Abracadabra!"

Jina: Look at the water! (B)어째서 그것이 그 유리잔 안으로 올라간 거지?

Ken: Air expands when it gets hot and creates higher pressure. When it gets cold, air contracts and creates lower pressure. When the flame burnt out, the air inside the glass cooled down. ⓔAs the air cooled down, the air pressure dropped. So the air outside the glass was at a higher pressure. It pushed the water into the glass.

17 위 글의 밑줄 친 (A), (B)의 우리말 표현을 조건에 맞도록 영작하시오. (6점)

(A): _____

　　(조건: 'it, out, for'를 반드시 포함할 것)

(B): _____

　　(조건: 'How, rose'를 반드시 포함할 것)

18 위 글의 밑줄 친 (가)와 용법이 다른 것은? (3점)

① It's fun to do a science experiment.

② It's not safe to play with fire at home.

③ It's important that we eat healthy food.

④ It's important to wear sunscreen to prevent sunburn.

⑤ It's convenient to take a subway in Seoul.

19 위 글의 밑줄 친 ⓐ∼ⓔ에 대한 설명으로 바르지 <u>않은</u> 것은?

(3점)

① ⓐthem: 'magic tricks'를 대신한다.

② ⓑKen, a member of the School Magic Club: Ken이 학교 마술 동아리 회원임을 알 수 있다.

③ ⓒcan't wait to see: '시간이 없어 기다릴 수 없다'는 의미이다.

④ ⓓa glass: '유리잔'을 의미한다.

⑤ ⓔAs: 접속사로 '∼할 때'를 의미한다.

---

20 다음 대화의 B에 대한 A 문장을 'how come'을 이용하여 각각 작성하시오. (6점)

(1)
A: _____?
B: He didn't go to school today because he had a cold.
(2)
A: _____?
B: They have big ears to stay cool.

(1) A: _____?
(2) A: _____?

[21∼26] 다음 글을 읽고 물음에 답하시오.

The Secret of the Disappearing Water

Ken: Now, ⓐI'm going to fill one of these cups with water. ⓑI will move them around (가)to confuse you. (A) Jina, which cup has the water in it?

Jina: That's easy! It's the middle one.

Ken: Okay, let's check. See? No water.

Jina: Show me the other cups.

Ken: See? There's no water. (B)

Jina: Wow! (나)_____

Ken: ⓒBefore the trick, I put a special material into one of the cups. (C) The material absorbed the water and ⓓturned it into jelly. (D) If you want to try this trick, ⓔit's necessary to use cups that you can see through. (E)

Jina: Thank you for your great performance. It was really amazing!

---

21 위 글의 (A)∼(E) 중 주어진 문장이 들어갈 알맞은 곳은? (3점)

Then the jelly stuck to the bottom.

① (A)　　　② (B)　　　③ (C)

④ (D)　　　⑤ (E)

---

22 위 글의 밑줄 친 ⓐ~ⓔ 중 문맥상 <u>어색한</u> 것은? (3점)

① ⓐ   ② ⓑ   ③ ⓒ

④ ⓓ   ⑤ ⓔ

25 위 글의 마법의 순서를 〈보기〉에서 찾아 알맞게 배열한 것은? (3점)

> (A) Ask your friends, "Which cup has the water in it?"
> (B) Fill a cup with water.
> (C) Move the cups around.

① (B)-(C)-(A)

② (A)-(C)-(B)

③ (B)-(A)-(C)

④ (C)-(A)-(B)

⑤ (C)-(B)-(A)

23 위 글의 밑줄 친 (가)to confuse와 같은 용법으로 사용된 것은? (3점)

① I like <u>to go</u> fishing.

② I study hard <u>to pass</u> the test.

③ <u>To speak</u> English is not easy.

④ My hobby is <u>to play</u> the guitar.

⑤ It is interesting <u>to read</u> comic books.

26 위 글의 내용으로 바르지 <u>않은</u> 것은? (3점)

① Ken filled one of the cups with water.

② Ken moved a cup around to confuse you.

③ You must use the cups that you cannot see through.

④ The water was turned into jelly due to the special material.

⑤ Ken put the special material into one of the cups.

24 위 글의 빈칸 (나)에 가장 알맞은 표현은? (3점)

① Why did the water disappeared?

② Why the water did disappeared?

③ How come the water disappeared?

④ How come did the water disappear?

⑤ How come the water did disappeared?

The Amazing Rising Water

Ken: Hello, everyone. Today, I'm going to show you something amazing. Here's a dish with water in it. Now, put a candle in the middle of the dish. Next, I'll light the candle and cover it with a glass, "Abracadabra!"

Jina: Look at the water! (A)[How come / Which] it rose into the glass?

Ken: Air expands when it gets hot and creates higher pressure. When it gets cold, air contracts and creates lower pressure. When the flame burnt out, the air inside the glass cooled down. As the air cooled down, the air pressure (B)[rose / dropped]. So the air outside the glass was at a (C)[lower / higher] pressure. It pushed the water into the glass.

Jina: Thank you for your great performance. (가)To see magic tricks is always exciting.

[충북 ○○중]

28 위 글을 참고하여 다음 질문에 대한 답을 주어진 표현으로 시작하는 영어 문장으로 작성하시오. (4점)

Q: What happened to the water after the flame burnt out?
→ The water _____.

→ _____

[부산 ○○중]

29 위 글의 밑줄 친 (가)를 주어진 단어로 시작하는 문장으로 바꾸어 쓰시오. (3점)

<Directions>
• 기존의 문장과 뜻이 같도록 쓸 것

(가)To see magic tricks is always exciting.

→ It _____.

[충북 ○○중]

27 위 글의 괄호 (A), (B), (C) 안에서 알맞은 표현으로 짝지어진 것은? (3점)

	(A)	(B)	(C)
①	How come	dropped	lower
②	Which	dropped	higher
③	How come	rose	lower
④	How come	dropped	higher
⑤	Which	rose	higher

[부산 ○○중]

30 위 글을 읽고 질문에 답할 수 없는 것은? (3점)

① Who lights the candle?
② When did Ken learn the trick?
③ What do you need to show the trick?
④ What happens when the flame burns out?
⑤ Did the air pressure inside the glass change?

반		점수	
이름			

문항수 : 선택형(25문항) 서술형(5문항) 　20．　．　．

◎ 선택형 문항의 답안은 컴퓨터용 수정 싸인펜을 사용
하여 OMR 답안지에 바르게 표기하시오.
◎ 서술형 문제는 답을 답안지에 반드시 검정 볼펜으
로 쓰시오.
◎ 총 30문항 100점 만점입니다. 문항별 배점은 각
문항에 표시되어 있습니다.

[울산 ○○중]

01 다음 빈칸에 들어갈 말로 알맞지 <u>않은</u> 것은?　　(3점)

- My friends always _____ at my jokes.
- I'm _____ worn out from all the exercise.
- People _____ dry sticks to make a fire.
- She is _____ of her sons because they passed the exam.

① laugh
② practice
③ gather
④ proud
⑤ completely

[울산 ○○중]

02 다음 문맥상 〈보기〉의 빈칸에 들어갈 가장 알맞은 단어는?
　　(3점)

> 보기
> It is _____ to study hard to pass the exam.

① compare
② necessary
③ practice
④ sign
⑤ excited

[울산 ○○중]

03 다음 글의 빈칸에 공통으로 들어갈 단어로 가장 알맞은 것은?
　　(3점)

> Have you heard about the movie "McFarland, USA?" It's about a cross-country team. The boys had no experience _____ cross-country. So people thought that they were a weak team. However, the team won _____ the end.

① for
② by
③ from
④ in
⑤ with

[부산 ○○중]

04 다음 우리말에 맞게 주어진 단어를 배열하시오.　(4점)

> 그 선생님은 학생들이 밖에서 놀게 허락하셨다.

> play / the students / let / outside

→ The teacher _____.

[울산 ○○중]

05 다음 중 어법상 옳은 것은?　　(3점)

① I want to make my mom laughed.
② Mike's teacher had his go home early.
③ The teacher made them finish their project.
④ Nancy helped her sister doing the dishes.
⑤ My mom let me to play computer games.

06 다음 우리말에 맞게 문장을 영작하시오. (5점)

> **조건**
> • 'although'를 반드시 사용할 것

> (1) 비록 늦게 일어났지만, 나는 버스를 놓치지는 않았다.
> (2) 비록 피곤했지만, 나는 열심히 공부했다.

(1)_____

(2)_____

08 다음 우리말을 영어로 바르게 옮긴 것은? (3점)

> 그는 비록 일찍 떠났지만, 기차를 놓쳤다.

① He left early and he missed the train.

② Although he missed the train, he left early.

③ Because he left early, he missed the train.

④ Although he left early, he missed the train.

⑤ He left early although he missed the train.

09 다음 〈조건〉에 맞추어 (A)와 (B)를 우리말에 맞게 영어로 쓰시오. (5점)

> Today was my dad's birthday. My mom prepared a party. (A)_____ with chocolate cream. Then we bought some gifts. Lastly, (B)_____ to him.

> (A) 엄마는 내가 초콜릿 크림이 있는 케이크를 굽게 했다.
> (B) 엄마는 내가 아빠에게 편지를 쓰게 만들었다.

> **조건**
> • 각 문장의 의미에 맞는 사역동사를 사용하시오.

(A) _____ with chocolate cream.

(B) _____ to him.

07 다음 문장 중 어법상 <u>어색한</u> 것은? (3점)

① I'll let you know the secret.

② I want to make him studies hard.

③ My mom made me wash the dog.

④ Please let us stay in this country.

⑤ He made me come to school early.

10 다음 밑줄 친 ⓐ의 우리말을 영어로 가장 바르게 옮긴 것은?

(3점)

> Koh Panyee was a small floating village in the middle of the sea. ⓐ비록 마을 소년들이 전에 축구를 해본 적이 없을지라도, they loved watching it on TV. One day, the boys decided to make their own soccer team. However, people laughed at their idea.

① After the boys in the village never played soccer

② Before the boys in the village never played soccer

③ As the boys in the village never played soccer before

④ But the boys in the village never played soccer before

⑤ Although the boys in the village never played soccer before

11 위 대화의 밑줄 친 ⓐ~ⓔ의 설명으로 옳은 것은? (3점)

① ⓐ have you heard of: ~에 대해 들어본 적 있어?

② ⓑ who crossed the desert: 누가 그 사막을 건넜니?

③ ⓒ on foot: 발 위에

④ ⓓ took: 가져갔다

⑤ ⓔ experience: 경험

12 위 대화의 빈칸 (A), (B)에 각각 공통으로 알맞은 표현으로 짝 지어진 것은? (3점)

	(A)	(B)
①	about	in
②	about	at
③	of	on
④	of	in
⑤	about	on

[11~13] 다음 대화를 읽고 물음에 답하시오.

> G: Tim, ⓐhave you heard of the Gobi Desert?
> B: Yes, I have. Isn't it in Mongolia and China?
> G: Yes, it is. Yesterday, I saw a TV show (A)_____ people ⓑwho crossed the desert on foot.
> B: Only ⓒon foot?
> G: Yes, it ⓓtook them (A)_____ 51 days.
> B: Wow, that's amazing. I want to ⓔexperience life (B)_____ the desert but I don't want to cross it on foot.
> G: Well, I want to try and cross the Gobi Desert (B)_____ 50 days.
>
> *G: girl, B: boy

13 위 대화를 읽고 주어진 문장의 빈칸을 완성할 때 가장 알맞은 단어는? (3점)

> Tim wants to _____ life in the Gobi Desert.

① walk

② hear

③ cross

④ experience

⑤ change

14 Choose the correct order. (3점)

> ⓐ No, what is it?
> ⓑ Oh, it sounds interesting.
> ⓒ Have you heard of cross-country?
> ⓓ It's a sport. In cross-country, people run across an open field.

① ⓐ - ⓒ - ⓓ - ⓑ
② ⓒ - ⓐ - ⓓ - ⓑ
③ ⓒ - ⓓ - ⓑ - ⓐ
④ ⓓ - ⓑ - ⓒ - ⓐ
⑤ ⓓ - ⓒ - ⓐ - ⓑ

15 다음 대화의 내용으로 옳지 <u>않은</u> 것은? (3점)

> G: Hojun, are you going to try out for the school ice hockey team? The new season is about to start.
> B: I'm not sure.
> G: Why not?
> B: I heard that Tony and Brad are also trying out for the team. They're so good.
> G: Well, you're also good at ice hockey, so don't give up!
> B: Okay, I'll try my best. Thanks a lot.

① Hojun won't give up and do his best.
② Hojun thinks that Brad plays hockey well.
③ The girl thinks Hojun is a good ice hockey player.
④ The new season of ice hockey is going to start soon.
⑤ Hojun is a member of the school ice hockey team.

[16~18] 다음 글을 읽고 물음에 답하시오.

> What can you do to be healthy? First, try to exercise every day. Second, try to eat healthy food. Don't eat too much fast food. Third, wash your hands before meals. Do (가)<u>these tips</u> sound hard to do? Well, take one step at a time and (A)<u>don't give up</u>. Then you'll live a healthy life.

16 위 글의 밑줄 친 (A)가 의도하는 것은? (3점)

① 선물 주기
② 칭찬하기
③ 주의 끌기
④ 격려하기
⑤ 감사하기

17 위 글의 밑줄 친 these tips가 의미하는 것이 <u>아닌</u> 것은? (3점)

① Exercise regularly.
② Don't eat too much fast food.
③ Sleep enough at night.
④ Eat fresh vegetables and fruits.
⑤ Wash hands before you have a meal.

18 위 글의 제목으로 적절한 것은? (3점)

① Good Tips for Exercise

② How to Eat Healthy Food

③ The Reason Why You Exercise

④ The Things to Do for a Healthy Life

⑤ Washing Your Hands before Breakfast

[19~24] 다음 글을 읽고 물음에 답하시오.

Koh Panyee was a small floating village in the middle of the sea. ⓐAlthough the boys in the village never played soccer before, they loved watching it on TV. One day, the boys decided to make their own soccer team. ⓑHowever, people laughed at their idea.

(A)

"That's impossible."

"What makes you say so?"

"Look around. Where are you going to play soccer?"

The villagers were right. The boys had no place to play soccer. They were discouraged.

"Don't give up! We can still play soccer."
"How?"

"Let's make our own soccer field."

(B)

They had no shoes so they had to play in bare feet. ⓒStill, they didn't care. ⓓIn fact, they built excellent skills and enjoyed playing soccer more.

(C)

㉠When they were about to leave, the villagers gave them new shoes and uniforms.

㉡One day, a boy brought a poster about a soccer tournament.

㉢They decided to give it a try.

㉣Some even came to watch the game.

(D)

On the day of the semi-final, it was raining hard. They were losing by two goals and it looked impossible to win.

(E)

The other team is so strong," they thought. But the boys didn't give Ⓐ_____. They took Ⓑ_____ their shoes during the second half and the game changed completely. They played better in the rain. ⓔBecause they lost by a score of three to two, they felt proud Ⓒ_____ themselves. They didn't give Ⓐ_____ when they were losing. They tried their best until the end.

19 위 글의 (A)~(E) 중 다음 글이 들어갈 곳으로 가장 적절한 곳은? (3점)

The boys gathered old boats and pieces of wood. They put the boats together and nailed the wood to them. After much hard work, they finally had a floating field. It was shaky and had nails everywhere. The balls and the boys would often fall into the sea, so the field was always wet and slippery.

① (A)　　　② (B)　　　③ (C)

④ (D)　　　⑤ (E)

20 위 글의 ㉠~㉣를 글의 흐름에 맞도록 배열한 것은? (4점)

① ㉡ - ㉢ - ㉣ - ㉠

② ㉡ - ㉢ - ㉠ - ㉣

③ ㉡ - ㉠ - ㉢ - ㉣

④ ㉠ - ㉡ - ㉢ - ㉣

⑤ ㉠ - ㉡ - ㉣ - ㉢

23 위 글의 밑줄 친 ⓐ~ⓔ 중에서 자연스럽지 <u>않은</u> 것은? (3점)

① ⓐ   ② ⓑ   ③ ⓒ

④ ⓓ   ⑤ ⓔ

21 위 글의 Ⓐ~Ⓒ에 들어갈 말로 올바르게 연결된 것은? (4점)

	Ⓐ	Ⓑ	Ⓒ
①	on	off	about
②	on	away	about
③	up	off	to
④	up	away	about
⑤	up	off	of

24 위 글을 읽고 작성한 독서록의 내용 가운데 올바른 것은? (3점)

I was very impressed by the story about the boys in Koh Panyee. In the beginning, ⓐ the villagers were very helpful in making their own team. ⓑThey also made their own soccer field with the help of the villagers. They practiced hard and participated in a soccer tournament. ⓒPeople thought they were very good from the start. ⓓOn the rainy day, they were losing by two goals in the semi-final. ⓔThey played better in the slippery field and finally won.

*impressed 감명 받은
*participate 참여하다

① ⓐ   ② ⓑ   ③ ⓒ

④ ⓓ   ⑤ ⓔ

22 위 글의 내용과 일치하는 것은? (3점)

① 소년들은 축구를 좋아해서 오래 전부터 축구를 해 왔다.

② 마을 사람들은 소년들이 축구를 하는 것에 대해서 긍정적이었다.

③ 소년들은 축구공 없이 나무 조각으로 축구를 연습했다.

④ 몇몇 마을 사람들은 소년들을 응원하러 토너먼트에 함께 가 주었다.

⑤ 소년들은 결승전에서 3대 2로 패배했다.

One day, a boy brought a poster about a soccer tournament. They decided ⓐto give it a try. When they were about ⓑto leave, the villagers gave them new shoes and uniforms. Some even came ⓒto watch the game. This made the boys ⓓto feel better. (가)At first, people saw them as the weakest team. However, when the tournament started, the soccer team surprised everyone.

On the day of the semi-final, it was raining hard. (나)They were losing by two goals and it looked impossible ⓔto win.

"The other team is so strong," they thought.

But the boys didn't give up. They took off their shoes during the second half and the game changed completely. (다)They played better in the rain thanks to the slippery field at home. Although (라)they won by a score of three to two, still, they felt proud of themselves. (마)They didn't give up when they were losing. They tried their best until the end.

26 위 글의 (가)~(마) 중 흐름상 <u>어색한</u> 것은? (3점)

① (가) ② (나) ③ (다)

④ (라) ⑤ (마)

27 위 글을 참고하여 다음 질문에 대한 답을 주어진 표현으로 시작하는 문장으로 영작하시오. (5점)

(1) What did the villagers give to the boys?
→ They _____.

(2) How did the boys feel after the semi-final?
→ They _____.

(1) _____

(2) _____

25 위 글의 ⓐ~ⓔ 중 쓰임이 바르지 <u>않은</u> 것은? (3점)

① ⓐ ② ⓑ ③ ⓒ

④ ⓓ ⑤ ⓔ

Koh Panyee was a small floating village in the middle of the sea. (A) ⓐ_____ the boys in the village never played soccer before, they loved watching it on TV. (B) One day, the boys decided to make their own soccer team. (C)

"That's impossible."

ⓑ"Why do you say so?"

"Look around. Where are you going to play soccer?" (D)

The villagers were right. The boys had no place to play soccer. They were discouraged. (E)

"Don't give up! We can still play soccer."

"How?"

"Let's make our own soccer field."

[충북 ○○중]

29 위 글의 빈칸 ⓐ에 가장 알맞은 표현은?   (3점)

① Because

② Although

③ If

④ When

⑤ As

[충북 ○○중]

28 위 글의 (A)~(E) 중 다음 문장이 들어갈 곳으로 가장 알맞은 곳은?   (3점)

| However, people laughed at their idea. |

① (A)   ② (B)   ③ (C)

④ (D)   ⑤ (E)

[충북 ○○중]

30 위 글의 밑줄 친 ⓑ와 같은 의미가 되도록 한 문장으로 영작하시오.   (4점)

조건
• 'what', 'make'(변형 가능)를 반드시 사용할 것

→ _____

2학년 영어 2학기 기말고사(8과) 2회

반		점수	
이름			

문항수 : 선택형(25문항) 서술형(5문항) | 20 . . .

◎ 선택형 문항의 답안은 컴퓨터용 수정 싸인펜을 사용하여 OMR 답안지에 바르게 표기하시오.
◎ 서술형 문제는 답을 답안지에 반드시 검정 볼펜으로 쓰시오.
◎ 총 30문항 100점 만점입니다. 문항별 배점은 각 문항에 표시되어 있습니다.

01 다음 〈보기〉의 영영 풀이 중 올바른 것만을 있는 대로 고른 것은? (4점)

보기

(A) bare: covered by clothes
(B) wide: measuring a large distance from one side to the other
(C) courage: no longer having the confidence you need to continue doing something
(D) nail: to fasten something to something else with nails
(E) proud: feeling pleased about something that you have done or something that you own

① (A), (B)
② (B), (D)
③ (C), (E)
④ (A), (C), (D)
⑤ (B), (D), (E)

03 다음 글의 흐름상 빈칸에 들어갈 단어가 바르지 못한 것은? (3점)

What can you do to be healthy? First, try to ⓐ_____ every day. Second, try to eat ⓑ_____ food. Don't eat too much ⓒ_____ food. Third, wash your hands before ⓓ_____. Do these tips sound hard to do? Well, take one step at a time and don't give up. ⓔ_____ you'll live a healthy life.

① ⓐ: exercise
② ⓑ: healthy
③ ⓒ: fast
④ ⓓ: meals
⑤ ⓔ: But

04 다음 중 어법상 옳은 것은? (3점)

① He made me to laugh.
② We didn't let the other team win.
③ Mom will let he go to the movies.
④ His sad story made me crying loudly.
⑤ The woman had the children to play outside.

02 다음 괄호 안에서 가장 적절한 말을 고르시오. (3점)

What makes you (say / saying / to say) so?

→ _____

05 다음 문장을 although를 이용하여 바꿔 쓰시오. (4점)

It rained a lot, but I took a walk in the park.

→ _____.

06 다음 우리말에 맞게 빈칸에 알맞은 말을 쓰시오. (4점)

> 그는 나에게 그의 가방을 옮기게 했다.

> **<Directions>**
> • 'make'를 반드시 활용할 것
> • 필요시 시제나 형태 변형 가능
> • 칸 수에 맞게 쓸 것

→ _____ _____ _____ _____

   _____ _____ .

07 다음 중 어법상 올바른 것은? (3점)

① I had cut her my hair.

② My mom decided my dog go to hospital.

③ We enjoyed to dance very much.

④ The teacher will let us use our cell phones.

⑤ The situation made us laughed.

08 다음 중 어법상 올바르지 <u>않은</u> 것은? (3점)

① Even if they are poor, they look happy.

② I played soccer in spite of the bad weather.

③ He is quite so strong even though he is old.

④ Although the heavy rain, we had to go to school.

⑤ Though she got up early, she was late for school.

09 다음 짝지어진 대화 중 <u>어색한</u> 것은? (3점)

① G: Tom, have you heard of the Gobi Desert?

  B: Yes, I have.

② G: Jun, are you going to try out for the soccer team?

  B: I'm not sure.

③ G: Let's meet in front of the Student Center this Friday.

  B: Sure. See you then.

④ G: Have you heard about "Ugly Sweater Party?"

  B: Of course, I haven't.

⑤ G: You will be a good player, so don't give up!

  B: Okay, thanks a lot.

10 다음 Tom의 말에 이어질 대화의 순서가 바르게 나열된 것은? (3점)

> Tom: I want to be a basketball player but I'm too short. Should I give up?
>
> (a) No, I haven't. Who is he?
> (b) He was a basketball player. He was short, but he won the 1986 Slam Dunk Contest.
> (c) No, don't give up! Have you heard of Anthony Webb?

① (a)-(b)-(c)

② (a)-(c)-(b)

③ (b)-(a)-(c)

④ (b)-(c)-(a)

⑤ (c)-(a)-(b)

[11~12] 다음 대화를 읽고 물음에 답하시오.

> G: (가)너 고비 사막에 대해서 들어본 적 있니?
> B: Yes, I have. Isn't it in Mongolia and China?
> G: Yes, it is. Yesterday, I saw a TV show about people who crossed the Gobi Desert on foot.
> B: Only on foot?
> G: Yes, it took them about 51 days.
> B: Wow, that's amazing. I want to experience life in the desert but I don't want to cross it on foot.
> G: Well, I want to try and cross the Gobi Desert in 50 days.
>
> G= Jane / B= Tim

12 위 대화의 밑줄 친 우리말 (가)를 영어 문장으로 바꾸어 쓰시오. (4점)

> **조건**
> • 단어 of를 사용하시오.

→ _____

11 위 대화의 내용과 일치하는 것을 <u>모두</u> 고른 것은? (3점)

> (A) The Gobi Desert is in Mongolia and China.
> (B) Tim saw a TV show about people who crossed the desert on foot yesterday.
> (C) The people in the TV show crossed the desert in 51 days,
> (D) The people in the TV show crossed the desert only on foot.
> (E) Tim wants to cross the desert in 50 days to experience life in the desert.

① (A), (B), (D)
② (A), (C), (D)
③ (A), (D), (E)
④ (B), (C), (E)
⑤ (C), (D), (E)

13 다음 대화가 자연스러운 대화가 되도록 주어진 문장에 이어질 내용을 순서에 맞게 배열한 것은? (4점)

> G: Hojun, are you going to try out for the school ice hocky team? The new season is about to start.
> B: I'm not sure.
>
> (A) Well, you're also good at ice hocky, so don't give up!
> (B) Why not?
> (C) Okay, I'll try my best. Thanks a lot.
> (D) I heard that Tony and Brad are also trying out for the team. They're so good.

① (A) - (D) - (C) - (B)
② (A) - (C) - (B) - (D)
③ (B) - (D) - (A) - (C)
④ (B) - (A) - (C) - (D)
⑤ (C) - (B) - (A) - (D)

14 다음 대화의 내용으로 알 수 <u>없는</u> 질문은? (4점)

> G: Alex, have you heard about this year's "Ugly Sweater Party?"
>
> B: Of course, I have. It's on December 5th, right?
>
> G: That's right. Are you going to go?
>
> B: I want to, but I don't have an ugly sweater.
>
> G: I have one that I don't wear at home. You can have it if you want.
>
> B: Thanks. That would be great.
>
> G: Let's meet in front of the Student Center and go inside together.
>
> B: Sure. See you then.

① Where is Alex going to meet the girl?

② Where will this year's "Ugly Sweater Party" be held?

③ When will this year's "Ugly Sweater Party" be held?

④ What time is this year's "Ugly Sweater Party" going to begin?

⑤ Did Alex already know about this year's "Ugly Sweater Party" before the girl told him about it?

15 다음 짝지어진 대화가 <u>어색한</u> 것은? (3점)

① A: What are you reading, Jiwon?
　 B: I'm reading a book about magic.

② A: I can show you a ballon trick now.
　 B: Great! I want to see it now.

③ A: Which sport do you want to learn?
　 B: Yes, I learned some before.

④ A: It hasn't rained for a long time.
　 B: Yes. The dry season is lasting too long.

⑤ A: Which class did you sign up for?
　 B: I signed up for a science class.

[16~18] 다음 글을 읽고 물음에 답하시오.

> On the day of the semi-final, it was raining hard. They were losing by two goals and it looked impossible to win.
>
> "The other team is so strong," they thought.
>
> But the boys didn't give up. They (A)_____ their shoes during the second half and the game changed completely. They played better in the rain (B)_____ the slippery field at home. (가)<u>그들은 비록 3대 2라는 점수에 의해 패배했지만, 여전히 그들은 그들 자신들이 자랑스러웠다.</u> They didn't give up when they were losing. They tried their best (C)_____ the end.

16 위 글의 빈칸 (A), (B), (C)에 내용상 들어갈 말로 올바르게 연결한 것은? (4점)

	(A)	(B)	(C)
①	put off	instead of	since
②	put off	thanks to	until
③	took off	thanks to	until
④	took off	instead of	since
⑤	took off	except for	through

18 위 글의 내용과 일치하는 것은? (3점)

① The boys played in bare feet during the second half.

② The boys finally won the game by a score of two to one.

③ Although the boys gave up the game, they felt proud of themselves.

④ Because it wasn't raining hard, it looked possible to win.

⑤ The other team played better thanks to the slippery field.

17 위 글의 밑줄 친 (가)의 우리말과 일치하도록 영작할 때 ★에 들어갈 단어로 가장 알맞은 것은? (3점)

> (가)그들은 비록 3대 2라는 점수에 의해 패배했지만, 여전히 그들은 그들 자신들이 자랑스러웠다.
> → _____ they _____ _____ a _____ _____★_____ three to two, still, they felt proud of themselves.

① score

② by

③ of

④ lost

⑤ although

19 다음 빈칸에 들어갈 말이 바르게 짝지어진 것은? (3점)

> One day, a boy brought a poster about a soccer tournament. They decided to give it a try. When they were about (A)_____, the villagers gave them new shoes and uniforms. Some even came to watch the game. This made the boys (B)_____ better. At first, people saw them as the weakest team. However, when the tournament started, the soccer team surprised everyone.

	(A)	(B)
①	to leave	to feel
②	to leave	feeling
③	to leave	feel
④	leave	to feel
⑤	leave	feel

"That's impossible."

"Why do you say so?"

"Look around. Where are you going to play soccer?"

The villagers were right. ⓐThe boys had no place to play soccer. ⓑThey were discouraging.

"Don't give up! We can still play soccer."

"How?"

"Let's make our own soccer field."

The boys gathered old boats and pieces of wood. ⓒThey put the boats together and nailed the wood to them. After much hard work, they finally had a floating field. It was shaky and had nails everywhere. The ball and the boys would often fall into the sea, so the field was always wet and slippery. ⓓThey had no shoes so they had to play in bare feet. Still, they didn't care. ⓔIn fact, they built excellent skills and enjoyed playing soccer more.

Koh Panyee was a small floating village in the middle of the sea. (A)_____ the boys in the village never played soccer before, they loved watching it on TV. One day, the boys decided to make their own soccer team. (B)_____, people laughed at their idea.

"(가)That's impossible."

"What makes you say so?"

"Look around. Where are you going to play soccer?"

The villagers were right. The boys had no place to play soccer. They were discouraged.

"Don't give up! We can still play soccer."

"How?"

"Let's make our own soccer field."

[울산 ○○중]

20 위 글의 밑줄 친 ⓐ~ⓔ 중 어법상 어색한 문장은? (3점)

① ⓐ   ② ⓑ   ③ ⓒ

④ ⓓ   ⑤ ⓔ

[울산 ○○중]

21 위 글의 내용과 일치하는 것은? (3점)

① 소년들은 장소가 없어 축구를 포기했다.

② 소년들의 축구장은 무거워서 물에 가라앉았다.

③ 소년들은 축구를 즐겼지만 훌륭한 기술은 쌓지 못했다.

④ 소년들은 종종 바다에 빠져서 축구장은 항상 물에 젖어 미끄러웠다.

⑤ 소년들은 축구장을 만들기 위해서 낡은 공과 나무 조각을 사용했다.

[울산 ○○중]

22 위 글의 빈칸 (A), (B)에 들어갈 말로 가장 알맞게 연결한 것은? (3점)

	(A)	(B)
①	As	Also
②	Although	However
③	As	However
④	Although	Also
⑤	While	Finally

[울산 ○○중]

23 위 글의 내용과 일치하는 것은? (3점)

① Koh Panyee was a small village that was floating on the river.

② The boys in the village have ever played soccer before.

③ The boys in the village didn't like to watch soccer on TV.

④ The villagers encouraged the boys when they decided to make their soccer team.

⑤ The boys were discouraged because there was no place to play soccer in the village.

[25–27] 다음 글을 읽고 물음에 답하시오.

The boys gathered old boats and pieces of wood. ⓐThey put the boats together and nailed the wood to them. ⓑAfter many hard work, they finally had a floating field. It was shaky and had nails everywhere. ⓒThe ball and the boys would often fall into the sea, so the field was always wet and slippery. They had no shoes so they had to play in bare feet. Still, they didn't care. ⓓIn fact, they built excellent skills and enjoyed playing soccer more.

One day, a boy brought a poster about a soccer tournament. They decided to give it a try. ⓔWhen they were about to leaving, the villagers gave them new shoes and uniforms. Some even came to watch the game. ⓕThis made the boys feel better. At first, people saw them as the weakest team. However, when the tournament started, the soccer team surprised everyone.

[울산 ○○중]

25 위 글의 밑줄 친 ⓐ~ⓕ 중, 어법상 옳은 문장만을 있는 대로 고른 것은? (3점)

① ⓐ, ⓑ

② ⓑ, ⓒ, ⓔ

③ ⓐ, ⓓ, ⓕ

④ ⓐ, ⓒ, ⓓ, ⓕ

⑤ ⓑ, ⓒ, ⓓ, ⓔ

[서울 영등포구 ○○중]

24 위 글에서 마을 사람들이 (가)라고 말한 이유를 쓰시오. (4점)

> **조건**
> • 주어와 동사를 갖춘 영어 문장으로 쓰시오.

→ _____

[울산 ○○중]

26 위 글의 내용을 나타내는 표현으로 가장 알맞은 것은? (4점)

① A piece of cake.

② No pain, no gain.

③ Out of sight, out of mind.

④ No news is good news.

⑤ A little knowledge is dangerous.

27 위 글을 읽고, 질문에 대답할 수 <u>없는</u> 것은? (3점)

① What was the floating field made of?

② Why was the floating field always wet?

③ What did people think of the boys' team?

④ Who bought the boys new shoes and uniforms?

⑤ How many villagers went to the stadium to watch the soccer game?

28 위 글의 밑줄 친 ⓐ~ⓔ 중에서 문맥과 관계<u>없는</u> 문장은? (3점)

① ⓐ ② ⓑ ③ ⓒ

④ ⓓ ⑤ ⓔ

29 위 글의 내용과 일치하는 것은? (3점)

① My family members are big fans of Poston Rivers.

② My family and I went to watch the game last weekend.

③ I couldn't wait to get gifts on my birthday.

④ My parents were upset because I supported a different team.

⑤ I hid my team's uniform in the wardrobe.

[28~30] 다음 글을 읽고 물음에 답하시오.

I had to (A)<u>do</u> a secret for a long time. Although my family members were all Poston City fans, I supported a different team, Poston Rivers. My parents believed that I was also a big fan of Poston City. I had to (B)<u>shoot</u> for my team secretly when both teams played against each other. I couldn't shout in joy (C)<u>because</u> my team scored. ⓐ<u>I had to go to the bathroom and celebrate there.</u> ⓑ<u>I had a secret place in the wardrobe, too.</u> ⓒ<u>I hid my favorite team's clothes.</u> ⓓ<u>Blue and black are the colors of my favorite team's uniform.</u> ⓔ<u>Birthdays were the worst time of all.</u> I always got soccer gifts for Poston City's team. But then my life changed. A rich mart bought both teams and (D)<u>pushed</u> them play together, as one big team, Poston United. Now I can (E)<u>excite</u> all the matches with my family.

30 위 글의 (A)~(E) 중에서 바르게 고친 것을 2개 고른 것은? (4점)

① (A) do → get

② (B) shoot → root

③ (C) because → if

④ (D) pushed → made

⑤ (E) excite → extend

정답 및 해설

Lesson 5 (중간)

---

01 ① **02** ② **03** ① **04** ⑤ **05** ②

06 Can you explain how to use the buttons?

07 ② **08** ②, ④

09 (1) The sound can be heard by you from far away.
　(2) Is this car driven by your father?

10 ③ **11** ⑤ **12** ⑤ **13** ⑤ **14** ① **15** ②, ③

16 Can you explain how to move everything

17 ④ **18** ④ **19** ① **20** ③

21 Mr. Doodle was hit by a car. **22** ④ **23** ③ **24** ②

25 ⑤ **26** ② **27** ② **28** ⑤ **29** ⑤ **30** ⑤

---

01 delete는 '삭제하다'라는 뜻을 가진 동사이다. 따라서 영영 풀이의 빈칸에 들어갈 말로 가장 적절한 것은 ① remove(제거하다)이다.

02 위에서부터 순서대로, suspect(용의자), detective(탐정), clue(단서), accident(사건, 사고)를 가리키는 영영 풀이이다.

03 ① 'TV나 컴퓨터를 켜기 위해 누를 수 있는 작고 동그란 것'이라는 영영 풀이가 가리키는 것은 button이다.

04 '~하기 위해서'란 의미로 '목적'을 나타내는 to부정사의 부사적 용법을 이용해 ⑤ 'Fold a piece of paper in half to make a triangle.'이라고 영작할 수 있다.

05 ① was found by → was found / ③ hear → heard / ④ must is washed → must be washed / ⑤ was → were로 고쳐야 어법상 적절한 문장이 된다.

06 상대방에게 무언가를 하는 방법을 물을 때, '~하는 방법'이라는 의미의 'how to+동사원형' 구문을 사용하여 'Can you explain[tell] me how to+동사원형 ~?'이라고 물어볼 수 있다.

07 ⓐ is → are / ⓓ grew → grown / ⓕ by she → by her / ⓖ beat → beaten / ⓗ cancel → canceled로 고쳐야 어법상 적절한 문장이 된다.

08 ② can being seen → can be seen / ④ send → sent로 고쳐야 어법상 적절한 문장이 된다.

09 수동태 문장을 만들 때는 본래의 동사를 be+p.p(과거분사형)로 고치는 것 뿐만 아니라 시제를 본래 문장과 일치시켜 표현해야 한다. 또한 본래 문장에서 주어 자리에 있던 행위의 주체는 by를 붙여 문장 뒤에 쓴다. 또한 조동사가 포함된 수동태는 「조동사+be+과거분사」의 형태로 나타내며, 수동의 의미에 조동사의 의미를 더해 해석한다.

10 수동태 문장을 만들 때는 본래의 동사를 be+p.p(과거분사형)로 고치는 것 뿐만 아니라 시제를 본래 문장과 일치시켜 표현해야 한다. 또한 본래 문장에서 주어 자리에 있던 행위의 주체는 by를 붙여 문장 뒤에 쓴다.

11 (A) 주어가 Bright stars이므로 동사는 수동형인 be seen이 적절하다.
(B) 영화가 오후 9시에 공원에서 상영된다는 것을 들었다는 내용이고 종속절의 주어가 a movie이므로 동사는 수동형인 will be shown이 적절하다.
(C) 주어가 delicious food이므로 동사는 수동형인 can be bought가 적절하다.

12 위 대화에 따르면, 종이여우를 만드는 첫 번째 단계는 종이를 반으로 접어 삼각형을 만드는 것('First, fold a paper in half to make a triangle.')이다.

13 "Kelly, 수수께끼 낼게. 일주일에 두 번, 일 년에 한 번, 하루에는 한 번도 볼 수 없는 건 뭘까?"라는 A의 질문에 대해 "난 정말 수수께끼를 좋아해."라는 B의 대답은 흐름상 자연스럽지 않다.

14 '우선, 농부가 여우 한 마리와 오리 한 마리, 콩 한 자루를 산다.'라는 문장이 들어가기에 가장 적절한 곳은 그런 다음 농부가 강을 건너야 한다고 말하고 있는 곳 앞인 (A)이다.

15 위 대화에 따르면, 준수는 해결 방안으로 오리를 여우보다 먼저 강 건너로 옮기라고 말하고 있다. 또한 Emily는 농부가 없으면 여우가 오리를 먹을 것이므로 한 곳에 남겨둬선 안 된다고 말했다.

16 상대방에게 무언가를 하는 방법을 물을 때, '~하는 방법'이라는 의미의 'how to+동사원형' 구문을 사용하여 'Can you explain[tell] me how to+동사원형 ~?'이라고 물어볼 수 있다.

17 A가 민수에게 학생 탐정에 대한 TV쇼를 알고 있는지 물어보자, 민수가 그 쇼를 좋아한다고 말하면서 이번 주에는 시청하지 못했는데 무슨 내용이었냐고 물어본다(ⓓ). A는 학교의 모든 자전거가 사라진 내용이었다고 설명하고(ⓐ), 민수는 그래서 학생 탐정이 어떻게 했냐고 질문한다(ⓒ). A는 학생 탐정이 학교 주위를 살펴보고 용의자 몇 명을 만나 질문을 했다고 한다. 그리고 마침내 도둑을 찾아냈다고 말한다(ⓔ). 이에 민수가 나중에 볼 거라고 말하면서 도둑이 누군지 얘기하지 말라고(ⓑ) 말하는 순서로 이어지는 것이 흐름상 가장 자연스럽다.

18 위 글에서는 탈출의 탑에 온 걸 환영한다고 말하면서 탈출하기 위해서는 수수께끼를 풀어야 하며 셜록 홈즈처럼 생각해서 수수께끼의 단서를 찾으라고 말하고 있다.

19 (A)like는 '~처럼'이라는 뜻의 전치사로 사용되었다. ①like는 '좋아하다'라는 뜻의 동사로 사용되었다.

20 ⓒ was questioned → were questioned로 고쳐야 어법상 적절한 문장이 된다.

21 수동태는 '주어+be동사+동사의 과거분사+by+행위자'의 형식

을 가지며 '...에 의해 ~되다[당하다]'라는 의미로 주어가 동사가 나타내는 행위를 당하거나 행동의 영향을 받는 것을 나타낸다. 수동태 문장의 주어 자리에는 능동태 문장의 목적어가 오고, by 다음에는 능동태 문장의 주어를 쓴다.

22 위 글에 따르면, Mr. Doodle은 교통 사고를 당했지만 심각하게 다치지는 않았다고('Luckily, he wasn't badly hurt, but he didn't see the driver.') 언급되어 있다.

23 위 글에 따르면, C씨가 Mr. Doodle을 차로 치었는데, 자동차 사고가 난 것은 일요일 오후인데 C씨는 사고 당시 아침 식사를 만들고 있다고 대답했기 때문이다.

24 위 글에서는 ② Where was Mr. B at the time of accident?(B씨는 사고 당시 어디에 있었는가?)에 대해서는 언급된 바 없다.

25 위 글에 따르면, 자동차 사고가 난 것은 일요일 오후인데 C씨는 사고 당시 아침 식사를 만들고 있다고 대답했기 때문에 가장 의심스러운 용의자이다.

26 (A) 비교급을 강조할 때는 비교급 앞에 much, still, even, far, a lot 등의 부사(구)를 쓰며 '(...보다) 훨씬 더 ~ 한'이라는 의미를 갖는다. very는 원급의 형용사(또는 부사)를 수식하며, 비교급은 수식하지 않는다.
(B) Jay가 놀랐다는 의미이므로 surprising(놀라게 하는)이 아니라 surprised(놀란)가 적절하다.

27 Jay가 좋아하는 가게의 이벤트에 당첨되었다는 이메일을 받고 놀랐지만 그 이벤트가 사실이 아니라고 생각해서 이메일을 지웠다고 설명하고 있다. 따라서 빈칸에 들어갈 말로 가장 적절한 것은 ② However(그러나)이다.

28 위 글에 따르면, Jay가 좋아하는 가게의 이벤트에 당첨되었다는 이메일을 받고 놀랐지만 그 이벤트가 사실이 아니라고 생각해서 이메일을 지웠다고 설명하고 있다.

29 (나)that은 두 문장을 연결하는 접속사로 사용되었다. ⑤that은 목적격 관계대명사로 사용되었다.

30 Jay가 좋아하는 가게의 이벤트에 당첨되었다는 이메일을 받고 놀랐지만 그 이벤트가 사실이 아니라고 생각한 이유는 11월은 30일까지 있기 때문이다.

Lesson 5 (중간)

01 ③ **02** ④ **03** ④ **04** ③ **05** ①
06 (A) (These houses) were built by (Jake).
(B) (The song) is sung by (the boy).
07 (1) A lot of flies can be seen around the food in summer.
(2) A speech will be given by the president next week.

---

08 ③
09 The second room is much[even, far] harder to escape than the first one.
10 ① **11** (1) was written by (2) will be washed by
12 ② **13** ④ **14** ⑤ **15** ⑤ **16** ② **17** ③
18 (A) the man is short so he can't reach the top button
19 ⑤ **20** 그는 그의 우산으로 그것을 누를 수 있다
21 ⑤ **22** ⑤ **23** November has (only) 30 days
24 ② **25** ③ **26** ③ **27** ⑤ **28** ①, ②
29 (1) Ms. C (2) afternoon (3) she was making breakfast
30 ⑤

01 ① thief: 도둑
② detective: 탐정
④ straight: 똑바로; 솔직하게
⑤ escape: 탈출하다

02 hide의 수동형은 be hidden이다.

03 '컴퓨터로 작성된 것 또는 저장된 것을 제거하다'라는 영영 풀이가 가리키는 것은 ④ delete(삭제하다)이다.

04 빈칸에 공통으로 들어갈 단어는 to부정사인 to가 적절하다.

05 ① build → built로 고쳐야 어법상 적절한 문장이 된다.

06 수동태 문장을 만들 때는 본래의 동사를 be+p.p(과거분사형)로 고치는 것 뿐만 아니라 시제를 본래 문장과 일치시켜 표현해야 한다. 또한 본래 문장에서 주어 자리에 있던 행위의 주체는 by를 붙여 문장 뒤에 쓴다.

07 조동사가 포함된 수동태는 「조동사+be+과거분사」의 형태로 나타내며, 수동의 의미에 조동사의 의미를 더해 해석한다. 조동사가 포함된 수동태의 부정은 조동사 뒤에 not을 써서 나타낸다.

08 ① sang → sung / ② will been bought → will be bought / ④ is lead → is led / ⑤ took → taken으로 고쳐야 어법상 적절한 문장이 된다.

09 비교급을 강조할 때는 비교급 앞에 much, still, even, far, a lot 등의 부사를 쓰며 '(...보다) 훨씬 더 ~ 한'이라는 의미를 갖는다. very는 원급의 형용사(또는 부사)를 수식하며, 비교급은 수식하지 않는다.

10 ⓒ will send → will be sent / ⓔ was planted → planted / ⓕ was invited → invited로 고쳐야 어법상 적절한 문장이 된다.

11 수동태 문장을 만들 때는 본래의 동사를 be+p.p(과거분사형)로 고치는 것 뿐만 아니라 시제를 본래 문장과 일치시켜 표현해야 한다. 또한 본래 문장에서 주어 자리에 있던 행위의 주체는 by를 붙여 문장 뒤에 쓴다. 조동사가 포함된 수동태는 「조동사+be+과거분사」의 형태로 쓴다.

12 위 대화에서 B는 Kelly에게 수수께끼를 내고 있다. 따라서 빈칸 (가)에 들어갈 말로 가장 적절한 것은 ② riddle(수수께끼)이다.

13 B가 Kelly에게 수수께끼를 냈고, Kelly가 이해하지 못하자 자세하게 설명해주고 있다. 따라서 빈칸 (A)에 들어갈 말로 가장 적절한 것은 ④ Can you explain why?(왜인지 설명해 주겠니?)이다.

14 위 대화에서 G는 B에게 게임을 같이 하자고 말하면서 게임에 대해서 설명하고 있다. 따라서 빈칸에 들어갈 말로 가장 적절한 것은 ⑤ Can you explain how to use these buttons?(이 버튼을 어떻게 사용하는지 설명해 주겠니?)이다.

15 위 대화에 따르면, G는 민수에게 둘 다 좋아하는 학생 탐정이 나오는 TV쇼에 대해서 이야기하고 있다. 민수는 그 TV쇼를 이번 주에 시청하지 않았기 때문에 나중에 볼 것이라고("I'll watch it later.") 말하고 있다.

16 위 글에 따르면, 남자가 키가 작기 때문에 엘레베이터에 사람이 없거나 우산이 없으면 자신의 집인 12층의 버튼을 누를 수 없었고, 반대로 엘레베이터에 사람이 있으면 버튼을 눌러달라고 부탁하거나 우산이 있으면 12층에 갈 수 있다는 내용으로 해석할 수 있다.

17 위 글은 남자가 키가 작기 때문에 엘레베이터에 사람이 없거나 우산이 없으면 자신의 집인 12층의 버튼을 누를 수 없었고, 반대로 엘레베이터에 사람이 있으면 버튼을 눌러달라고 부탁하거나 비가 와서 우산이 있으면 12층에 갈 수 있다는 내용의 글이다. 따라서 제목으로 가장 적절한 것은 ③ The man who was too short이다.

18 그 남자가 키가 작아서 12층 버튼을 누를 수 없었다는 문장으로 영작할 수 있다. 인과 관계를 나타내는 'so+형용사/부사+that+주어+동사' 구문을 쓸 수 있다.

19 (A) 비가 오거나 엘레베이터에 사람이 있으면 12층에 가지만, 엘레베이터에 사람이 없거나 비가 오지 않는 날이면 10층에 간다는 내용이다. 따라서 However(그러나)가 적절하다.
(B) 남자가 키가 작아서 12층 버튼을 누를 수 없지만 엘레베이터 안에 사람이 있거나 비가 와서 우산이 있으면 사람에게 부탁하거나 우산을 이용해 버튼을 누를 수 있었다는 애용이다. 따라서 But(그러나)이 문맥상 자연스럽다.

20 with: ~으로, ~을 가지고

21 '그러나 Jay는 그 이벤트가 진짜라고 생각하지 않고 이메일을 삭제했다.'라는 문장이 들어가기에 가장 적절한 곳은 이메일을 읽고 난 후인 (E)이다.

22 ⓔ의 'can't wait to'는 "빨리 ~하고 싶다"라는 뜻으로 어떤 일에 대한 기대감을 나타내는 표현이다.

23 Jay가 좋아하는 가게의 이벤트에 당첨되었다는 이메일을 받고 놀랐지만 그 이벤트가 사실이 아니라고 생각한 이유는 11월은 30일까지 있기 때문이다.

24 위 글에 따르면, Jay는 좋아하는 옷가게의 이벤트에 당첨되어 특별한 상품을 받을 수 있다는 이메일을 받았다.

25 '누가 Doodle 씨를 쳤는가?'라는 문장이 들어가기에 가장 적절한 곳은 세 명의 용의자를 심문해서 각각의 알리바이를 들은 후인 (C)이다.

26 ⓒ answered → questioned로 고쳐야 문맥상 적절한 문장이 된다.

27 위 글에서 누가 Mr. Doodle을 자동차로 쳤는지 용의자를 알아내려고 하고 있고, 세 명의 용의자의 알리바이에 대해서 이야기하면서 그것을 적어보라고 말하고 있다. 따라서 밑줄 친 (가)it이 가리키는 것은 ⑤ the answer(정답)이다.

28 위 글에 따르면, Mr. Doodle의 자동차 사고가 난 것은 일요일 오후였으며, 경찰은 세 명의 용의자를 심문했다.

29 위 글에 따르면, 자동차 사고가 난 것은 일요일 오후인데, 심문 받을 때 C씨는 사고 당시 아침 식사를 만들고 있다고 대답했기 때문에 가장 의심스러운 용의자이다.

30 위 글에 따르면, Mr. Doodle의 자동차 사고가 난 것은 일요일 오후이고 용의자 중 한 명인 B씨는 그 당시 개를 산책시키는 중이었다고 대답했다.

Lesson 6 (중간)

01 ④ **02** ② **03** ② **04** as **05** is as cheap as the red hat
06 ⑤ **07** ② **08** ③, ④
09 The question was so hard that I couldn't solve it.
10 (A) The dog is not as heavy as the cat.
(B) Kevin is not as slow as a turtle.
11 ④ **12** dance to show their love to female birds **13** ①
14 ③ **15** ③ **16** I'm sure we'll have a lot of fun. **17** ①
18 (1) In Korea, Buchaechum is so popular that people can see it in many traditional festivals.
(2) 한국에서 부채춤은 아주 인기 있어서 사람들은 그것을 많은 전통 축제에서 볼 수 있다.
19 ② **20** ③ **21** ②, ⑤ **22** ⑤ **23** ⑤
24 Let's take a look at different kinds of dance around the world.
25 ③ **26** ③ **27** ① **28** ⑤ **29** ⑤ **30** ②

01 빈칸에 공통으로 들어갈 말로 가장 적절한 것은 ④ through(~을 통해)이다.

02 '그 자동차의 엔진은 너무 강력해서 언덕도 쉽게 올라간다.'라는 의미의 문장이다. 따라서 빈칸에 들어가기에 적절한 단어는 powerful(강력한)이다.

03 위에서부터 순서대로, allow(~가 …하게 허락하다), colorful (형형색색의), busy(바쁜), detective(탐정), attention(주목, 주의)이 들어가는 것이 문맥상 가장 자연스럽다.

04 '~만큼 …한'이라는 동등 비교 표현은 'as (형용사/부사) as ~'의 형태로 쓸 수 있다. 이때 형용사와 부사는 모두 원급으로 쓰는 것이 어법상 적절하다.

05 '~만큼 …한'이라는 동등 비교 표현은 'as+형용사/부사+as ~'의 형태로 쓸 수 있다. 이때 형용사와 부사는 모두 원급으로 쓰는 것이 어법상 적절하다.

06 ① that I can't drink → that I can't drink it / ② can't → couldn't / ③ such big shirt → such a big shirt / ④ so that stupid → so stupid that으로 고쳐야 어법상 적절한 문장이 된다.

07 준호와 아버지의 키가 모두 172cm로 동일하다. 따라서 ② Junho is as tall as his father.(준호는 아버지만큼 키가 크다.) 라고 쓸 수 있다.

08 ① cleverer → clever / ② they look → they look like / ⑤ people can see → people can see it으로 고쳐야 어법상 적절한 문장이 된다.

09 'so+형용사/부사+that+주어+동사' 구문은 '너무 ~해서 …하다' 라는 의미로 인과 관계를 나타낸다.

10 비교 대상의 동등함을 나타내는 원급 비교는 형용사나 부사의 기본형과 함께 as를 이용해 표현할 수 있다. 'as+형용사/부사+as ~'의 형태로 쓴다.

11 위 대화에서 두 화자는 감상하고 있는 그림에 대해서 의견을 나누고 있다. 따라서 빈칸에 들어갈 말로 알맞지 않은 것은 ④ In the end(마침내)이다.

12 위 대화에 따르면, B는 수컷 새들이 왜 춤을 추는지 물어보았고 G는 "They dance to show their love to female birds."라고 대답했다.

13 위 대화에서는 새 또는 벌과 같은 춤을 추는 동물들에 대해서 이야기를 나누고 있다.

14 "쿠키 만드는 법을 설명해 주실 수 있나요?"라는 A의 질문에 대해 "물론이지, 난 고양이가 그 쿠키를 먹어버렸다고 생각해."라는 B의 대답은 흐름상 자연스럽지 않다.

15 위 대화에서는 학교 축제의 댄스 대회에서 무엇을 선보일지에 대해서 이야기하고 있다. 미나는 부채춤을 언급하면서 부채춤이 배우기 쉽고 아름답다고 말하고 있다.

16 "I'm sure (that) 주어+동사 ~."는 "난 ~일 거라고 확신해."라는 뜻으로 어떤 일에 대한 확신을 나타내는 표현이다.

17 '많은 사람들의 호감을 받는'이라는 영영 풀이가 가리키는 것은 ① popular(인기가 많은)이다.

18 '너무 ...해서 ~하다'라는 의미의 문장은 'so+형용사[부사]+that +주어+동사'의 형태로 쓸 수 있다.

19 위 글에서는 중국에서 새해에 추는 용 춤에 대해서 설명하고 있다. 따라서 (B)Different cultures have many difference events for New Year's day.는 흐름상 자연스럽지 않다.

20 ⓒ rise → raise로 고쳐야 어법상 적절한 문장이 된다.

21 위 글에 따르면, 용 춤은 중국의 춤이다(The dragon dance is an important part of the New Year Festival in China). 또한 용 춤의 댄서들은 금색, 빨간색, 노란색, 초록색의 의상을 입는다고 (The costume is colored gold, red, yellow and green.) 언급되어 있다. 용 춤의 댄서들은 의상 위에서가 아니라 아래에 서 있으면서 춤을 춘다고('Dancers stand under the dragon costume and hold it up high.') 언급되어 있다.

22 ⓐ happy → happiness / ⓑ though → through / ⓒ which → who / ⓓ Interesting → Interestingly로 고쳐야 어법상 적절한 문장이 된다.

23 위 글에서는 ⑤ What kinds of clothing do Kathakali dancers wear?(Kathakali 댄서들은 어떤 옷을 입는가?)에 대해서는 언급된 바 없다.

24 take a look at: ~를 살펴보다

25 Haka 댄서들이 야생 동물만큼 무섭게 보였다는 내용이므로 원급 비교 표현인 'as+형용사/부사+as ~'를 이용해 ③ 'The dancers looked as scary as wild animals'라고 쓸 수 있다.

26 위 글에 따르면, 마오리 족의 춤인 haka는 무서운 얼굴로 추는 춤으로 전투 전에 추었던 춤이며 적에게 자신들의 힘을 보여주기 위해 추었다고 언급되어 있다. 따라서 빈칸에는 ③ strength(힘)가 적절하다.

27 (B) 대명사 They는 앞서 언급된 복수명사인 the Maori를 가리킨다.
(C) 대명사 it은 앞서 언급된 단수 명사인 Buchaechum을 가리킨다.

28 원급 비교 표현인 'as+형용사/부사+as ~'를 이용해 'as beautiful as flowers or flying birds'라고 쓸 수 있다.

29 두 번째 문단에 'In Korea, Buchaechum is so popular that people can see it in many traditional festivals.(한국에서 부채춤은 너무 인기가 많아서 사람들은 많은 전통 축제에서 그것을 볼 수 있다.)'라고 언급되어 있다.

30 위 글에 따르면, 마오리족 사람들은 이야기를 전달하는 것이 아니라 자신의 힘을 적에게 보여주기 위해 춤을 춘다고 언급되어 있다.

Lesson 6 (중간) 2회

---

01 ③ **02** ③ **03** ③ **04** not as[so] tall as **05** ①

06 (A) She is so smart that she can solve the puzzles.
  (B) I was so happy that I sang (a song) all day.

07 ①

08 (1) She is bright enough to solve all the puzzles.
  (2) He is too young to read the book.

09 It was raining so heavily that the school cancelled the field trip.

10 he is as smart as an owl **11** ③ **12** ⑤ **13** ④ **14** ②

15 ④ **16** ⑤ **17** ③ **18** ③ **19** ④ **20** ③ **21** ④ **22** ⑤

23 ③ **24** only men are allowed to dance

25 ① **26** ① **27** ⑤ **28** ② **29** ③

30 Their movements look as beautiful as flowers or flying birds.

---

01 위에서부터 순서대로, field(들판), gracefully(우아하게), originally(원래), totally(완전히)가 들어가는 것이 문맥상 가장 자연스럽다.

02 originally: 원래, 본래 brave: 용감한
  express: 표현하다 allow: ~를 허용하다

03 (B) agree of → agree with / (D) what → where / (E) doing → having으로 고쳐야 어법상 또는 문맥상 적절한 문장이 된다.

04 '~만큼 …한'이라는 동등 비교 표현은 'as+형용사/부사+as ~'의 형태로 쓸 수 있다. 이때 형용사와 부사는 모두 원급으로 쓰는 것이 어법상 적절하다.

05 ② that keeps yelling → that they kept yelling / ③ happily → happy / ④ that cry so much → that she cried so much / ⑤ wisely → wise로 고쳐야 어법상 적절한 문장이 된다.

06 'so+형용사/부사+that+주어+동사' 구문은 '너무 ~해서 …하다'라는 의미로 인과 관계를 나타낸다.

07 ① lighter → light로 고쳐야 어법상 적절한 문장이 된다.

08 (1) '너무 ~해서 …하다'라는 의미의 표현 'so+형용사/부사+that+주어+동사' 구문은 '~할 만큼 충분히 …한'이라는 뜻의 '형용사/부사+enough to+동사원형' 구문으로 바꿔 쓸 수 있다.
  (2) 'so ~ that 주어+can't(couldn't)' 구문은 '너무 ~해서 … 할 수 없다'라는 의미로 'too ~ to+동사원형' 구문으로 바꿔 쓸 수 있다.

09 'so+형용사/부사+that+주어+동사' 구문은 '너무 ~해서 …하다'라는 의미로 인과 관계를 나타낸다.

10 '~만큼 …한'이라는 동등 비교 표현은 'as+형용사/부사+as ~'의

형태로 쓸 수 있다. 이때 형용사와 부사는 모두 원급으로 쓰는 것이 어법상 적절하다.

11 "난 다음주 주말에 우리 동네의 문화 행사에 갈 거야. 같이 갈래?"라는 A의 질문에 대해 "그거 아니? 앞으로도 열심히 해."라는 B의 대답은 흐름상 자연스럽지 않다.

12 조동사가 포함된 수동태 문장은 '조동사+be+과거분사(p.p)'의 순서대로 쓴다.

13 부채춤을 배우는 것을 도와주기로 한 것은 준수가 아니라 Mina이다("Mina is good at traditional dances. Can you help us, Mina?").

14 "그 후에, 그녀는 많은 어려움을 겪었어."라는 문장이 들어가기에 가장 적절한 곳은 세 살 때 부모님을 잃었지만 댄서의 꿈을 포기하지 않았다고 말하고 있는 곳인 (B)이다.

15 위 대화에 따르면, Michaela DePrince는 여러 어려움에도 불구하고 댄서의 꿈을 포기하지 않았다고("But she never gave up on her dream of becoming a dancer.") 언급되어 있다.

16 위 대화에 따르면, 민수는 그림 속의 사람들이 즐거워 보인다고("The people look like they're having fun.") 말하고 있다.

17 위 대화에서 화자들은 그림에 대해서 어떻게 생각하는지 묻고 대답하면서 대화하고 있다. 따라서 빈칸에는 ③ what do you think about(~에 대해서 어떻게 생각하니?)가 들어가는 것이 적절하다.

18 위 글에서는 ③ Why did dancers in Adumu jump high and cheer with loud noises?(왜 Adumu의 댄서들은 높이 뛰고 시끄러운 소리로 응원하는가?)에 대해서는 언급된 바 없다.

19 '악역을 연기하는 사람들은 검은색 화장을 한다.'라는 문장이 들어가기에 가장 적절한 곳은 선한 역할의 사람들은 초록색으로 화장을 한다는 곳 뒤인 (D)이다.

20 ⓒ paints → paint로 고쳐야 어법상 적절한 문장이 된다.

21 (가) 사람들이 춤을 추는 이유에 대해서 이야기하고 있으므로 빈칸에는 Why가 적절하다.
  (나) Kathakali 댄서들은 신체의 움직임을 통해서 이야기를 전달한다고 말하고 있다. 따라서 through가 적절하다.
  (다) Kathakali 댄서들이 하는 이야기가 선과 악에 대한 이야기라고 설명하고 있다. 따라서 about이 적절하다.

22 위 글에 따르면, 악역을 연기하는 Kathakali 댄서들은 검은색 화장을 한다고('Dancers who are playing good characters paint their faces green. Those who are playing evil characters wear black make-up.') 언급되어 있다.

23 선행사가 사람인 Those이므로 (C)에는 주격 관계대명사 who가 적절하다.

24 allow A to B: A가 B하도록 허용하다

25 위 글의 초반에 'The dancers tell stories through their body movements.(댄서들은 그들의 신체의 움직임을 통해 이야기를

말해 준다)'라고 언급되어 있다.

26 ⓐ performing → performed / ⓑ scarily → scary / ⓒ traditionally → traditional / ⓔ painting → painted / ⓕ graceful → gracefully로 고쳐야 어법상 적절한 문장이 된다.

27 (가): haka dancers　　　(나): the Maori
　　 (다): rugby players'　　(라): The dancers

28 위 글에서는 뉴질랜드와 한국의 전통 춤에 대해서 소개하고 있다. 따라서 제목으로 가장 적절한 것은 ② Dances of New Zealand and Korea(뉴질랜드와 한국의 춤들)이다.

29 위 글에 따르면, 럭비 선수들이 시합 전에 다른 팀의 선수들에게 자신들의 강함을 보여주기 위해 haka를 춘다고('Nowadays, in New Zealand, rugby players usually perform a haka before a game to show their strength to the other team.') 언급되어 있다.

30 비교 대상의 동등함을 나타내는 원급 비교는 형용사나 부사의 기본형과 함께 as를 이용해 표현할 수 있다. 형태는 'as+형용사/부사 +as ~'의 형태로 쓸 수 있다.

Lesson 7 (기말)

01 ③	**02** ④	**03** ④	**04** ⑤	**05** ⑤	**06** ④	**07** ①	**08** ③
09 ③	**10** ③	**11** ⑤	**12** ①	**13** ①	**14** ④	**15** ⑤	**16** ②
17 ②	**18** ⑤	**19** ⑤	**20** ⑤	**21** ④	**22** ②	**23** ⑤	**24** ④
25 ⑤	**26** ⑤	**27** ①	**28** ④	**29** rose into the glass		**30** ③	

01 ③ put on과 wear는 모두 '입다'라는 뜻을 가진 표현으로 유의어 관계이다. 나머지 단어들은 모두 반의어 관계에 있는 단어들이다.

02 '크기나 수 또는 양이 커지거나 어떤 것을 크게 만들다'라는 영영 풀이가 가리키는 것은 ④ expand(확장시키다, 확대하다)이다.

03 위 글의 안전 규칙에서는 선생님의 말씀을 주의깊게 듣고 실험 후에는 손을 깨끗이 씻어야 한다고 말하고 있다. 따라서 빈칸에는 ④ Science(과학)가 들어가는 것이 적절하다.

04 <보기>의 It은 to부정사가 이끄는 구문을 대신하는 가주어이다. ①~④는 모두 비인칭 주어 It이다.

05 주어진 우리말에 따라 단어를 배열하면, 'I can't wait to see your clock.'이 된다.

06 ① for → of / ② of → for / ③ of → for / ⑤ of → for로 고쳐야 어법상 적절한 문장이 된다.

07 ② Why flying fish jump → Why do flying fish jump / ③ Why was Sujin missed → Why did Sujin miss / ④ How come do they work → How come they work / ⑤ broke → break로 고쳐야 어법상 적절한 문장이 된다.

08 위 그림에 따르면, 병을 차갑게 한 다음 동전을 병의 입구에 올려놓

고 병을 따뜻하게 하면 병 입구의 동전이 올라갔다 내려갔다 하는 모습을 볼 수 있다. 따라서 각각 (A) cool, (B) Put, (C) Hold가 들어가는 것이 적절하다.

09 "어떤 음식을 먹고 싶니?"라는 A의 질문에 대해 "난 식당에서 먹고 싶어."라는 B의 대답은 흐름상 자연스럽지 않다.

10 Brian의 말에 대한 Mina의 대답이 "난 마술 수업에 등록했어. 거기서 빨리 마술 속임수들을 배우고 싶어."였다. 따라서 빈칸에 들어갈 Brian의 말로 가장 적절한 것은 ③ Which class did you sign up for?(넌 어느 수업에 등록했니?)이다.

11 위 글에서는 딸기 아이스크림을 만드는 방법에 대해서 설명하고 있다. 따라서 문맥상 빈칸에 들어갈 말로 가장 적절한 것은 ⑤ mix everything together and put it in the freezer(모두 섞어서 냉동고에 넣어라)이다.

12 위 대화에 따르면 한동안 비가 내리지 않고 있고 건기가 너무 길다고 말하고 있다. 따라서 빈칸에 들어갈 말로 가장 적절한 것은 ① worried(걱정하는)이다.

13 ⓐ는 비가 지금까지 오랫동안 오지 않았다는 내용이므로 현재완료 시제인 hasn't rained가 적절하다.

14 위 글에서는 ④ What do farmers do during dry season?(농부들은 건기 동안에 무슨 일을 하는가?)에 대해서는 언급된 바 없다.

15 '달걀이 물에 뜨면, 그것은 신선하지 않은 것이다.'라는 문장이 들어가기에 가장 적절한 곳은 물에 잠기는 달걀은 신선한 것이라고 말한 곳 뒤인 (C)이다.

16 위 글에 따르면, 달걀이 물에 뜬다면 달걀 안에 가스가 생겨서 신선하지 않기 때문이다.

17 ⓐIt은 to see magic tricks를 대신하는 가주어이다.

18 위 글에 따르면, 마술 속임수를 선보이는 것은 교내 마술 동아리의 회원인 Ken이라고 언급되어 있다.

19 위 글에서 Jina는 마술 동아리 회원인 Ken이 마술을 선보일 것이라고 소개하고 있다.

20 위 글에서는 Death Valley의 바위들이 어떻게 움직일 수 있는지에 대해서 이야기하고 있다. 따라서 제목으로 가장 적절한 것은 ⑤ The Moving Rocks in Death Valley(Death Valley의 움직이는 바위들)이다.

21 (D)it's necessary to use cups that you can see through는 it's necessary to use cups that you cannot see through로 고치는 것이 문맥상 자연스럽다.

22 ⓐit은 to부정사 구문을 대신하는 가주어로 사용되었다. 따라서 이와 쓰임이 같은 것은 ② '아침 식사를 하는 것은 중요하지 않니?'이다.

23 위 글에서는 Ken은 물을 사라지게 하는 마술을 선보이고 속임수에 대해서 설명하고 있다. 따라서 제목으로 가장 적절한 것은 ⑤이

다.

24 위 글에서는 Ken은 물을 사라지게 하는 마술을 선보이고 그 마술이 어떻게 가능한지에 대해서 설명하고 있다.

25 (가)light는 '불을 피우다'라는 뜻으로 사용되었다. 따라서 이와 쓰임이 같은 것은 ⑤ '난 불을 피우려고 노력했지만 나무가 축축했다.'이다.

26 "How come ~?"은 "어째서 ~인 거니?"라는 뜻으로 어떤 상황에 대한 정황을 알고 싶을 때 쓸 수 있는 표현이다. "What is the reason ~?" 또는 "Why ~?"로 바꿔 쓸 수 있다.

27 (A) it은 앞서 언급된 a dish를 가리킨다.
(B) it은 앞서 언급된 접시 속의 the water를 가리킨다.

28 (C) 공기가 뜨거워지면 팽창해서 높은 압력을 만든다고 했으므로 공기가 차가워지면 더 낮은 압력(lower pressure)을 만든다는 내용이 적절하다.
(D) 공기가 차가워지면 공기의 압력은 떨어진다(dropped).
(E) 유리병 안의 압력이 높아졌다 낮아지는 동안 바깥의 압력은 높은 상태(higher pressure)여서 유리병 안으로 물을 밀어낸다고 설명하고 있다.

29 위 글에 따르면, Ken이 "Abracadabra!"라고 외치자 물이 위로 올라갔다고("Look at the water! How come it rose into the glass?") 언급되어 있다.

30 위 글에서 Ken은 'Air expands when it gets hot and creates higher pressure.(공기가 뜨거워지면 팽창해서 더 높은 압력을 만든다.)'라고 설명하고 있다.

Lesson 7 (기말)

01 ⑤   02 ⑤   03 ④   04 ⑤   05 ②   06 ①

07 (1) It is fun to learn a K-pop dance.
(2) It is difficult to run 100 meters in 15 seconds.
(3) It is boring to stay home all day.

08 ③   09 ③   10 ②   11 ②   12 ②   13 ③   14 ①, ③
15 ①   16 ③

17 (A) It's more exciting for you to find out the secrets.
(B) How come it rose into the glass?

18 ④   19 ③

20 (1) How come he didn't go to school today?
(2) How come they have big ears?

21 ④   22 ⑤   23 ②   24 ③   25 ①   26 ②   27 ④

28 rose into the glass

29 is always exciting to see magic tricks   30 ②

01 give it a try: ~를 시도하다

02 위에서부터 순서대로, pressure(압력), absorb(흡수하다), experiment(실험), flame(불꽃)이 들어가는 것이 문맥상 가장 자연스럽다.

03 '점점 작아지거나 좁아지다'라는 영영 풀이가 가리키는 것은 ④ contract(줄어들다, 수축하다)이다.

04 위 문장에는 가주어 It이 사용되었으므로 빈칸에는 to부정사 구문이 들어가는 것이 적절하다.

05 ②to drink는 to부정사의 형용사적 용법으로 쓰여서 something을 수식한다. 나머지는 모두 to부정사의 명사적 용법으로 사용되었다.

06 ① for → of로 고쳐야 어법상 적절한 문장이 된다.

07 문장의 주어로 쓰인 to부정사가 수식어로 인해 길어진 경우, 보통 to부정사를 뒤로 보내고 대신 주어 자리에 가주어 it을 둔다. 이때 쓰인 it은 가주어이므로 구체적인 뜻이 없으며, '...하는 것은 ~하다'로 해석한다.

08 "어느 마술 속임수를 배워보고 싶니?"라는 A의 질문에 대해 "나는 마술 수업에 등록했어요."라는 B의 대답은 흐름상 자연스럽지 않다.

09 ⓐ와 ⓔ에는 why, ⓑ와 ⓒ에는 Which, ⓓ에는 if가 들어가는 것이 문맥상 자연스럽다.

10 위 대화에 따르면, 상한 계란을 골라내고 있는 사람은 Nojun이가 아니라 Kyuwon이다.

11 ⓑlast는 '지속하다', '지속되다'라는 의미의 동사로 사용되었다.

12 (A) them은 앞서 언급된 the farmers를 가리킨다.
(B) that은 앞서 언급된 장영실이 발명하려고 하는 the clock를 가리킨다.

13 위 대화에 따르면, 농부를 위한 특별한 물건을 발명하려고 하는 것은 세종대왕이 아니라 장영실이다.

14 위 대화에 따르면, 농부들이 비가 오지 않아 건기가 길어져서 걱정을 하고 있다. 이에 장영실이 농부들이 건기에 대비할 수 있는 특별한 시계를 만들려고 하고 있다.

15 "I can't wait to ~"는 "빨리 ~하고 싶다"라는 뜻으로 어떤 일에 대한 기대감을 나타내는 표현이다.

16 위 대화에 따르면, 위 실험의 과정에서 무게는 총 두 번 재야 한다.

17 (A) 문장의 주어로 쓰인 to부정사가 수식어로 인해 길어진 경우, 보통 to부정사를 뒤로 보내고 대신 주어 자리에 가주어 it을 둔다. to부정사의 의미상 주어는 'for+목적격'으로 쓴다.
(B) "How come ~?"은 "어째서 ~인 거니?"라는 뜻으로 어떤 상황에 대한 정황을 알고 싶을 때 쓸 수 있는 표현이다. "What is the reason ~?" 또는 "Why ~?"로 바꿔 쓸 수 있다.

18 (가)to see는 to부정사의 명사적 용법으로 사용되었다. ④to prevent sunburn(햇빛에 의한 화상을 예방하기 위해)은 부사적 용법으로 사용되었다.

19 "I can't wait to ~"는 "빨리 ~하고 싶다"라는 뜻으로 어떤 일에 대한 기대감을 나타내는 표현이다.

20 "How come ~?"은 "어째서 ~인 거니?"라는 뜻으로 어떤 상황에 대한 정황을 알고 싶을 때 쓸 수 있는 표현이다. "What is the reason ~?" 또는 "Why ~?"로 바꿔 쓸 수 있다.

21 '그러면, 젤리는 바닥에 달라붙는다.'라는 문장이 들어가기에 가장 적절한 곳은 특별한 재료를 넣어 물을 흡수해 젤리로 변한다고 말하고 있는 곳인 (D)이다.

22 ⓔ it's necessary to use cups that you can see through는 it's necessary to use cups that you cannot see through로 고치는 것이 문맥상 자연스럽다.

23 (가)to confuse는 to부정사의 부사적 용법으로 사용되었다. 따라서 이와 쓰임이 같은 것은 ② '나는 시험에 통과하기 위해 열심히 공부한다.'이다.

24 위 글에서는 물이 사라지는 마술을 보여주고 그 속임수에 대해서 설명하고 있다. 따라서 빈칸에는 ③ How come the water disappeared?(어째서 물이 사라진 거니?)가 적절하다.

25 위 글에 따르면, 마술을 보여줄 때 컵에 물을 채우고(B), 그 컵을 이리저리 움직인 다음(C), 친구에게 물이 어디 있는지 물어보는 (A) 순서로 이어지고 있다고 언급되어 있다.

26 위 글에 따르면, Ken은 컵 여러 개를 이리저리 움직일 것이라고 ("I will move them around to confuse you.") 말하고 있다.

27 (A) Jina는 Ken이 보여준 마술에서 물이 어떻게 위로 올라가는지에 대해서 묻고 있으므로 How come이 적절하다.

(B) 공기가 차가워지면 공기의 압력도 떨어진다(dropped)고 언급되어 있다.

(C) 유리병 안의 공기의 압력이 줄면 반대로 유리병 바깥 공기의 압력이 높아진다(higher pressure)고 언급되어 있다.

28 위 글에 따르면, Ken이 "Abracadabra!"라고 외치자 물이 위로 올라갔다고("Look at the water! How come it rose into the glass?") 언급되어 있다.

29 문장의 주어로 쓰인 to부정사가 수식어로 인해 길어진 경우, 보통 to부정사를 뒤로 보내고 대신 주어 자리에 가주어 it을 둔다. 이때 쓰인 it은 가주어이므로 구체적인 뜻이 없으며, '...하는 것은 ~하다'로 해석한다.

30 위 글에서는 ② When did Ken learn the trick?(Ken은 그 마술 속임수를 언제 배웠는가?)에 대해서는 언급된 바 없다.

Lesson 8 (기말) 〔1회〕

01 ② **02** ② **03** ④ **04** let the students play outside
05 ③
06 (1) Although I got[woke] up late, I didn't miss the[a] bus.
(2) Although I was tired, I studied hard.
07 ② **08** ④
09 (A) She had me bake a cake
(B) she made me write a letter
10 ⑤ **11** ① **12** ① **13** ④ **14** ② **15** ⑤ **16** ④ **17** ③
18 ④ **19** ② **20** ② **21** ⑤ **22** ④ **23** ⑤ **24** ④ **25** ④
26 ④
27 (1) They gave them[the boys] new shoes and uniforms.
(2) They felt proud of themselves.
28 ③ **29** ② **30** What makes you say so?

01 위에서부터 순서대로, laugh(웃다), completely(완전히), gather(모으다), proud(자랑스러워하는)가 들어가는 것이 문맥상 가장 자연스럽다.

02 <보기>의 주어진 문장은 가주어 It - 진주어 to부정사 구문이다. 문맥상 빈칸에는 보어인 ② necessary(필요한)가 들어가는 것이 가장 적절하다.

03 have no experience in ~: ~에 경험이 없다
in the end: 결국, 마침내

04 행동의 주체가 자발적으로 어떤 행동을 하는 것이 아니라 '주어가 목적어로 하여금 ~하게 하다'라는 뜻으로 쓰이는 동사를 사역동사라고 한다. 사역동사에는 make(~하게 하다), let(~하도록 허락하다), have(~하게 하다), help(~하게 돕다) 등이 있다. 이때 「사역동사+목적어+목적격보어(동사원형)」의 순서로 쓴다.

05 ① laughed → laugh / ② his → him / ④ doing → do 또는 to do / ⑤ to play → play로 고쳐야 어법상 적절한 문장이 된다.

06 접속사 even if, even though, although, though 등은 모두 '~이긴 하지만'이라는 뜻으로, 주절과 종속절이 반대되는 내용일 때 사용할 수 있다.

07 ② studies → study로 고쳐야 어법상 적절한 문장이 된다.

08 접속사 although는 '~이긴 하지만'이라는 뜻으로, 주절과 종속절이 반대되는 내용일 때 사용할 수 있다.

09 행동의 주체가 자발적으로 어떤 행동을 하는 것이 아니라 '주어가 목적어로 하여금 ~하게 하다'라는 뜻으로 쓰이는 동사를 사역동사라고 한다. 사역동사에는 make(~하게 하다), let(~하도록 허락하다), have(~하게 하다), help(~하게 돕다) 등이 있다. 이때 「사역동사+목적어+목적격보어(동사원형)」의 순서로 쓴다.

10 접속사 even if, even though, although, though 등은 모두 '~이긴 하지만'이라는 뜻으로, 주절과 종속절이 반대되는 내용일 때

사용할 수 있다.

11 ⓑ: '사막을 건넌'이라는 뜻으로 선행사 people을 수식하는 관계대명사절이다.

ⓒ on foot: 걸어서

ⓓ took: (시간이) 걸렸다

ⓔ experience: 경험하다

12 (A) about: ~에 관해; 약, 대략

(B) in the desert: 사막에서, in 50 days: 50일 동안에

13 위 대화에 따르면, Tim은 사막에서의 삶을 경험해보고 싶지만 걸어서 사막을 건너고 싶지는 않다고("I want to experience life in the desert but I don't want to cross it on foot.") 언급하고 있다.

14 A가 크로스컨트리에 대해서 들어보았냐고 묻자(ⓒ), B는 그게 무엇이냐고 되묻는다(ⓐ). A는 그것이 스포츠이며 크로스컨트리에서 사람들이 들판을 달린다고 말한다(ⓓ). 이에 B가 흥미롭게 들린다고(ⓑ) 말하는 순서로 이어지는 것이 흐름상 가장 자연스럽다.

15 위 대화에 따르면, Hojun이는 아이스하키 팀에 가입할 것이냐고 묻는 상대방의 질문에 아직 확실하지 않다고 대답한다.

16 (A)"don't give up."은 "포기하지 마."라는 뜻의 문장이다.

17 위 글에 따르면, 건강을 위한 조언으로 매일 운동하고 패스트 푸드가 아닌 건강한 음식을 먹으며 식사 전에 손을 닦으라고 조언하고 있다.

18 위 글에서는 건강을 위한 조언들을 전달하고 있다. 따라서 제목으로 가장 적절한 것은 ④ The Things to Do for a Healthy Life(건강한 삶을 위해 할 일들)이다.

19 주어진 문단은 소년들이 나무 조각을 모아서 직접 축구 연습장을 만들었다는 내용이다. 따라서 주어진 문단이 들어가기에 가장 적절한 곳은 자신들 스스로 축구 연습장을 만들자고 말하고 있는 (B)이다.

20 축구팀을 만들어 훈련하던 소년들이 축구 경기에 대한 포스터를 보게 되었고(ⓛ), 경기에 참여하는 시도를 하기로 결정했다(ⓒ). 소년들이 경기하러 떠나려 할 때 마을 사람들이 신발과 유니폼을 선물했고(ⓐ), 몇몇은 경기장에 갔다는(ⓔ) 순서로 이어지는 것이 흐름상 가장 자연스럽다.

21 Ⓐ give up: 포기하다

Ⓑ take off: ~를 벗다

Ⓒ feel proud of ~: ~를 자랑스럽게 느끼다

22 위 글에 따르면, 소년들이 축구팀을 만들어 토너먼트를 하기 위해 떠나려 했을 때 마을 사람들이 새 신발과 유니폼을 선물했고 몇몇은 경기를 보러 경기장에 갔다고 언급되어 있다.

23 ⓔ Because → Although로 고쳐야 문맥상 적절한 문장이 된다.

24 위 글의 (E) 문단에 따르면, 준결승날 비가 왔고 Koh Panyee 소

년들의 팀은 지고 있었다고 언급되어 있다.

25 ⓓ to feel → feel로 고쳐야 어법상 적절한 문장이 된다.

26 (라) they won by a score of three to two, still, they felt proud of themselves.는 '그들은 3대 2의 점수로 이겼지만, 여전히 자신들 스스로를 자랑스럽게 여겼다.'는 그들이 경기에서 졌지만 포기하지 않았다는 내용상 적절하지 않다.

27 (1) 위 글에 따르면, 마을 사람들은 소년들에게 새 신발과 유니폼을 주었다고 언급되어 있다.

(2) 위 글에 따르면, 준결승에서 소년들은 경기에 졌지만 자신 스스로를 자랑스럽게 여겼다고 언급되어 있다.

28 '그러나 사람들은 그들의 생각을 비웃었다.'라는 문장이 들어가기에 가장 적절한 곳은 축구를 해본 적 없는 소년들이 자신들만의 축구팀을 만들기로 결정했다는 내용 뒤인 (C)이다.

29 소년들이 이전에 한번도 축구를 해본 적이 없지만 텔레비전으로 축구를 보는 것을 좋아했다는 내용이다. 따라서 빈칸에는 Although(~일지라도)가 가장 적절하다.

30 "Why do you say so?"는 "왜 그렇게 말을 하니?"라는 의미의 문장으로 "What makes you say so?"로 바꿔 쓸 수 있다.

Lesson 8 (기말) 2회

> **01** ⑤ **02** say **03** ⑤ **04** ②
> **05** Although it rained a lot, I took a walk in the park.
> **06** He made me move his bag. **07** ④ **08** ④ **09** ④
> **10** ⑤ **11** ② **12** Have you heard of the Gobi Desert?
> **13** ③ **14** ④ **15** ③ **16** ③ **17** ④ **18** ① **19** ③ **20** ②
> **21** ④ **22** ② **23** ⑤
> **24** Because the boys had no place to play soccer.
> **25** ④ **26** ② **27** ⑤ **28** ④ **29** ⑤ **30** ②,④

01 (A) bare: 아무것도 걸치지 않은 (C) courage: 용기

02 행동의 주체가 자발적으로 어떤 행동을 하는 것이 아니라 '주어가 목적어로 하여금 ~하게 하다'라는 뜻으로 쓰이는 동사를 사역동사라고 한다. 사역동사 make(~하게 하다)는 「사역동사+목적어+목적격보어(동사원형)」의 순서로 쓴다.

03 위에서부터 순서대로, exercise(운동하다), healthy(건강에 좋은), fast food(패스트푸드), meals(식사), Then(그러면)이 들어가는 것이 문맥상 가장 자연스럽다.

04 ① to laugh → laugh / ③ he → him / ④ crying → cry / ⑤ to play → play로 고쳐야 어법상 적절한 문장이 된다.

05 접속사 Although는 '~이지만'이라는 뜻으로, 주절과 종속절이 반대되는 내용일 때 사용할 수 있다.

06 행동의 주체가 자발적으로 어떤 행동을 하는 것이 아니라 '주어가

목적어로 하여금 ~하게 하다'라는 뜻으로 쓰이는 동사를 사역동사라고 한다. 사역동사에는 make(~하게 하다), let(~하도록 허락하다), have(~하게 하다), help(~하게 돕다) 등이 있다. 이때「사역동사+목적어+목적격보어(동사원형)」의 순서로 쓴다.

07 ① had cut her → had her cut / ② My mom decided my dog go to hospital. → My mom decided that my dog should go to hospital. / ③ to dance → dancing / ⑤ laughed → laugh로 고쳐야 어법상 적절한 문장이 된다.

08 ④ Although the heavy rain → Although it rained heavily 또는 Despite the heavy rain으로 고쳐야 어법상 적절한 문장이 된다.

09 "못생긴 스웨터 파티에 대해서 들어본 적 있니?"라는 A의 질문에 대해 "물론이지. 들어본 적 없어."라는 B의 대답은 흐름상 자연스럽지 않다.

10 Tom이 자신은 농구선수가 되고 싶지만 키가 작아서 포기를 해야 하는지 묻고 있다. A는 포기하지 말라고 말하면서, Anthony Webb이라는 선수를 아냐고 묻는다(c). Tom이 들어본 적 없다고 말하면서 그가 누구냐고 되묻자(a), A는 그가 농구선수로 키가 작지만 1986년 슬램덩크 대회에서 우승했다고(b) 말하는 순서로 이어지는 것이 흐름상 가장 자연스럽다.

11 (B) 위 대화에 따르면, 어제 걸어서 사막을 건너는 사람이 나오는 TV쇼를 본 것은 Tim이 아니라 Jane이다.
(E) 50일 동안 고비 사막을 건너는 경험을 시도해 보고 싶다고 말한 것은 Tim이 아니라 Jane이다.

12 상대방에게 어떤 일에 대해 들어보았는지 물어볼 때 "Have you heard ~?"라고 질문할 수 있다. 의미는 '~을 들어본 적이 있냐?'는 의미이다.

13 여학생이 호준이에게 아이스하키 팀에 지원해 볼 것이냐고 묻자, 호준이는 확실히 모르겠다고 대답한다. 이에 여학생이 왜냐고 이유를 묻자(B), 호준이가 아이스하키를 잘하는 Tony와 Brad가 지원한다고 대답한다(D). 여학생이 호준이 너도 아이스하키를 잘한다고 말하면서 포기하지 말라고 격려한다(A). 이에 호준이가 최선을 다해 보겠다고 말하면서 고맙다고(C) 말하는 순서로 이어지는 것이 흐름상 가장 자연스럽다.

14 위 대화에서는 ④ What time is this year's "Ugly Sweater Party" going to begin?(올해 못생긴 스웨터 파티는 몇 시에 시작할 예정인가?)에 대해서는 언급된 바 없다.

15 "어느 스포츠를 배워 보고 싶니?"라는 A의 질문에 대해 "응, 난 이전에 몇 가지를 배웠어."라는 B의 대답은 흐름상 자연스럽지 않다.

16 (A) 비가 와서 경기장이 미끄러워서 신발을 벗고 경기를 했다는 내용이므로 took off(벗었다)가 적절하다.
(B) thanks to: ~ 덕분에
(C) until the end: 끝까지

17 주어진 우리말에 맞게 영작하면, 'Although they lost by a score of three to two, still, they felt proud of themselves.'가 된다.

18 위 글에 따르면, 비가 와서 경기장이 미끄러웠기 때문에, 소년들은 신발을 벗고 맨발로 후반전 경기를 뛰었다고 언급되어 있다.

19 (A) be about to: 막 ~할 참이다
(B): 사역동사 make는 목적보어로 동사원형을 취한다.

20 ⓑ They were discouraging. → They were discouraged. 로 고쳐야 어법상 적절한 문장이 된다.

21 위 글에 따르면, 'The ball and the boys would often fall into the sea, so the field was always wet and slippery.'라고 언급되어 있다.

22 (A) 소년들이 이전에 축구를 해 본 적이 없지만 TV에서 축구를 보는 걸 좋아했다는 내용이므로 Although(~일지라도)가 적절하다.
(B) 소년들이 자신들만의 축구팀을 만들기로 했지만 사람들이 그들의 생각을 비웃었다는 내용이므로 However(그러나)가 적절하다.

23 위 글에 따르면, 소년들은 마을에 축구를 할 곳이 없었기 때문에 낙담했다고('The boys had no place to play soccer. They were discouraged.') 언급되어 있다.

24 위 글에 따르면, 사람들이 축구팀을 만들려고 하는 소년들의 의견을 불가능하다고 말한 이유는 마을에 축구를 할 곳이 없었기 때문이라고('The boys had no place to play soccer.') 언급되어 있다.

25 ⓑ many → much / ⓔ to leaving → to leave로 고쳐야 어법상 적절한 문장이 된다.

26 위 글에서 소년들은 열악한 환경에도 불구하고 최선을 다해 축구장을 만들고 훈련을 했다고 언급되어 있다. 따라서 위 글의 내용을 나타내는 표현으로 가장 알맞은 것은 ② No pain, no gain.(고통 없이는 얻는 게 없다.)이다.

27 위 글에서는 ⑤ How many villagers went to the stadium to watch the soccer game?(몇 명의 마을 사람이 소년들의 축구 경기를 보기 위해 경기장에 갔는가?)에 대해서는 언급된 바 없다.

28 위 글에 따르면, 글쓴이는 가족들과 응원하는 팀이 달라서 자신이 응원하는 팀이 점수를 냈을 때도 소리를 지를 수 없었다고 이야기하고 있다. 따라서 ⓓBlue and black are the colors of my favorite team's uniform.(파란색과 검은색은 내가 가장 좋아하는 팀의 유니폼 색깔이다.)는 문맥상 자연스럽지 않다.

29 위 글에 따르면, 글쓴이는 부모님과 응원하는 팀이 달라서 자신이 응원하는 팀의 유니폼을 숨겼다고('I hid my favorite team's clothes.') 언급하고 있다.

30 (A) do → keep / (C) because → although / (E) excite → enjoy로 고쳐야 어법상 적절한 문장이 된다.